RESEARCH METHODS

RESEARCH METHODS

CONCEPTS AND CONNECTIONS

2
•EDITION

Michael W. Passer

University of Washington

worth publishers
Macmillan Learning
New York

Vice President, Social Sciences and High School: Charles Linsmeier
Senior Acquisitions Editor: Daniel DeBonis
Development Editor: Elsa Peterson
Assistant Editor: Katie Pachnos
Executive Marketing Manager: Katherine Nurre
Marketing Assistant: Morgan Ratner
Executive Media Editor: Noel Hohnstine
Senior Media Editor: Laura Burden
Media Editorial Assistant: Nik Toner
Media Producer: Joseph Tomasso
Director, Content Management Enhancement: Tracey Kuehn
Managing Editor: Lisa Kinne
Senior Project Editor: Jodi Isman
Senior Production Supervisor: Sarah Segal
Photo Editor: Sheena Goldstein
Photo Researcher: Teri Stratford
Director of Design, Content Management: Diana Blume
Senior Design Manager: Vicki Tomaselli
Cover Designer: Paula Jo Smith
Interior Designer: Patrice Sheridan
Art Manager: Matthew McAdams
Illustrations: Network Graphics, Eli Ensor, Charles Yuen
Composition and Illustrations: codeMantra
Printing and Binding: King Printing Co., Inc.
Cover Image: Aniwhite/Shutterstock

Library of Congress Control Number: 2015958994

ISBN-13: 978-1-319-29265-2
ISBN-10: 1-319-29265-8

Printed in the United States of America
First printing

Worth Publishers
One New York Plaza
Suite 4500
New York, NY 10004-1562
www.macmillanlearning.com

To my wife Bev,
for her endless love, support, and grace,

and to Harold Sigall,
my undergraduate mentor and friend,
who nourished my interest in psychology and introduced me to
the exciting enterprise of conducting psychological research.

ABOUT THE AUTHOR

MICHAEL W. PASSER is Senior Lecturer in Psychology at the University of Washington, Seattle. Born and raised in Brooklyn, New York, he entered the University of Rochester fully expecting to be a physics or chemistry major, but he became hooked on psychological science after taking introductory psychology and a seminar course on the nature of the mind. He got his start as an undergraduate researcher under the mentorship of Dr. Harold Sigall, was a volunteer undergraduate introductory psychology teaching assistant, and received a Danforth Foundation Fellowship that partly funded his graduate studies and exposed him to highly enriching national conferences on college teaching.

Dr. Passer received his PhD from UCLA, where he conducted laboratory research on attribution theory under the primary mentorship of Dr. Harold Kelley and gained several years of field research experience studying competitive stress, self-esteem, and attributional processes among boys and girls playing youth sports, mainly working with Dr. Tara Scanlan in the Department of Kinesiology. At the University of Washington, he has conducted hypothesis-testing field research on competitive stress with youth sport participants, collaborated on several applied research projects in the field of industrial-organizational psychology, and for the past 26 years has been a Senior Lecturer and faculty coordinator of U.W.'s introductory psychology courses. In this role, he annually teaches courses in introductory psychology and research methods, developed a graduate course on the teaching of psychology, and is a U.W. Distinguished Teaching Award nominee. With his colleague Ronald Smith, he coauthored five editions of the introductory textbook *Psychology: The Science of Mind and Behavior* (McGraw-Hill), and has published more than 20 scientific articles and chapters, mostly on attribution theory and competitive stress.

CONTENTS IN BRIEF

CONTENTS

PART IV   EXPERIMENTS: SPECIALIZED DESIGNS

Chapter 11 Quasi-Experimental Designs   345

PREFACE

Welcome to the research methods course and to the second edition of this textbook. I wrote this book for the same core reasons that I choose to teach the research methods course each year. First, I believe that regardless of a student's major or intended career, a research methods course in psychology or other behavioral science is among the most important classes an undergraduate can take. The course content is tailor-made to sharpen students' critical thinking skills and help students become savvier lifelong information consumers. The concepts they learn in this course should foster their ability and motivation to evaluate the soundness of conclusions and other claims they encounter, whether in scientific articles, textbooks, media reports, pseudoscientific writings, or advertisements.

The methods course can deepen students' appreciation of the scientific method and scientific values by enhancing their understanding of methodological concepts, different types of research and research design, and ethical and other challenges confronting behavioral scientists. While this methodological foundation has obvious benefits for students who take more advanced science courses or intend to become researchers, it also prepares all students to be knowledgeable citizens and professionals in an increasingly science-oriented world. Even if few of our students plan to pursue an academic research career, many hope to become practitioners in clinical or counseling psychology, industrial-organizational psychology, school psychology, social work, medicine or nursing, physical therapy, law, or business. As professionals, they will need to draw upon knowledge of research methods as they stay current with the literature in their chosen field and evaluate its implications for the way they conduct their work.

My second reason for writing this book is that, to put it mildly, teaching the methods course is a formidable challenge. Years ago, when the opportunity to teach it first arose, I was thrilled and eagerly prepared. A few days before the start of classes I ran into a colleague who asked, "What are you teaching?" "Research methods," I replied. "Oh," he said as he rushed off, "too bad!" Surprised but undaunted, I gave his comment little thought. (After all, while in graduate school, I had volunteered to be a teaching assistant for the course, loved the experience, and had enthusiastic students.)

The next day I encountered another colleague who asked what course I was teaching. "Methods," I said. Her reply? "Too bad!" This time I had to ask why. The course, she said, was a tough sell. Up to half the students weren't psych majors and took it to satisfy a science distribution requirement. Among the psych majors, many were seniors who had kept putting the course off, and few students aspired to research careers. The bottom line, she said, was that the course content didn't intrinsically interest most students. I told her I already had heard about these issues and looked forward to the challenge of teaching such a diverse group.

During the course, there were days when my students were highly engaged and others when their facial expressions suggested the end-of-class bell couldn't ring soon enough. Although I was an experienced and well-regarded instructor, teaching the methods course for the first time was a wake-up call. Still, when the official anonymous student evaluations arrived weeks later, I was pleased. Although many invoked the "tough sell" theme, most students found the class engaging and worthwhile. As one student memorably remarked, "I expected this course to suck swamp gas, but it was really pretty interesting." Importantly, another theme frequently emerged: "This course changed the way I look at information / evaluate information / think about claims / think about evidence / judge whether something causes something else." To this day, there is no student feedback that inspires me more than such comments about enhanced critical thinking.

My hope is that this textbook will provide students with a solid foundation of methodological concepts that honors the importance of the methods course by promoting the learning goals discussed more fully below. I hope that the textbook's balance of breadth and depth, topic selection and diverse examples, personal writing style, chapter-opening vignettes and pedagogical features, and supporting materials will enhance students' interest and engage them in the material. In addition, except for instructors who absolutely require methodological and statistical coverage to be interwoven throughout the narrative, I believe that the modular statistics approach used in this book will facilitate students' learning and engagement by allowing instructors to tailor the amount and placement of statistics coverage easily and flexibly.

LEARNING GOALS: CONCEPTS AND CONNECTIONS

The American Psychological Association (2013), in its document *APA Guidelines for the Undergraduate Psychology Major: Version 2.0,* describes five broad learning goals for undergraduate psychology programs. These are curricular goals, and there is no assumption that an individual course will focus on all of them. Still, the research methods course has the potential to address them all. In-class exercises and demonstrations, class research projects, labs, and discussion sections are among the components that can support these learning goals. I hope that this textbook and its supplements will help instructors to promote the goals that they deem most important. Here are some ways in which this package links to APA's undergraduate learning goals.

APA Learning Goal 1: Knowledge Base in Psychology. This learning goal includes enhancing students' understanding of psychology's goals as a discipline, and why psychology is a science. These topics are addressed in depth starting with the book's first chapter. Promoting students' understanding of key psychological terms, concepts, principles, and themes is another component of Learning Goal 1, and naturally this occurs throughout the textbook in relation to methodological topics. Key concepts and broad themes include systematic empiricism, operational definitions, validity and reliability, correlation versus causation, experimental control, confounding and plausible alternative explanations, and quantitative and qualitative approaches to studying behavior. Approximately 350 key terms and concepts are boldfaced and discussed in the chapter narratives.

The ability to evaluate theories, and to understand the complexity of studying behavior, are other aspects of Learning Goal 1 to which the textbook contributes. Moreover, this goal also includes fostering students' knowledge about major content domains in psychology, and of practical and societal applications of psychological findings and principles. By highlighting basic as well as applied research, and by drawing examples from diverse psychological subfields—including experimental, clinical, cognitive, developmental, social, comparative, educational, industrial–organizational, health, and biological psychology—the textbook can contribute to these subgoals.

APA Learning Goal 2: Scientific Inquiry and Critical Thinking. This learning goal corresponds to a core goal of this textbook and the research methods course. It involves promoting students' ability to understand and evaluate various research methods, and enhancing students' scientific reasoning and problem-solving skills. These skills include the ability to frame problems in operational terms and evaluate conclusions in light of principles of good research design. Learning Goal 2 also calls for enhancing students' information literacy, including their ability to search psychological databases, evaluate the quality of information sources, and interpret graphs and research findings. The textbook addresses these topics.

Science is a grand exercise in critical thinking, and an orientation toward deeper critical thinking is perhaps the most important lifelong outcome that most students will take away from the methods course. In line with specific components of Learning Goal 2 discussed by APA, I hope this textbook will boost students' ability to think critically about scientific, pseudoscientific, anecdotal, and other types of information that they encounter in educational contexts and everyday life. This includes the ability to evaluate the appropriateness of different research approaches, designs, and procedures for addressing particular questions; to judge the soundness of causal inferences and other conclusions and identify plausible alternative explanations for research findings; to understand that not all evidence is equal; and to weigh the quality of conflicting pieces of evidence.

This book supports critical thinking goals from the outset—for example, note the Chapter 1 opening scenario that illustrates different bases upon which people form beliefs. It also employs critical thinking as a recurrent theme woven into the narrative and illustrated by examples drawn from research, the media, and daily life. Each chapter concludes with critical thinking and application exercises, and critical thinking exercises also are provided in the Instructor's Manual. In addition, the topics of correlation and correlational research receive full-chapter treatment, with considerable attention devoted to the distinction between correlation and causation—a core critical thinking concept that can't be overemphasized, as many students continue to fall into the "correlation equals causation" trap. To support the APA learning goal of helping students to recognize the influence of sociocultural factors in scientific inquiry, the textbook uses several studies on sociocultural issues to illustrate various methodological concepts.

APA Learning Goal 3: Ethical and Social Responsibility in a Diverse World. Awareness of the need for ethical conduct in conducting research, and familiarity with the principles and standards of research ethics addressed in the APA Ethics Code, are key aspects of this APA learning goal. These topics and federal research ethics regulations are discussed in a meaty chapter on research ethics. This chapter goes beyond a mere description of ethics principles and regulations. It highlights how ethics codes and ethics review committees shape the process of conducting research, how ethics codes cannot address every ethical issue a researcher might face, and thus how striving to be an ethical researcher is itself an exercise in critical thinking. The chapter uses examples to stress how psychological scientists and other behavioral researchers must often grapple with thorny ethical dilemmas that result from conflicting ethical principles or ambiguities inherent in ethical standards. The chapter comes early in the book, but for instructors who prefer to address this topic later in the course, the chapter is easily assigned out of sequence.

APA Learning Goal 3 also emphasizes the importance of academic integrity. In a research methods course where students may conduct projects and write research reports or other scientific papers, this learning goal fuses with scientific integrity, which is discussed in depth in the research ethics chapter. Plagiarism is discussed in the research ethics chapter and also in Appendix A, Communicating Research Results, which is oriented toward student report writing.

The social responsibility component of Learning Goal 3 includes enhancing students' understanding of psychology's potential to enhance human welfare and affect social policy.

The textbook's discussions of topics such as quasi-experimental designs, program evaluation, the use of correlational findings for applied prediction, the importance of measurement reliability and validity, and reducing threats to internal validity reinforce connections between methodological concepts and the application of psychological science to societal, organizational, and other problems.

APA Learning Goal 4: Communication. This learning goal focuses on enhancing students' writing and oral communication skills, including the ability to write clearly and concisely in APA style. Cognitive psychologist Pam Marek, a professor at Kennesaw State University and associate editor of the journal *Teaching of Psychology,* has written an outstanding guide on scientific communication and APA style. Produced specifically for this textbook and presented in Appendix A, Communicating Research Results, it expands upon basic information on scientific communication in Chapter 2. This communication guide discusses how to conduct a scientific literature search, key elements of good scientific writing and of an APA style research report, essentials of APA writing style, and how to create an effective poster presentation. The guide includes an annotated manuscript of a research report and is supplemented online with additional information by Dr. Marek on grammar.

The textbook addresses quantitative literacy, another component of this learning goal, by discussing basic concepts in analyzing, graphing, and interpreting data. For instructors whose courses contain more statistical depth, the textbook's Statistics Modules unit, presented after the book's main chapters, contains more detailed conceptual discussion and shows how to perform various statistical calculations and tests.

APA Learning Goal 5: Professional Development. Finally, the textbook supports students' professional development by helping them enhance knowledge and skills, such as critical thinking skills, information literacy, and communication skills, that are relevant to a broad range of careers. Chapter 1 discusses ways in which taking a methods course can be relevant to psychology majors who plan to become researchers, to those who don't, and to students who don't major in psychology. For students who are considering a career in psychology, Worth Publishers has compiled an excellent collection of original essays in which leading psychological scientists discuss a major area of their research, its contribution to society, and how they became interested in the topic. This collection, *Psychology and the Real World,* can be packaged with new copies of the textbook.

TEXTBOOK FEATURES

Chapter Opening Vignettes and Examples From Diverse Subfields. Each chapter begins with one or more vignettes based on research studies or events in the media. My goals in using this approach are to engage students from the outset and draw them into the chapter, and provide opening examples that are periodically referred to later in the chapter to illustrate one or more key concepts.

Research methods instructors are in the enviable position of being able to draw research examples from diverse subfields. Certainly, boundaries between psychology's traditional subfields have increasingly blurred, but even so, drawing examples from diverse subfields illustrates how research methods are brought to bear on a wide variety of topics. It also broadens students' knowledge about exciting and important work being done by psychologists across many subfields and might help spark an interest—even a research interest—in a particular subfield.

Examples run the gamut from classic to recent studies. It's important to show that psychological science wasn't built in a day, but at the same time, to avoid having students feel that a textbook is dated. This textbook also covers topics, such as Internet research and the ethical issues it involves, that reflect our changing times.

Research Ethics Coverage. The detailed chapter on research ethics reflects the paramount importance of conducting ethical research. I seek to highlight how ethics codes and regulation affect the process of designing and conducting research, that ethics codes are not cookbooks that provide concrete steps for solving every ethical issue a researcher might face, and how the desire to be an ethical researcher and adhere to ethics codes can generate difficult ethical dilemmas. The chapter stands independently and easily can be assigned at any point during the course.

Flexible Sequence of Chapters. Most methods textbooks, including this one, devote their earliest chapters to core topics such as characteristics of science, measurement, and so forth. Many books then cover descriptive (nonexperimental) research before experimentation, whereas many others cover experimentation before descriptive approaches. This textbook can easily be adapted to either sequence. Moreover, with some exceptions (e.g., covering basic experimental designs before factorial designs), instructors can easily adapt the sequence of chapters within each part of the book to their particular preferences.

Pedagogy. I have endeavored to provide the amount and types of pedagogy necessary to help students gain understanding and assess their progress, while maintaining a clear focus on the main text content.

Key terms are boldfaced and each term is immediately accompanied by an italicized definition in the narrative. A list of key terms also is presented at the end of each chapter, along with its page location in the chapter, and a glossary of key terms for the entire text is found at the end of the book. To reinforce the importance of central concepts, many key terms introduced in the early foundational chapters—such as Chapter 2, which provides an overview of the research process—are presented again in boldface in subsequent chapters, where these concepts are explored in greater depth.

A Concept Check feature is placed at the end of each main section of every chapter. End-of-chapter pedagogy includes a Chapter Summary, a list of open-ended Assess Your Knowledge questions, and a set of Thinking Critically and Applying Your Knowledge (CTAYK) exercises. Answers to the Concept Check questions are presented at the end of each chapter, and answers to the odd-numbered CTAYK exercises are presented in Appendix D. Answers to the even-numbered CTAYK exercises are available as part of the Instructor's Resource Manual, providing instructors with the option to use these exercises as in-class critical thinking exercises or homework assignments, or to provide the answers to students for independent study.

Enhanced Graphics. Many reviewers of the first edition noted that the quality of this textbook's graphics program (i.e., graphs, photos, and other artwork) exceeded that of their current textbook. In this second edition, the graphics program has been further enhanced by the addition of a full-page infographic in every chapter. Each infographic focuses on one or more key concepts discussed in the chapter, either expanding on those concepts or summarizing them with a mix of graphics and text. Other new figures have been added to several chapters, and some existing figures have been modified to achieve greater clarity.

Flexible Statistics Coverage: Statistics Modules. Some instructors separate statistics coverage from the methods course almost entirely, whereas others teach statistics and methodology in a highly integrated manner. No approach to covering statistics in a methods book will satisfy everyone, but I hope that the modular approach in this book will enable instructors to easily emphasize or deemphasize statistics coverage, as they see fit. Several chapters introduce basic statistical concepts (e.g., descriptive statistics, statistical significance), and instructors who want more statistical depth can select from among 16 statistics modules (SM) presented after Chapter 12. Each module, and each subsection within, are numbered so that instructors can easily supplement chapter assignments with specific modules.

For example, in the context of providing an overview of the research process, Chapter 2 presents a simple introduction to the concepts of inferential statistics, statistical significance, and Type I and Type II error. Instructors who want their students to learn more fully about null hypothesis testing early in the course might specify a reading assignment of "Chapter 2, SM 9." Those who want students to learn about null hypothesis testing later in the course, such as in conjunction with covering single-factor experimental designs, could assign "Chapter 8, SM 9."

For greater convenience in listing reading assignments, every statistics module has numbered subsections. Thus, if an instructor only wants students to learn about the basic concept behind a *t* test, but not about calculating a *t* test, the reading assignment would specify module SM 12.1 rather than SM 12 as a whole. Some modules are cited in certain chapters (e.g., "For more details, see Statistics Module 2") but, of course, can be assigned at whatever time the instructor best sees fit.

A Final Comment. I look forward to the possibility that through this textbook, I may have an opportunity to contribute to students' education and intellectual growth. Above all, I hope instructors and students will have a great, rewarding experience in the research methods course.

CHANGES TO THE SECOND EDITION

The graphics program for this edition has been enhanced, the presentation of some topics has been reorganized, new research examples and key terms have been added, some material from the first edition has been deleted, and many references have been updated or added. Here are some of the major changes in each chapter.

Chapter 1. The sequence of material linked to the three-door-problem opening vignette has been changed to enhance clarity. The answer to the problem is now explained immediately after the problem's history is discussed, rather than several pages later. The table that accompanies this explanation has been streamlined, and the Molyneux problem has been dropped as an additional example of the use of reason and logic. The section "Goals of Science" now includes two new examples, one discussed in the narrative and another illustrated in a new full-page infographic. A new figure highlights the relation between basic and applied research, and a discussion of anecdotal evidence has been added to the section "Skepticism, Science, and Everyday Life."

Chapter 2. A cautionary paragraph about relying on popular media sources has been added to the discussion of conducting a scientific literature search. The section "Approaches to Conducting Research" now mentions between-subjects and within-subjects experimental designs, and the concepts of random assignment, counterbalancing, and extraneous variables are now introduced as key terms. A new figure complements the discussion of cross-sectional, longitudinal, and sequential designs, and the section on sampling now distinguishes between representative and nonrepresentative samples. The nontechnical overview of how scientists draw conclusions from data analyses now links the terms *Type I error* and *Type II error* to this discussion. A full-page infographic that summarizes major steps in the research process has been added.

Chapter 3. Three new figures are introduced: One highlights how research ethics are central to science, another presents the criteria used to assess whether an activity is considered human subjects research, and a full-page infographic presents a case example to illustrate the key concept of minimal risk. Additional narrative information is presented about the ethics review committee process, and about judging minimal risk. The discussion of informed consent now includes highly publicized controversies about online research (e.g., Facebook, OkCupid).

Chapter 4. The opening vignettes have been streamlined and integrated more extensively into the chapter narrative. Two new figures, including a full-page infographic, provide additional examples and other information about independent and dependent variables. A discussion of interobserver reliability has been added to the section "Reliability of Measurement," and the section "Validity of Measurement" includes new research-based examples of assessing criterion and construct validity. Respectively, two new figures summarize the different types of reliability and validity discussed in the narrative.

Chapter 5. A full-page infographic replaces a previous figure in highlighting why correlation does not establish causation, and carries through on the research theme established in the chapter opening vignette. The discussion of how researchers try to reduce causal ambiguity in correlational studies pays more attention to the importance of anticipating and measuring possible third variables. The example of popular media reporting of correlational findings has been updated with a more recent study.

Chapter 6. The coverage of case study research has been doubled and now discusses qualitative, quantitative, and mixed-methods approaches. Intrinsic, instrumental, and collective case studies are described, as are single-case and multiple-case study designs. There is a new section on gathering and analyzing data from case studies, including coverage of semistructured interviews and focus groups. Discussion of the advantages and limitations of case studies has been expanded. Observational research coverage receives a new full-page infographic illustrating different ways to record observations; these include narrative records, field notes, behavioral coding systems, behavior checklists, rating and ranking scales, and diaries.

Chapter 7. A revised exercise/vignette opens the chapter to illustrate how survey data are used for different purposes. In covering types of sampling, the description of cluster sampling has been refined and multistage sampling is now included. A new full-page infographic summarizes eight types of probability and nonprobability sampling covered in the chapter. Greater emphasis is given to issues concerning the wording and sequencing of questionnaire items, and an illustration of context effects in question placement has been added. The discussion of current issues facing survey researchers, such as the challenge cell-phone-only users pose to obtaining representative national samples, has been updated. The topic of being a critical consumer of surveys now includes a discussion of push polls.

Chapter 8. The concept of extraneous variables is discussed and illustrated more explicitly prior to the discussion of confounding. The coverage of order effects in within-subjects designs now presents fatigue effects and practice effects as boldfaced key terms, and adds the concept of sensitization. The section on addressing order effects, while still focusing on counterbalancing, now includes a discussion of temporal spacing. A new, full-page infographic illustrates how a specific research question could be investigated using either a between-subjects or within-subjects design, highlights differences between the two approaches, and is used in the chapter narrative to expand the discussion of special issues in designing within-subjects experiments.

Chapter 9. The topic sequence has been reorganized: Detailed coverage of understanding main effects and interactions in 2×2 designs now precedes the discussion of specific issues in designing a factorial experiment. To enhance clarity, an explicit distinction is now made between how the terms "levels" (of an independent variable) and "conditions" (specific cells within a factorial design) are used in the chapter. A new full-page infographic, "Understanding Interactions," presents three data graphs to illustrate the general patterns of interaction that can occur in a 2×2 factorial design. It also pinpoints for the student why each set of findings represents an interaction. These graphs are contrasted to one in an earlier figure that has been revised in this edition to show main effects but no interaction.

Chapter 10. The discussion of inferences about generalizability and of statistical conclusion validity has been expanded. A new full-page infographic caps the material on construct, internal, statistical conclusion, and external validity by applying these concepts to an additional research example. The coverage of placebo effects is reorganized, with separate sections on the scope of placebo effects, assessing versus controlling placebo effects, and double-blind and single-blind procedures. New sections have been added to the coverage of replication, focusing on independent versus nonindependent replications, and two approaches to "big replication" illustrated by the Many Labs Project (Klein et al., 2014) and Psychology Reproducibility Project (Open Science Collaboration, 2015). The discussion of complete and partial replication also has been expanded.

Chapter 11. The opening vignette has been simplified by eliminating one of the three examples of a quasi-experiment, leaving one applied research and one basic research example. Two figures that, respectively, portray hypothetical outcomes from a simple interrupted time series design and a time series design with a nonequivalent control group, have been modified to more clearly illustrate the interpretation of trend lines. A new full-page infographic highlights a progression of weaker to stronger quasi-experimental designs.

Chapter 12. Coverage of the history of single-case research in psychology, the multiple baseline design across behaviors, and extending single-case designs to social units has been shortened. The section "Combined Designs" has been restructured; a new full-page infographic now contrasts ABAB and multiple baseline designs, and illustrates how they can be combined to assess the effectiveness of a treatment.

Statistics Modules. The number, sequence, and topics covered by these modules remains the same. Module 1 (Descriptive and Inferential Statistics) now explicitly notes that some statistics are used in both descriptive and inferential analyses. More guidelines for creating grouped frequency intervals and for graphing frequency distributions have been added to Module 2 (Frequency Distributions). Symbols and Greek characters used to represent sample and population statistics are more fully described in Modules 4 (Measures of Dispersion) and 6 (The Normal Curve). Module 9 (Null Hypothesis Testing) continues to focus on nondirectional hypotheses, but the example of a directional null and alternative hypothesis has been added. The concept of degrees of freedom is now discussed more fully, using the chi-square test for goodness-of-fit test as a simple example (Module 10).

MEDIA AND SUPPLEMENTS

FOR INSTRUCTORS

Research Methods: Concepts and Connections comes with a robust package of supplemental materials to support teaching. All the instructor resources are available to download from the Macmillan Learning catalog at **www.macmillanlearning.com**.

- The **Instructor's Resource Manual** features a variety of teaching tips and activities to support the topics discussed in the text, including learning outcomes, extended chapter outlines, lecture and discussion guides, classroom exercises, web resources, and film suggestions.
- The **Test Bank** by Chrysalis Wright of University of Central Florida includes multiple-choice, essay, and critical thinking questions, totaling more than 120 items for each chapter. A special set of scenario-based multiple-choice questions for each chapter targets students' ability to think critically about specific studies.
- The **Diploma Downloadable Test Bank** allows instructors to add an unlimited number of new questions, edit questions, format a test, scramble questions, and include figures, graphs, and pictures. Student grades can be reported to an accompanying Gradebook.
- **Lecture Slides** by Megan McLaughlin and Pauline Davey Zeece provided in PowerPoint give teachers all the figures and images from the text in addition to a full-lecture accompaniment for each chapter. Each lecture includes questions and activities to augment the material in the book and bring concepts to life.
- **Macmillan Community** is an online forum where teachers can find and share favorite teaching ideas and materials, including videos, animations, images, PowerPoint slides, news stories, articles, web links, and lecture activities. It is also home to Worth's abundant social media content, including tweets, blog posts, webinars, and more! Browse the site and share your favorite materials for teaching psychology at **community.macmillan.com**.

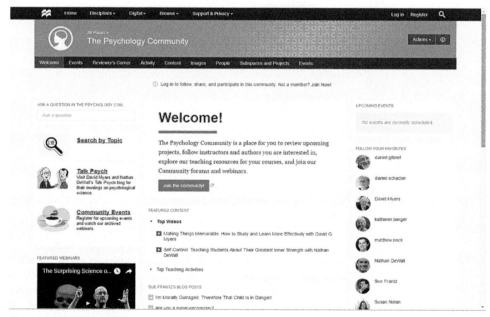

Community.Macmillan.com

LAUNCHPAD SOLO FOR RESEARCH METHODS

The LaunchPad Solo for Research Methods is an interactive course space that enhances and assesses students' understanding of research methods concepts. The system features a selection of video clips and two sets of activities: Research in Action and Data Visualizations.

The **Research in Action** activities provide users with direct experience in planning and designing studies. Each one puts the user in the role of a scientific investigator and asks that person to make decisions in planning and executing a study from idea to results. Instructors can use Research in Action as an in-class or take-home activity. Pre-built multiple-choice and essay quizzes make it easy to assess students' knowledge.

Is SAT performance related to family income and education level? How do concussion rates for high school sports differ? How important is a good night's sleep? The **Data Visualization** activities invite readers to consider these questions as scientists by looking at real experimental data. Each activity is based on an interactive graph that displays actual data from a published study. After reading a description of the study, students have to answer questions that test their ability to understand and reason about the data. Integrated lessons in statistical concepts further build students' quantitative reasoning skills.

The LaunchPad Solo for Research Methods is available to preview and purchase at launchpadworks.com.

Access to the LaunchPad Solo for Research Methods can be ordered together with *Research Methods: Concepts and Connections* using the ISBNs below.

Clothbound: ISBN-10: 1-319-06160-5 / ISBN-13: 978-1-319-06160-9

Loose-leaf: ISBN-10: 1-319-06161-3 / ISBN-13: 978-1-319-06161-6

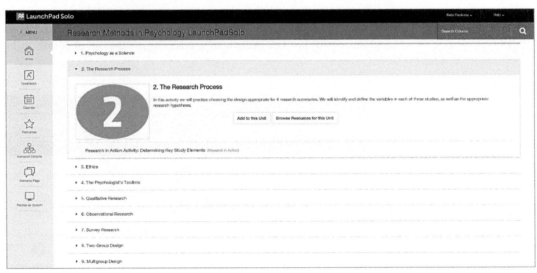

LaunchPad Solo for Research Methods

RESEARCH IN ACTION ACTIVITIES

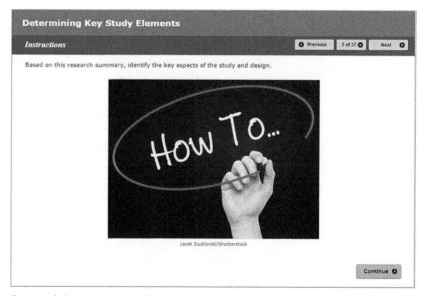

Research in Action Activity

DATA VISUALIZATION ACTIVITIES

ADHD Diagnosis Rates Over Time
Comorbidity: The Relationship Between Related Disorders
Concussion Rates in High School and College Athletes
Does Personality Remain Stable Over Time?
Does SAT Performance Correlate to Family Income and Education Level?
Do "Learning Styles" Exist?
Do Men and Women Differ in the Way They Remember Location Information?
Finding the Best Way to Describe Experimental Data
Have BMI and Food Consumption Changed Over Time?
Is There a Cognitive Decline With Age Regardless of Cognitive Stimulation?
The Relationship Between Stress and Eating Habits
The Relationship of Sleep to Other Variables (Academics, Mood, Illness, Personality)
The Size of Social Groups
Understanding How to Read and Use (or Misuse!) Data

ADDITIONAL STUDENT SUPPLEMENTS

- The **iClicker** Classroom Response System is a versatile polling system developed by educators for educators that makes class time more efficient and interactive. iClicker allows you to ask questions and instantly record your students' responses, take attendance, and gauge students' understanding and opinions. iClicker is available at a 10% discount when packaged with *Research Methods: Concepts and Connections*.

- *SPSS: A User-Friendly Approach* by Jeffery Aspelmeier and Thomas Pierce of Radford University is an accessible introduction to SPSS. Using a proven teaching method, statistical procedures are made accessible to students by building each section of the text around the storyline from a popular cartoon. Easing anxiety and giving students the necessary support to learn the material, *SPSS: A User-Friendly Approach* provides instructors and students with an informative guide to the basics of SPSS: available for Versions 17, 18, and 22.

- *Psychology and the Real World: Essays Illustrating Fundamental Contributions to Society,* **Second Edition**, is a superb collection of essays by major researchers that describe their landmark studies. Published in association with the not-for-profit FABBS Foundation, the new edition of this engaging reader includes Alan Kazdin's reflections on his research on treating children with severe aggressive behavior, Adam Grant's look at work and motivation, and Steven Hayes's research on mindfulness and acceptance and commitment therapy. A portion of all proceeds is donated to FABBS to support societies of cognitive, psychological, behavioral, and brain sciences.

- *The Psychology Major's Companion: Everything You Need to Know to Get Where You Want to Go*, by Dana S. Dunn (Moravian College) and Jane S. Halonen (University of West Florida), helps students to decide whether to declare psychology as their major, to learn strategies for producing an optimal experience in the major, and to prepare for graduate school or a psychology-related professional life.

- *The Critical Thinking Companion for Introductory Psychology,* **Third Edition**, by Jane S. Halonen (University of West Florida) and Cynthia Gray (Beloit College), contains a guide to critical thinking strategies as well as exercises in pattern recognition, practical problem solving, creative problem solving, scientific problem solving, psychological reasoning, and perspective taking.

- ***The Worth Expert Guide to Scientific Literacy: Thinking Like a Psychological Scientist***, by Kenneth D. Keith (University of San Diego) and Bernard Beins (Ithaca College), helps students foster solid habits of scientific thought, learning to apply an empirical attitude and data-driven decision making in their lives. With this increased level of scientific literacy, students will be better able to make sense of complex scientific information and to recognize pseudoscientific claims that are not only invalid but also potentially harmful.

- ***The Horse That Won't Go Away: Clever Hans, Facilitated Communication, and the Need for Clear Thinking*** by Thomas E. Heinzen, Scott O. Lilienfeld, and Susan A. Nolan is a fascinating series of case studies in confirmation bias. The authors engage and inspire students with true stories of how psychological research methods led to some surprising truths.

ACKNOWLEDGMENTS

I would like to thank the many people who have contributed to the writing and production of this textbook. First and foremost, I am indebted to my wife, Bev Wilson, a developmental psychologist and fellow academic, who has given me tremendous support and encouragement during this project. I also want to thank my past and present undergraduate students and graduate teaching assistants at the University of Washington for their feedback about the research methods course that has kept me on my academic toes and inspired me to keep the course fresh. My former colleague, Dr. Beth Kerr, also taught the methods course for many years. From lively discussions about the course to concrete assistance with course components, her support was invaluable.

I wish to express my gratitude to Dr. Laura Little, our faculty coordinator of the research methods course and a distinguished statistics instructor, for her detailed review of the textbook's Statistics Modules and her invaluable constructive feedback. I also am grateful to Dr. Little, my colleagues Dr. Jacquie Pickrell and Dr. Ann Culligan, and Dr. Michael Rader of Johnson County Community College, for their feedback about various infographics. To Dr. Pam Marek of Kennesaw State University, who wrote an excellent appendix for the book on communicating research results, my sincere thanks. And, of course, throughout the writing of the first and second editions of this textbook, I relied on thoughtful feedback from reviewers, focus group attendees, and survey respondents. My thanks go to them for their expertise and for the time they set aside to help develop this textbook.

Patricia Alexander
Long Beach City College

Kathryn Anderson
Our Lady of the Lake University

David Alfano
Community College of Rhode Island

Elizabeth Babcock
Augustana College

Jason Barker
University of Illinois at Springfield

Lisa Bauer
University of Missouri

Michael Becker
Penn State University at Harrisburg

Elizabeth Brondolo
St. John's University

Sarah Brosnan
Georgia State University

Hiram Brownell
Boston College

Dan Bucknam
Saint Mary's University of Minnesota

Jennifer Carlin-Dawgert
City College of San Francisco

Mary Jo Carnot
Chadron State College

Robert Cassidy
Concordia University

Ricardo Castillo
Santa Ana College

Alexandra Corning
University of Notre Dame

Clare Conry-Murray
Penn State Beaver

Anastasia Dimitropoulos
Case Western Reserve University

Nicole Dudukovic
Trinity College

Kimberly Duff
Cerritos College

Cathy Forestell
College of William & Mary

Rod Fowers
Highline Community College

Art Frankel
Salve Regina University

Edwin Gantt
Brigham Young University

Kathy Geher
State University of New York at New Paltz

Marcie Goeke-Morey
Catholic University of America

Chris Goode
Georgia State University

Paula Goolkasian
University of North Carolina at Charlotte

Angela Gutchess
Brandeis University

Kellie Hagewen
College of Southern Nevada

Kristina Hardy
Duke University

Robert Harvey
Virginia Polytechnic Institute and State University

Robin Howse
Bryant University

Debra Hull
Wheeling Jesuit University

Jean Humphreys
Dallas Baptist University

Jessica Irons
James Madison University

Katie Jacobs
University of Central Missouri

Rosalyn King
Northern Virginia Community College

Sean Laurent
University of Oregon

Fabio Leite
The Ohio State University at Lima

Mei-Ching Lien
Oregon State University

Linda Lockwood
Metropolitan State College of Denver

Chris Logan
Southern Methodist University

Stella Lopez
University of Texas at San Antonio

Rebecca Lundwall
Brigham Young University

Noah MacKenzie
University of Cincinnati

Stephen Madigan
University of Southern California

Thomas Malloy
Rhode Island College

Daniel McConnell
University of Central Florida

Kai McCormack
Spelman College

Todd McKerchar
Jacksonville State University

Meredith Minear
The College of Idaho

Joseph Morrissey
State University of New York at Binghamton

Brendan Morse
Bridgewater State University

Katie Mosack
University of Wisconsin at Milwaukee

Helga Noice
Elmhurst College

Roisin O'Connor
Concordia University

Blaine Peden
University of Wisconsin at Eau Claire

Jason Piccone
Nova Southeastern University

Michael Rader
Johnson County Community College

Chrislyn Randell
Metropolitan State College of Denver

Maria Reid
Florida International University

Rachel Ritchie
Florida International University

Michael Roberts
DePauw University

Rachael Robnett
University of California at Santa Cruz

Michelle Samuel
Mount St. Mary's College

Dan Sass
University of Texas at San Antonio

Tom Schmitt
Eastern Michigan University

Pamela Joyce Shapiro
Temple University

Elizabeth Ann Sheehan
Georgia State University

Tamar Shovali
Eckerd College

Joseph Simons-Rudolph
North Carolina State University

Tony Stantucci
Manhattanville College

Waylin Sternglanz
Nova Southeastern University

Stephen Truhon
Austin Peay State University

Nicholas Turiano
West Virginia University

G. Turner
Texas State University at San Marcos

Peter Vernig
Suffolk University

Joanne Walsh
Kean University

Christopher Warren
California State University, Long Beach

Amira Wegenek
Saddleback College

Karen Yanowitz
Arkansas State University

Tammy Zacchilli
Saint Leo University

It has truly been a pleasure to work with Worth Publishers. Bill Davis encouraged me to pursue this project, and Charles Linsmeier, now Vice President, Social Sciences and High School, provided excellent and greatly appreciated direction as this project's Editor in its early years. Dan DeBonis, who spearheaded the project since taking over as Editor, has simply been tremendous in his passionate support of the project, in providing me with numerous resources that have enhanced the book, and in his sincere desire to understand the needs of research methods instructors. Development Editor Elsa Peterson, with whom I have worked on prior textbook projects, has—as always—made many invaluable suggestions about the textbook's content, style, and artwork that go well beyond the normal call of duty. Her careful editing and attention to detail—along with similarly invaluable editing by Copy Editor Patti Brecht—are reflected on every page of the textbook.

I would also like to express my appreciation to Tracey Kuehn, Director of Content Management Enhancement, and Lisa Kinne, Managing Editor, for their wonderful support and input, and to the employees at codeMantra for their excellent production work. I want to thank Jodi Isman, the book's Senior Project Editor, for her tremendous effort in coordinating the many facets of the book's scheduling, copyediting, proofreading, typesetting, and production. I also wish to thank Katie Pachnos, Assistant Editor, who handled the reviews, production paperwork, and other miscellanea with the utmost speed and grace; Sarah Segal, Production Manager, who assisted with the production scheduling and was our liaison with the printer; and Sheena Goldstein, Photo Editor. Finally, I owe a tremendous debt of gratitude to Macmillan Learning's leadership, for fostering an organizational culture and commitment to quality that makes members of the Worth team—authors included—feel supported and appreciated. The passion, dedication, and expertise of everyone I have known at Worth are truly impressive. Thank you so much.

SCIENCE AND PSYCHOLOGY

CHAPTER OUTLINE

S arah is about to make a decision and wants your help. She is a contestant on a TV game show and is looking at three doors, labeled 1, 2, and 3. There is a fabulous prize behind one of the doors: a brand-new car. Behind each of the other two doors there is only a booby prize: a goat. Sarah doesn't want a goat, and her college roommate isn't thrilled about that prospect either. Here are the game rules:

- Monty is the game show host. He knows which door reveals the car and which two doors reveal the goats. Sarah does not know.

- Sarah picks a door. The door will remain closed for now.

- Monty will then open one of the other two doors and show her what's behind it. For example, if Sarah picks Door 1, then Monty will open either Door 2 or Door 3.

- The door Monty opens will *always* have a goat behind it. No matter what door Sarah picks, at least one of the other two doors has to have a goat behind it. If Sarah picks Door 1 and the car is behind Door 3, then Monty will open Door 2. If the car is behind Door 2, then Monty will open Door 3. If the car is behind Door 1 (the door she chose), then Monty will open either Door 2 or Door 3.

- The moment of suspense arrives. Monty has just shown Sarah a door with a goat behind it, so there are only two doors left. He offers Sarah a choice: She can keep the original door that she chose (Door 1) *or* she can switch to the other door.

Sarah isn't sure what to do. She really wants that car. If Sarah's goal is to maximize her chance of winning the car, what advice would you give her: Should she stay with her original choice, or should she switch to the other door?

Before discussing your advice, I want to welcome you to the research methods course. No matter your reason for enrolling, the principles covered in your methods class can have many important connections to your life: They will give you the power to change how you evaluate information and think about the world around you. I sincerely hope you will find the course intellectually stimulating and educational. Now let's get back to Sarah.

HOW DO WE KNOW?

Learning Objectives

After studying this section, you should be able to:

- Explain how tenacity, authority, reason, empiricism, and systematic empiricism differ as methods of acquiring knowledge and beliefs.
- Illustrate these ways of knowing, using the three-door problem or another example.

Sarah's hypothetical game show scenario is called the three-door problem. As you will see, its solution highlights several themes central to science and the research process: the need for sound reasoning, the importance of gathering relevant data in an organized manner, and the willingness to modify our beliefs when it becomes apparent that they are wrong. These themes will emerge as we use the three-door problem to illustrate basic concepts about how we acquire knowledge and beliefs. In turn, these concepts will establish a foundation for discussing goals and characteristics of science.

THE THREE-DOOR PROBLEM

When I pose the three-door problem to my own students, about 90% of them say that it makes no difference whether Sarah stays or switches. "It's 50–50 either way," they confidently assert. Smirks and eye rolls accompany comments such as "It's a trick question. With two doors left, she has a 50% shot with each one."

Was "it makes no difference" your response as well? When I first read the three-door problem in *Parade Magazine* years ago, I confidently concluded that the odds of winning would be the same regardless of staying or switching: "Hah—it's obviously 50–50." Obvious, yes; but also wrong. In fact, the odds will be 2 to 1 in Sarah's favor if she switches doors. At least that's the claim made by the famous magazine columnist who brought this brain teaser to the public's attention. Is she right?

To find out, let's cover some history. The three-door problem is loosely based on the original (1960s–1970s) version of a current American TV game show called *Let's Make A Deal*. In 1990 a reader of *Parade Magazine* posed the problem to Marilyn vos Savant, who has written the "Ask Marilyn" column for the weekly magazine since 1986. Readers send her brain teasers, trying to stump her, and vos Savant invariably solves them. On her website, vos Savant notes that she was listed for 5 years in the *Guinness Book of World Records* under the category of "Highest IQ."

Vos Savant's answer to the three-door problem touched off such a firestorm of controversy that, to this day, many websites discuss how to solve it. In her column, vos Savant stated that the contestant (our "Sarah") should switch doors because a "switch strategy" will result in a two-thirds probability of winning the car, whereas a "stay strategy" produces only a one-third chance of winning. In the following months, despite further explanation by vos Savant for her answer, letters of disbelief and complaint flooded in to *Parade Magazine* from mathematicians, statisticians, scientists, and other readers. Table 1.1 shows excerpts from several letters.

Table 1.1 Feedback Sent to vos Savant Following Her "Switch" Solution to the Three-Door Problem

Each of the first three comments was sent in response to vos Savant's initial or expanded answer, both of which were published in *Parade Magazine* in 1990. The last response was sent following further discussion of the problem in the magazine a year later. All responses are from college faculty members (PhDs), except for the last one.	You blew it, and you blew it big! . . . Shame!
	I'm very concerned with the general public's lack of mathematical skills. Please help by confessing your error and in the future being more careful.
	You are utterly incorrect. . . . How many irate mathematicians are needed to get you to change your mind?
	I still think you're wrong. There is such a thing as female logic.

Source: vos Savant (2006, paras. 3, 4, 9, 58).

The following year, vos Savant explained her answer further, and suggested that readers conduct an experiment to discover the solution for themselves (more on this shortly). Although many readers now wrote to say they agreed with her, others continued to say she was wrong. Publicity about the three-door controversy spread and the problem made its way into an episode of a popular prime-time TV show (*NUMB3RS*) and a Hollywood movie (*21*).

So who was correct: vos Savant or her critics? If you believe that Sarah's odds of winning the car are 50/50 regardless of whether she stays with her choice or switches to the other door, it is likely because you—like so many experts—have overlooked a key element of the problem: Once Sarah chooses Door 1, the sequence of events that follows is not random. Monty does not randomly open one of the three doors to show Sarah what's behind it. Rather, to maintain suspense, he must open one of the doors she did not choose (i.e., either Door 2 or Door 3). Furthermore, if the car happens to be behind Door 2 or Door 3, then he has only one choice: to open the door that reveals a goat. This nonrandom sequence of events makes it more likely that Sarah will win if she switches doors, and Table 1.2 provides a step-by-step analysis to show why this is so. Now, let's consider the three-door problem in the context of several methods of acquiring knowledge and forming beliefs.

TENACITY: KNOWING BY FORCE OF HABIT

Despite vos Savant's logical analysis of the three-door problem and other evidence that we'll discuss soon, some readers tenaciously maintained that her answer was wrong, as if stating, "I don't care about your evidence. It's like flipping a coin. It simply has to be 50–50 because there are only two doors left." The last quote in Table 1.1 reflects such a response, inanely dismissing vos Savant's arguments because, as the letter writer confidently knows, women have their own brand of logic.

Philosopher and scientist Charles Peirce (1877), in an article titled "Illustrations of the Logic of Science: The Fixation of Belief," described four methods by which people come to

Table 1.2 The Use of Reason: A Logical Analysis of All Possible Outcomes in the Three-Door Problem, When Initially Selecting Door 1

	Door 1	Door 2	Door 3	Outcome
Possibility 1	Car	Goat	Goat	If you stay, you win. Switch, you lose.
Possibility 2	Goat	Car	Goat	If you stay, you lose. Switch, you win.
Possibility 3	Goat	Goat	Car	If you stay, you lose. Switch, you win.

Analysis

In our example, Sarah has chosen Door 1. Each of the three doors has a one-third probability of having the car behind it.

A. Possibility 1: The car is behind Door 1. Monty cannot show Sarah Door 1 (it's the door she picked), so he shows Sarah the goat behind either Door 2 or Door 3. Sarah now chooses whether to switch to the other unopened door or stay with Door 1. If she switches, she loses the car. If she stays with Door 1, she wins the car.

B. Possibility 2: The car is behind Door 2. Monty cannot show Sarah Door 1 (it's the door she picked) or Door 2 (it has the car behind it). He must show her the goat behind Door 3. If Sarah switches and takes the other unopened door (Door 2), she wins the car. If she stays with Door 1, she loses the car.

C. Possibility 3: The car is behind Door 3. Monty cannot show Sarah Door 1 (it's the door she picked) or Door 3 (it has the car behind it). He must show her the goat behind Door 2. If Sarah switches and takes the other unopened door (Door 3), she wins the car. If she stays with Door 1, she loses the car.

D. Conclusion: In two out of three possible cases—if the car randomly happens to be behind Door 2 or Door 3—Sarah will win the car if she switches doors. In only one out of the three possible cases—if the car randomly happens to be behind Door 1—Sarah will win if she sticks with Door 1. Her odds of winning are twice as great if she switches.

hold beliefs about the world: tenacity, authority, reason, and science. **Tenacity** *involves believing something simply because it is what we have long believed.* With tenacity, there is no exploration of one's beliefs, no contemplation of opposing viewpoints. Rather, it entails closing oneself off to information that threatens a firmly held belief. Although Peirce viewed tenacity as a poor method upon which to base one's knowledge, he noted that it possessed "strength, simplicity, and directness" (1877, V, para. 12).

Of course, tenaciously held beliefs may be correct. We can distinguish between the method upon which knowledge is based and the accuracy of that knowledge. But tenacity, says Peirce, is like the proverbial ostrich putting its head in the ground and then, no longer seeing danger, assuming that everything is all right. Refusing to consider contrary evidence reduces the likelihood of forming accurate beliefs. And this brings us to Hawthorne, the cranky crab in Figure 1.1. Despite mounting evidence in support of global warming, some scientists' weighing of the evidence still leaves them unconvinced. That's well and good; scientific dissent often provides the spark for further and even more rigorous evidence gathering. Hawthorne's broad skepticism, however, seems based merely on tenacity, as his views on a "round earth" make clear.

AUTHORITY: KNOWLEDGE GAINED FROM OTHERS

Authority *involves relying on other people as our source of knowledge and beliefs,* and it's pervasive throughout our life. In childhood, we begin to rely on parents, other caregivers, siblings, teachers, members of the clergy, friends, television, radio, the web, books—you name it—for all sorts of knowledge. As a college student, you rely on authority when you acquire

Sherman's Lagoon

Figure 1.1 An example of tenacity. ("Sherman's Lagoon" used with the permission of Jim Toomey, King Features Syndicate and the Cartoonist Group. All rights reserved.)

knowledge from your professors and textbooks. If you decide not to take a course from a particular instructor because a friend says, "Don't do it, his lectures are really boring," then you have relied on your friend as an authority.

We are more likely to rely on others for information when we perceive them as *credible*, and, in general, we are most likely to view someone as credible when the following are true:

- We believe that the person has expertise on the subject.

- We perceive the person as trustworthy.

Relying on authority can be highly efficient. It's how society passes down knowledge from one generation to the next so that each new generation doesn't have to reinvent the wheel. Authority also has limitations and pitfalls. For one thing, experts may disagree. Second, even if they agree, it's still possible that they are wrong. This is what made the controversy over the three-door problem so fascinating. Many mathematicians, statisticians, and scientists who wrote to vos Savant claimed she was wrong.

Authority's other pitfalls occur when we attribute expertise to sources that don't merit it or dismiss expert sources as being untrustworthy because their message contradicts our beliefs. In this modern age when you can access the web, type in a few search terms, and instantly be linked to tons of information, there are additional dangers in uncritically relying on authority. First, people who are not experts can pass themselves off as such and post inaccurate information or quack advice that readers accept as valid. Second, we can be swayed by quackery and nonsense even if a source claims no special expertise. For some people, just seeing information "on the web" or "on TV" may lead them to assume that the information is accurate.

Given that we all rely on authority at times, how do we minimize these dangers? One key is to evaluate the source carefully, to try to assess the person's credentials. Another key is to think critically about the information itself. What evidence is provided to support the claim? Are there other explanations that could account for the evidence? We'll discuss critical thinking more fully later in the chapter.

REASON: RELYING ON LOGIC AND RATIONALITY

In everyday life, the word *reason* has many meanings. As Peirce (1877) employed it, **reason** *rests on the use of logic and rational (i.e., intellectually sound) argument to reach a conclusion about how things "must be."* He focused on reason in the sense that many philosophers would try to resolve questions about the nature of reality through systems of logical argument. For example, his contemporaries would use reason to consider the question of whether the mind is an entity separate from the body.

Logic and rational argument are integral to science, in the form of *reasoning,* the process of forming judgments (e.g., inferences, conclusions) based on facts or premises. Scientists use reasoning when they construct theories to account for known facts and when they derive hypotheses from theories in order to test those theories. But scientific knowledge is not based on the method of reason. The primary limitation of the method of reason is that different logical conclusions can be drawn depending on the premises one begins with. Consider the following example about infants' understanding of *object permanence*, the concept that objects continue to exist even when they are out of sight.

	1	2
Premise	Infants are not capable of understanding the concept of object permanence until they are 9 months old.	All infants understand the concept of object permanence by the time they are 7 months old.
Premise	Alice is a 7-month-old infant.	Alice is a 7-month-old infant.
Conclusion	Therefore, Alice is not capable of understanding the concept of object permanence.	Therefore, Alice understands the concept of object permanence.

Although opposite conclusions are reached, both conclusions are logically valid as long as their respective premises are true. But in reality, both conclusions cannot be true. Moreover, in the real world of human behavior, it may be that neither premise is true. Perhaps 70% of infants understand object permanence by 7 months of age (thus, Premise 1 is wrong), but it is not until 12 months of age that all infants understand it (thus, Premise 2 is wrong). In this case, we would have to phrase our conclusion in probabilistic terms: There is a 70% chance that Alice understands the concept of object permanence.

Pure reason is a poor basis for understanding behavior: It cannot establish the age at which children understand object permanence, nor the variability in their age of understanding. Nor can reason alone establish the functions of different brain structures, what type of psychotherapy is most effective for treating depression, or countless other answers to questions about how and why we think, feel, and behave as we do.

With regard to the three-door problem, you might expect that vos Savant's logical analysis would have ended the controversy. But this is not what happened. Many readers still doubted her answer, a response consistent with findings from many decision-making experiments that indicate people often draw incorrect conclusions on tasks that require basic logical and statistical reasoning (Toplak, West, & Stanovich, 2014). It was not until readers systematically gathered evidence and saw the results with their own eyes, that almost all of their letters to vos Savant acknowledged that her answer was correct. This leads us to two other ways of knowing: empiricism and science (systematic empiricism).

EMPIRICISM: KNOWLEDGE BASED ON EXPERIENCE

A great deal of what we know comes directly from our senses: from what we see, hear, touch, and so forth. *Knowledge based on the senses—on experiences with the world—is called* **empirical knowledge.** The related term, **empiricism,** *is the process of acquiring knowledge directly through observation and experience.* Empiricism also has another common meaning: *It is the philosophical viewpoint that all knowledge is derived from experience.*

Empiricism is a central building block of science—but for each of us, as we individually learn about the world and form beliefs based on our direct experiences, empiricism has limitations and risks. First, no matter how full and varied our lives are, none of us experience everything. It's not likely that in our lifetime we will experience prolonged weightlessness from months spent in outer space. Instead, we acquire knowledge about the bodily and psychological effects of prolonged weightlessness by relying on scientific research and credible experts (e.g., rigorously selected and trained astronauts) who have had those experiences.

Second, our experiences may not be representative of other people's experiences or, more broadly, of the general state of affairs in the world. Based on differing interactions with a job supervisor, you and another employee may believe that she is a mean-spirited, poor leader, while the other 10 employees in your department may believe she is a kind, helpful, effective leader. If you assume that all your fellow employees feel the way you do, you'll be sorely mistaken. Their knowledge may be different because they've had different experiences.

Third, even if our experiences are representative, we may interpret or remember them in a biased manner. Your supervisor may act fairly toward all her employees, but you and your colleague might be hypersensitive to criticism. Therefore, remarks she makes that you interpret as critisicm may be interpreted by most employees as constructive feedback. Moreover, perhaps there were times when your supervisor was genuinely helpful, but now you only make the effort to recall instances of perceived criticism or only talk about the supervisor with your one colleague who shares your negative opinion. Psychologists use the term **confirmation bias** to refer to *the tendency to selectively gather or interpret information in a manner that supports our views, thereby reducing exposure to disconfirming information* (Rajsic, Wilson, & Pratt, 2015).

Unrepresentative outcomes, biased memory, and confirmation bias illustrate a broader problem with relying on our own or other people's (even experts') personal experiences as a basis for drawing accurate conclusions about the natural world. There may be **plausible alternative explanations,** *credible reasons for why something has occurred, that differ from our belief or conclusion about it.*

In the three-door game, an empirical approach would be to play the game, or observe others playing it, and see what happens. So you observe Sarah playing: She stays with her original choice, and she wins the car. You observe three more contestants: One "stays" but doesn't win, one "switches" and wins, and one "switches" and loses. "OK," you say, "I was right after all: It's 50–50. Two people stayed, two people switched, and with each strategy one lost and one won." But even though this conclusion is empirically based, it is flawed because it is based on only four observations, too few to establish a reliable pattern of results.

SCIENCE: RELYING ON SYSTEMATIC EMPIRICISM

Science represents a field of study, a body of knowledge, and a process for acquiring knowledge. Here, we are interested in the process of science. Broadly speaking, **science** *is a process of systematically gathering and evaluating empirical evidence to answer questions and test ideas.* The phrase "systematically gathering and evaluating empirical evidence," or *systematic empiricism* for short, reveals three important aspects of science:

- Science relies on empirical evidence. Reason alone does not constitute sufficient evidence, nor do claims made by authorities without good empirical evidence to back up those assertions.

- Evidence is not gathered and interpreted haphazardly. Although informal observations often play a key role in stimulating scientists' curiosity and lead to important questions and ideas, the evidence to answer those questions or test those ideas is gathered according to a system or plan.

- Collecting evidence without evaluating it and drawing conclusions will not get us very far; we need to use *reasoning*. Reasoning plays a key role in science, both in evaluating evidence and in forming questions and ideas.

Our grand finale to the three-door problem illustrates the value of systematic empiricism. Vos Savant (2006) reported that after publishing her initial answer to the three-door problem, she received thousands of letters from the general public. Of these, 92% stated that her advice to switch doors was wrong. Among letters from people at universities and colleges, 65% stated that she was wrong. After the publication of her 1991 article that provided more details about the logic behind her answer (see Table 1.2), 44% of the letters received from the general public and 29% from people at academic institutions still contended she was wrong.

In that 1991 article, vos Savant (2006) also called upon her readers to perform a nationwide experiment to test the issue. She asked students in math classes across the country to simulate the three-door problem. Students were to pair up, with one member of each pair playing the role of the game show host and the other the role of the contestant. Each pair was asked to simulate 200 trials in which they adopted a "stay" strategy and 200 trials using a "switch" strategy. This would generate thousands of trials per class. Many classes did this, and other people performed computer simulations. Vos Savant reported that among the letters she received from people who conducted the simulation "by hand," virtually 100% now believed that she was correct and that switching increased the odds of winning. Among people who simulated the game on a computer, 97% of them now believed she was correct. One scientist wrote:

> After considerable discussion and vacillation here at the Los Alamos National Laboratory, two of my colleagues independently programmed the problem, and in 1,000,000 trials, switching paid off 66.7% of the time. The total running time on the computer was less than one second. (DeVault, cited in vos Savant, 2006)

If you still doubt that switching doors is the best strategy, you can systematically gather your own evidence. Type "Monty Hall problem simulation" into your web browser and see what simulations are available (several are, as of this writing). Select one and try to play a minimum of 100 trials; it usually takes only a few seconds per trial.

✓ CONCEPT CHECK 1.1 HOW DO WE KNOW?

Does each example below best illustrate reliance on tenacity, authority, reason, empiricism, or systematic empiricism as a way of knowing? Answers appear on page 29 at the end of the chapter.

1. Trevor wants to buy a new smartphone, so he reads phone reviews by experts on cnet.com and endgadget.com.
2. Four-year-old Shonda has a watercolor paint kit. She's curious about what color she will get if she mixes red and green paint, so she does it a few times to find out.
3. Claire takes her first multiple-choice test in junior high. When the graded test is returned to her, she pays attention only to the items she got wrong. She notices three questions for which she had initially chosen the correct answer but, after reconsidering, switched to a wrong answer. She fails to notice even more items for which she initially picked the wrong answer but switched to the correct answer. She concludes that "on multiple-choice tests, you should always stick with your first instinct."
4. In college, Claire learns that research consistently suggests the advice to "always stick with your first instinct on multiple-choice exams" is wrong. On average, when switching answers, students are more likely to change a wrong answer to a correct answer than vice versa. Claire rejects this and sticks with her "first-instinct" belief.

GOALS OF SCIENCE

Learning Objectives

After studying this section, you should be able to:

- Discuss four goals of science.
- Describe the concepts of distal and proximal causation as well as criteria for drawing a causal inference.
- Describe two contexts in which prediction and control are scientific goals.

Scientists seek to describe, explain, predict, and control events. These events are often analyzed in terms of variables. A **variable** *is any factor or attribute that can assume two or more values.* The variables that psychologists typically study are characteristics that differ across individuals, situations, or time. For example, people differ from one another—and change within themselves over time—in height, cognitive abilities, hormone levels, sleep patterns, attitudes, and numerous other ways. Groups and cultures differ in social norms and ethnic composition. Daily temperature, the length of word lists, and sound decibel levels vary. Research typically involves describing variables and associations between variables, explaining what causes something to vary, and predicting and controlling variables.

DESCRIPTION

One of scientists' most fundamental tasks is to describe phenomena. This goal is sometimes stated as "describing or uncovering the laws of nature," but description assumes many forms. Identifying the existence of new stars, cataloging species of plants, measuring the prevalence of various mental disorders, and determining whether students' choice of college major is related to their gender all exemplify the goal of description. For most psychologists, description involves identifying how people behave, feel, and think in various settings. Other psychologists describe the behavior of nonhuman species. Description often involves developing coding systems that identify different types of behavior that could occur in a given situation. For example, psychologists use coding systems to record types of mental disorders, facial expressions, and parenting behaviors.

Psychologists often describe many aspects of behavior within a single study. For instance, developmental psychologists who study bullying might observe elementary-school children and describe (1) how frequently bullying occurs in various settings (e.g., the classroom, the playground), (2) the sex of the bully and victim, and (3) the form of bullying (e.g., verbal, physical). The researchers could also describe whether relations exist among these variables, to answer questions such as "Do boys differ from girls in the forms of bullying they use?"

EXPLANATION

Scientists want to understand why phenomena occur. Once we have described how people behave, the question arises: "Why do they behave that way?" Phrased differently: "What causes people to respond as they do?"

Scientists' initial explanations often take the form of a **hypothesis**, *which is a tentative proposition about the causes or outcome of an event or, more generally, about how variables are related.* Hypotheses are tentative statements about how the world operates, and they are subject to empirical testing. Scientific hypotheses are more than "mere hunches." Scientists form hypotheses by reasoning about events, taking into account relevant existing scientific knowledge and other background information.

Ultimately, as empirical evidence on a particular phenomenon accumulates, scientists build theories. A **theory** *is a set of formal statements that specifies how and why variables or events are related.* Theories are broader than hypotheses. For example, a theory can be used to derive many new, more specific hypotheses. But theories themselves differ in scope. Some theories cast a wide net. Sigmund Freud's psychoanalytic theory sought to explain the structure, development, and workings of human personality. In contrast, many theories have a relatively narrow scope: One theory may explain how we perceive color and another how we hear sounds.

People often misuse the term *theory* in everyday life, tossing the word about as if it means "It's only a guess." This may happen when people are arguing against or trying to dismiss a scientific position, such as "Evolution: It's only a theory." This usage reflects a complete lack of understanding about the nature of scientific theories. For an explanation to achieve the status of a theory, it must be consistent with evidence. As we will explore further in Chapter 2, theories may be revised as new evidence accrues and may ultimately be replaced by better theories, but this reflects a normal progression of scientific inquiry.

The tasks of developing theories and explaining behavior are complex for several reasons. First, psychologists view causes of behavior from different perspectives. Biopsychological explanations focus on the role of genes, hormones, and brain functioning. Environmental explanations focus on the causal effects of physical stimuli and social experiences. From what is broadly called a "psychological" perspective, explanations focus on the role of factors such as conscious and unconscious motivational and cognitive processes.

Second, even within a perspective, multiple causes may affect behavior simultaneously. Research can capture some of this complexity and examine the joint influence of several variables, but even so, an individual study can isolate only a few of many potential causes.

A third complexity involves the distinction between distal and proximal causes. If we view causality as a chain of interrelated events, then **distal causes** *are the remote causes* and **proximal** (or **proximate**) **causes** *are the immediate causes*. Consider **Figure 1.2**, which shows a simplified version of a biological causal chain proposed to help explain the development of schizophrenia (Walker, Shapiro, Esterberg, & Trotman, 2010). Genetic inheritance, genetic mutations, and prenatal insults represent the most distal causes in the proposed chain. They create a biological vulnerability to schizophrenia that is present at birth but typically is not activated until after puberty begins.

Next, maturational changes in hormonal activity during puberty represent an intermediate causal position. For biologically vulnerable people, there is an increased risk that these hormonal changes will eventually help trigger neuropathological processes (e.g., brain degeneration, dopamine hyperactivity) that produce the full onset of schizophrenia. Figure 1.2 portrays neuropathological processes as proximal causes of schizophrenia. Stress also plays a proposed role in these neuropathological processes because it can worsen abnormal brain functioning. In sum, in trying to explain behavior, scientists often must take multiple causes into account.

A fourth complexity in explaining behavior is the fact that the conditions needed to make a **causal inference**—*to conclude that one variable had a causal effect on another variable*—are more stringent than merely demonstrating that the two variables are associated with one another. For the moment, let's designate our two variables as X and Y, and then consider a concrete example. In practice, researchers infer that X has caused an effect on Y when three conditions are met:

1. *Covariation.* As X changes or varies, Y changes or varies.

2. *Temporal order.* The change or variation in X occurs before the change or variation in Y.

3. *The absence of plausible alternative explanations.* The presence of other factors that might plausibly have caused a result (in this case, the change or variation in Y) must be ruled out.

It is this third criterion that often proves most challenging in research. In science, as in everyday life, the failure to consider plausible alternative explanations can lead to false beliefs about how the world operates. Consider this example. Two researchers hypothesize that when teams perform tasks, stronger team cohesion (variable X) causes teams to perform better (variable Y). The researchers receive permission to study all the teams in a collegiate women's basketball conference. Preseason, all players rate their team's level of cohesiveness on a questionnaire by indicating how strongly they agree or disagree with items such as "we are a tight knit unit" and "I like all of my teammates." The researchers compute a total cohesion score for each team and,

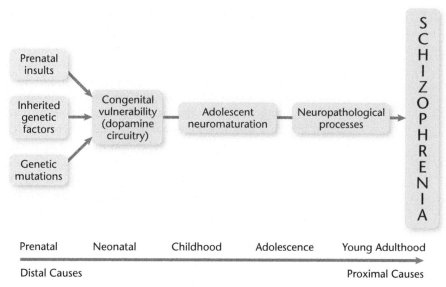

Figure 1.2 A proposed causal chain. In this proposed model, prenatal insults, inherited genetic factors, and genetic mutations are the most distal causes of schizophrenia. Neuropathological processes are the most promixate causes. (Adapted with permission from American Psychological Science from "Neurodevelopment and Schizophrenia: Broadening the Focus," by E. Walker, D. Shapiro, M. Esterberg, and H. Trotman, 2010, *Current Directions in Psychological Science, 19*, pp. 204–208 [Figure 1, p. 207].)

after the regular season ends, they record the percentage of games won by each team. Based on the hypothesis, they predict that, overall, teams with higher levels of preseason cohesion will win a higher percentage of games in the upcoming regular conference season. The findings support the prediction and the researchers conclude that stronger cohesion caused better performance.

Unfortunately, this causal conclusion is not justified because there are plausible alternative explanations for the researchers' findings. For instance, here is one factor the researchers did not take into account: the coaches' ability. Perhaps, before the season started, the better coaches were more skilled at creating tight knit, cohesive teams. And, throughout the season, these coaches may have fostered better team performance by having superior game plans and more effectively motivating players and improving players' skills. Thus, it is possible that although more cohesive teams won more games, team cohesion did not play any causal role in producing this greater success.

In sum, the alternative explanation is that better coaching caused stronger team cohesion and also greater team success, and this is why the researchers found a statistical relation between cohesion and success. Based on how the researchers conducted their study, we cannot rule out this alternative explanation, and this creates ambiguity in interpreting the results. The importance of thinking critically about plausible alternative explanations—whether in designing studies, interpreting research results, or evaluating claims in everyday life—will be a frequent theme throughout this book.

PREDICTION

Along with description and explanation, prediction is another key scientific goal. Prediction plays two major roles in scientific research: hypothesis and theory testing, and applied prediction. First, prediction is the strongest means by which scientists determine whether their explanations for events are correct. If we truly understand why an event occurs—what causes it—then we should be able to predict the circumstances under which that event will occur. For example, suppose we hypothesize that frustration is one factor that explains why people act aggressively. This hypothesis can be phrased in the form of an *if–then statement*: If people become frustrated, then they will be more likely to act aggressively. Likewise, the cohesion–performance hypothesis we discussed in the previous section could be rephrased as: If teams have stronger cohesion, then this will cause them to perform better than teams with weaker cohesion.

Next, we can use this if–then statement to generate a specific prediction about an expected outcome in a research study. For example, we might predict that in an experiment, "Compared to people who succeed in solving an important problem, people who fail to solve the problem will experience greater frustration and subsequently display greater verbal hostility toward another person." Similarly, the cohesion–performance hypothesis led to the prediction that in a women's collegiate basketball conference, teams with stronger preseason cohesion would have a higher regular season winning percentage. Evidence gathered by conducting a study might support our prediction, which would tentatively strengthen our belief that our hypothesized explanation is correct. We say "tentatively strengthen" rather than "prove" because it's always possible that a design limitation, procedural flaw, or other factor caused our results, or that evidence from future studies will not support our hypothesis. The results of the cohesion–performance study, for example, were consistent with the hypothesis, which supports the possibility that cohesion may have indeed influenced performance. But the study's design and procedures did not permit a clear causal conclusion to be drawn, due to the presence of plausible alternative explanations for the findings.

If the results of our initial study fail to support our prediction, then our hypothesis that "frustration causes aggression," or that team cohesion enhances team performance, may be incorrect or too simplistic. Perhaps frustration causes aggression, and cohesion boosts performance, under some circumstances but not others. If so, we'll need to develop a more sophisticated hypothesis about the relation between these variables and test its accuracy by conducting more research. Before doing so, we'll also need to reevaluate our initial study's methodology. Perhaps the study's design or procedures were flawed, and thus provided a poor test of our hypothesis. If so, we will want to improve the study and retest our hypothesis.

Testing hypotheses plays a critical role in building and assessing the validity of scientific theories. Scientists often develop hypotheses based on a theory and then put those hypotheses to the test. Evidence for or against a theory mounts as hypotheses are supported or not supported by empirical evidence. A hypothesis, however, does not have to be based on a theory. Especially in the early stages of research on a topic, no theory may exist. Instead, scientists may form hypotheses based on their knowledge about a topic and whatever evidence might already exist about it.

Prediction's second major role in science is more applied. If we know that two events or two variables are related to each other, then we can use our knowledge about one event or variable to make predictions about the other. In medicine, researchers have identified risk factors associated with developing particular diseases. Smoking is a well-established risk factor for developing lung cancer, in this case because research has demonstrated that smoking plays a causal role in producing lung cancer.

Predictions also can be used for practical purposes even when a causal relation between two variables does not exist or has not yet been established. To make such a prediction, all we need to know is that two variables are statistically associated with each other. For example, high-school grades are used to predict students' academic performance in college. Obviously, high-school grades don't *cause* college grades, but because they're associated with college grades, college administrators can use them to estimate (albeit imperfectly) how well college applicants are likely to perform. Moreover, in science and everyday life, prediction does not even require an understanding of why variables are associated. A child may not know why thunder follows lightning but can predict that when lightning flashes close by, it's time to cover the ears.

CONTROL

To control something is to exert influence over it, and there are two major contexts in which scientists attempt to achieve control. First, when conducting research, having control means being able to decide what variables to study, how and when to measure them, who the participants will be, and how many participants will be studied. When scientists want to examine whether one variable (X) has a causal effect on another variable (Y), they also achieve control by manipulating X and then measuring whether this produces a change in Y. For example, suppose we hypothesize that exposure to hot weather (X) increases people's aggression (Y). To test this hypothesis, we could examine official weather and police crime records from 20 cities, then calculate for the past year whether crime increased as daily temperatures increased. Although we would have some control in this situation (we choose the cities and time period to study), we certainly have no control over daily temperatures or the completeness of police crime records. Nor do we have control over many other factors (e.g., daily humidity, the number of people away on vacation) that might influence the daily amount of crime.

Similarly, the team cohesion–performance example illustrates how conducting research in a real-life setting usually reduces the ability to control, and thus eliminate, factors that might provide plausible alternative explanations for the findings. If we were to plan that study, we might try to obtain preseason measures of the coaches' ability (e.g., ratings by experts, such as scouts) so that we could assess whether this variable provides a credible alternative explanation for the cohesion–performance relation we expect to obtain. Still, there are many other factors, such as differences in the overall ability and the number of new players on teams and in the difficulty of nonconference opponents, that we can't directly control yet would have to try to rule out as possible alternative explanations. To gain the most control, researchers conduct laboratory experiments. For example, in a laboratory experiment, we can exercise control by manipulating the temperature of a room in order to expose people to different levels of heat. We can also exercise control by keeping the humidity and other environmental factors (e.g., noise level) constant. We will need to design a way to measure aggression, but that's under our control as well.

To study how team or group cohesion influences performance in a controlled laboratory experiment, we would face the challenging task of creating high- versus low-cohesion groups, such as by manipulating whether group members actually are, or perceive themselves to be, similar (high cohesion) or dissimilar (low cohesion) to one another on certain attributes (Karau & Hart, 1998). Moreover, we would need to manipulate group cohesion in a way that keeps the teams equivalent on other important factors (e.g., experience, task ability) that could affect how well they perform on the experimental task we choose. In this way, we could rule out those other factors as plausible alternative explanations for our findings. As you will learn in later chapters, experimental and nonexperimental methods have unique advantages and disadvantages, but the key point for now is that the laboratory experiment provides us with much greater control over our variables and the research setting.

The second context of control involves applying scientific knowledge to improve people's lives. Psychologists test the effectiveness of different psychotherapies, and the findings are used to help people overcome or cope with psychological disorders. Psychologists design programs to improve workers' job satisfaction, help prevent HIV/AIDS, enhance educators' ability to teach students, and improve aviation safety. In these and many other ways, psychologists and other scientists exert influence by creating interventions that, ideally, benefit people and society. In sum, taking both aspects of control into account, we can define **control** as *having influence over research settings and procedures and over the application of scientific knowledge.*

Before turning to our next topic, Figure 1.3 uses alcohol research to provide an overview of the goals of science we've discussed. Scientists gather data to describe people's alcohol consumption and factors (e.g., psychological attributes, behaviors) associated with it. They explain alcohol consumption and its effects by developing hypotheses and theories, deriving predictions, and gathering data to assess whether the predictions are accurate. Experiments test predictions under conditions of maximum control. For example, the balanced placebo design shown in Figure 1.3 has been used to test the prediction that people's alcohol expectations affect their behavior. In this design, the term *placebo* refers to a condition in which people consume a nonalcoholic drink but are convincingly led to believe they have consumed

GOALS OF SCIENCE

DESCRIPTION

Identify and describe the characteristics of a phenomenon.

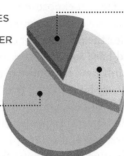

ALCOHOL USE IN THE UNITED STATES AMONG PEOPLE AGED 12 AND OLDER

≥ 5 binge episodes
16.3 million
Heavy Alcohol Users (11.7% of current users)

≥ 5 drinks on one or more occasions
60.9 million
Binge Alcohol Users (43.6% of current users)

Within past 30 days:
≥ 1 drink
139.7 million
Current Alcohol Users

National surveys find that alcohol is the most widely used recreational drug in the United States and Canada. Its use is often associated with decreased inhibition and greater risk taking (Jozkowski & Wiersma, 2015).

Center for Behavioral Health Statistics and Quality. (2015). Retrieved from http://www.samhsa.gov/data/

EXPLANATION

Develop hypotheses and theories about the causes of a phenomenon.

Image Source/DigitalVision/Getty Images

Scientists focus on biological, psychological, and situational factors to explain alcohol consumption and its behavioral effects. The concept of *alcohol expectancy* posits that one reason people may act less inhibited after drinking is that they expect alcohol to reduce their inhibitions.

PREDICTION

Formulate a testable prediction: If X, then Y.

Image Source/DigitalVision/Getty Images

Use the concept of alcohol expectancy to formulate a prediction: If people believe they have consumed alcohol, then their behavior will change in accordance with their alcohol expectations—even when the drinks they consumed were not alcoholic.

CONTROL

Isolate proposed causal factors; assess their effects on Y; rule out the potential influence of other factors.

BALANCED PLACEBO DESIGN

People are led to expect	Drink Administered	
	Alcoholic Drink (vodka + tonic)	Nonalcoholic Drink (tonic)
Alcoholic Drink	Examines joint influence of alcohol's physiological effects and people's alcohol expectancies	Examines influence of people's alcohol expectancies (placebo condition)
Non-alcoholic Drink	Examines influence of alcohol's physiological effects	Examines people's response when neither receiving nor expecting alcohol

In experiments, scientists manipulate the activation of alcohol expectancies. They may use a balanced placebo design to examine how alcohol expectations and alcohol's physiological effects separately and *jointly* influence behavior. Experiments find that people's alcohol expectations can influence their social behavior and judgments (Zawacki, 2011).

a low to moderate dose of alcohol. This mere expectation of consuming alcohol can cause people to behave in a way similar to people who have actually consumed alcohol (George, Gilmore, & Stappenbeck, 2012).

 CONCEPT CHECK 1.2 GOALS OF SCIENCE

What scientific goal—description, explanation, prediction, or control—is best illustrated by each of the following examples? Answers appear on page 30.

1. A cognitive psychologist develops a theory of human memory.

2. A company hires an industrial-organizational psychologist to develop a job aptitude test. The company will administer the test to job applicants and use the test scores to judge how well each applicant is likely to perform on the job.

3. A developmental psychologist chooses to study infants' emotional attachment by conducting a laboratory experiment rather than observing infants' natural behavior at home.

4. A team of clinical psychologists conducts a study to answer the question "Nationwide, what percentage of adults exhibit anxiety disorders?"

CHARACTERISTICS OF SCIENCE

Learning Objectives

After studying this section, you should be able to:

- Identify several scientific assumptions about the natural world.
- Describe eight other characteristics of science.
- Distinguish between empirical and nonempirical questions.

The scientific method, as it is often called, is not a single method of conducting research. Rather, it's a set of characteristics that typifies how scientists collectively go about acquiring and applying knowledge. Let's discuss a few of those characteristics.

SCIENCE INVOLVES ASSUMPTIONS

Imagine that every time you dropped or threw an object, it moved in a random path—sometimes up, sometimes down; at other times sideways, in zigzags or circles, and so forth. Now imagine that human behavior was completely random—that at any moment your actions and thoughts would be completely disconnected from what occurred the moment before. It's unthinkable, isn't it? And under such circumstances, it would be pointless to try to describe or explain the motion of objects or human behavior because the conclusion would always be that the phenomenon in question occurs randomly.

But evidence from our senses tells us that many events in the natural world—including how species behave—are not random. We know the sun will rise and set, and we can predict the timing of sunrise and sunset well in advance. We know that rivers run downhill, not uphill. And we can predict with a high degree of probability, though not absolute certainty, that during a physics or psychology lecture college students will be clothed and seated, not dancing naked in the aisles. Moreover, if events are not random, if they follow a pattern, then presumably some factor or factors are causing that pattern. And, finally, there would be little point to trying to study the causes of events unless we believed there was a way to identify those causes: to make nature give up its secrets. We have, then, three basic scientific assumptions about the natural world:

- Events are not random, but instead demonstrate regularity or pattern.

- These patterns have underlying causes.

- It is possible to discover these causes.

These three assumptions gel together into a single, more general assumption about the nature of our universe that might be stated this way in everyday language: The truth is out there, and it's waiting to be discovered.

SCIENCE IS EMPIRICAL AND SYSTEMATIC

We have already identified systematic empiricism as a cornerstone of science. This means that claims are based on evidence gathered and evaluated in a systematic manner. It means that scientific evidence gathering goes beyond the kind of casual observation that often occurs in everyday life. It's the difference between drawing a conclusion about the best "three-door problem" strategy based on noticing what happens on one or a few trials (empiricism) versus performing many trials with both the "stay" and "switch" strategies, carefully analyzing the outcomes, and then repeating the procedures to determine whether the results are the same (systematic empiricism).

SCIENCE FOCUSES ON TESTABLE QUESTIONS

On January 12, 2005, the National Aeronautics and Space Administration (NASA) launched an unmanned spacecraft called *Deep Impact*. Almost 6 months later, *Deep Impact* struck a scientific and literal bull's-eye when it released a smaller craft to collide with the comet Tempel 1, which was hurtling through space 83 million miles from Earth. Cameras on the main spacecraft recorded the collision, its aftermath, and the comet's newly revealed interior structure (NASA, 2008). It took humankind thousands of years to develop the knowledge and capabilities that made this remarkable achievement possible. Yet it only took one day for a Russian astrologer (that's *astrologer*, not *astronomer*) to slap NASA with a $300 million lawsuit for carrying out the *Deep Impact* mission. The astrologer's claim: The satellite–comet collision "ruins the natural balance of forces in the universe" (Associated Press, July 6, 2005, p. A4).

How could you possibly test the claim that the "natural balance of forces in the universe" is ruined? What forces? How many? What is their "natural balance" and what constitutes being "ruined"? The claim, as it is stated, is so vague and broad that it simply isn't testable. In contrast, the specific question of whether a spacecraft–comet impact will alter the comet's orbital path and, if so, by how much could be tested and, more importantly, measured using current technology.

Scientific research addresses questions that are testable within the limits of current technology. This does not prevent scientists, however, from asking questions or hypothesizing about events that might not be testable today but that, in principle, could be empirically studied in the future. As technology improves, scientists become capable of answering questions that their predecessors might only have dreamed about.

An **empirical question** (or **empirical claim**) *is one that, in principle, can be tested empirically: through observation.* Thus, the question of whether water ever existed on Mars was an empirical question even before spacecraft were sent there to find out, because scientists could envision a means to test it. Likewise, psychologists and other scientists can pose empirical questions about brain functioning and genetic influences on behavior that may not be testable today, but for which the necessary technology to test them can be envisioned.

How do we determine whether an assertion (i.e., a question, claim, hypothesis, or theory) is testable? There's no universally agreed-upon answer, but in practice a common criterion in science is one proposed by the eminent British/Austrian philosopher of science Karl Popper (1902–1994). Before reading further, take a few seconds to read the cartoon in Figure 1.4. Is the chemist's claim that he has discovered the potion of eternal life testable?

When I pose this question to my students, most say the claim isn't testable because we can never prove that the potion will make you live forever. After all, if we drink it and live for 5,000 years, we might still die the next day. And they're correct: We cannot prove the statement to be true. But if at any point after drinking it, we do die from natural causes, then we have shown the claim to be false. Popper's criterion for testability is called **falsifiability:** *In principle, an assertion*

"It may very well bring about immortality, but it will take forever to test it."

Figure 1.4 **Is this a testable claim?**

is testable if we can envision gathering some type of empirical evidence that will reveal the assertion to be false. In other words, although we can't prove that drinking the potion results in eternal life, we can *disprove* it. Try to apply the concept of falsifiability by looking at the 10 questions in **Table 1.3** and deciding whether each one represents an empirical or nonempirical question.

Table 1.3 Identifying Empirical and Nonempirical Questions

Ten questions appear below. Identify whether each is or is not an empirical question that science is capable of answering. The answers appear beneath the table.

1. Can money buy happiness?
2. Do humans have souls?
3. How should I live a good life?
4. Is it better to be wealthy or wise?
5. What determines our personality?
6. Is it ever moral to steal from someone else?
7. Are the mockingbird's and sparrow's songs part of their nature?
8. Is beauty in the eye of the beholder?
9. Should there be a death penalty for committing murder?
10. Does spanking children make them more aggressive?

Answers: The 1st, 5th, 7th, 8th, and 10th questions are empirical. The others are not.
To learn why, first do "Thinking Critically and Applying Your Knowledge," Exercise 1, on page 30; then see the explanations on page D-1 in Appendix D.

SCIENCE STRIVES FOR ACCURACY AND OBJECTIVITY

In everyday life, people often come away from the same event with different impressions or conclusions. This can happen because people enter those situations with divergent motives and preconceptions that serve as filters, coloring what they see and remember. Go to a sporting event and observe what happens when a referee or umpire makes a call on a close play:

Fans from one team boo and scream, "Hey, ref, open your eyes!" while fans from the other side cheer because the referee, in their view, obviously made a good call. Indeed, a classic social psychology experiment illustrated this point. Researchers showed Princeton University and Dartmouth College students the same film of an especially rough and bitter football game between the two schools and then measured the students' perceptions. According to the Princeton students, Dartmouth's team committed more than twice as many rule violations as the Dartmouth students reported seeing (Hastorf & Cantril, 1954). Whose view should we believe?

Scientists strive to measure variables accurately and conduct research in an objective, unbiased way. But scientists know they aren't robots and that, like everyone else, they have their own professional and personal outlooks that can influence the events they pay attention to and their interpretation of those events.

Fortunately, as you will learn throughout this book, when scientists collect data, they can use certain procedures to minimize the influence of their personal biases. For example, if a study tests a hypothesis, the observers who record data can be kept in the dark about the nature of that hypothesis. This can reduce the risk that the observers will form expectations about how the findings should turn out; such expectations could unconsciously bias their observations. Beyond precautionary steps that researchers can take in a particular study, the scientific process as a whole has features that promote the building of a body of knowledge that is as objective as humanly possible. Four of these characteristics are discussed next.

SCIENCE REQUIRES CLEAR DEFINITIONS

You will find three situations described in the bullets below. For each one, decide "yes" or "no": Did the person commit an act of aggression?

- An office manager screams at and repeatedly insults an employee for making an error on a project.

- A fifth-grader who doesn't like her teacher fantasizes about pushing the teacher down the stairs.

- A high-school student punches a classmate who shoved him first.

Next, present the three items to a few people and see whether their judgments agree with yours. You will likely find that people disagree about what constitutes aggression. A similar result would occur if we tried this exercise with examples illustrating concepts such as "stress," "intelligence," and "love." This illustrates that when people communicate with each other using the same terms, they may not actually mean the same thing. This can cause problems in science, just as it can in everyday life (e.g., two people who say they're in love but who differ on whether "in love" implies a monogamous commitment).

Many terms that behavioral scientists use, such as *stress* and *love,* are common in everyday life. Scientists also develop specialized terms to describe key concepts in their disciplines, terms such as *cognitive dissonance* and *semantic encoding.* Whether terms are borrowed from everyday language or are science-specific, scientists strive to define their terms clearly. Scientists may disagree about the meaning of various terms, but the key point is that if each scientist defines her or his terms clearly, then other scientists will know how the term is being used.

When scientists conduct a study, they must translate conceptual terms into specific procedures. For example, if we wish to measure the frequency of aggression among schoolchildren, we need to decide ahead of time what behaviors constitute aggression. Hitting and kicking would be examples. Should we include verbal taunts? What about intentionally damaging a student's property? Whatever we decide, the list of behaviors will represent the *operational definition* of aggression in our study. *An* **operational definition** *describes a variable in terms of the procedures (i.e., the operations) used to measure or manipulate it.* In other words, if scientists ask us, "How did you operationally define aggression in your study of schoolchildren?" they want to know the procedures we used to measure the children's aggression.

Operational definitions are central to science. As psychologists Joseph Durlak and Emily DuPre note, "Science cannot study what it cannot measure accurately and cannot measure what it does not define" (2008, p. 342). Likewise, operational definitions are important in other contexts, such as the workplace. For example, if you are an employee whose annual pay raise depends on whether you exhibited "good yearly performance," you'll want to know how the concept of "good performance" is operationally defined: How will it be measured?

SCIENCE INVOLVES PUBLIC REPORTING

Scientists publish their work in professional journals and books. This allows scientists to share their enthusiasm about their work with the scientific community, become recognized, and establish their reputations. But these are not the reasons why science, as a field, necessitates public reporting. Those reasons are threefold.

First, information must be made public if a body of knowledge about a topic is to grow. Second, when a scientist makes a claim based on a research finding, fellow scientists need to be able to evaluate the quality of that evidence. Were the operational definitions reasonable? Were there flaws in how the study was designed or executed? Were appropriate statistical analyses used? Has the researcher interpreted the findings in a reasonable manner? Are there plausible alternative explanations for what caused the findings to turn out as they did? Third, as we'll discuss shortly, public reporting enables other researchers to repeat the original study. Public reporting also obligates scientists to make their research data available to other scientists who wish to check the accuracy of the original analyses.

Different subfields within each science have their own professional journals. Scientists generally place more faith in research reports published in peer-reviewed journals than in reports published in journals that are not peer reviewed. A **peer-reviewed journal** *is a professional journal in which reports submitted for publication first undergo a screening process by several experts.* Usually two or three experts, called *reviewers*, evaluate each report in terms of its quality and importance. Each expert then sends a recommendation to the journal editor that the article should be accepted, rejected, or revised and resubmitted for further evaluation. In this last case, the researchers may be asked to gather more evidence, reanalyze their data, or consider alternative interpretations of the findings. This screening process is intended to operate as an initial quality filter. Many journals reject over 75% of the articles submitted to them; a few reject 85% or more (American Psychological Association [APA], 2016).

SCIENTIFIC KNOWLEDGE IS TENTATIVE, NOT ABSOLUTE

Until the 1960s, humans believed that they were the only species to use tools. Eventually, scientists discovered that some chimpanzee communities use tools; for example, they use rocks to break nutshells or sticks to "fish" for termites (Goodall, 1986; Ohashi, 2015). For generations, college and medical students were taught that the adult human brain did not produce new neurons. Today, we know that neurogenesis occurs in some regions of the adult human brain (Christian, Song, & Ming, 2014).

Most scientists are reluctant to claim that their evidence proves something to be true because there is always the possibility that new observations will contradict or qualify (i.e., set limits or restrictions upon) current conclusions and beliefs. As Albert Einstein once noted, "No amount of experimentation can ever prove me right; a single experiment can prove me wrong" (quoted in Calaprice, 2005). Chimpanzee tool use and adult neurogenesis are merely two of countless examples of how new information alters existing beliefs about the world. In short, this is a crucial part of what scientific progress is about: being receptive to the possibility that new knowledge may challenge or refine existing beliefs and theories.

SCIENCE IS SELF-CORRECTING

Scientific knowledge represents our current understanding of how the natural world works. New knowledge will cause some existing beliefs to be discarded or modified. Current scientific theories may need to be refined to account for new information, or they may be discarded if newer theories do a better job of explaining and predicting phenomena. In this way, the scientific approach is *self-correcting*: Our current understanding of the natural world and behavior has corrected our older understandings, just as some current understandings will be corrected by future discoveries.

Scientific self-correction also occurs in a narrower context that pertains to evaluating the validity of findings from individual studies. Sometimes researchers report a finding that, unknown to them, actually was produced by a flaw in the study's procedure or data analysis. Or the finding might be a fluke due solely to chance. Even if a report is published in a peer-reviewed journal, the experts who evaluated the article may not have detected the flaw. But once the article is published and reaches a wide scientific audience, a larger pool of current and future experts in that field can critically evaluate the soundness of the original researcher's procedures, analyses, and conclusions.

To assess the validity of the original results, scientists may decide to replicate the original study. **Replication** *is the process of repeating a study to determine whether the original findings will be upheld.* It is one of the cornerstones of science, because even when published research appears to be of the highest quality, replication allows scientists to determine whether the findings are reproducible. If replications fail to obtain results similar to those of the original study, this calls the validity of those results into question and may lead to additional research to sort things out. Ultimately, as research on the topic builds, the conclusions based on the original findings will be discarded, modified, or supported. In psychology, for example, researchers recently completed a worldwide project in which they conducted 100 replications of previous studies (Open Science Collaboration, 2015). We will discuss this project and strategies for replicating research in Chapter 10.

SCIENCE HAS LIMITATIONS

Science is hardly the only source of knowledge available to us. We gain knowledge by studying history, by reading works of literature, and through exposure to art. We acquire knowledge from our elders and from religious or other spiritual teachings. We learn from our daily experience and by expanding our horizons when we travel.

Although science has no monopoly on generating knowledge, those who work in science believe it is the best method humankind has developed for accurately understanding how the natural world operates and for distinguishing fact from fiction. But science has limitations, and chief among them is that there are important, nonempirical questions that science cannot answer. For example, science cannot tell us the meaning of life, whether God exists, or what moral values to live by. These types of questions involve value judgments or faith or other personal meanings that science cannot decide for us or dictate to us.

What science can examine, however, are questions such as "What do people think is most important in life?" and "What percent of people believe that God exists?" Science cannot tell you whether you should be religious or spiritual, but science can examine relations between people's degree of religiosity or spirituality and their age, sex, ethnicity, happiness, moral values, and beliefs about what matters most in life.

✔ **CONCEPT CHECK 1.3** CHARACTERISTICS OF SCIENCE

Fill in the blanks in the sentences below. Answers appear on page 30.

1. Three general scientific assumptions are that events _____ , _____ , and _____ .

2. Falsifiability is a criterion for judging whether a question is _____ .

3. When scientists define concepts in terms of specific procedures, such definitions are called _____ .

4. The process of repeating a study is called _____ .

BASIC AND APPLIED RESEARCH

Learning Objectives

After studying this section, you should be able to:

- Describe the primary purposes of basic and applied research.
- Discuss relations between basic and applied research.
- Recognize whether a study has basic, applied, or a mix of research goals.

Across the sciences, **basic research** *examines the fundamental nature of phenomena*. In psychology, basic research discovers principles that underlie behavior and mental processes, tests theories, and gathers other information about the fundamental nature of behavior. This research contributes to a core body of knowledge about countless topics, including genetics, brain functioning, sensation, learning, memory, life-span development, psychological disorders, social behavior, and cultural influences.

For example, psychologists from many areas—including cognitive, social, and biological psychology—conduct basic research on human decision making. They identify logical and illogical ways that decision makers think, examine brain processes that underlie decision making, and study how situational, personality, and cultural factors influence people's decisions. The primary focus of this basic research is not to solve practical decision-making problems. Rather, the focus is to explore the fundamental process of how people make decisions.

In science, **applied research** *directly focuses on helping to solve or evaluate a specific real-world problem*. A friend of mine has spent his career as an applied research psychologist. One of his projects sought to help the U.S. Army find ways to increase soldiers' enrollment in the army's college continuing education program (Orvis, McDonald, Raymond, & Wu, 2005). Similarly, when researchers developed parent-tutoring interventions to enhance the reading ability of schoolchildren who had learning disabilities, they were conducting applied research (Gortmaker, Daly, McCurdy, Persampieri, & Hergenrader, 2007).

Although research can often be clearly classified as basic or applied, to varying degrees many studies encompass both basic and applied goals. Consider this example.

When the twin 110-story towers of New York City's World Trade Center (WTC) opened for business in the early 1970s, they were the tallest buildings in the world. Before their construction, WTC engineers were concerned about whether people working on the highest floors would notice and be bothered by the expected sway of the buildings caused by winds (Benson, 2003). They searched for psychological research on this direct issue but found none. So the WTC's chief engineer contacted Paul Hoffman, a former University of Oregon psychology professor who had recently founded an independent research institute. The engineer asked Hoffman to perform the needed research, but Hoffman initially declined. Hoffman was interested in conducting basic research and viewed this project as applied research.

Upon reflection, Hoffman realized that this research would indeed involve basic science as well. It would address a fundamental question about human sensation and perception:

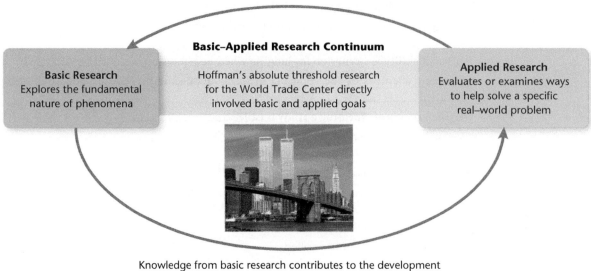

Applied problems and research may stimulate basic research, and provide valuable information about how well principles discovered through basic research apply to real–world settings.

Basic–Applied Research Continuum

Basic Research
Explores the fundamental nature of phenomena

Hoffman's absolute threshold research for the World Trade Center directly involved basic and applied goals

Applied Research
Evaluates or examines ways to help solve a specific real–world problem

Knowledge from basic research contributes to the development of interventions to solve real–world problems.

Photo by Jeff Overs/BBC News & Current Affairs via Getty Images

Figure 1.5 Basic and applied research. The distinction between basic and applied research can be viewed as a continuum.

What is the absolute threshold for detecting horizontal acceleration? To state this nontechnically, if you were in a room, how rapid would the acceleration of the floor's side-to-side motion have to be before you reliably noticed the floor swaying? Hoffman and psychology graduate student Paul Eskildsen conducted experiments and found that people were much more sensitive to a floor's horizontal acceleration than the engineers had anticipated (Benson, 2003). In sum, this research simultaneously had basic and applied goals.

Importantly, after the engineers replicated this finding in a subsequent experiment, they added structural reinforcement to the twin towers' design to reduce the amount of sway. After both towers were hit by commercial airliners in the September 11, 2001, terrorist attacks, thousands of people had time to escape before the buildings collapsed. Although we can't know for sure, it's possible that the structural reinforcements added in response to Hoffman and Eskildsen's research created precious extra minutes for people to escape (Benson, 2003).

There are important reciprocal relations between basic and applied research (see Figure 1.5). Knowledge acquired from basic research often provides the guiding framework for applied research. For example, psychologists have used principles discovered through basic research to develop therapies for psychological disorders, design programs that reduce workers' stress, and modify people's risky sexual behavior to reduce the risk of acquiring HIV/AIDS (Lemieux, Fisher, & Pratto, 2008).

Conversely, as the issue of WTC building sway illustrated, applied problems can stimulate research that uncovers basic scientific principles. Applied research can also provide feedback about whether basic scientific principles generalize to real-world situations. For example, basic psychological research has suggested principles for reducing conflict between groups. In turn, scientists have used these principles to create programs in order to reduce ethnic prejudice in schools, colleges, and other settings. An example is the "jigsaw classroom," in which schoolchildren are placed in multiethnic groups and assigned to work cooperatively to solve common problems (Aronson, 2004). Overall, applied research has yielded a mixture of supportive and unsupportive findings about these programs' effectiveness, providing useful information about the limitations of principles on which the programs were based (Lemmer & Wagner, 2015).

 CONCEPT CHECK 1.4 BASIC AND APPLIED RESEARCH

Titles of journal articles don't always indicate whether a study is primarily basic or applied, but the following do. Three titles from actual journal articles appear below. Decide whether each article primarily has a basic or applied focus. Answers appear on page 30.

1. Improving executive functioning in children with fetal alcohol spectrum disorders (Nash et al., 2015)
2. Narcissism, confidence, and risk attitude (Campbell, Goodie, & Foster, 2004)
3. Pilot navigation errors on the airport surface: identifying contributing factors and mitigating solutions (Hooey & Foyle, 2006)

BENEFITS OF LEARNING ABOUT RESEARCH METHODS

Learning Objectives

After studying this section, you should be able to:

- Describe potential benefits of learning about research methods.
- Reflect on how applicable these benefits are to you.

A course in research methods is among the most important courses that a college student can take. There are many benefits to learning about research methods, even if you don't plan on becoming a researcher. And yes, although a research career has many rewards—generating knowledge, benefiting society, and providing intellectual challenge—we instructors know that most students and even most psychology majors are not planning to become researchers. So what are some potential benefits?

Enhancing Critical Thinking Skills. Critical thinking has many components. It involves the ability to generate questions and state them clearly, to define problems precisely, to recognize when questions and problems formulated by other people are too vague or imprecise to be meaningfully answered, and to convert such questions or problems into more precise ones. Critical thinking involves the ability to efficiently search for and evaluate information pertaining to a question, problem, or claim. It requires sound reasoning skills, the ability to draw appropriate conclusions, and as Figure 1.3 on page 12 illustrates, the ability to identify plausible alternative explanations for why findings occur or events happen. This isn't an exhaustive list, but all of these skills play a central role in scientific research, and you can enhance them by taking a research methods course to heart. Beyond this course, these skills can serve you well throughout your life.

Reading About, Evaluating, and Conducting Research in Other Courses. Future coursework in psychology and many other fields will likely expose you to research studies and findings presented in textbooks, assigned articles, or lectures. You may also be asked to complete class projects or term papers that require summarizing and synthesizing studies published in scientific journals. Perhaps in a lab course or other class, your main project will be to conduct research. The skills and knowledge you acquire in your research methods class will put you in a better position to succeed in these assignments, to understand how the information you learn in other classes was generated, and to evaluate the quality of that information.

Reading About and Evaluating Research in a Nonresearch Career. Perhaps you're aiming for a career in psychology—maybe as a clinical, counseling, or educational psychologist—but have no desire to conduct research. Maybe you're planning to become a physician, physical therapist, or social worker. Your only desire is to provide therapy, counseling, medical treatment, or other services to help people. But how will you know what form of therapy, counseling, medical treatment, or other service is best? Throughout your career, to truly help people most effectively, you will need to stay abreast of new developments in your field. By attending professional conferences, reading journals, or taking continuing education classes, you will be exposed to new research findings and claims. Your knowledge of research methods will help you assess the validity of those claims.

What if your career has nothing to do with being a health provider? Perhaps you'll own your own company or become the director of human resources in a large organization. You may find yourself in a position of having to pay a lot of money to outside consultants in order to have personnel selection tests developed or the "latest and greatest" training programs implemented for your managers. How will you know whether a job selection or prepackaged management training program is scientifically sound or merely a costly fad? Knowledge of research methods can't guarantee that you'll make the right decisions, but it can increase your odds.

Preparing for a Research Career. If you're planning a career that involves conducting research—perhaps as a professor, consultant, or marketing researcher—then this course is one important step along the way. To become a proficient researcher, however, you will need to take more specialized coursework in methodology and statistics as well as become actively involved in doing research. One excellent way is to explore opportunities—often available for course credit—to join a faculty member's or graduate student's research team. If such opportunities are available, then it's important to have realistic expectations about the tasks you'll be performing: Always ask what your responsibilities will be and also be aware that many undergraduates may be competing for a limited number of such apprenticeship positions. In considering whom to select, a faculty member may want to know how well you've done in courses such as research methods and statistics.

Preparing for, and Gaining Entrance to, Graduate School. The analytic thinking, formal scientific writing, and other skills (e.g., searching psychological databases, conducting basic data analyses) emphasized in a research methods class are among the key skills required for success in graduate school, and in many careers as well. In psychology, directors of graduate-school admissions committees report that undergraduate transcripts are closely examined in deciding whom to admit (Landrum, 2003). Most graduate programs either require or prefer their applicants to have taken undergraduate courses in statistics and research methods (Norcross, Hanych, & Terranova, 1996).

Graduate admissions committees also view undergraduate research experience as an important criterion for admission into PhD programs and weight letters of recommendation heavily (Norcross, Kohout, & Wicherski, 2005). Performing well in a research methods course doesn't guarantee acceptance into graduate school, but it may help you gain acceptance to a research team as an undergraduate. A positive letter of recommendation from a faculty member who has had a real opportunity to evaluate your research-related work is likely to carry more weight than one from an instructor who, for example, only interfaced with you as a student in a large lecture class and never really got to know you.

Learning More About Psychology's Subfields. Exposing students to psychology's diverse subfields is a major goal of an introductory psychology course, not a methods course. Depending on the focus of your methods course, your instructor may illustrate concepts with examples from just one subfield or from many. Either way, the diverse examples in this book may give you some additional insight into psychology's breadth and help you decide what kinds of topics interest you the most.

 CONCEPT CHECK 1.5 BENEFITS OF LEARNING ABOUT RESEARCH METHODS

How would taking a research methods course benefit each of the following college students? Answers appear on page 30.

1. A company's website claims that a subliminal audio product can boost memory. Quotes from users praise the product's effectiveness. Felicia considers buying the product, hoping that better memory will enhance her grades.

2. Jon wants to attend graduate school in clinical psychology, become a licensed psychologist, and conduct psychotherapy.

3. Lavonne wants to obtain a PhD and conduct behavioral neuroscience research.

SKEPTICISM, SCIENCE, AND EVERYDAY LIFE

Learning Objectives

After studying this section, you should be able to:

- Discuss why skepticism and critical thinking are important in science and daily life.
- Describe basic critical thinking questions that we should ask when a claim is presented to us as fact.
- Apply critical thinking skills by evaluating a claim and the evidence offered to support it.

A popular men's lifestyle website informs readers that a survey it conducted found "63% of men and 60% of women admit that they would lie to their partner to avoid an argument" (*AskMen*, 2012, Part 1). A headline on a major British newspaper's website reads: "What does your handwriting say about you? Study finds more than 5,000 personality traits are linked to how we write" (Woollaston, 2013). A company offers over 1,000 self-help products for online purchase, noting that its special subliminal technology advances the mind's power and can help users effortlessly achieve their true potential (InnerTalk, 2016).

How should we react when reading claims such as these? For example, would it make a difference if we knew that the first quote was based on a national survey of 1,200 adults that used random sampling to select the participants, or instead was based on surveys of over 50,000 readers of *AskMen* and *TrèsSugar* online men's and women's magazines (*Brevard Times*, 2012)? It should, as you will learn in Chapter 7 . If the surveys were conducted as many magazine web surveys are (specific information about how participants were selected was not given), then despite having a sample of over 50,000 participants, it's risky to interpret the findings as representing the views of men and women in general. Of course, the magazines' websites don't claim that the surveys were scientific. But how many readers will interpret the findings as "facts" about men and women and pass this information on to friends with a comment like: "Hey, I read a survey that said most men and women would lie to their partners to avoid arguments"?

WHAT IS SKEPTICISM?

In science, **skepticism** *is an outlook that involves questioning the validity of claims before deciding whether to accept them.* It's a mind-set of "show me your evidence" when encountering a claim of fact. Skepticism is not identical to negativism or cynicism, which essentially are approaches of disbelieving or distrusting everything from the outset. Rather, a skeptical stance includes being open to accepting claims that are supported by valid evidence as well as refraining from accepting claims that are inadequately supported.

Skepticism is intimately related to the concept of *critical thinking*. A skeptical outlook leads scientists to use critical thinking skills in order to evaluate the soundness of the studies and conclusions presented in research reports. Scientists also employ critical thinking when encountering alleged facts about behavior and other psychological claims presented in the mass media, on the web, in popular magazines and books, and in other nonscientific sources.

For nonscientists as well, a skeptical outlook combined with good critical thinking skills can be strong assets in everyday life. The value of carefully evaluating information doesn't end when we step off campus or graduate from college. In our modern information age, claims about human behavior sprout rapidly and everywhere: on the web, in magazine and newspaper articles, in radio and TV news broadcasts, in advertisements and self-help books, and in comments by talk show hosts and politicians. How do we decide what's fact and what's fiction?

EVALUATING CLAIMS

Concern about the potential misrepresentation of scientific information to the public—and about the presentation of facts and claims that seem to be scientific but have no valid scientific basis—is nothing new. Consider the following:

> In a popular magazine, an excellent article based on sound work was published; but also published was an article by a "famous psychologist" who is not in the APA directory, telling how you can analyze your personality by knowing your favorite flower, and how dogs can know when their masters are dying in another state by ESP. What should we as psychologists do about such material? (American Psychological Association, 1953, pp. 33–34)

It's interesting that over a half-century ago, when TV was in its infancy and the web was nowhere in sight, the APA expressed serious concern about the dangers of exposing the public to inaccurate psychological claims. Today, the potential for such exposure is far greater, so what can we do to avoid being misled? There's no magic solution, but in the spirit of skepticism, an important step is to ask some basic critical thinking questions whenever a claim is presented to us. The list below expands on five critical thinking questions posed by Bernstein, Clarke-Stewart, Penner, Roy, and Wickens (2000):

1. What claim is being made?
2. What is the source of the claim?
3. Can I gather information about the credibility of that source?
4. What evidence is presented to support the claim?
5. What is the quality of the evidence?
6. Are there plausible alternative explanations for what caused the findings?
7. Are the interpretations of the findings reasonable?
8. What additional evidence is needed to reach a clearer conclusion?
9. Given the current state of the evidence, what conclusion is most reasonable?

SKEPTICISM AND ANECDOTAL EVIDENCE

One type of evidence that we frequently encounter in everyday life is **anecdotal evidence,** *in which anecdotes—brief stories or descriptions about personal experiences, other people, or events—are offered as facts to support or refute a claim.* "After only three weeks on the

Anecdotal Evidence 101 by Eric Perlin

Figure 1.6 The anecdotal evidence game.

EasyXYZ diet program, I lost 12 pounds. You can too" proclaims a customer quoted on the company's website. "Our new transportation initiative is working," says a city mayor in a reelection campaign speech. "Just ask the Evans family, who told us that it's easier now to get downtown." "I'm sorry to hear you're depressed," says a friend. "When I was really depressed and down on myself, I started listening to an audio product that contained subliminal messages to improve my self-esteem. In 3 months I felt a lot better. You should try it!" As for using anecdotal evidence to refute claims, **Figure 1.6** provides some examples.

Anecdotal evidence can be highly persuasive; compared to a pile of dry statistics based on large samples and controlled studies, it is vivid and memorable (Stanovich, 2013). And it might be correct: The XYZ diet, the transportation initiative, and the audio product may actually be performing as claimed. But from a skeptical, scientific viewpoint, there are serious problems with using or accepting anecdotal evidence in support of a causal claim. For one thing, an anecdote may represent an atypical case; perhaps only a few people lose weight on the EasyXYZ diet program or find it easier to get downtown this year versus last.

Another problem is that anecdotal evidence usually is based on unsystematic observation, and as noted in the sixth critical thinking question on the previous page, it is vital to think carefully about plausible alternative explanations for what is being claimed. Consider the friend, let's say a female friend, who said using a subliminal audio product improved her depression. Before you continue to the next paragraph, can you think of one or two plausible reasons why this anecdotal claim might be inaccurate?

Here are four of many possible reasons for skepticism about our friend's anecdotal evidence that the audio product lessened her depression:

- Her perception that the depression started to decrease only after she began to use the audio product may be incorrect. Perhaps it began to diminish, even slightly but consistently, before she began to use the product, and this trend continued on its own over the next 3 months.

- In many cases, people's depression ends on its own, even within 3 months (Whiteford et al., 2013). When a disorder, illness, or other condition ends on its own, this is called *spontaneous remission.*

- Other events that occurred in the 3-month period, and that had nothing to do with her use of the audio product—a change in season, receiving social support from friends—may have caused her improvement. When events unrelated to a treatment cause a change in the behavior of interest, this is called a *history effect.*

- If she had a positive expectation that the audio product would work, then this could have caused the improvement, even though the subliminal content of the product itself had no unique benefit. This type of response is called *a placebo effect*.

As you proceed through this textbook, you will learn more about these and other factors that may provide plausible alternative explanations for causal claims. You will also see how scientists design studies that control for such factors, permitting clearer causal conclusions based on their findings. For now, the key point is that in science, although anecdotal evidence may trigger interest in a topic and lead to more rigorous research (Siler, Lee, & Bero, 2015), by itself it is a weak form of evidence. You should treat it as such in everyday life as well.

As a final note, the value of asking critical thinking questions about the validity of claims extends well beyond sorting psychological fact from fiction. It comes into play when we search online for consumer product user evaluations and expert product reviews. It applies to how we gather and evaluate information before making career choices and what medical treatment to choose for an illness or injury. Skepticism and critical thinking can't guarantee that we'll always make the best decision, but they can increase the likelihood that we will.

 CONCEPT CHECK 1.6 SKEPTICISM, SCIENCE, AND EVERYDAY LIFE

Briefly answer each of the following questions. Answers appear on page 30.
1. Explain a key difference between skepticism and cynicism.
2. How are skepticism and critical thinking related?
3. Identify at least four critical thinking questions to ask when evaluating claims in everyday life. Then try to apply the questions to Exercise 3 on page 31.

CHAPTER SUMMARY

- Tenacity is a method of knowing that involves believing something simply because it is what we have long believed. Authority involves relying on other people for knowledge. The method of reason uses logic and rational argument to arrive at knowledge. In contrast, empiricism involves acquiring knowledge directly through observation and experience. As opposed to everyday observation and experience, science involves systematic empiricism: the systematic gathering and evaluation of empirical evidence.

- Description, explanation, prediction, and control are four main goals of science. Scientists describe phenomena and develop hypotheses and theories to explain why they occur. Hypotheses, which may be derived from a theory, are converted into if–then predictions and tested by gathering empirical data. When gathering data, scientists seek to maximize control over research settings so that the influence of extraneous factors can be ruled out. Prediction and control also have applied purposes. If two variables are associated, then knowledge about one variable can be used to predict the other; the concept of control includes the application of scientific knowledge to influence events or behavior in ways that benefit people.

- Science involves assumption that events are not random but have underlying causes that are capable of being discovered. Science is empirical, systematic, and focused on testable questions. Scientists strive for accuracy and objectivity in their work; they must clearly define concepts and operationalize those concepts when conducting research. Scientific knowledge is publicly reported and is tentative, which means that it is subject to revision as newer knowledge is acquired. In this manner, science is a self-correcting process. Finally, science has limitations, such as the inability to answer nonempirical questions.

- Basic research is conducted to examine the fundamental nature of phenomena. Applied research is conducted to help solve or evaluate a specific, real-world problem. Basic and applied research provide important benefits to each other.

- No matter the context, learning about research methods can enhance your ability to understand and critically evaluate information and claims. A research methods course can help prepare you to conduct research in other courses and is important in preparation for applying to graduate school in psychology. Examples covered in the course also can help you acquire more information about psychology's diverse subfields.

- Skepticism is an outlook that involves questioning the validity of claims before deciding whether to accept them. In combination with critical thinking skills, skepticism can help prevent you from being misled by anecdotal evidence and erroneous claims.

KEY TERMS

anecdotal evidence (p. 26)
applied research (p. 21)
authority (p. 4)
basic research (p. 21)
causal inference (p. 10)
confirmation bias (p. 7)
control (p. 13)
distal causes (p. 10)
empirical knowledge (p. 6)

empirical question (empirical claim) (p. 16)
empiricism (p. 6)
falsifiability (p. 16)
hypothesis (p. 9)
operational definition (p. 19)
peer-reviewed journal (p. 19)
plausible alternative explanations (p. 7)

proximal (proximate) causes (p. 10)
reason (p. 5)
replication (p. 20)
science (p. 7)
skepticism (p. 25)
tenacity (p. 4)
theory (p. 9)
variable (p. 9)

ASSESS YOUR KNOWLEDGE

1. Use the three-door problem to illustrate and contrast tenacity, authority, reason, empiricism, and science as ways of acquiring knowledge and forming beliefs.

2. Name the four main goals of science.

3. Describe two ways in which prediction is a goal of science. What are two ways in which control is a scientific goal?

4. What is the primary purpose of a theory? What is the relation between theories and hypotheses?

5. Explain and illustrate the difference between distal causes and proximal causes.

6. What is a causal inference? Name three criteria that need to be met in order to draw a causal inference.

7. What basic assumptions do scientists make about the natural world? Identify eight other major characteristics of science.

8. Explain how scientists determine whether a question is testable.

9. What is an operational definition? Provide an example to illustrate why operational definitions are necessary in science.

10. Discuss why scientific knowledge is tentative, and explain how science is self-correcting. What role does replication play in self-correction?

11. Use examples to illustrate the key difference between basic and applied research. How do basic research and applied research benefit each other?

12. Describe several benefits of learning about research methods.

13. What are some characteristics of critical thinking? What is skepticism? Why are critical thinking and skepticism important in today's world?

CONCEPT CHECKS: ANSWERS

1.1 How Do We Know?

1. Authority.   2. Systematic empiricism: Because Shonda intentionally manipulates (i.e., mixes) the colors and repeats her "paint-mixing test" several times, systematic empiricism would be a better answer than empiricism.   3. Empiricism: Claire's judgment is based on a personal experience, but she did not systematically evaluate the results of all her changed answers.   4. Tenacity.

1.2 Goals of Science

1. Explanation: A theory of memory's goal is to help explain how memory "works."   2. Prediction: The screening test is used as a predictor of job performance.   3. Control: The researcher chooses to conduct a laboratory experiment to maximize control over the research setting.   4. Description: The study is conducted to describe the national prevalence of anxiety disorders.

1.3 Characteristics of Science

1. have patterns (i.e., are not random); have underlying causes; these underlying causes are capable of being discovered   2. testable   3. operational definitions   4. replication

1.4 Basic and Applied Research

1. Applied: The main purpose is to enhance the children's social functioning.   2. Basic: The main purpose is to broaden knowledge about the relations among the three variables; no mention is made of any applied problem.   3. Applied: Identifying factors that contribute to pilot errors could enhance basic knowledge (i.e., about decision-making errors in general), but the main focus here is on using that information to test solutions for reducing those errors, an applied goal.

1.5 Benefits of Learning about Research Methods

1. Felicia: The methods course may enhance Felicia's appreciation of how important it is to critically evaluate claims, and it covers many concepts that will boost her ability to do so. The course may enhance concrete skills—such as knowing how to perform an effective search of the scientific literature—that will increase Felicia's odds of locating high-quality information about whether such products are effective.

2. Jon: The methods course will help Jon understand and evaluate research articles that he will read in other undergraduate courses and in graduate school. As a clinical psychologist, he will benefit from knowledge of research methods (i.e., if he plans to conduct research, the course provides one step in the educational process of becoming a researcher; moreover, enhanced knowledge of research methods will help him, as a practicing psychotherapist, critically evaluate new research on treatment methods). Enhanced critical thinking skills will be useful in his professional and daily life. As an undergrad, doing well in the methods course may help him gain entry onto a research team and, in turn (if he performs very well), get a good recommendation for graduate school.

3. Lavonne: Except for gaining knowledge to help assess the quality of future research on therapy effectiveness, all the benefits discussed for Jon also apply to Lavonne. Because she is planning a research career, the methods course is especially important in providing one step in the process of learning to become a researcher.

1.6 Skepticism, Science, and Everyday Life

1. Compared to cynicism, skepticism reflects more of an open-minded outlook ("show me your evidence") and a willingness to accept claims if good evidence supports them.   2. A skeptical mind-set should motivate us to ask critical thinking questions and evaluate the answers before accepting a claim or conclusion.   3. Nine critical thinking questions appear on page 26.

THINKING CRITICALLY AND APPLYING YOUR KNOWLEDGE

For each chapter, you will find answers to the odd-numbered "Thinking Critically and Applying Your Knowledge" exercises in Appendix D at the back of the book.

EXERCISE 1   Identifying Empirical and Nonempirical Questions

(a) On page 17, review the answers to the 10 items in Table 1.3. If you have answered any items incorrectly, reread the text section titled "Science Focuses on Testable Questions."

(b) For each question in Table 1.3 that is not empirical, revise it in a way that turns it into an empirical question.

EXERCISE 2   Identify the Research: Basic or Applied?

Four studies are briefly described below. For each study, identify whether it primarily represents basic or applied research.

(a) Dr. Gutiérrez, a biopsychologist (i.e., behavioral neuroscientist), conducts a study to examine whether emotionally positive and negative stimuli produce different levels of neural activation in various brain regions. Forty college students will be tested. Dr. Gutiérrez will expose each student to a series of photographs while using fMRI (functional magnetic resonance imaging) to record their neural response to each photograph. Each photograph depicts a stimulus that is emotionally positive (e.g., a flower bouquet) or emotionally negative (e.g., a filthy toilet bowl).

(b) Dr. Jackson, a clinical psychologist, designs a study to examine whether two types of therapy are effective in treating animal phobias in children. She creates three distinct conditions: a behavioral therapy condition, a cognitive-behavioral therapy condition, and a control condition in which the children do not receive therapy (until after the study is over). Out of a total of 60 children, 20 will be assigned at random to each of the three conditions and the severity of their phobias will be compared.

(c) Dr. Lieberman, an industrial-organizational psychologist, wants to test the hypothesis that people who are more satisfied with their jobs have higher job productivity than people who are less satisfied with their jobs. A large corporation allows Dr. Lieberman to administer a job-satisfaction questionnaire to 100 employees and provides him with the employees' job-productivity scores, based on ratings by their managers. Dr. Lieberman then examines the relation between job satisfaction and job performance.

(d) Dr. Wu is a cognitive psychologist who studies factors that distort eyewitness memory. The chief of police in a nearby town asks Dr. Wu to design a new procedure for police detectives to use when they interview eyewitnesses to crimes. The goal of the new interview procedure is to reduce the chances that the detectives, simply by the way they ask questions, will bias eyewitnesses' memory. Dr. Wu develops the new interview procedure. He then conducts a laboratory study in which college students watch a videotape of a crime, and actual police detectives from another town subsequently interview the student eyewitnesses. Each detective is assigned at random to use either the new interview procedure or the existing standard interview procedure. Dr. Wu compares the accuracy of the eyewitness information obtained from the two interview procedures.

EXERCISE 3 Claims, Comets, and Critical Thinking

In this chapter, you read about the *Deep Impact* mission, in which NASA used a small spacecraft to collide with a comet so that the comet's interior structure could be recorded. According to news reports the next day, a Russian astrologer filed a $300 million lawsuit against NASA for ruining "the natural balance of forces in the universe" (Associated Press, July 6,

2005, p. A4). We discussed how this claim was so vague that it would be viewed as scientifically untestable. Suppose, however, that the astrologer argues not only that this claim is testable but also that there is evidence to support it. Here is the evidence. Note that these are actual events.

- Merely 2 days after the *Deep Impact* collision, Indonesia was hit by a strong earthquake.

- The same day, just off the southern coast of Australia, a famous 150-foot rock formation that had stood against the pounding seas for ages collapsed into the ocean. The formation was part of a group of rock towers known as the "Twelve Apostles."

- Just a few days after the *Deep Impact* collision, Hurricane Dennis smacked into Cuba and headed toward the Florida and Louisiana coasts. It was unusually early in the summer for a massive hurricane to develop. The governor of Florida had to declare a state of emergency and urge residents to evacuate the coast.

Your task: Assume a skeptical attitude and use the nine critical thinking questions listed in "Evaluating Claims" to analyze this claim and the evidence above.

EXERCISE 4 Identify the Research Goal

Two studies are cited below. In each study, the researchers specify one or more questions that their study is investigating. Identify whether each question illustrates the scientific goal of (1) description, (2) explanation, (3) prediction, or (4) control. If you believe that an individual question illustrates more than one goal, then identify all the relevant goals.

Study A

Cavazos-Rehg, P. A., & DeLucia-Waack, J. L. (2009). Education, ethnic identity, and acculturation as predictors of self-esteem in Latino adolescents. *Journal of Counseling and Development, 87,* 47–54.

(a) Overall, do Latino students enrolled in traditional versus bilingual education programs differ in their self-esteem, ethnic identity, and acculturation?

(b) How well do grade point average, gender, acculturation, and other factors predict Latino students' level of self-esteem?

(c) Do the factors that predict self-esteem differ for Latino students enrolled in bilingual as opposed to traditional education programs?

(d) If ethnic identity and self-esteem are related, is acculturation a possible reason why they are related?

Study B

Logel, C., Walton, G. M., Spencer, S. J., Iserman, E. C., von Hippel, W., & Bell, A. E. (2009). Interacting with sexist men triggers social identity threat among female engineers. *Journal of Personality and Social Psychology, 96*, 1089–1103.

(a) When college male engineering students interact with a woman they believe is an engineering student, will the men who are more sexist display more dominance over and sexual interest in her?

(b) When college female engineering students interact with a man they believe is an engineering student (and who, unknown to them, has been instructed by the researcher to act in a sexist manner toward some women and a nonsexist manner toward other women), will exposure to sexist cues subsequently cause the women to perform more poorly on an engineering test?

LaunchPad
macmillan learning

To practice key concepts from this chapter, visit the LaunchPad Solo for Research Methods at **launchpadworks.com.**

2

CONDUCTING PSYCHOLOGICAL RESEARCH

CHAPTER OUTLINE

W hen Emily Rosa was 9 years old, she saw a video about a therapy technique called Therapeutic Touch (TT). According to the Therapeutic Touch International Association (2015), TT "is based on the idea that human beings are energy in the form of a field. When you are healthy, that energy is freely flowing and balanced. In contrast, disease is a condition of energy imbalance" (The Process of Therapeutic Touch, para. 1). TT practitioners claim that they can feel a human energy field surrounding a person's body and that, without touching the body, they can manipulate and rebalance the energy field to reduce stress, lessen pain, and promote healing.

Emily became curious about the claim that practitioners could feel a human energy field, so for her fourth-grade science fair project, she designed an experiment to test the claim. A year later, additional data were collected in a follow-up study. In total, 21 TT practitioners each performed 10 or 20 trials of a task in which Emily held her hand a few inches above each practitioner's left or right hand (see **Figure 2.1**). Emily selected the hand randomly on each trial. Their view of Emily blocked, the practitioners' task was to detect the location of Emily's hand. In 280 trials, the practitioners were accurate only 44% of the time, no better than a chance guessing rate of 50%. Emily's finding did not

Figure 2.1 Emily Rosa's experimental task. (L. Rosa et al., 1998.)

support the claim that TT practitioners could detect an energy field. Two years later, when Emily was 11, the study was published in the prestigious *Journal of the American Medical Association* (L. Rosa, E. Rosa, Sarner, & Barrett, 1998).

The study triggered a fierce debate. TT had already been controversial: Skeptics denounced it as quackery and proponents claimed it was valid. Some skeptics applauded Emily's study, but TT's supporters criticized her methodology and argued that her results didn't disprove that TT worked. Indeed, the study's purpose was not to test whether TT worked. Rather, it was designed to examine TT's basic assumption that practitioners could detect human energy fields. The journal received numerous complaints about publishing the results of a fourth-grader's science fair project, and the controversy hit the media. In a televised reply, the journal's editor stated: "Age doesn't matter. It's good science that matters, and this is good science" (Lemonick, 1998).

Emily's study actually addressed a very psychological topic: people's willingness to believe things about the natural world (e.g., the practitioners' belief that they could detect energy fields) that seemingly aren't so. More importantly, her work illustrates the classic steps in conducting scientific research: translate curiosity into a testable question, devise an ethical way to test it, systematically collect and analyze evidence, and report the findings. In this chapter, we'll discuss the process of performing research, albeit in a few more steps.

GENERATING RESEARCH IDEAS

Learning Objectives

After studying this section, you should be able to:

- Discuss sources for getting ideas about a research topic.
- Develop a research idea and identify the types of sources you used.

How do research ideas arise? Typically, the research process begins when we observe something that piques our curiosity or concern and ask a testable question about it. Sometimes a single observation triggers a research idea, as when Emily Rosa observed a claim made in a Therapeutic Touch video and asked, "Is the claim accurate?" Research ideas also evolve as we notice events over time and become increasingly curious about a topic. For example, clinical psychologist Susan Nolen-Hoeksema studied rumination, an interest that grew out of her professional interactions with depressed patients. She observed that these patients kept dwelling on negative events and problems in their lives and that this rumination seemingly had no useful purpose (Nolen-Hoeksema, 2011). Eventually, this observation, and the question of why depressed people ruminate, led her to conduct research on the emotional consequences of rumination.

As these examples illustrate, research ideas can form rapidly or slowly, and they derive from diverse sources, including personal experience and daily events, prior research and theory, real-world problems, and serendipity. Let's explore these diverse sources in more detail.

PERSONAL EXPERIENCE AND DAILY EVENTS

Personal experience can provide a wealth of questions to investigate. The key is to notice and reflect on something important, interesting, or perplexing about our own or other people's behavior. For example, have you ever tried *not* to think about something, only to have that unwanted thought keep popping back into your head? Social psychologist Daniel Wegner conducted experiments on this topic, called "thought suppression." His interest began when he noticed his own reactions to situations in which people denied accusations:

> I'd have to say that the early seed of this interest was a sleazy politician. I noticed that when a headline aired someone's denial of an accusation (for example, "Mayor claims she took no bribes"), I often ended up thinking the accusation was true anyway. This got me to wondering if denials ever really work—if you can erase ideas or possibilities with denials once they are known and the "cat is out of the bag." Eventually, this led to experiments on what happens when people are specifically asked not to think about something. (Wegner, 2011, p. 114)

Our interactions with other people, such as Nolen-Hoeksema's experiences with depressed patients, also provide fertile ground for generating research ideas. Cognitive psychologist Elizabeth Bjork studies memory and learning, including ways to help students learn more effectively. She notes that this interest was "triggered by interactions with students lamenting during office hours how hard they had studied, only then to perform poorly on a just-given exam. This motivated me to examine why students' study activities were sometimes so ineffective" (Bjork & Bjork, 2011, p. 56).

Daily events that we learn about indirectly, such as through media reports, provide another source of research ideas. For social psychologists John Darley and Bibb Latané (1968), years of research on the topic of bystander intervention grew out of an infamous news event—the 1964 murder of Kitty Genovese in New York City. The media reported that many of Genovese's neighbors heard her cries for help over a period of more than 30 minutes yet didn't call the police or otherwise intervene. This prompted Darley and Latané to ask, "Why did people fail to help?" and to conduct experiments to find an answer.

PRIOR RESEARCH AND THEORY

In science, one study often stimulates ideas for another. A researcher may conduct a series of studies on a topic, with each study testing a new question that builds upon the findings of the last. Similarly, as scientists learn of each other's work, they may observe something of interest that leads to new questions. For example, Darley and Latané's (1968) initial experiments tested the hypothesis that bystanders would be less likely to help someone during an emergency if they believed other bystanders were present. Whereas social commentators proposed that neighbors failed to help Kitty Genovese because they lacked concern, Darley and Latané's findings suggested that the presence of many bystanders led to collective inaction because, individually, bystanders assumed that someone else would intervene. Publication of Darley and Latané's (1968) findings sparked other scientists' interest in this topic. For over 45 years, this has led to new questions, more studies, and a growing body of knowledge on factors that influence bystander intervention (Dillon & Bushman, 2015).

To further illustrate how prior research can help generate new research questions, look at **Figure 2.2**, which shows one portion of the results from a developmental psychology study about lying to one's parents (Jensen, Arnett, Feldman, & Cauffman, 2004). These questionnaire data, collected from 490 high-school and college students, address the issue "How often do adolescents and emerging adults lie to their parents, and what do they lie about?" Can you

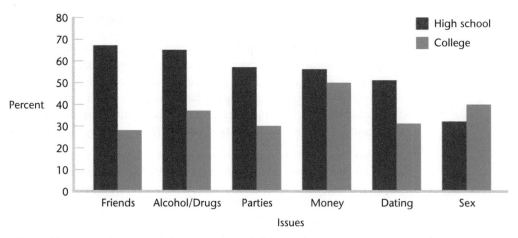

Figure 2.2 Lying to parents. The graph shows the percentage of students in Jensen et al.'s (2004) study who reported lying to parents about diverse issues. (Republished with permission of Springer Science and Bus Media B V, from "The Right to do Wrong: Lying to Parents Among Adolescents and Emerging Adults" by L. A. Jensen, J. J. Arnett, S. S. Feldman, and E. Cauffman, 2004, *Journal of Youth and Adolescence, 33*[2], pp. 101–112. Permissions conveyed through Copyright Clearance Center, Inc.)

generate other testable questions about lying that are related to this topic? After giving it a try, see footnote 1.[1]

Theories provide another key source of research ideas. Scientists test a theory by deriving predictions from it. Essentially, scientists ask, "What outcome does the theory predict should occur in this particular situation?" Scientists use reasoning to postulate an answer, and then they test their prediction. Theory development and testing have played an important role in psychology from its scientific infancy through the present (Stratton, 1896; Wondra & Ellsworth, 2015). We'll discuss an example later in the chapter.

REAL-WORLD PROBLEMS

Throughout psychology's history, the need to understand and solve real-world problems has generated countless research questions. Some, such as how to help astronauts psychologically cope with stresses of long-term space flight, arise from highly specific circumstances (Seaton, Bowie, & Sipes, 2009). Others arise from a long list of more widespread problems: addiction, depression, other psychological disorders, family dysfunction, prejudice, crime, school and workplace conflicts, and so forth. Here, questions such as "What causes it?", "How prevalent is it?", "What characteristics and consequences are associated with it?", and "How do we best treat or prevent it?" are the springboard for much basic and applied research.

Child-clinical psychologists Lauren Hensley and Enrique Varela (2008) were curious about why only some children develop post-traumatic stress disorder (PTSD) symptoms after experiencing a severe stressor. This prompted them to examine characteristics associated with a greater risk of children's developing PTSD symptoms after experiencing a natural disaster. About a half-year after Hurricane Katrina devastated the U.S. Gulf Coast, Hensley and Varela gathered data from 302 schoolchildren in New Orleans. They found that children who had greater overall exposure to Katrina, had experienced greater personal loss or disruption to their lives, and had more anxious personalities in general tended to develop more PTSD symptoms.

---

[1] Here are a few of many possible questions: (1) Why do adolescents and emerging adults lie to their parents? (2) How often do parents realize that their children are lying? (3) How often, why, and about what topics do parents lie to their children? (4) How do adolescents, emerging adults, and parents perceive the acceptability of various motives for lying? (5) For the previous four questions, are there sex, ethnic, and cross-cultural differences?

In today's scientific and fiscal climate, the American Psychological Association (APA), government agencies, and health insurance companies emphasize a related question: "How do we know that a treatment works?" Increasingly, mental health practitioners are being urged or required by health insurers to use **evidence-based treatments** (also called **empirically supported treatments**): *interventions that scientifically controlled studies have demonstrated to be effective in treating specific conditions* (Niu & Arean, 2015). This emphasis on establishing evidence-based treatments also extends to other interventions, such as antibullying and educational programs (Slavin, 2012). Even if you aren't planning a research career, asking the question "How do we know that this treatment, program, product, or service is effective?" will serve you well throughout your life.

SERENDIPITY

Research ideas also come about through *serendipity,* the accidental discovery of something important. Serendipity involves stumbling across something by chance—often while looking for something else—and having the wisdom and curiosity to recognize that you may be on to an important discovery (A. A. Baumeister, 2006). For example, lithium is prescribed to treat manic episodes in people diagnosed with bipolar disorder. The initial discovery in the 1940s that lithium salt has a calming effect occurred, by chance, in an experiment in which it was administered to guinea pigs for another purpose (A. A. Baumeister, Hawkins, & López-Muñoz, 2010). Similarly, drugs may be tested to determine whether they help to alleviate a particular disorder only to be found unexpectedly to benefit another condition.

 CONCEPT CHECK 2.1 GENERATING RESEARCH IDEAS

Decide whether each statement is true or false. Answers appear on page 68 at the end of the chapter.

1. In behavioral science, one's personal experiences are generally viewed as a poor source for generating research questions.
2. *Serendipity* refers to the process of using an existing theory to form a new research question.
3. Studies that establish evidence-based treatments address the general question "How do we know whether a treatment is effective?"

GATHERING BACKGROUND INFORMATION

Learning Objectives

After studying this section, you should be able to:

- Identify major online psychological databases.
- Broaden and narrow a search of the scientific literature.
- Extract the key information from a research article.
- Explain how qualitative and quantitative review articles differ.

After we form a research idea, we don't rush off and conduct a study. If research already exists on our topic, carefully examining it will provide valuable information about how other scientists have defined, measured, and examined the concepts we are interested in. This also makes us aware of existing findings and the limitations of those findings. If a relevant theory exists, we can use it to guide us in forming a hypothesis to test. To identify relevant research and theory, we perform a search of the scientific literature. Should you need to do so, such as for a class assignment, keep these two cautions in mind:

1. Do not assume that this search will "only take a few minutes" or that performing a good scientific literature search is the same as the casual web searching we do in daily life. Good searches take time, including time spent refining your topic, reading online abstracts (i.e., summaries) of publications, obtaining publications that seem relevant, and then reading them carefully to determine their appropriateness for your purposes. For example, returning to Emily Rosa's experiments on Therapeutic Touch, her colleagues searched several online scientific databases for prior research on TT (L. Rosa et al., 1998). They identified 853 reports that mentioned TT, of which 83 were research studies. They reviewed these studies and found that none had assessed the alleged ability of TT practitioners to detect human energy fields.

2. Popular media outlets, such as the news websites of major broadcast networks (e.g., NBC, CBS, CNN, BBC, CBC), and online or print versions of newspapers and news magazines such as *Time* and *Newsweek,* are not scientific sources. Nor are *Wikipedia,* other general encyclopedias such as *Encyclopædia Brittanica,* or *YouTube* videos. Informative popular media articles and videos, some authored by scientists themselves, routinely appear on many scientific topics. These items may stimulate your curiosity and become a source of research ideas. But a proper literature search should focus on primary (i.e., original) scientific sources, and to achieve this, we examine scientific databases.

SEARCHING SCIENTIFIC DATABASES

Even if you have been Googling since you were in preschool, this doesn't necessarily mean that you know how to perform an efficient and thorough scientific literature search. Many scientific databases, including the first two discussed below, offer a valuable "Help" link to assist with learning how to use them. The "Help" link pays big dividends in terms of saving time in the long run.

PsycINFO and PsycARTICLES

PsycINFO and PsycARTICLES are online databases from the APA. Each covers over 100 years of research. For each publication, these databases provide a record that includes the title, authors' names, publication source and date, and an abstract. **Figure 2.3** shows part of a PsycINFO record for an article on deceptive dating behavior.

Both databases provide plentiful options, called *parameters,* for tailoring a search. The screen menu on my campus allows users to restrict searches to keywords, titles, authors, dates, certain populations (e.g., human, nonhuman), and many other parameters. Users can choose how the search results are displayed (e.g., by date or author).

PsycARTICLES covers 110 journals from psychology and related fields (APA, 2015a). It includes all journals published by the APA and the Canadian Psychological Association. Overall, these journals are among the top periodicals in their subfields. A key feature of PsycARTICLES is that it contains a complete online version—called a full-text version—of almost every article it carries. If your campus library subscribes to PsycARTICLES, you should be able to access these online articles at no additional cost.

PsycINFO tracks almost 2,500 journals, including those covered by PsycARTICLES, as well as books and dissertations in psychology and related fields (APA, 2015b). Because PsycINFO is a larger database, it often identifies relevant articles not found in PsycARTICLES. This is a strong advantage, especially when examining topics on which there is little research. However, unlike PsycARTICLES, PsycINFO is a database of abstracts rather than online articles. Depending on your campus library's physical holdings and online subscriptions, it may be easy or difficult to access complete articles identified by a PsycINFO search.

Title:	**Dating deception:** Gender, online **dating,** and exaggerated selfpresentation.
Authors:	Guadagno, Rosanna E., Department of Psychology, University of Alabama, Tuscaloosa, AL, US Rosanna@ua.edu. Okdie, Bradley M., Department of Psychology, Ohio State University, Newark, OH, US. Kruse, Sara A., Department of Psychology, University of Alabama, Tuscaloosa, AL, US
Address:	Guadagno, Rosanna E., Department of Psychology, University of Alabama, P.O. Box 870348, Tuscaloosa, AL, US, 35487-0348, Rosanna@ua.edu
Source:	Computers in Human Behavior, Vol 28(2), Mar, 2012. pp. 642–647.
Publisher:	Netherlands:Elsevier Science
ISSN:	0747-5632 (Print)
Language:	English
Keywords:	**dating, deception,** gender differences, online **dating,** self-presentation, online social interactions
Abstract:	This study examined how differences in expectations about meeting impacted the degree of deceptive self-presentation individuals displayed within the context of **dating.** Participants filled out personality measures in one of four anticipated meeting conditions: face-to-face, email, no meeting, and a control condition with no pretense of **dating.** Results indicated that, compared to baseline measures, male participants increased the amount they self-presented when anticipating a future interaction with a prospective date. Specifically, male participants emphasized their positive characteristics more if the potential date was less salient (e.g., email meeting) compared to a more salient condition (e.g., face-to-face meeting) or the control conditions. Implications for self-presentation theory, online social interaction, and online **dating** research will be discussed. (PsycINFO Database Record (c) 2012 APA, all rights reserved) (journal abstract)
Subjects:	***Deception;** *Human Sex Differences; *Social **Dating;** *Online Social Networks; Expectations
Methodology:	Empirical Study; Quantitative Study
Copyright:	All rights reserved. Elsevier Ltd. 2011
Digital Object Identifier:	10.1016/j.chb.2011.11.010
Database: PsycINFO	

Figure 2.3 Portion of a record produced by a PsycINFO search.

Databases in Related Disciplines

Sociology, biology, medicine, and many other fields that overlap with psychology have their own online literature databases. Depending on your topic, consider supplementing your psychological database search with an online search of research in another field. For example, if your topic is on psychological disorders, searching the online medical research database MEDLINE may uncover useful references not identified by PsycINFO.

General Search Engines and Google Scholar

Google and other general search engines are marvelous tools for everyday browsing but are inefficient for conducting most scientific literature searches. They yield far too many irrelevant results (e.g., commercial websites, blogs). In contrast, Google Scholar is dedicated to searching for scholarly articles. Its "Advanced Scholar Search" option provides an interface for restricting searches by key terms, authors' names, dates, and publication titles. Google Scholar lists search results according to a "relevance" ranking, which it computes. The ranking appears to be most strongly influenced by the frequency with which an article has been cited in other publications (Beel & Gipp, 2009). At your college, check whether it is possible to interface Google Scholar with the campus library system. If so, then alongside each hit that Google Scholar yields, it will display a link if your library carries an electronic version of the article.

Choosing a Database

First, if you will be performing literature searches in your methods course, then determine whether your instructor wants you to use a particular database, possibly one not discussed here. Second, there is no overall "best" database because different users place different value on the features of each one. For example, compared to PsycARTICLES, some researchers prefer PsycINFO because of its wider journal coverage. Compared to Google Scholar, they prefer PsycINFO's broader list of built-in search parameters and ability to list search results by date. Conversely, other researchers prefer Google Scholar because of its relevance rankings and other features.

Narrowing and Broadening a Search

One key to performing an efficient database search is knowing what you're looking for. Another key is knowing how to broaden and narrow a search so that it will yield a reasonable number of relevant articles. Suppose we are interested in the topic of lying and deception. Typing the search term *lying* into PsycINFO produces 4,311 records, many of which don't examine lying as in deception (e.g., they focus on "lying" down). Using the search term *deception* generates 7,400 hits, including hundreds that deal with self-deception—an important topic, but not what we are searching for. Typing *lying* into one search window and *deception* into another window, then linking these terms with the operator OR, broadens the search because PsycINFO will identify publications associated with either word. Indeed, this yields 10,607 results. To restrict our search, we would link *lying* and *deception* with the operator AND, telling PsycINFO to return only results that include both terms. This yields 1,104 results.

Typing *lying* AND *deception* NOT *self-deception* reduces the hits to 1,060. The terms AND, NOT, and OR are called *Boolean operators,* and they are used to narrow or expand a search. We can further restrict our search by requesting records only from peer-reviewed journals. This yields 762 hits, which is still too many. Our problem, as **Figure 2.4** illustrates, is that we're not being specific enough in selecting our topic. Suppose our strongest interest is lying among adolescents. Selecting an option that further restricts our search to *adolescence (13–17 years)* reduces the list to 66 citations. This is a manageable number to review by examining the titles and abstracts, but we might want to further narrow our search. For example, if we are interested in lying between adolescents and parents, changing the search terms to *lying* AND *deception* AND *parent** yields 13 citations. The asterisk in *parent** is a *truncation symbol,* and by using it, we will pick up citations that use terms such as *parent, parents, parental,* or *parenting.*

Digital Skillet/Getty Images

Wavebreakmedia/Shutterstock

Rich Legg/Getty Images

Figure 2.4 Lying and deception: Narrowing a topic. A PsycINFO search for *lying AND deception* in peer-reviewed sources yields about 1,100 records, far too many to examine. For a more productive search, we need to think more specifically about the aspects of lying and deception we are most interested in: lying among adolescents (e.g., to parents or to each other), deception in online dating, lying in courtroom testimony, and so forth.

Conversely, if our interest involves finding peer-reviewed articles on lying and deception in the context of online dating, typing *lying* AND *online dating,* or typing *deception* AND *online dating,* yields only one or eight citations, respectively. In this case, we want to broaden our search. We try *decept** AND *online dat*,* so that the search will pick up citations that use either *deception* or *deceptive* and also either *dating, dates,* or *dater.* However, we still get only eight hits. Perhaps *online dating* as a single term is too restrictive, so we try *decept** AND *online* AND *dating.* This yields 12 hits, and broadening the search by removing the restriction to peer-reviewed journals yields 21 hits.

As you gain experience in using online scientific databases, pick up tips from tutorials, and become more familiar with key concepts and terms in psychology, your searches will become more efficient. Your search also may turn up many types of articles (e.g., editorials, letters, encyclopedia entries). Therefore, if possible (as with PsycINFO), at times you may want to limit your search to certain types of articles. The two types that you are likely to need most often are peer-reviewed research articles and review articles, so let's discuss how to obtain and read them.

OBTAINING ARTICLES

Many journals are published online and also in print. In a best-case scenario, once you identify an article using PsycINFO, Google Scholar, or another online search engine, you will be able to obtain a free online copy by clicking a link on the page of search results. For example, if your campus library subscribes to a journal's online version, then you may be able to access the article (or the journal issue containing the article) by clicking a "Check availability" or "PDF" icon adjacent to the article's title or abstract.

If a search engine or database doesn't link you to an online copy of the article, check your campus library's electronic and print journal holdings. You may find that your library holds the online journal you want. If the library subscribes only to the print version, you will need to go to the library in person. Your library may provide online access to the more recent years of some journals and have print versions from earlier years.

If you cannot access an article online and a print version of the journal is not in your campus library system, then you have several options:

- Your campus library may participate in an interlibrary loan program that enables you to request access to the article from another library. You may be able to find the journal in your public library system or the library of another college or university in your area.

- You can contact one of the article's authors (usually the first author) and request a copy. For example, each PsycINFO record provides the authors' email and physical addresses. When contacting an author, always write your request in a formal, professional manner.

- If you search online using the title of the journal, you'll probably obtain a link to the journal's publisher, who may provide an electronic copy of the article for a fee.

READING RESEARCH ARTICLES

The first thing you'll notice when you locate a research article is the *title, author names,* and *institutional affiliation* (e.g., University of Texas). Beyond that, the structure of a research report will vary somewhat depending on the journal. We'll focus here on APA journals; many other journals also use the APA format.

Structure of a Research Article

Research reports begin with a brief abstract. In the subsequent sections, the authors essentially say, "Here's the topic and purpose of our study, the method we used, the data analyses, our discussion of what we found, and our references."

Abstract. An *abstract* is a one-paragraph summary of the report. Typically, it mentions the study's purpose, hypotheses, methodology, and main findings and conclusions.

Introduction. There's no heading labeled "Introduction," but this section begins the narrative. The authors describe the general topic and specific questions they are studying, explain why the topic is important, and cite prior research and theorizing that bear on their questions. They also state any hypotheses that are being tested.

Method. This section is typically divided into subsections that describe the overall research design, the participants' general characteristics (e.g., "72 pairs of mothers and their 4- to 8-month-old infants"), how they were selected, the specific procedures used, and how variables were manipulated or measured. If subsections are short, the authors may combine them (e.g., "Design and Participants").

Results. The authors describe how they analyzed their data and present their results. Statistical findings may also be shown in tables and graphs.

Discussion. The authors expand on the key findings, but in less statistical terms. They discuss whether hypotheses were supported, implications of the findings, limitations of the study, and issues to be resolved in future research.

References. The authors list the sources they cited in the article, using a standard format specified in the *Publication Manual of the American Psychological Association* (APA, 2010b).

Understanding Research Articles

Research articles vary in complexity. The abstract is a good place to begin, to get an overview of the study. Then proceed to the introduction, paying particular attention to the study's purpose and hypotheses. The Method section is very important. Reading it carefully will help you understand how the study was done and broaden your understanding of the many details involved in conducting research.

The Results section is usually the most technical and difficult to read. Some studies involve relatively simple statistical analyses and present data in graphs or tables—based on percentages or mean (i.e., average) scores—that are fairly straightforward. Other studies involve advanced statistical techniques. Fortunately, there are two main ways to extract the important results of a study without having to know the complex statistical details. First, if a Results section is complicated, focus on the written descriptions within each sentence that spell out the findings, rather than on the numbers and technical statistical terms. Second, the Discussion section that follows the Results section is an excellent source for identifying the key findings. The authors may summarize them at the beginning of this section and discuss them further throughout the section. Thus, even when the methods and analyses used in a study are complicated, you can still discern the most central findings. As you progress in your methods course, terms in articles that might seem foreign right now (e.g., *interaction, main effect*) will become familiar to you. Likewise, as you learn about statistical analysis in your methods class or a statistics course, the Results section of many articles will become easier to understand.

Finally, the References section can be a good resource if you need to find more articles on the topic. For example, when the authors cite research in their introduction, if those studies sound relevant to your topic, the References section provides you with the information you need to locate those sources in a literature search.

READING REVIEW ARTICLES

As research on a topic accumulates, review articles written by experts in the field come in handy. One type of review article is the *qualitative review,* in which authors identify important articles on a topic and primarily integrate the findings in a nonstatistical manner, deriving major themes and conclusions from the literature. Annual Reviews is a publisher that specializes in reporting qualitative review articles in 37 disciplines. In addition to the *Annual Review of Psychology,* you may find their annual publications in clinical psychology, law and social science, neuroscience, and other fields relevant to your interests. In general, articles published by Annual Reviews are a good resource for undergraduates. Their reference sections may help you identify individual empirical reports relevant to the topic you're studying.

Other research reviews are more quantitative. In some, experts identify and review empirical reports on a topic, possibly categorizing the individual studies on the basis of their methodological quality. The authors then describe the number or percent of studies that support or fail to support a particular hypothesis or conclusion, and they discuss their findings (Mostert, 2001).

Another quantitative approach, **meta-analysis,** *is a statistical procedure for combining the results of different studies that examine the same topic.* In most empirical studies, each individual response from every participant becomes part of the data that are statistically analyzed. In a meta-analysis, the reviewer identifies empirical studies conducted on the same topic and variables. Each study (or, more precisely, each relevant statistical comparison made within each study) is treated as the unit of analysis. For example, Mark Frank and Thomas Feeley (2003) identified 11 experiments that examined whether training or feedback can improve people's ability to detect whether someone is lying. In total, these 11 studies involved 20 relevant statistical comparisons.

For each comparison in a meta-analysis, the reviewers examine a statistic called the **effect size,** *a statistical measure of the strength of a relation between two variables* (e.g., between receiving or not receiving training and the subsequent ability to correctly identify who is lying). The reviewers then calculate the average effect size for all the comparisons, which provides an overall estimate of whether the size of the relation between two variables is small, medium, or large. Frank and Feely (2003) concluded that training provided a small gain in the ability to accurately detect lying. (See Statistics Module 13 on pp. 446–448 for more details on effect size.)

CONCEPT CHECK 2.2 GATHERING BACKGROUND INFORMATION

Decide whether each statement is true or false. Answers appear on page 68.

1. PsycINFO is a broader database than PsycARTICLES.

2. Using standard Boolean search procedures, typing *memory loss* AND *dementia* will produce a broader search than typing *memory loss* OR *dementia*.

3. In APA journals, an abstract is the final section of an article; it is used to discuss the research findings in depth.

4. Meta-analysis is a statistical approach for combining the results of different studies on the same topic.

FORMING A HYPOTHESIS

Learning Objectives

After studying this section, you should be able to:

- Explain and illustrate how hypotheses are formed inductively and deductively.
- Describe characteristics of a good hypothesis.

As noted in Chapter 1, a **hypothesis** *is a tentative proposition about the causes or outcome of an event or, more generally, about how variables are related.* A hypothesis can be stated in an if–then form as a prediction about the relation between two or more variables (e.g., if X, then Y). Hypotheses should be based on a reasoned analysis of existing evidence relevant to the question being studied. A statement like "Well, my guess is that this is what will happen" would not be considered a scientific hypothesis. In contrast, if you make rational use of a theory or other findings from a literature search, your prior expert knowledge, or other relevant background information to specify how you expect variables to be related, then you've formed a hypothesis. Let's consider an example.

FORMING HYPOTHESES INDUCTIVELY AND DEDUCTIVELY

In their study on lying among high-school and college students, Lene Jensen and her colleagues tested five hypotheses (Jensen et al., 2004). Two hypotheses were:

1. Compared to adolescents, emerging adults will lie less frequently and find lying less acceptable (i.e., *if* an age group consists of emerging adults, *then* they will lie less frequently and find lying less acceptable than will an age group consisting of adolescents).

2. Compared to women, men will lie more frequently and find lying more acceptable (i.e., if students are male rather than female, then they will lie more frequently and find lying more acceptable).

Jensen et al. (2004) formed these hypotheses primarily through **inductive reasoning:** *using specific "facts" to form a general conclusion or general principle.* In this case, the "facts" were the findings from previous research. Police detectives use inductive reasoning when they gather specific clues and then form a tentative conclusion about who committed the crime and why. Likewise, physicians use inductive reasoning when they gather specific information about a patient's symptoms and then form a hypothesis about the nature of the illness (e.g., "It's likely you have a stomach ulcer").

Another common way to form a hypothesis is to derive it from a theory. Recall that a **theory** *is a set of formal statements that specifies how and why variables or events are related.* Theories are broader than hypotheses, and when we use a theory to derive a hypothesis, we are engaging in **deductive reasoning:** *using a general principle to reach a more specific conclusion.* For example, if a physician reaches a tentative decision that "you have a stomach ulcer," then the physician can reason deductively that "if you have a stomach ulcer, this additional medical test (e.g., a barium swallow) should yield the following result (e.g., the ulcer should be visible on an X-ray)."

Psychologists David Buss and David Schmitt (1993) used deductive reasoning to derive hypotheses about sex differences in human mating strategies. Buss and Schmitt work in the field of evolutionary psychology, which endeavors to explain how evolution has shaped modern human behavior. They developed a theory, called sexual-strategies theory (SST), which proposes that as a result of evolutionary processes, women and men are born with different predispositions (tendencies) regarding mating strategies and sexual behavior. To test their theory, they first derived nine hypotheses and then generated 22 specific predictions from those hypotheses. For example, their first hypothesis was that overall, short-term mating is a larger component of men's sexual strategy than of women's sexual strategy. They then used this hypothesis to make five specific predictions about men's and women's sexual strategies. Prediction 2 was: "For any given period of time (e.g., a month, a year, a decade, or a lifetime), men will desire a larger number of mates than will women" (p. 210). Therefore, we can trace their process of deductive reasoning as follows:

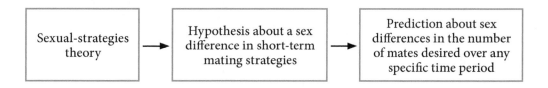

CHARACTERISTICS OF A GOOD HYPOTHESIS

Testability is a key criterion that a good hypothesis must satisfy. And, if you recall the concept of *falsifiability* from Chapter 1, then you will recognize that for a hypothesis to be testable, in principle, it must be possible to gather evidence that will disconfirm it. Of course, scientists typically hope that their hypothesis is supported, but a study must have some potential outcome that will refute the hypothesis.

To be testable, the hypothesis should not be vague; the concepts contained in it should be *clearly defined* and *based on sound reasoning*. A good hypothesis generates *specific predictions* so that it will be clear whether the data support the hypothesis or fail to do so.

A successful hypothesis is also *supported by the data* collected in studies that test it. As predicted, Jensen et al. (2004) found that on most issues, emerging adults reported lying less often and generally accepted lying less than did adolescents. Similarly, all five predictions that Buss and Schmitt (1993) deduced from their short-term mating strategy hypothesis were supported. For example, to test their prediction that men will desire a greater number of mates for any given period of time, Buss and Schmitt gathered responses from 75 men and 73 women to the following questions: "How many sexual partners would you ideally like to have over the next 1 month? 6 months? 1 year? 2 years? 3 years? 4 years? 5 years? 10 years? 20 years? 30 years? During your lifetime?" **Figure 2.5** shows the results. In general, for most time periods, men desired about 3 to 4 times as many sexual partners as women. There are, however, some twists to this story (and controversies about sexual-strategies theory), which we'll encounter later when talking about data analysis and the process of testing theories.

Testing hypotheses is an exciting affair. Yet in many cases, researchers conduct studies without explicitly forming a conceptual hypothesis. There may be no relevant theory or little prior information upon which to develop a hypothesis. This type of research, called *exploratory research,* also plays a key role in science and carries its own excitement. As in hypothesis-testing research, the questions asked in an exploratory study need to be stated clearly, specifically, and in a form amenable to gathering empirical evidence.

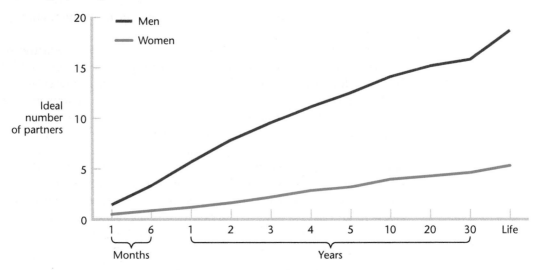

Figure 2.5 Short-term and long-term sexual strategies. The graph shows the number of sexual partners desired for various time periods by women and men in Buss and Schmitt's (1993) study. (Adapted with permission from the American Psychological Association from "Sexual Strategies Theory: An Evolutionary Perspective on Human Mating," by D. M. Buss and D. P. Schmidt, 1993, *Psychological Review*, *100* [2], p. 204.)

✓ **CONCEPT CHECK 2.3** **FORMING A HYPOTHESIS**

Select the correct answer (from inside the parentheses) for each question below. Answers appear on page 68.

1. Compared to theories, hypotheses are _____ (broader, narrower, the same) in scope.

2. A prosecutor uses evidence found at a crime scene to develop a hypothesis about a suspect's motive. This best illustrates _____ (inductive, deductive) reasoning.

3. For a hypothesis to be testable, there should be, in principle, some type of evidence that potentially would _____ (absolutely prove; falsify) that hypothesis.

DESIGNING AND CONDUCTING A STUDY

Learning Objectives

After studying this section, you should be able to:

• Contrast quantitative versus qualitative, and experimental versus descriptive, approaches to conducting research.

• Discuss the concepts of internal and external validity in relation to laboratory and field research settings.

• Explain the nature, pros, and cons of cross-sectional, longitudinal, and cohort sequential research designs.

• Discuss how the need to operationalize definitions, anticipate confounding variables, and use sampling plays a role in planning a study.

The next step in the research process is to gather empirical evidence by planning and conducting a study that adheres to the professional and governmental ethical standards described in Chapter 3. Performing good research can require a lot of patience and persistence. It takes careful planning and execution, and attention to the "big picture" as well as to minute details. Among the "big picture" items to consider are the general approaches that will be taken.

APPROACHES TO CONDUCTING RESEARCH

Psychological research assumes many forms—different types of experiments, surveys, observational studies, and so forth—that you will learn about in subsequent chapters. Research also can be viewed in terms of several general categories or dimensions. Here are some of them.

Quantitative and Qualitative Research

The data in psychological research are often numerical measurements that quantify a characteristic or behavior, such as the speed, frequency of occurrence, or duration of a response. Examples include the amount of time it takes to react to a stimulus, the number of correct responses made when performing a task, and answers to questions such as "This past week, on how many days (0 to 7) did you consume any alcoholic drinks?" **Quantitative research** *relies primarily on numerical data and numerical (e.g., statistical) analysis to describe and understand behavior.* Emily Rosa's experiments on Therapeutic Touch were quantitative. To assess whether TT practitioners could detect human energy fields, the researchers recorded the number of trials in which practitioners correctly located Emily's hand and then statistically analyzed the data (L. Rosa et al., 1998). This was the study's central focus.

Similarly, Jensen et al.'s (2004) study about lying to parents represents quantitative research. On a questionnaire, adolescents and young adults rated how frequently they lied to their parents about specific issues. The researchers relied heavily on statistical analyses to help them summarize the data and determine whether the responses of high-school students to each item differed, overall, from the responses of college students.

In contrast, **qualitative research** *seeks to achieve a relatively holistic or thematic description and understanding of behavior, primarily through the nonstatistical analysis of data.* Typically, qualitative researchers examine events that occur naturally in people's lives and try to capture the meaning or importance of these experiences from the participants' viewpoint. They often gather data by interviewing participants and asking them to discuss the events of interest (Hill et al., 2015). Other examples of qualitative data sources include audio-video recordings, live observers' descriptions of people's behavior, and the content of people's diaries.

Qualitative researchers may examine such data without using statistics, such as by identifying and describing patterns or themes that emerge. If statistics are reported, they play a secondary role and are used to support the main thematic analysis of the data. For example, to learn about the social reactions that survivors of domestic violence receive from their social network (e.g., family and friends), clinical/community psychologists Jennifer Trotter and Nicole Allen (2009) interviewed 45 female victims of recent domestic violence. They then performed a **content analysis,** *an analysis of the different types of content found within or represented by a set of data.* Specifically, they analyzed the content of the interviews, looking for themes in the data and also classifying the women's perceived social network reactions as positive, negative, or mixed.

Content analysis can yield numeric and nonnumeric information. Trotter and Allen briefly noted that 22% of these women reported receiving exclusively positive reactions from their family and friends, and 78% reported receiving positive as well as negative reactions. But their main analysis and discussion nonstatistically elaborated on four themes that emerged from the interviews, centering on reactions that (1) enhanced the victim's safety, (2) provided emotional support, (3) provided helpful advice or information, and (4) provided practical aid, such as assistance with childcare or transportation. They illustrated positive and negative examples of each theme by using quotes taken from interview transcripts. Table 2.1 shows the results of a portion of this qualitative analysis.

Table 2.1 Portion of the Data Analysis from a Qualitative Study

	Theme	
	Emotional Availability	**Aid**
Positive Reactions	Individual(s) provided emotional support (e.g., listening to concerns, validating feelings). [32]	Individual(s) provided survivor with practical forms of aid (e.g., housing, transportation, childcare, financial help). [28]
	Example: "The friends that have been the most supportive, I go over there once a week. And they're always willing to kind of take the burden like if I'm having a bad day . . . I come over and vent. . . they were always just there to listen."	Example: "I was in a situation and I called Mary at like 2 o'clock in the morning and I was like, 'come and pick me up,' and she got outta her bed and she came and got me."
Negative Reactions	Individual(s) not emotionally available; blamed the survivor for her abuse, distanced themselves, or minimized the impact of abuse. [23]	Individual(s) refused or failed to provide the practical assistance requested (e.g., childcare, help leaving the relationship). [16]
	Example: "My mom, she um, she kinda pushed me away. Because she felt like it was my fault, like I needed to do something. . . . I did not stay strong on my word, and so she kinda felt like, sorry, you keep letting [the abuse] happen."	Example: "He [Bob] came to me one day and said, 'I do not wanna watch your kids no more, and here they are.'"

The numbers in brackets indicate how many of the 45 participants mentioned an incident of this type during their interview. The full table in Trotter and Allen's (2009) study listed four themes, with two positive and two negative quotes for each theme.

Source: Adapted from "The Good, the Bad, and the Ugly: Domestic Violence Survivors' Experiences with Their Informal Social Networks," by J. L. Trotter and N. E. Allen, 2009, *American Journal of Community Psychology, 43,* pp. 221–231. Copyright © 2009 American Psychological Association. Reprinted by permission of Springer New York LLC.

The distinction between quantitative and qualitative research can be viewed along a continuum, because these approaches may be combined in various ways and degrees. Such combinations are sometimes called *mixed-methods research* (Teddlie & Tashakkori, 2009). In one mixed-methods study, psychologists interviewed 12 parents whose young children had type 1 diabetes (Monaghan, Sanders, Kelly, Cogen, & Streisand, 2011). The parents had participated in a program designed to provide psychological support as they cared for their children. The researchers qualitatively analyzed parents' comments about the program. Quantitative items included asking parents to rate the relevance of the information received, and the counselors' knowledge and helpfulness. Most parents rated the program positively, and the qualitative analysis identified themes concerning suggested improvements. For example, parents felt the program would have been more useful if it had been held closer to the time when their child had first been diagnosed with type 1 diabetes.

Experimental and Descriptive Research

Scientists conduct experiments to examine causal relations between variables. In an **experiment,** *the researcher manipulates one or more variables, attempts to control extraneous factors, and then measures how the manipulated variables affect participants' responses.* In an experiment, the **independent variable** *is the manipulated variable,* and the **dependent variable** *is* *the measured variable.* In Emily Rosa's experiment on Therapeutic Touch, on each trial she manipulated the placement of her hand by putting it above the participant's left or right hand. This was the independent variable. Emily then measured each participant's verbal report as to where her hand was located. Other aspects of the setting were kept constant. This allowed Emily to examine whether there was a causal relation between the actual placement of her hand and the participant's belief about its placement.[2]

As another example, Darley and Latané (1968) manipulated participants' perceptions of how many bystanders were present when a presumed emergency took place in a laboratory. This was the independent variable. The researchers then measured whether—and how quickly—each participant responded to help the victim. These represented two dependent variables. Their results indicated that the independent variable (perceived number of bystanders) had a causal influence on the dependent variables (likelihood and speed of helping the victim).

Some experiments are designed so that each participant engages in only one condition of the independent variable. This is called a *between-subjects design.* Imagine an experiment comparing the effectiveness of using rote memorization versus using mental imagery (our independent variable, which we manipulate) to learn college textbook material (the dependent variable, which we measure). Using a between-subjects design, we will instruct some participants to use rote memorization, and instruct different participants to use mental imagery, as they study the textbook material we provide them. Because the participants will differ, on their own, in many ways that could affect the outcome of the experiment (e.g., academic ability and motivation), we want to avoid bias in how we determine the learning strategy each participant will be assigned to use. Stated another way, we want to create equivalent groups of participants at the outset of the experiment, prior to exposing them to the independent variable. The most common way that researchers do this is to use **random assignment:** *a procedure in which each participant has an equal probability of being assigned to any one of the conditions in the experiment.* **Figure 2.6** portrays this research design.

An alternative experimental design, called a *within-subjects design,* is to have every participant engage in all the conditions. This way, even though participants will vary in academic

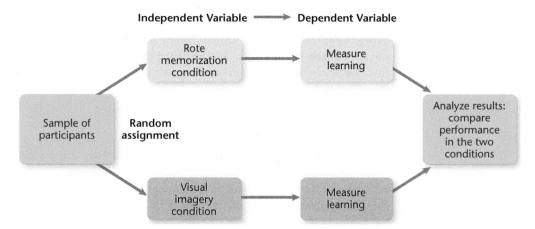

Figure 2.6 Experimental design. An experiment using a between-subjects design. Each participant engages in only one condition of the experiment.

---

[2] In later chapters, you will learn that under some circumstances, an independent variable can be a measured variable rather than a manipulated variable. For now, we will focus on independent variables only as manipulated variables.

ability and motivation, in personality, and so forth, we control for these preexisting differences by having the same participants engage in every condition. But in this approach, we need to minimize the risk that the order in which participants engage in the conditions will become a **confounding variable:** *an extraneous factor that systematically varies along with the variables we are studying and therefore provides a potential alternative explanation for our results.* For example, if the rote memorization condition always comes second and yields poorer performance than the visualization condition, we don't know whether this is because rote memorization is an inferior learning strategy, or because participants were fatigued after first engaging in the visualization condition.

To minimize this type of order effect we would use **counterbalancing:** *a procedure in which the order of conditions in an experiment is varied so that no condition has an overall advantage relative to the other conditions.* For example, half of the participants would engage in the mental imagery condition first, followed by the rote memorization condition. The other participants would engage in the rote memorization condition first, followed by the mental imagery condition. Additionally, given the nature of this particular experiment, we also would need to create two sets of equally difficult textbook readings and exams, because once participants engage in one condition, they will have become familiar with that set of materials. Chapters 8 and 9 provide detailed coverage of between-subjects and within-subjects experimental designs.

In **descriptive research** (also called **nonexperimental research**), *researchers measure variables but do not manipulate them.* The findings are used to describe characteristics of variables and associations between variables. Case studies, observational studies, surveys, and correlational studies are types of descriptive research that are discussed in upcoming chapters.

Trotter and Allen's (2009) qualitative study of women survivors of domestic violence was descriptive research. The researchers did not manipulate any variables. Instead, they asked these women to describe how other people responded to them in the aftermath of the domestic violence. Likewise, Jensen et al.'s (2004) quantitative study of lying among students was descriptive research. Jensen and her colleagues did not manipulate participants' gender or whether participants were in high school or college. Rather, they measured participants' school status and gender, and measured their responses to questions about lying. In this way, they could assess whether associations existed between participants' self-reported lying behaviors and their age status (adolescent, emerging adult) and gender. For reasons we will discuss in later chapters, descriptive research may yield insights into potential causal relations between variables, but it does not provide the clear causal conclusions permitted by properly conducted experiments.

Laboratory and Field Research

The *laboratory setting* offers researchers a key advantage: maximum control. In psychology, the overwhelming majority of basic experimental research is conducted in the laboratory. Because the laboratory essentially shuts out the external world, experimenters can isolate the independent variables of interest while keeping other factors as constant as possible. For example, if we wish to examine how room illumination (the independent variable) affects task performance (the dependent variable), we can expose people to different levels of lighting while making sure that everyone performs the same task. We can eliminate exposure to noise, prevent interruptions from other people, use climate control to keep the room's temperature and humidity nearly constant, and so forth. In this example, features such as room temperature, humidity, noise, and interruptions each represent an **extraneous variable:** *a factor that is not the focus of interest in a particular study, but that could influence the outcome of the study if left uncontrolled.*

The goal of exercising control in an experiment is simple: to achieve high internal validity. **Internal validity** *represents the degree to which we can confidently infer that our study demonstrated that one variable had a causal effect on another variable.* In an experiment, we want to be able to conclude that the independent variable caused the differences in the dependent variable. If we find that people perform a task more poorly when exposed to a low rather than high level of room illumination, we want to conclude that it was the lighting, not some extraneous variable (e.g., differences in noise, humidity, or temperature), that was responsible. By affording greater control over these extraneous factors, the laboratory environment increases the likelihood that causal inferences based on our experiment will have high internal validity.

What happens if we fail to adequately control an extraneous variable, such as the level of noise in the room? Essentially, if our experiment reveals that the results for the dependent variable (e.g., task performance scores) differ as a function of the independent variable (e.g., the levels of illumination that we manipulated), we now face a problem in interpreting our findings. What caused the differences in performance: Was it the independent variable, or was it the extraneous variable? In this case, the uncontrolled extraneous variable has become a confounding variable that provides a potential alternative explanation for our results.

Because the concept of a *confounding variable* is so important, let's consider this example more closely. In our illumination experiment, suppose half of our participants perform a task in a quiet, brightly lit room and the other half perform the identical task in a different, dimly lit room. Now imagine that the dimly lit room also happens to be next to a room with noisy machinery, and some of that noise filters through the walls. If we find that people in the dimly lit room perform more poorly, was it due to the lower amount of illumination or to the noise in that room? Noise is an extraneous variable that we have not adequately controlled, and therefore it has now become a confounding variable that provides a plausible alternative explanation for our findings. This ruins the internal validity of our experiment, because now we can no longer be confident in concluding that it was the independent variable (level of illumination) that caused the differences in the dependent variable (task performance).

Of course, we would be foolish to conduct our experiment this way. Because we can anticipate that different amounts of noise, humidity, and heat could affect our participants, we want to prevent these extraneous variables from potentially becoming confounding variables. Therefore, everyone will perform the task in the same climate- and noise-controlled room, and we'll dim or brighten the lights for each participant.

Countless aspects of behavior can likewise be studied in the laboratory under controlled conditions. Even when researchers are not conducting an experiment, they may prefer to study participants in the laboratory to achieve greater control. For example, rather than observe parents interacting with their children in the natural setting of their homes, researchers may choose to observe them in the laboratory. This way, the observational environment is the same for all participants, and distractions that might occur in the home are eliminated.

Although the laboratory environment has advantages, its artificiality is often viewed as a major limitation. The concern is that findings from the laboratory may have low external validity. **External validity** *refers to inferences about the generalizability of the findings beyond the circumstances of the present study.* Will the principles found in our study generalize to other populations, tasks, or settings? Conducting a **field study**—*research in a field (real-world) setting*—is often assumed to enhance the likelihood that the findings will have high external validity. More specifically, it's assumed that field study findings are more likely to generalize to other real-world settings because, at least, the initial findings were obtained "in the real world." Ultimately, however, the question of external validity is an empirical one: It is answered by conducting further research in different contexts to establish the generalizability of the initial findings. Plenty of findings from laboratory and field studies have demonstrated high external validity; other findings have not.

Unfortunately, field studies (which typically are not experiments) do not afford researchers the high degree of control found in the laboratory. In real-life situations, many factors vary simultaneously, making it difficult to disentangle their effects and draw a clear conclusion as to whether any particular factor had a causal effect. Thus, conducting research in the field increases the risk of low internal validity.

Sometimes, however, it is possible to conduct a **field experiment,** *a study in which researchers manipulate an independent variable in a natural setting and exercise some control over extraneous factors.* Evolutionary psychologist Tamsin Saxton and her colleagues examined whether exposing women to the odor of a particular human pheromone would increase their ratings of men's attractiveness (Saxton, Lyndon, Little, & Roberts, 2008). They conducted three field experiments involving speed-dating events, one that they arranged at a student union building and two that were held by a private speed-dating agency at a local bar. Prior to the speed-dating rounds, each female participant applied a very small amount of solution to the skin below her nose. The researchers controlled which of three solutions each woman received—the pheromone or one of two control solutions (clove oil, water)—and had each woman rate the attractiveness of each man immediately after their speed-dating encounter. Because these were speed-dating events, all women were exposed to the same men. Field experiments combine the advantages of experimental control with the benefit of gathering data in a real-world situation. The researchers found that, compared to clove oil, the pheromone exposure enhanced women's ratings of men's attractiveness at only one of three speed-dating events.

Cross-Sectional and Longitudinal Research

Many psychological questions focus on age differences and developmental processes. How, for example, do our perceptual and cognitive abilities, brain processes, personality, social values, and life satisfaction change as we grow older? In a **cross-sectional research design,** *people of different ages are compared at the same point in time.* In **Figure 2.7**, the blue rectangular-shaded area portrays a cross-sectional design with four age groups, called *age cohorts.* Jensen et al.'s (2004) study on lying to parents was cross-sectional: They compared two age cohorts—adolescents and emerging adults—and drew conclusions about the relation between age and lying behaviors.

An advantage to conducting cross-sectional research is that data can be gathered relatively quickly from many age groups. A key disadvantage is a potential confounding variable called *cohort effects:* Overall, different age groups have different environmental histories.

For example, suppose we measure how quickly 20-, 30-, 40-, and 50-year-olds can detect novel visual stimuli flashed on a computer screen. We find that the older the age cohort, the slower (i.e., poorer) the average reaction time. Does this reflect a biologically based decline in cognitive abilities that occurs with age? Or, might this reflect differences in the amount of time these age groups currently spend—or spent while growing up—playing sophisticated, fast-paced video games? A cross-sectional study cannot disentangle aging effects from potential cohort effects. Even if we measure the video game experience of the four groups and find that it is similar, there may be other important differences in the environmental histories of the four cohorts that could fully or partially account for the findings.

In a **longitudinal research design,** *the same participants are tested across different time periods,* as the oval green-shaded area of Figure 2.7 shows. We might measure the visual reaction time of 20-year-olds this year and then again once every 10 years, until they are 50 years old. This approach has the advantage of studying the aging process in the same people. Disadvantages include the greater length of time required to collect data, the likelihood that

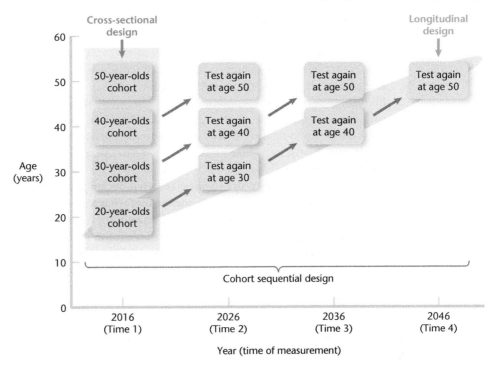

Figure 2.7 Cross-sectional, longitudinal, and cohort sequential designs.

some participants will drop out over time, and the possibility that due to this cohort's unique life experiences, the conclusions we draw about aging might not apply to past or future generations of 20-year-olds.

One way to combine the advantages of cross-sectional and longitudinal research in studying developmental processes is to use a **cohort sequential research design:** *Several age cohorts are tested longitudinally.* In one basic type of sequential design, we could measure the visual reaction time of 20-, 30-, 40-, and 50-year-olds in 2016, and then study each of the first three cohorts again, every 10 years, until they reach age 50. In Figure 2.7, the combination of all the elements (those inside the rectangular and oval shaded areas, plus those outside these areas) portrays this sequential design, which lets us examine whether multiple cohorts display a similar developmental pattern across various measurement periods. Using advanced statistical techniques, a sequential design helps researchers to separate aging-related difference from cohort effects, but it requires a much greater investment of time, effort, and money.

PLANNING AND PERFORMING THE STUDY

Because upcoming chapters provide much information relevant to planning and executing research, we'll only cover a few key points here. First, as Chapter 3 discusses, *we must plan an ethical study.* Whether a study involves human participants or other species, concern for their welfare plays a key role in shaping the types of studies that researchers can conduct. Ethical conduct is essential to becoming a good scientist.

Second, we will need to decide, if we haven't already, whether to employ a quantitative, qualitative, or mixed-methods research approach, and more specifically, the type of study we will conduct (e.g., experiment, observational study) and what the research setting will be. We must determine who our research participants will be, how many participants we hope to study, and how we will recruit them.

Third, we must carefully consider how we will measure or manipulate the variables we are studying. What specific procedures will we use to measure "lying behavior" or "helping a victim," or as Emily Rosa and her fellow researchers (L. Rosa et al., 1998) had to decide, how to measure whether a Therapeutic Touch practitioner is able to detect a presumed human energy field? If we plan to manipulate the level of illumination in an experiment, how many illumination (brightness) conditions will we have, and what will be the precise level of illumination in each condition? In sum, as noted in Chapter 1, for each variable we plan to study, we must decide upon an **operational definition:** *the specific procedures (i.e., specific operations) used to measure or manipulate a variable in a particular study.* Chapter 4 addresses measurement issues more fully.

Next, we will want to use the best research design possible given the resources we have and the constraints we face. "Best" means that we want our design and procedures to yield the clearest possible information to test our hypothesis or to answer our exploratory questions. In an experiment, our design should yield the highest possible internal validity. An important part of achieving this goal is to anticipate how extraneous variables could influence our results. We want to develop a research design and a specific **research protocol,** *a standardized set of procedures that the researcher will follow with each participant,* that will maximize control over extraneous variables and prevent them from becoming confounding variables. Recall that a confounding variable is an extraneous factor that systematically varies along with the variables we are studying and therefore provides a potential alternative explanation for the causal conclusions we hope to draw.

Anticipating how we can minimize potential confounding variables also is important in descriptive research. Recall that in Jensen et al.'s (2004) nonexperimental study, college students reported that they lied to their parents less often than did high-school students (refer back to Figure 2.2 on p. 36). The high school was located on the West Coast of the United States; the college was located in the Midwest. Should we conclude that emerging adults lie less often to parents than do adolescents or, instead, that young people in the Midwest lie less often than young people on the West Coast? Geographic region, unfortunately, is a confounding variable, as the researchers pointed out in their article. The differences in responses about lying might truly reflect an age difference, but we can't be sure of that. Anticipating this potential confounding variable, Jensen and colleagues gathered demographic data from the students and used that information to make certain adjustments to their statistical analysis. A stronger design would have been to study adolescents and emerging adults from the same city or town, but perhaps this wasn't an option available to the researchers.

As we plan our study, we also will need to determine who will administer the procedures to the participants, how we will train any research assistants, and the equipment and materials we will need. We also want to develop our plan for analyzing the data that we will collect.

THE ROLE OF SAMPLING

Research questions typically ask about a **population,** *which consists of all the cases or observations of interest to us in a given study.* Consider these questions: (1) Is cognitive-behavioral therapy an effective treatment for clinical depression? (2) Can 1-week-old infants distinguish between the voice of their primary caregiver and the voice of a stranger? (3) Among adults, is happiness related to monetary wealth? In these examples, the populations of interest are, respectively, all clinically depressed individuals, all 1-week-old infants, and all adults.

Unfortunately, researchers are usually unable to study an entire population. Doing so may be too costly, and access to population members may be limited. For these and other reasons, researchers typically gather data from a **sample,** *which is a subset of cases or observations from* *a population.* Thus, when we seek answers to the questions above by studying 112 clinically depressed people, 54 infants, or 1,200 adults, we are working with samples. Samples can be representative or nonrepresentative of the population. A *representative sample* is one that reflects important characteristics of the population, whereas a *nonrepresentative sample* does not. For example, if 54% of the students at a college campus identify themselves as female, but only 29% of the students in a sample identify themselves as female, then the sample is not representative of the campus population.

Planning a study may involve many sampling decisions. Who will be in our sample? How will we recruit them? How large a sample do we need? Furthermore, because researchers often can't observe a sample everywhere or all the time, sampling decisions may have to be made about times and locations. If we study bullying among schoolchildren, during what hours, days, and months will we observe our sample of children, and in which locations (e.g., hallways, schoolyards)? In several chapters of this book, we will discuss sampling issues, including why it is vital to obtain representative samples in some types of research, but not in other types.

Before moving on to the final three sections of the chapter, take a look at **Figure 2.8** on the following page. It will summarize the major steps in the research process we have covered thus far and give an idea of the final three sections to come.

 CONCEPT CHECK 2.4 DESIGNING AND CONDUCTING A STUDY

Select the correct answer for each question below. The answer options appear inside the parentheses. Answers appear on page 68.

1. In an experiment, the independent variable is _____ (manipulated, measured).

2. In an experiment, the dependent variable is _____ (manipulated, measured).

3. Qualitative research emphasizes a _____ (statistical, thematic) approach to studying behavior.

4. Dr. Lau uses a personality test to measure shyness. People's test scores represent the _____ (conceptual, logistical, operational) definition of shyness.

ANALYZING DATA AND DRAWING CONCLUSIONS

Learning Objectives

After studying this section, you should be able to:

- Contrast qualitative and quantitative data analysis.
- Discuss uses of descriptive and inferential statistics, and describe measures of central tendency and dispersion.
- Explain, in nontechnical terms, the concepts of "statistical significance" and Type I and Type II error.

After researchers collect data, they analyze those data and draw conclusions about their findings. This section introduces you to some basic concepts about these topics.

QUANTITATIVE AND QUALITATIVE ANALYSIS

Quantitative analysis *is mathematical and typically involves using statistics to aid in summarizing and interpreting data.* For example, in the studies we've discussed on Therapeutic Touch, lying to parents, and mating strategies, the researchers relied heavily on quantitative analysis to help them interpret their data. Keep in mind that when researchers employ quantitative analysis, they don't simply compute and report statistics; they evaluate the meaning of those statistical results and use them to describe and draw conclusions about their data (Bernard, 1996).

Infographic: **Figure 2.8**

THE RESEARCH PROCESS

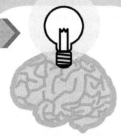

Start Here

Gather Background Information

Perform a scientific literature search and refine the research idea as needed.

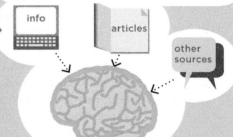

Generate a Research Idea

Observe something of interest and ask a testable question about it. Use personal experience, daily events, prior research and theory, real-world problems, and serendipity as sources for ideas.

Form a Hypothesis

State a prediction about an expected outcome, such as the expected relation between two variables.

Build Knowledge and Theories

The study contributes to scientific knowledge and may spur new research ideas.

The results may help build theories, from which new hypotheses are derived and tested by further research.

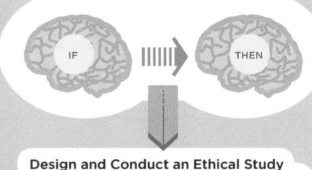

IF   THEN

Design and Conduct an Ethical Study

Gather data to test the hypothesis or answer other research questions.

Report the Findings

Write a research report that conforms to scientific publication style. Submit the report to a scientific journal for review.

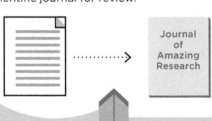

Journal of Amazing Research

Thematic Analysis

Analyze Data; Draw Conclusions

Perform quantitative (statistical) and/or qualitative (thematic) data analyses. Draw conclusions about the findings.

Qualitative analysis *is nonmathematical and often involves identifying, classifying, and describing different types of characteristics, outcomes, or behaviors.* For example, recall that Trotter and Allen (2009) asked female victims of domestic violence to discuss social reactions they received from friends and family. Trotter and Allen then verbally analyzed the transcripts of the women's responses, ultimately identifying four themes that they believed best captured the different types of reactions these women reported (see Table 2.1, p. 48).

Researchers also may combine qualitative and quantitative analysis approaches, as when Monaghan et al. (2011) quantitatively analyzed questionnaire data and qualitatively analyzed interview data to evaluate parents' reactions to a child-diabetes care program (p. 48). Another common example in behavioral research involves using content analysis to classify nonnumeric data into categories so that variables and associations between them can then be examined statistically. Here, qualitative analysis provides a foundation for subsequent quantitative analysis.

Consider that many advertisers try to use humor to get you to buy their products or services (**Figure 2.9a**). In a cross-cultural study, researchers analyzed the content of 3,056 advertisements obtained from similar types of popular magazines in China, France, and the United States (Laroche, Nepomuceno, Huang, & Richard, 2011). They hypothesized that due to different cross-cultural norms, humor would be employed most often in French advertisements and least often in Chinese advertisements. Two trained, independent coders from each country classified their country's ads as attempting or not attempting to use humor. This aspect of the content analysis was qualitative: It involved judging types of content (i.e., humorous, nonhumorous) in the ads.

Once the advertisements were classified, it became possible to count the number of ads in the humorous and nonhumorous categories (these are called *frequency counts*), calculate percentages, and perform statistical tests to help interpret the findings (**Figure 2.9b**). The researchers concluded that the American ads employed humor more often than the French and Chinese ads and noted that their hypothesis was not supported overall.

(a)

The Advertising Archives

(b)

	China	France	United States
Total number of advertisements	1,098	965	993
Number of humorous advertisements	171	150	234
Percent of advertisements that are humorous	15.6%	15.5%	23.6%

Figure 2.9 **A content analysis of advertisements in three countries.** (a) The researchers first classified each advertisement into one of two types: humorous or nonhumorous. This was a qualitative analysis that required a judgment as to whether an ad used humor or not. In this example, polar bears are portrayed drinking cola the way humans might—even though we know that polar bears don't drink cola—therefore we would likely classify this ad as humorous. (b) Once the ads were classified, the researchers statistically analyzed the frequency of the two types of ads across the three countries. This was a quantitative analysis. (Data from Laroche et al., 2011.)

DESCRIPTIVE AND INFERENTIAL STATISTICS

Descriptive statistics *organize and summarize a set of data.* Percentages and averages are familiar, everyday examples that are frequently used in research.

Measures of Central Tendency

Measures of central tendency are statistics that describe the "typical values" or "center" of a distribution of scores. A distribution is a set of scores organized either from highest to lowest or lowest to highest. Here's an example: 0 0 0 0 0 1 3 3 4 5 6.

The **mode** *is the most frequently occurring score in a distribution.* In our distribution, zero is the mode: It occurs five times. The **median** *is the midpoint of a distribution.* In our distribution of 11 scores, the sixth score is the midpoint (i.e., the middle score). Thus, the median is 1. The **mean** *is the arithmetic average of a distribution of scores.* It is the sum of all the scores divided by the total number of scores. In our distribution, the mean is 2.00. In psychology, the mean is the most frequently used measure of central tendency because it takes all the numeric information in a distribution into account. But one disadvantage of the mean is that it can be strongly influenced by a few extreme scores; these are called *outliers.*

Look again at Figure 2.5 (p. 46). Based on the mean scores for the 11 time periods, Buss and Schmitt's (1993) findings make it appear that women and men differ greatly in their ideal number of desired sexual partners. Evolutionary psychologist William Pedersen and his colleagues obtained similar results in a study of 266 female and male undergraduates (Pedersen, Miller, Putcha-Bhagavatula, & Yang, 2002). For example, on average, female and male students desired 2.78 and 7.69 sexual partners over the next 30 years, respectively. Now look at **Figure 2.10**, which displays the percentage of women and men who desired each particular number of partners over the next 30 years. Does the sex difference still seem as large? As Pedersen et al. anticipated, a few outlying scores—those of men who wanted 40, 45, or 99 sexual partners—inflated the men's mean. When the researchers analyzed women's and men's median scores (which are not influenced by outliers) for the 11 time periods, they

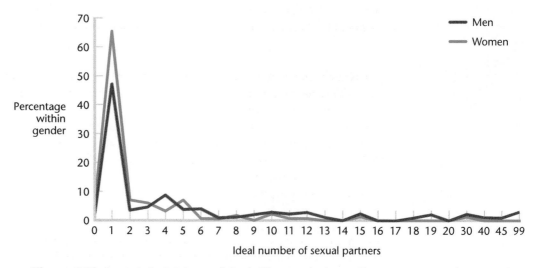

Figure 2.10 Sexual strategies revisited. The graph shows the percentage of men and women in Pedersen et al.'s (2002) study who desire various numbers of sexual partners over the next 30 years. (Adapted with permission from American Psychological Science from "Evolved Sex Differences in the Number of Partners Desired? The Long and the Short of It," by W. C. Pedersen, L. C. Miller, A. D. Putcha-Bhagavatula, and Y. Yang, 2002, *Psychological Science, 13*[2], 157–161.)

found few significant sex differences and concluded that sexual-strategies theory was not supported. In sum, the mean is usually the best measure of central tendency, but it's always important to examine data for outliers.[3] For more details about measures of central tendency, see Statistics Module 3 (pp. 419–422).

Measures of Dispersion

Measures of dispersion describe the degree of spread in a set of scores. Are the scores far apart or close to one another? For example, Table 2.2 shows the ages of eight guests at three parties. The mean age at each party is the same, but these data sets differ considerably. Party 1 is a night of revelry involving young adults. Party 2 is a dinner party with parents and their children. Party 3 is Billy's third birthday party, hosted by his grandparents. Thus, we need statistics that inform us about the variability in our data.

Table 2.2 Ages of People With the Same Mean Age at Three Parties

Person	Party 1	Party 2	Party 3
1	20	34	2
2	23	9	3
3	22	10	2
4	24	41	3
5	22	38	4
6	24	7	3
7	20	31	78
8	21	6	81
Mean age	22	22	22

The **range** *describes the highest and lowest scores in a distribution; it can also be expressed as the distance between them.* For example, the range in Party 3 can be stated as "81 years to 2 years" or as "79 years." The range is a crude measure because only the extreme scores affect it. For example, these two dissimilar sets of scores have the same range:

10 10 10 9 2   10 2 2 2 2

Fortunately, there are more sensitive measures of dispersion that take every score into account. The **variance** and the **standard deviation** (which is the square root of the variance) *reflect how much the scores in a distribution are spread out in relation to their mean.* Overall, if scores are spread far apart, the variance and the standard deviation will be greater than if scores are tightly clustered. For example, Parties 1, 2, and 3 in Table 2.2 have standard deviations of 1.50 years, 14.30 years, and 33.21 years, respectively.

Variance and the standard deviation are key statistical concepts in psychology. The standard deviation is the most commonly reported descriptive measure of dispersion, and both

---

[3] Buss and Schmitt (1993) did examine their data for outliers. If a participant reported wanting 100 or more sexual partners for any time period, that response was rescored to 99 so that it would not have a more severe effect on the data. Note that this rescoring actually worked against their hypothesis because it shrank the size of male–female mean differences (which still ended up being significant). Pedersen et al. (2002) followed the same procedure. They reported that had outliers not been treated this way, for the 30-year period, the mean for men would have been 64 sexual partners desired. Most notably, one participant in their study desired 6,000 sexual partners (see McBurney, Zapp, & Streeter, 2005). Clearly, outliers can have a huge effect on the mean!

the standard deviation and variance form the basis of important statistical tests. Statistics Module 4 (pp. 422–425) offers more detail about measures of dispersion.

Inferential Analysis and Statistical Significance

In most studies, researchers study samples rather than populations. Yet they typically want to draw conclusions—make inferences—that apply to populations. **Inferential statistics** *allow researchers to draw conclusions about a population based on data from a sample.* Inferential statistical analysis often involves using statistical tests to help determine whether the findings of a study are statistically significant. Let's briefly explore, in a nontechnical way, what statistical significance means. We'll use experiments as examples, but the concept of statistical significance also applies to other types of research. For a more detailed discussion of inferential statistics and the concept of statistical significance, see Statistics Modules 1 (pp. 411–414) and 9 (pp. 435–440), respectively.

Consider an experiment in which we randomly assign 20 college students to a control condition and 20 to a treatment condition. Each student flips a coin 10 times. In the treatment condition, we say "Boo!" to each student before the first flip. The results indicate that, on average, per 10 flips, there are 5.1 Heads in the treatment condition and 4.9 Heads in the control condition. Should we infer that saying "Boo!" causes college students to flip more Heads? Probably not; more likely, we would conclude that the difference reflects the random nature of flipping coins. In other words, the difference is due solely to chance, or what scientists call *random error:* random factors that influence an outcome.

Similarly, in any experiment, even if a treatment (i.e., the independent variable) has no effect, due to random factors it is unlikely that participants' responses in the different conditions will be identical. For example, imagine an experiment in which we examine whether consuming alcohol influences performance on a visual-search task. On a series of task trials, 60 symbols will suddenly appear on a computer monitor. Either all 60 symbols will be identical, or one "target symbol" will differ slightly from the others. On each trial, the goal is to decide whether a target symbol is present. Fifty adults participate; we randomly assign 25 to receive nonalcoholic drinks (the control condition) and 25 to receive alcoholic drinks (the treatment condition) prior to performing the task. In the treatment condition, participants consume a moderate dose of alcohol. We measure how accurately and quickly all participants perform the task.

Suppose we find that, in 30 task trials, the mean number of errors in the control and alcohol conditions are 6.34 and 8.70, respectively. How do we know that this difference in mean scores isn't due solely to random error—to chance fluctuations in participants' moods, attention, or energy level? Maybe, by chance, the 25 participants assigned to the alcohol condition just happened to be worse, overall, in their visual-search ability. Perhaps, even if they had not consumed alcohol, they would have performed more poorly than the participants in the no-alcohol condition. In sum, there are random, unpredictable factors operating in any study that might affect the data we obtain.

This is where inferential statistics enter the picture. Stated in nontechnical terms, inferential statistics let us determine the probability that the difference in mean scores is due solely to chance. The next question is: How low does this probability have to be to let us reject the idea that our findings are due solely to chance? Historically, in psychology, this criterion is set at 5%; when an inferential statistical analysis indicates that the probability chance alone could account for a finding is less than 5%, that finding is considered to be **statistically significant:** *unlikely to be due to chance.* We would say we have found a "statistically significant difference" in task performance between the alcohol and no-alcohol groups. In essence, we would conclude that it is implausible chance alone could have produced our results and that our findings better support the conclusion that consuming alcohol influences visual-search performance. In contrast, if our findings are not statistically significant, we would not be able to conclude that consuming alcohol influences visual-search performance.

Statistical significance only means it is unlikely that our findings are due solely to chance. Statistical significance does not tell us whether the findings are conceptually, theoretically, or practically important, or whether the findings might actually have been produced by confounding variables. These issues are addressed by evaluating other factors, such as the scientific or social contribution made by the study and the quality of the research design and procedures.

DRAWING CONCLUSIONS

Testing for statistical significance and drawing conclusions based on the test results form part of a data analysis approach called *null hypothesis testing*, described in Statistics Module 9 (pp. 435–440). Here, we will continue with a less technical discussion, introducing only two new terms below.

In our hypothetical alcohol experiment, if our findings are statistically significant, have we proven that alcohol affects visual-search performance? And, conversely, if our findings are not statistically significant, have we proven that alcohol doesn't affect visual-search performance? Unfortunately, we have not. When we use inductive reasoning and draw a general conclusion from samples of data, there is always a possibility that our conclusion will be incorrect. Similarly, in everyday contexts that involve inductive reasoning—medical diagnosis, criminal detective work, and courtroom trials, to name a few—there is a risk of drawing faulty conclusions based on samples of evidence. In these situations, we can distinguish between two general types of erroneous conclusions, what we'll informally call "false alarms" and "missed opportunities." Let's see how they apply to a courtroom trial, and then to research.

Suppose that a defendant is accused of committing a crime but proclaims his or her innocence. After considering the evidence, the jury reaches a verdict. In an ideal world, the verdict would always be correct: A defendant who truly committed the crime would be found guilty, and one who truly is innocent would be found not guilty. In both cases, justice is done. Unfortunately, there are two ways in which juries can err: (1) In reality, the defendant did not commit the crime, but the jury's verdict is guilty; and (2) in reality, the defendant did commit the crime, but the jury's verdict is not guilty. The first error means that an innocent person is convicted of a crime. In essence, the jury sounded a false alarm: "Guilty! We have a criminal here!" In contrast, the second error means that a truly guilty person has been set free. In essence, the jury missed an opportunity to put a real criminal in jail.

In research, in the context of performing an inferential statistical analysis to determine whether findings are statistically significant, the terms *Type I error* and *Type II error* correspond to the concepts of false alarms and missed opportunities, respectively. If we conclude that there is a relation between two variables when in fact there is not, this would be an example of a Type I error: a false alarm. In essence, we are proclaiming that "something is going on here in terms of how the natural world operates" when, in reality, nothing is. Suppose that in our alcohol experiment, we decide on the basis of a statistical test that our results support the conclusion that alcohol influences visual-search performance. If, in reality—in the way the world really operates—alcohol does not influence visual-search performance and the performance score differences in the alcohol versus no-alcohol conditions reflect only chance fluctuations, then our conclusion represents a Type I error. We have sounded a false alarm to the scientific community. Conversely, imagine instead that in our study, we decide on the basis of our statistical test that the findings fail to support the conclusion that alcohol influences visual-search performance. If, in reality, alcohol does affect visual-search performance, then our conclusion represents a Type II error. We have missed the opportunity to discover and report an actual relation between these variables.

In sum, even in properly designed, well-executed studies, random factors introduce some risk that a researcher's inductive conclusions will be in error. Recall that in inferential statistical analysis, if a finding is determined to be statistically significant, this means that it is unlikely (typically, less than 5% probability) the result was due solely to chance. Still, that probability is not zero and there remains a chance, however small, that the findings might simply be a fluke. As noted earlier, see Statistics Module 9 (pp. 435–440) to learn more about inferential statistical analysis and Type I and Type II error.

 CONCEPT CHECK 2.5 ANALYZING DATA AND DRAWING CONCLUSIONS

Match each concept on the left with the proper item on the right. Answers appear on page 68.

1. measures of dispersion
2. statistical significance
3. qualitative analysis
4. measures of central tendency

(a) the mean, median, and mode
(b) identifying different types of responses
(c) the range, variance, and standard deviation
(d) unlikely that a result obtained in a study is due solely to chance

REPORTING THE FINDINGS

Learning Objective

After studying this section, you should be able to:

- Describe diverse ways in which researchers communicate their findings to the scientific community.

Public reporting of research findings is a key component in the engine that moves science forward. Publishing research reports in scientific journals is the most common and professionally esteemed method of disseminating research findings, particularly if the journals are peer reviewed. Scientists also communicate their research by writing books or book chapters and by making oral or "poster" presentations at professional conferences. As **Figure 2.11** shows, a *poster presentation* is a visual summary, displayed on a poster, that is similar in structure to a research article. For undergraduates, research reporting commonly takes the form of delivering oral reports in class and submitting written reports to one's instructor. Undergraduates also make poster presentations at departmental and campuswide research fairs and sometimes at professional conferences. Some undergraduates publish research in professional journals.

The format for writing a research report varies across different sciences. In psychology, the *Publication Manual of the American Psychological Association,* Sixth Edition (APA, 2010b), establishes the most widely used writing standards. Its 253 pages cover a wealth of topics, from general writing style to precise elements of punctuation, spelling, and capitalization. Don't worry; psychologists don't spend weeks memorizing the guidelines. We do, however, learn the major elements of APA writing style and keep the manual at our side for guidance on specific issues.

Courtesy of Alicia Chong, Lisa Chong, and Jenna Olson

Figure 2.11 At conferences, poster sessions are a common method of reporting research.

Writing a research report is technical writing, with a premium on clarity, logical organization, parsimony, and precision. Although the *Publication Manual* is not what most people would call an exciting read, it contains valuable information to help sharpen your technical writing and even your general writing skills. In this textbook, Appendix A offers information on how to write a research report, covers major APA writing style guidelines, and examines a sample research report.

 CONCEPT CHECK 2.6 REPORTING THE FINDINGS

Decide whether each statement is true or false. Answers appear on page 68.

1. A "poster presentation" refers to posting the results of a study directly on the Internet rather than first publishing them in a scientific journal.

2. In general, peer-reviewed journals are the most prestigious outlets for publishing a study.

3. In psychology, the APA has developed the most widely used guidelines for writing a research report.

BUILDING KNOWLEDGE AND THEORIES

Learning Objectives

After studying this section, you should be able to:

- Explain the benefits of building theories and the characteristics of a good theory.
- Discuss whether the results of a study should be viewed as proving or disproving a theory.

It's often the case that a study ends up raising more questions than it answers. In our hypothetical alcohol experiment, if we find that a moderate dose of alcohol impairs visual-search performance, we might ask new questions such as these:

- Did alcohol's physiological effects produce this outcome, or was the cause people's expectations that consuming alcohol would impair their performance?

- What effects would different doses of alcohol have on performance?

- Does alcohol impair performance equally when performing easy, moderately difficult, and difficult tasks?

Either we or other researchers may conduct more studies to answer these questions. For example, experimental psychologist William Hoyer and his colleagues conducted two experiments that expanded on our hypothetical "no-alcohol versus alcohol" study (Hoyer, Semenec, & Buchler, 2007). They added another control group—called an alcohol placebo control group—in which participants were convincingly led to believe they had consumed alcoholic beverages when, in fact, their beverages were nonalcoholic. Their results suggested that the mere expectation of having consumed alcohol was sufficient to impair visual-search performance. Participants who consumed a moderate dose of alcohol (producing a .04% breath alcohol concentration, or BAC) also experienced performance impairment, but no more so than participants who merely thought they had consumed alcohol. In contrast, adults who consumed a higher dose of alcohol (.06% to .08% BAC) experienced more impairment than participants who merely believed they had consumed alcohol. In turn, these experiments raised additional questions about alcohol consumption and visual-search performance.

Eventually, as research on a topic accumulates, scientists may form a theory. As noted earlier, a *theory* is a set of formal statements that specifies how and why variables or events are related. The purpose of forming a theory is to explain some phenomenon, such as how color vision is possible, why prejudice occurs, or how memory functions. Forming a theory provides several important benefits:

- A theory provides a unifying framework that organizes existing knowledge about a topic into a coherent whole.

- A theory can help us understand and make predictions about new situations and events for which there currently may not be any empirical information.

- A theory can generate interest on a topic within the scientific community and provide a focus for new research.

CHARACTERISTICS OF A GOOD THEORY

Good scientific theories possess several characteristics. Let's examine some of them.

Testability and Specificity

To be considered scientific, a theory must be empirically testable. Extending the concept of falsifiability discussed in Chapter 1, in principle, a theory is testable if we can envision some type of empirical evidence that will reveal predictions derived from the theory to be false. To test a theory, we use deductive reasoning to form a hypothesis based on that theory. When we conduct a study to test the hypothesis, we convert the hypothesis into a specific prediction about the outcome we expect to find. Buss and Schmitt's (1993) research on mating strategies illustrated this progression, as we saw earlier. Based on their sexual-strategies theory, they derived the hypothesis that men would be more invested in a short-term mating strategy than would women. In turn, this hypothesis led to several specific predictions, including:

> *If* participants are male, *then* they will desire a greater number of sexual partners than will females over any particular period of time.

A good theory allows us to make predictions that are specific, not just general. Specific predictions are less likely to be correct due to chance. They're easier to falsify and thus they put the theory "on the line" to a greater extent than do general predictions.

Internal Consistency and Clarity

A good theory is *internally (i.e., logically) consistent:* Different components or principles of a theory should not contradict one another. A related feature of internal consistency is that a good theory does not make contradictory predictions about the outcomes that will occur in a particular situation. If we proposed a theory allowing us to hypothesize that "in situation X, Y will occur" and also "in situation X, Y will not occur," then we would have a problem: There would be no potential way to falsify the theory because no matter what the outcome is, the theory is "covered."

Clarity is another aspect of a good theory: Concepts and the links between them should be clearly specified. Clarity does not mean that any person should be able to read the theory and understand it. Rather, the theory's concepts and logic should be understandable to experts in the field. **Figure 2.12** illustrates a theory that would not meet this criterion.

Empirical Support

A good theory is supported by empirical evidence. First, when a theory is proposed, it must be consistent with the known empirical facts at that time (or it must explain why those facts are flawed). For example, for many centuries it was widely accepted that other planets, the Sun, and other stars revolved around Earth. This theory helped to explain, for example, why the Sun rises in the east and sets in the west. In 1543 the astronomer Nicolaus Copernicus published a theory stating not only that Earth and other planets revolve around the Sun, but also that Earth

"I think you should be more explicit here in step two."

Figure 2.12 **Example of an unclear theory.**

rotates and tilts on its rotational axis. Many scientists, philosophers, theologians, and others regarded this theory as radical, and it was accepted only slowly as new astronomical evidence was discovered. Although Copernican theory may have been radical, it still had to account for the known fact that the Sun seemingly "moves across the sky" in a predictable manner.

Second, a good theory can't rest on the laurels of preexisting evidence. Hypotheses that scientists logically generate from the theory should be consistently supported by new research. If new research fails to support those hypotheses, and if that research is judged to be of good quality, then our confidence in the theory's validity decreases. Ultimately, depending upon the breadth of disconfirming evidence, either a portion of the theory or the entire theory will need to be modified or discarded. We'll return to this issue momentarily.

Parsimony

In everyday usage, *parsimony* refers to being extremely frugal or economical. In science, parsimony is a guiding principle that is often called the **law of parsimony:** *Explanations should use the minimum number of principles necessary to account for the greatest number of facts.* This principle is sometimes tersely stated as "keep it simple" (or KISS—"Keep It Simple, Stupid!"), but this doesn't capture parsimony's full meaning. A more complex, less parsimonious explanation may be justified if it accounts for a greater number of facts or makes more accurate predictions than does a simpler explanation.

The law of parsimony implies that if two theories do an equally good job of accounting for known facts and predicting future outcomes, then the simpler theory—the one that uses fewer or simpler constructs—is the preferred theory. *Occam's razor*, the principle that entities should not be multiplied unnecessarily, is a centuries-old precursor to the law of parsimony. It's named after William of Ockham, a 14th-century English philosopher.

Scientific Impact

On a practical level, one measure of a good scientific theory is the degree to which it has an impact on the field. Does it stimulate research and contribute to the advancement of scientific knowledge? In this sense, even a theory that is eventually disconfirmed can generate scientific progress by sparking new ideas and research, ultimately leading to the development of better theories.

PROOF AND DISPROOF

The accumulation of supportive evidence for a theory does not absolutely prove a theory to be true. Scientific knowledge is regarded as tentative, rather than absolute. Even if many studies provide supportive evidence, the next study may not be supportive, or a new theory may be developed that better accounts for existing knowledge. For example, since the formulation of sexual-strategies theory in 1993, numerous studies by different researchers have supported predictions derived from the theory (see Buss & Schmitt, 2011). Some findings, however, have not been supportive and alternative theories—some focusing on different evolutionary factors and others on sociocultural factors—have been developed to explain gender differences in mating strategies and behavior (Eagly & Wood, 1999; Pedersen, Putcha-Bhagavatula, & Miller, 2011). Overall, the status of sexual-strategies theory remains the subject of scientific debate (Liesen, 2013).

Another reason why supportive research evidence does not absolutely prove a theory to be true stems from the nature of logical reasoning. To illustrate this, consider a statement (called a premise) that takes the following form: "If X, then Y." An example would be: "If an animal is a horse, then it has four legs." Based on this premise, it is not logical to reason in reverse: "If an animal has four legs, then it is a horse." After all, that animal might be a dog, cat, zebra, or some other four-legged species. This type of error in reasoning is called *affirming the consequent*: Given the initial premise "If X, then Y," it is logically incorrect to conclude that "if Y, then X."

Consider, then, the following premise: "If theory X is true, then outcome Y should occur in our study." Paralleling the example of the horse, we would be committing a logical error if we reasoned that therefore "if outcome Y occurs in our study, then theory X is true." After all, think back to the topic of statistical significance that we discussed earlier. There is always a possibility, however small, that outcome Y occurred in a study due solely to chance rather than the specific causal factor that is proposed in the theory and that we tested in our study.

It is also possible that outcome Y occurred because of a flaw in our study, a factor that we tried to control but did so inadequately. The better the quality of our study, the more unlikely it will be that confounding factors would account for our results. But even so, we cannot know with absolute certainty that the outcome in our study was caused by the theoretical variable we were testing. Therefore, when the findings of a study are consistent with the predictions of theory, we can conclude that the theory has been supported but not that it has been proven true.

What if the results of a study do not support a theory? Can we claim that our findings disprove the theory? Logically, we can—if the theory makes the strong prediction that if X is present, Y should always occur. In this case, if we expose research participants to X and Y does not occur, we have falsified the theory or at least the portion of it that led to the prediction. But in practice, when the results of a study fail to support a theory-based hypothesis, they are most likely to be viewed as "unsupportive" or "casting doubt" on the theory's validity. There is always a possibility that in conducting our study and data analysis, we missed an opportunity to detect a relation between two variables that actually does exist. Perhaps if we had studied more participants, designed our study differently, or used other procedures, we might have detected a relation.

In sum, the entire enterprise of psychological theorizing and research is more "probabilistic" than absolute (R. F. Baumeister, 2008). Thus, the scientific status of a theory becomes stronger or weaker as supportive or unsupportive findings keep emerging across different studies. Repeated unsupportive results may cause a theory to be modified or, if that proves unsuccessful, to be discarded.

✓ **CONCEPT CHECK 2.7** BUILDING KNOWLEDGE AND THEORIES

In each item below, other things being equal, which theory is the better theory? Answers appear on page 68.

1. Theory A and Theory B generate identical and equally accurate predictions. Theory A proposes eight concepts to achieve this; Theory B proposes three concepts.
2. Theory X predicts that when people experience fear, this will *influence* their desire to affiliate with others. Theory Y predicts that when people experience fear, this will *increase* their desire to affiliate with others. Research testing the theories finds that, overall, fear does influence affiliation by increasing the desire to affiliate.
3. Theory P generates hypotheses that are not falsifiable. Theory Q's hypotheses are capable of being falsified.

CHAPTER SUMMARY

- The research process begins when we generate a research idea by observing something of interest and asking a question about it. Personal experiences and daily events, prior research findings and current theories, real-world problems, and serendipity are sources for generating questions.

- After scientists form an initial question, they gather background information. Primarily, this takes the form of using online research databases to conduct a literature search.

- Research may be exploratory or conducted to test a hypothesis. Prior research findings and other evidence are used to form hypotheses inductively. Theories are used to generate hypotheses deductively. A good hypothesis is testable, specific in its predictions, and supported by research that tests it.

- General approaches to conducting research include quantitative, qualitative, and mixed-methods research; experimental and descriptive research; laboratory and field research; and cross-sectional, longitudinal, and cohort sequential research. Researchers must decide how to operationalize their variables, design an ethical study, and minimize the presence of potential confounding variables.

- Quantitative data analysis typically involves statistics; qualitative data analysis involves identifying types of things. Descriptive statistics summarize the characteristics of a data set. Inferential statistics allow researchers to draw conclusions about populations based on samples of data. Inferential statistics are often used to determine whether research findings are statistically significant. When researchers draw general conclusions from samples of data, there is some risk that those conclusions will be in error.

- Scientists report their findings in professional journals, in books and book chapters, and at professional conferences. In psychology, the *Publication Manual of the American Psychological Association* (APA, 2010b) describes the standards for writing style and formatting a report.

- A theory explains why a phenomenon occurs. It organizes existing information and provides a basis for generating new hypotheses. A good theory is testable, generates specific predictions, is internally consistent and clearly stated, is consistent with already known facts, and is supported by new evidence gathered via hypothesis testing. A good theory is also parsimonious.

KEY TERMS

cohort sequential research design (p. 53)
confounding variable (p. 50)
content analysis (p. 47)
counterbalancing (p. 50)
cross-sectional research design (p. 52)
deductive reasoning (p. 44)
dependent variable (p. 48)
descriptive research (nonexperimental research) (p. 50)
descriptive statistics (p. 58)
effect size (p. 43)
evidence-based treatments (empirically supported treatments) (p. 37)

experiment (p. 48)
external validity (p. 51)
extraneous variable (p. 50)
field experiment (p. 52)
field study (p. 51)
hypothesis (p. 44)
independent variable (p. 48)
inductive reasoning (p. 44)
inferential statistics (p. 60)
internal validity (p. 51)
law of parsimony (p. 65)
longitudinal research design (p. 52)
mean (p. 58)
median (p. 58)
meta-analysis (p. 43)

mode (p. 58)
operational definition (p. 54)
population (p. 54)
qualitative analysis (p. 57)
qualitative research (p. 47)
quantitative analysis (p. 55)
quantitative research (p. 47)
random assignment (p. 49)
range (p. 59)
research protocol (p. 54)
sample (p. 54)
standard deviation (p. 59)
statistically significant (p. 60)
theory (p. 44)
variance (p. 59)

ASSESS YOUR KNOWLEDGE

1. Describe some common sources of ideas for research.

2. What are PsycINFO, PsycARTICLES, and Google Scholar? How do they differ?

3. How do qualitative review articles differ from review articles based on meta-analysis?

4. Explain the difference between forming a hypothesis inductively and doing so deductively. Explain some characteristics of a good hypothesis.

5. Describe and illustrate the main difference between quantitative and qualitative research.

6. In an experiment, what is the purpose of randomly assigning participants to conditions?

7. How do experiments and descriptive studies differ?

8. Illustrate the difference between independent and dependent variables. What does it mean to operationally define a variable?

9. Explain the concepts of internal validity, external validity, and confounding. Why do confounding variables reduce internal validity?

10. Define the terms *population* and *sample*. Why do researchers typically study samples rather than populations?

11. How do quantitative and qualitative analysis differ? How might both be used in a single study?

12. Explain the general difference between descriptive and inferential statistics, and between measures of central tendency and measures of dispersion.

13. What does it mean when we say that a research result is statistically significant?

14. When researchers draw inductive conclusions from samples of data, what are two general types of error that can occur?

15. Explain the characteristics of a good theory and why scientists generally avoid saying that the results of a study absolutely prove or disprove a theory.

CONCEPT CHECKS: ANSWERS

2.1 Generating Research Ideas

1. false   2. false   3. true

2.2 Gathering Background Information

1. true   2. false   3. false   4. true

2.3 Forming a Hypothesis

1. narrower   2. inductive   3. falsify

2.4 Designing and Conducting a Study

1. manipulated   2. measured   3. thematic
4. operational

2.5 Analyzing Data and Drawing Conclusions

1. c   2. d   3. b   4. a

2.6 Reporting the Findings

1. false   2. true   3. true

2.7 Building Knowledge and Theories

1. Theory B   2. Theory Y   3. Theory Q

THINKING CRITICALLY AND APPLYING YOUR KNOWLEDGE

EXERCISE 1   Identify the Type of Research and the Main Variables

In Chapter 1, Exercise 2a–d, you determined whether each of four studies represented basic or applied research. Here, for these same studies:

• Determine whether each one is an experiment or a descriptive study.

• Identify the variables that are being examined. If a study is an experiment, try to identify the independent and dependent variables. (We'll cover independent and dependent variables more fully in Chapters 4 and 8.)

First try to base your decision on the brief descriptions of the four studies below. If you have trouble, read the full descriptions in Chapter 1.

(a) Dr. Gutiérrez exposes research participants to emotionally positive and negative stimuli, and measures whether these two types of stimuli produce different levels of neural activation in various brain regions.

(b) Dr. Jackson randomly assigns children who have an animal phobia to receive behavioral therapy, cognitive-behavioral therapy, or no therapy. Dr. Jackson measures the strength of the children's phobia at the beginning and end of the study.

(c) Dr. Lieberman tests the hypothesis that employees who are more satisfied with their jobs have higher job productivity than employees who are less satisfied with their jobs.

(d) Dr. Wu has college students watch a videotape of a crime and then serve as eyewitnesses. Actual police detectives interview the students about the crime. The detectives are randomly assigned to use either a new interview procedure developed by Dr. Wu or the standard old interview procedure. Dr. Wu compares the accuracy of the eyewitness information obtained from the two interview procedures.

EXERCISE 2   News from the Doctor; Driving Under the Influence (DUI)

Reread the chapter's section on "Drawing Conclusions." Apply the concepts discussed in that section to the following situations:

1. A few days ago, you went to see a physician because you had been feeling ill for several weeks. The doctor ordered a blood test to help determine whether your liver is functioning normally. The test results are back; based on these results and your other symptoms, the physician forms a conclusion about whether your liver is functioning normally. Describe two possible ways in which this conclusion could be **(a)** accurate or **(b)** in error.

2. A man is driving after having several drinks at a bar. A police officer pulls him over due to signs of erratic driving and administers a Breathalyzer test. Describe two possible ways in which the Breathalyzer test result could lead to **(a)** a correct conclusion and **(b)** an erroneous conclusion about whether the man is driving with a blood alcohol concentration over the legal limit in this jurisdiction.

EXERCISE 3   Searching for Something?

You are writing a paper on the topic of mental disorders and using PsycINFO to conduct a literature search. In the six examples below, will the search terms used in Search B produce a narrower or broader search than those used in Search A? Recall that the asterisk (*) is a truncation symbol.

Search A	Search B
1. *phobia*	*phobia* AND *depression*
2. *phobia*	*phobia* OR *depression*
3. *schizophrenia*	*schizophrenia* AND *2012*
4. *schizophrenia*	*schizo**
5. *schizo** AND *depression*	*schizo** AND *depress**
6. *phobia* AND *therapy*	*phobia* AND *therapy* AND *experiment*

EXERCISE 4   My Word! Identify the Confounding Variable

A junior high-school student designs a memory experiment for a class project. She creates word lists that contain 4, 6, 8, 10, 12, or 14 words. Each word has four letters (e.g., *bird, neck, slow, help*) and appears only once. There are 30 participants. Every participant first sees the 4-word list; then the 6-, 8-, 10-, and 12-word lists; and finally the 14-word list. For each list, the words appear on a computer monitor at a rate of one per second. After the last word on each list, a beep sounds and the participant tries to verbally recall the words. The student measures the percentage of words correctly recalled for each list. She finds that, overall, people performed more poorly as the lists became longer.

There is a blatant confounding variable in this experiment. Can you identify it, explain why it is a confounding variable, and redesign the study to control for it? Can you think of other potential confounding variables or ways to improve the experiment?

CONDUCTING ETHICAL RESEARCH

CHAPTER OUTLINE

A young woman reads a job advertisement and arranges an in-person interview. The meeting begins routinely with the male interviewer asking how she is, whether she found the location easily, and where she grew up. But next, he asks whether she has a boyfriend. Then, after inquiring about her education and work experience, he asks, "Do people find you desirable?" and "Do you think it is important for women to wear bras to work?" (Woodzicka & LaFrance, 2005, p. 76). Later, a researcher reveals that the interview was secretly videotaped and was actually part of a social psychology experiment designed to assess—under controlled but still realistic conditions—whether sexual harassment affects women's job interview performance. The researcher discusses the study and rationale for the deception and gives the woman the option to have her data and videotape erased. Did the goal of this study justify misleading the woman about the nature of the job interview? What other ethical concerns do the research procedures raise?

A clinical psychologist conducts a qualitative, longitudinal study of marital satisfaction in 73 couples. During an in-depth interview, a husband spontaneously and unexpectedly states that he has had an extramarital affair, was subsequently diagnosed as HIV positive, and doesn't plan to tell his wife.

The researcher has promised participants confidentiality: Their names will not be publicly linked to the information they provide. Yet the researcher is now aware that a husband intends a course of action that places his wife at risk for harm. Should a researcher break a promise of confidentiality if doing so may keep someone else from harm (Fisher & Vacanti-Shova, 2012)?

Psychologists Jennifer L. Perry and Nancy K. Dess (2012) note that "engaging in research of any kind is a privilege that carries with it weighty ethical responsibilities and opportunities" (p. 423). The two scenarios above illustrate just a few of many weighty ethical issues that psychologists may confront when conducting research.

THE IMPORTANCE OF RESEARCH ETHICS

Learning Objective

After studying this section, you should be able to:

• Explain why research ethics are important to science and society.

Ethics *represent a system of moral principles and standards.* In the United States, Canada, and other countries, national psychological organizations and federal agencies have published ethics codes to govern how psychologists conduct research with humans and nonhuman animals (APA, 2010a; Canadian Psychological Association, 2000, 2016). Unlike researchers in a field such as astronomy or geology, psychologists study people and other sentient beings. As such, they face the responsibility of respecting the participants in a study. Ethics codes promote such respect and ensure a standard of safety for participants. But becoming an ethical researcher involves more than just learning about ethics codes. It involves appreciating why ethical professional conduct is paramount in science and why conducting psychological research is often ethically challenging. Research ethics involve thinking about what constitutes moral behavior in research contexts and the principles behind why that behavior is moral (Perry & Dess, 2012).

Progress in psychological science depends on people's willingness to be studied. It depends on the public's and government's acceptance of the value and appropriateness of human and nonhuman animal research. It depends on scientists' ability to trust the integrity of one another's work. All this rests on an assumption that psychologists—whether based on their internal moral compass, formal regulations, or both—will conduct and report research ethically (see **Figure 3.1**).

Research ethics are also important because they are intertwined with methodological issues (Thurman, 2015). Ethics affect how scientists manipulate and measure variables, recruit and interact with participants, store and analyze data, report findings, and execute other aspects of their research. Ethical concerns also limit the types of studies that researchers can conduct. For example, it would be unethical to experimentally raise children in environmentally and socially deprived conditions to determine whether such deprivation impairs their cognitive, emotional, and social development. As a result, behavioral scientists wishing to study these issues, or examine children's resilience in the face of prolonged adversity, have used other approaches that do not violate ethical principles. For example, they have studied children who were rescued from abusive caregivers after years of physical and social deprivation (Koluchová, 1972, 1991).[1]

---

[1] In the 1930s, two psychologists conducted studies in which infants received routine care (e.g., feeding, cleaning), but were exposed to prolonged physical and social deprivation. One study exposed two twins to continuous deprivation for just over a year (Dennis, 1935); the other exposed one twin to deprivation during the 40-hour workweek for almost 2 years (McGraw, 1939). Clearly, such studies would not be permissible today (see Razel, 1988, for commentary and historical context).

Figure 3.1 Research ethics are central to the scientific enterprise. They affect many interrelated aspects of (a) how scientists conduct research (green-shaded areas), and (b) the public's and scientific community's faith in the value of scientific research (red-shaded areas).

Research ethics also affect the validity of scientific findings. The scientific imperative to gather, analyze, and report data honestly is one example. Adhering to ethical guidelines so that people don't feel coerced into research participation, and so that they understand when and how their identities will be kept confidential, are other examples. People whose participation has been blatantly or subtly coerced may be more likely to distort their responses (Sieber, 2012). Safeguarding confidentiality can enhance the validity of research findings by increasing participants' willingness to respond truthfully.

To maximize the validity of research findings, however, in certain situations ethics codes allow researchers to deceive participants about key aspects of a study. For example, in the "job interview" experiment described earlier, social psychologists Julie Woodzicka and Marianne LaFrance (2005) examined whether mild sexual harassment negatively affected women's interview performance. To undertake this research, they had to convince a university research ethics committee that the study's benefits to society outweighed the ethical costs of misleading the women about the interview's purpose, secretly recording the women's behavior, and exposing them to harassing questions without their prior consent. Using deception in research is ethically controversial, as we'll discuss later.

✓ CONCEPT CHECK 3.1 THE IMPORTANCE OF RESEARCH ETHICS

The following sentence contains five possible responses ("a" through "e"). Decide whether each is true or false. Answers appear at the end of the chapter on page 107.

1. Research ethics influence: (a) the public's trust in science; (b) scientists' trust in each other; (c) the research procedures used in a study; (d) whether a study can be conducted; (e) the validity of research findings.

CODES OF RESEARCH ETHICS

Learning Objectives

After studying this section, you should be able to:

- Identify events that led to the development of the Nuremberg Code and Belmont Report, and understand their major principles.

- Explain how the APA Ethics Code was developed and discuss its major principles.

- Evaluate whether the benefit of wording ethics principles and standards in broad terms is outweighed by its disadvantages.

The Hippocratic Oath, which came into existence more than 2,000 years ago, is one of the most famous professional ethics codes in history. Intended to guide medical practice rather than research per se, it enumerates several ethical principles that are found in research ethics codes today. These principles include acting with integrity and competence, benefiting others, avoiding doing harm and injustice, and protecting confidentiality (Pope, Tabachnick, & Keith-Spiegel, 1987). Before we see how these principles are embodied in the American Psychological Association (APA) Ethics Code, let's examine two watershed events in the evolution of research ethics.

THE NUREMBERG CODE

Following the end of World War II, some of the most famous war crime trials in history were held in the German city of Nuremberg. In one portion of these trials, 16 German physicians who had worked for the Nazi regime were convicted of crimes against humanity; they had conducted horrific medical experiments in which thousands of concentration camp inmates were involuntarily subjected to extremely painful procedures that injured or even killed them.

In some experiments, physicians removed nerve tissue, muscle, and bone to study the regeneration and transplantation of body parts. In other experiments, the inmates were intentionally infected with malaria, exposed to poison gas, placed in ice-water tanks for up to several hours, or burned on parts of their body (**Figure 3.2**). The purported medical rationale for these torturous and often lethal experiments was to obtain information on bodily responses and tolerance limits to such traumas, information primarily designed to benefit the German military (Nuernberg Military Tribunals, October 1946–April 1949).

In response to these gross violations of human rights, in 1947 the military tribunal judges enumerated the **Nuremberg Code,** *a set of ethical principles essential for a medical experiment to be "permissible."* The spirit of the Nuremberg Code principles also applies to behavioral research, as follows:

- People's consent to participate in a study must always be voluntary, and they should be free to withdraw from the study at any time.

- Prior to giving consent, people should be informed about the study's purpose and the potential risks to their personal welfare.

- All unnecessary risks to participants should be avoided.

Figure 3.2 War crimes: Nazi medical experiments. At the Dachau concentration camp in 1942, victims of a Nazi medical experiment were placed in a low-pressure chamber, and extreme altitudes were simulated. The experimenters wanted to identify the highest altitude from which German military aircraft crews could parachute and survive without oxygen equipment. In this photo, the man has lost consciousness. Many victims died during these experiments.

- The study should yield results whose benefit to society outweighs any potential risks to participants.

- Only qualified scientists should conduct the research.

In turn, the Nuremberg Code influenced the content of subsequent research ethics codes. One of these was the *Belmont Report*.

THE BELMONT REPORT AND FEDERAL REGULATIONS

The **Belmont Report** *is an ethics code that provides the foundation for U.S. federal regulations governing research on humans* . Such research is commonly called *human subjects research.* Federal agencies that fund this research require compliance with these regulations. Published in 1979, the Belmont Report was pivotal because it covered both biomedical and behavioral research. Historically, several infamous medical experiments played an important role in motivating the development of the Belmont Report. Let's briefly examine one of them.

The Tuskegee Syphilis Study

On July 25, 1972, the *Washington Evening Star* ran an article about an ongoing, 40-year medical study of syphilis. Beginning in 1932, researchers from the U.S. Public Health Service and Alabama's Tuskegee Institute had recruited 600 financially poor Black men from the rural South, many of whom were illiterate, as research subjects. Two thirds of these men had advanced syphilis, but they didn't know it and the researchers didn't tell them (Jones, 1993). The researchers never attempted serious treatment—even after penicillin became widely available around 1950—because doing so would have interfered with the study's goal of learning how syphilis spreads throughout the body, ultimately damaging the brain, heart, eyes, and other organs. The researchers had also asked the men's local physicians not to attempt treatment. And whenever a study participant died, the researchers offered to help pay for the burial as an incentive for the participant's family to give them permission to perform an autopsy (Jones, 1993).

The study continued until the *Washington Evening Star*'s news article brought it into the open with the headline "Syphilis Patients Died Untreated." As newspapers around the country carried the story, public shock and outrage spread until the government stopped the study (Brandt, 2000; Jones, 1993). In 1997, President Clinton offered the U.S. government's official apology to the Tuskegee study's survivors and the families of deceased participants (Figure 3.3).

The Tuskegee Syphilis Study was perhaps the most controversial of a number of studies involving human participants that elicited public outrage, leading the U.S. government in 1974 to update its regulations protecting human research subjects. The government also formed the National Commission for the Protection of Human Subjects of Biomedical and Behavioral Research (NCPHSBBR), and 5 years later the commission published *The Belmont Report: Ethical Principles and Guidelines for the Protection of Human Subjects* (NCPHSBBR, 1979).

Principles and Guidelines

The Belmont Report identified three primary ethical principles:

- respect for persons,

- beneficence, and

- justice.

Figure 3.3 Formal apology for the Tuskegee Syphilis Study. Herman Shaw, a 94-year-old survivor of the Tuskegee Syphilis Study, and President Bill Clinton, at the 1997 ceremony in which Clinton offered the government's official public apology for the study.

The first principle, respect for persons, focuses on respecting the autonomy and decisions of people who are capable of self-determination and protecting individuals who are not capable of self-determination. The second principle, beneficence, highlights researchers' obligation to maximize benefits and avoid, or at least minimize, possible harm to participants and society.

The third principle, justice, requires that all people—not just the wealthy or privileged—have access to therapies and other benefits derived from publicly funded research. Justice also requires that potentially vulnerable groups—such as people with mental health problems, prisoners, and the economically poor—not be exploited when selecting research participants. The Belmont Report notes that the forced participation of concentration camp inmates in the Nazi medical experiments grossly violated the principle of justice. In the Tuskegee Syphilis Study, most participants were economically poor. Critics charge that offering free meals and medical care to these men was exploitative and coercive: Given their personal circumstances, the men were hard pressed to turn down the offer.

From these three ethical principles, the Belmont Report derived guidelines for:

- obtaining consent from research participants,
- assessing the risks and benefits of research projects, and
- selecting participants in a just way.

The Belmont Report stressed the importance of establishing independent review committees to assess a proposed study's risks, benefits, and ultimate ethical justifiability. The **Common Rule,** *a United States federal policy that specifies ethics regulations for human subjects research,* builds strongly on the Belmont Report (U.S. Department of Health and Human Services [HHS], 2009). Figure 3.4 shows the Common Rule criteria for judging whether an activity constitutes *human subjects research.*

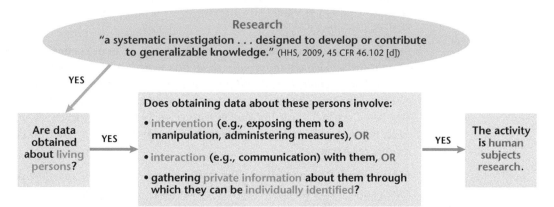

Figure 3.4 When is an activity considered to be human subjects research? The Common Rule specifies criteria for determining whether an act of collecting data about people constitutes human subjects research. (U.S. Department of Health and Human Services, Code of Federal Regulations, 2009.)

THE AMERICAN PSYCHOLOGICAL ASSOCIATION ETHICS CODE

Psychologists strive to meet a high standard of professional ethical conduct. Therefore, issues emphasized in the Belmont Report are also addressed in the ethics codes of many professional psychological organizations. We'll focus on the **American Psychological Association (APA) Ethics Code** (2010a), *which describes general ethical principles and specific ethical standards to guide psychologists' professional behavior.* The code's full title is *Ethical Principles of Psychologists and Code of Conduct.*

Development of the APA Code

When the APA was founded in 1892, it had no formal ethics code. By the late 1930s, as the number of American psychologists grew and as new areas of psychological science and professional services blossomed, the APA created a committee to evaluate cases in which charges of unethical behavior were raised about psychologists' professional conduct. After World War II, the APA (1953) published its first Ethics Code, titled *Ethical Standards of Psychologists,* which has been revised 10 times since.

Note that the 1953 APA Ethics Code was published only 6 years after the Nuremberg Code and predates the Belmont Report by 26 years. The 1953 code addressed ethical standards in client relationships, research, and other areas. In 1973—also prior to the Belmont Report—the APA published an expanded document that focused entirely on research, titled *Ethical Principles in the Conduct of Research with Human Participants.*

The APA committees that developed the 1953 and 1973 ethical guidelines began with a scientific, empirical method. They asked thousands of APA members to (1) describe "situations they knew of first-hand, in which a psychologist made a decision having ethical implications" (APA, 1953, p. vi) and (2) describe the key ethical issues involved. All told, the committees analyzed over 6,000 examples of potential ethical incidents. They grouped examples describing similar issues into categories that formed the basis for identifying major ethical themes. We'll encounter a few of the ethical incidents submitted to these committees.

General Principles

Expanding on the Belmont Report, the current APA Ethics Code (2010a) identifies several broad ethical principles to which all psychologists should aspire to adhere. Appendix A contains the full text of these principles. Here, we'll focus on how these principles apply to conducting psychological research.

Beneficence and Nonmaleficence. The principle of **beneficence** *means that psychologists "should strive to benefit those with whom they work"* (APA, 2010a, p. 3), and **nonmaleficence** *means that psychologists should be careful not to cause harm.* This tandem principle obligates psychologists to protect the welfare of research participants; moreover, beneficence also has a broader meaning that encompasses benefits to society. According to this principle, psychologists need to conduct their research in a way that maximizes benefits and minimizes harm.

Fidelity and Responsibility. The principle of **fidelity** *means that psychologists should behave in a trustworthy manner.* To earn others' trust, researchers need to behave responsibly. **Responsibility** *involves adhering to professional codes of conduct and not exploiting people.* It involves recognizing one's professional obligations to society, striving to act ethically, training one's assistants to act ethically, and caring about the ethical behavior of colleagues.

Integrity. The principle of **integrity** *means that psychologists should be honest and truthful, and should not engage in fraud.* Researchers should strive to record data accurately and analyze data appropriately. They should not misrepresent facts when drawing conclusions and discussing their findings. Researchers also should honor promises made to others.

Justice. A concern for **justice** *calls upon psychologists to recognize that the benefits of their research, and of psychological science as a whole, should be made available to all persons.* Justice also compels psychologists to treat each research participant fairly.

Respect for People's Rights and Dignity. The principle of **respect** *calls for psychologists to* "*respect the dignity and worth of all people, and the rights of individuals to privacy, confidentiality, and self-determination*" (APA, 2010a, p. 3). Researchers should take special steps to honor these rights when people's ability to make independent decisions is compromised—for example, when participants are children, prisoners, or individuals who suffer from psychological disorders. When studying people whose gender, ethnicity, culture, age, religion, or sexual orientation differs from the researcher's, the researcher should respect these differences.

ADHERING TO ETHICS CODES: AMBIGUITIES AND DILEMMAS

Beyond the aspirational principles we've just discussed, most of the APA code describes more specific ethical standards to which researchers must adhere. Still, the APA code and other ethics codes are not cookbooks that offer precise recipes for making all the moral decisions that a researcher could confront (Lefkowitz, 2012). Some terminology used in ethics standards is broad enough (e.g., "reasonably expected," "as early as feasible") to accommodate the unique circumstances of any particular study. This helps the standards cover the diversity of behavioral research, but such broad language also produces ambiguity (Joyce & Rankin, 2010; Kimmel, 2012). This ambiguity can create the following complications:

- greater potential difficulty for the researcher in deciding how a principle or standard applies to a particular case;

- a greater likelihood of disagreement between researchers and institutional research ethics review committees—all of whom are trying to be morally responsible—in deciding whether a proposed study satisfies ethics regulations;

- a greater possibility that different ethics review committees would reach different decisions about (1) whether to approve the same research proposal and (2) what changes to the researchers' procedures might be needed to gain committee approval. This situation has occurred, for example, when researchers at different institutions have collaborated on studies needing approval by each institution's ethics review committee (Ceci & Bruck, 2009; Pritchard, 2011).

In planning and executing their studies, researchers may also face ethical dilemmas in the following circumstances:

- Adhering to one principle or standard might call for a course of action that conflicts with another principle or standard.

- Different aspects of the same principle or standard might call for conflicting courses of action.

- Different participants or other parties involved in a study might have competing interests; thus, applying the same principle or standard to each party would require conflicting courses of action.

Consider the scenario described at the beginning of the chapter involving a study of marital satisfaction, where the clinical psychologist must decide whether to honor a promise to protect a husband's confidentiality after the husband reveals his HIV-positive status and his intent to conceal this information from his wife. Protecting the husband's confidentiality would be supported by the principles of *integrity* (i.e., honoring promises) and *fidelity and responsibility* (i.e., establishing trust). Yet the psychologist also has a professional relationship with the wife; she, too, is a research participant in this study of married couples. To what extent does having a relationship of trust with the wife imply a moral obligation to inform her of the potential risk to her health that her husband plans to conceal? (See Fisher & Vacanti-Shova, 2012.)

Turning to the principle of *beneficence and nonmaleficence,* the goal of avoiding harm would seem to support revealing the husband's HIV-positive status to his wife. This could reduce the potential for serious harm by allowing her to make informed decisions about future sexual activity with her husband. We also might ask whether the obligation to avoid harm would suggest this course of action even if the wife were not a participant in the study. Conversely, we also must consider harms that could result from informing the wife, such as violating the husband's trust (including his general trust of researchers) and possibly increasing marital distrust and conflict. Even though the potential harms involved in this ethical dilemma are not the direct result of research procedures to which the psychologist has actively exposed participants, as might occur when researchers expose participants to potentially stressful experimental tasks, the principle of avoiding harm would still apply.

 CONCEPT CHECK 3.2 **CODES OF RESEARCH ETHICS**

Match each principle on the left to its core concept on the right. Answers appear on page 107.

1. nonmaleficence   (a) displaying honesty in conducting research and reporting findings
2. respect   (b) using scientific knowledge to benefit all people, not just some
3. integrity   (c) being a trustworthy researcher; caring about research ethics
4. justice   (d) protecting the welfare of research participants
5. fidelity   (e) being mindful of gender, ethnic, and other individual differences, and of the dignity and worth of all people

ETHICAL STANDARDS IN HUMAN SUBJECTS RESEARCH

Learning Objectives

After studying this section, you should be able to:

- Explain the concept of minimal risk and make a reasoned judgment about whether a study involves no more than minimal risk.
- Evaluate the potential risks of a study, paying attention to various types of risk.
- Discuss major ethical issues pertaining to informed consent.
- Evaluate whether a study involves deception and discuss the controversy over deception.

As **Table 3.1** shows, the APA's ethical standards are organized into 10 major categories. We will examine several sections of Standard 8 ("Research and Publication") and other standards. Appendix A provides the complete APA text of Standard 8 and of sections from other standards relevant to conducting research. See http://www.apa.org/ethics/code/ to access the entire APA Ethics Code.

INSTITUTIONAL REVIEW

APA ethical standards obligate psychologists to comply with governmental policies concerning institutional approval of research. In the United States, many federal departments and agencies that fund and conduct human subjects research adhere to the ethics regulations set forth in the Common Rule. Whether domestic

Table 3.1 The 2010 APA Ethics Code: Ethical Standards

Standard 1. Resolving Ethical Issues	Standard 6. Record Keeping and Fees
Standard 2. Competence	Standard 7. Education and Training
Standard 3. Human Relations	Standard 8. Research and Publication
Standard 4. Privacy and Confidentiality	Standard 9. Assessment
Standard 5. Advertising and Other Public Statements	Standard 10. Therapy

or international, any college, university, or other institution that conducts human subjects research funded or otherwise supported by one of these federal agencies must ensure that this research complies with the Common Rule. Most of these institutions also choose to require that all their human subjects research—regardless of whether or by whom it is funded—conforms to all or major portions of the Common Rule.

In the United States, an **Institutional Review Board (IRB)** *is an independent institutional committee that evaluates whether proposed research with human participants complies with federal ethics regulations.*[2] An institution can create its own IRB or arrange for ethics reviews by an external IRB. Institutions that do not receive federal funding for human subjects research may choose to establish IRBs or other ethics review procedures, but are not required to do so by the Common Rule.

An IRB must comprise at least five members of varying backgrounds, including (1) at least one member who is not otherwise affiliated with the institution, (2) at least one member with a primarily scientific background, and (3) at least one member whose background is primarily *not* scientific. Upon completing its evaluation of the ethics compliance of each proposed study, an IRB has several options. These include (1) approving the study, in which case the research may begin; (2) disapproving the study, in which case it cannot be conducted; or (3) requiring the investigator to modify the study and resubmit the proposal for further review. If an IRB grants approval, an institution may still require a research proposal to undergo further review. For example, beyond an IRB review, a proposed project to study adolescent bullying in public high schools would likely be reviewed by each participating school and/or the local school district. If an IRB disapproves a study, however, other review committees or institutional officials cannot override the IRB's ruling.

When a research proposal is submitted, it will first be examined to determine which of three ethics review categories applies: (1) *exempt* from IRB review, (2) *expedited review*, or (3) *full IRB review*. First, certain types of proposed research are eligible for exemption from IRB review. For example, depending on the sensitivity of the information collected and whether it is recorded in a way that prevents participants' identities from being known, research based on surveys, interviews, naturalistic observations of people's public behavior, and the analysis of data sets that already exist (e.g., Census records) may be granted exempt status. So may the study of normal educational practices in common educational settings. "Exempt" does not mean "exempt from following ethics codes." *Exempt research* must still comply with ethics regulations.

Researchers apply for exempt status when they believe their proposed study qualifies. Each institution decides who is authorized to verify that a study meets the criteria for exemption. This usually will be a designated staff member who works in an administrative unit that oversees human subjects research, a qualified liaison, such as the chair of a departmental human subjects review committee, or an IRB member. Second, many studies

[2] Similar committees exist in many countries. They have different names, such as Research Ethics Board (REB) in Canada, Local Research Ethics Committee (LREC) in the United Kingdom, and Human Research Ethics Committee (HREC) in Australia.

that don't qualify for exempt status, but fall within a level of minimal risk to participants, may be eligible for expedited review. In an *expedited review,* one or more IRB members can approve a research proposal, require modifications to it, or forward it to the full IRB for a review. (A proposal can be disapproved only after a full IRB review.) Studies on a wide range of psychological topics are eligible for expedited review, including research on "perception, cognition, motivation, identity, language, communication, cultural beliefs or practices, and social behavior" (HHS, 1998, Applicability, F7). Proposals that don't qualify for exempt status or expedited review fall into the third category and must undergo a full IRB review.

ASSESSING RISKS AND BENEFITS

APA ethical standards require psychologists to take reasonable precautions against exposing research participants to harm. If harm cannot be avoided, then it must be minimized. To approve a study, an IRB must determine that two conditions are satisfied concerning potential risks of harm to participants. First, the IRB must be convinced that the researcher has minimized any scientifically necessary risks to participants. Second, regardless of the level of risk, it must be outweighed by the study's potential benefits. *This evaluation of risks relative to benefits is commonly called "weighing the* **risk/benefit ratio***."*

Minimal Risk Versus More Than Minimal Risk

Because the concept of "zero risk" calls for an absolute certainty that is typically impossible to guarantee, researchers and IRBs evaluate risk in terms of a standard called *minimal risk.* **Minimal risk** *"means that the probability and magnitude of harm or discomfort anticipated in the research are not greater in and of themselves than those ordinarily encountered in daily life or during the performance of routine physical or psychological examinations or tests"* (HHS, 2009, Section 46.102.i). But, in trying to estimate the risks of harm or discomfort "ordinarily encountered in daily life," whose life sets the standard? U.S. federal policy advises that the concept of minimal risk "should reflect 'background risks' that are familiar and part of the routine experience of life for 'the average person' in the 'general population'" (Secretary's Advisory Committee on Human Research Protections [SACHRP], 2008, "Interpretation of Minimal Risk," para. 5).

Minimal risk is a reference point against which the risks to participants in a particular study are judged as posing *no more than minimal risk* or, instead, *more than minimal risk.* For example, during an experiment you might become momentarily frustrated while performing a task. Although this is a risk, it likely would represent no more than minimal risk because in daily life, an "average person" might routinely experience brief frustration while performing a task at work, school, or elsewhere. Similarly, while engaging in an online experiment, the risk of your computer being hacked isn't zero, but this is a risk an average person would routinely face while using the Internet (SACHRP, 2013, March 12-13).

Figure 3.5 provides a more detailed example of judging a study's risk in relation to minimal risk. It is based on a case example provided by the U.S. government (SACHRP, n.d., Case 1). As you proceed through the figure, notice that in the third graph the level of risk that constitutes minimal risk is estimated in relation to the daily life of an average person in the general population. In contrast, the estimated risk to which participants will be exposed varies, depending on their characteristics (the first graph) and the specific procedures to be used, such as who will conduct the interviews (the second graph).

Risk estimates may be guided by reason, careful analysis, federal recommendations, and so forth. Ultimately, however, they are subjective judgments and different IRBs may reach different conclusions about whether a study involves more than minimal risk. Participants

Infographic: **Figure 3.5**

UNDERSTANDING MINIMAL RISK*

1 The Research Proposal

- **Researchers:** A clinical psychologist and medical psychologist.
- **Purpose:** To learn about the process of making end-of-life decisions (e.g., about whether and when to use hospice care) in the care of terminally ill cancer patients.
- **Participants:**

Group A: Adult close family members mourning the loss of a patient who has died recently

Group B: Adult patients newly diagnosed as being terminally ill

Group C: Adult patients diagnosed over a month ago, who have been attending a support group with other terminally ill patients

- **Procedure:** Each participant will be interviewed for one hour.

2 Estimated risk by an IRB (or other ethics review committee) of harm and discomfort from research participation, based on subject characteristics.

 Bereaved Family Members

Newly Diagnosed Patients

 Patients in Support Group

LOWER RISK   HIGHER RISK

3 Estimated risk of harm and discomfort from research participation, based on training and skill of the interviewer. Higher risk is judged if the interviewer is an assistant.

 Research Assistant

 Experienced Clinician

LOWER RISK   HIGHER RISK

4 Estimated risk from research participation (with a trained clinician as the interviewer) in relation to the estimated reference level of minimal risk.

 Bereaved Family Members

 Newly Diagnosed Patients

 Patients in Support Group

LOWER RISK   HIGHER RISK

Minimal Risk Threshold: Estimated probability and magnitude of the harm and discomfort of daily life for the average person in the general population.

5 Risk Status Conclusion: In this analysis, if the only participants studied were to be the previously diagnosed patients attending the support group, the proposed research might be classified by this IRB as posing no more than minimal risk. Otherwise, the study would be considered to involve more than minimal risk due to the inclusion of one or both of the other groups. Note that another IRB might decide that even for patients in a support group, the risks of participation exceed minimal risk. This would occur if another IRB estimates the minimal risk threshold to be lower, and/or the risks to participants to be greater, than the estimates by the IRB shown here.

*Adapted from a case example provided by SACHRP, Office of Human Research Protections, U.S. Department of Health & Human Services, (n.d.).

are said to be **at risk** *when a proposed study involves more than minimal risk;* in such cases, the proposal undergoes a full IRB review. Under a full review, stronger safeguards must be in place to protect participants' welfare. However, even when a study involves no more than minimal risk, the researchers must still take reasonable steps to minimize potential negative effects. For example, if some participants in an experiment find a task to be frustrating, a researcher could discuss their reactions with them after they complete the experiment and reassure them that many people find the task difficult.

Types of Harm

IRBs consider several types of potential harm in judging the degree of risk to participants. The harm may be physical, psychological, social, economic, legal, or some combination of these.

Risk of Physical Harm. This includes the potential for pain, physical injury, or other physical discomfort. Such risk can arise, for example, when researchers wish to examine how stressors such as sleep deprivation, noise, and heat influence people's behavior. Consider this case:

> I directed a series of studies concerning the effects of heat, noise, altitude, and vibration on human performance in physiology. All of these studies involved considerable discomfort for the subjects. Physical danger was also present . . .; there was also the possibility than an undiscovered medical defect . . . could render a subject unable to tolerate stresses that would be acceptable for normal subjects. (APA, 1973, p. 59)

To minimize risk, the equipment underwent a week of testing before it was used, and the researchers monitored equipment safety during the studies. Participants had to pass a full medical exam before being cleared to participate and were medically monitored during the study. Before giving consent, each person was required to observe someone else undergo the research procedures and listen to a lecture emphasizing the physical dangers that could arise if something went wrong.

Risk of Psychological Harm. This involves the experiencing of negative emotions, threats to one's self-esteem, and other types of psychological distress. For example, participants may perform tasks in which they are instructed to try to do well, and they may become frustrated, anxious, or sad if they perform poorly. Depending on the estimated intensity and duration of these responses, and the context (e.g., a study of older adults unaccustomed to such tasks), such research may be judged by IRBs as involving more than minimal risk.

In some studies, participants are exposed to environmental stressors or other aversive stimuli that may cause emotional distress. Recall that in Woodzicka and LaFrance's (2005) experiment, women in the sexual harassment condition were exposed to three sexually inappropriate job interview questions. If you were an IRB member, what would you judge potential participants' risk of emotional distress to be? The results of this study indicated that women indeed felt more sexually harassed and perceived the interviewer as more sexist than did women in a control job interview condition who were asked equally unusual but nonharassing questions. However, the harassment and control conditions produced little overall difference in reported emotional distress. IRBs, of course, must judge expected risks before knowing how the results of a study will turn out.

Risk of Social Harm and Loss of Privacy. This can occur when information obtained about a person becomes known, causing the person to experience undesirable social consequences. In some studies, for example, researchers may ask participants to disclose sensitive personal information. Participants might be embarrassed or even exposed to some type of jeopardy if their responses became public. In a job satisfaction study, for example, you might not want your manager to know that you rated him or her as an "extremely poor" leader.

Risk of social harm and loss of privacy can be minimized through procedures that ensure anonymity or confidentiality. **Anonymity** *means that a participant's identity is unknown, even to the researcher.* For example, in a survey conducted by mail, if there are no markings or information on the questionnaire or return envelope that could be used to identify the people who respond, then participation would be anonymous. More often, however, participants are not anonymous but are promised confidentiality. **Confidentiality** *means that participants' identities will not be released without their consent, and data from the study will be reported in a way that does not identify individual participants.*

Promises of anonymity or confidentiality not only protect participants but also are intended to enhance the validity of research findings by increasing participants' truthfulness in responding. In a study seeking to examine illegal or socially inappropriate behaviors such as drug use or extramarital affairs, if certain participants who are more likely to have engaged in such behaviors do not trust promises of anonymity or confidentiality, this could compromise their willingness to participate or reduce their willingness to respond honestly. If this distorts either the sample of people who agree to participate or participants' responses, it will reduce the validity of the findings.

In studies that promise confidentiality, researchers must have procedures in place to safeguard the confidentiality of the information they collect. Typically, they assign code numbers to identify each participant, and key research personnel are the only ones who have access to the list that matches the code numbers to participants' identities. After the data are collected, the list may be destroyed, leaving only code numbers associated with the data. However, as we'll discuss later, under certain circumstances researchers may be legally required or ethically obligated to release confidential information.

Risk of Economic or Legal Harm. These risks often overlap with considerations of privacy and social harm, as this case illustrates:

> I was doing a job-satisfaction survey for a local concern. The replies were to be anonymous. I was informed that the employer had secretly marked the questionnaire to locate "troublemakers." I burned the questionnaire and told the sponsor where to place his money. (APA, 1973, p. 90)

The risk of economic and legal harm can also overlap with physical and psychological harm. For example, consider that sleep deprivation adversely affects people's motor and cognitive performance (Taber & Hurley, 2006), and imagine an experiment in which participants are to be deprived of sleep for two nights. After the deprivation ends, will participants be free to drive home? What if a sleep-deprived participant causes an automobile accident, incurring financial and legal damages and causing harm to her- or himself and others? The researcher should take steps to minimize such risks.

Sensitive Information

Psychologists study many topics that involve gathering sensitive information from participants. According to U.S. federal guidelines:

> Sensitive information includes (but is not limited to) information relating to sexual attitudes, preferences, or practices; information relating to the use of alcohol, drugs, or other addictive products; information pertaining to illegal conduct; information that, if released, might be damaging to an individual's financial standing, employability, or reputation within the community or might lead to

social stigmatization or discrimination; information pertaining to an individual's psychological well-being or mental health; and genetic information or tissue samples. (HHS, 2011, B1)

Gathering sensitive information heightens ethical concerns about protecting participants' confidentiality. Research suggests that IRBs are less likely to approve research proposals that involve more sensitive, as opposed to less sensitive, topics (Ceci, Peters, & Plotkin, 1985). Some psychologists believe that IRB members overestimate the likelihood that asking research participants to discuss sensitive issues, such as personal traumas, will cause participants to experience long-term distress or be retraumatized (Legerski & Bunnell, 2010; Yeater, Miller, Rinehart, & Nason, 2012).

Incidental Findings

An *incidental finding* is an unexpected finding about a research participant that is not directly related to the purpose of a study, but that may be significant for the participant's or someone else's health or functioning. For example, suppose that during a home visit conducted for a study on children's language development, a researcher observes an instance of child physical abuse. This would be an incidental finding. As we will discuss later, the researcher's response would be governed by ethics codes and duty-to-report laws.

As another example, suppose that in a study, several psychologists measure female college students' brain activity while the students perform perceptual tasks. Unexpectedly, one student's brain scans reveal a possible tumor or lesion. Is it obvious that the researchers should tell the student? They are not physicians, and their suspicion might be wrong. Even if they are correct, the abnormality may not be clinically significant. Telling her might cause needless worry and lead her to misinterpret future medical or psychological symptoms as being related to this abnormality when, in fact, they are not. For the student, pursuing further medical diagnosis could have financial costs and decrease her future ability to obtain health insurance. Still, are these risks outweighed by the possibility the abnormality could be significant?

Psychologists and other neuroscientists are concerned about how to ethically respond to such incidental brain research findings. Currently, ethics codes do not provide a clear policy, and researchers handle such incidental findings in different ways (Phillips et al., 2015). Table 3.2 shows a sample incidental-findings policy for brain-imaging research.

Subjectivity in Risk Assessment

The subjectivity of risk assessment contributes to the challenge of research ethics. Researchers and IRB members may agree on the types and overall level of risk to participants, but disagree on whether the planned procedures adequately address those risks. Often, disagreements arise about the nature or degree of risk itself. Consider this actual example reported by Stephen Ceci and Maggie Bruck (2009).

Developmental psychologists from three different universities plan a study to test a theory-based hypothesis. The topic involves children as eyewitnesses. The researchers will ask 6- to 10-year-old children to make judgments about why a boy has not told the truth. Each child will watch a 4-minute video involving a firefighter, a police officer, and the boy (all played by actors). In one scene, the firefighter tells the boy to leave the firefighter's hat alone. A subsequent scene shows the police officer asking the boy leading questions about the boy's interaction with the firefighter. In response to these suggestive questions, the boy in the video falsely reports that the firefighter hit him. The children will then be asked why they think the boy in the video didn't tell the truth.

Table 3.2 Sample Incidental-Findings Policy

Unexpected Finding on Research Subject MRI

In the event an unexpected "oddity" or suspected abnormality is found on an MR study in the course of a research or test MRI, the images are to be reviewed by a faculty radiologist trained in MR Image interpretation as soon as reasonably possible. The reviewing radiologist will make a determination of either "possibly abnormal" or "non-significant" finding. If a non-significant finding, the PI should be notified but no other action is required. If a determination of "possibly abnormal" is made, that information needs to be conveyed to the PI and the subject. The physician reviewing the MR scan will discuss the concern with the PI. They will jointly formulate a plan of action to notify the subject and discuss the finding of concern with the subject. The physician discussing with subject will document this for the MR Lab records and will also provide a recommendation for follow-up for further evaluation (e.g., referral to subject's physician or to a UW physician).

At no time will the MR lab provide diagnosis or imaging workup of the clinical problem/question. Any diagnostic evaluation must be done in a clinical facility.

Although we make every attempt to review images by an experienced MR operator at the time they are acquired, the MR Lab is not responsible for medical diagnostic review of all images acquired. In the event that a PI desires a formal physician review of their study images, the PI is responsible for contracting with a MR trained physician to provide this service.

Note: PI = principal investigator (i.e., the lead researcher); MR = magnetic resonance.

Source: An Example of an Incidental Finding Policy for Brain Imaging Research. University of Washington Magnetic Resonance Research Laboratory (n.d.). Used by permission.

The three psychologists proposing the study must obtain approval from the IRBs at their respective institutions. Two IRBs approve it, but the third does not, deeming it "unethical to show children public servants in a negative light" (Ceci & Bruck, 2009, p. 28). The researchers appeal the decision and amass information to support their view that watching the video will not harm the children's perception of public servants. The IRB denies the appeal and will approve the study only if the researchers change their procedure. Do you agree with this IRBs' risk assessment?

Judging the Quality of the Research

Suppose you are a researcher in the area of visual perception, an expert in your field. You submit a research proposal to an IRB, which reviews it and decides that your proposed study contains flaws. The IRB asks you to modify your study and resubmit your proposal. Should an IRB be judging the quality of your proposed study—especially if none of its members are experts in visual perception or perhaps not even research psychologists?

Judgments that IRBs make about the methodological quality of a proposed study can be a sore point with researchers. Still, IRBs are obligated to decide whether investigators are minimizing risk "by using procedures which are consistent with sound research design" (HHS, 2009, Section 46.111.a1). IRBs also consider the soundness of a study in order to judge its scientific value and potential benefits, ultimately deciding whether those benefits outweigh potential risks (Rosenthal, 1994). As needed, IRBs can ask outside experts to evaluate technical aspects of a research proposal, although such experts would act only as consultants and would not vote on the proposal.

INFORMED CONSENT

In June 2014 a scientific journal published the findings of a massive online experiment that involved 683,003 Facebook users and had been conducted without users' knowledge (Kramer, Guillory, & Hancock, 2014). For one week, Facebook had intentionally omitted from half of these users' News Feeds some of the emotionally positive or negative posts sent by friends. Some News Feed posts were omitted randomly for users in control groups, regardless of emotional content. This experimental manipulation had a small (though statistically significant)

Figure 3.6 **Media reaction to (a) Facebook's emotion contagion experiment and (b) OkCupid's mismatch experiment.** Both experiments came to the public's attention in 2014 and generated debate about when, and how, informed consent needs to be obtained by online researchers.

effect on the emotional content of users' own posts, and it led to a public uproar about the study's ethics (see **Figure 3.6a**). The study's lead researcher was a Facebook data scientist; the other two were academic researchers at Cornell University involved in designing the study and writing the final report. This resulted in a heated debate about whether the study should have first undergone an IRB review at Cornell and whether Facebook users' consent to participate should have been obtained (Puschmann & Bozdag, 2014).

A month later, the founder of the online dating service OkCupid added fuel to this ethical fire by telling readers in a blog, "Guess what, everybody: if you use the Internet, you're the subject of hundreds of experiments at any given time, on every site. That's how websites work" (Rudder, 2014, July 28, para. 2). The blog described experiments OkCupid had conducted on unsuspecting members, including one that provided false information to pairs of members about how well their dating profiles matched (see **Figure 3.6b**). OkCupid's studies were industry research not subject to U.S. federal Common Rule regulations. But, as with Facebook's experiment, the revelation of these studies focused public attention squarely on the ethical concept of informed consent.

Informed consent, *the principle that people have the right to make a voluntary, informed decision about whether to participate in a study,* is a major element of the APA Ethics Code and federal regulations. An informed decision is one in which people "know what they are getting into" before freely agreeing to participate. With limited exceptions, APA standards and federal regulations require researchers to inform potential participants about the purpose, procedures, and duration of the study; possible discomfort, adverse effects, and other risks; benefits and incentives for participating; and limits of confidentiality, before they consent to be in a study. Participants must also be informed that they can decline to participate and, if they do agree to participate, can subsequently withdraw from the study at any time. Consent forms should avoid jargon, be easy for participants to understand, and vary in length and content depending on the particular study. Table 3.3 lists basic elements of an informed consent form.

Limits to Confidentiality

The APA Ethics Code obligates researchers to discuss limits of confidentiality with potential participants as part of obtaining informed consent. This is an important ethical safeguard. Recall once again the hypothetical study of marital satisfaction in which the researcher must decide whether to break a promise of confidentiality to a husband by informing the wife of his HIV-positive status. By informing participants of conditions that limit confidentiality, the researcher has stronger ethical grounds for breaking confidentiality if one of those conditions arises. This may reduce the chance of legal liability if researchers find themselves obligated to release confidential information.

When might researchers be obligated to do this? Unless a participant consents to the release of confidential information, psychologists may break confidentiality "only as mandated by law, or where permitted by law for a valid purpose such as to . . . protect . . . others from harm" (APA, 2010a, 4.05). Many American states mandate that *any person* who suspects child abuse must report it to a child protective or law enforcement agency (HHS, 2010). Researchers who study children need to consider how they will respond if, in the course of a study, they observe or are told something that leads them to suspect a child is being abused. Similarly, in some types of psychological studies, a researcher might anticipate the possibility

---

Table 3.3 Basic Elements of Informed Consent

1. **Purpose and Nature of the Research**
   State that this is a research study. Indicate how long participation is estimated to last. Describe the procedures and note any (e.g., treatments) that are experimental.

2. **Anticipated Risks, Discomforts, Adverse Effects**
   Describe the risks, discomforts, and other adverse effects that a participant may reasonably expect to encounter by engaging in the study.

3. **Anticipated Benefits**
   State the anticipated benefits of participation for the individual participant or other people.

4. **Alternative Procedures or Treatments**
   Indicate whether alternative procedures or treatments exist that may benefit the participant.

5. **Confidentiality and Limits to Confidentiality**
   Describe to what extent participants' identities will be kept confidential.

6. **Incentives and Compensation**
   Describe any incentives being offered for participation. If a study involves more than minimal risk, then describe whether compensation or treatment will be provided in the event that participation causes injury.

7. **Contact Information**
   Indicate whom the participant should contact with questions or concerns.

8. **Voluntary Participation and Freedom to Discontinue Participation**
   State that participation is voluntary, the participant may discontinue her or his participation at any time, and no penalty (e.g., taking away benefits to which the person otherwise would have been entitled) will result from declining or discontinuing participation. Describe whether there are other anticipated consequences to declining or discontinuing participation.

Sources: APA (2010a, Section 8.02); HHS (2009, Section 46.116a).

of learning about possible domestic violence, suicidal intent, or other circumstances that would place participants or other people in danger. Thus, psychologists need to be aware of "duty-to-report" laws that are relevant to their research context. However, the applicability of such laws to researcher–participant professional relationships is often less clear than it is to physician–patient or therapist–client relationships (Fisher & Vacanti-Shova, 2012). Moreover, unexpected events happen in research, and an investigator may not always be able to anticipate all the appropriate limits to confidentiality that should be stated in a consent form.

Avoidance of Coercion and Vulnerable Populations

Informed consent requires that people freely accept or decline a request to participate in research. To avoid potential coercion, psychologists should not offer people excessive incentives for participating in research (APA, 2010a, 8.06). Any compensation offered (e.g., money, services, extra credit toward course grades) should be appropriate and clearly described in the informed consent form.

Psychological research often involves participants from what are called *vulnerable populations*. Federal regulations identify children, prisoners, people with mental disabilities, people who are educationally or economically disadvantaged, and pregnant women as among the populations that are "likely to be vulnerable to coercion or undue influence" (HHS, 2009, Section 46.111, 7b; Figure 3.7). Ethics codes call on researchers to be sensitive to extra safeguards that may be needed when studying these and other vulnerable populations (APA, 2010a; HHS, 2009). In behavioral research, concerns about vulnerability most often pertain to people's ability to truly provide informed consent based on an absence of coercion and an ability to understand the risks and benefits of participation.

Vulnerability is a complex concept. There are different types of risks (e.g., physical, psychological, social) to which particular participants might be vulnerable in one study but not another. For researchers, the key ethical task is to carefully consider the characteristics of their intended participants, along with the risks and social context of the proposed research, and then determine whether extra safeguards are needed to protect participants' welfare (Sieber, 2012). For example, in research with prisoners, a consent form must avoid making any statement about participation increasing one's chance of parole. But if you were a prisoner and knew that a researcher either sat on or knew members of a parole board, might this affect your decision just a wee bit? Today, prisoners are afforded extra protections under

Figure 3.7 Vulnerable research populations. In research contexts, children (typically defined as individuals under the age of 18) and prison inmates are among several groups considered "vulnerable populations" that receive additional human subjects protections.

federal research guidelines (HHS, 2009). Among those protections: It must be made clear to each prisoner that parole decisions will not be influenced by research participation, and parole boards must ensure that their decisions will not be influenced by whether prisoners consented to participate in research.

Some individuals, such as children and adolescents under the legal age of adulthood, are not legally capable of giving consent. Similarly, an institutionalized adult patient diagnosed with schizophrenia, whose thinking is disorganized, cannot provide meaningful informed consent. In such cases, where permissible by law, the person's legal guardian must provide informed consent on behalf of the participant. Parents, for example, would provide informed consent for their children. Even so, researchers are still obligated to obtain the participant's assent. **Assent** *means that even though the person might not be able to comprehend the details of a study to the degree listed on a consent form, he or she provides some evidence of being willing to agree to participate in the study.*

Suppose that a developmental psychologist wants to observe how parents and children interact while playing. The parents provide informed consent for themselves and their children, and the researcher would explain the study to the children in age-appropriate language to seek their assent (e.g., "We would like you to go into this room with your mom and dad and play some games. Is this OK with you?"). Once the study begins, the researcher remains responsible for monitoring the children's welfare and their continued willingness to participate.

Experimental Treatments

Psychologists Celia Fisher and Karyn Vacanti-Shova (2012, p. 343) note that people have a "general misconception that 'experimental' treatment means 'better' treatment," and researchers must attempt to dispel this belief in obtaining informed consent. For studies testing the effectiveness of experimental treatments—such as a new therapy for a psychological disorder—researchers must make it clear to participants (1) that they will not necessarily be assigned to receive the experimental treatment and (2) that the experimental treatment may be less or no more effective than the procedures that other groups (e.g., control groups) receive. Potential participants must also be informed about possible financial costs and compensation, services the control group may receive, the procedure used to assign participants to treatment or control groups, and other treatments that would be available if they choose not to participate or, after agreeing to participate, withdraw from the study later on.

Informed Consent and Internet Research

The Internet is a major venue for human interaction and attracts the interest of scientists seeking to study human online social behavior. In addition, researchers use the Internet as a tool for conducting online surveys, experiments, and other types of studies on many issues, including prejudice, eating disorders, personality, drug use, and memory (Pan, Pashler, Potter, & Rickard, 2015). Some Internet studies, such as Facebook's emotion-contagion experiment and an earlier experiment in which researchers manipulated Facebook News Feed messages to enhance voter turnout in congressional elections, have hundreds of thousands, or even millions of participants (Bond et al., 2012). This growth of Internet research (also called *e-research*) has raised thorny ethical issues about informed consent, including: (1) When is informed consent required in e-research? (2) How should researchers obtain it? (3) How can the participant's informed consent be validated?

IRBs and scientific organizations, including the APA, have started to tackle these issues. In general, informed consent is less likely to be required in e-research when individuals' responses are anonymous, when the behavior asked about can be assumed to be public, and when the research involves no more than minimal risk (Kraut et al., 2004).

When informed consent is required, e-researchers can present an online consent form. Users can click a button to provide consent and acknowledge that they have read and understand the consent form.

But how can online researchers tell whether a participant truly understands the consent form or has even read it? This is particularly important because online participants, unlike participants who interact face-to-face with the researchers, don't have an easy, immediate opportunity to ask questions about the study. Moreover, if the consent form stipulates that a participant must be of legal adult age, how can researchers validate that an adolescent or child isn't clicking the form? Possible solutions include requiring participants to (1) provide consent by phone, (2) click "I understand and accept" for each of several sections of the online consent form, (3) pass a short online quiz about the consent form, and (4) provide additional information online that would verify their age (Hoerger & Currell, 2012; Kraut et al., 2004).

Dispensing With Informed Consent

Just as some forms of research can be exempt from IRB review, the APA Ethics Code (2010a, Standard 8.05) states that in some situations researchers are not obligated to obtain informed consent. For example, studies in which people complete anonymous questionnaires, or in which people's natural behavior is observed in public places, would be exempt as long as (1) the procedures are unlikely to cause participants distress or harm, (2) participants' responses will be kept confidential, and (3) their responses, if they were to be disclosed, would not cause them harm.

Similarly, when researchers make video or audio recordings of people's naturalistic behavior in public places, informed consent is not required if the recordings are to be used in ways that protect participants' identities and will not harm them. Otherwise, informed consent for electronic recordings must be obtained. Determining whether a setting is public or private, however, is not always easy. For example, Kevin Crowley and his colleagues (Crowley, Callanan, Tenenbaum, & Allen, 2001) videotaped parents interacting with their children at a museum. Is a museum a public setting? If so, is it as public as, say, a city sidewalk or a public park? Are people entitled to a reasonable expectation of privacy once inside the museum? In this study, the researchers did obtain informed consent from each participating family before their behavior was videotaped (see Figure 3.8).

Even when informed consent is required, researchers are not obligated to disclose every technical detail of the study. Such details might confuse or overwhelm participants. Researchers also do not routinely inform potential participants about the hypotheses being tested, for such knowledge might cause participants to alter their behavior and respond unnaturally. Informed consent does, however, obligate researchers to disclose all information that would reasonably be expected to influence people's decision about whether to participate.

Bill Aron/Photo Edit

Figure 3.8 Observational research: A public or private setting? Parents and their child explore an exhibit at a science museum. Is the inside of a museum a public or private setting? Where on the public–private continuum would you rate this setting as compared to being inside a sports stadium, movie theater, or department store, or sitting on the grass in a public park?

DECEPTION

Deception *occurs when researchers intentionally withhold information from potential participants that might influence their decision to provide informed consent (so-called* passive deception) *or intentionally mislead participants about some aspect of a study* (so-called active deception; Kimmel, 2012). The APA Ethics Code allows researchers to use deception when (1) a study is likely to yield significant potential benefits, (2) there is no feasible nondeceptive approach to obtain those same benefits, and (3) participants are unlikely to experience physical pain or substantial emotional harm. Nevertheless, the use of deception has been a thorny, hotly debated ethical issue for many decades (Baumrind, 1985; Kelman, 1967; Kimmel, 2012).

In certain types of studies, researchers justify deception on the grounds that the study's scientific validity and potential benefits would be compromised without it. This rationale underlies the use of deception in the supposed job interviews, mentioned at the beginning of the chapter, that were actually part of an experiment on sexual harassment. Participants were misled into believing that the interview and inappropriate questions were real (i.e., active deception) and were not informed that they were being videotaped (i.e., passive deception). Researchers Woodzicka and LaFrance (2005) note:

> Subtle sexual harassment was experimentally induced in a situation designed to be as realistic as possible. This goal posed several challenges, both practical and ethical. If participants perceived the harassment to be part of the study, we would likely not learn much about actual reactions, only about conjectured ones. (p. 69)

Deception studies have been most common in social psychology (Stark, 2010), but they also occur in other psychological subfields. Consider a cognitive psychologist who investigates the accuracy of eyewitness memory. The psychologist tells participants that an experiment's purpose is to study emotions. They will watch video clips from movies and report their emotional reactions to each one. One of the clips graphically portrays a pedestrian being mugged. Later, the participants are asked to describe the mugger's appearance and other crime details. In this study, the experimenter has provided a false *cover story* to mislead participants about the study's true purpose. In real life, crimes usually occur unexpectedly and eyewitnesses have no warning that their memory is about to be tested. Had participants been told the experiment's true purpose ahead of time, they would have anticipated that a crime would take place and possibly made a special effort to pay attention to its details. This could distort the results and decrease the study's validity.

The Milgram Obedience Studies

Perhaps the most famous psychological research involving deception is the series of experiments on obedience conducted in the 1960s by social psychologist Stanley Milgram (1963, 1974).[3] In these experiments, each participant was told that the study's purpose was to examine how punishment affected learning. By the chance of a draw, the participant was assigned to be the Teacher and another person, supposedly also a participant, became the Learner. Unknown to the participant, the draw was rigged and the Learner was actually a **confederate,** *an accomplice of the investigator who is trained to act a certain way.* The participant's task as the Teacher was to read a list of word pairs to the Learner, whose task was to remember them. Every time the Learner made an error, the participant was to administer an electric shock, each 15 volts stronger than the last (**Figure 3.9**). At any point, if the participant was reluctant to go on, the experimenter ordered the participant to continue

---

[3] Milgram's (1974) book described 18 studies, each representing a particular condition within an overall experimental program. Within each study, all participants were exposed to the same procedures; procedures varied only across the studies. Nevertheless, following Milgram's lead, each study historically has been referred to as an experiment.

(a) **(b)**

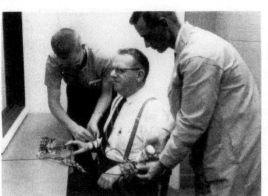

Figure 3.9 Milgram's obedience studies. (a) With the participant present, the experimenter straps the Learner's wrists "into an 'electric chair' apparatus" (Milgram, 1974, p. 19). (b) The shock generator.

increasing the shock—even as the Learner (in one of the procedures used) protested, screamed in agony, stated that he had a heart condition, and eventually fell silent and ceased to respond. In some conditions of the experiment, most participants fully obeyed the experimenter's orders.

After the experimental task was completed, Milgram assured each participant that the shocks had not been dangerous; he also had the Learner meet with the participant—a "friendly reconciliation" (Milgram, 1964, p. 849) to show that the learner had not been harmed. Milgram also attempted to reduce any stress the participant was feeling, and stated that a full description of the research would be sent to the participant after the research program ended. The debriefing portrayed in Milgram's famous 1965 documentary movie *Obedience* about his research also shows Milgram telling participants that the Learner was a confederate who did not really receive any shocks and who intentionally gave many wrong answers. Milgram reveals that the study's purpose was not to examine how punishment affects memory, but rather to determine whether people would obey the experimenter's orders to shock the Learner. This full debriefing, however, was not routine. It appears that many participants (especially those in the earlier experiments) were only fully informed about the true nature of the study after the entire research program was completed, via the mailed research report (Nicholson, 2011; Perry, 2013).

Unlike the participants in Woodzicka and LaFrance's (2005) experiment on sexual harassment, Milgram's participants knew from the start that they were engaging in psychological research. However, they still were deceived in several ways. First, the study's true purpose was disguised; they were misled into believing it was to investigate learning. Second, the study involved a confederate (the Learner), and numerous events were staged without the participants' knowledge. Third, in Milgram's early studies it became clear that many participants experienced substantial stress as they wrestled with the conflict of not wanting to harm the Learner versus obeying the experimenter's commands. Once this became known, not telling future participants about the potential for considerable stress constituted another deception. Had Milgram informed them of how stressful the experiment might be, potential recruits might have declined to participate. Fourth, many participants left the laboratory still believing that the shocks they had administered and the Learner's pained responses were real. For them, the deception was continued until the end of the research program.

The Ethical Controversy Over Deception

Milgram's studies took place after the APA's (1953) first Ethics Code had been developed, but before all subsequent codes were in place. His work highlights the ethical controversy concerning deception in research. The use of deception contradicts the APA's (2010a) *principle of respect for people's rights and dignity.* Deceiving participants denies them the right to provide fully informed consent and could be viewed as undermining their dignity. Deception also conflicts with the APA's *principle of fidelity and responsibility* and *principle of integrity,* which emphasize that psychologists should be trustworthy, honest, and truthful.

In addition, the *principle of beneficence and nonmaleficence* states that psychologists should take care to do no harm. Deceiving research participants may cause them to doubt the truthfulness of informed consent statements in future studies ("I wonder what this study really is about?") and even to question the honesty of behavioral researchers in general (Baumrind, 1985; Epley & Huff, 1998). It might also do harm by exposing people to emotionally stressful research procedures or leading to negative emotions when they are eventually told about the deception. Current APA guidelines permit deception in studies that involve a risk of emotional stress—as long as that stress is not substantial.

In contrast, ethical arguments can be made to support the use of deception. The *principle of beneficence and nonmaleficence* encompasses the broader benefits that research provides to society, and the *principle of fidelity and responsibility* states that psychologists must remain aware of their "scientific responsibilities to society" (APA, 2010a, p. 3). Finally, the *principle of integrity* calls on psychologists to "promote accuracy . . . in the science . . . of psychology" (APA, 2010a, p. 3). Gaining accurate scientific knowledge about behavior requires methodologically sound research. This brings us back to the argument that deception is sometimes necessary to obtain valid responses and maximize a study's potential benefits.

The issue of deception is perhaps the most complex and controversial aspect of research with human participants (Fisher, 2005; Kimmel, 2012). Opinions among psychologists run the gamut, from those who believe deception is never or only rarely appropriate to those who believe it is more broadly defensible when studying some types of behavior. The current APA code is a balancing act that allows deception to be used under limited circumstances. All major aspects of the deception must be fully explained to participants afterwards, and each participant must be allowed to have his or her data removed from the study. Full debriefing typically occurs immediately, at the end of each participant's session, but the code acknowledges that researchers may propose delaying full disclosure until after they've collected all their data.

A researcher should never make the decision to use deception lightly. Research that involves deception must undergo a full IRB review. Ultimately, the IRB decides whether using deception is ethically and scientifically justified in each case.

DEBRIEFING

When researchers finish gathering data from a participant, they don't simply say "thank you" and show the participant to the door. The APA code requires a **debriefing,** *a conversation with the participant that conveys additional information about the study.* Debriefing sessions have several goals, including the following:

- to provide participants with more complete information about the study, including information about any deception that occurred;

- to learn how participants perceived their research experience and to correct any erroneous perceptions about the study;

- to minimize adverse effects that participants may have experienced, and maximize the likelihood that they will feel positively about their participation;

- to enlist each individual's cooperation in not discussing the study with other people who might be future participants.

During debriefing, it is essential to respect participants' dignity and be sensitive to potential adverse effects they may have experienced. The researcher should also restate how participants' privacy will be safeguarded and remind them of any limits to confidentiality. Before telling them more about the study, the investigator might ask how they feel about it. If a participant's answers, current physical state, or prior behavior during the study suggest the presence of physical or psychological harm, the researcher will need to address these reactions. During debriefing, researchers may also explore how participants perceived the task. Perhaps the instructions were unclear, or the task was less engaging than anticipated. Such feedback may help researchers improve their future studies.

When the researcher describes the study in more detail, the scientific rationale for exposing participants to any deception and risk of harm should also be explained. Care must be taken to minimize the possibility of participants becoming angry or embarrassed because they were "fooled" or experiencing deflated self-esteem based on the experimental manipulation.

Debriefing provides an opportunity to enhance participants' understanding of the value of the study and of research in general. Debriefing also offers an opportunity to enlist participants' cooperation in maintaining the scientific integrity of the study. This occurs when the researcher asks each participant to avoid discussing the study—its purpose, procedures, and so forth—with other people who might become participants. The goal is to minimize **contamination,** *which occurs when future participants learn information from previous participants that they are not supposed to know until after data collection is completed.* Contamination may distort future participants' behavior and threaten the validity of the findings.

A skillful debriefing that respects and educates participants can help secure their cooperation in preventing contamination. It can make them feel that their research experience was worthwhile and that any deception or risk of harm they experienced was scientifically justifiable rather than capricious (Smith & Richardson, 1983). If a study involves deception, the researcher should explain its nature and rationale during the debriefing. In Woodzicka and LaFrance's (2005) experiment on sexual harassment, the researchers gave participants the option of having their data and videotape erased once they were debriefed about the deception in the study. Woodzicka and LaFrance reported that only one participant (of 50) requested that this be done. Given the substantial deception to which the participants were exposed, these data illustrate the value of careful debriefing.

 CONCEPT CHECK 3.3 ETHICAL STANDARDS IN HUMAN SUBJECTS RESEARCH

Decide whether each statement below is true or false. Answers appear on page 107.

1. All IRB members who review a research proposal must be scientists who are experts in, or are very knowledgeable about, the proposed topic.

2. In judging the risk to which participants may be exposed, researchers and IRBs take into account only two types of risk: physical and psychological.

3. If parents give informed consent for their children to participate in a study, the researcher is still obligated to obtain the children's assent.

4. The current APA Ethics Code prohibits deception under all circumstances.

ETHICAL ISSUES IN NONHUMAN ANIMAL RESEARCH

Learning Objectives

After studying this section, you should be able to:

- Explain why psychologists study nonhuman animals.
- Identify different viewpoints about nonhuman animals' moral standing.
- Describe the purpose of an IACUC, and explain the Three Rs.

Nonhuman animal research has a long history in psychology and has contributed to some of psychology's most important discoveries and applications. Note that we *Homo sapiens* are part of the animal kingdom and that the widely used term *animal research* actually refers to *nonhuman animal research*. Still, because *animal research* is the term often used in practice, we'll follow this convention.

ANIMAL RESEARCH IN PSYCHOLOGY

Consider one of many topics to which animal research has enormously contributed: learning. Over a century ago, American psychologist Edward Thorndike (1898, 1911) examined how cats learned new responses in order to obtain food. His work highlighted how the consequences of an organism's responses affect learning. Russian physiologist Ivan Pavlov (1923/1928) studied salivation responses in dogs and discovered basic principles of a type of learning called classical conditioning. Subsequent animal research by psychologists led to discoveries about other types of responses that could be classically conditioned (Ader & Cohen, 1975).

In the 1920s, German psychologist Wolfgang Köhler (1925) presented chimpanzees with novel tasks to determine whether they were capable of learning through insight. Around this time, American psychologist Edward Tolman studied spatial learning in rats, eventually proposing that they developed cognitive maps of their surroundings (Tolman, 1925, 1948). Köhler's and Tolman's research foreshadowed a surge of interest in cognitive models of learning and animal cognition.

In the mid-20th century, American psychologist B. F. Skinner (1938) and other behaviorists discovered many principles of operant learning (e.g., how patterns of reinforcement affect behavior) by studying rats and pigeons in laboratory experiments. Pioneering physiological psychologists such as Donald Hebb of Canada (1949) and Karl Lashley (1944) of the United States conducted animal research to explore the brain's role in learning and memory. Contemporary animal researchers who study learning continue to advance our knowledge about classical and operant conditioning, other learning processes, and biological bases of learning (Pace-Schott, Germain, & Milad, 2015).

According to the APA's Committee on Animal Research and Ethics (n.d.), animals are subjects in 7% to 8% of psychological research. Rats, mice, other rodents, and birds represent about 90% of the animals used in such studies, and roughly 5% are monkeys and other primates. Psychologists who conduct animal research do, however, study diverse species (including insects, fish, and snakes), and they work in diverse subfields. Researchers working in *comparative psychology* (also called *animal behavior*) seek to gain insights into evolutionary processes, and *experimental psychologists* study animals to investigate topics such as learning, memory, sensation, hunger, and thirst. Psychologists working in *behavioral neuroscience, behavioral genetics,* and *psychopharmacology* study animals to explore how the brain, hormones, genes, and drugs regulate behavior. These are just some of the many subfields in which psychologists study animals.

WHY STUDY ANIMALS?

Some psychologists study animals primarily to learn about other species, but most seek knowledge that may help explain human behavior or enhance human welfare. Why study other species to learn about human behavior? One reason is that animals typically mature and pass through the life cycle more quickly than humans. Thus, successive generations of rats or mice can be selectively bred relatively quickly, providing researchers with an important means of examining hereditary bases of behavior. Likewise, animals' shorter life cycles enable researchers to examine the long-term effects of environmental factors that affect development without having to wait decades to gather all the data.

Researchers also study animals to achieve a level of experimental control that is typically not feasible with human participants. Suppose that, to study whether a drug impairs learning, researchers administer the drug to an experimental group of adult rats but not to a control group. They then measure how long it takes the rats to learn a maze. The rats have come from several litters, and the researchers have made sure that within each litter, half the rats were randomly assigned to the experimental group and half to the control group. This enables the researchers to create experimental and control groups that, overall, have more similar genetic histories than would be possible in typical human experiments. The researchers have also done their best to ensure that from birth until the time the rats were tested in the maze as adults, all of them were exposed to the same environmental conditions (e.g., cage size, type of food). By controlling these extraneous genetic and environmental variables that are not of interest in this particular study, the researchers have reduced the "background noise" in their experimental procedure and increased the likelihood of detecting any real effects of the drug.

A third reason for studying animals is that there are many important issues that, for ethical reasons, cannot be investigated experimentally using human participants. For example, real-world observations may indicate that women who drink alcohol during pregnancy are at increased risk for giving birth to children who have cognitive impairments, but animal experiments can assess whether prenatal alcohol exposure actually *causes* such impairments. Similarly, the use of animal subjects allows psychologists to manipulate genes, specific brain structures and pathways, and neurotransmitter and hormonal activity to assess how this affects behavior. Such experiments have yielded vast knowledge about the brain's role in regulating learning, memory, reward and addiction, hunger and obesity, sex, sleep, and other functions (Kanoski et al., 2011; **Figure 3.10**).

In these and countless other examples, experiments cannot be conducted ethically with human participants. But this raises a parallel question: Can such research be conducted ethically with animals?

Courtesy of Dr. Sebastien G. Bouret, University of Southern California

Figure 3.10 Obesity research with nonhuman animals. Research with strains of genetically obese mice helped scientists to learn about leptin, a hormone secreted by fat cells. Leptin influences general appetite. Due to a gene mutation, the fat cells of the mouse on the right do not produce leptin, causing it to overeat and become obese. Psychologists and other scientists continue to conduct experiments with laboratory mice and rats to examine the role of leptin in regulating food intake.

ETHICAL PERSPECTIVES AND ATTITUDES

Psychologists John Gluck and Jordan Bell (2003) note that conflicting attitudes about animal research pivot around the fundamental philosophical question of whether animals have moral standing—that is, whether animals have "the status necessary to access the protections provided by the moral and ethical standards of a society" (p. 7). Gluck and Bell identify several secular ethical viewpoints that include the following:

- *Inherent-rights perspectives.* All sentient beings have inherent value and moral standing, and thus they cannot be used by humans for whatever purpose humans wish. Because animals are incapable of providing informed consent, they cannot be subjected to experiments or studied in other ways that would routinely require informed consent.

- *Utilitarian perspectives.* All sentient beings have moral standing but not necessarily equal standing. Moral standing increases along with an organism's greater capacity to experience pleasure and pain, which in turn is related to cognitive abilities such as greater self-awareness. Following the principle of utility (i.e., making decisions to maximize the collective good), research on animals would be justified when the projected benefits to humans or animals clearly outweigh the risks to the animal subjects. The higher an organism's moral standing, the greater the justification needed.

- *Pro-use perspectives.* Humans are strongly obligated to treat animals humanely, but animals are not people and don't have the same moral standing. Humans' strongest moral obligation is to fellow humans, and humans have the right to decide the status of animals. The potential benefits of animal research to human welfare justify such work.

Surveys of psychologists, students, and the general public reveal varying levels of support within each group for different types of animal research (Hagelin, Carlsson, & Hau, 2003). For example, Scott Plous (1996a) conducted a national survey of 3,982 psychologists who were members of the APA (few were animal researchers). When asked their overall opinion of using animals in behavioral research, 80% of the psychologists supported it, 14% opposed it, and the rest were unsure. Naturalistic observation research and research involving the confinement of rats and pigeons were strongly supported. When it came to research involving pain or death, however, about 60% of the psychologists opposed the use of primates and dogs and about 46% opposed the use of rats and pigeons.

ANIMAL RESEARCH AND ANIMAL-RIGHTS ACTIVISM

In the public and political arena, many animal-rights groups work within the law to sway opinion against animal experimentation and to promote legislation banning it. The APA and other scientific organizations likewise work within the law to oppose such bans and to inform the public and politicians about the benefits gained from animal research. Partisans on each side sincerely believe in the morality of their positions, and their counteracting efforts have sculpted a political landscape in which behavioral and biomedical animal experimentation is permitted but heavily regulated.

Although the vast majority of animal-rights activists continue to work nonviolently to achieve their goals, some have resorted to intimidation and even physical violence. Animal researchers have received threats and their research laboratories have been vandalized. In 2006 a climate of intimidation surrounded the construction of a major new facility for animal research at Oxford University in England. One member of an animal-rights group declared, "We must target professors, teachers, heads, students, investors, partners, supporters and anyone that dares to deal in any part of the university in any way. There is no time for debate . . . from now on, anything goes" (Allan, 2006, p. 4). Threats of this nature scared away the original company contracted to build the facility, and workers for the new company wore face masks to conceal their identities while on the job.

Scientists and law enforcement agencies obviously take issue with such tactics. Researchers also contend that some animal-rights groups grossly misrepresent the nature of animal research while denying its many benefits. In 1984, for example, leaflets published by an animal-rights group accused experimental psychologists of cruelty toward animals. One of six accusations was that animals "are deprived of food and water to suffer and die slowly from hunger and thirst" (Direct Action Program 1984, p. 3, as cited in Coile & Miller, 1984). Psychologists D. Caroline Coile and Neal Miller (1984) examined all of the scientific articles published in the prior 5 years in APA's leading animal research journals and did not find a single study that entirely supported any of the accusations. In no study, for instance, did animals starve to death or die of thirst.

Although there were studies involving food or water deprivation (e.g., to ensure that animals would be hungry prior to a learning task in which food was the reward for successful performance), 99% of such studies used a deprivation period of 24 hours or less, and in no study did the deprivation period exceed 48 hours. Coile and Miller (1984) noted that 24-hour food deprivation essentially parallels the common situation in which pets are fed once daily. It's also important not to sugarcoat the fact that, as Coile and Miller acknowledged, in some behavioral experiments animals are indeed exposed to pain, stress, other suffering, or surgery. Still, they found the claims made by the animal-rights group to be untrue and designed to inflame public opinion.

DOES ANIMAL RESEARCH YIELD BENEFITS?

Neal Miller (1985) also refuted a claim by animal-rights activists that animal experiments in psychology had no value. He identified many ways in which knowledge from behavioral animal experiments enhanced human and animal welfare, including the following:

- treating phobias and compulsions;

- training companion animals to assist people who have disabilities;

- understanding biological mechanisms associated with mental disorders;

- saving the lives of wild animals by applying behavioral techniques rather than lethal control to reduce problem behaviors;

- reducing self-injurious behaviors among children diagnosed with autism spectrum disorder;

- treating anorexia and chronic ruminative vomiting, which can be life-threatening (**Figure 3.11**).

Behavioral animal research also has fostered the development of entirely new scientific subfields. Today, the notion that emotional stress can impair our immune system is widely accepted. But until recent decades, medical science rejected this belief and the broader principle it reflects—that your brain and immune system communicate with one another (Pincock, 2012). Groundbreaking research by experimental psychologist Robert Ader and his colleagues with laboratory rats and mice slowly changed medical and scientific opinion (Ader & Cohen, 1975). This research established that immune system responses could be classically conditioned and helped give birth to the field of *psycho-neuroimmunology,* which examines how the brain, immune system, and behavior affect one another (Ader & Kelley, 2007). Animal research in this field is contributing to our understanding of how psychological factors affect illness, health, and aging (Desbonnet et al., 2012).

In sum, animal research has yielded many benefits, and those benefits continue to grow. Still, whether such benefits outweigh the costs to animals, whether animal research is ethical, and if so under what conditions are questions we each must answer for ourselves. Society's current answer allows animal research but strongly regulates its conduct.

(a) (b)

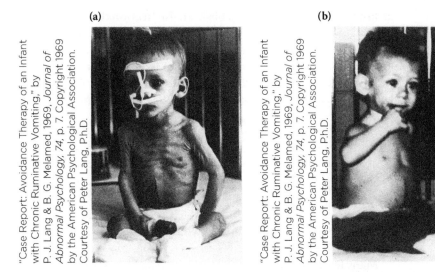

"Case Report: Avoidance Therapy of an Infant with Chronic Ruminative Vomiting," by P. J. Lang & B. G. Melamed, 1969, *Journal of Abnormal Psychology, 74*, p. 7. Copyright 1969 by the American Psychological Association. Courtesy of Peter Lang, P.h.D.

"Case Report: Avoidance Therapy of an Infant with Chronic Ruminative Vomiting," by P. J. Lang & B. G. Melamed, 1969, *Journal of Abnormal Psychology, 74*, p. 7. Copyright 1969 by the American Psychological Association. Courtesy of Peter Lang, P.h.D.

Figure 3.11 Applying principles from nonhuman animal research. In his article describing the benefits of animal experimentation, psychologist Neal Miller (1985) included these two photographs of a 9-month-old boy taken before and after the boy was successfully treated for ruminative vomiting. The repetitive vomiting had left the boy severely dehydrated and malnourished, thus threatening his life. The treatment was based on behavioral principles discovered in animal experiments.

HUMANE CARE AND USE

The APA established its first animal research guidelines in the 1920s, about 30 years before publishing its first Ethics Code regarding human subjects. In 1966 the U.S. Congress passed the **Animal Welfare Act,** *which regulates the use of warm-blooded vertebrates (except for mice, rats, and birds) in scientific research.* The act was last amended in 2008. Scientists who conduct animal research at institutions that receive funding from the U.S. Public Health Service must also conform to its policies, which do cover mice, rats, and birds. These policies are set forth in the extensive *Guide for the Care and Use of Laboratory Animals* (Committee for the Update of the Guide for the Care and Use of Laboratory Animals [CUGCULA], 2011).

Animal Research and the APA Ethics Code

The APA Ethics Code (APA, 2010a) requires psychologists to comply with all appropriate governmental regulations concerning animal research. You can find Standard 8.09 of the code, which focuses on animal research, in Appendix A. The APA also sets forth more specific conditions for animal researchers in its *Guidelines for Ethical Conduct in the Care and Use of Animals* (APA, 2012). These guidelines address (1) the need to justify the study; (2) the nature and training of personnel involved in the study; (3) the care, housing, and acquisition of laboratory animals; (4) the experimental procedures to be used; and (5) field research with animals. The guidelines also address the educational use of animals, such as in laboratory courses or classroom demonstrations.

Government Regulations, the IACUC, and the Three Rs

The U.S. Department of Agriculture (USDA) enforces the provisions of the Animal Welfare Act. USDA veterinarians conduct unannounced inspections of all animal research facilities at least once a year. In addition, each institution that conducts research on the animal species covered by the Animal Welfare Act, or that receives U.S. Public Health Service funding for animal research, must establish an **Institutional Animal Care and Use Committee (IACUC),** *which reviews animal research proposals for compliance with federal regulations.* The IACUC can approve a proposal, deny approval, or require the researchers to modify the proposal. It also inspects research facilities twice a year and can halt a previously approved study if it is found to be violating federal regulations. U.S. Public Health Service policy requires the IACUC's membership to include the following:

- a Doctor of Veterinary Medicine either certified . . . or with training and experience in laboratory animal science and medicine or in the use of the species at the institution;

- at least one practicing scientist experienced in research involving animals;

- at least one member from a nonscientific background, drawn from inside or outside the institution;

- at least one public member to represent general community interests in the proper care and use of animals (CUGCULA, 2011, p. 24).

Many federal ethical standards and regulations pertain to three general principles known as the **Three Rs:** *reduction, refinement, and replacement* (CUGCULA, 2011; Russell & Burch, 1959).

1. Reduction means that a researcher should reduce the number of animals being studied to the minimum number possible needed to achieve the scientific objectives of the study.

2. Refinement means that an investigator should refine the experimental procedures to expose animals to the least possible amount of pain or suffering necessary to achieve the study's objectives.

3. Replacement means that when it is scientifically and ethically feasible, a researcher should replace the use of nonhuman animals with alternative methods (e.g., using human volunteers) or replace more sentient animals with less sentient ones as subjects.

The Office of Laboratory Animal Welfare at the National Institutes of Health has an excellent website that provides links to many animal research regulations: (http://grants.nih.gov/grants/olaw/olaw.htm). If you look at these links even briefly, you will see that the federal regulations governing animal research are extensive, and they are so for good reason. We've seen in this section that animal research contributes to important scientific discoveries and societal applications. At the same time, we've also seen that the landscape for conducting animal research is morally complex and politically charged. APA and federal regulations on animal research reflect our society's current solution to a difficult balancing act between competing moral viewpoints.

✓ **CONCEPT CHECK 3.4** ETHICAL ISSUES IN NONHUMAN ANIMAL RESEARCH

Select the correct answer for each question below. Possible responses appear inside the parentheses. The correct answers are given on page 107.

1. According to the _____ (inherent-rights, utilitarian, pro-use) perspective, animal research is justifiable only when the projected benefits to humans or animals clearly outweigh the risks to the animal subjects.

2. The principle of _____ (reduction, refinement, replacement) obligates researchers to use procedures that expose animals to the minimal amount of pain or suffering necessary to achieve a study's objectives.

3. The principle of _____ (reduction, refinement, replacement) obligates animal researchers to study the minimum number of animals necessary to achieve a project's objectives.

SCIENTIFIC INTEGRITY

Being an ethical researcher requires not only familiarity with research ethics codes, but also ethical commitment—"the desire to do the right thing" (Fisher & Vacanti-Shova, 2012, p. 336). Consider the following incident, submitted to the committee charged with developing APA's first Ethics Code. It reflects behavior that rarely gets noticed by the public because it's part of the norm of professional scientific conduct.

> Some years ago a large advertising agency asked a research man to conduct a market survey to determine the maximum potential market for a common household product. The client who manufactured this product was planning an extensive promotion to increase sales. The investigation revealed that . . . the product was [already] . . . in almost every home that was checked—and that the client's brand accounted for nearly all of the amount in use. . . . [T]he agency executive . . . ordered the research man to doctor the results so the need for the promotion campaign would not be eliminated. The research man refused to do this. . . . (APA, 1953, p. 118)

This behavior reflects a good scientist's most important professional quality: integrity. Integrity means that psychologists are truthful. Such honesty is vital to science because, collectively, it enables scientists to trust one another and the accuracy of their colleagues' work. Integrity pertains to all aspects of the research process, and it is the cornerstone of the public's trust in science.

Now consider a second incident that, rightfully, made international headlines. In August 2011, at Tilburg University in the Netherlands, three junior researchers working in the laboratory of social psychologist Diederik Stapel informed the chair of their department and a key university administrator that Stapel had committed scientific fraud. Within two weeks, Stapel admitted that the allegation was true, was suspended, and later lost his job (Enserink, 2011, September 7; Tilburg University, 2011, October 31).

The administrator formed a distinguished committee to further investigate Stapel's scientific misconduct. Seven weeks later, it filed a scathing report, concluding that Stapel had committed extensive fraud over several years (Tilburg University, 2011, October 31). This fraud included completely fabricating the data in many studies that were later published. Stapel had hidden this data fabrication from his research colleagues. The committee noted:

> The fact is that the fraud with data has been on a large scale and has persisted for a lengthy period . . . . This conduct is deplorable, and has done great harm to science, and the field of social psychology in particular. To the best of our knowledge, misconduct of this kind by a full professor in his position is unprecedented. (Tilburg University, 2011, October 31, p. 5)

Stapel's gross misconduct goes to the heart of two ethical standards that we'll now discuss: avoidance of false or deceptive statements, and honesty in reporting research results. We'll also examine another key aspect of integrity—avoidance of plagiarism—and discuss plagiarism further in Appendix A.

AVOIDING FALSE OR DECEPTIVE STATEMENTS

The APA Ethics Code (2010a, Standard 5.01, p. 8) obligates psychologists to avoid making deceptive and fraudulent statements when publishing or discussing the results of their research. It doesn't matter whether the outlet is a scientific journal or book, a popular magazine, a blog, or a news interview. Research reported in all of these venues constitutes a "public statement," and the people who read or hear about it must be able to trust the accuracy of the researcher's statements.

Diederik Stapel's data fabrication obviously meant that the journal articles reporting those data contained false statements about how data were collected and about the findings. In cases like this, published articles that result from scientific misconduct must either be publicly corrected or fully retracted (i.e., withdrawn and stricken from the record), depending on the nature of the misconduct. This may not completely undo the scientific damage, however, because those articles may have already been used by other researchers as sources for ideas or as references to support theories or hypotheses.

Avoidance of false and deceptive statements also means that psychologists must portray their training, credentials, and areas of expertise accurately. At times researchers are asked and paid to be expert witnesses in legal proceedings or are hired by organizations to serve as consultants. They may be invited to appear on a television talk show or news segment. In all these contexts, psychologists and other scientists must represent themselves honestly.

REPORTING RESEARCH RESULTS ETHICALLY

Fabricating or falsifying data are among the most unethical things a researcher can do. Fraudulent recording or reporting of data undermines scientists' confidence in the body of knowledge that past and present colleagues have built and erodes the spirit of trust essential to scientific progress. It also undermines the public's trust in science.

In research, data falsification can have direct public consequences, such as causing businesses to invest money, a drug to be marketed, or a social program to be continued or discontinued based on distorted data. For example, in 2012, allegations were made that Anil Potti, a prominent cancer researcher, falsified findings in some of the research he had conducted while previously at Duke University (Hart, 2012, February 18). Lung cancer patients subsequently participated in experimental treatments based, in part, on this allegedly fraudulent research. As a result, in 2011 several patients and family members of deceased patients sued Potti and Duke University. Although this is a medical example, it's easy to imagine how similarly severe consequences could arise from fraudulent data reporting in psychological research (e.g., the development of a treatment for a psychological disorder based on prior, fraudulent findings.)

Prevalence and Detection of Data Fraud

How common is data fraud? In one 10-year study of federally funded American institutions that file annual reports on research integrity, only 0.2% of almost 37,000 reports included a case where a misconduct allegation (data fraud or other misconduct) was upheld (Rhoades, 2004). More recently, John, Loewenstein, and Prelec (2012) surveyed 2,155 research psychologists from American universities. Participants responded to either a standard questionnaire or one accompanied by special incentives to encourage honest responding. Respectively, 0.6% and 1.7% of participants admitted to falsifying data at least once in their career. These findings suggest that data falsification is uncommon, but also that its prevalence is underestimated. In science, any rate of data fraud above zero is a matter of serious concern.

Several hallmarks of science aid in uncovering data fabrication and falsification. First, science is a public process. Once a research report is published, other scientists can dissect it. Moreover, the APA Ethics Code, and research ethics across the sciences in general, obligate researchers to provide their original data to other scientists who wish to verify those data. Thus, scientists know that data that look suspicious may invite re-analysis or further scrutiny. An unwillingness or inability to share one's data in this way invites suspicion.

This occurred in a 2015 case of alleged fraud that received widespread media attention. It began when the prestigious journal *Science* published a study by two political scientists (LaCour & Green, 2014; retracted May 28, 2015). Later, other researchers identified what they believed to be statistical irregularities in that study's findings. They reported this to the senior author of the original study, a faculty member, who ultimately asked that the article be retracted from *Science*. One of several reasons this author gave for the retraction request was that the other author, a graduate student who collected the data, said he had accidentally deleted the raw data file and thus could not produce the original data (Green, 2015, May 19). The second author disputed the fraud allegation and asserted the original data file had been intentionally destroyed to comply with IRB regulations to protect the confidentiality of the participants (LaCour, 2015, May 29).

Fraud may also come to light when scientists publish their reports and other scientists fail to replicate the original findings. Published findings can fail to replicate for many reasons that have nothing to do with fraud, but multiple failures to replicate—especially when the original research procedures are closely followed—can raise concerns about the integrity of the original research. Fraud is also uncovered when scientists allege that a colleague known to them (e.g., a mentor or research team member) is engaging in misconduct. In Stapel's fraud case, junior researchers he was mentoring informed officials of his misconduct (Tilburg University, 2011, October 31).

Explaining what motivates data fraud or other misconduct isn't simple. Pressures to publish research, obtain grant funding, and establish and maintain a professional reputation are often cited, but most scientists face these pressures yet don't resort to misconduct. Moreover, to say after the fact that fraud occurred because the person has a "character flaw" offers only an unsatisfactory, circular explanation. Instead, federal agencies have increasingly focused on the socialization process by which scientists develop their ethical values. For instance, the National Institutes of Health (2000) will not award researchers a monetary grant until those investigators have documented that everyone involved in designing and carrying out the research has completed an authorized program of coursework on research ethics. These special training courses, which last several hours, typically can be taken by attending in-person seminars or via a web-based tutorial.

Steroids of Science: Questionable Research Practices

Data fabrication and falsification are extreme ethical breaches and deserve all the attention and sanctions they receive. Psychologists and other scientists have also expressed concern about other research practices that, because they occur more often, may have a greater cumulative potential to distort the body of scientific knowledge. For example, John and colleagues (2012) found that overall, about 40% of the 2,155 psychologists they surveyed admitted to, at least once, "deciding whether to exclude data after looking at the impact of doing so on the results" (p. 21). Moreover, on average, they believed that this practice was somewhat ethically defensible.

John et al. (2012) call such behaviors "QRPs": questionable research practices that exist in a gray zone of what is scientifically acceptable. They argue that "QRPs are the steroids of scientific competition, artificially enhancing performance" (p. 3) because such practices increase the odds of obtaining statistically significant findings. This makes it more likely that a research report will be published. In contrast, sometimes data legitimately may have to be dropped from a study, such as when recording equipment clearly malfunctions. The key issue is that individual observations should be dropped only when they meet criteria of "bad data" that, ideally, have been decided upon before the study begins. In this way, decisions to drop data will bear no relation to whether those data are consistent with a hypothesis under study.

QRPs have become a topic of increasing ethical debate (Fiedler & Schwarz, 2016). Overall, research psychologists believe that such practices are justifiable in at least some circumstances, but John et al. (2012) argue that such beliefs are primarily rationalizations for ethically questionable behavior.

PLAGIARISM

As a student, you probably have heard many warnings to avoid plagiarism when writing a paper or conducting a class project. **Plagiarism,** *taking credit for someone else's work or ideas,* is a serious ethical violation in science as well as in academics. The APA Ethics Code obligates psychologists to avoid plagiarizing other people's work or data. What constitutes plagiarism, and how can it be avoided?

Properly Citing Other People's Written Work

Just as you would expect other people to acknowledge ideas and work that you originated, the essence of avoiding plagiarism is giving credit to other people where credit is due. One form of plagiarism is copying text written by someone else, failing to put that text in quotation marks, and failing to cite the source, thus making it appear as if those words are one's own. Even if the original source is cited, failure to put the copied text in quotation marks constitutes plagiarism: It makes it appear that the researcher or student came up with those precise words, whereas in fact the original author did. Thus, *the first basic rule for avoiding plagiarism is: When copying material from another source, place the material in quotes or offset it as a block quotation; acknowledge the authors' names and the date of their work; specify as precisely as possible the location (e.g., page numbers) where the original material can be found; and include a full reference for that source, typically at the end of your scientific or academic report.*

Paraphrasing someone else's work also can constitute plagiarism if it is not done properly. The paraphrasing must be different enough from the author's original text so as not to copy the structure and wording of the original. To write a good paraphrase, you need to thoroughly understand the *ideas* in the original so that your paraphrase expresses those ideas clearly and in your own words. Finally, although quotation marks are not used for a paraphrase, the source must still be credited just as if it were quoted verbatim. Therefore, *the second basic rule for avoiding plagiarism is: When paraphrasing someone else's work, make sure you have expressed the author's ideas in your own words, and credit the source by citing the authors' names and the date of their work and providing a full reference for that source.*

Properly citing your sources ensures that when people read your report, they don't erroneously believe that you originated someone else's material or idea. Moreover, you've given the original authors the credit they are due. In psychology, research reports must conform to the official writing and publication style set forth by the APA; this style contains many rules about how to properly cite other people's work. You'll learn more about how to avoid plagiarism and cite other people's work in Appendix A, which addresses scientific writing and communication.

Properly Citing Other Types of Work

Plagiarism also occurs when presenting other people's data and findings as if they were one's own. Consider this case:

> My predecessor in this institute had been engaged in a certain research project. When he left he expressed an interest in continuing that research, particularly a phase of the project which he was planning to report in print. The data were the property of the institute and I was paid to exploit that area of the data collection program. When I took over his research responsibilities in that area I found myself wondering how

much I should utilize his unpublished findings, whether it would be ethical for me to continue where he had left off, or whether I should develop a different approach to the problem. I chose the last alternative, and several years later, when it was clear that he was not going to continue his interests in the project, I wrote a monograph in which the objective data he had planned to employ was utilized, giving him full credit. (APA, 1953, p. 134)

Was the researcher's solution ethical? The institute owned the data and hired the psychologist to continue analyzing those data. It could be argued that the psychologist was obligated to the institute to analyze and publish the data in the most expedient way possible; this might have been to follow his predecessor's path directly. But given the limited information we have about this case, the psychologist—by creating a new approach, giving his predecessor ample time to pursue the research, and giving his predecessor credit in the report—struck a reasonable balance between his obligations to the institute and his commitment to act with scientific integrity.

 CONCEPT CHECK 3.5 SCIENTIFIC INTEGRITY

Decide whether each statement below is true or false. Answers appear on page 107.

1. If a hypothesis has previously been supported by a lot of research, then it is ethical to withhold new data that are inconsistent with it.

2. The APA Ethics Code obligates researchers to provide their original data to other scientists who wish to verify those data.

3. In writing reports, if you paraphrase other people's ideas rather than directly quoting them, then you don't need to cite the original authors' names and source.

Now that we've reached the end of this chapter, I hope you have gained a deeper appreciation of why research ethics are important and challenging. Keep their importance in mind as you learn more about research methods, and display the utmost ethical commitment if you conduct research.

CHAPTER SUMMARY

- Ethics represent a system of moral principles and standards. Research ethics are essential to scientific progress, influence how psychologists design and perform their studies, and generally facilitate the validity of scientific findings.

- The Nuremberg Code evolved in response to heinous medical experiments by Nazi physicians during World War II. It contains 10 ethical principles governing biomedical research. The Belmont Report was developed, in part, as a response to unethical American medical research, including the Tuskegee Syphilis Study. The Belmont Report provides the basis for the federal ethics policy, called the *Common Rule,* that governs human behavioral and biomedical research.

- The APA Ethics Code highlights the principles of beneficence and nonmaleficence, fidelity and responsibility, integrity, justice, and respect for people's rights and dignity. In conducting research,

psychologists may face challenges in interpreting ethics codes or resolving conflicts between different provisions of ethics codes.

- The APA code and federal regulations provide ethical standards for conducting research to which psychologists must adhere. An IRB evaluates whether proposed human subjects research complies with federal regulations. To approve a study, an IRB must believe that the researcher has minimized any scientifically necessary risks to participants and that the potential benefits of the study outweigh its potential risks. Researchers usually must obtain people's written informed consent prior to gathering data about them. Ethics codes call upon researchers to be sensitive to extra safeguards that may be needed when studying and obtaining informed consent from vulnerable populations.

- Deception involves withholding information or misleading people in ways that might influence their decision to participate. Deception is ethically controversial, but is allowed under limited conditions. It is used to reduce the risk that participants will act unnaturally during the study.

- Debriefing occurs at the conclusion of a research session. The investigator provides participants with more complete information about the nature of the study, explains any deception, and addresses any adverse effects that the participants may be experiencing.

- Animal research has contributed to some of psychology's most important discoveries and applications. Researchers working with laboratory animals can typically achieve high levels of control and study issues that, due to potential harm, would be unethical to study with humans.

- Debate over whether and when animal research is ethical centers around the question of whether animals have moral standing. Three ethical perspectives—inherent rights, utilitarianism, and pro-use—address this issue. Claims by animal-rights activists that animal experiments in psychology yield no meaningful benefits are untrue.

- Psychologists who conduct animal research must adhere to APA's ethics standards and governmental regulations. IACUCs review whether proposed animal research complies with these regulations. Most standards and regulations pertain to three principles, known as the Three Rs: reduction, refinement, and replacement.

- Psychologists are obligated to avoid false and deceptive statements, including statements regarding their research findings, publications, and areas of expertise. They must treat scientific data with the utmost care and never fabricate or falsify data. Data fraud is one of the most unethical acts that a researcher can commit. When writing papers or reports, scientists (and students) should not plagiarize the work or ideas of other people and should properly cite their sources.

KEY TERMS

American Psychological Association (APA) Ethics Code (p. 76)
Animal Welfare Act (p. 99)
anonymity (p. 83)
assent (p. 89)
at risk (p. 82)
Belmont Report (p. 74)
beneficence, principle of (p. 76)
Common Rule (p. 75)
confederate (p. 91)

confidentiality (p. 83)
contamination (p. 94)
debriefing (p. 93)
deception (p. 90)
ethics (p. 71)
fidelity, principle of (p. 76)
informed consent (p. 86)
Institutional Animal Care and Use Committee (IACUC) (p. 100)
Institutional Review Board (IRB) (p. 79)

integrity, principle of (p. 77)
justice, principle of (p. 77)
minimal risk (p. 80)
nonmaleficence, principle of (p. 76)
Nuremberg Code (p. 73)
plagiarism (p. 104)
respect, principle of (p. 77)
responsibility, principle of (p. 76)
risk/benefit ratio (p. 80)
Three Rs (p. 100)

ASSESS YOUR KNOWLEDGE

1. Discuss how research ethics and the validity of scientific findings are related.

2. Describe, in general, different types of conflicts that can produce ethical dilemmas for researchers.

3. What historical events led to the development of the Nuremberg Code and Belmont Report? What major ethical principles do they share? Explain the five major sets of ethical principles set forth in the APA Ethics Code.

4. Describe the functions and composition of an IRB. What are the major rulings an IRB can make when reviewing a research proposal? Explain the concepts of minimal risk, at risk, and the risk/benefit ratio, and identify four major types of potential harm.

5. Discuss the concept of informed consent and how it applies to experimental treatments. How does assent differ from informed consent? What special problems concerning informed consent arise in conducting Internet research?

6. Describe the general controversy over deception and how this controversy applies to Milgram's obedience research. Identify several major goals of debriefing.

7. Describe several reasons why psychologists study nonhuman animals.

8. What position do inherent-rights, utilitarian, and pro-use perspectives take on the issue of whether animals have moral standing?

9. Identify major animal research issues addressed by the APA standards and guidelines, and describe the purpose of an IACUC.

10. What do the Three Rs mean in the context of animal research?

11. Describe why data fraud is one of the most serious ethical violations a researcher can commit and how scientists may uncover it.

12. Define plagiarism. To avoid plagiarism, how should the work of other people be cited and paraphrased?

CONCEPT CHECKS: ANSWERS

3.1 The Importance of Research Ethics

1. (a) true   (b) true   (c) true   (d) true   (e) true

3.2 Codes of Research Ethics

1. d   2. e   3. a   4. b   5. c

3.3 Ethical Standards in Human Subjects Research

1. false   2. false   3. true   4. false

3.4 Ethical Issues in Nonhuman Animal Research

1. utilitarian   2. refinement   3. reduction

3.5 Scientific Integrity

1. false   2. true   3. false

THINKING CRITICALLY AND APPLYING YOUR KNOWLEDGE

EXERCISE 1   Shyness and Help: A Deception Experiment

Read the following summary, written by Celia Fisher and Denise Fyrberg (1994), of an experiment conducted by DePaulo, Dull, Greenberg, and Swaim (1989). It is used with the permission of C. Fisher (personal communication, April 17, 2012). Identify ways in which participants were deceived and then think about these issues:
(a) Was the hypothesis important?   (b) Did the procedures effectively test the hypothesis?
(c) Was it likely that participants experienced psychological discomfort during the task or when they were debriefed?   (d) To obtain valid results, was it important to use deception?   (e) Did the study's scientific benefits outweigh its costs to participants?   (f) If you were an IRB member, would you have approved this study?

Purpose of Study: Psychologists have hypothesized that individuals who are shy may suffer interpersonal and personal disadvantages. This experiment was conducted to examine whether shy individuals are less likely than not-shy individuals to ask a stranger for help and whether their help-seeking is influenced by the sex of the stranger.

Participants: [Seventy-six] male and female undergraduates (half of whom were identified as shy by the Stanford Shyness Survey and half of whom scored not-shy) participated for Introductory Psychology course credit.

Procedure: At the beginning of the experiment participants were told that the experiment was concerned with how individuals perceive height and were introduced to a male or female stranger described as a student who had just finished the perception part of the experiment. They were told that if they needed assistance they should ask this other student. They were not told that the true purpose of the study was to observe their help-seeking behaviors nor were they told that the other "student" was really [a confederate].

Participants were then asked to stand several sticks on a table, take a picture of each stick and then draw a line of the same height. Unbeknownst to the participant, one of the sticks was purposely cut so that it would not stand up. To elicit as much help-seeking as possible, the [confederate] did not directly answer any questions.

Measurement of Participant Reactions: The experimenter secretly recorded whether or not the participants asked for help when they could not stand up the stick. After the participants had completed the stick measuring task they answered questions about their comfort level during the experiment. Their self-ratings were compared with the tape recordings of the experiment.

Debriefing: After participants completed the questions they were thanked and told the true purpose of the experiment. The experimenter answered questions and discussed any distress the participants might be experiencing.

Results: When the participants' behavior and responses were analyzed, it was found that compared to not-shy participants, shy participants were less likely to seek help from members of the opposite sex and described themselves as more uncomfortable in the help-seeking situation. This was especially true for shy women when they had to seek help from a male stranger.

EXERCISE 2   Memory for Word Lists

A cognitive psychologist plans to conduct a theory-testing laboratory experiment that examines how people's ability to remember new information depends on the amount of information, the rate at which the information is presented, and the presence or absence of performance feedback. Sixty college students will voluntarily participate in exchange for course extra credit. In each experimental session, a single participant will be exposed to monosyllabic word lists (e.g., *ball, talk*) consisting of 4, 6, 8, 10, 12, and 14 words per list. All words in each list will be presented at the same rate, but this rate will vary across lists from one word per second up to one word every 3 seconds. Half the participants will receive immediate, accurate performance feedback after each list; the other half will not. In total, each student will be exposed to 36 lists (6 list lengths × 6 word rates), with the list order randomly determined for each student.

The psychologist will measure how many words students can correctly remember immediately after exposure to each list. No personally identifying information will be stored with the data; participants' names will be recorded on a separate list only to enable them to receive extra course credit.

Evaluate the   **(a)** potential benefits of this study and   **(b)** potential risks to which participants might be exposed. Then make an overall judgment on whether this research   **(c)** places participants at no more than minimal risk, or at risk, and   **(d)** provides benefits that outweigh the risks.

EXERCISE 3   A Great Research Idea

Darla, an honors program psychology major at Hypothetical University (HU), meets at length with a psychology professor to discuss an idea for her senior honors project. The professor is impressed with Darla's preparation and familiarity with prior research on this topic and thinks that Darla's idea and proposed research design show great insight. The professor feels, however, that it would not be feasible for Darla to conduct the study within her remaining time at college. Darla is disappointed but agrees that the time frame probably isn't realistic. She mentions in leaving that she has applied to graduate psychology programs (in other geographic regions) and hopes to conduct the study if she gets into graduate school. The professor and Darla never meet again, and she graduates in the spring. That summer, a psychology graduate student at HU meets with the professor to discuss possible topics for a master's thesis. The professor tells him about his meeting with Darla and describes the idea that Darla had proposed. The graduate student thinks it's a great idea and uses it as the basis for his thesis.

Does this situation raise any ethical issues? Should the professor and/or graduate student have acted differently? If so, how?

4

DEFINING AND MEASURING VARIABLES

CHAPTER OUTLINE

Sam is 10 years old and has a long history of conduct problems (Rote & Dunstan, 2011). He has been repeatedly suspended at school for breaking rules, disobeying teachers, and disrupting classes. At home he has been defiant and broken objects, and his mother and sister have been frequent targets of his physical and verbal aggression. Such problem behaviors are called *externalizing* because they are directed outward.

Based on prior research and theory, a team of clinical and developmental psychologists hypothesizes that parental depression increases children's risk of developing externalizing problems (Callender, Olson, Choe, & Sameroff, 2012). They conduct a longitudinal study to test a conceptual model on which their hypothesis is based. Parents of 245 3-year-olds complete a set of questionnaires in their homes. They rate how much distress they have experienced from various depressive symptoms in the past week, and how often their child has displayed specific externalizing behaviors in the past two months. Ratings of the children's externalizing behaviors are obtained again, 2½ years later, from parents and kindergarten teachers.

In a markedly different setting, at a National Aeronautics and Space Administration research center, an airline cockpit crew sits inside a flight simulator that is reproducing the layout of Chicago's O'Hare Airport. They are one of 34 crews participating in experiments that assess whether modern cockpit information-display technologies can reduce crew navigation errors during taxiing maneuvers

AP Photo/Ives

Figure 4.1 Tenerife air disaster. In foggy conditions, a Pan Am 747 taxied on a runway. Its crew failed to identify a runway exit and turn off as instructed by air traffic control (ATC). At the far end of the runway, a KLM 747 initiated takeoff after its captain mistakenly believed he had ATC clearance. Upon spotting each other, the Pan Am flight tried to steer off the runway. The KLM flight tried to lift off, but hit the Pan Am 747's fuselage and crashed to the ground. Both planes caught fire and almost all aboard died.

(Hooey & Foyle, 2006). Human-factors psychologists study how people interact with each other, technology, machines, and tools as components of an overall performance system. In these experiments, the researchers classify different types of crew navigation errors made during taxiing simulations. They use live observations, audio-video recordings of the flight crews, and simulation replays to identify when navigation errors have occurred (Hooey & Foyle, 2006).

Such errors can have serious consequences. In 2013, in Johannesburg, a cockpit crew mistakenly steered a Boeing 747 jet onto a narrow perimeter taxiway. Its right wing sliced into an office building, injuring several people (Kitching, 2015, June 20). In 1977, in foggy weather on Spain's island of Tenerife, 583 people were killed when a Boeing 747 prematurely initiated takeoff and crashed into another 747 that was taxiing toward it from the other end of the runway. Miscommunication between flight crews and air traffic control, and failure by the taxiing crew to turn onto a runway exit, were among the causes of the crash (Weick, 1990; **Figure 4.1**).

Psychologists who explore child development seem worlds apart from those who study aviation safety. So, too, do experimental psychologists who examine hunger in laboratory animals and social psychologists who study why people fall in love. Yet these diverse scientists share with all researchers the core tasks of defining and measuring the factors they are studying.

TYPES OF VARIABLES

Learning Objectives

After studying this section, you should be able to:

- Identify variables as qualitative or quantitative, and discrete or continuous.
- Contrast and illustrate independent and dependent variables.
- Explain what constructs, mediator variables, and moderator variables are.

In this chapter you'll encounter several concepts (e.g., independent and dependent variables) that we briefly touched upon in prior chapters. Here, we'll explore these topics further and discuss other aspects of how researchers define and measure variables.

Recall that a **variable** *is any factor or attribute that can assume two or more values.* For example, among college students at a party, hair color (values of black, brown, red, blonde, and so forth) and the number of alcoholic drinks consumed (values of 0, 1, 2, 3, or higher) can vary across students. The number of times a child disrupts class can vary from one class to another, or from one child to the next within the same class. The intensity of feelings of depression can vary across different people and within the same person over time. When a plane taxis to or from a runway, the number of navigation errors made by cockpit crews can vary. Moreover, different types of errors can occur, such as planning a taxi route incorrectly or making an incorrect turn even if the planned route is correct. Environmental conditions (e.g., day or night, wind direction and speed, degree of visibility) also change. All of these examples illustrate variables.

In short, variables are about the wondrous differences that occur in our universe: ways in which people differ from each other; ways in which the same people change over time or act differently across diverse settings; and ways in which other species, objects, and environments differ. Nature contains a seemingly infinite number of variables for scientists to explore, and the task of accounting for the variability in people's behavior and characteristics—being able to describe, explain, and predict it—is fundamental to psychological science and other behavioral sciences.

QUALITATIVE AND QUANTITATIVE VARIABLES

Qualitative variables *represent properties that differ in "type"* (i.e., a type of attribute or quality), such as biological sex, religious affiliation, eye color, and marital status. Thus, people may be categorized as biologically male or female and as Buddhist, Christian, Hindu, Jewish, Muslim, and so forth. These categories represent differences in the "kind" of some attribute. In their study of children's externalizing behavior, Callender and colleagues (2012) classified children as boys or girls and parents as mothers or fathers. In their aviation study, Hooey and Foyle (2006) broke down navigation errors into three categories: planning errors, decision errors, and execution errors. They also experimentally manipulated the type of navigation technology that cockpit crews were able to use during taxiing maneuvers. Type of navigation error and type of navigation technology are qualitative variables.

Quantitative variables *represent properties that differ in "amount."* People differ quantitatively in their height, weight, degree of shyness, time spent learning a task, and blood alcohol levels on a Saturday night. Sounds vary quantitatively in intensity and perceived loudness. In Callender et al.'s (2012) longitudinal study, parents differed quantitatively in their level of depression, and children differed quantitatively in their degree of externalizing behavior.

Task performance is a common quantitative variable in behavioral research. In the aviation experiments reported by Becky Hooey and David Foyle (2006), flight crews performed a series of "land and taxi-to-the-gate" simulations. The different *types* of errors that could be made—planning, decision, and execution errors—represent a qualitative variable. But when we count the *number of errors* that flight crews make, we are examining a quantitative variable. Thus, for example, we might find that one crew makes twice as many planning errors as another crew.

Note that qualitative variables, like quantitative variables, can generate numerical data and be statistically analyzed. With qualitative variables, we can count the number of instances that occur within each category; report that information as frequencies, percentages, or proportions; and perform statistical tests as needed. For example, in Callender et al.'s (2012) research on externalizing behavior, 48% of the children studied were girls and 52% were boys. In the control condition of Hooey and Foyle's (2006) aviation experiments, in which flight crews relied on traditional navigation technology (e.g., paper charts of the airport layout), 23% of the 150 navigation errors were planning errors, 42% were decision errors, and 35% were execution errors.

DISCRETE AND CONTINUOUS VARIABLES

Now let's think about five quantitative variables: the number of children in different families, the number of navigation errors that cockpit crews make during taxiing maneuvers, the time it takes to complete a task, people's blood alcohol level, and the intensity of parents' feelings of depression. A family might have 0, 1, 2, 3, or more children. But it cannot have 1.5 or 2.76 children. A cockpit crew might make 0, 1, 2, 3, or more navigation errors while taxiing to an arrival gate, but they can't make 1.5 or 3.789 errors. Quantitative variables such as these are called **discrete variables:** *Between any two adjacent values* (e.g., 0, 1, 2, 3 children), *no intermediate values are possible.*

In contrast, no matter how close the times are that two people take to finish a task, it is always possible for another score to exist in between. If their times are 4.0 and 5.0 seconds, respectively, then times of 4.1, 4.2, 4.3, 4.4, and so on are possible. If their times are 4.1 and 4.2 seconds, then times of 4.11, 4.12, 4.13, and so on are possible. We can always obtain new intermediate values by considering one additional decimal place. Likewise, no matter how close two blood alcohol levels or two parents' degree of depression are, it is possible to imagine another blood alcohol level or degree of depressed emotion that falls in between. Such variables are called **continuous variables:** *In principle, between any two adjacent scale values, intermediate values are possible.*

Realize that in practice, when we study continuous variables, they are of necessity converted into discrete variables. We may choose to measure time to the hour, minute, second, tenth or hundredth of a second, and so on. But no matter to how many decimal places we carry out our measurement, we must have a cutoff somewhere. This creates discrete values beyond which we simply round up or down. Similarly, Callender et al. (2012) asked parents to rate how distressed they had felt during the prior week in relation to six symptoms of depression (e.g., sadness, hopelessness). Each rating was made on a 5-point scale that ranged from 0 (*not at all*) to 4 (*extremely*), and ratings were combined to create an overall depression score for each parent. This measurement procedure converted intensity of depression, a continuous variable in principle, into a discrete variable.

When scientists design their research and analyze their data, they consider whether the variables they are studying are qualitative or quantitative, and discrete or continuous. As a simple example, look at the graphs in **Figure 4.2**. Suppose that these graphs display the results of two experiments. In the first experiment, students perform a reading-comprehension task while being exposed to different intensities of street noise (expressed in decibels, a measure of relative sound intensity). Note that in the graph, the decibel values on the *x*-axis

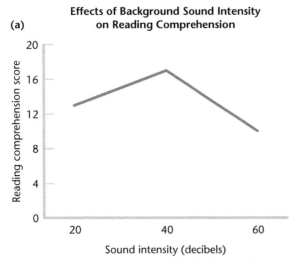

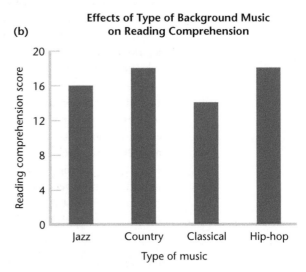

Figure 4.2 Example of a line graph and a bar graph. (a) A line graph. The variable plotted along the *x*-axis, sound intensity, is a quantitative variable that is continuous in principle, even though in operational form it is discrete. (b) A bar graph. The variable plotted along the *x*-axis, type of music, is a qualitative variable.

represent an ordered progression from lower to higher sound intensities. Furthermore, because sound intensity, in principle, is a continuous quantitative variable, it is appropriate to display the data in a *line graph*. That is, even though we represented sound intensity by a discrete number of decibel values in our experiment, the line in the graph can be used to interpolate the reading-comprehension scores at other sound levels that fall within the range of decibels examined in our study.

In the second experiment, we ask college students to perform a reading-comprehension task while they listen to one of four types of music: jazz, country, classical, or hip-hop. Here, we have a qualitative variable along the *x*-axis. Unlike the other graph, the order of the values—in this case, the four categories of music—on the *x*-axis is arbitrary. For example, "classical music" could be placed in the leftmost, rightmost, or one of the inner positions. A line graph could be viewed as implying a continuum of "type of music" that does not exist. For qualitative variables, it is more appropriate to display the findings in a *bar graph*.

When the variable on the *x*-axis is quantitative but discrete (e.g., family size), a bar graph appropriately avoids implying that the variable has intermediate scale values (e.g., 3.4 or 5.7 family members). However, especially when a graph presents many findings (e.g., the *x*-axis variable has many values), it is often easier to grasp the overall pattern of how two variables are related in a line graph than in a bar graph. In memory experiments, for example, researchers may expose people to word lists of different lengths and examine how list length influences the ability to correctly recall the words. Or researchers may examine how the position of an item within a list (e.g., 1st, 2nd, 3rd, . . . 15th position) affects recall. List length, or item position (called serial position), would be plotted on the *x*-axis and recall scores on the *y*-axis. Line graphs are often used to highlight the nonlinear or linear relations between such variables and memory performance (Ward, Grenfell-Essam, & Tan, 2010). In sum, both types of graphs are used to portray discrete quantitative variables along the *x*-axis.

INDEPENDENT AND DEPENDENT VARIABLES

The distinction between independent and dependent variables is one of the most basic concepts in the behavioral sciences. An **independent variable** *is the presumed cause in a cause–effect relation; in experiments, it is a factor that researchers manipulate or systematically vary in order to assess its influence on some behavior or outcome.* A **dependent variable** *is the presumed effect in a cause–effect relation; in an experiment, it is the behavior or outcome that the researcher measures to determine whether the independent variable has produced an effect.* Let's examine the first part of these definitions, which concerns presumed causes and effects.

Whether developing theories, models, and hypotheses about behavior, or simply posing questions about it, we can distinguish conceptually between variables proposed to be causes and those proposed to be effects. For example, each of the following questions asks whether a causal relation exists between two variables. Before you look at Figure 4.3, test your understanding by trying to identify the presumed cause and effect represented in each question. Then determine and create labels for the independent and dependent variables.

- Compared to traditional navigation technologies, will modern technologies reduce the number of navigation errors that cockpit crews make during taxiing maneuvers?

- Is the speed with which people react to stimuli affected by the intensity of those stimuli?

- How effective are different types of psychotherapy in treating agoraphobia?

- Does being religious or spiritual help protect people against disease and promote longer life?

- Does people's level of self-esteem influence how hard they try to succeed at achievement tasks?

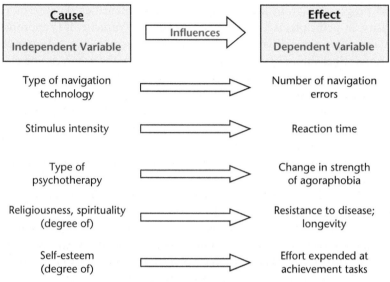

Figure 4.3 Independent and dependent variables at a conceptual level. Based on the phrasing of the bulleted questions on page 113, the factors that are conceptually viewed as the independent variable and dependent variables are shown in this figure. You may have chosen different labels for the variables, which is fine, as long as your label captures the gist of the factor and is properly placed as the presumed cause or the effect.

The independent and dependent variables conceptually represented in these questions are shown in Figure 4.3. You can see how the word *dependent* means just what it says: The outcome of a dependent variable is presumed to *depend on* the value of (also called the *level of* or the *condition of*) an independent variable. The number of navigation errors that cockpit crews make may depend on the type of navigation technology made available to them. Reaction times to stimuli may depend on the intensity of those stimuli. Reductions in the strength of people's agoraphobia may depend on the type of psychotherapy that they receive.

Note that in each of these three examples, the independent variable—type of navigation technology, stimulus intensity, and type of therapy—is a **situational variable:** *a characteristic that differs across environments or stimuli.* In contrast, in the last two examples, each independent variable—people's degree of religiousness or spirituality and their degree of self-esteem—is a **subject variable:** *a personal characteristic that differs across individuals.* The two questions ask whether these personal characteristics influence people's health outcomes and their achievement behavior, respectively.

Now let's address the part of the definition of independent and dependent variables that focuses on experiments. We saw in Chapter 2 that experiments are best suited for identifying cause–effect relations because they provide researchers with a high degree of control over the variables being examined. In an experiment, the researcher creates different levels or conditions of the independent variable and then exposes participants to those conditions. The key aspect of participants' behavior—the dependent variable—is then measured in each of the conditions and compared to determine whether the independent variable influenced the participants' behavior.

Hooey and Foyle (2006), for example, examined whether flight-crew navigation errors could be reduced by introducing new information-display technologies into the cockpit. Thus, the research question became, "Do different navigation technologies (the independent variable; the cause) influence the number of navigation errors (the dependent variable; the effect) that cockpit crews make during taxiing maneuvers?" In two experiments, Hooey and Foyle manipulated this situational independent variable by having flight crews perform a series of "land and taxi-to-the-gate" flight simulations in which they—Hooey and Foyle—controlled the types of technologies that were made available to the flight crews. Then, in each technology condition, they *measured the dependent variable* by recording the navigation errors that crews made while taxiing. In fact, they actually measured how the various technologies influenced three types of navigation errors: planning errors, decision errors, and execution errors. Thus, as in many experiments, there were several dependent variables.

Manipulating independent variables is the hallmark of experimentation. In some experiments, however, researchers also include independent variables (usually subject variables) that are selected rather than manipulated. For example, in the cockpit-crew navigation experiments, we could measure the captains' and first officers' years of flying experience. We could then select cockpit crews to participate based on their experience in order to create conditions of high, moderate, or low experience. We can now examine how navigation performance (the dependent variable) varies as a function of different cockpit technologies (an independent variable we manipulate) and crew experience (an independent variable we create by selecting people who already differ in their experience). You will learn more about this research approach in Chapter 9. Until that point, unless specifically noted otherwise, when you come across the term *independent variable* in this book, you should assume that it refers only to a variable that is manipulated by the experimenter.

In nonexperimental studies, researchers may conceptualize and discuss certain variables as if they were independent variables, but these variables are not manipulated as in an actual experiment. For example, we can ask whether religiousness and spirituality causally influence people's physical health and longevity (Powell, Shahabi, & Thoresen, 2003). We also can ask, as Callender et al. (2012) and other researchers have done, whether parental depression influences the development of children's conduct problems. But for ethical and practical reasons, we're not likely to manipulate whether or how deeply people are religious. Instead, we can use interviews or questionnaires to *measure* people's religiousness and spirituality and also measure their health and longevity. Then we can perform statistical analyses to determine whether religiousness and spirituality are associated with health and longevity. Similarly, Callender et al. (2012) did not manipulate parental depression; they measured it, measured children's subsequent externalizing behaviors, and statistically examined whether these variables were associated with one another. Recall from Chapter 2 that studies like these, in which relations between variables are examined but all of the variables are measured and none are manipulated, represent *descriptive research*. More specifically, Callender et al.'s research was a longitudinal correlational study. It is more difficult to draw unambiguous causal conclusions from correlational and other descriptive studies than from experiments, as we will explore in later chapters.

Before moving on, keep several points about independent and dependent variables in mind. First, the same factor can be either an independent or dependent variable depending on the particular research question being studied. For instance, self-esteem represents a dependent variable in the question "Does failure at an important task decrease people's self-esteem?" But if our research question is "Does self-esteem influence how well people perform at a novel task?," then in this context self-esteem is an independent variable. Second, researchers often want to know how an independent variable (e.g., different amounts of sleep deprivation) influences multiple dependent variables (e.g., people's daytime sleepiness, moods, and task performance). And third, researchers may examine how two or more independent variables simultaneously influence the same dependent variable or variables. Thus, in an experiment we can examine how talking or not talking on a cell phone (which we manipulate), along with having or not having a passenger in the car (which we also manipulate), jointly influence people's driving performance. **Figure 4.4** illustrates these points, using examples from experiments about alcohol.

HYPOTHETICAL CONSTRUCTS

If I ask you to count the number of times a rat presses a lever in 10 minutes, or to identify how many words a college student correctly recalls immediately after being read a list of 15 words, you would likely have little difficulty knowing what to do. You can observe the rat and record a checkmark for each lever press. You can compare the words recalled by the student to the actual words on the list. But if I had asked you instead to "measure motivation in a rat" or "measure a person's memory," your task of deciding how to proceed would become more challenging.

Infographic: **Figure 4.4**

INDEPENDENT AND DEPENDENT VARIABLES: ALCOHOL EXPERIMENTS

INDEPENDENT VARIABLE (CAUSE)	DEPENDENT VARIABLE (EFFECT)

The same variable can be an independent variable or dependent variable, depending on the research question.

1 Does stress affect people's craving for alcohol? (Nesic & Duka, 2014)

stress

desire for alcohol

2 Does alcohol influence the strength of people's stress response when they are in a threatening situation? (Moberg, Weber, & Curtin, 2011)

alcohol consumption

stress

A study may examine how an independent variable influences two or more dependent variables.

3 Does alcohol affect people's altruism and willingness to take risks? (Corazzini, Filippin, & Vanin, 2015)

alcohol consumption

altruism

risk taking

A study may examine how multiple independent variables simultaneously influence one or more dependent variables.

4 What effects do consuming alcohol (independent variable #1) and energy drinks (independent variable #2), individually and mixed together, have on people's subsequent desire to drink more alcohol? (Marczinski, Fillmore, Henges, Ramsey, & Young, 2013)

alcohol alone

energy drink alone

both

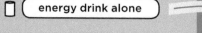
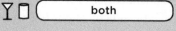

desire for alcohol

Many of the concepts that behavioral scientists are interested in—motivation, aptitude, memory, stress, personality, intelligence, self-esteem, happiness, depression, mental imagery, and so on—represent psychological states or processes that are hypothesized to exist but cannot be directly observed. Rather, what we observe are measurable responses that are presumed to reflect these psychological attributes. Such concepts are called **hypothetical constructs:** *underlying characteristics or processes that are not directly observed but instead are inferred from measurable behaviors or outcomes.* For example, I can observe you eating a huge amount of food, or observe you wolfing down food quickly, or note that you just said to me, "I'm famished; time for pizza!" I can take any of these measurable behaviors as indicators of an underlying psychological state that we call "hunger"—but I cannot see your "hunger" in the direct way that I can see your eye color. Similarly, I can read you 15 words and then immediately ask you to recall as many as you can, assess whether you can accurately recall a personal event that took place a month ago, and even record your brain activity while you perform these tasks. All of your responses are measurable, but each reflects a different aspect of a broader, inferred psychological construct that we call "memory."

MEDIATOR AND MODERATOR VARIABLES

As you likely know, there is considerable evidence that talking on a cell phone impairs driving performance (Ferdinand & Menachemi, 2014). In this analysis, talking or not talking on a cell phone while driving represents an independent variable, and driving performance represents a dependent variable. **Figure 4.5a** shows a hypothesized direct causal link between these two variables.

As for *why* cell phone conversations might adversely affect driving performance, the physical act of having to drive with one hand while holding a phone has been viewed as one culprit. This can't explain, however, why using a hands-free device impairs driving performance. In contrast, distraction of attention can at least partly account for driving impairments resulting from handheld and hands-free cell phone conversations. For example, experiments by cognitive psychologist David Strayer and his colleagues found that talking on a hands-free cell phone while driving interfered with drivers' ability to pay attention to visual information and impaired driving performance (Strayer, Drews, & Johnston, 2003). Strayer et al. proposed a causal sequence in which talking on a cell phone diminishes the ability to notice visual information, which in turn impairs driving performance.

Suppose we take the model in Figure 4.5a and expand it by adding the concept of distraction of attention. **Figure 4.5b** illustrates one way we can diagram this causal sequence. Distraction of attention occupies an intermediate position in which it is influenced by cell phone use and, in turn, influences driving performance. This type of variable is called a

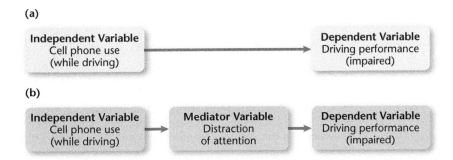

Figure 4.5 Example of a mediator variable. (a) A direct link is proposed between an independent variable and dependent variable. (b) A mediator variable is added, providing an explanatory causal link between the independent and dependent variable.

mediator variable: *a variable that provides a causal link in the sequence between an independent variable and a dependent variable* (Baron & Kenny, 1986; MacKinnon & Fairchild, 2009).

Let's consider another example: the model proposed in **Figure 4.6** by Callender et al. (2012). Parental depression is an independent variable, and child externalizing behavior is a dependent variable. There are two mediator variables—negative appraisals and harsh parenting—that link the independent variable to the dependent variable. That is, depression is hypothesized to cause parents to appraise their children's behavior more negatively, which then causes those parents to discipline their children more harshly. In turn, this leads the children to display greater externalizing behavior.

Callender et al.'s (2012) longitudinal findings supported this model, but they appropriately cautioned that because their study was correlational, clear cause–effect conclusions could not be drawn. Moreover, this model focused on only one hypothesized path by which conduct problems develop. There are additional reasons why parental depression might promote children's conduct problems, and there are developmental factors beyond parental depression that may cause conduct problems (Goodman, 2007).

You can see that in behavioral research, mediator variables are often internal psychological constructs—such as "distraction of attention" in Figure 4.5 and "negative appraisals of child behavior" in Figure 4.6—that are hypothesized to represent a mechanism by which an independent variable influences a dependent variable. However, external factors can also serve as mediator variables. In Figure 4.6, for example, the mediator "harsh parenting behavior" is a directly observable external factor.

Whereas a mediator variable helps explain *why* an independent variable influences a dependent variable, a moderator variable informs us about *when* and *for whom* an independent variable produces a particular effect. More formally, a **moderator variable** *is a factor that alters the strength or direction of the relation between an independent and dependent variable.* Returning to our cell phone example, suppose we find that (1) when traffic is heavy, cell phone conversations moderately impair driving performance, but (2) when traffic is light, cell phone conversations either don't influence driving performance, impair it much less, or (just hypothetically, mind you) have the opposite effect and improve driving performance. In this case, the variable of traffic density moderates (i.e., alters, changes) the relation between our independent variable and dependent variable. In one type of situation (high traffic density), talking on a cell has a certain effect on performance; in another type of situation (low traffic density), talking on a cell phone has a different effect (in strength and/or direction) on performance. Similarly, suppose future research reveals that the use of modern navigation technologies reduces cockpit-crew taxiing errors during nighttime hours, but not during daylight hours. In this case, nighttime/daytime is a moderator variable: it alters the relation between an independent variable (type of navigation technology) and a dependent variable (navigation errors).

As in our cell phone and cockpit navigation technology examples, moderator variables are often situational factors, but they can also be personal attributes. For example, an independent

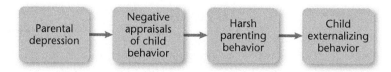

Figure 4.6 Parental depression and child conduct problems. This model proposes one possible route by which parental depression may increase children's externalizing behaviors. In this model, the mediator variables are parents' negative appraisals of their children's behaviors, and harsh parenting behavior. (Republished with permission of Springer from "The Effects of Parental Depressive Symptoms, Appraisals, and Physical Punishment on Later Child Externalizing Behavior," by K. A. Callender, S. L. Olson, D. E. Choe, and A. J. Sameroff, 2012, *Journal of Abnormal Child Psychology, 40*[3], 471–483. Permission conveyed through Copyright Clearance Center, Inc.)

variable might have different effects on people's behavior (the dependent variable) depending on whether they are female or male, old or young, have high or low self-esteem, and so on. The degree to which modern cockpit navigation technologies reduce navigation errors might differ for highly experienced versus less experienced cockpit crews. In these cases, biological sex, age, self-esteem, and crew experience would be moderator variables. In sum, mediator and moderator variables are central to building psychological theories and models. To reiterate, they help us understand *why* (mediators) and *when and for whom* (moderators) independent variables influence dependent variables.

✓ **CONCEPT CHECK 4.1 TYPES OF VARIABLES**

Fill in the blank for each item below. Answers appear at the end of the chapter on page 137.

1. The different values of a(n) _____ variable represent different "types" of an attribute, such as different college majors or ethnic groups.

2. The different values of a(n) _____ variable represent different amounts of some attribute, such as height, weight, or the speed of a response.

3. In terms of cause and effect, the _____ variable represents the cause and the _____ variable represents the effect.

4. A(n) _____ variable is a variable that helps to explain why an independent variable influences a dependent variable.

DEFINING VARIABLES

Learning Objectives

After studying this section, you should be able to:

- Explain why it is important for scientists to be explicit about how they conceptually define their variables.

- Discuss what it means to operationally define a variable and illustrate how the same construct can be operationally defined in several ways.

I'm going to assume that at some point in your life you have experienced stress. If you haven't, I'd like to know your secret. How would you define the concept of "stress"? (A circular definition, such as "stress is when you feel stressed," would not be acceptable!) If each of your classmates defined stress and we compared everyone's definitions, would they be the same? Perhaps one classmate might define stress as "being in a situation that puts pressure on you," while another might state that stress is "feeling anxious about something." I suspect that we would find many differences in how you and your classmates would define stress.

CONCEPTUAL DEFINITIONS

Scientists, like anyone else, may disagree about how to define certain concepts or variables. For example, the construct of intelligence has been conceptualized in significantly different ways by various theorists and researchers. Some view intelligence as representing a general mental capacity to think, reason, and adapt to the environment (Spearman, 1923). Others view intelligence as a set of distinct cognitive skills (Thurstone, 1938) or as a set of distinct abilities that extend beyond cognitive skills and into arenas such as musical, physical, and interpersonal skills (Gardner, 2006).

Disagreements about how best to define concepts, although sometimes frustrating for students, do not create the stumbling block to scientific progress that you might expect. Rather, they can spark healthy debate and lead to new research. Such disagreements, however, place a premium on making one's definitions clear. When a theorist, researcher, or classmate explicitly defines a term, this provides you with the opportunity to agree with that view or disagree and suggest an alternative. But in any event, at least you will know what the person means when using a particular term.

Hooey and Foyle (2006), for example, explicitly defined key concepts in their flight-crew navigation experiments. They conceptually defined pilot navigation errors as "failure to comply with the taxi clearance issued by air traffic control" (p. 52). Moreover, after systematically gathering information from several sources—a large survey of pilots, live observations of cockpit crews during actual commercial flights, and focus groups held with pilots and air traffic controllers—Hooey and Foyle identified and conceptually defined three subtypes of navigation errors. These were (1) planning errors, which "occur when the crew formulates an erroneous plan or intention, but carries out the plan correctly"; (2) decision errors, which "occur when the clearance has been properly received, communicated, and planned, but the pilot makes an erroneous choice at a decision point along the route"; and (3) execution errors, which occur when "the clearance is correctly communicated, pilots identify the correct intersection and direction of the turn, but they err in carrying out the maneuver" (pp. 55–56).

OPERATIONAL DEFINITIONS

In addition to defining variables conceptually, scientists must decide on the specific procedures for measuring those variables in their research. If the research is an experiment and thus involves manipulating a variable to create different conditions to which participants will be exposed, then the researchers also must decide on the procedures to create those different conditions. We can view the set of procedures—the *operations* that scientists use to measure and manipulate variables—as a concrete, nuts-and-bolts way of defining those variables. The term **operational definition** *refers to defining a variable in terms of the procedures used to measure or manipulate it.* In the case of hypothetical constructs, operational definitions translate abstract concepts that cannot be directly observed into tangible, measurable variables. Let's consider three examples.

First, suppose that we're interested in studying stress that can occur when people compete against one another. There are many possible ways that we might operationally define stress, such as (1) people's self-ratings of worry and tension assessed by a questionnaire just before competition begins; (2) scores on a psychological test that measures people's typical level of stress in competitive situations; (3) the frequency of behaviors representing "nervous habits" (e.g., fidgeting, fingernail biting), based on observing people before and during competition; (4) measures of muscle tension, heart rate, respiration rate, sweating, and stress hormones recorded before, during, and after competition. The full operational definitions of stress would contain more information, such as specifying the procedures used to make physiological recordings or describing the ratings scales that were used (e.g., a 5-point scale in which 1 = *I don't feel stressed at all* and 5 = *I feel extremely stressed*).

In an actual study, we might use several of these measures. Moreover, in an experiment, we might operationally define stress by manipulating the environmental conditions—the situational demands—to which participants are exposed. For example, we can create conditions in which people compete for a valued prize against a difficult or easy opponent. These manipulated conditions would operationally represent conditions of high and low stress.

As a second example, let's return to Hooey and Foyle's (2006) flight-crew experiments. A navigation error was operationally defined as "taxiing on a portion of the airport surface on which the aircraft had not been cleared, and deviating from the cleared taxiway center line by at least 50 ft" (p. 60). The operational definitions of planning, decision, and execution errors were represented by a list of specific, observable flight-crew behaviors that were organized into a flowchart. **Figure 4.7** shows the portion of the flowchart that operationally defines one of the three dependent variables: decision errors.

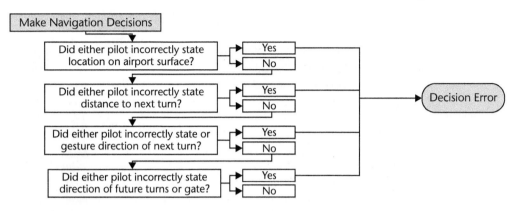

Figure 4.7 Operationally defining crew navigation errors. This flowchart represents how Hooey and Foyle (2006) operationally defined navigation decision errors. It is a portion of a larger flowchart that also operationally defined navigation planning and execution errors. (Copyright 2006. From Pilot navigation errors on the airport surface: Identifying contributing factors and mitigating solutions. *The International Journal of Aviation Psychology* by Hooey, B. L. et al. Reproduced by permission of Taylor & Francis LLC [http://www.tandfonline.com].)

Similarly, the independent variable in their experiments, type of navigation technology, involved making various cockpit information technologies available or unavailable to the flight crews during their simulated flights. Hooey and Foyle (2006) identified three modern navigation technologies that, at the time, were "the most likely candidates for cockpit integration" (p. 56). Traditional navigation methods represented a fourth technology. Thus, four navigation technologies were used, either individually or in combination:

- *Traditional technology.* This was a control condition in which crews used typical cockpit technology, such as paper charts of the airport layout.

- *Datalink.* In this text-messaging system, communications between the air traffic controller and cockpit crew were displayed as text readouts on a screen.

- *Electronic moving maps.* Similar to the GPS or smartphone navigation apps that people use when driving, these maps displayed the airport layout and the aircraft's moment-to-moment location.

- *Head-up displays.* Navigation information was displayed on the front window of the cockpit.

Along the *x*-axis of the graphs in **Figure 4.8**, you can see the specific technology conditions that Hooey and Foyle (2006) created for their experiment. These conditions represent their operational definition of the independent variable. Other researchers might have created different conditions, but the key point is that you know precisely what Hooey and Foyle did, and if you wish to replicate their study, you have a detailed road map for doing so. As you can see in Figure 4.8a, the text-messaging and electronic-map technologies, each of which provided cockpit crews with unambiguous information about taxiway clearances from the control tower, were sufficient by themselves to eliminate all planning errors. In contrast, it took a combination of technologies to eliminate all decision errors (Figure 4.8b) and all execution errors (graph not shown in Figure 4.8). Based on the findings of these and other human-factors experiments, such technologies have been incorporated into the latest generation of commercial aircraft (Neville & Dey, 2012).

For our third example, we return to Callender et al.'s (2012) study of children's externalizing behaviors. The researchers had to operationally define all of the conceptual variables contained in their proposed model (refer back to Figure 4.6 on page 118). They did this by having parents and teachers provide ratings on numerous items from psychological

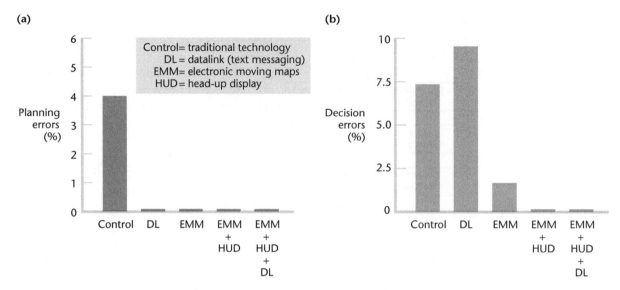

Figure 4.8 Pilot navigation errors on the airport surface. The percentage of simulated flights on which crews made a planning or decision error, as a function of the cockpit technology that was available. (a) Planning errors. (b) Decision errors. (Copyright 2006. From Pilot navigation errors on the airport surface: Identifying contributing factors and mitigating solutions. *The International Journal of Aviation Psychology* by Hooey, B. L. et al. Reproduced by permission of Taylor & Francis LLC [http://www.tandfonline.com].)

inventories. The scores on these measures represented the operational definitions of the four variables, as follows:

- *Parental depression.* Parents completed the six-item Depression scale from a broader test called the Brief Symptom Inventory (Derogatis, 1993). They used a 5-point rating format (ranging from 0 = *not at all* to 4 = *extremely*) to indicate whether they had felt distressed during the past week from experiencing each of six symptoms of depression (e.g., sadness, disinterest, suicidal thoughts).

- *Negative appraisals of child behavior.* Using a 5-point rating format (ranging from 1 = *strongly agree* to 5 = *strongly disagree*), parents rated 11 items that assessed their attitudes about their child's degree of affection and social responsiveness toward them (e.g., "I wish my child were more affectionate to me"). These items were drawn from the Maternal Perceptions Questionnaire (Olson, Bates, & Bayles, 1982) and the Parenting Stress Index (Abidin, 1995).

- *Harsh parenting behavior.* Parents completed the Harshness of Discipline scale (Dodge, Pettit, & Bates, 1994). They used a 5-point rating format (ranging from 0 = *never* to 4 = *several times a day*) to report how frequently they had physically punished their child (e.g., spanking, shaking) in the past 3 months.

- *Child externalizing behavior.* Parents completed the Child Behavior Checklist (CBCL) for children ages 2 to 3 (Achenbach, 1992) at the start of the study, and they and the children's kindergarten teachers completed the CBCL for children ages 6 to 18 (Achenbach & Rescorla, 2001) at the end of the study. These CBCL versions list about 100 child behaviors. Each item is rated on a 3-point scale (ranging from 0 = *not true* to 2 = *very true* or *often true*) to indicate how well it describes the child's behavior over the last 2 months (for 2- to 3-year-olds) or 6 months (for 6- to 18-year-olds). Child externalizing behavior was measured by items from the Externalizing subscale (e.g., defiant, hits others, cruel to animals).

OPERATIONAL DEFINITIONS IN EVERYDAY LIFE

Although the term *operational definition* may not be a part of everyday discourse, operational definitions play a role in many facets of daily life. As a student, when you ask, "What does it take to get a grade of 4.0 in this course?" or "to get an A on this assignment?" you are seeking an operational definition. Course syllabi and homework handouts that describe grading criteria represent one form of operational definitions. Legal contracts, including the lengthy "Terms of Use" that you typically have to agree to when downloading software or accessing services via the web, are essentially operational definitions that spell out agreements between the different parties.

In the workplace, job descriptions act as operational definitions of the tasks employees are expected to perform. Moreover, many organizations conduct formal, annual performance reviews of their employees. If you have held a part-time or full-time job, you may have undergone such a review. These reviews often determine annual salary increases or promotions based on whether each employee has met various performance goals. These specific performance goals act as operational definitions for judging what constitutes "excellent," "good," "average," or "poor" job performance.

In everyday discourse, we typically take it for granted that when other people express concepts, those words have the same meaning for them as for us. But at times this assumption is not just false, it's potentially dangerous. The reason often boils down to differences in how, essentially, people operationally define concepts in their own minds. Consider the concept of "sex," as in "having sex." In a study of 839 college students in the U.S. Midwest, vaginal intercourse was the only one of many behaviors that 100% of students agreed was "having sex" (Gute, Eshbaugh, & Wiersma, 2008). Students' opinions were divided as to whether other behaviors constituted "having sex"; for example, only 36% of women and 45% of men said that a person having "oral contact with your genitals" constituted "having sex." Several studies of college students in other countries (e.g., Australia, Canada, the United Kingdom) have found similar results (Pitts & Rahman, 2001).

Why might such disagreement about definitions of "sex" matter? As Gute et al. (2008) note, imagine someone who wants to know whether a potential dating or marital partner has practiced sexual abstinence, or has refrained from "risky sex," only to be told "yes" because the partner doesn't consider activities other than vaginal intercourse to be "sex." As they also note, in medical contexts, "without asking questions about specific sexual behaviors, a physician may not be able to assess a patient's risk of sexually transmitted infection" (Gute et al., 2008, p. 336). Some students may report to a health-care provider that they are sexually inactive not because they intentionally seek to lie, but because they don't consider the sexual behaviors in which they are engaging to actually constitute "sex." In sum, whether we're consciously aware of it or not, operational definitions play an important role in everyday life.

✓ CONCEPT CHECK 4.2 DEFINING VARIABLES

Three definitions of *love* appear below. Indicate whether each definition best represents a conceptual or operational definition. Answers appear on page 137.

1. A rating on a scale from –2 (*strongly disagree*) to +2 (*strongly agree*) in response to the statement "I am in love with my current partner."

2. A feeling of deep longing for, and sense of commitment to, another person.

3. An emotion in which the presence or thought of another person triggers arousal, desire, and a sense of caring for that person.

SCALES OF MEASUREMENT

Learning Objectives

After studying this section, you should be able to:

- Explain the basic characteristics of nominal, ordinal, interval, and ratio scales.
- Provide examples of measures that reflect these four measurement scales.

Measurement *is the process of systematically assigning values (numbers, labels, or other symbols) to represent attributes of organisms, objects, or events.* The term *systematic* means that values are assigned according to some rule. Here, we'll focus on scales of measurement (rules) used for assigning values to variables.

Although some form of the "thumb scale" may have first attained prominence with Roman emperors who decided the fate of gladiators, two movie critics, Gene Siskel and Roger Ebert, made it famous in modern times. If both critics liked a movie, it received two thumbs up. If both disliked it, the movie got two thumbs down. The film received one thumb up if the critics' opinions were split. Other film critics simply use a four- or five-star rating scale, as do many reviewers of restaurants and consumer products.

The concept of **scales of measurement** *refers to rules for assigning scale values to measurements.* For movie critics, the scale values are the number of thumbs or stars that represent the measure of "movie quality." For psychologists, the scale values are numerical scores or category labels that represent the variables being measured. For example, scale values of 0, 1, 2, 3, 4, and so on can be used to represent the number of navigation errors made by flight crews. If we conduct a study and wish to measure college students' academic majors, the scale values would represent the names of each academic major.

Note that for purposes of recording data, just as numbers are assigned to represent the frequency of errors on a task, we could assign numbers to different college majors: 1 = *biology,* 2 = *physics,* 3 = *psychology,* 4 = *anthropology,* 5 = *business,* and so on. But those numbers are merely substitute symbols devoid of any quantitative information. We could assign those numbers any way we wish, such as alphabetically: 1 = *anthropology,* 2 = *biology,* 3 = *business,* and so forth.

Why are scales of measurement important? Although numbers can be assigned to any variable, the mathematical operations that researchers can meaningfully perform on those numbers (e.g., add, subtract, multiply, or divide them), and thus the ways in which researchers analyze and interpret their data, are influenced by the scale of measurement used. There are four measurement scales to consider: nominal, ordinal, interval, and ratio. As we progress from nominal to ratio scales—or, as some scientists prefer to say, from nominal to ratio *levels* of measurement—progressively more information is conveyed about the variable being measured.

NOMINAL SCALES

When measurement occurs at the level of a **nominal scale,** *the scale values represent only qualitative differences (i.e., differences of type rather than amount) of the attribute of interest.* Thus, for the attribute of political affiliation, classifying people as Republicans, Democrats, or Independents represents a nominal scale of measurement. So does classifying students according to their college major, or classifying people as having different types of anxiety disorders. In Callender et al.'s (2012) study of children's externalizing behavior, classifying parents as mothers or fathers, and children as girls or boys, represented a nominal scale of measurement. In Hooey and Foyle's (2006) cockpit-crew experiments, classifying each navigation error as either a planning, decision, or execution error represents a nominal level of measurement.

Nominal scaling involves creating a set of labels or names for categories that are mutually exclusive and assigning each case into one of those categories (Siegel & Castellan, 1988). All cases within a category must be equivalent on the attribute represented by that category. In other words, all people assigned to the political category of Independents must be Independents.

Nominal scaling abounds in science and everyday life. For example, behavioral researchers have developed coding systems for classifying many characteristics, such as different types of emotional facial expressions, parenting behaviors, group interactions, and even dream content (Yu, 2015). In daily life, restaurants divide their menu offerings into different categories (appetizers, main courses, desserts) and subcategories (main courses: fish, poultry, meat, vegetarian). Computer users categorize items into different folders (e.g., photos, video games, documents, music). And in many offices, steel filing cabinets store folders of categorized paper documents.

Nominal scales, although common and very important, are considered to be the weakest level of measurement in the sense that they provide the least amount of information about the cases that were measured. All we can assume is that cases within a category are equivalent to one another and different from the cases in other categories. Although numbers can be assigned to represent categories, such as using numeric codes to represent academic majors (e.g., 1 = *biology*, 2 = *physics*, 3 = *psychology*), the numbers themselves are arbitrary. They provide no information about "greater than" or "less than" and are not amenable to the basic arithmetic operations of addition, subtraction, multiplication, or division. What would "3 minus 2" or "2 minus 1" mean, in terms of academic majors? Statistically, in a sample of 400 students, if 100 major in biology, 100 in physics, and 200 in psychology, it likewise makes no sense to say that the average major is 2.25.

But, as we discussed early in the chapter, researchers do obtain quantitative data from qualitative variables. They can count the number of instances in each category, use that to compute the mode (e.g., the most common college major in the sample), proportions and percentages (e.g., 50% of the sample majored in psychology), and can statistically analyze those results. Such quantitative data would allow us to examine, for example, whether there are significant differences in the percentage of female versus male college students majoring in a given subject.

ORDINAL SCALES

In an **ordinal scale,** *the different scale values represent relative differences in the amount of some attribute.* For example, in an elementary-school class of 25 children, we can measure social status by ranking the children from most popular (rank = 1) to least popular (rank = 25). Athletic teams' performance can be measured by looking at their place in the standings (first place, second place, etc.). Each year the magazine *U.S. News & World Report* publishes a list that ranks "America's Top Colleges." In a marketing survey, I might present you with the names of 10 ice cream flavors and ask you to rank them from 1 to 10, starting with your most preferred flavor.

Values on ordinal scales can be represented by numbers or category labels that imply an ordering on some quantitative dimension. If we categorize people as children, adolescents, and adults based on their age, we are using an ordinal scale. Similarly, if we categorize tasks or documents as top priority, priority, and low priority, we are using an ordinal scale (see **Figure 4.9**).

Figure 4.9 An example of unusual category labels that appear to represent an ordinal scale.

In science and everyday life, we often use rank ordering to measure attributes of people, other organisms, social groups, objects, and other stimuli. In contrast to nominal scales, ordinal scales provide information about how different people or other entities stand relative to one another on dimensions such as greater than, less than, better than, or worse than. For example, if Claire is more popular than Elissa, and Elissa is more popular than Alice, we know that Claire is more popular than Alice. But ordinal scales do not tell us whether the "distance"—the amount of difference—between rankings is equivalent across the entire scale range. Claire may be much more popular than Elissa, who in turn is just barely more popular than Alice. Similarly, the difference in institutional scholastic performance between a first- and a fifth-ranked college cannot be assumed to be the same as the difference between a sixth- and tenth-ranked college.

As another example, consider the rating format of the individual items from the Use of Physical Punishment scale (Dodge et al., 1994) that Callender et al. (2012) employed to assess harsh parenting behavior. Parents rated how often they physically punished their child in the past 3 months. The response options were: 0 = *never,* 1 = *once a month,* 2 = *once a week,* 3 = *every day,* and 4 = *several times a day.* Clearly, although physically punishing a child every day represents more frequent punishment than doing so once a week, with this rating format the distances between the numeric values cannot be considered to represent equal distances in the frequency of punishment.

INTERVAL SCALES

Measurement occurs on an **interval scale** *when equal distances between values on the scale reflect equal differences in the amount of the attribute being measured.* For example, suppose for the moment that we are able to measure shyness on an interval scale (let's say, with higher scores on a personality test representing a greater amount of shyness) and that Sarah, Robin, and Janet, respectively, have scores of 20, 23, and 26. In this event, the scores inform us that Janet is more shy than Robin, who in turn is more shy than Sarah. Additionally, because Janet's and Robin's scores differ by three units, and because Robin and Sarah's scores differ by three units, the amount of difference in shyness between Janet and Robin is the same as the amount of difference in shyness between Robin and Sarah. Thus, the information yielded by an interval scale is more precise than the information we obtain at the nominal and ordinal levels of measurement.

Temperature, as recorded on a Fahrenheit or Celsius scale, is a classic example of an interval scale of measurement. As the readout of a thermometer increases from 70 °F to 78 °F, the amount of temperature change is the same as when the thermometer changes from 65 °F to 73 °F. Similarly, on a Celsius scale, a change from 0 °C to 5 °C represents the same amount of increase in temperature as a change from 15 °C to 20 °C.

Researchers often analyze scores from certain types of psychological measures as if these scores reflect an interval scale of measurement. Examples include scores from various intelligence and aptitude tests, tests that assess personality traits and psychological disorders, and rating scales that assess people's attitudes. There are long-running debates, however, about whether the scores generated by such measures truly represent an interval scale and, if not, how the scores should be statistically analyzed (Carifio & Perla, 2007; Gardner, 1975; Scholten & Borsboom, 2009). In the shyness example above, can we indeed assume that test scores of 23 versus 20 and of 26 versus 23 convey psychologically equal intervals in the extent to which people are shy? If not, then are the scores only ordinal data, telling us merely that someone is more or less shy than someone else? Details of these debates are beyond our scope, but be aware that many psychological measures are treated in statistical analyses as interval data and that there are differences of opinion about whether doing so is appropriate.

RATIO SCALES

Measurement occurs on a **ratio scale** *when equal distances between values on the scale reflect equal differences in the amount of the attribute being measured and the scale also has a true zero point.* Compared with nominal, ordinal, and interval scales, ratio scales provide the most information about the attribute being assessed.

As compared to an arbitrary zero point, a true zero point exists when a score of zero represents the absence of an attribute. Let's return to temperature as an example. The Fahrenheit and Celsius scales contain arbitrary zero points. On the Celsius scale, 0 °C was chosen to represent the temperature at which water freezes. On both scales, temperatures below zero degrees occur. Because neither scale has a true zero point, we cannot say in either system that 20° is twice the temperature of 10°, or that 75° is 3 times the temperature of 25°. Although the scale intervals may be equal in each system, we cannot use the scale values to create meaningful ratios.

In contrast, time, length, and annual income are examples of variables that can be measured on a ratio scale. A person who watches 10 hours of television a week watches twice as much TV as a person who watches 5 hours. A reaction time of 500 milliseconds is twice as fast as a reaction time of 1,000 milliseconds. Eight millimeters is twice the length of 4 millimeters. Whether measured in dollars, pounds, euros, or any other currency, an annual income of 30,000 is twice that of 15,000, and a score of zero represents an absence of annual income. **Figure 4.10** summarizes the various measurement scales.

Scale	Key Characteristic	Example
Nominal	Different scale values only represent different qualities.	Olympic team (e.g., China, Great Britain, Nigeria, France), primary color of jersey (e.g., green, blue)
Ordinal	Scale values represent quantitative ordering.	Order of finishing the race (e.g., first, second, third)
Interval	Equal scale intervals represent equal quantitative differences.	Temperatures in the stadium throughout the day (e.g., 20 °C, 28 °C)
Ratio	Equal scale intervals represent equal quantitative differences, and there is a true zero point.	Time to finish the race, in seconds (e.g., 12.91, 13.18)

Photo by Streeter Lecka/Getty Images

Figure 4.10 Scales of measurement at the 2012 Olympic Games.

CONCEPT CHECK 4.3 SCALES OF MEASUREMENT

Three variables related to college life are listed below. Decide whether each one best represents an interval, ordinal, ratio, or nominal scale of measurement. Answers appear on page 137.

1. Place of residence (e.g., dormitory, sorority/fraternity house, off campus)
2. Number of college credits completed
3. Current standing of intramural softball teams (first place, second place, etc.)

MEASUREMENT ACCURACY, RELIABILITY, AND VALIDITY

Learning Objectives

After studying this section, you should be able to:

- Explain what is meant by the accuracy and reliability of a measure.
- Illustrate different ways of estimating a measure's reliability.
- Discuss how validity differs from reliability, and contrast various types of validity.

Suppose that you assist me in collecting some data during a class meeting. We ask a student named Jim to leave his seat, come to the front of the room, and stand on a digital bathroom scale. Once the digital readout appears, he gets off the scale. A minute later, he gets on and off the scale again. We repeat this process until we have a total of five measurements. In collecting these data, we use a *standardized procedure* in which each measurement is taken under conditions that are as equivalent as possible. For example, we have Jim approach the scale from the front and stand on it each time with his right foot first, sit down and not eat or drink or move about in between measurements, and so forth. Now let's use this example to help us examine three aspects of measurement: accuracy, reliability, and validity.

ACCURACY OF MEASUREMENT

The **accuracy** *of a measure represents the degree to which the measure yields results that agree with a known standard.* Suppose that, in weighing Jim 5 times, the bathroom scale readouts are 174.8, 175.2, 175.0, 175.1, and 174.9. We say, "Jim, based on the average readout, you weigh 175 pounds." If Jim's true weight is indeed 175.0 pounds, then we have a measure that, at least for casual home use, yields reasonably accurate scores. But suppose Jim replies, "Gee. I weigh myself 3 times a week at the Intramural Center before exercising, using one of those fancy balance scales. For the last 2 months I've always been around 167." If Jim's true weight is 167 pounds, then our measure is considerably inaccurate. To make this determination, we need to have a known standard against which to compare the readout of our bathroom scale. For example, if we can verify that the scale in the Intramural Center is accurate because it has been properly calibrated, then we can compare the results of our scale to that one.

Suppose we find that in comparison to an accurate, known standard, our scale readout consistently adds 4 pounds to Jim's and to other students' true weight scores. Or, alternatively, suppose the scale repeatedly overestimates everyone's weight by 3%. These types of inaccuracies represent **systematic error** (also called **bias**): *a consistent degree of error that occurs with each measurement.* We would try to eliminate this bias by recalibrating our scale against a known standard (and, if we can't, taking it back to the store for a refund).

In behavioral science, the accuracy of physical instruments used to measure many variables (e.g., speed, duration, and frequency of response; force; weight; blood chemical concentrations) can be calibrated against known standards. Measurement accuracy, however, cannot be determined for many psychological variables because known standards do not exist.

For example, if I measure your personality or IQ with a psychological test, what is the known standard against which I can compare the accuracy of those measuring instruments? In such cases, as well as with measures where accuracy can be determined, researchers devote their attention to two other aspects of measurement: reliability and validity.

RELIABILITY OF MEASUREMENT

The **reliability** *of a measure is assessed by examining its consistency.* Does a measure yield consistent scores under conditions where consistency would be expected? We weighed Jim five times over a period of a few minutes, using standardized measurement procedures, and obtained scores of 174.8, 175.2, 175.0, 175.1, and 174.9. Under these conditions—Jim didn't binge on cookies and wash them down with a can of soda in between each weighing—we would expect the scale readouts to be consistent. Indeed, the five scores varied within +/−0.2 pounds. For a home-use bathroom scale, it appears to have adequate reliability. Notice, however, that just because our scale is a reliable measure, this does not necessarily mean that it is accurate. If Jim's true weight is 167 pounds, as he claimed, then our bathroom scale would be reliable—it yields consistent numbers—but it would be inaccurate because those numbers repeatedly overestimate Jim's weight.

For simplicity, let's assume that Jim's true weight is 175 pounds and that we have a properly calibrated scale in which systematic measurement error has been eliminated. Even so, our measurements still contain error, which we see in the fluctuations of +/−0.2 pounds in the scale readouts. These variations are said to reflect **random measurement error:** *random fluctuations that occur during measurement and cause the obtained scores to deviate from a true score.* Perhaps the score is affected by minor changes in where Jim stands on the scale or by whether he remains still or moves even slightly at the moment when the scale assesses his weight. Each time Jim stands on the scale, the operation of its mechanical guts (only the readout is digital) will not be precisely the same. All of these and other factors could contribute to random error and cause any particular score to deviate up or down from Jim's true weight. When studying behavior, random measurement error can be introduced by:

- participants' characteristics (e.g., momentary fluctuations in moods and attentiveness),

- the measurement setting or procedures (e.g., chance variations in room conditions and how instructions are delivered),

- the measuring instrument itself (e.g., ambiguously worded test items, ambiguous criteria for classifying people's behavior into different categories, fluctuations in the attentiveness of observers who are recording people's behavior), and

- other factors (e.g., random mistakes in transcribing data).

The greater the random error, the less reliable a measuring instrument will be. Returning to the example of Jim's weight, if Jim's five scale readouts were 182, 172, 174, 179, and 168, even though these average to his true weight of 175 pounds, those large fluctuations surely would lead us to return the scale to the store and complain that it was unreliable. Indeed, according to one approach to the study of measurement, known as *classical test theory* (Novick, 1966), the reliability of a measure reflects the degree to which it is free from random measurement error. In practice, researchers estimate the reliability of measures by assessing their consistency. **Figure 4.11** portrays several methods for doing this, which we will now discuss.

Test–Retest Reliability

One common way of measuring reliability, **test–retest reliability,** *is determined by administering the same measure to the same participants on two or more occasions, under equivalent*

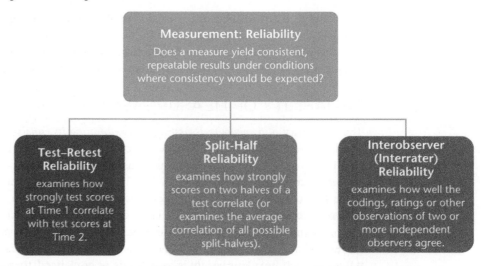

Figure 4.11 Measurement reliability. Researchers can estimate the reliability of a measure in several ways. This figure highlights three approaches.

test conditions. This is basically what we did when we measured Jim's weight five times over a period of a few minutes, although in a reliability study we would use a larger sample of participants.

Suppose we want to assess the test–retest reliability of a psychological measure such as a test of personality or intelligence. Because personality traits and intelligence are, in theory, relatively stable characteristics that should not change substantially over a short period of weeks, we could give the test to participants at Time 1 and then again at Time 2, which would be perhaps 1, 2, or a few weeks later. We would then use statistical analysis to determine how well participants' scores at Time 1 correlate with their scores at Time 2. The stronger the correlation between the two sets of test scores, the higher the reliability of the measure.

Recall that in Callender et al.'s (2012) study of parental depression and children's externalizing behavior, parents completed a nine-item Depression scale from a psychological test called the Brief Symptom Inventory (BSI). The researchers who developed the BSI obtained initial data on the test–retest reliability of its various subscales (e.g., depression, phobic anxiety, obsessiveness-compulsiveness) by administering the BSI to 60 adults twice, 2 weeks apart (Derogatis & Melisaratos, 1983). High test–retest correlations in this and subsequent studies provide one measure of the BSI's reliability.

Split-Half Reliability

In contrast to administering the same test twice to the same people, some ways to estimate reliability involve a single test administration. One example is **split-half reliability:** *the items that compose a test are divided into two subsets, and the correlation between subsets is determined.* For example, suppose we have developed a 40-item test that we claim measures shyness. We give the test to 500 participants. In analyzing the data, we randomly split the test in half, essentially creating two 20-item tests that we'll call Subtest A and Subtest B. Now we correlate people's scores on Subtest A with their scores on Subtest B. The two halves of the test should correlate highly with each other if the test is reliable. Thanks to the availability of computers, researchers often use a variation of this procedure in which a test's items are split into two halves in every possible way, and the average correlation between the halves is determined.

Split-half reliability is one example of an overall approach to estimating reliability that is often called *internal reliability* or *internal-consistency reliability*. Essentially, this approach assesses the interrelatedness of the items within a measure, and researchers interpret stronger interrelatedness as evidence of higher test reliability. For example, a frequently reported statistic called *Cronbach's alpha* reflects how strongly the individual items in a test or in a subset of a test correlate with one another overall. The developers of the BSI, in addition to assessing it test–retest reliability, used data from a different sample of 719 people to compute Cronbach's alpha for each of the BSI's nine scales (i.e., different subsets of items that measured depression, hostility, anxiety, and six other attributes). They found that the Depression scale had good internal reliability (Derogatis & Melisaratos, 1983).

Interobserver (Interrater) Reliability

In many studies, human observers must make judgments about people, other organisms, or other types of stimuli. Their task may be to use a coding system to classify people's facial expressions as representing emotions of happiness, sadness, anger, and so forth. Or, they may be asked to use rating scales to measure the intensity of people's responses or the degree to which people exhibit various personality characteristics. The content of people's diaries, dream reports, or of books or television shows may need to be examined and classified into different categories (e.g., violent versus nonviolent content).

Interobserver reliability (also called **interrater reliability**) *represents the degree to which independent observers show agreement in their observations.* Various statistics are used to calculate interobserver reliability, depending on the type of data being recorded and the number of observers recording the same event. For example, where each instance of behavior is classified into one qualitatively different category or another (e.g., different types of emotions), the percentage of times that two observers agree, over and beyond the degree of agreement that would be expected to occur by chance, is often used as a measure of interobserver reliability (Cohen, 1960).

In Hooey and Foyle's (2006) cockpit-crew navigation experiments, three trained observers identified when a crew navigation error occurred and then classified the type of error using specific behavioral criteria, as illustrated in the flowchart in Figure 4.7 on page 121. To do this, the observers examined the flight simulations (both live and via replay) as well as video and audio recordings of the cockpit crews. Hooey and Foyle reported 100% agreement among the observers in identifying the occurrence of navigation errors.

In other studies, participants may be the ones who are asked to make judgments about other people. For example, in Callender et al.'s (2012) study, parents were asked to use the Child Behavior Checklist (CBCL) for children ages 2 to 3 (Achenbach, 1992) to rate how often their 3-year-old children exhibited numerous behaviors, including externalizing behaviors such as defiance and getting into fights. By having different observers, such as mothers and fathers, independently rate the same children, researchers have found that good interobserver reliability is obtained when using the CBCL (Koot, Van Den Oord, Verhulst, & Boomsma, 1997). We'll take a further look at interobserver reliability in Chapter 6, when we discuss observational research.

VALIDITY OF MEASUREMENT

Let's consider one final scenario involving our bathroom scale. Suppose that when Jim is weighed five times during class, the readouts are 175.0, 175.1, 175.1, 174.8, 175.0. I then tell Jim that based on these data, he has above-average intelligence. Jim graciously refrains from calling me a fool in front of the class, but he—like you—should legitimately wonder how on earth I drew that conclusion from those numbers.

The issue here is one of measurement **validity:** *Can we truthfully infer that a measure actually does what it is claimed to do?* If the developers of a psychological test claim that it measures shyness, does evidence indicate that the test actually measures shyness and not some other psychological characteristic? If a company claims that scores on a job aptitude test can be used to predict managerial success, can we indeed draw valid conclusions based on job applicants' test scores about who is likely to be successful or unsuccessful as a business manager?

Historically, much of the work devoted to establishing validity has focused on the development of psychological tests, such as intelligence tests, personality tests, tests used to diagnose psychological disorders, aptitude and achievement tests, and personnel-selection tests. In this context, it's common for researchers to use the term *validity* as representing a property of the measure itself, as in "Does this shyness test have good validity?" We'll adhere to this conventional usage, but keep in mind that, more technically, the concept of validity refers to the inferences that we draw about a measure and the results we obtain from it (Shadish, Cook, & Campbell, 2002). Thus, based on people's test scores, is it valid for us to draw inferences about their degree of shyness?

For a measure to be valid, it must first have good reliability. Suppose that 1000 adults take a shyness test today, and again next week. We find that the 300 people who score highest in shyness this week score in the middle or bottom of the pack next week, and that the 300 people who have the lowest shyness scores this week score in the middle or top of the pack next week. Given the fact that shyness presumably is a relatively stable personal characteristic, such results indicate poor test–retest reliability. Thus, how can we possibly draw valid inferences about people' degree of shyness based on this test? Our conclusions about who is shy and who is not will differ considerably, depending on whether we use the first or second set of test scores.

Although a measure must be reliable in order for it to be considered valid, reliability by itself is not sufficient to establish a measure's validity. Notice that, earlier, when I used the bathroom scale to draw a conclusion about Jim's intelligence, the readouts on the scale were consistently close to 175.0. But this only indicates that our measuring device seems to be reliable. It does not indicate that consistent scores on the bathroom scale display are a valid basis for judging someone's intelligence. Similarly, if shyness test scores are highly consistent when people take that test twice in a week, this excellent reliability does not let us infer that those scores actually represent shyness, as opposed to some other psychological characteristic. In sum, *just because a measure is reliable, this does not necessarily mean it is valid.* So how is validity established?

To answer this question, imagine that we are developing a new test that we claim measures students' scholastic aptitude, and that will be faster to complete than the current, widely used SAT college admissions test. We'll call it the Quick Scholastic Aptitude Test (QSAT), and use it to explore several aspects of validity. **Figure 4.12** provides an overview of the coming discussion.

Face Validity and Content Validity

One type of validity, **face validity,** *concerns the degree to which the items on a measure appear to be reasonable.* Thus, if the QSAT consists of questions that assess logical reasoning skills, reading comprehension, and the ability to solve abstract problems, then on the surface the QSAT would have greater face validity than if it solely contained items that asked about people's favorite ice cream flavors, fruits, and colors. Face validity is not a scientific form of validity (and thus doesn't appear in Figure 4.12), but from a practical standpoint, it can be important. If items don't seem reasonable to the people taking a test, this may decrease their motivation to respond carefully. Face validity also may influence how readily people accept the results of a test as being valid. Nevertheless, it is possible for a test to have low face validity yet still measure what it claims to measure. Conversely, just because a test "looks good" (i.e., it has face validity) does not mean that it is scientifically valid.

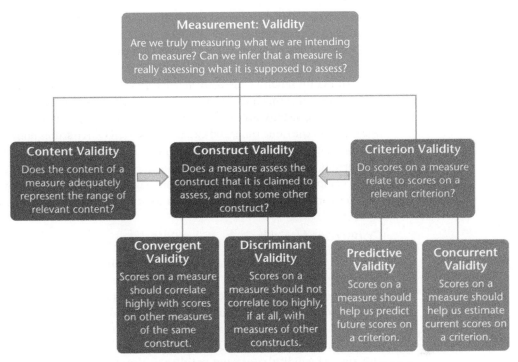

Figure 4.12 Measurement validity. Researchers want to draw valid inferences based on the measures they use. They gather several types of evidence to establish measurement validity.

Content validity *represents the degree to which the items on a measure adequately represent the entire range or set of items that could have been appropriately included.* For example, suppose I tell students in my introductory psychology class that Exam 2 will cover the textbook chapters on learning, memory, and language. I then develop an exam that contains questions based only on the learning chapter. In this case, my sample of test items does not adequately represent the variety of possible items that would have been appropriate to include (i.e., it is missing items on memory and language). Similarly, when constructing the QSAT, if we are being guided by a theory that conceptualizes academic aptitude as having verbal, mathematical, logical reasoning and other components, then the QSAT should include items that adequately represent each of those components.

Criterion Validity

Criterion validity *addresses the relation between scores on a measure and an outcome* (Cronbach & Meehl, 1955). If we claim that QSAT scores can predict students' college grades, then we will need to establish the criterion validity of our QSAT. If an industrial/organizational (I/O) psychologist is developing a test that will be used to hire business managers, she will need to establish that her test has criterion validity: that it actually can predict how well managers perform. In these examples, college grades and managerial performance are outcomes, called *criteria* (singular: *criterion*).

One type of criterion validity, called *predictive validity,* is demonstrated when a measure recorded at one time predicts a criterion that occurs in the future. To examine whether the QSAT has predictive validity, we could administer the test to high-school seniors and examine how well, among those students who go to college, their QSAT scores help us to predict their first-year college grade point averages. Similarly, an I/O psychologist can administer a personnel-selection test to many job applicants. For those applicants who are hired by the company, she can examine whether higher scores on the selection test predict better on-the-job performance.

Of course, as we are developing the QSAT, we may not want to wait a year or more to gather initial data on how well QSAT scores predict college grades. Therefore, we can examine another type of criterion validity, called *concurrent validity:* the relation between scores on a measure and an outcome, when that measure and outcome are assessed at the same time (i.e., concurrently).

We could give the QSAT right now to a sample of college students, obtain those students' college grades at the same time, and examine how well QSAT scores allow us to estimate students' current grade point averages. Similarly, the I/O psychologist can identify a sample of managers who already work for the company, administer the screening test to them, and at the same time obtain company ratings of how well each manager is performing. She can then examine how well the scores on the screening test enable her to determine managers' current performance ratings.

Construct Validity

In developing the QSAT, we are doing more than simply claiming that it can predict students' grades; we are claiming that the QSAT measures a construct—in this case, an underlying psychological attribute—called scholastic aptitude. We believe that scholastic aptitude involves something broader than just getting good grades. It reflects a person's more general capability to successfully engage in, and contribute to, all manner of scholastic work. How can we demonstrate that the QSAT is a valid measure of the construct of scholastic aptitude? This type of validity, **construct validity,** *is demonstrated when a measure truly assesses the construct that it is claimed to assess.*

Evidence that our QSAT has content validity and criterion validity will help to establish its construct validity as well (Cronbach & Meehl, 1955). For example, if we demonstrate that high-school students' QSAT scores help us to predict their college grades, this would be consistent with the claim that the QSAT measures scholastic aptitude. But other types of evidence also are important. For example, if validated psychological tests that measure scholastic aptitude already exist, then students' scores on the QSAT should correlate well with their scores on those other tests. Additionally, in high schools and colleges where teachers get to know students well, we could have teachers rate their students' scholastic aptitude. We would then expect students' QSAT scores to correlate well with teachers' ratings. Such findings would provide support for a component of construct validity called **convergent validity:** *scores on a measure should correlate highly (i.e., converge) with scores on other measures of the same construct* (Campbell & Fiske, 1959).

It will also be important for us to demonstrate that our QSAT has another component of construct validity called **discriminant validity:** *scores on a measure should not correlate too strongly with scores on measures of other constructs* (Campbell & Fiske, 1959; Schry, Roberson-Nay, & White, 2012). For example, suppose that based on existing theories, scholastic aptitude is hypothesized to be unrelated to traits such as shyness and agreeableness. Suppose as well that there is theoretical justification for expecting that attributes such as intelligence and creativity contribute moderately to scholastic aptitude. Therefore, if we correlate QSAT scores with validated measures of these other traits, we should find either no correlation or only weak correlations with shyness and agreeableness, and relatively moderate correlations with intelligence and creativity. In particular, the QSAT correlations with intelligence and creativity should not be so high as to suggest that the QSAT, instead of measuring scholastic aptitude, is really measuring intelligence or creativity. Imagine, for example, that the QSAT correlates more strongly with intelligence tests than with other validated psychological tests that measure scholastic aptitude. This would not be good!

In sum, construct validity is the broadest and most theoretically based type of validity. It is established by the pattern of how a particular measure relates to other measures that, in theory, should or should not be related to it (Campbell & Fiske, 1959; Cronbach & Meehl, 1955). Evidence for the construct validity of a measure also builds as the results of studies support its content validity and criterion validity (Cronbach, 1970).

To further illustrate these points, consider the measure that Callender et al. (2012) used to assess parental depression in their study of parenting and children's externalizing behavior: the Depression scale of the Brief Symptom Inventory (BSI; Derogatis & Melisaratos, 1983). The test developers, in presenting their initial evidence about the BSI's validity, focused on its construct validity. They correlated people's scores on the BSI with their scores on other psychological tests. High correlations with scores on two psychological tests of depression supported the convergent validity of the BSI Depression scale. Lower correlations with psychological tests measuring other constructs—such as anxiety, obsessiveness-compulsiveness, schizophrenia, and resentment and aggression—provided some evidence for the discriminant validity of the BSI Depression scale.

Other researchers evaluated the BSI Depression scale as a screening test for depression. They examined its validity by assessing the relation between BSI scores and a diagnostic criterion: the outcome of clinical interviews. In one study of 177 adults, 24 participants were diagnosed as depressed based on clinical interviews (Stukenberg, Dura, & Kiecolt-Glaser, 1990). Participants also were classified as depressed or not depressed based on their BSI Depression scale scores. The BSI classification agreed with the clinical interview outcome in 76% and 77% of the cases in which interviewees were diagnosed, respectively, as depressed and not depressed. In providing support for the Depression scale's criterion validity, these results also are consistent with the claim that the BSI's Depression scale measures the construct of depression.

SOME FINAL THOUGHTS

Researchers in all psychological subfields are concerned with measurement issues, and there are some subfields—such as *quantitative psychology* and *psychometrics*—whose members specialize in measurement issues and their relation to statistical analysis.

As a student interested in a particular psychological topic—for a term paper, for a research project, or out of sheer curiosity—how can you begin to learn about the ways psychologists have defined and measured (or, for that matter, manipulated) the variables of interest to you? For some topics, one way to start is by looking at specialized reference books, such as the *APA Dictionary of Psychology* (VandenBos, 2007). Another approach is to read journal articles on the topics that interest you. For each article, pay particular attention to the introductory section (which, typically, presents and defines key concepts) and the Method section (which describes the procedures used to measure those concepts). To find relevant articles, use the literature search tips discussed in Chapter 2 and Appendix A. Remember that many journal articles are highly technical, so don't expect to understand every detail right away. Such understanding comes as you develop expertise in an area.

✓ **CONCEPT CHECK 4.4** MEASUREMENT ACCURACY, RELIABILITY, AND VALIDITY

Decide whether each statement below is true or false. Answers appear on page 137.

1. The speedometer on Bill's car consistently overestimates the car's true speed by 5%. This type of error is called random measurement error.

2. Test–retest reliability and split-half reliability are different methods of assessing whether a psychological test yields consistent measurements.

3. Predictive and concurrent validity both represent types of criterion validity.

4. Construct validity is the most theoretical type of validity.

CHAPTER SUMMARY

- Variables are characteristics of organisms or environments that can assume two or more values. Qualitative variables represent properties that differ in *type*. Quantitative variables represent properties that differ in *amount or number*.

- An independent variable is the presumed causal factor in a cause–effect relation. In an experiment, it is the factor that the researcher manipulates or systematically varies. A dependent variable is the presumed effect in a cause–effect relation. In an experiment, it is the behavior or outcome that the researcher measures to determine whether the independent variable has produced an effect.

- Many concepts that behavioral scientists study represent psychological attributes that cannot be directly observed. Rather, we observe measurable responses that are presumed to reflect these underlying attributes. Such concepts are called hypothetical constructs.

- A mediator variable is a variable that provides a causal link between an independent and dependent variable. A moderator variable alters the strength or direction of the relation between an independent and dependent variable.

- Operational definitions translate hypothetical constructs into tangible, measurable variables. Operational definitions involve defining a variable in terms of the procedures used to measure or manipulate it.

- Different scales of measurement reflect different rules for assigning scores to variables. With nominal scales, the various scale values represent qualitative differences of some attribute. When using ordinal scales, the different values represent relative differences—rankings—in the amount of some attribute. Measurement occurs on an interval scale when equal distances between values on the scale reflect equal differences in the amount of the attribute being measured. Ratio scales have the properties of an interval scale, but also have a true zero point.

- Good measures of variables are accurate, reliable, and valid. Accuracy represents the degree to which a measure yields results that agree with a known standard. Reliability—including test–retest reliability and split-half reliability—refers to the consistency of a measure. Validity refers to whether a measure actually assesses the attribute that it is claimed to assess.

- Face validity concerns the degree to which the items on a measure appear to be reasonable. Content validity represents the degree to which the items on a measure adequately sample the entire set of items that could have been included. Criterion validity focuses on how well a measure can predict or estimate a criterion. Predictive validity and concurrent validity represent two types of criterion validity.

- Construct validity is demonstrated when a measure has consistently been shown to assess the underlying construct that it is claimed to assess. Convergent validity and discriminant validity, along with content and criterion validity, provide evidence for the construct validity of a measure.

KEY TERMS

accuracy (p. 128)
construct validity (p. 134)
content validity (p. 133)
continuous variable (p. 112)
convergent validity (p. 134)
criterion validity (p. 133)
dependent variable (p. 113)
discrete variable (p. 112)
discriminant validity (p. 134)
face validity (p. 132)
hypothetical construct (p. 117)
independent variable (p. 113)

interobserver reliability (interrater reliability) (p. 131)
interval scale (p. 126)
measurement (p. 124)
mediator variable (p. 118)
moderator variable (p. 118)
nominal scale (p. 124)
operational definition (p. 120)
ordinal scale (p. 125)
qualitative variable (p. 111)
quantitative variable (p. 111)
random measurement error (p. 129)

ratio scale (p. 127)
reliability (p. 129)
scales of measurement (p. 124)
situational variable (p. 114)
split-half reliability (p. 130)
subject variable (p. 114)
systematic error (bias) (p. 128)
test–retest reliability (p. 129)
validity (p. 131)
variable (p. 110)

ASSESS YOUR KNOWLEDGE

1. What is the key difference between a qualitative variable and a quantitative variable, and between a discrete variable and a continuous variable?

2. Explain the meaning of the terms *independent variable* and *dependent variable*.

3. What is a hypothetical construct? Give an example.

4. What are mediator and moderator variables?

5. Why are variables operationally defined? Provide an example of an operational definition for an independent and dependent variable.

6. What is measurement? When measuring a variable, how do systematic error and random measurement error differ? Provide an example.

7. What are the properties of a nominal scale of measurement? Provide two examples.

8. How do measurements on an ordinal scale differ from those on a nominal scale? What new information is provided? Give an example.

9. Explain the key properties of interval and ratio scales. Provide an example of each.

10. Explain what it means for a measure to be accurate and to be reliable. Describe some different ways to determine the reliability of a measure.

11. Define the general concept of validity and briefly explain what is meant by face validity, content validity, and criterion validity. Describe two subtypes of criterion validity.

12. What is construct validity? Describe the types of evidence that can be used to establish the construct validity of a measure.

CONCEPT CHECKS: ANSWERS

4.1 Types of Variables

1. qualitative   2. quantitative   3. independent; dependent   4. mediating

4.2 Defining Variables

1. operational   2. conceptual   3. conceptual

4.3 Scales of Measurement

1. nominal   2. ratio   3. ordinal

4.4 Measurement Accuracy, Reliability, and Validity

1. false   2. true   3. true   4. true

THINKING CRITICALLY AND APPLYING YOUR KNOWLEDGE

EXERCISE 1   Independent and Dependent Variables

From the way that each of the following statements is phrased, identify the variables that conceptually are viewed as the independent and dependent variables.

(a) How does sleep deprivation affect people's mood?

(b) How does people's reaction time to visual stimuli in a driving-simulator task change as a function of the amount of alcohol that they have consumed in the preceding hour?

(c) Does the ease with which people can acquire a second language depend on the age at which they are first exposed to that second language?

(d) As people practice a physical task, such as playing a musical instrument, do physical changes occur in the structure of brain neurons that are involved in regulating such behavior?

(e) Does smoking while pregnant increase the risk that the newborn will have a low birth weight?

(f) Are people who grow up in an individualistic culture more likely to prefer participating in individual rather than team sports, as compared to people who grow up in a collectivistic culture?

(g) Does the number of words that a person can recall from a word list depend on the rate at which the words were presented?

(h) Does the number of bystanders present when a victim needs help affect the likelihood that someone will aid the victim?

(i) How does the schedule of reinforcement under which a response is acquired influence the degree to which that response will be resistant to extinction?

(j) When it comes to physical attraction, do opposites attract?

EXERCISE 2   Scales of Measurement

Identify whether the way in which each of the following variables is measured represents a nominal, ordinal, interval, or ratio scale.

(a) In a study examining the relation between depression and sunshine, the 12 months of the year are ranked from *most sunny* to *least sunny*.

(b) Children solve a puzzle while their mothers watch. Whenever a mother speaks to her child, the researcher codes the comment as *praise, criticism, instruction, asks question,* or *other*.

(c) To examine the relation between aggression and daily temperature, a researcher determines whether people in a large city commit more crimes on hotter days. Based on official police and weather data for a full year, the researcher records (1) the number of crimes reported each day and (2) the high temperature reached each day (in degrees Fahrenheit or Celsius).

(d) In a national survey, people are asked to respond to the following question: "On average, how many nights per week do you have difficulty falling asleep? Please write down a number from 0 to 7."

(e) In a national survey, people are asked to respond to the following question: "Please identify your annual income: 1 = 0 to $19,999; 2 = $20,000 to $39,999; 3 = $40,000 to 59,999; 4 = $60,000 to $79,999; 5 = $80,000 to $99,999; 6 = $100,000 or more."

(f) A researcher observes a troop of chimpanzees in the wild and identifies the dominance hierarchy of the troop.

(g) In a sleep-deprivation experiment, a researcher measures how much weight laboratory rats lose or gain during a 24-hour period.

(h) On a questionnaire examining leisure behavior, people are asked to report their favorite recreational activity by choosing among options such as sports, arts, reading, gardening, travel, and so on.

EXERCISE 3   Reliability and Validity

Three short scenarios are described in the next column. Each scenario *most directly* illustrates one of the following 10 qualities of a measure. Identify that single quality and explain your answer.

good reliability	poor reliability
good face validity	poor face validity
good content validity	poor content reliability
good criterion validity	poor criterion reliability
good construct validity	poor construct validity

Scenario A

Dr. Jones administers a job-skills test to 100 job applicants. The company then hires the 50 applicants who had the highest scores on the test. Among these 50 applicants, after they have been employed at the company for 6 months, those who scored higher on the job-skills test are performing substantially better on the job.

Scenario B

A psychologist administers a computer-based test to 140 college students. The test is designed to measure the students' unconscious prejudice toward certain groups. Each student takes the same test a second time, 3 weeks later. There is a very high correlation between students' test scores on the two occasions: higher scores on the first administering of the test are strongly associated with higher scores on the second administering of the same test.

Scenario C

Dr. Suzuki has developed a psychological test to measure people's general level of optimism. Research consistently shows that scores on Dr. Suzuki's optimism test are most highly correlated with scores on other psychological tests of optimism and, as predicted by theory, are only weakly correlated with scores on tests that measure the degree to which people tend to give socially desirable answers to questions (i.e., answers that they think are socially appropriate and that other people "want to hear").

CORRELATION AND CORRELATIONAL RESEARCH

CHAPTER OUTLINE

Crime dramas have long been a staple of evening TV. Major networks collectively devote many hours of prime-time evening programming to dramas focusing on fictional murders, rapes, robberies, kidnappings, and other crimes. Current or recent crime dramas on evening TV include *Criminal Minds, Law & Order: Special Victims Unit, Blue Bloods, Castle, Hawaii 5-O, NCIS, Chicago P.D., Bones, Sherlock, CSI: Crime Scene Investigation,* and *The Mentalist.* For more crime coverage, you can stream or tune in to reality crime shows (*COPS*), cyber-crime shows (*Mr. Robot, CSI: Cyber*), original cable channel crime dramas (*Sons of Anarchy*), endless crime drama reruns, and of course local and national nightly news.

If TV viewers think that it's a dangerous world out there, who can blame them? Is it possible, then, that people who consume a steady diet of TV might overestimate their chances of being crime victims and develop a distorted fear of crime? Scientists began investigating this issue decades ago and continue to do so (Gerbner & Gross, 1976; Kort-Butler & Sittner Hartshorn, 2011). As we'll see, their research highlights some important lessons about the major topics of this chapter: correlation and correlational research.

Just as we can ask whether people's TV-watching habits and perceptions of crime are associated, most psychological research examines relations between variables. This is the purpose of experiments, and it's a primary or secondary goal of most descriptive (i.e., nonexperimental) studies, including types of observational and survey research discussed in Chapters 6 and 7. In this chapter, we'll explore key issues about conducting nonexperimental research to examine relations between variables.

CORRELATION: BASIC CONCEPTS

Learning Objectives

After studying this section, you should be able to:

- Contrast the major procedures used in experimental versus correlational research.
- Explain the concepts of positive correlation and negative correlation.
- Discuss key properties of a correlation coefficient.
- Analyze findings portrayed in scatter plots.

A **correlation** *is a statistical association between variables.* A correlation exists between two variables (X and Y) when the scores or values of X are associated with the scores or values of Y in a nonrandom fashion. Thus, among adults, height and weight are correlated: Taller people tend to weigh more than shorter people. Likewise, childhood intelligence is correlated with adulthood intelligence; people with higher scores on intelligence tests in childhood also tend to have higher scores in adulthood (Deary & Brett, 2015). And as the headline in **Figure 5.1** indicates, in a long-term British study of 20,951 women and men, eating more chocolate over the course of a year—up to an average daily amount of about 100 grams (3.5 ounces)—was associated with a reduced risk of developing heart disease or having a stroke over the next 12 years (Kwok et al., 2015).

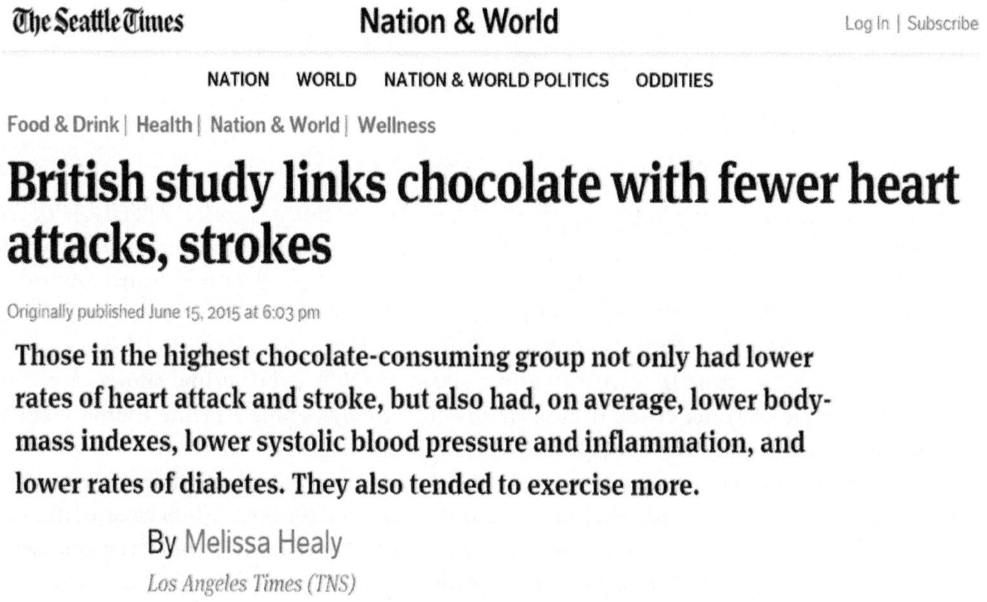

The Seattle Times

Nation & World

Log In | Subscribe

NATION   WORLD   NATION & WORLD POLITICS   ODDITIES

Food & Drink | Health | Nation & World | Wellness

British study links chocolate with fewer heart attacks, strokes

Originally published June 15, 2015 at 6:03 pm

Those in the highest chocolate-consuming group not only had lower rates of heart attack and stroke, but also had, on average, lower body-mass indexes, lower systolic blood pressure and inflammation, and lower rates of diabetes. They also tended to exercise more.

By Melissa Healy

Los Angeles Times (TNS)

Figure 5.1 Chocolate consumption and cardiovascular disease. A correlational study of men and women living in England found that consuming more chocolate was linked to a lower subsequent risk of having a heart attack or stroke within the following 12 years. (Source: *The Seattle Times.*)

CORRELATIONAL RESEARCH

The word *correlation* also occurs in the context of discussing correlational research and distinguishing such research from experiments. When scientists conduct experiments, their goal is to examine cause–effect relations between variables. When they conduct correlational research, their ultimate goal often is similar: to understand potential cause–effect relations. There are some key distinctions, however, between correlational research and experiments. In the simplest form of an *experiment,* the researcher takes the following steps:

- *Manipulate* an independent variable, X.

- *Measure* a dependent variable, Y.

- *Statistically analyze* whether the different conditions of X have produced differences in Y.

- *Attempt to eliminate confounding variables* by controlling the experimental environment.

Recall from Chapter 2 that confounding variables are extraneous factors that systematically vary with X and may influence Y. They are undesirable because they provide potential alternatives to the conclusion we wish to draw, namely, that X influenced Y.

In contrast, **correlational research** (also called **relational research**) *involves examining potential associations between naturally occurring variables by measuring those variables and determining whether they are statistically related.* Let's take the simplest case: a correlational study of two variables, X and Y. Here, the researcher takes the following steps:

- *Measure* variable X.

- *Measure* variable Y.

- *Statistically analyze* whether there is an association between X and Y.

- *Attempt to reduce the influence of confounding variables* through statistical control and, where possible, through special research designs.

It is extremely important to remember that *in correlational research, variables are measured, not manipulated.*

In psychology, correlational research most often examines the following three possible sources of associations:

1. *X and Y are characteristics of the same people.* Is there a correlation between people's level of self-esteem (X) and level of anxiety (Y), or between how stressed they feel (X) and how much they exercise (Y)?

2. *X and Y are characteristics of different, but related, sets of people.* Is there a correlation between children's level of self-esteem (X) and their parents' level of self-esteem (Y), or between workers' job satisfaction (X) and their managers' level of experience (Y)?

3. *X is a personal characteristic and Y is an environmental characteristic.* Are people more likely to act aggressively (X) on hotter days (Y)? Is students' satisfaction with college (X) related to the overall size of their institution (Y)?

To illustrate, let's return to the question of whether watching TV might distort people's perceived risk that they will become crime victims. In the 1970s, by analyzing U.S. government reports, police records, and other data, George Gerbner and his colleagues found that television portrayals of crime distorted reality (Gerbner & Gross, 1976; Gerbner et al., 1977). For example, whereas the actual crime rate was 0.41 crimes per 100 people, almost two thirds of television characters were involved in or exposed to violence. Whereas 10% of actual crimes were violent (e.g., murder, rape, assault), TV shows portrayed 77% of criminals as engaging in violent crime.

The researchers proposed that watching a lot of television increased people's perceived risk of being a victim of violent crime. To test their hypothesis, they analyzed data from a national survey in which American adults were asked, "During any given week, what are your chances of being involved in some type of violence?" Two choices were given: "About 1 in 100" (reasonably close to the odds based on national crime statistics) and "About 1 in 10" (a gross overestimation of the odds). Gerbner and Gross (1976) classified people who reported watching 4 or more hours of TV per day as "heavy TV viewers" and those who reported watching 2 hours or less per day as "light TV viewers." They found that 52% of heavy TV viewers selected the "1 in 10" odds of being a crime victim, whereas only 38% of light TV viewers did so. In other analyses, they found that heavy TV viewers were less trusting of other people than were light TV viewers.

Procedurally, in this correlational study:

- The average number of hours of TV that people watched per day (variable X) was *measured* using a survey item.

- People's perceived crime risk (variable Y) also was *measured* by a survey item.

- Statistical analyses revealed an association between these two variables: Overall, people who watched more TV perceived a higher risk of becoming a crime victim. The researchers also examined associations among other variables (e.g., TV watching and trust).

- Statistical procedures (which we will discuss later) were used to reduce the influence of potential confounding variables.

POSITIVE AND NEGATIVE CORRELATION

Variables can be positively or negatively correlated. **Positive correlation** *means that higher scores or levels of one variable tend to be associated with higher scores or levels of another variable.* As X increases, Y also tends to increase; as X decreases, Y also tends to decrease. As noted earlier, taller adults tend to weigh more, and higher scores on intelligence tests in childhood are associated with higher scores in adulthood. These are examples of positive correlations.

Returning to the relation between watching TV (variable X) and perceived crime risk (variable Y_1), for simplicity, **Table 5.1** shows data from a hypothetical study with only 10 participants. (In real research we would want many more participants.) Focus on these two scores for each participant: the average weekly number of hours of TV watched this month, and a rating of the perceived probability of becoming a crime victim (ranging from zero to 100%, in increments of 10 percentage points).

Notice that participants who watched more hours of TV per week, overall, have higher perceived crime-risk scores. For example, Wilma, Jacob, Carlos, and Shonda watched between 2 and 4 hours of TV per week, and their perceived crime-risk scores ranged from 10% to 40%. In contrast, Mike, Kyoko, Robert, and Deborah watched between 9 and 19 hours of TV per week, and their risk scores ranged from 60% to 80%. Also notice that the relation between X and Y scores is not perfect. For example, Wilma and Jacob each watched 2 hours of TV per week, yet their perceived risk scores differ. Jacob watched less TV than Carlos, Alex, and Shonda, but has a higher perceived crime risk score. Still, the overall trend is clear: X and Y are positively correlated. In fact, these data portray a strong positive correlation. (In the actual study described earlier, the correlation between TV watching and perceived crime risk was positive but weak.)

Negative correlation *means that higher scores or levels of one variable tend to be associated with lower scores or levels of another variable.* Scores on X and Y tend to move in opposite directions: As X increases, Y tends to decrease. As X decreases, Y tends to increase. To illustrate, let's focus on the relation between watching TV (variable X) and the degree to

Table 5.1 Understanding Positive and Negative Correlation

Participant	Variable X, Weekly Hours of TV Watched	Variable Y_1, Perceived Crime Risk (%)	Variable Y_2, Trust in Other People
Wilma	2	10	22
Jacob	2	40	11
Carlos	4	20	18
Shonda	4	30	14
Alex	5	30	10
Rita	6	50	12
Mike	9	70	7
Kyoko	11	60	9
Robert	11	80	10
Deborah	19	70	6

This table presents a set of hypothetical data for 10 participants. Perceived crime-risk scores can range from a probability of zero to 100% in increments of 10 percentage points. Trust scores can range from 5 to 25, with higher scores indicating greater trust.

which people generally trust others (variable Y_2). Assume that trust is measured by combining scores of five 5-point survey items, such that higher scores indicate greater trust (e.g., 1 = *I never trust people*; 5 = *I always trust people*). Table 5.1 reveals that as TV-watching scores increase, trust scores generally decrease. As another example, some studies have found a negative correlation between perceived social support and psychological distress, such that people who report having less social support tend to report more psychological distress (Peng et al., 2012). The relation between chocolate consumption and the risk of cardiovascular disease also represents a negative correlation: Eating more chocolate, as measured by questionnaire items that asked people to recall how often and how much chocolate they consumed over the past year, was associated with a lower risk of subsequently developing or dying from heart disease or stroke, as measured by hospital records (Kwok et al., 2015).

MEASURING AND GRAPHING CORRELATIONS

Even with the simple data set in Table 5.1, mere visual inspection is inadequate to precisely judge how strongly the variables are correlated. Moreover, in real research, the data are usually not so straightforward; there may be hundreds or thousands of participants, and researchers may examine correlations among many variables. Fortunately, statistics and graphs help us identify correlations.

The Correlation Coefficient

Pearson's *r* (the **Pearson product-moment correlation coefficient**) *is a statistic that measures the direction and strength of the linear relation between two variables that have been measured on an interval or ratio scale.* Pearson's *r* can range from values of +1.00 to −1.00, with the plus or minus indicating a positive or negative correlation, respectively. The strength of a correlation is reflected by the absolute value of the coefficient. A correlation of |1.00| indicates a perfect linear relationship between X and Y: +1.00 represents a perfect positive correlation and −1.00 represents a perfect negative correlation. The closer the absolute value of a correlation is to 1.00, the stronger the relation. Thus, if variables X and Y are correlated −.47, and variables A and B are correlated +.39, then X and Y are more strongly correlated than

A and B. Similarly, the following five correlations are correctly listed in descending order of strength: −.91, +.82, −.65, +.34, +.17. From this you can see how important it is to be careful not to confuse the words *positive* and *negative* with the notions of "good" and "bad."

Also note that thus far, positive correlations have been designated with a plus sign. In psychology, the typical approach for reporting correlations is to present positive correlations without a plus sign and to use a minus sign to indicate a negative correlation. Therefore, from this point forward, we will omit the plus sign when reporting a positive correlation.

Researchers compute Pearson's *r* when they assume that both X and Y have been measured on an interval or ratio scale. Another statistic, **Spearman's rho** (the **Spearman rank-order correlation coefficient**), *is used to measure the relation between two quantitative variables when one or both variables have been measured on an ordinal scale (i.e., the scores represent ranks.)*

Please note two key points. First, when a correlation coefficient is computed, the way in which the measurement scales have been coded affects whether the statistical analysis yields a plus or minus sign for that coefficient. In Table 5.1, TV watching and perceived crime risk were positively correlated because the higher numbers of hours of TV watched corresponded to higher perceived probabilities of being a crime victim. But suppose we had measured perceived crime risk differently, say, by an item on a 5-point rating scale worded such that higher scores represented less perceived risk (e.g., 1 = *very high risk,* 5 = *very low risk*). In this case, the correlation statistic between TV watching and perceived risk would switch from positive to negative. To avoid the confusion that can occur in cases like this, researchers will often code their variables initially, or recode them prior to analyzing them, so that higher values for each variable conceptually reflect a greater amount of the underlying attribute. Thus, higher scores in Table 5.1 reflect more TV watching, a greater perceived crime risk, and a greater trust of other people.

Second, realize that the way a researcher conceptualizes a variable affects whether a correlation emerges as positive or negative. In Table 5.1, TV watching is negatively correlated with trust. But suppose we conceptualized our variable as "mistrust" rather than "trust," and on the five questionnaire items that measure mistrust higher scores represent greater mistrust (e.g., 1 = *I never mistrust people*; 5 = *I always mistrust people*). In this case, our analysis would reveal a positive correlation between TV watching and mistrust: People who watch more TV tend to be more mistrustful of other people.

Scatter Plots

A **scatter plot** (also called a **scattergram**) *is a graph in which data points portray the intersection of X and Y values.* **Figure 5.2** shows a scatter plot of the strong positive correlation between TV watching and perceived crime risk, based on the hypothetical data in Table 5.1. The numerical values of one variable are represented along the horizontal axis (*x*-axis), and the numerical values of the other variable are represented along the vertical axis (*y*-axis). Each point on this scatter plot represents the intersection of a pair of values for hours of TV watched and perceived crime risk. Thus, the data point at the coordinates X = 2, Y = 10 represents Wilma's responses. Robert's responses are plotted at coordinates X = 11, Y = 80.

Figure 5.3 illustrates scatter plots for correlations of $r = 1.00$, $r = 0.00$, and $r = −1.00$. When a correlation is perfect, the pairs of X and Y scores form data points that fall precisely onto a straight line, sloping upward from left to right ($r = 1.00$) or downward from left to right ($r = −1.00$), as in Figures 5.3a and 5.3c. When there is no correlation ($r = 0.00$), variations in X scores don't correspond to variations in Y scores in a linear fashion, and the overall pattern of data points has no upward or downward slope, as in Figure 5.3b. In between values of $r = 0.00$ and $r = +/− 1.00$, a correlation becomes stronger as the data points increasingly

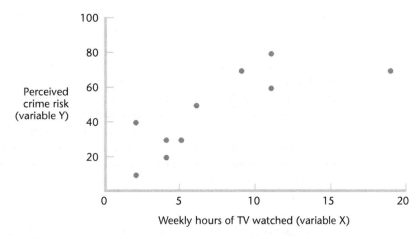

Perceived crime risk (variable Y)

Weekly hours of TV watched (variable X)

Figure 5.2 Scatter plot of the hypothetical data in Table 5.1.

converge onto a sloped straight line. Scatter plots are valuable because they provide a visual feel for the data and can reveal nonlinear relations between variables that the Pearson *r* statistic cannot detect.

Interpreting the Strength of a Correlation

How can you tell when a correlation is "weak," "moderate," or "strong"? Researchers apply such labels all the time. Although there is no universally agreed-upon standard for these terms, Cohen (1988) provides an often-cited set of guidelines for judging whether associations between variables are of small, medium, or large size. He proposes that absolute values of Pearson's *r* of .10 to .29 reflect a small association, .30 to .49 reflect a medium-sized association, and .50 to 1.00 represent a large association. Still, as Cohen notes, these guidelines are not set in stone, and it is arbitrary to say that the .01 difference in strength between absolute values of *r* = .29 and *r* = .30 suddenly transforms a small association into a medium-sized one.

Moreover, across different areas of psychology, the subjective criteria for judging the strength of a correlation may vary. For example, psychologists working in the field of *psychometrics* examine the statistical properties of psychological tests. When assessing the reliability of a new personality test by having the same people take the test twice, 2 weeks apart, psychometricians would be unlikely to consider a test–retest correlation coefficient of .50 to

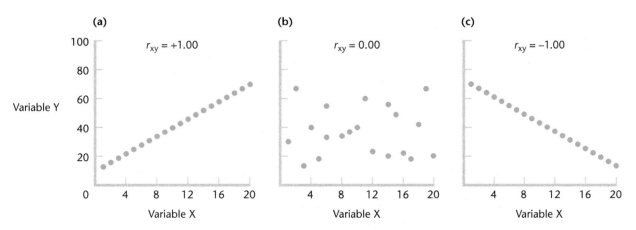

Figure 5.3 Three scatter plots.

indicate strong (in the sense of "acceptable") reliability. Rather, it would indicate that the test needs further work to enhance its reliability.

Although the absolute value of a correlation reflects its strength, it *cannot* be interpreted directly as representing the "percentage" that two variables are related. For the data in Table 5.1, the correlation between TV watching and perceived crime risk is $r = .79$, but this does *not* mean that these variables are "79% related" or that their scores "match up" or "change in the same direction" 79% of the time. Rather, to interpret the strength of the correlation, first consider that in Table 5.1, the scores for hours of TV watched are not all the same; they demonstrate variability. Within the set of 10 scores for perceived crime risk, there also is variability: Those scores are not all the same. Recall from Chapter 2 (p. 59) that there are different ways to measure variability. One measure is called the *variance*. For a set of scores, the variance takes into account how far the scores are spread apart from their mean (see Statistics Module 4 for details).

An important aspect of Pearson's r is that when you square the correlation coefficient, the resulting value (r^2) represents the proportion of variance in Y that is accounted for by the variance of X. In our TV–crime example, $r = .79$ and $r^2 = .62$; thus, 62% of the variance in the scores for perceived crime risk is statistically accounted for by the variance in the scores for TV watching. This value, r^2, is called the *coefficient of determination*. Another way to think of this is that, for two variables, X and Y, the coefficient of determination (r^2) informs us about the extent to which differences among the X scores predict—statistically account for—differences among the Y scores, based on the linear relation between the two variables.

Figure 5.4 visually portrays the concept of "variance accounted for." The circle in Figure 5.4a represents the total variance in the Y scores. If $r = 0.00$, then differences among X scores do not account for—do not help us predict—any of the variance in the Y scores. However, if $r = .20$, then the variance in X accounts for 4% of the variance in Y (i.e., $r^2 = .04$), portrayed by the small green slice in Figure 5.4b. As Figures 5.4c and 5.4d show, the stronger the correlation between X and Y, the bigger the slice of Y's variance accounted for by the variance of X.

The coefficient of determination helps us appreciate how differences in numerical values of correlations actually translate into larger differences in the ability of one factor to account for variability in another factor. Compared to a correlation of .20, correlations of .40 and .80 may seem 2 times and 4 times stronger. Figure 5.2 shows, however, that X will account for 4 times (16% vs. 4%) and 16 times (64% vs. 4%) more of the variance in Y, respectively.

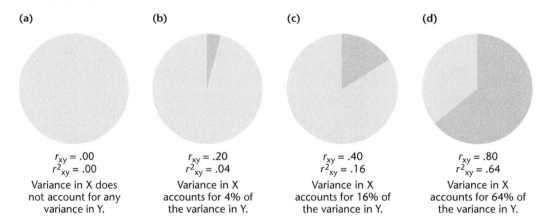

(a)	(b)	(c)	(d)
$r_{xy} = .00$	$r_{xy} = .20$	$r_{xy} = .40$	$r_{xy} = .80$
$r^2_{xy} = .00$	$r^2_{xy} = .04$	$r^2_{xy} = .16$	$r^2_{xy} = .64$
Variance in X does not account for any variance in Y.	Variance in X accounts for 4% of the variance in Y.	Variance in X accounts for 16% of the variance in Y.	Variance in X accounts for 64% of the variance in Y.

Figure 5.4 Differences in the strength of correlations. In each of these four diagrams, the entire circle represents the total variance in Y (i.e., perceived crime risk). The part of the entire circle shaded in pink represents the proportion of variance in Y that is accounted for by the variance in X (weekly hours of TV watched).

CONCEPT CHECK 5.1 CORRELATION: BASIC CONCEPTS

Select the correct words to complete each sentence below. Possible responses are given inside the parentheses. Answers appear at the end of the chapter, on page 170.

In a correlational study that examines variables X and Y,

1. X is _____ (measured, manipulated) and Y is _____ (measured, manipulated).
2. A negative correlation means that higher scores on X are associated with _____ (higher, lower) scores on Y.
3. A correlation of .43 is _____ (stronger, weaker) than a correlation of −.58.
4. A correlation of .43 _____ (does, does not) mean that X and Y scores match 43% of the time.

CORRELATION DOES NOT ESTABLISH CAUSATION

Learning Objectives

After studying this section, you should be able to:

- Explain why correlation does not establish causation.
- Discuss how researchers try to reduce bidirectionality and third-variable problems in correlational studies.
- Analyze the general design used in a particular correlational study.
- Evaluate the quality of media reports that discuss correlational research.

Let's return to the relation between watching TV and perceived crime risk. Gerbner and Gross (1976) proposed that consuming a heavy diet of TV would increase people's sense of danger about crime and erode their willingness to trust other people. The premise, then, is that watching TV has a *causal influence* on people's beliefs and emotions. Unfortunately, as reasonable as this premise may seem, the correlational nature of their research does not allow us to draw such a clear conclusion.

Stated differently, if we find that TV watching and perceived crime risk are *correlated,* this does not necessarily imply that TV watching has a causal effect on perceived crime risk. *Correlation does not establish causation.* The reason why leads us back to a major theme of learning about research methods and of critical thinking in general: the need to consider plausible alternative explanations for why something has occurred. Let's explore this in more detail.

THE BIDIRECTIONALITY PROBLEM

Recall from Chapter 1 that there are three key criteria used in drawing causal inferences:

1. *Covariation of X and Y.* As X changes, Y changes.
2. *Temporal order.* Changes in X occur before changes in Y.
3. *Absence of plausible alternative explanations.* Other than the changes in X, there are no changes in other factors that might reasonably have produced the changes in Y.

Now, as **Figure 5.5** illustrates, let's apply these criteria to the correlational research by Gerbner and Gross (1976; Gerbner et al., 1977) on TV watching (variable X) and perceived crime risk (variable Y). The researchers had a causal hypothesis: Watching TV influences perceived crime risk. Their analysis of survey data revealed that these two variables were correlated. Thus, the first criterion for drawing a causal inference, covariation of X and Y, appears to have been met: Statistical tests indicated that this relation, though weak, was not likely due to chance. Correlation, by definition, means that X and Y covary.

Infographic: **Figure 5.5**

WHY CORRELATION DOES NOT ESTABLISH CAUSATION

Hypothesis

Influences

Variable X: Watching TV

Variable Y: Perceived Crime Risk

Testing the Hypothesis: A Correlational Approach

Prediction: In a national survey, overall, adults who report watching more TV will perceive that they have a higher risk of being a crime victim than will people who report watching less TV.

Results: Number of hours of TV watched and perceived crime risk are positively correlated.

We Cannot Draw a Clear Causal Conclusion

✓ **Covariation**

Watching TV and perceived crime risk are associated.

⊘ **Temporal order**

There is no clear temporal order because amount of TV watched and perceived crime risk were measured at the same time.

⊘ **Absence of plausible alternative explanations**

Bidirectionality and third-variable problems exist.

(a) The Bidirectionality Problem

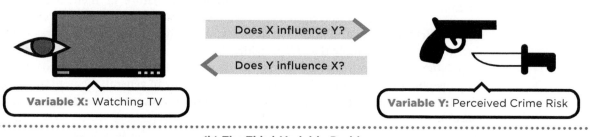

Does X influence Y?

Does Y influence X?

Variable X: Watching TV

Variable Y: Perceived Crime Risk

(b) The Third-Variable Problem

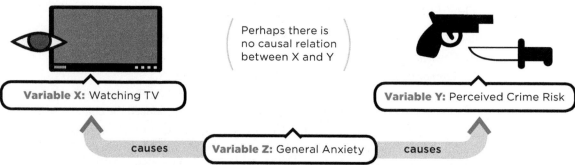

Perhaps there is no causal relation between X and Y

Variable X: Watching TV

Variable Y: Perceived Crime Risk

causes   **Variable Z:** General Anxiety   causes

Stronger general anxiety may cause people to a) watch more TV (e.g., as a distraction), and b) perceive a greater risk of crime. Thus, the correlation between X and Y really is due to Z.

But when we examine the criterion of temporal order, we run into a problem. Remember that in a correlational study, the researcher measures variables but does not manipulate them. This often creates ambiguity about the temporal order of variables X and Y. And, in turn, this temporal ambiguity opens the door to a possible alternative explanation for why a correlation between X and Y exists. In a survey, for example, if people who report watching more TV also report a higher perceived crime risk, one possible interpretation is that, indeed, watching more TV (variable X) has caused these individuals to believe that they are more likely to become crime victims (variable Y).

Yet, as Figure 5.5 shows, we must also consider the alternative possibility that Y has caused X. Think of it this way: If some people perceive a high risk of being a crime victim and others perceive a low risk, which group is more likely to stay inside in the evening rather than go out for a walk or a night on the town? Thus, perhaps TV watching and perceived crime risk are correlated because perceiving greater risk causes people to stay home and watch more TV. This predicament is called the **bidirectionality problem** (also called the **two-way causality problem**): *ambiguity about whether X has caused Y or Y has caused X.* Moreover, it is also possible that each variable influences the other. Perhaps people's concern about crime causes them to stay inside and watch more TV, and watching TV causes their concern to grow.

Although the bidirectionality problem is common in correlational research, in some correlational studies it can be ruled out on logical grounds. For example, *seasonal affective disorder* (SAD) is a form of depression that is associated with the changing seasons of the year. Most typically, people who suffer from SAD develop more symptoms or more intense symptoms of depression in the fall and winter. As spring and summer return, their symptoms lessen (Kim et al., 2015). Thus, among SAD sufferers, for any 12-month period there is a strong negative correlation between the average number of minutes of daylight per month (variable X) and the intensity of their depression (variable Y): The fewer the minutes of monthly daylight, the more intense the depression. Here, we can safely assume that Y cannot possibly cause X: As SAD sufferers' degree of depression changes, this does not cause the amount of monthly daylight to change! So can we now confidently conclude that X (changes in monthly daylight) is the cause of Y (changes in the intensity of depression) among people with SAD? Unfortunately not, as we will now see.

THE THIRD-VARIABLE PROBLEM

Even when we can rule out the bidirectionality problem, to reasonably conclude that X has caused Y, we must still be confident that there are no other plausible alternative explanations for why variable Y has changed. Here, we run into another problem when trying to causally interpret a correlation. It is possible that X and Y are not causally linked in any way: neither X causing Y, nor Y causing X. Instead, perhaps there is another variable—a confounding variable that we'll call Z—that is lurking behind the scenes and is the real cause of why scores on variable X and/or variable Y change. In correlational research, this ambiguity is often called the **third-variable problem:** *A third variable, Z, may be the true cause of why X and Y appear to be related.*

To illustrate, let's return to Figure 5.5 and the TV–crime risk correlation. As the figure shows, general anxiety might be a third variable. Day to day, some people are simply more anxious than others. Perhaps people who have higher levels of general anxiety are more likely to watch TV than people who are less anxious. Perhaps they watch TV because it temporarily takes their minds off their own worries. At the same time, perhaps higher general anxiety also causes people to worry more about crime. If so, it could be that higher levels of general anxiety (Z) cause people to watch more TV (X) and to overestimate the risk of being a crime victim (Y). In a study, if we fail to measure Z, then all we see when analyzing the data is the association between higher scores on X and higher scores on Y.

But higher scores on Z are really what's driving up the scores on X and Y. Thus, X and Y may be related statistically (i.e., they are correlated), but there may be absolutely no causal link between them, as the bottom component of Figure 5.5 illustrates. In this case, the relation between X and Y is *spurious* (i.e., not genuine), and their correlation is often called a *spurious correlation*.

General anxiety is only one of many possible confounding third variables. Here's another example: age. Compared to younger adults, perhaps older adults like to watch more TV, and perhaps older adults also tend to worry more about crime. Thus, the reason TV watching (X) and perceived crime risk (Y) are correlated may have nothing to do with one of them causing the other. Rather, perhaps age (Z) is the key underlying factor.

As another example, consider the daylight–SAD correlation. **Figure 5.6a** illustrates the point we discussed earlier about bidirectionality: We can eliminate the bidirectionality problem because we know that changes in SAD don't cause changes in monthly daylight. But even when bidirectionality can be ruled out, we need to ask whether there are any third variables (Z) that change from season to season and might provide a plausible alternative explanation for why SAD sufferers become more depressed in fall and winter. Might people's eating habits, levels of physical activity, work patterns, or sleep habits change with the seasons? While it would take additional research to answer those questions, we do know for certain that seasonal changes in daylight are accompanied by changes in average daily temperature. Perhaps it is the colder temperatures of fall and winter, not changes in daylight, that cause increases in depression. This third-variable analysis is diagrammed in Figure 5.6b.

Notice that in Figure 5.6b, the arrow from variable Z to variable Y indicates the possibility that variation in seasonal temperature is the true cause of the seasonal changes in SAD symptoms. Notice also that the link from variable Z to variable X is not an arrow. This is because we know that colder seasonal temperatures do not cause seasonal changes in daylight; they are merely correlated with such changes. This example illustrates that a third variable, Z, does not need to be a presumed cause of both X and Y in order to provide an alternative causal explanation for a correlation between X and Y. Rather, Z may be hypothesized as the cause of X *or* Y and merely be correlated with the other variable. In practice, however, third variables are often postulated to cause both X and Y.

Merely proposing a third variable that might account for a correlation between X and Y does not, of course, automatically make it so. For example, some experiments have found that early-morning exposure to intense artificial lights improves the symptoms of many SAD patients (Pail et al., 2011). This finding is consistent with the hypothesis that seasonal changes in light (X) influence these individuals' depression (Y). Nevertheless, potential third variables should always be considered when interpreting correlational findings. To reinforce this point, try to identify the third variables responsible for the correlations described in **Table 5.2**.

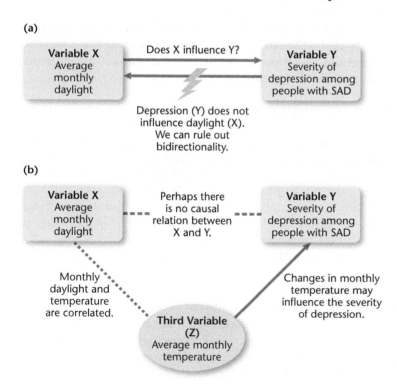

Figure 5.6 SAD and monthly daylight. (a) For some correlations, bidirectionality can be ruled out. (b) The third-variable problem must still be considered.

Table 5.2 Identifying Potential Third Variables

For each item, identify a third variable that could completely account for the correlation between X and Y. See answers on page 170, last section of "Concept Check: Answers."

Correlation 1: For each of the 40 largest North American cities:

$$X = \text{total attendance at religious services in 2016, per city}$$
$$Y = \text{total annual alcohol consumption in 2016, per city}$$

Result: Religious attendance is positively correlated with alcohol consumption.

Correlation 2: For the past 24 months:

$$X = \text{the amount of ice cream consumed each month in North America}$$
$$Y = \text{the number of drownings each month in Europe}$$

Result: As North Americans consume more ice cream, drownings in Europe tend to increase.

Correlation 3: Vista Elementary School has 380 first- through sixth-graders.

$$X = \text{each child's height}$$
$$Y = \text{each child's vocabulary size}$$

Result: Height is positively correlated with vocabulary size.

CAN WE GAIN A CLEARER CAUSAL PICTURE?

Scientists who conduct correlational studies often attempt to reduce the causal ambiguity that accompanies the correlational method through special statistical analyses and research designs. These two approaches can also be combined.

Statistical Approaches

We noted earlier that age might be a third variable that would account for the correlation between watching TV and perceived crime risk: Perhaps, with increasing age, people watch more TV and also perceive a greater risk of being a crime victim. If we could somehow remove participants' age from the picture, we would be left with a better test of whether TV watching and perceived crime risk are related.

In correlational studies, the most common way that researchers try to remove the influence of potential third variables is by measuring them when the data are collected and then statistically adjusting for those variables in the data analysis. Gerbner and Gross (1976; Gerbner et al., 1977), in fact, anticipated that age might be a confounding third variable, and they attempted to filter out the role of age in two ways. First, they divided survey respondents into two age groups (under 30 years old; 30 years and older) and examined the relation between TV watching and perceived crime risk for each age group. **Figure 5.7** shows that regardless of age, heavy TV viewers were more likely than light TV viewers to overestimate their chances of being a crime victim. Figure 5.7 also shows that Gerbner and Gross conducted similar analyses for three other potential third variables: gender, education, and reading newspapers. The relation between TV watching and perceived crime risk held across these analyses as well.

Gerbner et al. (1977) also used another statistical approach, called **partial correlation,** *in which a correlation between variable X and variable Y is computed while statistically controlling for their individual correlations with a third variable, Z.* In this approach, the correlations between X and Z, and between Y and Z, are statistically "partialed out" (i.e., filtered out) of the analysis between X and Y. The more strongly Z correlates with X and Y, the more likely it is that the strength of the correlation between X and Y will change considerably after their shared association with Z is statistically controlled. In many cases, after a partial correlation analysis is conducted, what originally was a statistically significant simple correlation

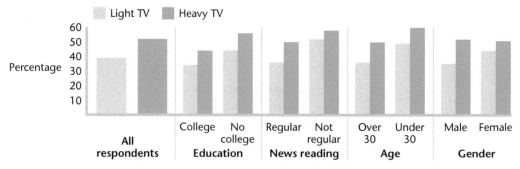

Figure 5.7 Percentage of light- versus heavy-TV viewers who greatly overestimated the risk of being a crime victim. Perceived risk and TV viewing were related, even after accounting for several potential third variables. (Information from Gerbner & Gross, 1976.)

between X and Y may be reduced enough in strength so that it is no longer statistically significant. Based on their partial correlation analyses, however, Gerbner et al. (1977) concluded that third variables such as age, sex, and education were not responsible for the correlation between TV watching and perceived crime risk.

In trying to address the problem of drawing causal conclusions from correlational data, partial correlations are merely the tip of the statistical iceberg. There are more advanced statistical techniques that build on the principle of partial correlation and can examine complex patterns of correlated variables. The key point is that researchers use these statistical techniques—such as *path analysis* and *structural equation modeling*—to test hypotheses about *possible* causal links among sets of correlated variables.

Research Design Approaches

In a correlational study that employs a **cross-sectional research design** (also called a **one-shot correlational study**), *each person participates on one occasion, and all variables are measured at that time.* The surveys that provided the data on TV watching and perceived crime risk illustrate this common research approach. Within a single survey, participants answered questions about their age, sex, education, TV-watching habits, perceptions of crime, and so on. Then the correlation between TV watching and perceived crime risk was examined. In such research, the bidirectionality problem typically sticks out like a sore thumb because X and Y are measured at the same time.

Longitudinal Designs. Other correlational studies employ a **longitudinal research design,** *in which data are gathered on the same individuals or groups on two or more occasions over time.* In one type of longitudinal design, called a **prospective design,** *variable X is measured at an earlier point in time than variable Y,* thereby reducing the likelihood that variable Y is a cause of variable X. For example, suppose that a developmental psychologist measures the parenting practices to which young children are exposed. Later, when those children become adolescents, the psychologist assesses their social adjustment. If a relation is found between these two variables, we can rule out the bidirectionality problem: Adolescents' degree of social adjustment cannot retroactively influence how they were parented as children. (This doesn't rule out the third-variable problem, however, which we'll address shortly.)

In fields such as clinical psychology, health psychology, and medicine, prospective correlational studies are used to identify personality traits, lifestyle habits, and life experiences that may be risk factors for developing mental disorders or physical illnesses. The chocolate–cardiovascular disease study highlighted in Figure 5.1 was a prospective correlational study based on data from a sample of 20,951 women and men living in England and who did not have a known history of heart attack or stroke. Their chocolate consumption habits (X) were measured by questionnaire when they enrolled in the study between 1993 and 1997 (Kwok et al., 2015). Information from hospital records as to whether they subsequently were diagnosed with or died from heart disease or stroke (Y) was collected from their time of enrollment through March 2008, an average follow-up period of 11.9 years. Using this research design, the bidirectionality problem—but not the third-variable problem—presumably can be ruled out. It does not make sense to propose that newly developed heart disease and strokes (or death from these causes) could operate backward in time and causally influence the participants' earlier chocolate consumption habits.

As another example, consider the intriguing question of whether being a religious or spiritual person helps to promote a healthy, longer life. Many prospective studies have found that people who attend religious services or other religious meetings more often than their peers tend to live longer lives (Powell et al., 2003). **Figure 5.8** portrays this association as reported by Susan Lutgendorf and her colleagues (Lutgendorf, Russell, Ullrich, Harris, & Wallace, 2002). These researchers examined data from a sample of 557 healthy adults from Iowa who were aged 65 or older at the start of the study in 1982, at which time their religious attendance was measured, and who were still alive when blood tests were taken (for another aspect of this study) in 1988. Mortality data were then gathered for the following 6-year period ending in 1994.

The statistically significant attendance–mortality correlation was weak ($r = -.15$), but when we are talking about a variable as overridingly important as death, even such a weak association can take on considerable meaning. As you can see in Figure 5.8, among people who never attended religious services or meetings in 1982, 34% died during the 6-year measurement period. Among those who attended twice or more per week, 14.5% died during the same time period. Obviously, whether people did or did not die from 1988 to 1994 could not retroactively influence their religious attendance in 1982, and thus the bidirectionality problem (but again, not the third-variable problem) can be ruled out.

Cross-Lagged Panel Studies. Now consider another longitudinal design, the **cross-lagged panel design,** which involves three steps: (1) *measure X and Y at Time 1;* (2) *measure X and Y again, at Time 2;* and (3) *examine the pattern of correlations among X_1, X_2, Y_1, and Y_2.* One of the most well-known uses of this design concerns research on whether watching violence on TV increases viewers' aggressive tendencies. Conducting perhaps the first cross-lagged panel

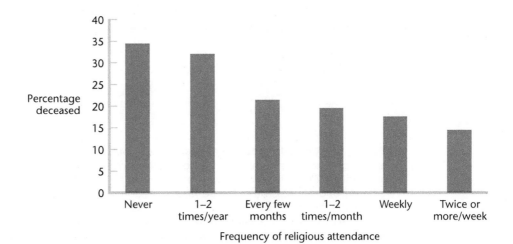

Figure 5.8 Association between religious service attendance and 6-year mortality rates. This study used a prospective longitudinal design. (Adapted with permission from APA from "Religious Participation, Interleukin-6, and Mortality in Older Adults," by S. K. Lutgendorf, D. Russell, P. Ullrich, T. B. Harris, and R. Wallace, 2004, *Health Psychology, 23*[5], p. 465.)

study on this topic, Leonard Eron and his colleagues measured third-graders' TV-watching preferences and aggressive behavior in 1960 (Eron, Huesmann, Lefkowitz, & Walder, 1972). At the time, all of the boys and girls in the study lived in a semirural area of New York State. Ten years later the researchers contacted the children, now in their teens, and measured these two variables again. No significant correlations between TV-watching preferences and aggressive behavior were found among the 216 girls who participated at both time periods. In contrast, **Figure 5.9a** shows some of the key results for the 211 boys.

The statistics in Figure 5.9a are simple correlations. First, on the far left, you see a weak correlation ($r = .21$) between preference for violent TV and aggression in 1960. By itself, this would be a one-shot correlation, and the bidirectionality problem would be in full play: Watching more violent TV may have caused the children to behave more aggressively, or a greater preexisting tendency to behave aggressively may have caused the children to watch more violent TV shows. Now focus on the two diagonal lines that cross each other. These are called *cross-lagged correlations* ("lagged" for the time lag between the two measurement periods). You can see that preference for violent TV in 1960 was moderately correlated with aggression in 1970 ($r = .31$), whereas aggression in 1960 was not significantly correlated with preference for violent TV in 1970 ($r = .01$). This cross-lagged, longitudinal pattern suggests that it is more plausible that watching violent TV (in childhood) causes aggression (in adolescence) than the other way around.

Combining Statistical and Design Approaches

One problem that you can see in Figure 5.9 is that aggression in 1960 is correlated with preference for violent TV in 1960 ($r = .21$, as already noted) and also with aggression in 1970 ($r = .38$). Thus, perhaps aggression in 1960 is a causal third variable: Maybe being more aggressive in 1960 caused the children to prefer violent TV shows in 1960 (X), and the more aggressive children in 1960 developed into more aggressive teenagers 10 years later (Y). This alternative causal possibility, which is diagrammed in Figure 5.9b by the solid and dashed gray lines, suggests that there may be no causal link between watching violent TV in 1960

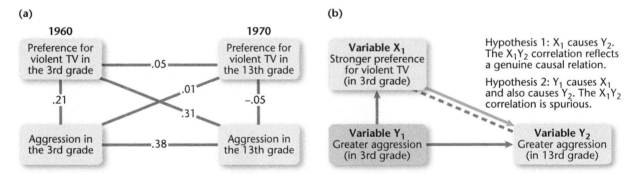

Figure 5.9 Cross-lagged panel design. (a) Correlations between violent TV preference and aggression in a sample of 211 boys. The correlations between aggression in Grade 3 and violent TV preference, measured in Grade 13, and between violent TV preference in Grade 3 and aggression in Grade 13, are called cross-lagged correlations. (b) Two causal hypotheses. Focusing only on this portion of the cross-lagged panel design highlights the potential third-variable problem. Children's aggression, as measured in Grade 3, would be the third variable. The pattern of findings from the complete cross-lagged panel design indicates, however, that violent TV preference in Grade 3 remains correlated with aggression in Grade 13, even after statistically controlling for the possible influence of this third variable. (Adapted with permission from APA from "Does Television Violence Cause Aggression?" by L. D. Eron, L. R. Huesmann, M. M. Lefkowitz, and L. O. Walder, 1972, *American Psychologist, 27,* pp. 253–263 [Figure 1, p. 257].)

and subsequent aggression in 1970. Here is where partial correlation analysis becomes useful. The researchers examined the cross-lagged correlation between 1960 violent TV preference and 1970 aggression, while statistically controlling for each of their correlations with 1960 aggression (Eron et al., 1972). The resulting partial correlation between 1960 violent TV preference and 1970 aggression remained statistically significant, albeit weaker (.25). In addition, the researchers conducted further partial correlation analyses, adjusting for possible third variables such as fathers' and mothers' aggressiveness, parental punishment of children, and children's IQ. None of these analyses eliminated the significant cross-lagged correlation between preference for violent TV in the third grade and level of aggression 10 years later.

Huesmann and his colleagues subsequently combined a cross-lagged design and advanced statistical analyses in a study of 6- to 10-year-old children from the Chicago area who were assessed in 1977 and again 15 years later (Huesmann, Moise-Titus, Podolski, & Eron, 2003). The findings indicated that, for boys and girls, watching more TV violence in childhood was associated with behaving more aggressively in young adulthood. This cross-lagged link remained significant even after analyses statistically controlling for several other possible third variables, including the children's level of aggressiveness at the start of the study. In contrast, for both sexes, the other cross-lagged link—between childhood aggression and adulthood watching of violent TV—was not statistically significant.

In correlational research, the strategy of combining longitudinal designs with partial correlational analyses or related statistical techniques has become increasingly common. All of the longitudinal correlational studies we've discussed thus far have included this statistical approach. Researchers try to anticipate various potential confounding variables and measure them at the start of the study, so that they can statistically control for these variables in later analyses. For example, in the chocolate–cardiovascular disease study, when the researchers measured participants' chocolate consumption habits (X) at the start of the project, they also assessed several other characteristics of the participants, such as their age, gender, smoking and exercise habits, and alcohol consumption (Kwok et al., 2015). Participants also underwent a medical exam and blood tests at that time to measure factors such as their weight, blood pressure, and cholesterol levels. The association between greater chocolate consumption and lower subsequent risk of cardiovascular disease remained statistically significant even after the analyses were adjusted to take many of these potential confounding variables (i.e., third variables) into account.

Now Can We Draw Clear Causal Conclusions?

Recall that in Gerbner and Gross's (1976) research on the perceived risk of being a crime victim, they anticipated that several factors, such as participants' age and gender, might act as third variables. Because their partial correlation analyses did not eliminate the association between TV and perceived crime risk, our confidence that this association may reflect a direct causal relation between X and Y increases. Still, not only does the bidirectionality problem remain because of the cross-sectional research design, but an even more pervasive problem persists regarding potential third variables. This problem applies to all correlational studies, even those that use special research designs and advanced statistical techniques to adjust for third variables. Social psychologist Anthony Doob and experimental psychologist Glenn Macdonald (1979), who conducted a follow-up study on TV watching and perceived crime risk, state the problem well:

> No list of confounding variables can be complete. The worry of any researcher doing correlational research and wishing to make a causal statement is that some other variable would, in fact, account for the effect apparently demonstrated. (p. 171)

Doob and Macdonald (1979) felt that Gerbner and Gross (1976) overlooked a plausible third variable: the actual amount of violent crime in participants' neighborhoods. They proposed that "people who watch a lot of television may have a greater fear of being victims of violent crimes because, in fact, they live in more violent neighborhoods" (p. 171). To test their hypothesis, they studied adults living in high-crime and low-crime neighborhoods of Toronto and nearby suburbs. Doob and Macdonald measured the number of all TV programs and violent TV programs that participants watched in a week; they then asked participants questions about crime victimization that were combined into an overall victimization score.

Ignoring neighborhood crime rates, they replicated the simple correlation between TV watching and perceived crime risk. But when they examined this correlation separately for each of four neighborhoods, only in one neighborhood did TV watching significantly correlate with perceived crime risk. Moreover, the overall relation between TV watching and perceived crime risk disappeared when statistical adjustments were made to simultaneously control for third variables such as neighborhood crime rate and participants' age and sex. "Thus," said Doob and Macdonald, "it would appear that television itself is not likely to be a direct cause of people's fear of being victims of crime" (p. 177). Overall, more recent correlational research supports this conclusion (Gross & Aday, 2003; Kort-Butler & Sittner Hartshorn, 2011).

In correlational research, even the most sophisticated statistical procedures and the best longitudinal designs do not provide the type or degree of control over potential confounding factors that experiments make possible. Despite the high quality of their cross-lagged panel design and advanced statistical analyses examining the link between children's watching of TV violence and subsequent aggressive behavior in adulthood, Huesmann et al. (2003) noted that "longitudinal nonexperimental data do not provide a strong test of causation" (p. 218). Still, as these researchers also noted, longitudinal correlational research "can be used to compare the relative plausibility of alternative causal perspectives" (p. 218). They concluded that their findings were more consistent with (1) the theoretically based hypothesis that watching TV aggression increases people's aggressive behavior than with (2) the alternative hypothesis that greater aggressiveness leads people to prefer violent TV programs. Cross-lagged panel designs and analyses continue to be used in many scientific fields to assess how well patterns of longitudinal correlations fit the predictions of competing causal hypotheses (Rieger, Göllner, Trautwein, & Roberts, 2016).

MEDIA REPORTS OF CORRELATIONAL RESEARCH

In Figure 5.1, you saw the headline of a newspaper article titled "British study links chocolate with fewer heart attacks, strokes" (Healy, 2015, June 15). In the original scientific journal article describing this study, the researchers emphasized the importance of their prospective longitudinal design. They also statistically controlled for many potential third variables. Still, the researchers appropriately pointed out that because this study was correlational, other third variables could have accounted for the results. For example, they noted that people who consumed more chocolate might have had other lifestyle habits that the researchers did not measure and that may have contributed to a lower risk of developing cardiovascular disease (Kwok et al., 2015).

Such appropriate cautions can also be found in well-written news articles and TV news segments in which reporters describe findings from correlational research. The journalist who wrote the newspaper article on the chocolate–cardiovascular disease study informed readers that this research did not establish a causal link. She interviewed an independent researcher who described how aspects of a generally healthy lifestyle might have been a confounding third variable, and that experiments were necessary to determine whether chocolate consumption influenced cardiovascular disease risk.

Unfortunately, such high-quality reporting is not always evident in the news media. At times, the results of correlational studies are presented in ways that can give the public a false impression that a causal relation was found. And, even if the body of a news report appropriately cautions against clear cause–effect conclusions, people browsing through the news may read no further than eye-catching headlines that imply causality, such as "Chocolate, chocolate, it's good for your heart, study finds" (Aubrey, 2015, June 19).

Whether you are reading scientific articles, writing a report, digesting the news, or being exposed to commercial advertisements, always appreciate that a correlation between X and Y may suggest the *possibility* of a causal relation. At the same time, keep the bidirectionality and third-variable problems in mind and remember the cardinal rule: By itself, correlation does not establish causation.

 CONCEPT CHECK 5.2 CORRELATION DOES NOT ESTABLISH CAUSATION

Decide whether each statement is true or false. Answers appear on page 170.

1. To conclude that variable X influences variable Y, we need to satisfy only two criteria: covariation and temporal order.

2. If X and Y are correlated and we eliminate the bidirectionality problem, then we can clearly conclude that X has caused Y.

3. In general, correlational studies yield clearer causal conclusions when they use one-shot designs rather than longitudinal designs.

CORRELATION AND PREDICTION

Learning Objectives

After studying this section, you should be able to:

- Discuss the general concept of using regression analysis to predict the scores of a variable.

- Explain why, if two predictor variables (X_1 and X_2) each correlate significantly with a criterion variable (Y), only one of those predictors might end up being retained in a regression equation.

As I sat down to write this section, my wife came by and asked: "Do you know why they plant rosebushes at the end of the rows in wine vineyards?" When I replied that I had no clue, she told me she had just learned that rosebushes serve as an early warning system for danger to the grapevines. So, for example, if mildew begins to infest the field, the signs of infestation will show up first on the rosebushes, giving workers several days of lead time to try to control the infestation before damage occurs to the grapevines.

One of the most important properties of correlation is that if two variables are correlated, knowing the scores on one variable helps us to estimate (i.e., predict) the scores on the other variable. Correlation enables prediction even when no causal relation between the two variables is assumed. Infested rosebushes don't cause grapevines to become infested. Rather, winemakers assume that these factors are correlated and use one to predict the other. Likewise, although high school students' SAT scores don't cause their college grades, those factors are correlated; therefore, college administrators use SAT scores to estimate how students will perform in college. The stronger the correlation between two variables, the more accuracy we gain in predicting one from the other. If two variables are not correlated, then there is no predictive advantage.

USING ONE PREDICTOR

Regression analysis (also called **simple linear regression**) *explores the quantitative, linear relation between two variables,* and is often used to predict the scores of one variable based on the scores of another variable. Suppose we want to use high school students' composite SAT scores (i.e., math + reading + writing scores) to estimate their first-year college GPA (henceforth, "college GPA"). In this case, GPA is the **criterion variable:** *the variable that we are trying to estimate or predict.* SAT scores represent the **predictor variable:** *a variable whose scores are used to estimate scores of a criterion variable.* The predictor variable is designated as X and the criterion variable as Y. For simplicity, assume we have data from 50 students. In actual research, we would want a much larger sample.

If SAT scores are not correlated (or not significantly correlated) with college GPA, there is no point in proceeding with a regression analysis. We find, however, as much research has, that these two variables are moderately and positively correlated (Berry & Sackett, 2009). The scatter plot in **Figure 5.10a** shows our data, for which *r* = .45. We use a statistical software program to perform the regression analysis; it produces an equation, called a *regression equation,* that allows us to use SAT scores to estimate college GPA (for more detail, see Statistics Module 5.3).

When we plug the SAT score for each of our 50 students into the regression equation, we end up with 50 estimated college GPA scores. For example, for an SAT score of 2050, the predicted college GPA would be 3.0. If we now plot the 50 pairs of SAT scores and *estimated* GPA scores on a graph (as in a scatter plot), we will find that the data points fall on a straight line, as in Figure 5.10b. The line will be straight because there is a perfect correlation between the X scores and the *estimated* Y scores (i.e., after all, we used the X scores to create the Y scores). This straight line is called a *regression line,* and if we overlay this line on top of the scatter plot, it will now look as it does in Figure 5.10b.

In essence, the regression line is a visual representation of the regression equation: It represents the overall best fit between X and Y. "Best fit" means that according to a certain statistical criterion, this line does the best possible job (of any straight line) of most closely fitting the overall pattern of the 50 data points in the scatter plot. The stronger the correlation between X and Y, the better the overall fit. When two variables are perfectly, linearly correlated, the actual data points will fall exactly onto the regression line.

You may wonder why we would use SAT scores to estimate these 50 students' college GPAs. After all, we already know these students' actual college GPAs! The idea is that once we have conducted our regression analysis, we can now plug future high school students' SAT scores into the regression equation to estimate how well they will likely perform in college. College admission committees take this information into account when deciding whom to

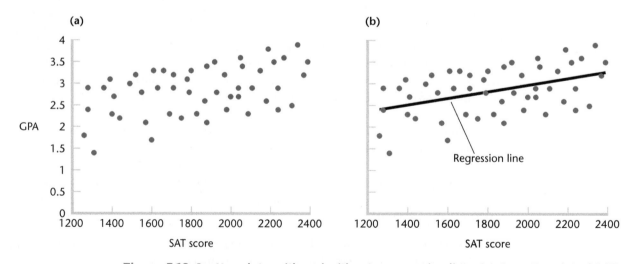

Figure 5.10 Scatter plots, with and without a regression line. (a) A scatter plot of SAT scores and first-year college GPA for a hypothetical sample of 50 students. (b) A scatter plot with a regression line added. The SAT–GPA correlation is .45.

admit. Be aware that, in practice, the process of developing a regression equation based on one sample and then applying the equation to other (e.g., future) samples is more complex than portrayed here.

USING TWO OR MORE PREDICTORS

When estimating college GPA, we don't have to limit ourselves to one predictor variable. Suppose we want to add a second predictor (X_2) to our regression equation: high school GPA. Our hope is that with two predictors, we will achieve more accurate estimates of college GPA than we would by using either predictor alone. This type of analysis, **multiple regression,** *explores the linear relation between one variable* (e.g., college GPA) *and a set of two or more other variables* (e.g., SAT scores, high school GPA). Once again, we would use computer software to determine a regression equation. For each of the 50 students, the SAT and high school GPA scores would be entered into the equation and used to predict that student's college GPA. We could also evaluate the utility of adding more predictors to the equation. As the number of predictors grows, it becomes increasingly important to have a large sample of data.

Here is a key concept about multiple regression: To be retained in the final regression equation, each new predictor must enhance our ability to estimate Y beyond what can be achieved by the other predictor variables already in the equation. To illustrate, imagine that SAT scores correlate $r = .45$ with college GPA, and high school GPA correlates $r = .50$ with college GPA. If we calculate r^2 for each predictor, we find that SAT scores account for 20% of the variance in college GPA, and high school GPA accounts for 25% of the variance in college GPA. If we use both predictors in our equation, will we now account for 20% + 25% = 45% of the variance in students' college GPA? It depends.

If our two predictors do not correlate at all with each other, then each predictor will contribute completely unique information to the prediction of students' college GPA, and in combination they will account for 45% of the variance in Y. But if SAT scores and high school GPA are themselves correlated with each other (which they are, moderately; Berry & Sackett, 2009), then some of the information contributed by the second predictor will be redundant with information already contributed by the first predictor. In this case, combined in our regression equation, students' SAT scores and high school GPA will account for less than 45% of the variance in college GPA.

Indeed, it often happens that a predictor will correlate significantly with the criterion variable on its own, but after being entered into a multiple regression analysis, it is found not to add a statistically significant amount of new information to the prediction of Y (i.e., the amount of additional variance in Y that it accounts for is not statistically significant). In this case, the predictor would be dropped from the final regression equation. By the way, beyond its use in practical applications such as college student admission and personnel selection, multiple regression is also used extensively in basic research.

✓ **CONCEPT CHECK 5.3** CORRELATION AND PREDICTION

Dr. Locklear studies 100 dating couples. For each couple, she measures the number of months they have dated as well as each partner's age and relationship satisfaction. Based on this scenario, fill in the blanks for each item below. Answers appear on page 170.

1. Dr. Locklear uses "months dating" to predict partners' relationship satisfaction. This would be an example of _____ analysis. "Months dating" would be the _____ variable, and relationship satisfaction would be the _____ variable.

2. Dr. Locklear uses "months dating" and "age," together, to predict relationship satisfaction. This would be an example of _____ analysis.

BENEFITS OF CORRELATIONAL RESEARCH

Learning Objectives

After studying this section, you should be able to:

- Generate additional examples of how correlational findings are used to predict outcomes in daily life.

- Explain why the convergence of correlational and experimental findings is important.

- Discuss the value of correlational research in test validation and hypothesis testing.

Although correlational research does not permit clear causal conclusions, it provides many benefits. You already know one of them from this chapter: Correlation enables prediction. And, if you have read Chapter 4, you know another: Correlation plays an important role in the development and validation of psychological tests.

PREDICTION IN DAILY LIFE

There are many practical applications in which correlational findings are used to predict behavior. Using standardized tests such as the SAT and ACT to help select students for college admission is one example. Remember, SAT and ACT scores are not the cause of better college performance. Rather, as **Figure 5.11a** illustrates, there are presumed, underlying third variables such as academic aptitude, prior learning, motivation, and others factors that influence both SAT and college performance.

A similar rationale holds for using personnel tests to select among job candidates in business, industry, government, and the military (Figure 5.11b). Many organizations invest heavily in commercially available tests or in developing their own personnel selection tests; these are used to select candidates who are most likely to succeed on the job. Historically, industrial-organizational psychologists have played a major role in developing and assessing the validity of such personnel selection tests (Van Iddekinge, Roth, Raymark, & Odle-Dusseau, 2012).

In fields such as clinical psychology, clinical neuropsychology, and counseling psychology, practitioners use psychological tests and other measures to diagnose mental disorders, assess impairments following brain damage, assess people's personality traits and aptitudes, and so forth. These data lead to recommendations—essentially, predictions—about issues such as: "What type of therapy or training would be most effective for this person?" "Would this person function best in an assisted-living facility?" "What type of career is this person best suited for?" The usefulness of diagnostic tests in such individual cases rests, in part, on broader correlational research demonstrating that test scores do, in fact, help predict people's real-world functioning or other outcomes (Gould, Bowie, & Harvey, 2012).

If you have automobile, renter's, homeowner's, or life insurance, correlational data

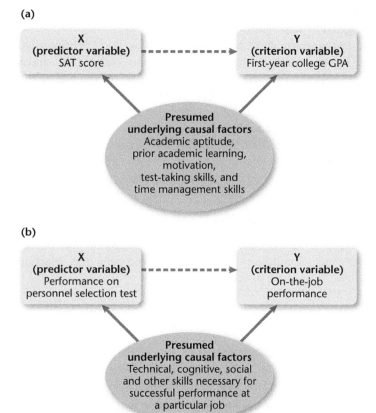

Figure 5.11 Predictors need not be causes. (a) Using SAT scores to predict first-year college GPA. (b) Using personnel-selection test scores to predict job performance.

help determine the premiums you pay. For example, your age, sex, and marital status are predictive of your risk of having an automobile accident. Knowing this, companies adjust insurance premiums accordingly. Making such predictions (e.g., of your "risk") based solely on statistical data is called *actuarial prediction,* and judging from the annual profits of most insurance companies, they appear to have it "down to a science."

TEST VALIDATION

Tests used for personnel selection, college admission, psychological assessment, career counseling, and the like must possess several qualities to be considered valid. Recall from Chapter 4 that one quality is called *criterion validity:* The test should be able to predict relevant criteria, such as college grades or the quality of job performance. As we've just seen, correlation establishes a basis for prediction, and correlational research is the primary approach for establishing the criterion validity of tests.

For many types of tests, construct validity is an essential quality. There must be evidence that a test truly measures the particular construct (e.g., a personality trait, intelligence, depression) it is claimed to measure. A test that purportedly measures self-esteem must be shown to primarily measure self-esteem, not some other quality such as self-confidence or narcissism. Moreover, for a test to be valid, it must also be reliable: It must yield consistent measurements. Correlational research plays a central role in establishing the construct validity and reliability of tests. One strategy for establishing construct validity is to see how well a new test correlates with other, already validated tests that measure the same attribute. One strategy for establishing test reliability is to examine how well items or subsets of items within the test correlate with each other or with overall test scores (see Chapter 4 for more details).

VENTURING WHERE EXPERIMENTS CANNOT TREAD

Correlational research can be employed in circumstances where, due to practical or ethical considerations, highly controlled experiments cannot be conducted. Consider the following questions:

- Does parental divorce increase the risk that children will develop psychological difficulties later in life?

- Does being a religious or spiritual person benefit one's physical health and contribute to a longer life?

Although each of these questions asks about causal relations between variables, it is difficult to imagine how controlled experiments could be carried out to examine them. Practically and ethically, we cannot randomly assign married couples to "divorce" and "remain married" conditions to assess how this affects children's psychological health. Nor can we experimentally control numerous real-world factors (e.g., number of biological and stepsiblings) that might confound any presumed causal connection between marital/divorce status and children's long-term psychological adjustment. Likewise, we cannot experimentally manipulate whether people are religious.

To explore questions like these, correlational studies offer a great advantage because they only involve measuring variables rather than manipulating them. This does not mean, however, that correlational studies are easier to conduct than experiments or that thorny ethical issues never surface in correlational studies. This simply is not the case. Correlational studies and experiments run the gamut from being extraordinarily difficult and time consuming to design and execute, to being relatively straightforward to conduct.

HYPOTHESIS AND MODEL TESTING

Although clear causal inferences cannot be drawn from correlational research, correlational findings do indicate whether the obtained associations between variables are *consistent with the possibility* that a cause–effect relation might exist. Thus, correlational research can provide information about whether a hypothesized causal model is more or less plausible than an alternative causal model, as illustrated earlier by the cross-lagged panel research on TV watching and aggression (Eron et al., 1972; Huesmann et al., 2003). Similarly, in Chapter 4, we discussed a prospective correlational study by Callender and his colleagues (2012) that examined the following hypothesized model: (1) Depression causes parents to judge their children's behavior more negatively, (2) this leads parents to punish their children more harshly, and (3) this increases the risk that children will subsequently display conduct problems. Their correlational study could not demonstrate causality, but the results were consistent with the pattern of findings predicted by the causal model.

Let's consider the value of correlational research in examining possible causal relations between religion or spirituality and physical health. In reviewing this topic, Lynda Powell and her colleagues identified several causal hypotheses proposed by various researchers; these are shown in **Table 5.3** (Powell et al., 2003). Powell and her colleagues then reviewed high-quality correlational studies on this topic. These were prospective studies that statistically adjusted for the potentially confounding effects of many demographic, lifestyle, and preexisting health factors. Taking Hypothesis 1 as an example, Powell and colleagues found that in six of nine studies, people who attended religious services more frequently than their peers early in the study were less likely to die during the remainder of the study (representing about a 25% mortality reduction, on average). They concluded that, overall, current evidence was "persuasive" in support of the hypothesis that church/service attendance protects against earlier death.

More conservatively, we can say that these correlational findings are consistent with what we would expect if the hypothesized causal relation between attendance and delayed mortality actually existed. By using longitudinal designs and statistically filtering out the potential influence of several plausible confounding variables (e.g., third variables such as preexisting health status), the researchers increased the likelihood that their correlational findings reflect an underlying causal relation. Still, it is possible that the researchers failed to take into account other third variables that might be the true causes of why attendance at religious services and mortality are correlated.

Conversely, Table 5.3 shows that Powell et al. (2003) failed to find support for Hypothesis 4. If we begin with the premise that the causal relation proposed in this hypothesis

Table 5.3 Hypotheses About the Relation of Religiousness/Spirituality and Health

Hypothesis[1]	Strength of Evidence[2]
1. Religious service attendance protects against death.	Persuasive
2. Religion or spirituality protects against cardiovascular disease.	Some
3. Religion or spirituality protects against cancer mortality.	Inadequate
4. Religion or spirituality improves recovery from acute illness.	Consistent failures

[1] The phrase "protects against death" refers to the specific time period in a study during which mortality rates were measured.

[2] "Studies include statistical adjustments for potential confounding variables such as age, gender, ethnicity, education, disability status, health behaviors (e.g., smoking, exercise, diet), social support, and depression" (Powell et al., 2003, p. 39).

Source: Adapted with permission from Powell et al. (2003). Use does not imply endorsement.

exists—that being religious or spiritual influences people's recovery from acute illness—then we should at least find a correlation between religiosity/spirituality and recovery from acute illness. The reason: Conditions for establishing a correlation between two variables are less rigorous than those needed to establish causality. Consistent failures to find even a correlation between two variables cast doubt on the possibility that a causal relation between those variables exists.

CONVERGENCE WITH EXPERIMENTS

Because correlational studies reveal potential cause–effect links between naturally occurring variables, they can provide an impetus for researchers to conduct experiments that subsequently examine such possible causal links under more controlled laboratory conditions. Moreover, when experiments uncover causal relations between independent and dependent variables, correlational research can help establish the external validity of those experimental findings by examining whether the variables in question are at least correlated under naturally occurring conditions. Thus, there is often a synergistic relation between these two research methodologies, and a convergence of correlational and experimental findings increases our confidence that scientists have identified a causal relation that applies to real-life circumstances.

The scientifically established link between smoking and lung cancer represents one of the most publicly visible examples of the convergence of correlational and experimental findings. If the only evidence supporting this link came from laboratory animal experiments, questions about the generalizability of this finding to humans would loom large. If the only evidence supporting a smoking–cancer link came from correlational studies with humans, questions about the causal ambiguity of those findings would persist. Together, the two sources of evidence converge powerfully.

Similar cases abound throughout behavioral science. Consider an intriguing study on whether learning experiences physically change the brain. The researchers used brain imaging to compare the size of a particular brain region in nonmusicians versus musicians who averaged nearly 12 years of experience playing stringed instruments such as the violin (Elbert, Pantev, Wienbruch, Rockstroh, & Taub, 1995). To play their instruments, these musicians use their right hand to draw the bow across the strings and their left hand to finger the strings rapidly and precisely. This sends a tremendous amount of sensory information from the fingertips of the left hand to a specific area of the somatosensory cortex in the brain's right hemisphere, which receives and processes this stimulation. The researchers found that, overall, this right-brain somatosensory area was (1) larger among musicians than nonmusicians and (2) larger among musicians who started playing music at a younger rather than an older age.

It is tempting to conclude that many thousands of hours of musical practice and play caused the musicians' brains to change physically, but because this was a correlational study, we need to resist that temptation. Perhaps these brain differences were present at birth or developed during childhood and were caused by a third variable, such as heredity, that also influenced whether these people became musicians and the age at which they started playing.

The findings do, however, converge with the results of laboratory animal experiments that have demonstrated a causal effect of environmental stimulation on the brain's structure (Rosenzweig, 1984). Most directly, some experimenters have trained rats to use their paws, and monkeys to use their fingers, to perform skilled movements at laboratory tasks. Their experiments have found that these learning experiences produce structural changes to areas of the animals' brains involved in controlling such movements (Kleim et al., 2002).

These experimental findings do not negate the problems of causal interpretation inherent in the correlational study of musicians, but they place those results within a broader network of evidence on how experience affects the brain.

 CONCEPT CHECK 5.4 BENEFITS OF CORRELATIONAL RESEARCH

Decide whether each statement below is true or false when it completes the opening phrase. Answers appear on page 170.

Correlational research

1. is often used to establish the reliability and validity of psychological tests.
2. provides a basis for actuarial prediction in everyday life.
3. is often used to test theories and hypotheses.

SPECIAL ISSUES

Learning Objectives

After studying this section, you should be able to:

- Provide examples of nonlinear relations between two variables.
- Discuss why range restriction can pose a problem in determining the correlation between two variables.
- Explain why associations involving qualitative variables need to be viewed differently from associations involving quantitative variables.

Many factors affect the measurement of a relation between two variables. We'll discuss three factors here: nonlinear relations, range restriction, and associations involving qualitative variables.

NONLINEAR RELATIONS

Pearson's r measures the degree of linear relation between two variables. Some variables, however, have a nonlinear relation. In such cases, Pearson's r will underestimate or possibly fail to detect the relation between two variables.

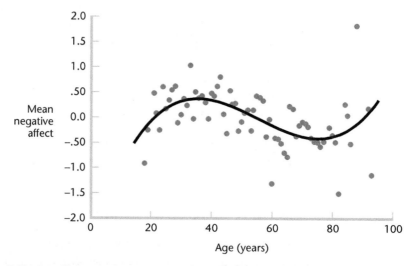

Figure 5.12 Curvilinear relation between age and overall negative affect. Higher values on the y-axis indicate greater overall negative emotion. Each data point represents the average negative emotion score at a particular age. (Adapted with permission from APA from "Aging and Negative Affect: The Rise and Fall and Rise of Anxiety and Depression Symptoms," by B. A. Teachman, 2006, *Psychology and Aging, 21,* pp. 201–207 [Figure 1].)

Consider a study by clinical psychologist Bethany Teachman (2006), from an article whose title captures the nonlinear relation portrayed in **Figure 5.12**: "Aging and Negative Affect: The Rise and Fall and Rise of Anxiety and Depression Symptoms" (p. 201). In this cross-sectional study, 335 Americans aged 18 to 93 completed psychological tests that measured depressive symptoms, general anxiety, and general negative emotionality. Teachman also combined the scores on these measures to create an overall "negative affect" score for each participant. Each measure had a significant nonlinear relation with age, even when statistically adjusted for several possible third variables, including participants' health status. Without discussing complexities of the data analysis, the key point is that the solid line in Figure 5.12 provides the best overall fit to the data. On average, comparing across different age groups, negative affect increased throughout early adulthood, decreased during middle adulthood and the beginning of late adulthood, and then increased again.

Figure 5.13 shows another nonlinear relation. This study, from community psychology, examined the relation at people's workplaces between the proportion of co-ethnic coworkers and job satisfaction. Noemí Enchautegui-de-Jesús and her colleagues asked 648 Dominican, Mexican, Puerto Rican, and non-Hispanic Black adults to use a 6-point scale (1 = *none*, 6 = *all*) to identify the proportion of their colleagues at work who were of the same ethnicity as they were (Enchautegui-de-Jesús, Hughes, Johnston, & Oh, 2006). Participants, 57% of whom were immigrants, also rated their degree of job satisfaction on an 11-point scale (0 = *the worst possible*, 10 = *the best possible*). The simple linear correlation between these two variables was near zero and not statistically significant. In contrast, a statistically significant nonlinear relation was found: As the proportion of co-ethnic coworkers increased, job satisfaction initially increased but then changed direction and decreased. The highest levels of job satisfaction were associated with job environments in which an intermediate proportion of coworkers shared the participants' ethnicity.

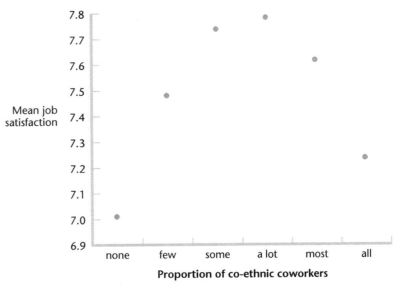

Figure 5.13 Curvilinear relation between employee job satisfaction and the proportion of co-ethnic coworkers. Each data point represents the average job satisfaction rating of participants who reported having a particular proportion of co-ethnic coworkers. (Information from Enchautegui-de-Jesús et al., 2006.)

Keep in mind that, as with correlational research in general, this study and Teachman's (2006) research on age and negative emotionality do not demonstrate causality. We cannot clearly conclude that the degree of coworker co-ethnicity influences job satisfaction or that the aging process causes negative emotionality to change. Thinking critically, in your opinion is bidirectionality a feasible alternative explanation for the results of each of these studies, and are there third variables that might plausibly explain the results?

RANGE RESTRICTION

In correlational research, **range restriction** *occurs when the range of scores obtained for a variable has been artificially limited in some way.* Range restriction can lead to erroneous conclusions about the strength, direction, and linear versus nonlinear nature of the relation between two variables.

Looking again at Figure 5.13, imagine a different scenario. If each of the Black, Mexican, Dominican, and Puerto Rican participants had worked in job settings where there were none, few, or at most only some coworkers of the same ethnic background as theirs, what would the graph look like? In this case, there would be no right half of the graph, and based solely on the data from the "none," "few," or "some" categories along the *x*-axis, we would conclude that there was a positive correlation between the proportion of co-ethnic workers and job satisfaction. In another scenario, if all the participants had come from job settings in which "a lot," "most," or "all" of their coworkers shared the same ethnicity, there would be no left half of the graph and we would likely conclude that there was a negative correlation between the proportion of co-ethnic workers and job satisfaction. It was only by studying a more complete, varied sample of participants whose work environments spanned the whole range of possibilities that the more complex relation could be detected (Enchautegui-de-Jesús et al., 2006).

When a relation is linear, range restriction can distort its strength. **Figure 5.14** shows data from 40 hypothetical job applicants, with X representing their scores on a newly developed personnel-selection test that is being evaluated by the company's industrial-organizational psychologist. To optimally assess the test's criterion validity, the psychologist convinces the company to hire all 40 applicants provisionally. Six months later, their job performance is rated by supervisors. The Pearson correlation for the entire data set, *r* = .51, indicates that

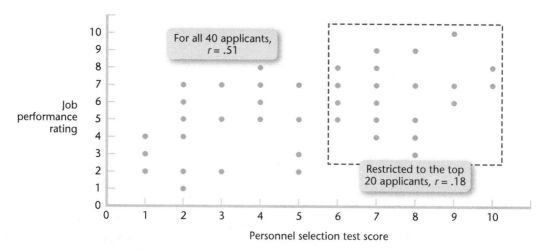

Figure 5.14 Range restriction and correlation, based on hypothetical data from 40 job applicants. In this example, range restriction substantially reduces a correlation's strength.

higher scores on the selection test predicted better job performance. The test appears to hold promise. Suppose, however, that the company had only been willing to hire the 20 applicants who had the highest scores on the screening test, whose scores are shown within the dashed rectangle in the scatter plot. This would have created a more homogeneous sample of participants by restricting the range of scores of variable X, and the correlation for this data set would have dropped to a much weaker value of $r = .18$.

ASSOCIATIONS INVOLVING QUALITATIVE VARIABLES

Is college students' choice of major related to their ethnicity and gender? In one study, Catherine Riegle-Crumb and Barbara King (2010) analyzed data from a nationally representative sample of 3,946 sophomores. The researchers focused their study on three racial/ethnic groups, categorizing female and male students as Black, Hispanic, or non-Hispanic White. They also grouped college majors into three categories: (1) STEM, which stands for "sciences, technology, engineering, and math" (in this study, physical sciences, computer science, engineering, and math); (2) biological sciences; and (3) non-STEM (all other majors).

In this example, you cannot use Pearson's r or Spearman's rho to analyze the association between ethnicity and college major, or between gender and college major, because all of these variables have been measured on a nominal scale (see Chapter 4, p. 124). That is, the data about people's ethnicity, gender, and major represent qualitative categories—different names of groups and majors—rather than quantitative dimensions involving different amounts of some characteristic. Although we can ask whether there is an association between ethnicity and college major, and between gender and college major, the absence of ordinal, interval, or ratio scaling makes it impossible to say that such variables are positively or negatively correlated. The concept of "direction" of a relation between ethnicity and major, and gender and major, simply does not apply in this case.

Figure 5.15 shows the percentage of students within each ethnic–gender group who majored in each of the three fields. The researchers conducted two analyses, one for women and another for men, to examine whether ethnicity and choice of major were significantly associated. In each analysis, they used a statistical test appropriate for this type of data (see Statistics Module 11 for more detail). These associations were not statistically significant. In contrast, the researchers noted that among men, the percent majoring in STEM fields is about 4 times greater than among women, a disparity that occurred for each of the three ethnic groups.

As another example involving a qualitative variable, consider a study by clinical psychologist George Bonanno and his colleagues, which examined psychological resilience among adults in New York City and nearby areas 6 months after the terrorist attacks of September 11, 2001 (Bonanno, Galea, Bucciarelli, & Vlahov, 2006). By telephone, they randomly surveyed adults in New York City and adjacent areas of New Jersey and Connecticut, obtaining a final sample of 2,752 participants. In addition to asking participants about their demographic background, the researchers assessed each participant's exposure

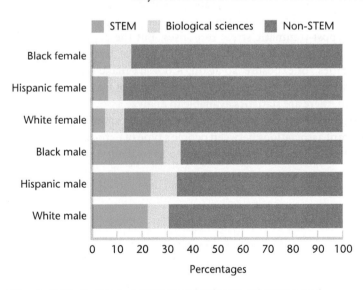

Figure 5.15 College majors in relation to ethnicity and gender. Each horizontal bar shows the percentage of students from a particular ethnic/gender group majoring in various fields. (Adapted with permission from American Psychological Science from "Questioning a White Male Advantage in STEM Examining Disparities in College Major by Gender and Race/Ethnicity," by C. Riegle-Crumb and B. King, 2010, *Educational Researcher, 39,* pp. 656–664 [Figure 1].)

Table 5.4 Psychological Responses to Trauma Six Months After the 9/11 World Trade Center Attacks

Exposure Category	Prevalence of Response to Trauma Exposure		
	Resilience (%)	Recovery from Trauma (%)	Probable PTSD Related to the Attack (%)
Saw attacks in person from outside the World Trade Center ($n = 798$)	55.6	31.9	12.5
Friend or relative killed ($n = 392$)	53.9	34.9	11.2
Involved in rescue ($n = 296$)	51.2	37.0	11.8
Lost employment ($n = 147$)	39.1	43.4	17.5
Friend or relative killed and saw attack ($n = 142$)	33.4	35.4	31.3

The percentages in each row may not add up to 100% due to rounding error.

Source: Data from "Psychological Resilience After Disaster: New York City in the Aftermath of the September 11th Terrorist Attack," by G. A. Bonanno, S. Galea, A. Bucciarelli, and D. Vlahov, 2006, *Psychological Science, 17,* p. 184. Copyright © 2006 by Association for Psychological Science. Reprinted by permission of SAGE Publications, Inc.

to the 9/11 World Trade Center attacks. For example, participants were asked whether they had a friend or relative killed in the attacks, had been involved in the rescue, and so forth. In total, the researchers identified nine exposure categories, five of which are listed in the first column of Table 5.4. In addition, based on a detailed clinical phone interview, the researchers assessed the presence of post-traumatic stress disorder (PTSD) symptoms. They classified each participant's current psychological status as falling into one of three categories: (1) resilience (the person displays zero or one symptom of PTSD); (2) recovery from trauma (the person displays two or more symptoms, but does not meet the clinical criteria for a diagnosis of PTSD); and (3) probable PTSD related to the attack.

In this case, the categories of resilience, recovery, and probable PTSD can be considered as representing an underlying ordinal scale, as each successive category reflects a progressively more substantial set of post-traumatic stress responses. But the exposure categories are nominal: Overall, the nine categories represent different "types" of exposure rather than different "amounts" or "severities" of exposure, so again, it doesn't make sense to think of there being an overall positive or negative correlation between type of exposure and PTSD status. Fortunately, once again, there are statistics available to analyze associations when one or both variables are nominal, and Statistics Module 11 discusses an example. In this study, the researchers found significant associations between people's type of exposure to the World Trade Center attacks and their likelihood of being diagnosed as resilient, recovered, or having probable PTSD.

 CONCEPT CHECK 5.5 SPECIAL ISSUES

Decide whether each statement below is true or false. Answers appear on page 170.

1. The Pearson's r correlation statistic measures the strength of both the linear and nonlinear relation between two variables.

2. Range restriction can distort conclusions about both the strength and direction of a relation between two variables.

3. It is possible to examine associations between variables even if one or both variables are measured on a nominal scale.

CHAPTER SUMMARY

- Two variables, X and Y, are correlated when the scores or values of X are systematically associated with the scores or values of Y.

- In correlational studies, the researcher (1) *measures* variable X, (2) *measures* variable Y, (3) statistically examines whether X and Y are associated, and (4) attempts to minimize potential confounding factors through statistical control and special research designs.

- Positive correlation means that higher X scores are associated with higher Y scores. Negative correlation means that higher X scores are associated with lower Y scores.

- Pearson's *r* measures the direction and strength of the linear association between two variables. Pearson's *r* can range from values of +1.00 to −1.00. The plus or minus sign indicates the correlation's direction; the absolute value of *r* represents the correlation's strength. The coefficient of determination (r^2) represents the proportion of variance shared between two variables. A correlation can be graphed on a scatter plot.

- Correlation does not establish causation. The bidirectionality problem refers to the principle that when X and Y are correlated, X may have caused Y or Y may have caused X. The third-variable problem refers to the possibility that a third variable, Z, may be the true cause of why X and Y appear to be related, and thus there may be no causal link between X and Y.

- To reduce the bidirectionality problem, researchers may conduct longitudinal research, such as a cross-lagged panel study. Researchers also may try to statistically remove the influence of potential third variables. The simplest approach, partial correlation, computes a correlation between X and Y while statistically filtering out their association with a third variable (Z). Even so, it is always possible that researchers have overlooked other plausible third variables. Thus, correlational studies do not provide as clear a test of causal relations as experiments do.

- If X and Y are correlated, knowing the scores of X helps us predict the scores of Y. Simple regression analysis uses a single predictor to estimate scores of a single criterion variable. Multiple regression uses two or more predictors to estimate the scores of a single criterion variable.

- Correlational research is used for applied prediction and in test validation. It can examine topics that for practical or ethical reasons cannot be investigated via experiments. By revealing potential cause–effect links between naturally occurring variables, correlational studies can spur researchers to conduct experiments that examine such links under controlled conditions. Conversely, when experiments uncover causal relations, correlational research can help establish the external validity of those experimental findings.

- If two variables have a nonlinear relation, Pearson's *r* will underestimate or fail to detect the relation between them. Range restriction occurs when the range of scores obtained for a variable has been artificially limited. It can lead to false conclusions about the relation between two variables. For associations involving qualitative variables, the concept of linear relation (i.e., of positive and negative correlation) does not apply.

KEY TERMS

bidirectionality (two-way causality) problem (p. 149)
correlation (p. 140)
correlational (relational) research (p. 141)
criterion variable (p. 158)
cross-lagged panel design (p. 153)
cross-sectional research design (one-shot correlational study) (p. 152)

longitudinal research design (p. 152)
multiple regression (p. 159)
negative correlation (p. 142)
partial correlation (p. 151)
Pearson's *r* (Pearson product-moment correlation coefficient) (p. 143)
positive correlation (p. 142)
predictor variable (p. 158)

prospective design (p. 152)
range restriction (p. 166)
regression analysis (simple linear regression) (p. 157)
scatter plot (scattergram) (p. 144)
Spearman's rho (Spearman rank-order correlation coefficient) (p. 144)
third-variable problem (p. 149)

ASSESS YOUR KNOWLEDGE

1. Describe and contrast the core characteristics of the experimental versus correlational methods.

2. How does research on the topic of TV watching and perceived crime risk illustrate the correlational method?

3. Explain the concepts of positive correlation and negative correlation. Provide an example of each.

4. What does Pearson's *r* measure? Describe the range of numbers that can be obtained with this statistic, and how this statistic reflects the strength and direction of a correlation.

5. What is a scatter plot? Describe how a scatter plot is created.

6. Identify three key criteria that are used in drawing inferences about cause and effect.

7. Discuss whether correlational studies meet the criteria for inferring causality. Be sure to explain and illustrate the bidirectionality and third-variable problems.

8. Explain the concept of partial correlation and the purpose of using this technique in correlational research. Give an example.

9. How do longitudinal correlational designs attempt to reduce the causal ambiguity of interpreting correlational data?

10. What is an applied purpose of regression analysis? Identify two key types of variables in regression analysis.

11. How do simple regression and multiple regression differ from each other?

12. Discuss advantages of the correlational method.

13. What is range restriction and what problem can it cause? Give an example.

14. Is it possible for two qualitative variables to be positively or negatively correlated? Explain your answer.

CONCEPT CHECKS: ANSWERS

5.1 Basic Concepts

1. measured; measured   2. lower   3. weaker   4. does not

5.2 Correlation Does Not Establish Causation

1. false   2. false   3. false

5.3 Correlation and Prediction

1. simple linear regression (or just "regression analysis"); predictor; criterion   2. multiple regression

5.4 Benefits of Correlation Research

1. true   2. true   3. true

5.5 Special Issues

1. false   2. true   3. true

Questions From Table 5.2

1. size of city population; overall, as city population size increases, more people are available to attend religious services and to consume alcohol. 2. daily temperature; on hotter days (i.e., summer months) more North Americans go swimming, and more Europeans eat ice cream. 3. age; overall, older children are taller and know more words than younger children.

THINKING CRITICALLY AND APPLYING YOUR KNOWLEDGE

EXERCISE 1   Happiness and Friendships

Dr. Alvarez is a development psychologist who examines whether college students' degree of happiness is related to how much time they spend with friends. On a questionnaire, 383 women and 364 men report: (a) their current, overall level of happiness on an 11-point scale (0 = *low happiness,* 10 = *high happiness*), and (b) the number of minutes, on average, that they spent interacting with friends (e.g., in person, online, by phone) per day, for the past week. Dr. Alvarez analyzes the women's and men's data separately. For simplicity, the data for 10 female students are shown.

(a) Based on visually inspecting these data, do happiness and time spent with friends appear to be positively correlated, negatively correlated, or uncorrelated?

(b) Create a scatter plot: Plot scores for happiness (variable X) along the *x*-axis and time spent with friends (variable Y) along the *y*-axis. Based on the scatter plot, do happiness and time spent with friends appear to be positively correlated, negatively correlated, or uncorrelated?

(c) Assume the data reveal a strong positive correlation between happiness and amount of time spent with friends. *Based solely on this study,* which one of the following four conclusions is most appropriate? (1) Greater happiness causes people (i.e., motivates them) to spend more time with their friends. (2) Spending more time with friends causes people to become happier. (3) Happiness and amount of time spent with friends are causally related, but we can't tell which causes which. (4) We cannot conclude that happiness and amount of time spent with friends are causally related.

(d) After answering the question in part (c), apply the bidirectionality and third-variable problems to the results of this study. For the third-variable problem, identify at least one factor that would plausibly explain why happiness and the amount of time spent with friends are correlated even though there might be no causal link between these two variables.

Student	Happiness	Minutes per Day With Friends
Erin	2	40
Claire	3	20
Sheridan	3	50
Maliah	5	20
Shih-Fen	5	40
Kristen	6	50
Lavonne	7	60
Anika	7	50
Rachel	8	80
Camila	9	70

EXERCISE 2   The Planet Grog

In a galaxy far, far away, a total of eight inhabitants live on the planet Grog. Here are the heights (in inches) and weights (in pounds) of those inhabitants, called Grogarians.

(a) Looking at the data, do you believe that there is a correlation between the Grogarians' height and weight? If your answer is yes, how strong would you subjectively estimate the correlation to be? Is it a perfect correlation, strong correlation, moderate correlation, or weak correlation?

(b) Create a scatter plot of these data. Plot height (variable X) along the *x*-axis. Plot weight (variable Y) along the *y*-axis. Based on the scatter plot, do you wish to change your answer in part (a)?

(c) Don't read further until you have completed parts (a) and (b) above. Have you completed them? Now, to predict the Grogarians' weight based on their height, can you figure out the simple mathematical relation between these two variables?

Grogarian	Height (inches)	Weight (pounds)
Zork	60	30
Kryg	62	31
Oikr	66	33
Frox	68	34
Blix	70	35
Pzzr	74	37
Yhizi	76	38
Luxx	78	39

EXERCISE 3   Correlation and Causation

Three examples of hypothetical correlations between two variables, X and Y, are described below. For each example: (1) Describe how the bidirectionality problem applies. (2) Identify at least one third variable that could reasonably account for the correlation between X and Y.

(a) In a sample of 1,000 families, a positive correlation is found between the frequency with which parents use corporal punishment (e.g., spanking) and the frequency with which their children misbehave at school.

(b) In a sample of 200 pairs of business managers and employees, a positive correlation is found between the quality of employee performance and the frequency with which managers praise their employees.

(c) In a sample of 300 teenagers, a negative correlation is found between the number of friends they each have and the number of hours per week they spend playing video games.

6

CASE STUDIES AND OBSERVATIONAL RESEARCH

CHAPTER OUTLINE

A t the age of 22, a young man known as N.A. had completed a year of junior college and was serving in the U.S. Air Force. One day, in a fleeting instant, a freak accident changed his life forever. N.A. was sitting at a table while, behind him, his roommate was handling a miniature fencing foil. His roommate tapped N.A. and then made a forward, upward thrust of the foil to N.A.'s side. Responding to the tap, N.A. turned his head around, directly into the path of the foil. It entered N.A.'s right nostril and pierced his skull, causing damage to portions of his thalamus, hypothalamus, and neural connections between them (see **Figure 6.1**; Squire, Amaral, Zola-Morgan, Kritchevsky, & Press, 1989).

Amazingly, N.A. survived. Following surgery and a half year of hospitalization, he was able to return home. His abilities to use language, to perceive the world, and to move remained intact. His IQ remained well above average. Initially, however, N.A. had profound difficulty remembering events from his life that had occurred in the 2 years prior to his accident, a condition called *retrograde amnesia*. This condition improved greatly over time, but the accident also left him with another form of amnesia, *anterograde amnesia*: N.A. had great difficulty forming long-term memories of new experiences. For example, if N.A. met you for the first time and then spent several hours with you, the following day he likely would say that he had never met you. This type of amnesia, portrayed in popular movies such as *50 First Dates, Memento, Finding Nemo,* and *Finding Dory,* improves over time in some cases. N.A.'s anterograde amnesia lessened somewhat in the first 7 years after his accident, but showed little improvement after that and remained severe. With some exceptions, N.A.'s memory of the daily events in his life since 1960—the year of the accident—is hazy and often blank.

When N.A. was in his late 30s and early 40s, neuropsychologist Philip Kaushall and his colleagues studied him closely for 6 years (Kaushall, Zetin, & Squire, 1981). They met with N.A. many times at his home and at a Veteran's Administration hospital where he was a patient. They administered tests to assess N.A.'s cognitive and intellectual functioning. They observed him carefully and conversed with him and his mother, with whom N.A. lived.

Kaushall et al. (1981) noted that N.A. was bright, polite, friendly, optimistic, and relaxed. He spoke clearly and did not exhibit general mental confusion. At his home, N.A. proudly showed the researchers his collections of model airplanes, rocks, shells, and guns. Yet, as Kaushall et al. also reported:

> Within a short time span, he does not repeat himself or show the same objects twice; but, after the third or fourth visit, after he asks each time whether he has shown you his collections, his remarks and activities come to reveal a devastated life and an isolated mental world. . . .
>
> He suffers from a severe loss of memory for the events of each day, especially for incidental happenings. Even significant events are recalled vaguely, if at all. Accordingly, he accumulates an inadequate record of the past, including public events like the news as well as personal experiences. For example, after a telephone interruption, he may not remember what he was doing just before. He can also forget his intentions while performing a task involving a sequence of steps, even without an interruption. He says that he cannot watch TV satisfactorily, because he will forget the story narrative during the commercial break. (Kaushall, Zetin, & Squire, 1981, p. 384)

From "A Psychosocial Study of Chronic, Circumscribed Amnesia," by P. I. Kaushall, M. Zetin, & L. R. Squire, 1981, *Journal of Nervous & Mental Disease, 169*(6), p. 384. Copyright 1981 by Wolters Kluwer Heath, Inc. Reprinted by permission.

Scientists studied N.A. for many years after his accident in 1960 (Squire et al., 1989), and we will discuss more about his case soon. Today, memory researchers continue a long tradition of intensively studying individual cases of amnesia, and cases of truly exceptional memory as well (Ally, Hussey, & Donahue, 2013; Luria, 1968). But why devote so much effort to observing a single case? As with every other type of research, you will see that this approach has important strengths, as well as limitations.

Yogi Berra, a famous baseball player widely known for his puzzling yet oddly insightful remarks, once commented that "you can observe a lot by watching" (DeVito, 2008, p. 230). This chapter focuses on two important types of descriptive research, case studies and observational research, that squarely place the scientist in the role of systematic observer. It also examines several ways in which behavior can be observed indirectly.

Observation, of course, is fundamental to all scientific inquiry, and when scientists conduct experiments they surely are observing how participants behave. This chapter, however, focuses on nonexperimental methods. Let's first examine case study research and then turn to observational research.

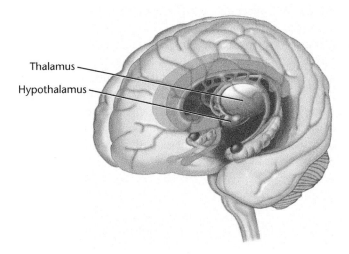

Thalamus

Hypothalamus

Figure 6.1 Damage to N.A.'s brain. In a freak accident, a miniature fencing foil was thrust upward and entered N.A.'s right nostril, penetrating his skull. The accident damaged portions of his hypothalamus and several regions of the thalamus in his left hemisphere. (From *Psychology* [p. 98], by D. L. Schacter, D. T. Gilbert, D. M. Wegner, & M. K. Nock, 2014, New York: Worth. Copyright 2014 by Worth Publishers. Modified with permission.)

CASE STUDIES

Learning Objectives

After studying this section, you should be able to:

- Describe basic characteristics and advantages of case study research.
- Discuss qualitative and quantitative approaches to conducting a case study.
- Explain how intrinsic, instrumental, and collective case studies differ.
- Illustrate ways that data are gathered and analyzed in case studies.
- Discuss limitations of case study research.

Kaushall et al.'s (1981) detailed analysis of amnesia patient N.A. illustrates a research approach called a **case study:** *an in-depth analysis of an individual, social unit, event, or other phenomenon.* Case studies are conducted in many fields of psychology and across other disciplines in the natural and social sciences, humanities, and professional fields (e.g., medicine, law, business).

BASIC CHARACTERISTICS

Case studies vary greatly in scope and in how data are collected, analyzed, and reported. Still, their core feature remains the researchers' focus on comprehensively examining a particular case (Stake, 1994). The *case* in a case study may be an individual person or nonhuman animal, a larger unit (e.g., a married couple, work group, organization, community, nation), a past or current event, a program, or even an activity (Creswell, Hanson, Clark, & Morales, 2007). For example, Moore and Prentice (2013) wanted to examine how nurse practitioners and registered nurses who work in Canadian outpatient oncology facilities collaborate with one another. They gathered data at a single oncology care facility in Ontario, but noted that "the *case* or main unit of analysis for this study was the process of collaboration" (p. 1576). In other words, they chose to define their case as an activity or process (collaboration) because this best suited their research goals.

When the case in a case study is a social unit, such as a family, sports team, high school, or business organization, researchers usually collect data either from all members or a sample of individual members from that social unit. For example, an interdisciplinary team of researchers, including health psychologist Kathrin Cresswell (Sheikh et al., 2011), examined the nationwide implementation of an electronic patient–health record system in England. Each of 12 hospitals was treated in the research design as a separate case study site. Among the many types of data collected (e.g., observations, documents), researchers conducted 431 interviews with individual health-care providers, hospital administrators, and other people. This may seem like a far cry from the type of case study of N.A. conducted by Kaushall et al. (1981), but the common thread is that an individual—whether an individual person or hospital—was the focus of an in-depth analysis in each case study.

WHY CONDUCT CASE STUDIES?

Flexibility is one among many strengths of the case study approach. As we will see, this approach allows researchers to draw upon a wide variety of techniques to gather data. Further, as data collection proceeds, it may give rise to new questions that the researcher might decide to explore, or indicate limitations in the study's design or execution that the researcher is able to remedy, within the remainder of the study.

Another strength of case studies is that they can offer a unique window into the nature of a person's behavior and mental life. They can provide considerable detail about unusual events and people who have rare psychological abilities or disorders. Case studies also provide insight into more common psychological experiences and afflictions. Although we can learn many important things by statistically comparing groups of people who are diagnosed with amnesia or depression versus those who are not, it's the rich narrative provided in a compelling case study that gives us the sensation of peering into the psychological world of amnesia or depression—or, for that matter, of extraordinary memory or creative genius.

Using N.A.'s case, Kaushall et al. (1981) painted a picture of how amnesia can affect a person's everyday life. They highlighted how "the outstanding feature of N.A.'s life style is its constricted regularity. Only those routines learned through years of living in the same place can be performed reliably" (p. 386). For example, they described how N.A. eventually was able to drive himself from home to the V.A. hospital for his weekly visits through a general sense of feel and trying to recognize landmarks. Yet N.A. could not draw a clear map of the route, or remember the name of his highway exits or streets along the way, and sometimes would fail to turn off at the correct exit.

The researchers also described how N.A. would challenge his own memory by taking solo daytime walks in his neighborhood, deriving great pride from his ability to find his way home. They wrote of N.A.'s sense of humor and steadfast optimism, while at the same time pointing out how his amnesia devastated his once active social life. Friendships and dating are difficult to maintain when it's a struggle just to remember the theme of a long ongoing conversation; when it's difficult to talk about what you did today, or yesterday, or for the past month, because you have no memory of it. Details such as these are what a case study reveals.

Another advantage of case studies is that they can provide insight into the possible causes of behavior and lead to hypotheses that are tested using other research methods. As an example, for centuries, case studies have enabled scientists to assess changes in psychological functioning that occur following damage to particular brain areas. These case studies of people who have experienced brain injuries, including those of amnesia victims such as N.A., often lead to hypotheses about the role of specific brain structures in regulating normal behavior.

Case studies can also test hypotheses and provide evidence that supports or contradicts a theory or scientific viewpoint. For example, suppose a theory of memory proposes that whenever we can't remember something, it is because of retrieval failure. According to this theory, the memory is permanently stored in the brain, but we can't access the correct code to "pull it out" of storage. Such a theory would have a hard time explaining N.A.'s case:

> . . . a general retrieval deficit cannot explain why N.A.'s memory is poor for events that have occurred since his accident in 1960 but good for events that occurred before 1960. (Kaushall et al., 1981, p. 388)

Case studies also can provide support for the external validity of findings obtained in experiments or other types of research. Recall that external validity concerns the degree to which the findings of a study can be generalized to other populations and settings. N.A.'s case and similar amnesia cases supported the external validity of animal laboratory studies in suggesting that before a memory is stored in the brain as a long-term memory, a period occurs during which the brain must first consolidate that memory; the damage to N.A.'s brain seemingly prevented this consolidation of new memories from taking place. N.A.'s case study also supported an emerging theoretical viewpoint that the human brain has different long-term memory systems, including procedural memory (remembering "how") and declarative memory (remembering "what"). The existence of distinct memory systems would explain why, for example, N.A. could remember how to perform newly learned skills (procedural memory) while being unable to consciously recall those learning experiences or most of his other new daily experiences or facts (declarative memory).

TYPES OF CASE STUDIES

Researchers may adopt a qualitative, quantitative, or mixed-methods approach to conducting a case study. Within these approaches, the reasons for selecting a particular case as the focus of study, and the number of cases the researcher chooses to examine, can vary. Different types of case studies have been described based on each of these factors.

Qualitative, Quantitative, and Mixed-Methods Approaches

For researchers who adopt a qualitative orientation, the essence of a case study—what is commonly called a **qualitative case study**—*is to examine an individual case in depth, within its real-life context* (Creswell et al., 2007; Crowe et al., 2011). The qualitative researcher typically seeks to gain a multifaceted, holistic understanding of the case, including an awareness of how the participant or participants (e.g., if the case is a group) perceive their situation or the phenomenon being studied. The researcher attempts to gather multiple types of data in order to understand the individual and the surrounding context from the individual's point of view (Stake, 1994).

Kaushall et al.'s (1981) case study of N.A had a qualitative emphasis. The goals were to explore how severe amnesia could influence a person's daily activities and personality development, to examine how N.A. perceived his amnesia and everyday life, and to do so outside the confines of the laboratory. Their narrative description of N.A.'s case is organized around themes such as the nature of his memory impairment and his awareness of it, his social relationships and sleep-related dreams, places he goes to outside the home and how he independently travels to them, and his recreational pastimes and other daily activities. By including portions of transcripts of conversations they had with N.A., and many other quotations of comments that N.A. made, Kaushall et al. provide the reader with a window into N.A.'s world.

Although Kaushall et al. (1981) repeatedly administered neuropsychological tests to N.A. over the 6 years they studied him, discussion of these findings was minimal, nontechnical, and took a back seat to the far more extensive narrative discussion based on their home observations of N.A. and conversations with him. This stands in contrast to—and nicely complements—important prior case reports about N.A. by other scientists who took a more quantitative or mixed-methods approach to data collection and analysis.

In a **quantitative case study,** *researchers rely primarily on numerical assessments and analysis to describe and understand a case.* In a **mixed-methods case study,** *researchers rely substantially on both qualitative and quantitative data and analyses to explore a case.* The mixed-methods approach is best viewed along a continuum, blending qualitative and quantitative components to varying degrees. To describe the nature and severity of N.A.'s memory impairment, these earlier reports presented numerous quantitative findings: detailed neuropsychological test results and many graphs comparing N.A.'s task performance with that of individuals who had no brain damage or damage to other brain areas (Teuber, Milner, & Vaughan, Jr., 1968). Although secondary to such quantitative analyses, these researchers also gathered qualitative information during multiple home visits that involved observations of N.A. and conversations with him and his mother. They used this information to describe how N.A.'s accident affected his daily behavior and other aspects of his psychological functioning at home.

Intrinsic, Instrumental, and Collective Case Studies

Psychologist Robert Stake (1994) identifies three types of case studies based on the study's purpose and number of cases examined. Although Stake's focus is on qualitative case studies, these distinctions can also be applied to quantitative and mixed-methods case studies.

Researchers may study an individual case because of some intrinsic interest in that particular case, such as because it represents something unique. For example, we might want to study the leadership practices or corporate culture at Apple Inc. because of the company's extraordinary fame, success, and impact on society. We're curious about what makes Apple tick, and we are less concerned or even unconcerned with uncovering principles of successful leadership that we hope might generalize to other companies. Stake (1994) calls this type of study an **intrinsic case study:** *A case is examined in depth due to some inherent interest in learning about that particular case.*

There also are many instances in which a researcher wants to learn about a broader phenomenon, such as leadership success, and describe it or develop or test a hypothesis about it. Among many successful organizations we could choose to study in order to learn about leadership, we select one as a case because it is instrumental in enabling us to achieve this broader goal. In this type of case study, an **instrumental case study,** *a case is analyzed in depth because it is an example of, or otherwise provides information about, a broader phenomenon.*

A case study also may reflect both purposes (Stake, 1994). In psychology, individual cases are most often studied for instrumental purposes or a blend of intrinsic and instrumental reasons. That is, even when a case is intrinsically compelling, psychologists typically study it to illuminate some process, activity, or condition (Creswell et al., 2007). At the time when N.A.'s accident occurred, it presented psychologists with an opportunity to study anterograde amnesia in a rare case where brain damage did not also produce other substantial cognitive or perceptual deficits. Thus, N.A.'s unique case was of intrinsic interest and also of instrumental value to researchers. By exploring the nature of N.A.'s amnesia in depth, Kaushall et al. (1981) hoped "to learn something about both the impact of amnesia and about the role of memory in the organization of normal behavior" (p. 383).

Stake (1994) also describes a third approach to case study research, a **collective case study,** *in which each of several cases is studied in depth for the purpose of learning about a broader phenomenon.* For example, to learn about leadership success or anterograde amnesia, we could study three organizations or three amnesia patients, each of which would be the focus of its own in-depth, instrumental case study (Stake, 1994). Then, in addition to reporting our in-depth analysis of each organization or patient, collectively we could compare and contrast these cases, looking for commonalities and differences that help us better understand the nature of leadership success or anterograde amnesia. Stake's (1994) concept of a collective case study is similar to that of a multiple-case study design, which we discuss in the next section.

Single-Case Study and Multiple-Case Study Designs

Case studies can be distinguished in terms of whether they represent a single-case or multiple-case study design (Yin, 2003). In a **single-case study design,** *researchers analyze one case in depth.* This allows researchers to concentrate their available resources (e.g., funding, time) on that case, enabling a more in-depth analysis than might be possible if they studied multiple cases. Kaushall et al.'s (1981) research focused on N.A. as a single case.

Single-case study designs are often used in fields such as clinical psychology and neuropsychology, as well as in medical science, in which published case studies detail the symptoms, current situational context and history, and treatment of an individual who has a particular disorder. A single-case study design in social or industrial-organizational psychology, or in disciplines such as sociology, anthropology, and business, might be used to examine a single social clique, a work group, a community, or a business organization.

In a **multiple-case study design,** *researchers examine two or more cases and perform an in-depth analysis of each case.* Despite the use of the singular *study* in *multiple-case study,* this design refers to performing a set of case studies within an overarching investigation of a topic (Yin, 2003). As Stake (1994) notes, "We may simultaneously carry on more than one case study, but each case study is a concentrated inquiry into a single case" (p. 237).

For example, as noted earlier, Sheikh et al. (2011) studied the implementation of a nationwide electronic patient–health record system in England. Within the overall investigation, a separate case study was conducted at each of 12 hospitals (the cases) who were early adopters of the new record-keeping system. This represents a multiple-case study design. Their analyses uncovered implementation difficulties and limited initial benefits from the new record-keeping system among these early adopters.

A potential disadvantage of the multiple-case study design is that researchers may need more resources to conduct the study; or, if those are not available, they may have to scale back on how deeply they plan to analyze each case. An advantage of this design is that researchers may choose to study the multiple cases sequentially, gathering and analyzing the data from one case before moving on to the next. Insights learned from one case may help the researchers refine their topic and measures (e.g., interview questions) before gathering data about the next case (Yin, 2003).

A multiple-case study design also allows researchers to compare and contrast cases, a technique called *cross-case comparison*. Yin (2003) proposes that in studies where generalization is a goal, a multiple-case study design may allow researchers to examine whether the findings they obtain for one case replicate across other cases. In the study of hospitals mentioned previously, Sheikh et al. (2011) selected 12 cases to represent different regions of England and different sizes and types of facilities (e.g., teaching hospitals vs. nonteaching hospitals). This enabled the researchers to identify implementation difficulties and benefits of the new electronic records system that were localized to specific cases, and others that occurred more generally across cases.

GATHERING AND ANALYZING DATA

Although the methods used to gather data can vary widely, case studies in psychology typically include direct observation and questioning. Two approaches to observation discussed later in the chapter, *naturalistic observation* and *participant observation,* are often used in qualitative case studies, while a third approach, *structured observation,* is often seen in quantitative case studies. In clinical case studies, psychologists often base much of their analysis on observing and talking with their patients or clients in therapy sessions. In the case of N.A., as noted earlier, researchers met with him during visits he regularly made to a nearby hospital, and also repeatedly visited him at his home, where he spent almost all his time. This provided the opportunity to gather data in different settings and to observe N.A. in his daily life. Case study researchers also may gather data in other ways, such as talking with family members and others who know the participant, as Kausall et al. (1981) did through conversations with N.A.'s mother.

In qualitative case studies, questioning often is done via semi-structured interviews, especially in instances when the case represents a larger social unit (e.g., school, hospital, work group) from which multiple members will be interviewed. In a **semi-structured interview,** *the researcher identifies in advance a set of topics or themes to be discussed with the interviewee, but the way and sequence in which questions are asked remain flexible.* Questions are typically open ended (i.e., "Tell me about. . .), rather than the more structured rating scale questions used by quantitative researchers, and the question sequence is flexible to enable the interviewer to explore issues raised by the interviewee in more detail. To provide some structure to the interview, the interviewer usually has a written guide that lists the topics to be covered.

Focus groups also may be used to gather data. In a **focus group,** *a moderator leads a group of people through an interview and discussion of a set of topics.* Depending on a researcher's goal, focus group members may be selected because they are similar to one another on some key characteristic (e.g., all managers in a particular unit of a company), or instead, selected to create a diverse group (e.g., managers in different units, or employees working in different jobs). As in a semi-structured individual interview, a set of topics or questions is determined in advance, but allowance is made for open-ended group discussion.

Individual interviews or focus group sessions can be video- or audio-recorded, and these records can be used to generate a written transcript of the session that provides the basis for qualitative and quantitative analyses (Stewart, Shamdasani, & Rook, 2007). For example, researchers may perform a thematic content analysis of the session to identify major ideas or

Figure 6.2 Communication board: Psychological case study of locked-in syndrome. Tracey, a patient diagnosed with locked-in syndrome, communicates with people using this board. She used it to respond to questions posed by psychologists in a case study. First, as someone starts to name the colors on the board, Tracey selects a row by raising her eyes to signal "yes" in response to hearing the color she wants. Then, the person speaks the letters (or digits) in the row until Tracey selects the item she wants by again raising her eyes. There also are selections for "end word" and "new word." (Copyright 2011 from "A Case Study of Locked-In-Syndrome: Psychological and Personal Perspectives," *Brain Injury*, by B. A. Wilson, A. Hinchcliffe, T. Okines, G. Florschutz, & J. Fish. Reproduced by permission of Taylor & Francis LLC [http://www.tandfonline.com].)

problems raised during the session, they may measure the amount of time participants spent talking about various issues, or they may use session video recordings to assess the frequency and intensity of different emotional responses that participants made in response to specific items raised during the interview or focus group session.

Case study researchers may also gather many other types of data. They may use physiological measures and brain imaging. Psychological assessments may be given: These might include personality tests; intelligence tests; and also neuropsychological tests, which help diagnose normal and abnormal psychological and brain functioning by examining how a person performs on various tasks. For example, clinical psychologist Barbara A. Wilson and her colleagues conducted a case study of a young woman named Tracey, who had developed locked-in syndrome (LIS) following an accident in a gym (B. A. Wilson, Hinchcliffe, Okines, Florschutz, & Fish, 2011). In LIS, people are fully conscious but experience total voluntary-muscle paralysis except for the ability to blink or make vertical eye movements. This case study focused on in-depth assessment of Tracey's psychological and emotional functioning, as measured by 16 neuropsychological tests. Tracey communicated her responses by using vertical eye movements to indicate her selection of a particular letter or number on a specially designed communication board that she had already learned to use (see **Figure 6.2**).

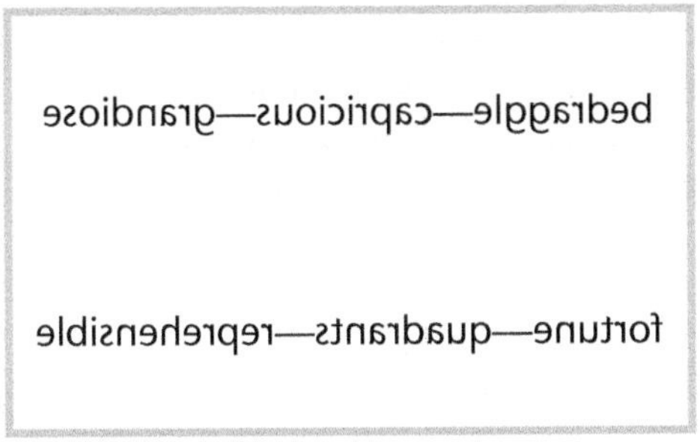

Figure 6.3 A mirror-reading task. Two mirror-reading word sequences, each consisting of three words. The top example was used in the case study of subject N.A. (Republished by permission of *Science* from "Preserved Learning and Retention of Pattern-Analyzing Skill in Amnesia: Dissociation of Knowing How and Knowing That," by N. J. Cohen & L. R. Squire, 1980, *Science*, *210*[4466], pp. 207–210. Permission conveyed through Copyright Clearance Center, Inc.)

By examining these quantitative test results and qualitative data they gathered about Tracey, the researchers were able to assess her psychological functioning, feelings about her medical condition, quality of life, and hopes for the future (B. A. Wilson et al., 2011). Their analysis drew a portrait of a woman whose psychological functioning was either average or above average (compared to test norms) in almost all respects, and who felt that her current quality of life was reasonable. The researchers noted, however, that Tracey was frustrated by some people's unwillingness to "take the time, effort, and energy to communicate with her" (p. 536).

Similarly, researchers administered many neuropsychological tests and other tasks to amnesia victim N.A. For example, psychologists Neal Cohen and Larry Squire (1980) assessed his performance on a mirror-reading task. This is a difficult task that requires reading words presented in a reversed image, as they would appear in a mirror (see **Figure 6.3**). Mirror reading is a skill typically learned with practice, as measured quantitatively by the decreased time it takes people to mirror-read both new and repeated words over a series of trials. Exposed to multiple trials each day for 3 consecutive days, N.A. improved his mirror-reading skills for both new and repeated words at a rate similar to that of healthy adults who did not suffer from amnesia. And 3 months later, he retained his skill learning. Yet despite clearly improving with practice, each time N.A. performed the task, he had either no conscious memory or only a vague memory of ever having performed it before. Moreover, although many words had been repeated 20 times, N.A. believed that all the words were new.

Thus, N.A. was apparently able to learn how to perform some new skills, but unable to consciously remember ever performing them. This result was critically important because it paralleled a finding obtained a few years earlier in another case of even more extensive anterograde amnesia, that of a man referred to as H.M., whose amnesia developed after surgical removal of his hippocampus and adjacent tissue in order to relieve his severe epilepsy. Together, these results suggested that human memory is organized in the brain as different systems, such as one system involving memory for procedural skills, and another for memory—called *episodic memory*—involving the conscious recall of personal experiences. Beyond that, the general similarity of H.M.'s and N.A.'s anterograde amnesia, and the fact that it resulted in each case from damage to different but nearby interconnected areas of the brain, suggested that the hippocampus and its adjacent areas (H.M.'s damage) and certain areas within the thalamus and hypothalamus (in particular, two small clusters of nuclei near the rear of the hypothalamus called the mammillary bodies) might be part of an overall neural circuit key to the formation of new long-term episodic memories. Subsequent memory research, based on experiments and additional case studies, offers general support for this conclusion (Child & Benarroch, 2013; Matthews, 2015).

Case studies are reported in diverse ways. An entire article or book may be devoted to a single case study, or a publication may present findings from several case studies. For example, the well-known neurologist Oliver Sacks wrote books such as *The Man Who Mistook His Wife for a Hat and Other Clinical Tales,* in which each chapter presents the case report of a patient who had a different brain disorder that produced remarkable psychological symptoms (Sacks, 1985). And yes, one of those cases involves a man who, while searching for a hat to wear, literally mistook his wife for a hat, grabbing her head and trying to place it on his own. The man's condition is called *visual agnosia,* an inability to visually recognize objects.

LIMITATIONS OF CASE STUDIES

Every research method has limitations as well as strengths, and discussions about the limitations of case studies often center around three issues: (1) the difficulty of drawing clear causal conclusions, (2) the generalizability of the findings, and (3) the potential for observer bias. First, case studies are not well suited to drawing clear causal conclusions about how one variable affects another (Yin, 2003). There are usually many factors that could be responsible for causing a person or a group to act a certain way, or for causing an event or other outcome to occur. These potential causes may operate individually or in various combinations, and in a case study it is difficult to sort them out. In an experiment, single factors and specific combinations of factors can be isolated and manipulated as independent variables. Other factors that might affect behavior—and that therefore could provide alternative explanations for any findings—can be controlled. The effects of the independent variable on behavior are then measured. In case studies, researchers simply do not have the high degree of control over variables needed to rule out alternative explanations.

In the case of N.A., for example, the researchers noted that he spent much of his time at home arranging items in his closets and tidying things. They observed that he was often irritable, stubborn, and seemed "to express obsessive concern that everything be in its right place and becomes irritated, according to his mother, if even the telephone is placed askew" (Kaushall et al., 1981, p. 386). N.A.'s mother strongly stated that N.A. had not been irritable, stubborn, or obsessive prior to his accident. If that is true, then what caused these personality changes? As the following quote illustrates, the researchers drew conclusions, but appropriately highlighted the issue of multiple potential causes and the difficulty in sorting them out:

> It is our impression that N.A. strives for a rigorously stable environment as an aid to his memory. A constant environment would be the least disconcerting and would help him keep track of where things are. It is possible, too, that these characteristics are related to his dependence on his mother and to denial of anger toward her and the world from which he has been separated. In cases of brain injury, it is often difficult to know whether a behavior develops as a way of mitigating the deficit itself or because it copes with the feelings that the deficit produces. (Kaushall et al., 1981, p. 387)

In fact, as critical thinkers, we need to entertain at least two other causal possibilities beyond those suggested above. First, perhaps N.A.'s personality had not changed, and his mother's perception is incorrect. Perhaps N.A. had been irritable and stubborn as a child or teenager, and perhaps somewhat obsessive about things other than tidying up—but those qualities stand out more now that he is an adult. Second, if we indeed assume that his personality has changed, how do we know whether the change occurred in response to the specific brain injury and resulting amnesia, to the feelings produced by the amnesia, to some combination of these, or in fact to none of these factors? Even adults without brain injuries and amnesia can become more irritable, stubborn, and obsessive as they age. Just ask my wife; she's observed such a case.

A second limitation of cases studies is a potential lack of generalizability. This applies to all research, but the question is whether findings based on only a single case or small number of cases are especially likely to have low external validity. Would other people injured in the same way as N.A. display the same personality changes and, most importantly, the same memory deficits? Proponents of case study research note that the answer to such a question depends on the particular case being studied (Flyvbjerg, 2006). In some instances, for example, a researcher may attempt to select cases for study that, based on some measurable criterion, appear to be typical of a broader population. Still, in any study, there is always a risk that the sample of people studied may be atypical, even highly atypical, of the population from which they are drawn. This is more likely to happen with a sample of one person or a few people rather than many people, but it's essential to remember that this doesn't necessarily mean the results from a particular case study will fail to generalize. As with other types of studies, psychological principles suggested by case studies need to be validated by further research.

Another potential limitation of case studies, **observer bias,** *occurs when researchers have expectations or other predispositions that distort their observations.* For example, two researchers with different theoretical frameworks and expectations might selectively focus their attention on different behaviors or perceive the same behaviors differently. The latter point is analogous to how our brains can organize different perceptions of the same physical stimulus, as happens with so-called ambiguous or reversible stimuli (see **Figure 6.4**).

Researchers' expectations can also influence the behavior of the people they are studying. In experiments and some

Necker cube

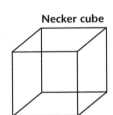

This image can be viewed in different ways.

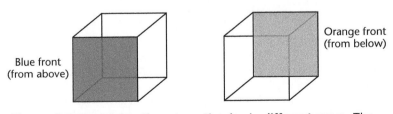

Blue front (from above)

Orange front (from below)

Figure 6.4 Perceiving the same stimulus in different ways. The Necker cube illusion illustrates that it is possible to perceive the same physical stimulus in multiple ways. Look at the top drawing. Are you able to perceive the cube as if looking down at it, and also as if looking up at it? The cube will have a different front face, depending on your perception.

other types of research, procedures can be used that will reduce the influence of such biases. For example, researchers can have trained assistants observe participants, and those assistants can be kept "blind"—uninformed—about the hypotheses being investigated. But in many case studies, the strong reliance on the researcher's direct observations, and the prolonged and often intensive direct contact between the researcher and participant (e.g., in clinical case studies where the researcher also is the therapist), enhance the potential influence of observer bias.

The potential ethical difficulty of maintaining participant anonymity is an important issue across many types of research, but especially so in case study research. First, a wealth of detailed information, some or much of it highly personal, may be collected about the case. Second, the large amount of detail presented in the research report may increase the risk that other people—especially "insiders" such as other members of a group—will be able to piece together the identity of the case (Crowe et al., 2011). The case study researcher needs to consider these risks carefully, take strong precautions to prevent the loss of anonymity, and specify the nature of any social risk when obtaining participants' informed consent.

 CONCEPT CHECK 6.1 CASE STUDIES

Decide whether each statement is true or false. Answers appear at the end of the chapter on page 206.

1. A case study can involve more than one person; it can be a study of a family or larger social unit.
2. A limitation of case studies is that their results do not allow clear causal conclusions to be drawn.
3. In certain instances, the results of one case study can disconfirm a hypothesis or currently accepted scientific "fact."
4. Major concerns about case studies include the potential for observer bias and the risk of poor external validity.

OBSERVATIONAL RESEARCH

Learning Objectives

After studying this section, you should be able to:

- Discuss basic characteristics and purposes of observational research.
- Identify and illustrate different types of observational research, and explain the pros and cons of each.
- Illustrate different ways that observational researchers record behavior.
- Explain different types of sampling used in observational research.
- Discuss limitations of observational research.

The term **observational research** *encompasses different types of nonexperimental studies in which behavior is systematically watched and recorded.* After discussing the basic characteristics and benefits of observational research, we'll examine several types of observational studies, approaches used to sample and record observations, and concerns about observing behavior.

BASIC CHARACTERISTICS

In most observational studies, researchers measure the behavior of multiple people or nonhuman animals, either in real time as the behavior unfolds or upon reviewing electronic records (e.g., video recordings) of the behavior. As with case studies, some researchers who conduct observational studies adopt a qualitative approach, in which the goal is to achieve a holistic description and understanding of behavior primarily through nonstatistical means. Others take a quantitative approach that relies heavily on numerical measurements and statistical analyses to describe and

Clive Bromhall/Oxford Scientific/Getty Images

Figure 6.5 The hammer/anvil technique. Some communities of chimpanzees have learned the hammer/anvil technique to crack open nuts. A heavy piece of wood or a stone is used as a hammer, and a relatively flat stone is used as an anvil, on top of which the nut is placed.

understand behavior. Researchers may also combine these in a mixed-methods approach, as the following study illustrates.

Beginning with anthropologist Jane Goodall's (1986) pioneering observational research of chimpanzee communities in their natural habitats, studies have found that we humans are not the only primates to use tools. Psychologists, anthropologists, and other scientists have seen chimpanzees crumple up leaves to mop up ants, use leaf spines to fish inside small openings for termites, and use sticks to dig for insects (Whiten et al., 2001). Christophe Boesch (1991) observed chimpanzees living in a rain forest in Ivory Coast, focusing on one type of tool use: the hammer/anvil technique, in which chimpanzees use a piece of wood or a stone as a hammer to crack nuts that they place on an anvil (e.g., a tree root or a flat stone). This technique takes up to 10 years for a chimpanzee to master (see **Figure 6.5**).

In observing the Ivory Coast chimpanzees, Boesch's goal was to examine whether mothers help their young acquire this hammer/anvil technique. Boesch defined three potential types of maternal influence: (1) stimulation (e.g., a mother leaves some nuts next to the anvil, increasing the opportunity for an infant to use its hammer); (2) facilitation (e.g., a mother lets her infant use her own hammer, which typically has a better weight and shape than the infant's); and (3) active teaching (e.g., an infant is experiencing a problem with the technique and the mother demonstrates how to do it correctly).

The quantitative aspect of Boesch's (1991) approach is seen in his statistical analyses conducted to examine the association between different types of maternal influence and the infants' ages. Boesch gathered data on 19 chimpanzee mothers, each with one offspring ranging in age from less than 1 year to 8 years. In approximately 70 hours of observation, he recorded 387 instances of stimulation and 588 of facilitation. Boesch found that maternal assistance in the form of stimulation peaked when the infants reached age 3, at which time they are just beginning to acquire basic nut-cracking skills. Maternal facilitation peaked among 5-year-olds.

The qualitative aspect of this research is illustrated by Boesch's (1991) reliance on the content of his personal observations in ways that the numbers alone do not capture. To support his conclusions, he provides examples that describe instances and contexts of maternal assistance. The most detailed descriptions are devoted to the two instances in which Boesch concluded that active maternal teaching had occurred. Here's a portion of one description involving a mother and her 5-year-old, whom researchers named Ricci and Nina. The daughter, Nina, was struggling mightily with different hammer grips in a vain effort to crack a nut:

> After 8 min of this struggle, Ricci joined her and Nina immediately gave her the hammer. Then, with Nina sitting in front of her, Ricci, in a very deliberate manner, slowly rotated the hammer into the best position with which to pound the nut effectively. As if to emphasize . . . this movement, it took her a full minute to perform this simple rotation. With Nina watching her, she then proceeded to . . . crack 10 nuts. . . . Then Ricci left and Nina resumed cracking. Now, by adopting the same hammer grip as her mother, she succeeded in opening four nuts in 15 min. . . . In this example, the mother corrected an error in her daughter's behaviour and Nina seemingly understood this perfectly, since she continued to maintain the grip demonstrated to her. (Boesch, 1991, p. 532)

From "Teaching Among Wild Chimpanzees," by C. Boesch, 1991, *Animal Behaviour, 41*(3), p. 532. Copyright 1991 Elsevier. Reprinted by permission.

Boesch concluded that the mothers in this chimpanzee community demonstrated concern about their offspring's tool learning and varied their guidance techniques according to their offspring's age. We'll come back to this point later in the chapter, when discussing some concerns about observational research.

WHY CONDUCT OBSERVATIONAL RESEARCH?

Like case studies, observational research is well suited to describing behavior. Because it involves recording the behavior of many participants, observational research affords excellent opportunities to examine relations among variables. For example, by observing 19 mother–offspring chimpanzee pairs in which the offspring varied in age, Boesch (1991) was able to examine whether there was an association between offsprings' age and the frequency of maternal stimulation and facilitation of tool use. If, instead, Boesch had conducted a case study of one or two mother–offspring pairs, he would have had to follow those pairs for years in order to examine whether the overall frequency of maternal stimulation and facilitation varied as each infant aged. Any findings might have been idiosyncratic to those one or two particular mother–offspring pairs.

As another example, suppose you are studying human children and seeking to find out whether an association exists between children's gender and the frequency with which they bully or are bullied. You would be better off observing bullying behavior among several groups of children, as opposed to conducting a case study of one girl and one boy.

Both in describing behavior and in examining relations among naturally occurring variables, observational research can be exploratory or—as we'll see shortly—it can be used to test hypotheses and theories. Moreover, although observational research is poorly suited to drawing clear causal conclusions, observational findings may suggest possible causal relations that can subsequently be examined using controlled laboratory experiments. Observational studies also help to establish the generalizability of principles previously discovered in experiments. Finally, when practical and ethical constraints make it difficult or impossible to conduct experiments on a particular issue, observational studies often remain a viable approach for gathering information.

TYPES OF OBSERVATIONAL RESEARCH

Observational studies vary in the naturalness of their settings (e.g., a city street or tropical rain forest vs. a laboratory or zoo), in whether participants are aware or unaware that their behavior is being observed, and in the degree to which the observer intervenes in the situation (such as avoiding or interacting with participants). Of the many possible types of observational studies, we'll examine five here: naturalistic observation (disguised and undisguised), participant observation (disguised and undisguised), and structured observation.

Naturalistic Observation

As young children and their parents entered a children's science museum, a researcher approached them. Video cameras and wireless microphones had been temporarily installed at 18 museum exhibits, and the researcher asked for the family's consent to video-record them. Then the family explored some "hands-on" exhibits, which demonstrated principles from several sciences, including psychology. Each exhibit was simple enough for the children to manipulate by themselves.

In video recordings made on 26 days spread out over a period of 2.5 years, Kevin Crowley and his fellow researchers focused on the conversations that parents had with their 1- through 8-year-olds as the children interacted with the exhibits (Crowley, Callanan, Tenenbaum, &

Table 6.1 Coding Parent–Child Interactions at a Science Museum

Behavior	Definition	Example
Explanation	Parent talks about "causal connections within the exhibit interface. . . , relations between observed phenomena and more general principles. . . , or analogies to related phenomena."	"You see all those colors because the bubble reflects different kinds of light."
Giving directions	Parent gives "directions on exhibit use."	"Put your hands on those sensors."
Talking about evidence	Parent speaks about something that is observable, but the statement does not include an explanation.	"There's the crankshaft!"

Source: Information from "Parents Explain More Often to Boys Than to Girls During Shared Scientific Thinking," by K. Crowley, M. A. Callanan, H. R. Tenenbaum, & E. Allen, 2001, *Psychological Science, 12*(3), p. 259. Copyright 2001 by the American Psychological Society.

Allen, 2001). In particular, they were interested in whether parents would exhibit a gender bias by providing fewer explanations of scientific principles to their daughters than to their sons. The researchers reasoned that if a gender bias exists in family settings where children informally learn about science, this might be one factor contributing to the gender gap in American children's science achievement, in which girls on average fall behind boys.

Crowley and his colleagues (2001) analyzed parent–child interactions from 298 families, and as **Table 6.1** shows, they recorded how frequently parents made three types of comments to the children. They also recorded whether a parent or child initiated each interaction with an exhibit, whether the child actively manipulated the exhibit, and whether the parents' remarks were a response to a question asked by the child. The results were dramatic. Overall:

- Boys and girls did not differ significantly in how often they initiated contact with the exhibits, and almost all the boys and girls actively manipulated the exhibits.

- No gender bias occurred in how often parents gave instructions or talked about evidence to their sons and daughters.

- In contrast, regardless of the children's age or which parent was present, boys were much more likely than girls to receive explanations (see **Figure 6.6**).

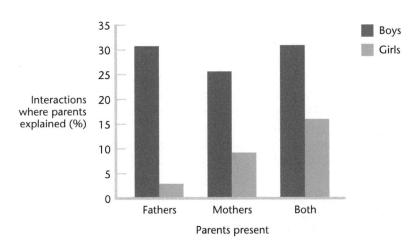

Figure 6.6 Naturalistic observation in a children's museum. No matter whether only the father, only the mother, or both parents were present, boys received substantially more scientific explanations from their parents than girls. (Crowley, K., Callanan, M. A., Tenenbaum, H. R., & Allen, E. (2001). Parents explain more often to boys than to girls during shared scientific thinking. *Psychological Science, 12*(3), pp. 258-261.)

- Finally—and importantly—the gender bias did not occur because boys asked their parents questions more often than did girls; in general, few children asked questions.

This study by Crowley and his colleagues (2001) illustrates a research approach called **naturalistic observation,** *in which researchers passively observe behavior in a natural setting.* The word *passively* means that researchers try to avoid direct involvement with the individuals who are being observed. In the science museum study, the researchers' only interaction with them was to obtain their informed consent to participate. When parents and children interacted at the exhibits, the researchers were not involved with them.

Disguised Versus Undisguised Naturalistic Observation. Naturalistic observation can be classified as **disguised versus undisguised observation,** *based on whether the individuals being studied are aware that they are being observed.* The science museum study is an example of *undisguised naturalistic observation:* The fact that participants were being observed was not hidden from them, and video cameras and wireless microphones were placed at the exhibits. Other examples of undisguised naturalistic observation occur in studies where researchers are visible while passively observing animals in the wild, or children in their homes or at school (Karasik, Adolph, Tamis-LeMonda, & Zuckerman, 2012).

Disguised naturalistic observation occurs when individuals are not aware of the observer's presence. For example, Martin Remland and his colleagues wanted to examine cross-cultural differences in people's "interpersonal space," that zone of "private space" around our bodies that each of us maintains when interacting with other people (Remland, Jones, & Brinkman, 1995). In your own experiences, when you talk one-on-one with another person, you have probably encountered some people who stand closer to you or who touch you more often than others. Remland and his colleagues set out to test the hypothesis that people from southern European countries have smaller interpersonal space boundaries than people from northern European countries. They video-recorded 386 instances of two people (adults or older teens) standing and talking with one another. Each social interaction took place at a shopping mall, or near a train or bus station, in one of several small to moderately sized cities in England, France, Greece, Ireland, Italy, the Netherlands, or Scotland.

The recordings were made in a disguised manner, so people would not be aware that they were being observed, and the findings only partially supported the researcher's hypothesis. As expected, touch occurred in a significantly greater percentage of Greek (32%) and Italian (24%) dyads than among English (11%), French (8%), or Dutch (4%) dyads; but contrary to the hypothesis, touch did not occur in significantly more Greek and Italian dyads than Scottish (18%) and Irish (17%) dyads. Also contrary to the hypothesis, for the dependent variable of standing distance, it was the Irish and Scots who stood closest to one another, and no statistically significant differences in distance were found among the other cultural groups.

Advantages and Disadvantages. One advantage of naturalistic observation is that, by definition, it examines behavior under what are sometimes called "ecologically valid" conditions. One aspect of ecological validity addresses the similarity between the research setting and settings that occur in real life. With naturalistic observation, the research setting is "real life." Disguised naturalistic observation has the added advantage that the behaviors observed have not (in principle) been distorted by the presence of the observer.

Typically, the far more important issue is whether the findings obtained from naturalistic observation will have external validity. Do parents give more scientific explanations to boys than to girls in other contexts, such as when their children watch science shows on television or do science homework? Does this gender bias in scientific explanation occur in families representing various ethnic or cultural groups? Does Remland et al.'s (1995) cross-cultural finding that urban Greeks and Italians are more likely than urban English, French, and Dutch to engage in touch while conversing apply to people from the countryside? Does it apply to settings other than malls, train stations, and bus stations? It is often assumed that just because people are initially studied in a real-world setting rather than in a laboratory, the findings will automatically have greater external validity. To be sure, with naturalistic research we know from the start that the findings apply to at least one real-world setting, which is something we can't say about findings from a laboratory experiment. But ultimately, the external validity of both observational and experimental findings needs to be established by conducting new studies in diverse settings and with different populations.

The chief disadvantages of naturalistic observation stem from the complexity of behavior, the lack of control over the research setting, and the practical difficulties of observing every important behavior that takes place. Many factors are likely to influence participants' behavior at any given time, and the observer does not have the ability to control the research setting in order to isolate some factors while holding others constant. If observations are being recorded live, as behavior is unfolding, it will usually be impossible to observe all participants and everything they do. Even if observations are video- or audio-recorded so that they can be examined and reexamined, the sheer volume of behavioral responses to record may be overwhelming. Therefore, as we'll discuss later, the researcher will need to sample certain individuals, certain times, certain types of behaviors, or all of the above.

Conducting observational research of any type also involves ethical issues. As discussed in Chapter 3, under most circumstances researchers must obtain people's voluntary informed consent prior to studying them. The American Psychological Association (APA) Ethics Code permits naturalistic observation research without informed consent (making disguised observation possible) if several conditions are met:

1. The study is not expected to cause participants harm or distress;
2. confidential information is protected; and
3. if participants' responses were to become known, this would not expose them to social, economic, or legal risks (APA, 2010a).

Additional ethical requirements govern disguised video and audio recording. (See Appendix B, Sections 8.02, 8.03, and 8.05, for more details about informed consent.)

Finally, undisguised naturalistic observation enhances the risk that the observer's presence will cause participants to alter their behavior. This problem, called **reactivity,** *occurs when the process of observing (or otherwise measuring) behavior causes that behavior to change.* Even if the observer is not physically present, if participants are aware that their behavior is being recorded, they may not act naturally. Fortunately, as you'll see later in the chapter, there are techniques that researchers can use to minimize reactivity.

Participant Observation

Researchers who conduct naturalistic observations attempt to avoid interacting with their subjects. In contrast, with **participant observation,** *the observer becomes a part of the group or social setting being studied.* The thought of a cultural anthropologist or sociologist living among remote tribal villagers may be the first image that crosses your mind when you think of participant observation. In fact, however, participant observation has been used to study behavior in a great variety of settings, including psychiatric hospitals, climbing expeditions on Mount Everest, senior living centers, and gambling locations (Griffiths, 2011).

Disguised Participant Observation. In 2005, national surveys indicated that about one quarter of adults in the United States, and one fifth of adults in Canada and Great Britain, believed that space aliens have already visited Earth (Lyons, 2005, November 1). Back in the 1950s, Mrs. Keech was among the believers. Who was Mrs. Keech? A homemaker living in Chicago, she was the leader of a small UFO cult. Mrs. Keech (a cover name substituted by researchers) told her followers that aliens from the planet "Clarion" had repeatedly traveled to Earth in flying saucers. What's more, through mental telepathy, these aliens had been sending messages to her that she recorded through "automatic writing." And the latest messages weren't good; they foretold that in several months, on December 21, 1954, a catastrophic flood would destroy much of North America. But there was hope: Mrs. Keech told her followers that the aliens would arrive at her house on the midnight before the flood and take them all to safety in their flying saucer. Some highly committed believers sold their possessions and left their jobs to prepare for their Doomsday rescue.

When social psychologist Leon Festinger heard about this cult and its prophecy, he and two colleagues conducted a participant observation study that has since become a classic (Festinger, Riecken, & Schachter, 1956). They joined the cult, without revealing that they were researchers, and made notes of their observations as the predicted Doomsday supposedly approached. The purpose of their study was to provide a real-life test of a theory that Festinger was formulating, the *theory of cognitive dissonance.* Its essential premise is this: People have a psychological need for their cognitions to be consistent with one another. When two cognitions are inconsistent, people will experience an unpleasant psychological state of tension that Festinger called "cognitive dissonance." In the case of the UFO cult, inconsistent cognitions might be: "I wholeheartedly trust Mrs. Keech and the Clarions" versus "The Clarions didn't show up as foretold."

Dissonance theory would go on to become a highly influential social psychological theory; one reason for its appeal was that it made predictions that were supported by research, but that also seemed to fly in the face of everyday common sense. In this case, starting with the assumption that there would be no Clarions and no cataclysmic flood, Festinger accurately predicted that following this failed prophecy, Mrs. Keech and the cult members—rather than disband in the face of reality—would instead reduce dissonance by increasing their efforts to recruit new members, thereby validating the legitimacy of the group.

Festinger et al.'s (1956) study is an example of disguised participant observation: The researchers became a part of the group they were studying and they withheld from other group members the fact that they were observing the group's behavior for scientific purposes. Their method raises two important issues:

- How might their presence in the group have influenced the group's behavior, particularly given the group's relatively small size? Might a smaller group have disbanded? The researchers' account, detailed in their book *When Prophecy Fails,* makes this seem unlikely, but of course there is no way to know for sure.

- No informed consent was obtained from the cult members, and deception clearly occurred due the fact that the researchers pretended to be believers and withheld the true purpose of their presence in the group. APA's first set of ethical guidelines for psychologists had just been released in 1953. Was Festinger et al.'s research method ethical?

Similar ethical issues were involved in a study by psychologist David Rosenhan (1973), published in the journal *Science* under the title "On Being Sane in Insane Places." Along with the Festinger et al. (1956) study about the UFO cult, Rosenhan's is one of the most famous disguised participant observation studies in psychology. To gain insights into the experience of being an institutionalized psychiatric patient, and to address "the question of whether the sane can be distinguished from the insane" (p. 251), Rosenhan and seven other mentally healthy people gained admittance to a total of 12 hospitals by falsely reporting that they were hearing voices. Once admitted, they stopped reporting any symptoms and acted "normally" for the duration of their stay, making observations and taking notes about their experiences. Rosenhan addressed the necessity of the deception by noting, "However distasteful such concealment is, it was a necessary first step to examining these questions. Without conceal-ment, there would have been no way to know how valid these experiences were. . ." (p. 258).

And what were the pseudopatients' experiences? Rosenhan reported that in 11 of the 12 cases, the pseudopatients were diagnosed as schizophrenic; that on average they were kept in the hospital for 19 days, with a range of 7 to 52 days; and that many of the actual psychiatric patients recognized that the researcher-pseudopatients were behaving normally, whereas the staff failed to recognize this. Rosenhan's conclusion that psychiatric diagnosis was invalid drew heated criticism from psychologists and psychiatrists, much of it detailed in rebuttals to Rosenhan's work published in a 1975 issue of the *Journal of Abnormal Psychology* (Spitzer, 1975).

Undisguised Participant Observation. Both disguised and undisguised participant obser-vation run the risk that the researcher's presence in the group—and likely interactions with group members—may influence the group's behavior. Undisguised participant observation, however, avoids the ethical issue of deception that arises when researchers conceal their iden-tity. The tradeoff concerns whether participants' explicit knowledge that this "new person among us" is a researcher will, by itself, cause participants to become more self-conscious and alter their behavior.

Undisguised participant observation is often combined with other methods of gathering data directly from participants. (After all, the participants already know about the research-er's presence.) For example, **ethnography** *is a qualitative research approach that often com-bines participant observation with interviews to gain an integrative description of social groups.* A key goal of ethnography, which is used by psychologists, sociologists, and anthropologists, is to explore the contexts in which behaviors occur and the meaning of those behaviors as perceived by group members (Suzuki, Ahluwalia, Mattis, & Quizon, 2005). Results from eth-nographic research typically are described in a narrative, storylike form, rather than through statistical analyses of numeric data.

For example, sociologist Susan Rosenbloom and developmental psychologist Niobi Way (2004) used undisguised participant observation and interviews to examine ethnic discrimination at an urban high school composed almost entirely of Latino (48%), Asian American (36%), and African American (15%) students. Rosenbloom had previously worked at the school and assisted a teacher during part of this study. For over half a year, she observed interactions in hallways and several classrooms, and at extracurricular func-tions. Rosenbloom and Way found that, among the 20 Latino and 20 African American students who were interviewed, discrimination was perceived primarily in their interac-tions with adults. The students felt that the police harassed them, and that the police and shopkeepers didn't trust them and exposed them to extreme surveillance. They believed that teachers had low expectations of them, didn't care about them, and made deroga-tory remarks. Participant observations—which were limited to school-related settings—supported the conclusion that some teachers discriminated against Latino and African American students.

Interestingly, none of the 20 Asian American students interviewed (almost all of whom were of Chinese descent) reported discrimination by adults. Instead, they focused on fre-quent physical and verbal harassment from Latino and African American students. Partici-pant observations indicated many instances where Asian American students were subjected to ethnic slurs and, seemingly at random, were given quick "pop" slaps to the head by non-Asian male and female students. Asian American students talked of being pushed, punched, and teased as "geeks"; the researchers' observations confirmed all these behaviors on the part of the non-Asian students.

Based on their qualitative analysis, which also included discussions with teachers, Rosenbloom and Way (2004) proposed that teachers' discriminatory treatment of African

American and Latino students—and their more favorable treatment and expectations of Asian American students—helped set the stage for ethnic conflicts within the school by pitting the different ethnic groups against one another. At the same time, Rosenbloom and Way noted that the students expressed beliefs in the ideal of equality. As one student put it, "I just feel that everybody's the same no matter what [race] they are" (p. 441). Students also described cross-ethnic friendships, with one saying, "Well, I get along with everybody, you know. It's like, the friends I have, they don't have to be a certain color. . . . I don't care where they're from" (p. 442). Ironically, however, the authors noted that just as students argued against stereotypes of their own ethnic group, they nevertheless applied stereotypes to the other ethnic groups at the school.

Advantages and Disadvantages. To researchers who value participant observation, its key benefit is the opportunity to study people's behavior from the viewpoint of an insider. Compared to naturalistic observation, participant observation provides a greater opportunity to gain insights about the personal meaning of behavior to group members, particularly when the observation is undisguised and the researcher is thus free to supplement observations with interviews or other data collection methods. As for disguised participant observation, in some situations it may be the only way for psychologists to gain access to a group. For example, it's difficult to see how Festinger and his colleagues (1956) could have gained access to a secretive UFO cult without posing as members.

Compared to naturalistic observers, however, participant observers—whether disguised or undisguised—run a greater risk of influencing the behavior they are studying because their involvement in the situation is more active. The fact that participant observers are interacting with group members, and doing so for time periods that may last for months or even a few years, also raises the risk of losing objectivity and can make it difficult to maintain appropriate boundaries with group members. Counseling psychologist Liza Suzuki and her colleagues (Suzuki et al., 2005), focusing on ethnographic research (in which undisguised participant observation is a key ingredient), sum up the issue well:

> There are often difficulties in establishing and maintaining distance, given prolonged contact with participants and the close relationship that may need to be established in order for researchers to establish trust with participants. Despite this, the ethnographer is expected to establish and maintain substantive and genuine relationships with participants, be ever mindful that their goal is to create scientifically rigorous scholarship, and be careful not to cross lines of intimacy that would compromise the integrity of their scholarly work. (Suzuki et al., 2005, p. 207)

Structured Observation

In **structured observation,** *a researcher fully or partly configures the setting in which behavior will be observed.* For example, unlike what takes place in naturalistic observation, the researcher may present participants with specific tasks, or expose them to a social situation that the researcher has created, and observe their responses. These tasks and situations are often designed to be analogues—representations—of circumstances that occur naturally. In such cases, this type of structured observation is sometimes called *analogue behavioral observation.*

Suppose we want to test a hypothesis that parenting behaviors play a role in why children develop high or low levels of achievement motivation. As a first step in testing our hypothesis, we plan to observe how parents and children interact while the children perform achievement tasks (e.g., attempt to solve novel puzzles). So, with parental permission (and the children's agreement), we use psychological tests to identify children who have relatively high or low achievement motivation.

Figure 6.7 An example of structured (analogue behavioral) observation. A mother interacts with her daughter during a task situation created by the researcher.

Next, to examine parent–child interactions, we could try to observe the children in their homes, wait for naturally occurring instances when they perform achievement tasks (e.g., homework or video games), and hope that the parents interact with their children during these tasks. Depending on the family, however, perhaps it will be days or weeks before an appropriate situation to observe occurs spontaneously. Using structured observation instead, we would create a situation in which we bring together parents and their children, give the children achievement tasks, and ask the parents and children to interact in any way they wish (see **Figure 6.7**).

The structured setting could be a laboratory or the families' homes. In either location, we could video-record the parent–child interactions for later coding and analysis. Even if the study is done at the families' homes, it would still be structured observation; because we are determining the tasks and times for the parent–child interactions, it would not be naturalistic observation. It would not be participant observation, either, because once the session begins, we would only observe. And, it would not be an experiment because we are not manipulating any independent variables. We are examining whether parent–child interactions differ depending on whether the children have higher or lower achievement motivation, but we are not manipulating the children's achievement motivation; we are only measuring it and examining it for possible associations with parent–child interactions.

Advantages and Limitations. In general, compared to naturalistic and participant observation, the chief advantages of structured observation are greater efficiency and control. By structuring the observational setting, the researcher can expose participants to the same tasks, make things happen at a specific time and place, and save time and money by eliminating potentially long waits for the target behaviors to occur spontaneously. Moreover, if the setting is a laboratory, this exposes all participants to the same physical environment and eliminates sources of distraction (e.g., siblings, visitors, or calls to the families' homes) that might interrupt the observation process or affect participants' behavior.

To some, the chief disadvantage of structured observation arises from the fact that the setting, especially in the laboratory, is only an analogue of real life. This raises the question: Do the patterns of behavior and the associations between variables that were observed under structured circumstances represent what actually occurs under natural circumstances? Moreover, structured observation is rarely disguised, which increases the potential for reactivity to occur.

Structured observation has a long history in many psychological subfields. Developmental psychologists use structured observation to study children's cognitive, social, and emotional development; examine parent–child interactions; and gain insight into how parenting behaviors might contribute to the development of children's psychological traits (Piaget, 1927/1930; Volbrecht & Goldsmith, 2010). They also use structured observation to study child–child interactions. For example, in everyday life, children diagnosed as having cognitive disabilities often have difficulty gaining peer acceptance. Developmental psychologist Beverly J. Wilson (1999) created an analogue play entry situation to examine specific social skills of children diagnosed as cognitively delayed (IQ scores ranging from 50 to 85) or nondelayed (IQ 95 to 127). Each child was led into a room where two other children were

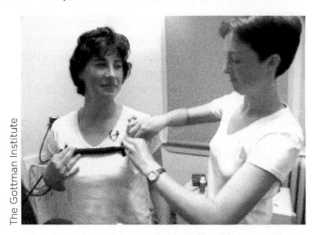

Figure 6.8 Structured (analogue behavioral) observation of marital interaction. In married couples, equipment is attached to each partner so that physiological responses can be recorded while the couples are interacting. Each couple is led into a room, seated, and then asked to talk about two important sources of disagreement in their relationship. While physiological measures are taken, their conversation is video- and audio-recorded. Researchers subsequently analyze these recordings, trying to identify patterns of behavior that predict marital satisfaction or dissatisfaction, and continuation of the relationship versus divorce (Gottman, Coan, Carrere, & Swanson, 1998).

interacting (e.g., playing together with toys). These other children were actually confederates who (according to plan) repeatedly rebuffed the child's attempts to join in and then eventually accepted the child into the group.

Wilson (1999) found that, as compared to children who did not have cognitive delays, children with cognitive delays were more intrusive when they tried to join in. For example, their timing was poorer; they were less likely to wait for a break in other children's interaction before trying to enter the situation. In further research, B. J. Wilson and her colleagues used this analogue play entry setting to observe children who had conduct and social problems (B. J. Wilson, Petaja, Stevens, Mitchell, & Peterson, 2011). After initial rejection by the two playmates, children who had better attention skills and more emotional control were better able to persist in their attempts to join the play group.

In a similar vein, clinical and health psychologists have used structured observation to identify patterns of behavior in adults that may contribute to good versus poor psychological and social functioning. For example, imagine coming into the laboratory with a dating partner or spouse. Your task will be straightforward: The two of you are asked to talk about one or more relationship issues on which you disagree. You choose the issues. While you're talking, the researchers video-record the interaction and measure your stress hormones and other indices of physiological arousal (**Figure 6.8**). Later, the researchers code and analyze the content of your discussions and your facial expressions. Using this procedure, psychologists have identified many differences in how happily and unhappily married or dating partners interact with one another (Robles, Shaffer, Malarkey, & Kiecolt-Glaser, 2006). In one structured observation study, using the data collected from newlywed couples, the researchers were able to predict with 83% accuracy which couples would be divorced 6 years later (Gottman, Coan, Carrere, & Swanson, 1998).

RECORDING OBSERVATIONS

Observations of behavior can be recorded in many ways. A researcher may use one approach or combine several.

Bill Aron/Photo Edit

Figure 6.9 Field notes summarize a researcher's impressions. A child psychologist records field notes while observing children in a Los Angeles playground.

Narrative Records and Field Notes

In observational research, detailed descriptions of behavior typically come from narrative records or field notes. *Narrative records* provide an ongoing description of behavior that is used for later analysis. Using a laptop computer, old-fashioned pen and paper, a voice recorder, or some other device, an observer writes down or narrates an extensive, continuous description of participants' behavior as it unfolds. Narrative records also come in the form of video and audio recordings of participants' behavior during observation sessions, from which transcripts of behavior can later be generated and analyzed. In general, *field notes* are less comprehensive than narrative records; observers use them to record important impressions or instances of behavior (**Figure 6.9**). In some cases, field notes are written soon after observation is finished rather than while it is in progress.

Narrative records are used for both qualitative and quantitative analyses. For example, educational psychologist Diane Kellegrew (2000) studied mothers whose 2-year-old children had disabilities such as Down's syndrome or cerebral palsy. Kellegrew combined interviews with videotaped sessions of naturalistic observations at home to examine how mothers developed self-care routines (getting dressed, eating meals, etc.) for their children and used these routines as opportunities to socialize their children. Kellegrew adopted a qualitative approach in her research "because this form of inquiry is uniquely suited to explore the ways in which people make meaning and negotiate their lives" (p. 254).

Kellegrew (2000) created narrative records by developing transcripts of the interviews and of segments of the videotapes that captured daily routines. She then coded information from the transcripts in terms of the type of daily routine, the people who were present, the goals the mothers were trying to achieve, and other meanings that the situation held for the mothers. Rather than present statistical analyses of coded data, qualitatively oriented researchers typically examine their data visually to identify patterns and themes. When Kellegrew did this, it enabled her to paint a picture of how self-care routines evolved and functioned within the lives of the family.

As we first saw in Chapter 2 (see Table 2.1, p. 48), qualitative analyses often include quotes from participants that illustrate key themes. For example, one mother, who worked during the day and relied on her own mother (the child's grandmother) to care for the child during the day, commented:

> She [the grandmother] doesn't expect him to do anything. She doesn't think he can do certain things, mostly self-help skills. I don't know that I agree with it. But, I can't be there really to teach him lessons. I've come to the realization that certain things are not worth fighting over. Certain things I am particular about. Those are the things I will fight for. (Kellegrew, 2000, p. 256)

Compare the flavor of that quote with one from another mother:

> I just expect things and whether or not she can do them or not, I at least expect her to try. Like I ask her to make the bed, and if Karen at least tries to tug on it, I know she's comprehending that I want her to do something with the bed. (Kellegrew, 2000, p. 257)

Behavioral Coding Systems

Behavioral coding systems, *which involve classifying participants' responses into mutually exclusive categories,* are a major component of many observational studies. Let's consider an example. When you were growing up, did you participate or know someone who participated in organized youth sports? In the United States, about 44 million 5- to 18-year-olds do (National Council on Youth Sports, 2008). In Canada, about 60% of 3- to 17-year-olds participate in organized sports (Solutions Research Group, 2014, June 10). Back in the 1970s, enrollment in youth sports programs mushroomed and younger children began participating. Most coaches were parents who volunteered but had no training as coaches. Not much was known about how coaches treated children or the psychological consequences of sports competition on children.

Personality psychologist Ron Smith and his colleagues (Smith, Smoll, & Hunt, 1977) developed a coding system to assess the game behaviors of Little League Baseball coaches (see **Table 6.2**). The broadest distinction exists between spontaneous coaching behaviors and coaches' reactions to things players do. In turn, these reactions are broken down into responses to players' desirable performance, responses to players' mistakes, and responses to

Table 6.2 Coding the Behavior of Youth Sports Coaches: The Coaching Behavior Assessment System[1]

Reactive Coaching Behaviors	
Behavior	**Definition**
Responses to Desirable Performance	
1. Reinforcement	Positive, rewarding verbal/nonverbal reactions to good plays or good effort
2. Nonreinforcement	Failure to respond to a good performance
Responses to Mistakes	
3. Encouragement after a mistake	A positive, consoling reaction to a player following a mistake
4. Technical instruction after a mistake	Instructing a player how to correct a mistake that he or she just made
5. Punishment	A negative verbal/nonverbal reaction following a mistake
6. Punitive technical instruction	Technical instruction, following a mistake, given in a harsh or sarcastic manner
7. Ignoring a mistake	Failure to respond to a player's mistake
Response to Misbehavior	
8. Keeping control	Reactions intended to restore or maintain order among team members
Spontaneous Coaching Behaviors	
Behavior	**Definition**
Game Related	
9. General technical instruction	Spontaneous instruction in the techniques and strategies of the sport (not following a mistake)
10. General encouragement	Spontaneous encouragement that does not follow a mistake
11. Organization	Administrative behaviors that set the stage for play (e.g., assigning responsibilities, positions)
Game-Irrelevant	
12. General communication	Interactions with players unrelated to the game

[1] The 12 specific behaviors coded within this system are consecutively numbered.

Source: From "Scrutinizing the Skipper: A Study of Leadership Behavior in the Dugout," by B. Curtis, R. E. Smith, & F. L. Smoll, 1979, *Journal of Applied Psychology, 64,* p. 393. Copyright 1979 by the American Psychological Association. Modified with permission. Use does not imply endorsement.

players' misbehavior. Spontaneous coaching behaviors are broken down into those that are game related or are game irrelevant. Several categories have further subdivisions, resulting in a total of 12 categories.

During a game, each time a coach directs a behavior toward a player, an observer could use a behavior tally sheet (a type of behavior checklist) to mark that behavior down within one of the 12 categories. So, for example, if a player makes an error fielding a ground ball and the coach says, "Johnny, next time remember to bend deeper at the knees," this would be marked as an instance of "technical instruction after a mistake." If instead the coach said, "Johnny, you never listen! How many times do I have to tell you to bend deeper at the knees!," this would be classified as punitive technical instruction because it conveys technical information but in a punitive way. If you have ever played youth sports, many of these categories will no doubt seem familiar.

It takes a great deal of work to develop a reliable and valid coding system. Among other things, the coding categories must be clear and mutually exclusive, and the observers well trained, so that different observers watching the same behavior will assign it the same codes. Coding systems exist for numerous types of behavior, such as parenting behaviors, types of infant temperament, marital interactions, facial expressions, emotional responses, schoolchildren's classroom behavior, and ape behavior. Boesch's (1991) classification of chimpanzee mothers' stimulation, facilitation, and active teaching behaviors represents a three-category coding system. A coding system and the observers who use it constitute a measurement device. I'll say more about coding systems shortly.

Rating Scales, Ranking Scales, and Diaries

Observer rating and ranking scales *are used to evaluate participants' behavior or other characteristics.* In observational research, the primary observers are typically the researchers themselves or their highly trained assistants. Other people who have had the opportunity to observe participants, such as teachers and classmates of schoolchildren, may also be asked to rate or rank participants on various dimensions, such as popularity, aggressiveness, or helpfulness. *Peer nominations* ask members of a group to name fellow members who best meet some criterion. Peer nominations can be in the form of a ranking scale ("Name the most popular, second most popular, and third most popular kids in your class") but they don't have to be ("Name the most popular kids in your class").

Acting as self-observers, participants may be asked to rate or rank themselves, or to keep diaries of their behavior. A **diary** *asks participants to record their behaviors or experiences for defined periods of time or whenever certain events take place.* Thus, schoolchildren might be asked to make a diary entry once per day, week, or month; or each time they are involved in a bullying incident. Diaries may contain general and specific questions that call for unstructured responses (e.g., "Describe what you did today," "Describe any incidents in which someone teased you today"), they may include a checklist to record the frequency of certain behaviors, and they may even contain rating scales (e.g., "Overall, rate how happy you felt today").

Thus, in a study of sixth-grade school bullying by educational psychologist Anthony Pellegrini and Maria Bartini (2000), bullies and victims were identified in several ways:

- Trained observers used behavioral coding to assess how frequently each child bullied another or was the victim of bullying.

- The trained observers also used rating scales to evaluate each child (e.g., "This child bullies or threatens to get his/her own way"; p. 363).

- Teachers completed the same rating scales for each child.

- Classmates made peer nominations (e.g., they named kids who start fights, say mean things, or get picked on).

- Throughout the school year, children made monthly diary entries about bullying/victimization incidents they directly experienced.

Studies that collect data solely through participant diaries, or through ratings made by people who know the participants, are typically not considered observational research. Such research might be called a "diary study," a "questionnaire study," or a "correlational study." It is the presence of trained observers and a focus on recording ongoing behavior that make research "observational." Nevertheless, rating and ranking scales, peer nominations, diaries, and other forms of data collection (e.g., interviews) may be used to supplement narrative records, field notes, or ongoing behavioral observations (see **Figure 6.10**).

Observer Training and Reliability

Suppose that you and I are independently observing and coding the behavior of the same coach at a Little League Baseball game, using the categories shown in Table 6.2. We might be at the game, making our observations in real time. Or, we might be watching and listening to a recording of the game. Afterward, we compare our observations: You've recorded 75 instances of general encouragement, 52 of general technical instruction, three of punishment, and so on. For me, the corresponding figures are 41, 54, and 22. We're in close agreement on the amount of general technical instruction that took place, but as for encouragement and punishment, were we observing the same coach? Some of the discrepancy in our observations is likely due to random error. Perhaps at different times, each of us had a few brief lapses in attention, and therefore we each missed a few behaviors that the other saw. Observer bias may be another culprit. You and I may consistently differ in our criteria for judging what constitutes encouragement or punishment. Perhaps I'm a lot more sensitive—maybe overly sensitive—to the slightest harshness in the tone of the coach's voice and thus am more likely than you to rate the same behaviors as punitive.

For the researchers conducting the study, our data represent a problem: a lack of consistency—that is, poor reliability—in how behavior is measured by different observers. The researchers simply could not be confident of what actually occurred during the game. If such coding discrepancies occurred game after game, and across many observers, the data from the study would be useless.

Interobserver reliability (also called **interrater reliability**) *represents the degree to which independent observers show agreement in their observations.* Various statistics are used to calculate interobserver reliability, depending on the type of data being recorded and the number of observers recording the same event. For example, with coding systems like the one above, where each instance of behavior is assigned to one qualitatively different category or another (e.g., encouragement, punishment, instruction), *Cohen's kappa* is one of the most common statistics for calculating the reliability between two observers. Cohen's kappa represents the percentage of times that two observers agree, over and beyond the degree of agreement that would be expected to occur by chance (Cohen, 1960).

Obtaining high interobserver reliability requires a well-developed coding system (or other measure of behavior) and extensive observer training. Researchers may take years to develop and refine their behavioral coding systems. If the categories do not accurately reflect the types of behavior that are occurring, if each category is not clearly defined, or if the different categories of a coding system overlap, then observers will become confused about how to code certain behaviors and will more likely disagree in their coding. If there are too many categories, given the circumstances under which observers will be implementing the system, then more errors in coding are likely to occur and reliability will decrease.

SOME WAYS TO RECORD OBSERVATIONS

Narrative Records

Provide an ongoing description of behavior. Record observations longhand or shorthand, type into computer, or audiorecord narration or notes. For narrative records, may instead audio-video record behavior and then transcribe data; may supplement with field notes.

EXAMPLE: Researcher observation of work group.

Friday 3:42 p.m.:
Maria tells group,
emergency project.
All must be at office
Sat/Sun.

Robert objects. Maria
firm. Robert agrees.
Mood of group: mix of
dejection, anger.

Friday 3:42 p.m.: Maria [job supervisor] walks into room, calls for all workers' attention. Has them gather in front of her. Matter-of-factly informs them of emergency task they must complete.
Maria: The VP passed this down to me 5 minutes ago. Our company just got a chance to land a major client. We have to develop a marketing proposal and have it on the VP's desk first thing Monday.
Robert: I'm away this weekend. Big trip with the family.
Maria: Cancel it.
Robert: This isn't going to sit well with my wife.
Maria: Tell her it's on me. There's no choice.
Robert [shakes head]: I'll be here, but this stinks.

Field Notes

Record key impressions or instances of behavior. Less comprehensive than narrative records.

EXAMPLE: Researcher observation of work group.

Behavioral Coding System

Classify responses into mutually exclusive categories:

Record each instance of a behavior with a tally mark, or enter each time of day it occurs.

Use codes to record behavior sequences.

EXAMPLE: Researcher observation of a youth sport coach during a game.

A Frequency Tally

Coach Behavior	Frequency
(R): Reinforcement	~~卌~~ ~~卌~~
(NR): Nonreinforcement	~~卌~~ ~~卌~~ |||
(P): Punishment	|||

A Coding Sequence (left to right)

NR NR R NR P P R R NR R NR R R

Behavior Checklist

For a list of behaviors, place a mark to record that a behavior has occurred during a particular event or time period.

EXAMPLE: A woman participates in a job skills training program. An observer records her behavior during a simulated job interview.

Upon Meeting Interviewer:

made eye contact	✓
extended hand to greet	
stated appreciation for interview	✓
smiled	✓
did not sit until invited	✓

Rating and Ranking Scales

Evaluate a behavior (its frequency or quality) or a characteristic by rating it or ranking it.

EXAMPLE: A researcher asks elementary school teachers to rate their students.

name: Carol

Attribute	Strongly Agree	Agree	Neutral	Disagree	Strongly Disagree
Attentive in Class	1	(2)	3	4	5
Work Done on Time	1	2	(3)	4	5
Gets Along w/Classmates	(1)	2	3	4	5

Diaries

Participants describe (and may also rate) their own behaviors or experiences for a certain time period, or whenever a certain event occurs (e.g., a researcher beeps them at random times).

10/12 11:00 am Library between classes

Working on math homework. Tired due to lack of sleep and moderately anxious because I'm behind. Due tomorrow and not sure if I can complete it, or at least do a good job. mood = 4

10/12 8:45 pm Homework done! texting friend about big party in 2 weeks. Have been working on party plans for the last 20 minutes. It'll be awesome. mood = 1.

All photos: ©Charles Yuen

For example, if you are making live observations of coaches, or of parent–child or child–child interactions, you will be harder pressed to accurately code an entire rapid sequence of behaviors into 40 categories than into 10. A coding system with many categories would be more feasible when working from written transcripts, from video recordings than can be paused and reexamined, or when having the responsibility to make live recordings of only a sample of behaviors (e.g., record only a single behavior occurring at the start of each 30-second interval).

No matter how good the coding system, it will be worthless if observers aren't trained to use it properly. Training may take weeks or months. Trainees (often, college undergraduates or graduate students) typically study written or online manuals of the coding system, receive hands-on instruction either individually or in groups, and practice using the system extensively by coding behavior from video recordings or transcripts. They are then tested by being asked to code segments of videotaped or live behavior, and the reliability of their codings is assessed. Researchers typically set a minimum standard that trainees must achieve before they will be allowed to begin making actual observations, and once a study begins, reliability is periodically assessed to ensure that the observers are still using the system properly. For example, in one naturalistic observation study, observers had to attain 90% agreement in their codings from training videotapes before they were permitted to visit families' homes and record infants' behavior (Fouts, Roopnarine, Lamb, & Evans, 2012). During the data collection phase, their observations were periodically checked to make sure that reliability remained high.

SAMPLING BEHAVIOR

In observational research, it is often impossible to observe every person or nonhuman animal of interest, or even to observe a subset of participants all the time in all relevant situations. And even if behavior is video- or audio-recorded so that it can be viewed repeatedly for analysis, it typically is not possible—nor is it necessary—to detail every minute response they make. Thus, before conducting a study, researchers ask themselves some basic questions: Who will be observed, what are the key behaviors to observe, in what situations will subjects be observed, and how often and for how long will they be observed? The answers to these questions will necessitate different types of sampling, with the ultimate goal being to obtain a set of representative data.

Focal sampling *is used to select a particular member (or unit, such as a parent–infant dyad) who will be observed at any given time.* In this method, if you were observing a class of children in a schoolyard during recess, or families of monkeys, you would focus your attention on observing one child or monkey continuously for a specified time period. That time period might be short, say, 3 minutes (Pellegrini & Bartini, 2000), or much longer, such as 20 minutes (Zahed, Prudom, Snowdon, & Ziegler, 2008). During the next time period, you would then observe another focal child or monkey. With enough time relative to the size of the group, you would be able to observe each member several times, for the same or a similar total amount of time. The sequence of members selected for focal sampling could be determined randomly or chosen on some other basis.

With **scan sampling,** *at preselected times the observer rapidly scans each member of a group so that the entire group is observed within a relatively short period.* Multiple scans of the entire group are taken throughout the study. The preselected times may be hours or only minutes apart. As the members are scanned, the observer records instances in which a particular behavior (e.g., one child bullying another) occurs. Experienced observers can perform scans of human and nonhuman animal groups with 40 or fewer members in less than a minute (Altmann, 1974). To be effective, however, the behavioral coding system should have only a small number of categories so that the researcher can rapidly shift observations and data recording from one member to another.

Situation sampling *is used to establish diverse settings in which behavior is observed,* which in turn increases the external validity of the findings as compared to sampling behavior in only one setting. For example, in their study of school bullying, Pellegrini and Bartini (2000) observed children in classrooms, school hallways, the cafeteria, and some outdoor settings. This creates a more representative sampling of behavior than would be the case if behavior were only observed in one location.

When researchers are unable to record behavior continuously throughout the entire period of a study, **time sampling** *is used to select a representative set of time periods during which observations will occur.* Once again, turning to Pellegrini and Bartini's (2000) school bullying study, the decision was made to observe the children a minimum of once per week for an entire academic year. Moreover, observations were made in the mornings and afternoons. Had observations been made, say, only in the fall, or only in the morning, the children's behavior might not have been representative of how they behave at other times.

LIMITATIONS OF OBSERVATIONAL RESEARCH

Although observational research has many benefits, it also has limitations. We'll focus on three issues here: causal inference, observer bias, and reactivity.

Problems with Drawing Causal Conclusions

As with case studies, it is difficult to draw clear causal conclusions from observational studies. Many variables may simultaneously affect participants' behavior and the researcher does not have the capability to isolate one or two key factors while controlling for the rest. A researcher may, however, anticipate some possible alternative explanations for the expected findings and gather data to rule them out. For example, recall that when children interacted with science exhibits at a museum, boys were much more likely than girls to receive explanations from their parents (Crowley et al., 2001). The researchers suggested that this was evidence of a parental gender bias, but it would hardly reflect a bias if boys received more explanations merely because they asked their parents more questions than did girls. By analyzing the frequency of questions asked by boys and girls and finding no statistically significant gender difference, Crowley and his colleagues were able to rule out this potential alternative explanation and make a more compelling case for the existence of parental gender bias. But, without denying the descriptive fact that boys received far more explanations than girls, it is still possible that other variables unexamined by the researchers—rather than a conscious or unconscious motivational bias by the parents—could account for the findings.

As another example, take a few seconds and reread Boesch's (1991) description of the hammer/anvil teaching incident involving the chimpanzee Ricci and her offspring, Nina (p. 183). Do you feel comfortable with the conclusion that Ricci "corrected an error in her daughter's behavior" and, more generally, that the mothers in this chimp community demonstrated concern about their infants' tool learning and provided their infants with guidance? I suspect that many research psychologists, especially those favoring a strict behavioral perspective, would not.

The difficulty here is that inferences are being drawn about the causes for the mother chimpanzee's actions. Can we be sure, for example, that Ricci was intentionally attempting to demonstrate the proper hand position to Nina? Perhaps the reason Ricci joined Nina and took the hammer was not to correct Nina's technique; perhaps Ricci simply was hungry and wanted to crack and eat some nuts. And once done, she sat back down. Perhaps Nina at that point did indeed try to copy her mother's hand position on the hammer. Or perhaps Nina got it right just by chance, or if not by chance, by trial and error (i.e., after 8 prior minutes of futility, maybe she was about to correct her technique on her own, even without Ricci's intervention). Similarly, how do we know that what Boesch called "stimulation" (e.g., mothers leaving uncracked nuts on the anvil) was really intended to stimulate the infants' practice of the hammer/anvil technique?

One additional piece of information described by Boesch (1991)—that Ricci took a full minute to slowly rotate the hammer, whereas this normally might be something she could do in a few seconds—adds a compelling element to support the idea that Ricci was attempting to demonstrate the proper way of holding the hammer. Nevertheless, the possibility remains that there may be alternative explanations for such an action.

Observer Bias

As we've discussed earlier, *observer bias* occurs when researchers have expectations or other predispositions that distort their observations. It can occur in any type of research—case studies, experiments, correlational studies—in which observers record behavior. For example, if I have an expectation that youth sports coaches treat their young athletes harshly in a drive to win at all costs, then this may unconsciously color how I perceive and thus code specific responses that are ambiguous—those that fall in the "gray zone" between being punitive or merely nonsupportive. This aspect of observer bias ties into the perceptual demonstration earlier in the chapter (p. 181): The same physical stimulus (whether a Necker cube or someone's behavior) may be perceived in different ways.

Observer bias can manifest itself in other ways, too. If I only selected playoff games to observe (at which time pressures on coaches to win would likely be stronger), or only chose to observe coaches with a known reputation of being "harder on their kids," then I would be stacking the deck in favor of confirming my expectations. Assuming I don't have the resources to observe all coaches for all games, then an unbiased approach would be to observe all coaches who agreed to participate an equal number of times throughout the entire season, using random selection to determine which coaches are observed any particular weekend.

How can observer bias be minimized? In studies that involve behavior coding, it's essential to have:

1. a well-developed coding system with clear operational definitions of the various behavior categories,

2. rigorous observer training, and

3. periodic checks to make sure that observers (who may be the investigators themselves or trained assistants) are using the system reliably.

I'll say more about these precautions in a moment.

Whenever possible, data should be gathered using **blind observation:** *Observers should be kept unaware of (i.e., blind to) all hypotheses being tested and any key information about participants that relates to those hypotheses.* For example, suppose I want to test the hypothesis that the parents of high-self-esteem children give their kids more encouragement than do the parents of low-self-esteem children. I receive permission to administer a psychological test measuring self-esteem to the children at school, and to observe them at home interacting with their parents. If I've trained 10 assistants to perform the home observations, I will not tell them about my hypothesis. Nor will I tell them which children have high or low self-esteem. In this case, if the results support the hypothesis, it would be implausible for another scientist to argue that the observers intentionally or unconsciously biased their behavioral coding in such a way as to help me achieve those results.

Suppose, however, that I don't have any assistants—that due to budget or other constraints, I have to be the one making the observations. Obviously, I know my own hypothesis. But by having someone else do the self-esteem scoring, I can keep myself blind as to whether each child that I observe has high or low self-esteem. And if I didn't know which kids had high or low self-esteem when I observed them, it would be implausible for someone to argue that I biased my observations to support my hypothesis.

Reactivity

Recall that *reactivity* occurs when the process of observing (or otherwise measuring) behavior causes that behavior to change. Sensing potential threat from a human observer, an animal in the wild may stop feeding, maintain vigilance, move away, or make aggressive gestures. More than a few schoolchildren and office workers have been known to quickly stop goofing off when a teacher or boss enters a room. No doubt you can think of many social situations in which you modified your behavior because you were aware that someone else was (or might be) watching. And at skill-related tasks, over a hundred years of research indicate that the mere presence of observers can alter a person's performance (Uziel, 2007).

Reactivity is undesirable because the behavior being recorded no longer represents how people truly behave when they are not being observed or monitored. Of course, reactivity is a concern in all types of behavioral research, not just in observational studies. Surveys and experiments, for example, have the potential to be reactive because people are aware that their behavior is being measured. And reactivity can happen when people are asked to self-observe, such as recording their behavior in diaries.

Still, it would be incorrect to assume that significant reactivity automatically occurs whenever people know they are being monitored. It doesn't (Hufford, Shields, Shiffman, Paty, & Balabanis, 2002). And there are some procedures that researchers can use to minimize the potential for reactivity. In observational research, one approach—when practical and ethically permissible—is to keep the observer disguised.

When disguised observation can't be used, another approach to minimizing reactivity takes advantage of the principle of habituation. **Habituation** *is a decrease in the strength of a response, over time, to a repeated stimulus.* When you sleep in a new locale (e.g., a hotel room, a new dorm room or apartment), strange noises may startle you the first few nights, but over time you barely notice them: You habituate to them. Similarly, an observer who sits in the back of a classroom or who observes wild animals while in plain view will at first attract attention, but over time (and it may take a long time) the children or animals will generally ignore the observer (**Figure 6.11**). Observers can delay recording behavior until after the children or animals have habituated to their presence. Habituation, though generally reliable, isn't always perfect. It may take a long time for some people or nonhuman animals to habituate, and once habituated, instances may still occur when the subject reacts to the presence of an observer (de Waal, 1982).

In addition to disguised observation and habituation procedures, there are other ways to avoid reactivity when measuring behavior. The final section of the chapter briefly addresses some of them.

Spencer Grant/Science Source

Figure 6.11 Habituation in observational research. When disguised observation is not possible, observers can reduce reactivity by taking advantage of the principle of habituation.

✓ CONCEPT CHECK 6.2 OBSERVATIONAL RESEARCH

Fill in each of the blanks below. Answers appear on page 206.

1. A researcher who observes children from afar and whose presence is hidden is engaging in _____ observation. A researcher who observes parents interact with children in their homes, and who selects a specific set of tasks for them to work on together, is engaging in _____ observation. A qualitative research approach called _____ often combines participant observation with interviewing.

2. In recording observations, _____ provide a comprehensive, ongoing written description of behavior. In contrast, _____ involve classifying participants' responses into mutually exclusive categories. Researchers use _____ sampling to observe behavior in diverse settings and increase the _____ validity of their findings.

3. People may change their behavior when they know they are being observed. This general problem is called _____. One approach to reducing this problem is to use the principle of _____, in which the strength of responses to repeated stimuli decreases over time.

UNOBTRUSIVE MEASURES AND ARCHIVAL RECORDS

Learning Objectives

After studying this section, you should be able to:

- Describe several types of unobtrusive measures and archival records.
- Discuss the limitations of using unobtrusive measures and archival records.

The word *unobtrusive* means "inconspicuous" or "not blatant." An **unobtrusive measure** *assesses behavior without making people aware that the behavior is being measured.* Researchers use unobtrusive measures to reduce the problem of reactivity.

The degree to which measures are unobtrusive or obtrusive is probably best conceived as a continuum rather than as an either-or situation (Kazdin, 1979). With some unobtrusive measures, such as disguised naturalistic observation, people remain completely unaware that any aspect of their behavior is being recorded for research purposes. **Physical trace measures,** *which unobtrusively examine traces of behavior that people create or leave behind,* are another example (Webb, Campbell, Schwartz, Sechrest, & Grove, 1981). We could indirectly measure people's eating behavior or alcohol consumption at home by painstakingly sifting through the garbage and recyclables (e.g., the contents of trash cans or dumpsters). Or, we could use the amount of litter that people drop on the ground in public parks as one measure of the effectiveness of an anti-littering campaign. The products that people create are another type of physical trace measure, and to examine the gender, ethnic, and religious stereotypes in a society, we could analyze the content of current television shows, movies, comic books, and best-selling novels.

In other forms of unobtrusive measurement, people may be aware that they are participating in a research study, but remain unaware of the actual behaviors being measured and/or the times at which their responses are measured. Telling participants in a laboratory study that they are working on a perceptual task, when in fact the task measures unconscious prejudice, is one example (Towles-Schwen & Fazio, 2003). Once the experiment commences, participants certainly know that they are being observed, but they are unaware that behaviors reflecting prejudice are being measured.

Similarly, social-personality psychologist Matthias Mehl and his colleagues sought to examine how people's personality characteristics are expressed in everyday life (Mehl,

Gosling, & Pennebaker, 2006). In addition to administering a personality test to 96 college students and asking them to keep a diary at the end of each day, the researchers used Electronically Activated Recording (EAR) to observe the students as they went about their daily lives. The EAR is

> . . . a modified digital voice recorder that periodically records brief snippets of ambient sounds. Participants wear the EAR attached to their belt or in a purse-like bag while going about their daily lives. The method is unobtrusive because the EAR operates imperceptibly. (Mehl et al., 2006, p. 863)

In this study, students signed a consent form and were fully aware that their verbal behavior would be monitored periodically for 2 days. In fact, they had to clip an external microphone to their shirt collars so that the EAR could function. But the EARs had been programmed to record 30-second sound intervals about 5 times per hour, and students were not aware of—and could not detect—when the EAR was actually recording. Although not as unobtrusive as completely disguised naturalistic observation, the EAR method avoids the ethical issues associated with covert observation, and it certainly is less obtrusive than following participants around with a notepad or camcorder throughout the day. It's also less obtrusive than the "beeper methodology" used in some observational studies, in which participants wear beepers and are signaled several times a day, at which point they record responses in a diary or on a behavior checklist. (Beeper studies have their own advantages, though, in that they aren't limited to measuring audio responses. Participants in beeper studies are typically asked to record their current behavior, thoughts, or emotions.)

Another possibility for measuring behavior unobtrusively is through archival records. **Archival records** *are previously existing documents or other data that were produced independently of the current research.* Archival records can include collections of government documents (e.g., crime, economic, and census reports), corporate files, personal letters and photographs, popular media (e.g., newspaper, TV, film, and literary archives), and many other kinds of records.

To examine whether gender, ethnic, and other stereotypes in a society have changed over time, I can use archives maintained by major film studios and several universities to access TV shows and films from the past half century, and analyze changes in their content. To test the hypothesis that aggression increases when people are more frustrated, I might operationally define aggression by measuring the frequency of violent crimes (e.g., murder) and operationally define frustration by various economic indicators (e.g., unemployment rate). I would then examine federal, state/provincial, or local government archives for the past 50 years to gather year-by-year data on the economy and frequency of violent crimes. I could also gather data from the archives of newspapers from around the country. In both of these examples, as a scientist, I would be gathering data about people's current and past behavior unobtrusively; my presence obviously had no influence on people's behavior at the time the data originally were recorded.

Unobtrusive measures and archival records also carry their share of concerns and limitations. First, disguised observation, any withholding of information or active deception that keeps participants unaware of the true behaviors being measured, and any use of archival records must be ethically permissible. Second, physical trace measures or archival records are not available or even a plausible option for many variables that psychologists study. And third, if physical trace or archival measures are available, there may be alternative viewpoints as to what those physical traces or records actually represent. Is my assumption valid that harder economic times can be used operationally as a measure of "greater frustration" on the part of the public? If violent crime does increase during harder economic times, what explanations other than "greater frustration" might plausibly account for this development?

Finally, although a researcher's use of physical trace or archival measures may be unobtrusive, the original data collection may not have been. For example, archives of major national surveys are kept by several governmental agencies as well as university and private survey research centers. Often free of charge, and sometimes for a fee, researchers are able to access all the data from these past surveys for their own current use. These archival survey records are unobtrusive in terms of the current researcher's use, but whether the data were originally gathered by in-person or telephone interviews or a mail-in questionnaire, at the time the survey was conducted, it was an obtrusive procedure because participants were aware that their responses were being measured. The bottom line is that when examining some topics, researchers may be able to find creative ways to measure behavior inconspicuously, and such measures are best used in conjunction with other measurement techniques. Within a study, if different measures yield similar conclusions, the researcher can be more confident in the validity of the findings.

✓ CONCEPT CHECK 6.3 UNOBTRUSIVE MEASURES AND ARCHIVAL RECORDS

Decide whether each statement is true or false. Answers appear on page 206.

1. Researchers use physical trace measures to reduce the problem of reactivity.
2. Archival records are unobtrusive in the sense that the researcher who is currently using them does not influence the original responses that were recorded.
3. Archival records are always unobtrusive at the time they were initially produced.

CHAPTER SUMMARY

- Case studies are in-depth analyses of an individual, social unit, event, or other phenomenon. In an intrinsic case study, a case is examined in depth because the researcher has an inherent interest in learning about that particular case. In an instrumental case study, a case is selected for analysis to learn about a broader phenomenon. In a collective case study, researchers seek to learn about a broader phenomenon by studying two or more cases in depth and drawing comparisons between them.

- Case study researchers may employ a single-case or multiple-case design, and gather and analyze data using qualitative, quantitative, or mixed-methods approaches. Direct observation and questioning are two common methods for gathering case study data, but psychological assessments and other measures may also be used.

- Case studies excel at describing behavior. They enable data to be collected about rare events and people who have rare abilities or experiences. They can be used to test hypotheses and theories, provide insight into possible causes of behavior, stimulate experimental research, and help establish the external validity of findings from experiments.

- It is difficult to draw clear causal conclusions from case studies. A second limitation is that findings based on a single case may not generalize to other cases. The potential for observer bias is a third limitation.

- Observational studies are well suited to describing behavior and examining associations between variables. They can be used to test hypotheses and theories, suggest possible causal relations that are subsequently examined in experiments, and examine the external validity of experimental findings. When ethical constraints make experiments impossible, observational research may be a viable alternative.

- In naturalistic observation, participants are observed in their natural environment and the researcher attempts to minimize involvement with the participants. In participant observation, the observer becomes a part of the group being studied. This provides the opportunity to study people's behavior from an insider's viewpoint but increases the risk of reactivity. Naturalistic and participant observation may be disguised or undisguised.

- With structured observation, a researcher creates an analogue of a situation that would occur naturally.

Structured observation can take place inside or outside of the laboratory. Control is gained by exposing all participants to the same tasks and (if in the laboratory) the same general setting.

- Observations can be recorded in many ways. A narrative record provides a continuous description of behavior, which is then analyzed at a later time. Observers may use less comprehensive field notes to record their impressions or important instances of behavior.

- Behavioral coding systems are used to classify participants' responses into mutually exclusive categories. Observer rating and ranking scales are used to evaluate characteristics of participants' behavior. To establish high interobserver reliability, it is important to develop a high-quality coding system. Participants may also be asked to keep a diary in which they categorize or rate their own behavior or feelings.

- Researchers use sampling when it is not possible to observe or analyze continuous responses from every participant. With focal sampling, the observer focuses attention on each participant one at a time, often for a lengthy time period. With scan sampling, at preselected times the observer rapidly scans each member of a group so that the entire group is observed within a relatively short period. Researchers use situation sampling to establish diverse settings in which behavior is observed, and time sampling to select a representative set of time periods during which observations occur.

- Three major issues of concern in conducting observational research are: (1) the difficulty of drawing clear causal conclusions; (2) the potential for observer bias; and (3) reactivity.

- Reactivity can be reduced or avoided by using unobtrusive measures, which assess behavior without making people aware that their behavior is being measured. Disguised naturalistic observation, physical trace measures, and some types of archival records are examples of unobtrusive measures.

KEY TERMS

archival records (p. 203)
behavioral coding systems (p. 194)
blind observation (p. 200)
case study (p. 174)
collective case study (p. 177)
diary (p. 195)
disguised versus undisguised observation (p. 186)
ethnography (p. 189)
focal sampling (p. 198)
focus group (p. 178)
habituation (p. 201)

instrumental case study (p. 177)
interobserver reliability (interrater reliability) (p. 196)
intrinsic case study (p. 176)
mixed-methods case study (p. 176)
multiple-case study design (p. 177)
naturalistic observation (p. 186)
observational research (p. 182)
observer bias (p. 181)
observer rating and ranking scales (p. 195)
participant observation (p. 187)

physical trace measure (p. 202)
qualitative case study (p. 176)
quantitative case study (p. 176)
reactivity (p. 187)
scan sampling (p. 198)
semi-structured interview (p. 178)
single-case study design (p. 177)
situation sampling (p. 199)
structured observation (p. 190)
time sampling (p. 199)
unobtrusive measure (p. 202)

ASSESS YOUR KNOWLEDGE

1. Is the focus of a case study always an individual person? Explain.

2. How do intrinsic and instrumental case studies differ in purpose?

3. Explain some reasons for using a multiple-case study design?

4. Describe three general advantages and three limitations of case studies.

5. What are some of the general advantages of conducting observational research?

6. Describe key differences between naturalistic, participant, and structured observation, and provide one example of each approach.

7. What are focal, scan, situation, and time sampling? Why would a researcher use each type of sampling?

8. Explain the key difference between qualitative and quantitative approaches to observing behavior, and illustrate each approach with an example.

9. Describe some specific ways in which observers can record what they observe. How can participants be asked to observe their own behavior?

10. Discuss the concept of reactivity and some ways to reduce it.
11. Identify several ways in which observer bias can influence the results of a study.
12. What is interobserver reliability, and how can it be maximized?

13. What is an unobtrusive measure? Define and illustrate physical trace measures and archival records.
14. Describe three limitations of unobtrusive measures, including archival records.

CONCEPT CHECKS: ANSWERS

6.1 Case Studies

1. true   2. true   3. true   4. true

6.2 Observational Research

1. disguised naturalistic; structured; ethnography

2. narrative records; behavioral coding systems; situation; external 3. reactivity; habituation

6.3 Unobtrusive Measures and Archival Records

1. true   2. true   3. false

THINKING CRITICALLY AND APPLYING YOUR KNOWLEDGE

EXERCISE 1   Spaced Out: Regional Differences in Interpersonal Space

Dr. Zola wants to use naturalistic observation to study whether people living in diverse regions of the United States differ, overall, in their interpersonal space boundaries. Her research team will observe 400 pairs of adults—100 in each of four geographic regions—while the adults in each pair talk to each other. We will focus here on her sampling of locations. (Assume that the study will comply with ethical regulations and valid procedures will be used to assess how far apart people stand while conversing.)

Dr. Zola plans to record observations during the final week of July, as follows:

Northeast	New York City: various sites in Central Park, Manhattan
South	Atlanta: Hartsfield-Jackson Airport, various sites in the main domestic passenger terminal
Midwest	Bloomington, Minnesota (near Minneapolis—St. Paul): various sites inside the Mall of America (an indoor shopping and entertainment complex with over 500 stores)
West	Anaheim (near Los Angeles): various sites inside the Disneyland theme park

Address these two questions:

(a) If Dr. Zola only has the resources to study one setting in each region, did she choose these four settings wisely? If yes, explain why. If no, explain why and suggest improvements.
(b) Suppose that Dr. Zola has the resources to observe behavior in more settings. What do you think her top priority should be in adding more locations? Explain your answer.

EXERCISE 2   Parenting Behaviors and Children's Self-Esteem

Dr. Brunell believes that parenting behaviors influence children's self-esteem. He will first conduct a case study, and then observational research, to examine this issue. He is particularly interested in whether children with high self-esteem have parents who provide more support (e.g., encouragement, praise) than do parents of children with low self-esteem. However, he also wants to gain insight from the case study about other aspects of parent–child interactions that may shape the development of children's self-esteem, and use that knowledge to help design his observational research. In his observational research, Dr. Brunell first plans to observe 100 families where two parents are raising a single child, and then conduct another observational study of single-parent households.

(a) In his case study, taking the goal of this research into account, would you recommend that Dr. Brunell use a single-case or multiple-case (i.e., collective case) study design? Why?

(b) What would be some benefits of taking a qualitative approach to conducting this case study? What would be some benefits of a quantitative and mixed-methods approach? What approach would you recommend to Dr. Brunell, and why?

(c) In his observational research, how might Dr. Brunell use undisguised naturalistic observation and, alternatively, structured observation? Describe the advantages and disadvantages of each approach.

(d) Suppose that Dr. Brunell finds that, overall, parents of high-self-esteem children encourage and praise their children more often than do parents of low-self-esteem children. Dr. Brunell concludes that parental support produces higher self-esteem in children. (He doesn't believe that support is the only causal factor, but he concludes that it is *a* causal factor.) Discuss whether this conclusion is appropriate, given the types of studies conducted.

EXERCISE 3   Evaluating a Behavioral Coding System

Suppose that in Dr. Brunell's observational study of parenting behaviors and children's self-esteem, described above, he decides to record behavior by using a behavioral coding system. He develops a system with the following three categories: (1) Parental Praise (parent praises child); (2) Parental Encouragement (parent encourages child, other than by praise); (3) Parental Criticism (parent criticizes child).

(a) If you were advising Dr. Brunell, what feedback would you give him about his coding system? Does the system do a good job of capturing the concept of parental "support" for the children? Would you change any of these three categories, or add any other categories? You might look at the coding system in Table 6.2 and consider whether it contains any categories or concepts that might be useful and adaptable to Dr. Brunell's study.

(b) What would be the advantages and disadvantages of expanding the coding system?

LaunchPad
macmillan learning

To practice key concepts from this chapter, visit the LaunchPad Solo for Research Methods at **launchpadworks.com.**

CHAPTER OUTLINE

To begin this chapter, think of how you would respond to these survey items.

1. For each of the items below (a, b, and c), indicate whether you believe in it or not (Answer options: believe in, don't believe in, not sure).

    a. Ghosts   b. Astrology   c. Witches

2. Generally speaking, would you say that most people can be trusted, or that you cannot be too careful in dealing with people?

3. Generally speaking, do you think that most people would try to take advantage of you if they got the chance, or would they try to be fair?

Although it might be interesting to examine whether belief in paranormal phenomena is associated with the degree to which people are trusting or cynical about human nature, the items above actually come from two different surveys. People's belief in ghosts, astrology, and witches were assessed by Harris Poll researchers in a nationally representative U.S. sample of teenagers and adults, as part of a larger survey (Shannon-Missal, 2014). Respectively, among teens and adults, 46% and 42% said they believed in ghosts, 36% and 29% in astrology, and 23% and 26% in witches. The general finding that a substantial percentage of people believe in paranormal phenomena was consistent with the results of earlier surveys, such as a highly publicized study conducted by Gallup researchers of nationally representative samples of adults in Canada, Great Britain, and the United States (Lyons, 2005). Beyond the findings shown in **Figure 7.1**, one third of U.S. adults believed in mental telepathy and almost three quarters believed in at least one paranormal phenomenon (Moore, 2005).

Harris Poll and Gallup are two of many commercial organizations that specialize in conducting a type of survey called an *opinion poll,* which assesses people's beliefs, values, or attitudes about a topic. Harris Poll and Gallup surveys also ask people about their demographic characteristics, lifestyle habits, and other behaviors. The primary goal of such surveys, and of many surveys conducted by researchers at academic institutions and government agencies, is to determine the percentage of a sample (e.g., of adults in a particular nation) that holds a certain view or reports a particular characteristic, and then use this information to estimate the percentage of the broader population (e.g., of all adults in the nation) that has that particular attribute. Particularly in the context of political election campaigns, this may be the type of survey, or reason for conducting surveys, with which you are most familiar: Based on the results of a sample, researchers estimate the percentage of voters in a broader population that say they will vote for a particular candidate.

In contrast, there are many instances in which scientists put survey data to other uses and are not primarily concerned with describing the percentage of a population that thinks or behaves a certain way or has some other attribute. Consider the second and third survey items presented at the beginning of the chapter. In a series of four studies, psychologists Olga Stavrova and Daniel Ehlebracht (2016) used these items or ones like them to measure the degree to which people held cynical attitudes about human nature. They did so to test the hypothesis that greater cynicism about people, in general, would be associated with lower current and future economic earnings. They reasoned that cynical people, as opposed to those who are less cynical, are less likely to cooperate with others, and this in turn would hinder opportunities for economic advancement. They analyzed data that had been collected from nationally representative samples in Germany and the United States. Four surveys were conducted longitudinally, across a period of up to 9 years. These surveys also contained measures of people's self-reported annual income.

Cynicism, current income, and future income were all associated with one another, and with other demographic factors. Although the relation was weak, in each set of survey data, cynicism remained a predictor of future income even after the relation between future

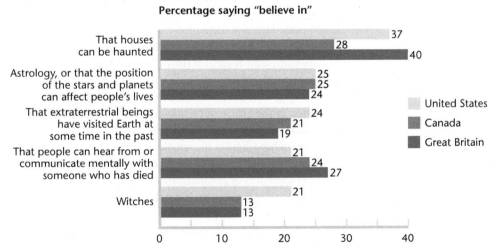

For each of the following items I am going to read you, please tell me whether it is something you believe in, something you're not sure about, or something you don't believe in. How about:

Figure 7.1 Paranormal beliefs among American, Canadian, and British adults. (Adapted from "Paranormal Beliefs Come (Super)Naturally to Some" by L. Lyons, page 1, http://www.gallup.com/poll/19558/Paranormal-Beliefs-Come-SuperNaturally-Some.aspx.)

income and these other variables was statistically controlled. Although clear causal conclusions can't be drawn from such correlational data, Stavrova and Ehlebracht's (2016) research illustrates how survey data are often used for the sole or primary goal of testing hypotheses or exploring associations among variables, rather than for reporting the percentage of a population that thinks or responds a certain way.

Survey research makes important contributions to science and society. Psychologists and other behavioral scientists conduct surveys for basic as well as applied purposes. Survey research also is a global, multi-billion-dollar commercial enterprise. In this chapter, we explore how and why surveys are conducted, the challenges that survey researchers face, and the qualities of good and poor surveys. This knowledge should help you become a more critical consumer of survey information.

BASIC CHARACTERISTICS OF SURVEYS

Learning Objectives

After studying this section, you should be able to:

- Illustrate how a population, sampling frame, and sample differ from one another.
- Provide an example of a representative and nonrepresentative sample.
- Discuss benefits and limitations of survey research.

In behavioral science, a **survey** *uses questionnaires and interviews to gather information about people.* Surveys can gather many types of information and serve many purposes, but before addressing those topics, it will first be helpful to cover some basic concepts.

POPULATIONS AND SAMPLES

The term **population** *refers to all the cases or observations of interest to us.* For example, suppose an instructor wants to ask the students in her undergraduate research methods course to answer a brief questionnaire about course issues. The students in that class are the population of interest, and the instructor can feasibly administer the questionnaire to the entire population. In contrast, if the population of interest to the instructor is "North American college students," it's not practical to gather data from everyone. Realistically, the instructor can survey a **sample,** *a subset of cases or observations from the population.*[1]

Consider another example. Suppose I ask you to assist me in conducting a survey to learn about the lifestyles and opinions of undergraduates on my campus. We will conduct in-depth interviews to gather data. Because my campus has approximately 30,000 undergrads, the population is too large for us to interview everyone. So, to select a sample, we first ask the registrar for a list of the names and contact information of all currently enrolled students. This represents a **sampling frame,** *a list—of names, phone numbers, addresses, or other units—from which a sample will be selected.*

The sampling frame represents the operational definition of the population. In principle, the population is the entire currently enrolled student body, but in practice, the population is operationally defined by the names on the registrar's list. By the time the interviews begin, some students whose names are on the list may have dropped out, and the names of some current students won't be on the list because they enrolled late. Sampling frames typically are imperfect measures of populations. Our goal is to develop a sampling frame that does the best possible job of representing the population.

Let's imagine that we interview a sample of 600 students and, based on the findings, we draw conclusions—make *inferences*—about the lifestyles and opinions of the entire population

---

[1] In psychological research, it's common to talk about populations and samples of people. In statistics, *population* and *sample* refer to sets of scores. See Statistics Module 1.2 for details.

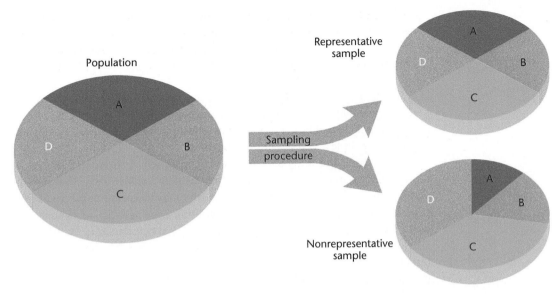

Figure 7.2 Representative and nonrepresentative samples. A representative sample reflects the important characteristics of the population. A nonrepresentative sample does not reflect these characteristics; its composition on important attributes differs significantly from the population's composition on those attributes.

of 30,000 students. Is it really valid to do that? Similarly, by interviewing a mere thousand or even 3,000 people, is it valid for Gallup Poll researchers (McCarthy, 2016) to make inferences about the opinions and lifestyle habits of approximately 245 million American adults?

Fortunately, the answer is yes, but only if the sample is representative of the population. As **Figure 7.2** illustrates, a **representative sample** *reflects the important characteristics of the population.* In our campus survey, if 85% of the students we interview are Caucasian males, but 52% of the undergraduates on campus are female and 57% represent other ethnic groups (which is the case), then we have a problem. This would be a **nonrepresentative** (or **biased**) **sample** *that does not reflect important characteristics of the population.* Later we'll discuss different methods for selecting representative samples.

Finally, researchers are usually unable to contact some of the people selected to be in a survey (e.g., people who are out of town, or not answering their phones). Moreover, some people who are contacted will decline to participate. A survey's *cooperation rate* represents the percentage of individuals, households, or other units who participate in the survey out of all those who are contacted (American Association of Public Opinion Research [AAPOR], 2011). Suppose that 1,000 students are selected to be in the survey, interviewers make contact with 900 of them, 300 decline to participate, and 600 do participate. In this instance, the cooperation rate will be 66.7% (600 participants divided by 900 students contacted). In contrast, a survey's **response rate** *represents the percentage of cases who participate in a survey out of all those who were selected to participate* (AAPOR, 2011). Thus, in the example above, the response rate would be 60% (i.e., 600 of 1,000 selected people participated; 100 couldn't be contacted and 300 refused).

WHY CONDUCT SURVEYS?

From A (alcohol use) to Z (zero-tolerance discipline policies), surveys address an enormous range of topics. Basic researchers conduct surveys to advance scientific knowledge about human behavior. Applied researchers collect survey data to address practical issues. Surveys, such as opinion polls based on representative samples, also give people a voice and inform the public. Psychologist Jon Krosnick, an expert in survey methodology, notes that everybody has come to realize that in order to stay in touch with the realities of the marketplace, in order for government to be responsive to its citizens and in order for academics to understand what drives people's behavior, surveys are an incredibly efficient way of getting at data. (quoted in Trei, 2006, Sept. 27, para. 5)

Indeed, efficiency is a great advantage of survey research. Data from representative samples permit reasonable estimates about entire populations. Moreover, regardless of whether a researcher seeks to obtain a representative sample, a single survey can be used to gather data from many people about dozens of variables.

Surveys are commonly used to assess people's self-reported preferences, attitudes, beliefs, lifestyle habits, and other behaviors. They usually include items that measure demographic variables (e.g., sex, age, ethnicity, income) and may assess other personal characteristics (e.g., people's relationship, job, and life satisfaction). Especially in fields such as clinical psychology, psychiatry, and health psychology, survey participants may be asked to describe or rate aspects of their mental and physical health. They also may be administered psychological tests (e.g., spatial tasks, memory tests) by trained interviewers so that researchers can study people's mental functioning (Mograbi et al., 2012).

Here are some common uses of survey data:

- *To describe the characteristics of a population.* What percent of college students use cocaine? How prevalent are various disorders (e.g., depression, phobias, dementia) in the adult population? How do voters feel about Candidate X?

- *To describe and compare the characteristics of different populations or different demographic groups within a population.* What percent of male and female college students use cocaine? Does the prevalence of psychological disorders significantly vary across different ethnic groups? How do voters of different ages feel about Candidate X?

- *To describe population time trends.* In recent decades, how has the rate of cocaine use among college students changed? Has the prevalence of psychological disorders changed over time? As the election approaches, is Candidate X becoming more popular or less so?

- *To describe relations among psychological variables, (self-reported) behaviors, and other characteristics.* Are people's overall happiness and life satisfaction correlated with self-esteem and beliefs in personal control versus fate? Is cynicism about human nature related to people's current and future income?

- *To test hypotheses, theories, and models.* We hypothesize "that holding cynical beliefs about human nature can be detrimental for individuals' income" (Stavrova & Ehlebracht, 2016).

Data from a single survey are often used for several purposes. For example, the Institute for Social Research (ISR) at the University of Michigan annually conducts a nationally representative survey, called *Monitoring the Future*, which examines drug use among American high school students, college students, and other groups (Johnston, O'Malley, Bachman, Schulenberg, & Miech, 2015). Based on participants' response to the item "What is your sex?," Figure 7.3 compares recent cocaine use among male and female college students (see the second bulleted item above) and also reveals changes in students' cocaine use over time (the third bulleted item).

LIMITATIONS OF SURVEYS

Like other nonexperimental methods, surveys are generally not well suited for examining cause–effect relations. Surveys can ask people for their opinions about why they behave the way they do, but the findings reflect only that—people's opinions. Survey data also serve as input for correlational analyses that examine potential causal relations between variables.

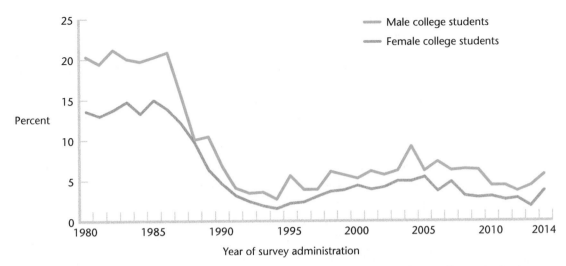

Figure 7.3 Annual cocaine use among male and female American college students, 1980–2014. The percentage of American male and female college students who used cocaine at least once within the most recent year (as of the date of each survey). The graph also shows how cocaine use has changed over time. (Data from *Monitoring the Future national survey results on drug use, 1975–2014: Volume 2, College students and adults ages 19–55*, by L. D. Johnston, P. M. O'Malley, J. G. Bachman, J. E. Schulenberg, and R. A. Miech, 2015, p. 403. Ann Arbor: Institute for Social Research, The University of Michigan.)

But as Chapter 5 discusses, such correlational analyses do not match the ability of experiments to draw clear causal conclusions.

Another limitation of surveys stems from the fact that there are many ways to select samples, some better than others. Poor sampling can generate highly misleading results. Even with the best sampling methods, unrepresentative samples can occur once in a while, for reasons we'll explore later.

Finally, because surveys assess people's self-reports, the validity of survey data depends on participants' willingness to treat the survey seriously and respond to questions honestly, a point illustrated in **Figure 7.4**. Although some people might be motivated to radically distort their answers, a more general concern is that people's responses to questionnaires can be unintentionally influenced by limitations and biases that pervade human thinking. When responding to survey items, people may inaccurately perceive their own current behavior (e.g., overestimate how long it takes them to fall asleep) or inaccurately recall their past behavior. Even without conscious awareness, people's answers may be distorted by **social desirability bias,** *a tendency to respond in a way that a person feels is socially appropriate,*

Figure 7.4 An extreme case of response distortion. CALVIN AND HOBBES © 1995 Watterson. Dist. by UNIVERSAL UCLICK. Reprinted with permission. All rights reserved.

rather than as she or he truly feels. Some people's responses may be swayed by biases in how questions are worded, particularly if the wording suggests that one opinion or behavioral pattern is more socially acceptable than another. Fortunately, there are ways to conduct surveys and design questions that can minimize these problems. In sum, like other types of research, conducting high-quality surveys is a painstaking endeavor that requires a lot of knowledge, skill, and dedication.

✓ **CONCEPT CHECK 7.1** **BASIC CHARACTERISTICS OF SURVEYS**

Dr. Kim surveys registered voters in your region. Fill in each of the blanks below. Answers appear at the end of the chapter, on page 240.

1. In this survey, the _____ is the entire set of registered voters in your region. The subset of voters selected to participate in the survey represents the _____. To select this subset, Dr. Kim first must obtain a _____, which represents an operational definition of registered voters in your region.

2. If the subset of selected voters properly reflects key characteristics (e.g., ethnic composition) of the entire set of voters, then this subset is called a(n) _____. If it doesn't reflect these key characteristics, then the subset is a(n) _____.

SELECTING A SAMPLE

Learning Objectives

After studying this section, you should be able to:

- Describe different types, benefits, and drawbacks of probability and nonprobability sampling.
- Explain the concepts of sampling error and confidence level.
- Discuss major factors that affect decisions about sample size.

There are two general methods for selecting a survey sample. With **probability sampling,** *each member of the population has a chance of being selected into the sample, and the probability of being selected can be specified.* With **nonprobability sampling,** *each member of the population either does not have a chance of being selected into the sample, the probability of being selected cannot be determined, or both.* Nonprobability sampling is scientifically useful in many situations, but in surveys probability sampling is typically preferred. Let's explore why.

PROBABILITY SAMPLING

Probability sampling relies on statistical theory to select a sample from a population. It is the only approach that reliably allows us to use certain statistics from a sample (e.g., the percentage of participants who expressed a certain opinion) to estimate the responses of a population. We'll examine three probability sampling methods.

Simple Random Sampling

Let's return to the undergraduate opinion/lifestyle survey that we are conducting on my campus. We have already obtained our sampling frame of 30,000 names from the registrar, and we plan to sample 1,000 students. To do this, we could use an approach called **simple random sampling,** *in which every member of the sampling frame has an equal probability of being chosen at random to participate in the survey.* Thus, with a sample of 1,000 students and a sampling frame of 30,000 students, the probability that any individual student would be selected to participate in the survey is 1 in 30.

Stratified Random Sampling

Demographic sex-ratio statistics reported by my university state that 52% of the undergraduates on campus are women and 48% are men. With simple random sampling, the percentage of women and men selected for our sample will likely be close to those figures, but probably won't match that sex distribution exactly. The situation is analogous to having a supersized jar filled with 30,000 marbles, 52% of which are green. If we randomly select 1,000 marbles from the jar, it's possible—but unlikely—that precisely 520 will be green. What is likely, however, is that the number of green marbles in our sample will be close to 52% (say, between 49% to 55%). And of course, rarely, we might by chance select a sample of marbles that badly overestimates or underestimates the number of green marbles in the jar.

In our survey, to maximize the probability that our sample of 1,000 students will accurately reflect the sex composition of the student body, we can allocate 520 spaces in our sample to women and 480 to men. Once we have divided our sampling frame into these groups (female/male), we would then use simple random sampling to select the female and male students for our study. This procedure is called **stratified random sampling:** *A sampling frame is divided into groups (called strata; singular = stratum), and then within each group random sampling is used to select the members of the sample.*

In practice, sampling may involve several strata. For example, we might first identity the percentage of first-year, sophomore, junior, and senior students. This would be one stratum. Then, within each of these four groups, we could create a second stratum based on students' sex. Now we have eight groups (senior women, senior men, junior women, etc.), with the number of spaces in the sample allocated to each group based on the female-to-male student sex ratio within the first-year, sophomore, junior, and senior classes, respectively. We would then use random sampling to select the members within each group.

Cluster and Multistage Sampling

Now let's suppose we wish to conduct a survey, but there is no ready-made sampling frame (such as a registrar's list of students' names) to represent the population. Is it still possible to use probability sampling?

Survey researchers often face this situation, and fortunately they can use a form of probability sampling named **cluster sampling:** *Units (e.g., geographic regions, schools) that contain members of the population are identified. These units—called "clusters"—are then randomly sampled.* When cluster sampling is used in just one stage—what is sometimes called **single-stage cluster sampling**—*all the participants in the randomly selected clusters are chosen to participate in the survey.*

Once an initial sample of clusters is selected, however, researchers may perform one or more additional stages of sampling to obtain their final sample of selected participants. This process is called **multistage sampling,** *the use of two or more stages to select progressively smaller samples.* In the simplest case, which involves two stages, once the first set of clusters has been randomly selected, a subset of members within those clusters is then randomly selected. Let's consider an example.

Social psychologist Scott Plous (1996b) wanted to know how undergraduate psychology majors attending colleges in the United States felt about the use of nonhuman animals in psychological research. No sampling frame—no master list of "undergraduate psychology majors"—was available. So, to obtain a sample of psychology majors, Plous used a cluster sampling procedure that involved two stages. In Stage 1, he created a sampling frame of American colleges and universities. To be included in this sampling frame, a college or university had to (1) be an independent, state, or state-related institution, and (2) have an enrollment of 1,000 or more students. Plous then used the 1994 *Peterson's Guide to Four-Year Colleges* to identify 708 academic institutions that met these criteria. Because he wanted a geographically diverse sample of psychology majors, Plous added an additional criterion that no more than two schools could be located in the same state. Plous then randomly selected and contacted 50 colleges and universities from this sampling frame. Of these institutions, 42 agreed to participate.

The Department of Psychology in each of these 42 colleges or universities constitutes a cluster. Using information received from each participating department, Plous (1996b) then constructed another sampling frame: this time, of the individual psychology majors within each cluster. In departments with fewer than 50 psychology majors, all majors were asked to participate in the survey. In larger departments, 50 students were randomly chosen to participate. All told, of the 2,002 students randomly chosen for the sample, 59% participated.

Plous's cluster sampling procedure (1996b) yielded a national probability sample of undergraduate psychology majors. Because his initial sampling frame excluded some types of institutions (e.g., those with less than 1,000 students), we cannot assume that his final sample of participants represented the entire population of undergraduate psychology majors. We can assume, however, that it represented the large population of psychology majors attending the types of colleges and universities included in the study. His survey found, by the way, that most psychology majors supported animal research, except in cases where the research exposed animals to pain or death.

In fact, Plous's sampling procedure (1996b) was a hybrid approach that had elements of single-stage cluster sampling and multistage sampling. He used single-stage cluster sampling with psychology departments that had fewer than 50 psych majors: Once a department (cluster) had been randomly selected, all the members (psych majors) were chosen to be in the sample. With psychology departments that had more than 50 psych majors, Plous used multistage sampling. In Stage 1, psychology departments (clusters) were randomly selected. In Stage 2, a sample of psych majors from within the department was then randomly selected for inclusion in the survey.

Multistage sampling may involve more than two stages. To identify a nationwide sample of high school students, for example, researchers might first create a sampling frame of all counties or school districts in the nation. After randomly selecting counties (first-stage clusters), they may randomly select high schools within those counties (second-stage clusters), and then homerooms within those schools (third-stage clusters). Finally, they may select all students in those homerooms to be in the sample, or, in a fourth stage of sampling, randomly select students within each homeroom. Note that, although this example focused on using multistage sampling to select successive samples of clusters, multistage sampling also may involve two or more stages of stratified random sampling, or combinations of simple random sampling, stratified random sampling, and cluster sampling.

NONPROBABILITY SAMPLING

Unlike probability sampling, nonprobability sampling does not rely on statistical theory to select a sample from a population. Nonprobability samples are common in survey research because they are easier and less costly to obtain. As we'll see, this creates problems if the researcher's intent is to use certain statistics obtained from a sample (e.g., the percentage of participants who say they consume alcohol daily) to estimate the response of an entire population (e.g., to estimate the percentage of people in the population who say they consume alcohol daily). If this is not the researcher's intent, then nonprobability sampling may be well suited or at least adequate for the purpose of a study.

Convenience Sampling

The most common form of nonprobability sampling is called **convenience** (or **haphazard**) **sampling:** *Members of a population are selected nonrandomly for inclusion in a sample, on the basis of convenience.* To illustrate, to conduct a survey of student opinions at my university, suppose that I stand in the main quadrangle on campus from 10 a.m. to 4 p.m. every day for a week, and as students walk by, I ask them to participate in my survey.

The essential technique here is "grab whomever you can." Unfortunately, although convenient, this technique introduces potential biases into the sampling procedure. For example, students whose classes or other campus activities don't take them through the main quad would have no chance of inclusion in my sample. At my university, classes in the arts, humanities, and social sciences are more likely to be held in buildings on the main quad than are classes in engineering and the natural sciences. So, even if students taking the latter classes occasionally walked through the quad, they almost surely would be underrepresented in my convenience sample. If I try to broaden the sampling procedure by recruiting a few assistants and stationing them, say, in front of each cafeteria on campus, our sample will underrepresent students who eat off-campus.

Even if I were to station 100 interviewers all around campus, biases could creep into how they selected students passing by. They may be more likely to approach students who are walking more slowly, who appear less rushed, who seem happier, or who look "friendlier" and perhaps more likely to agree to participate. In these and other ways, convenience sampling is likely to generate a nonrepresentative sample of students.

Quota Sampling

On the surface, a type of convenience sampling procedure called *quota sampling* seems similar to the stratified random sampling procedure that we discussed earlier. In **quota sampling,** *a sample is nonrandomly selected to match the proportion of one or more key characteristics of the population.* Thus, if 52% of the students on my campus identify their sex as female, we could set a quota such that 52% of the sampled students would be female. Likewise, we could set quotas for our sample to match the percentage of first-year, sophomore, junior, and senior students on campus, the percentage of different ethnic groups in the student body, and so on.

Although quota sampling matches the sample to the population on particular characteristics, the problem is that it still relies on convenience sampling to select the sample members within each of the quota groups. Thus, although 52% of our sample will be female, we have no way to estimate the likelihood that their responses will represent those of all female students on campus. Our quota sample may still underrepresent female students from certain majors, those taking classes at certain times of day, or those students whose interests or income levels lead them not to eat on campus, and so forth.

Stated differently, in stratified random sampling, each member of the population has some chance of being selected for the sample, and that probability can be quantified. With quota sampling, although female students may constitute 52% of our sample, the probability of individual students being selected to participate cannot readily be determined. For some students, however, the probability may be zero if the student's campus routine does not coincide with the locations where the convenience sampling is taking place.

Self-Selected Samples

In surveys, **self-selection** *occurs when participants place themselves in a sample, rather than being selected for inclusion by a researcher.* If you're browsing the web, come across a link that asks you to take a survey, and choose to participate, you've self-selected into that survey.

The same situation holds when a TV news anchor or host of a talent show (e.g., *The Voice*) says, "To participate in our poll/To vote for your favorite performer . . . text this number." Likewise, TV stations, newspapers, and magazines may ask you to go to their website, link to their survey, and "let your opinion be known." All these surveys rely on self-selected samples. Essentially, this is a form of convenience sampling in which the researcher casts a wide net and hopes for people to respond.

Many self-selected samples have a huge number of participants, but don't let this impress you. If a magazine with 5 million readers includes a survey questionnaire within its latest issue and 250,000 readers submit a completed questionnaire, that's only 5% of the readership. But even if a million readers participated, we could not use the results to reliably estimate how a population would respond. Why? Because we can't assume that people who read that magazine are representative of the general population. In fact, we can't even assume that the people who respond are representative of the population of readers of the magazine! Thus, although it's acceptable to say that "38% of people who took the poll had a certain opinion," it's not acceptable to use the results from a self-selected sample to claim that this opinion is held by "38% of our readers"—or, even worse, "38% of the general population."

Note that most psychological research, whether descriptive or experimental, involves self-selected convenience samples. For example, participants often are recruited from college classes, or via advertisements from the local community, because these usually are the most convenient sources available. The participants are not randomly selected from either the general or local population, or even from the population of students on campus or in a particular class. Rather, they are people who happen to learn of the opportunity to be in a study and choose to sign up.

This use of convenience sampling, however, is adequate for most psychological research. A longitudinal study discussed in Chapter 4, which tested the hypothesis that parental depression is correlated with the subsequent development of conduct problems in children, illustrates this point (Callender et al., 2012). The research team of clinical and developmental psychologists did not seek to use statistics from their sample to estimate a numerical value about the strength of this correlation in the general population (e.g., "Based on our sample, we conclude that in American families with children, there is a correlation of .23 between parental depression and child conduct problems"). Rather, their goal was more along these lines: "If this hypothesis is accurate, then even with a convenience sample, we should find a depression–conduct problem correlation. This is our starting point, and if the hypothesis is supported, we or other researchers can conduct further research to establish the external validity of our findings." A similar logic underlies the use of convenience samples in most descriptive studies and experiments.

Purposive Sampling

In **purposive sampling,** *researchers select a sample according to a specific goal or purpose of the study, rather than at random.* For example, using a cultural psychology framework, Nicole Stephens and her colleagues hypothesized that institutional norms at American universities and colleges emphasize independence over interdependence, and that these norms place first-generation college students at an achievement disadvantage relative to other students from families where one or both parents are college graduates (Stephens, Fryberg, Markus, Johnson, & Covarrubias, 2012). A series of surveys and experiments supported these hypotheses; their initial study was a survey that used purposive sampling.

Stephens et al. (2012) asked high-level college and university administrators (primarily, undergraduate deans) to identify the most important student learning goals that their schools emphasized (e.g., independent research, collaborative research, leadership, being a team player). Rather than select a random sample of administrators from all American higher education institutions, they used *U.S. News & World Report* rankings to identify the top 50 "national universities" and top 25 "liberal arts colleges." They purposefully chose this sample of schools because "administrators employed at top institutions would be good representatives of the current cultural ideals or standards of the mainstream American system of higher education" (p. 1183). In a second survey, they studied less elite schools.

Expert sampling and snowball sampling are two common types of purposive sampling. In **expert sampling,** *researchers identify experts on a topic and ask them to participate.* Stephens et al.'s (2012) rationale for selecting "top schools" represents expert sampling. In **snowball sampling,** *people contacted to participate in a survey are asked to recruit or to provide contact information (names, locations) for other people who meet the criteria for survey inclusion.* For example, the Pew Research Center conducted a series of surveys to assess Internet experts' opinions regarding how the Internet would socially, politically, and economically influence people's lives in the year 2020 (Anderson & Rainie, 2010, p. 4). Expert sampling was initially used to select several hundred people that the researchers identified as Internet leaders and builders. These Internet experts, in turn, were asked to identify and recruit other experts to participate. Thus, the sample size grew or "snowballed." Figure 7.5 summarizes the various type of sampling we have discussed.

MARGIN OF SAMPLING ERROR AND CONFIDENCE LEVEL

The only way to be absolutely certain about how a population would respond to a survey item is to study the entire population. Results from probability samples allow us to estimate how a population would respond, but those estimates come with uncertainty.

To understand this uncertainty, first consider a concept called **sampling variability:** *chance fluctuations in the characteristics of samples that occur when randomly selecting samples from a population.* Suppose that in a national drug use survey, we ask a nationally representative sample of 1,200 adults whether they have consumed alcohol during the past week, and 48.0% say "yes." Now imagine that, starting over with the entire population each time, we had drawn a second random sample, and a third, and fourth. It is unlikely that in each sample, precisely 48.0% of participants would have said "yes." To draw an analogy, suppose you flip a coin 10 times and obtain 7 Heads. This represents one sample of flips. Now, take a second sample by flipping the coin another 10 times, and a third sample, and a fourth. Are you going to get 7 Heads each time? It's unlikely. The number of Heads you obtain with each sample of 10 flips (or 100, or 1,000 flips) will fluctuate as a result of chance factors. Similarly, in our survey, had we repeatedly drawn samples of 1,200 adults, simply due to chance variations in the characteristics of each sample, we would expect some differences in the results obtained from these samples (e.g., 49.1%, 48.5%, 45.7% report consuming alcohol).

These chance fluctuations introduce a degree of error—called *sampling error*—when we use statistics from a sample to estimate numerical values in a population. In other words, our population estimates will differ depending on the particular sample we happen to select. You might wonder, why not draw several samples, average the findings, and use those averages to estimate population values? A major problem with such an approach is that the costs would be prohibitive. Fortunately, however, thanks to statistical theory and probability sampling, we don't need to select multiple samples of people every time we conduct a survey. Instead, we can use the results from our one sample (e.g., 48.0% consumed alcohol) to estimate a range of values within which the true population value is likely to reside.

In everyday language, such as in media reports of surveys, this range of values is commonly called the *margin of error.* The technical term, however, is **margin of sampling error:** *a range of values within which the true population value is presumed to reside.* Thus, based on the finding that 48.0% of our sample consumed alcohol, we could estimate that "48.0% of the population consumed alcohol within the past week, with a margin of sampling error of

Infographic: **Figure 7.5**

SURVEYS AND SAMPLING METHODS

PROBABILITY SAMPLING

PURPOSE: to obtain a representative sample of the population.
- Based on statistical theory.

- Each member of the sampling frame has a chance of being selected.
- Each member's probability of being selected can be specified.

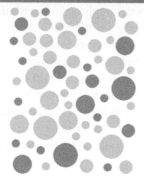

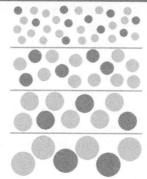

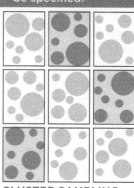

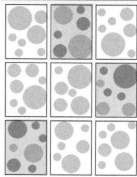

SIMPLE RANDOM SAMPLING
Members are chosen at random from the sampling frame. Each member has an equal probability of being selected. Here the chance of being selected is one third.

STRATIFIED RANDOM SAMPLING
Divide the sampling frame into groups, such as age groups. Allocate spaces in the sample to proportionately represent each group. Randomly select members within each group.

CLUSTER SAMPLING
Clusters of members, such as schools, are randomly selected. In each chosen cluster, all the members (students) are included in the sample.

MULTISTAGE SAMPLING
Probability sampling occurs in multiple stages. Clusters are randomly selected. Then members within each cluster are randomly selected.

- selected to be in the sample
- not selected to be in the sample

NONPROBABILITY SAMPLING

PURPOSE: To obtain samples when probability sampling is not feasible or convenient. To obtain specialized samples.
- Nonrandom selection; not based on statistical theory.

- Often there is no formal sampling frame. The probability of being selected varies and/or cannot be specified.
- Cannot reasonably assume the sample is representative of the population.

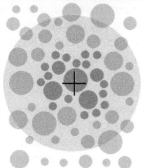

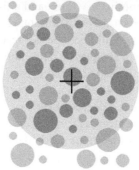

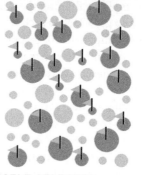

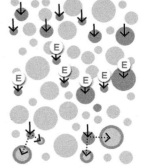

CONVENIENCE SAMPLING
Sample selection is based on convenience. Select participants who happen to pass by or are otherwise available.

QUOTA SAMPLING
Create groups based on an attribute, such as age. Set quotas to represent each group proportionately in the sample. Then select whomever happens to be available to fill the quotas. This is a type of convenience sampling.

SELF-SELECTED SAMPLING
People place themselves in the sample, such as respondents to a survey posted on a website. This is a type of convenience sampling.

↓ **PURPOSIVE SAMPLING**
Hand pick sample to achieve a specific purpose.

Ⓔ **EXPERT SAMPLING**
Ask experts on a topic to participate.

↓ **SNOWBALL SAMPLING**
Ask people with certain attributes to participate and help recruit similar others to participate.

+/−3%." In other words, we are estimating that nationally between 45.0% to 51.0% of adults drank alcohol during the past week.

There is, however, one crucial qualification to this estimate. We can be highly confident, but cannot be absolutely certain, that the true population value lies within the margin of sampling error. In other words, we cannot be sure that between 45% and 51% of the population would have reported using alcohol. The chance always exists that, for any given variable (e.g., alcohol consumption), our particular sample may diverge enough from the population to result in a population estimate that misses the mark, even when the margin of error is taken into account.

Fortunately, when using probability sampling, statistical theory is once again our ally. It allows us to determine a **confidence level,** *a degree of confidence that the true population value resides within a particular margin of error.* Thus, for example, we can estimate that 48.0% of the population would have responded "yes" to using alcohol within the past week, with a margin of sampling error of +/−3% and a confidence level of 95%. This means that, based on the results from our sample of 1,200 participants, we are 95% confident that between 45% and 51% of American adults would have reported consuming alcohol within the past seven days. (For more details on sampling error and the concept of confidence, see Statistics Modules 8 and 15, respectively.)

WHY NOT AIM FOR MORE PRECISE ESTIMATES?

Perhaps you're wondering why we should accept a +/−3% margin of sampling error. Why not aim for a narrower margin like +/−1%? Similarly, why not aim for a higher confidence level, say, 99%? If we did this, based on our survey results, we would be 99% confident that between 47% and 49% of the population drank alcohol during the previous week. Surely that's a more powerful statement than saying we're only 95% confident that between 45% and 51% of the population drank alcohol during this time.

The answer is that the required sample size grows substantially as we seek to narrow the margin of error or increase our confidence level. This may make the costs (e.g., money, effort, time) of conducting the survey prohibitive. Look at Table 7.1. You will see that the desired margin of sampling error strongly influences the needed sample size. For example, with a 95% confidence level, to achieve a margin of sampling error of +/−3% (see Column 2) with a population of 25,000,000 (Row 3), we need a sample of 1,068 people. To narrow the margin of sampling error to +/−1% (Column 1), we would instead need to sample at least 9,600 people.

Table 7.1 also shows that if we hold the margin of sampling error and population size constant, we need a larger sample size if we are seeking a 99% rather than 95% confidence

Table 7.1 Sample Size Needed to Achieve Various Margins of Sampling Error and Confidence Levels

| Size of Population | 95% Confidence Level | | | 99% Confidence Level | | |
| | Margin of Sampling Error | | | Margin of Sampling Error | | |
	+/−1% (1)	+/−3% (2)	+/−5% (3)	+/−1% (4)	+/−3% (5)	+/−5% (6)
2,500	1,984	748	333	2,173	1,061	525
25,000	6,939	1,024	379	9,972	1,717	647
25,000,000	9,600	1,068	385	16,578	1,843	664
250,000,000	9,604	1,068	385	16,588	1,844	664

Sample sizes were calculated using the online Survey Random Sample Calculator (CustomInsight.com, n.d.) and online Sample Size Calculator (National Statistical Service, n.d). In some cells, estimates from the two calculators differed by a sample size of 1; the larger estimate is shown. These sample sizes are general guidelines: Population and survey design characteristics will affect the required sample size.

level. For example, to attain a 99% confidence level and a +/−1% margin of sampling error for a population of 25,000,000, we would need to sample at least 16,578 people (Column 4). In practice, a 95% confidence level has become the standard for survey research. Margins of error between +/−3% and +/−5% are common.

Frequently, survey data are also used to estimate the responses of groups within the overall population, such as women, men, and ethnic and political groups. In such cases, the margin of sampling error depends on the sample size of the group, not the size of the total sample. Suppose that our national sample of 1,200 adults consists of 600 women. Assuming a 95% confidence level, Column 2 in Table 7.1 shows that a sample size of 600 women is insufficient to support a margin of sampling error of +/−3% for a population size of 25,000,000 or more. The sample of 600 women does, however, meet the size requirement of 385 needed for a margin of sampling error of +/−5% (see Column 3). If prior to conducting our survey, we know we will want to maintain a margin of error of +/−3% when separately analyzing the responses of women and men, then we would select a larger sample.

 CONCEPT CHECK 7.2 SELECTING A SAMPLE

Decide whether each statement is true or false. Answers appear on page 240.

1. Quota sampling is a type of probability sampling.
2. Cluster sampling is a type of probability sampling.
3. In probability sampling, it is important that the sample be self-selected.
4. In surveys, sampling error is caused by mistakes that interviewers make in recording people's responses.

CONSTRUCTING THE QUESTIONNAIRE

Learning Objectives

After studying this section, you should be able to:

- Describe the general steps in developing a questionnaire.
- Identify different types (i.e., formats) of questions.
- Explain major issues that arise in the wording and placement of questions.

Whether delivered orally in an interview or in written form, a questionnaire is a scientific measuring device. Creating one may seem easy, but in fact the opposite is true. We may take for granted the expertise needed to construct a good questionnaire, at least until we come across one with ambiguous, biased, or otherwise poorly written items.

STEPS IN DEVELOPING A QUESTIONNAIRE

Developing a good questionnaire requires clarity of goals, preparation, and attention to detail. Here are some of the major steps.

- *Reflect upon your research goals and convert them into a list of more specific topics that you want to learn about.* If your general goal is to learn about alcohol use among college students, specific topics could include: extent of use, attitudes toward use, relation between use and students' demographic and psychological characteristics.

- *Identify variables of interest within each topic.* Within "extent of alcohol use," variables could include: use (yes/no) of alcohol within the past day, week, and month; binge drinking (yes/no) within the past day, week, and month; number of drinks consumed this week.

- *Consider the practical limitations of the survey.* For example, will people have the time and patience to answer all the questions you plan to ask? If not, prioritize and reduce the number of items.

- *Develop your questions, decide on their order, and get feedback from mentors or colleagues.* Do the items really measure the variables that you intend them to? Are they clear? Have someone help you proofread the questions for errors.

- *Pretest your questionnaire.* Administer it to a small sample of people from the population you're studying. Obtain feedback about whether the instructions and items are clear. Assess how long it takes to complete the questionnaire. In pretesting, as in the survey itself, adhere to ethical practices (see Chapter 3).

- *Revise the questionnaire as needed and if possible pretest the revised version before conducting your survey.*

TYPES OF QUESTIONS

You have probably filled out many questionnaires in the past. If so, you know that questionnaire items can be formatted in many ways. Let's examine some commonly used formats.

Open-Ended and Closed-Ended Questions

An **open-ended question** *asks people to respond in their own terms,* whereas a **closed-ended question** *provides specific response options* (Table 7.2). An open-ended format maximizes people's freedom of response. This benefit may be especially important in the preliminary stages of a research project. For example, to develop the closed-ended question that you see in Table 7.2B, you might first present a preliminary sample of students with the first of the two open-ended questions in Table 7.2A. Then you would identify the most common open-ended responses and include them as response options in the closed-ended question.

Unfortunately, open-ended responses can be difficult and time-consuming for researchers to convert into usable data (AAPOR, n.d.). Researchers often need to develop a coding system to classify the responses into mutually exclusive categories. If Bill answers the college satisfaction question by saying "the opportunity to learn new ideas and skills," and Marion says "being able to learn skills that help prepare me for my career," do these responses represent the same or different categories? Researchers must also train people (called "raters") to use the coding system in an accurate and consistent manner. A key goal of such training is to achieve high **interrater reliability,** which occurs when *different raters using the same coding system agree on how they classify or otherwise score participants' responses.*

Closed-ended items have many benefits. The response options are already coded (either by numbers or letters), making it relatively easy to enter the data into a computer file. For theoretical or other reasons, researchers can choose to restrict the response options to the most important or relevant categories. With an open-ended item question, some students might say they are most satisfied with "the athletic facilities" or "the chance for a summer break," responses that may not be theoretically relevant to the purpose of the study.

Closed-ended questions are not perfect, however. A major disadvantage is that, by only being allowed to choose among a limited number of options, some participants may feel that their true answer (e.g., "the athletic facilities," in response to Table 7.2B) isn't included. One solution is to include a response option that says "Other." Researchers also must consider whether to add a response option for "Don't Know."

Multiple-Choice, Ranking, and Forced-Choice Questions

There are many types, or formats, of closed-ended items. *Multiple-choice questions* are commonly used to measure many variables, including demographic characteristics such as level of education, marital status, annual income, family composition, ethnicity, and religious

Table 7.2 Question Formats

A. Open-Ended Questions

Please describe the one aspect of being a college student that you find most satisfying.

In the past week, on how many days did you engage in online social networking?

B. Closed-Ended Question: Multiple-Choice, One Response Allowed

Which of the following aspects of being a college student do you find most satisfying?
Please circle one:

1. the opportunity to challenge myself intellectually

2. the opportunity to be exposed to new ideas

3. the opportunity to make progress toward a career

4. the opportunity to meet new people

5. the opportunity to participate in campus social life

C. Closed-Ended Question: Multiple-Choice, Multiple Responses Allowed

How did you learn about our product? Check as many sources as apply.

❏ TV   ❏ Internet   ❏ Newspaper ad   ❏ Family member

❏ Radio   ❏ Magazine   ❏ Friend   ❏ Other source

D. Closed-Ended Question: Ranking Scale

The world faces many problems today. Ten problems are listed alphabetically below. Please place the number 1 next to the problem that you believe is the most important. Then place a 2 next to the problem you believe is second most important, and so on, until you have ranked all 10 items.

——————— AIDS crisis   ——————— overpopulation

——————— armed conflict   ——————— pollution

——————— global warming   ——————— poverty

——————— hunger   ——————— prejudice

——————— natural resource depletion   ——————— terrorism

E. Closed-Ended Question: Forced-Choice

Select only one response from each pair of statements below. If you feel that neither statement exactly matches your opinion, then choose the response that best represents what you believe.

Statement One: Having a strong military is the best way to guarantee lasting peace.

OR

Statement Two: Using skillful negotiation and diplomacy is the best approach to guarantee lasting peace.

Source: Information from the Pew Research Center (2016, para. 2 and item 14).

F. Closed-Ended Question: Likert-Type Rating Format

Would you support or oppose a federal law that bans the death penalty?

1	2	3	4	5
Strongly Support	Support	Neutral	Oppose	Strongly Oppose

---

affiliation. Here's an example: "What is your current marital status? Never been married, married, living with a partner, divorced, separated, widowed." Questions B and C in Table 7.2 are other multiple-choice items.

Multiple-choice items often require respondents to choose just one answer, such as the item they consider most important or most desirable. Question B in Table 7.2 illustrates this format. Here's another example of a question that calls for only one answer: "Which of the following issues is the most important problem facing the world today?" Alternatively, multiple-choice items may allow respondents to select as many answers as they wish; Question C in Table 7.2 is an example of this format.

Ranking scales present a list of items and ask people to order them along some dimension, such as degree of importance. Question D in Table 7.2 provides an example. With ranking scales, you can ask people to rank all the response options (e.g., rank all 10 problems from most to least important), or just a subset of them (e.g., rank the three problems you feel are most important by writing a 1, 2, or 3 next to the item, with 1 representing your top choice).

Forced-choice questions, such as Question E in Table 7.2, require people to choose between two options. One reason that researchers use forced-choice questions and ranking scales is to avoid the possibility that people might express the same opinion or preference toward each side of an issue. If the question on ensuring peace had been split into two questions, perhaps a person might agree equally with each statement. If asked to judge each global problem separately, perhaps a person would rate each problem as "extremely important." Forced-choice items and ranking scales help to tease out people's priorities and relative preferences.

Rating Scales and Formats

Many survey items, such as Question F in Table 7.2, ask people to report their attitudes, beliefs, and behaviors along a quantitative dimension. One of the best known types of rating scales, the **Likert scale,** *measures people's attitudes by combining scores on several items, each of which records how positively or negatively a person feels about a statement.* Social-organizational psychologist Rensis Likert (1932) developed this approach. Each individual item in a Likert scale is called a *Likert item.*

Suppose we want to measure people's attitudes about the death penalty. We could pose several statements, such as:

Item 1 Do you agree or disagree that the death penalty should be allowed as a punishment for committing murder?

Item 2 Do you agree or disagree that there should be a national law banning the death penalty?

Item 3 Do you agree or disagree that the death penalty should be allowed for some crimes other than murder?

Each item would be answered using a 5-point response format, as follows:

1	2	3	4	5
Strongly Disagree	Disagree	Neither Agree Nor Disagree	Agree	Strongly Agree

The "negative" and "positive" response options are balanced around a neutral point, and each option is labeled by a number and verbal statement (e.g., "Strongly Agree") called an "anchor." Ratings on the individual Likert items would be added to compute a total score that represents a person's overall attitude about the death penalty. Recognize that unlike Items 1 and 3, for Item 2 higher ratings indicate a stronger attitude against the death penalty. Therefore, before computing a total attitude score, we would *reverse score* (i.e., recode) Item 3 as follows: $1 = 5, 2 = 4, 3 = 3, 4 = 2$, and $5 = 1$.

Likert's 5-point balanced rating format became famous—so famous that the format itself is often called a Likert rating scale, even though the term *Likert response format* is more appropriate (Carifio & Perla, 2007). This format has spawned many variations: For example, some researchers use a 7-point format, created by adding options such as "Slightly Disagree" and "Slightly Agree." Likert's response format can also be used with labels other than "Agree–Disagree," such as "Approve–Disapprove" and "Support–Oppose," as Question F in Table 7.2 illustrates.

WORDING THE QUESTIONS: IT'S HARDER THAN YOU THINK

Survey questions should be kept as simple and short as possible in order to make them easy to understand and to keep the overall length of the survey manageable. Each question should be clear, balanced, and free of jargon (AAPOR, n.d.; Dillman, Smyth, & Christian, 2014). Here are some common pitfalls to avoid:

- **Leading questions** *are items presented in an unbalanced way that can overtly or subtly suggest that one viewpoint or response is preferable to another.* For example, first consider a balanced question: "Do you support or oppose the university's proposal to raise tuition by $100 per year in order to modernize campus computer facilities?" Now consider two leading versions: (1) "You support the university's proposal to raise tuition . . . don't you? (2) "Do you support the university's proposal to raise tuition. . . ?" The first version, which could be asked in a face-to-face or telephone interview, overtly suggests that supporting the tuition raise is the desirable response. The second version is more subtle, although asking "Do you support. . ." would still be leading. To avoid this bias, the question should be balanced: "Do you support or oppose. . . ?"

- **Loaded questions** *are items containing emotionally charged words that suggest one viewpoint or response is preferable to another, or containing assumptions with which the option to disagree is not provided.* For example: "Would you favor or oppose a law banning restaurants from serving foods that contain dangerous, heart-damaging trans-fats?" The last part of the question should be rephrased as "from serving foods that contain trans-fats?" Questions also are loaded when they contain an assumption that, by virtue of the answer options provided, forces the respondent to go along with the assumption. For example, suppose you are asked: "From 1 to 12 months, how many months should our new college president be given to clean up the administration's wasteful spending?" By answering this question, you are implicitly acknowledging that the administration's spending is wasteful, even if you don't believe or don't know whether this is the case. A fairer approach would be to ask people whether they do or don't believe that the administration's spending is wasteful, and then for those who do, follow that up with a question about the time frame for addressing this situation.

- **Double-barreled questions** *are items that ask about two issues within one question, forcing respondents to combine potentially different opinions into one judgment.* For example: "Do you agree or disagree that alcohol use and marijuana use are a problem among today's college students?" If someone strongly agrees that marijuana use is a problem, but strongly disagrees that alcohol use is a problem, what should this person mark on a 5-point Likert-style item: "Neither Agree Nor Disagree"? The solution is to ask separate questions: one about alcohol, the other about marijuana.

- **Double negatives,** *which are items whose phrasing contains two negative words,* often cause confusion. For example: "Do you agree or disagree that, once people reach the age of adulthood, it is not possible for them to change their undesirable personality traits?" Combining "not possible" with "undesirable" creates a double negative. Toss in the "disagree" phrasing and we actually have a triple negative. The question also is needlessly long. Here's a better version: "Do you believe it is possible or impossible for adults to change their basic personality traits?"

PLACING THE QUESTIONS IN ORDER

After writing the individual questionnaire items, we must now decide on their sequence. Such decisions can be difficult because the particular placement and grouping of items can affect people's responses to them.

Order Effects

The general placement of an item, such as whether it comes toward the beginning or end of a questionnaire, is one factor that can influence people's responses. For example, boredom or fatigue may reduce people's attentiveness in responding to items placed near the end of a survey. Krosnick and Pressor (2010) note that, at least with self-administered questionnaires (such as those in mail or online surveys, where a live interviewer is not presenting the items), people may provide less detail in their answers to open-ended questions, or may be more likely to skip items or simply respond "agree" when those items appear later rather than earlier in a questionnaire.

Context effects, *which occur when responses to a survey item are influenced by the particular items that occur directly or soon before it,* are another type of order effect. Consider this example provided by the Pew Research Center (2015, January 29). In October 2003, Pew researchers conducted a poll that included two items in which people were asked whether they favored or opposed (a) gay marriage, and (b) legal agreements (civil unions) affording the same rights to gays and lesbians as those given to married couples. At that time, gay marriage was not legal in any of the 50 states in the United States. Within the overall poll, the researchers experimentally manipulated the order of these two items.

The influence of item order on responses to the question about gay marriage was not statistically significant. In contrast, as you can see in Table 7.3, 37% of people who were first presented with the question about civil unions said that they favored such legal agreements, whereas 45% of people expressed support for civil unions when that question was asked immediately after the question about gay marriage.

In case you feel that a swing of eight percentage points based on item order does not seem particularly large, consider this: Given the first sequence of items, a newspaper headline in 2003 might have read "New poll finds that U.S. adults clearly oppose civil unions." Based on the second sequence, that headline might have been "New poll finds that almost half of U.S. adults support civil unions."

Context effects are more likely to occur when adjacent items in a questionnaire focus on related rather than unrelated topics, but overall it is not easy to predict when a significant context effect will occur (Krosnick & Presser, 2010) and researchers disagree on whether they are common or relatively infrequent (Tourangeau, Singer, & Presser, 2003). The potential for

Table 7.3

More People Favor Civil Unions When First Asked About Gay Marriage					
	Sequence 1			Sequence 2	
Asked first	*Legal agreements*	%		*Gay marriage*	%
	Favor	**37**		Favor	33
	Oppose	55		Oppose	61
	Don't know	8		Don't know	6
Asked second	*Gay marriage*			*Legal agreements*	
	Favor	30		Favor	**45**
	Oppose	58		Oppose	47
	Don't know	12		Don't know	8
Sample size		780			735

PEW RESEARCH CENTER Oct., 2003 (as cited in Pew Research Center, 2015, January 29).

context effects to occur, however, has especially important implications for researchers who periodically (e.g., annually) conduct surveys—such as those asking about lifestyle habits, drug use, or political or social attitudes—to examine changes in public opinion or in people's behaviors over time. Whether the samples in these surveys include the same participants studied longitudinally over time, or a new probability sample selected for each survey, it is important for the researchers to keep the sequence of items as similar as possible over time in each successive survey questionnaire (Pew Research Center, 2015, January 29).

General Guidelines

When determining the sequence of items in a questionnaire, one rule of thumb is to group together items that deal with a similar topic or subtopic (Dillman et al., 2014). Suppose we are conducting a broad survey of adults' lifestyle habits: their jobs, shopping routines, sleep habits, recreational activities, and eating patterns. If we want to ask multiple questions about each of these topics, it will generally be better to group those questions by topic than to skip around and ask one question about sleep, the next question about eating, the next about shopping, and so forth. Grouping questions by topic allows survey participants to focus their attention more easily on one aspect of their lives at a time.

Another rule of thumb, within a set of questions on the same or related topics, is to place open-ended questions before closed-ended questions (Pew Research Center, 2015, January 29). The rationale for this is to avoid having the response options listed in closed-ended questions influence participants' answers to open-ended items. For example, if we want to know which of today's many global problems young adults believe is most important, it would be better to ask them an open-ended question before, rather than after, presenting a multiple-choice or ranking item that lists specific problems, such as Question D in Table 7.2. This way, they would say what's on their mind—and possibly mention a global problem that is not on the list—without having their attention or memory influenced by the 10 world problems identified in the ranking item.

A third rule of thumb is to place more general items (whether open-ended or closed-ended) before more specific ones. For example, suppose that a survey contains a question asking college students to rank order the importance of several planning goals on their campus, such as reducing class sizes, offering required courses more frequently, upgrading student computer facilities, and improving campus safety. Let's imagine that the survey also will contain several specific questions about campus crime, such as (1) "Within the past year, how many incidents of physical assault do you believe were reported on campus?" and (2) "A rape in a dormitory was reported to campus police last week. Were you aware of this (yes/no)?" If specific items like these were to come before the item asking students to rank the importance of campus issues, they might heighten students' awareness of and fears about campus crime, and thus bias their response to the ranking scale item (AAPOR, n.d.).

A fourth guideline is to place personally sensitive questions after those that are less personally sensitive, and certainly to avoid starting the survey with highly sensitive questions (Dillman et al., 2014). In face-to-face and telephone interviews, this will give the interviewer more time to build rapport with the participant. For any survey format, the time already invested in responding to earlier questions may increase the participant's subsequent willingness to answer deeply personal questions.

A fifth guideline concerns items placed at the beginning of a survey. Krosnick and Pressor (2010) note that, to boost participants' motivation to respond to the survey attentively, "a questionnaire's initial items should usually bear a strong connection to the topic and purpose that were described in the survey introduction, engage respondent interest, and impose minimal respondent burden" (p. 291). Krosnick and Pressor point out that, to achieve this, researchers often avoid putting a slew of boring demographic questions at the beginning of a questionnaire and instead start with relatively nonsensitive, closed-ended items that are easy for respondents to answer and ask about their attitudes or factual information (e.g., about lifestyle habits).

Depending on the particular items in each survey, there may be many times when following one of these rules of thumb conflicts with another. Ultimately, the researchers' expertise on the topics and questionnaire construction will determine the item order they choose.

CONCEPT CHECK 7.3 CONSTRUCTING THE QUESTIONNAIRE

Decide whether each statement is true or false. Answers appear on page 240.

1. "Tell me about the personal qualities that you look for in a close friend" is an example of an open-ended question.

2. Ranking scales and forced-choice items are examples of closed-ended questions.

3. A Likert scale combines ratings on several items, and each item uses a balanced response format.

4. Double-barreled questions are desirable because they allow the researcher to ask about two issues by using just one question.

ADMINISTERING THE SURVEY

Learning Objectives

After studying this section, you should be able to:

- Describe face-to-face and telephone interviewing and the advantages and disadvantages of each.
- Describe mail and Internet surveys and the advantages and disadvantages of each.
- Explain nonresponse bias and discuss its relation to response rates.

Historically, surveys have been administered in three ways: through face-to-face interviews, through telephone interviews, and by mail. More recently, electronic methods such as websites and email have joined the list. Some surveys, called *mixed-mode surveys,* use multiple approaches (Dillman et al, 2014). In one national survey, students in the United States were interviewed in person at the start of their first year of college (Fischer, 2007). During the rest of their college careers, these same students participated in a series of follow-up telephone interviews. In another survey, face-to-face interviews were conducted in the homes of randomly selected adults in England, Scotland, and Wales before and after a political election (Johnson, Thomson, & Scholes, 2007). For some participants, the Internet was used to administer a follow-up questionnaire.

FACE-TO-FACE INTERVIEWS

Face-to-face interviews, also called *in-person interviews,* occur in many settings. As you shop in a mall or stroll through town, an interviewer using convenience sampling might ask you to participate in a consumer survey. Other surveys, including some that involve randomly selected national samples, employ face-to-face interviews conducted at people's residences (Johnson et al., 2007).

Because of their many advantages, face-to-face interviews are often considered the gold standard of how to administer a survey (Ball, 2007, March 5). First, they generally achieve higher response rates than telephone or mail surveys (Holbrook, Green, & Krosnick, 2003). Second, in a face-to-face meeting, the interviewer has the best chance of establishing personal rapport with the participant. Rapport can be important when it comes to ask sensitive questions that a participant might otherwise be reluctant to answer. Rapport can also help the interviewer motivate the participant to complete the survey, particularly if the questionnaire is long. Third, an in-person interviewer can ensure that the questions are presented to all participants in the same order. Fourth, if participants have difficulty interpreting some items or give ambiguous responses, the interviewer can clear this up. Finally, in a face-to-face situation, interviewers have access to respondents' verbal and facial cues that may indicate uncertainty about items, inattention, fatigue, and so on.

One major drawback to face-to-face interviews is their high cost. Interviewers must be trained, in many surveys they are paid, and there are time and transportation costs associated with traveling to people's homes or workplaces. If the participant is not available, one or more return trips may be required. By some estimates, in the United States it costs about $1,000 to conduct a one-hour in-person interview in a participant's home (Ball, 2007, March 5).

A second concern is that, if questions are delivered verbally by the interviewer, complicated items or those containing many response options may tax participants' memory capabilities. For example, suppose I ask you: "Of the following global problems, which do you think is the most important?" I then read aloud a list of 10 problems (global warming, poverty, etc.). Unfortunately, this amount of information exceeds the typical storage capacity of human working memory (i.e., short-term memory). The first few items and those toward the end of the list are likely to be remembered best, thereby biasing the probability that respondents will pick one of these issues (Krosnick, 1999). To avoid this problem, an interviewer might give the participant a card to look at, on which the question and answer options are printed.

Another concern with face-to-face interviews is the possibility of **interviewer effects:** *aspects of the interviewer's presence that distort participants' true responses.* One potential source of distortion is *interviewer bias.* With or without conscious awareness, when interviewers read questions out loud, they may exhibit subtle changes in facial expression or voice inflection that influence people's responses. Upon hearing a person's response, an interviewer may make a facial expression or utter a verbal response ("hmmm") suggesting approval or disapproval; this, in turn, may shape the participant's responses to subsequent items.

Interviewer characteristics, such as gender, ethnicity, and age, are another set of factors that may distort how participants respond. For example, one study examined national survey data to assess whether the racial attitudes expressed by Black participants differed depending on whether the interviewer was Black or White (Anderson, Silver, & Abramson, 1988). The findings indicated that Black participants were more likely to express greater warmth toward Whites when the interviewer was White. In another study, researchers examined data from a pre-election poll taken in Virginia in which one of the candidates for governor was Black (Finkel, Guterbock, & Borg, 1991). Compared to White participants questioned by White interviewers, White participants questioned by Black interviewers were more likely to indicate an intention to vote for the Black candidate.

Rigorous interviewer training is an important part (and cost) of survey research. It helps standardize interviewers' procedures for administering the questionnaire. Increasingly, computer-assisted personal interviewing (CAPI) systems have been used to further standardize interviewers' behavior and increase the efficiency of data collection. With CAPI, the questionnaire is loaded onto a laptop or touchscreen tablet computer. In one approach, the interviewer follows the sequence of questions that appear on the computer screen, reads each one, and records participants' answers. In another approach, the computer may be turned over to the participants, who then read the questions and enter their responses to each item. In a hybrid approach, the interviewer reads most of the items but turns the computer over to participants for questions of an especially sensitive nature, allowing them to respond with greater privacy.

TELEPHONE INTERVIEWS

In Canada and the United States, telephone interviewing became widely accepted by the early 1980s, at which time almost all households had landline telephones. Before then, telephone surveys ran a substantial risk of creating nonrepresentative samples: Many households didn't have telephones and they differed in important ways—such as having less income—from households that had telephones. Note that survey researchers in Canada and the United States are allowed to call phone numbers registered with national "do not call" lists, which allow people to block calls from some types of telemarketers.

As with face-to-face interviews, telephone interviews—at least those that aren't completely automated and conducted by a voice-synthesized computer—have the advantage of a "human touch." A human interviewer can clarify people's questions about the survey, explain items that participants may find confusing, and establish some rapport with respondents. Compared to face-to-face surveys, in phone surveys it is easier for researchers to monitor whether interviewers are following standardized instructions and correctly handling any problems (e.g., one supervisor can monitor and assist many interviewers).

Most telephone surveys employ *random digit dialing (RDD),* which uses computers to randomly determine the phone numbers that will be dialed. RDD surveys have been called "the workhorse of the survey industry" (Link, Battaglia, Frankel, Osborn, & Mokdad, 2008). A key advantage of using RDD is that many people have unlisted numbers. As a group, if people with unlisted numbers differ in important ways from people who list their numbers, then their exclusion will produce a biased sample. With RDD, both listed and unlisted numbers are covered. For survey researchers, federal regulations allow automated dialing of phone numbers generated by RDD for both landline and cell phones in Canada, but only for landlines in the United States (Public Works and Government Services Canada, 2014). In the United States, RDD cell phone numbers must be dialed by a human caller.

Many telephone surveys use computer-assisted telephone interview (CATI) systems. The questionnaire is entered into a computer, the interviewer sits at a computer terminal, and as the survey instructions and items appear on the computer monitor, the interviewer reads them to the participant. The interviewer can enter participants' answers directly into the computer, which greatly enhances the speed and ease of gathering and storing the data.

Telephone surveys also have disadvantages. Interviewers may not be able to establish the same level of rapport over the phone that they could in person. For participants, it may be more mentally taxing to listen to survey items being read over the phone than it would be to see the items on a computer screen or printed questionnaire. Thus, to maintain participants' attention and patience, phone interviews typically last no more than 30 minutes (Holbrook et al., 2003). Although facial cues are eliminated, interviewer effects may still occur. People can still be influenced by an interviewer's verbal cues, and they may respond to items differently based on their perception of the interviewer's sex, ethnicity, or age (Cotter, Cohen, & Coulter, 1982).

The Cell-Phone-Only Problem

Another concern regarding telephone surveys is that for ethical, practical, and financial reasons, they are more difficult to implement for cell phones. Because many people have only cell phones and no landline phones—47% of American adults and 21% of Canadian households, with those numbers growing yearly (Blumberg & Luke, 2015; Statistics Canada, 2014)—such individuals would not be sampled in a traditional landline random digit dialing survey. To complicate matters, cell-phone-only use is more common among younger than older people, and among people in low- rather than middle- or high-income households. For example, a recent national probability survey of adults in the United States estimated that 60% of 25- to 29-year-olds, but only 9% of adults 65 and older, live in cell-phone-only households (Blumberg & Luke, 2015).

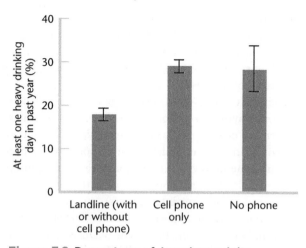

Figure 7.6 Percentage of American adults, by telephone status, who reported having a heavy drinking day at least once during the past year. Data were collected from 17,762 people, using in-person interviews that measured participants' phone status. In this sample, 8,581 people lived in households that had landlines, 8,610 lived in cell-phone-only households, and 571 people had no phone in their household. (Based on data in S. J. Blumberg and J. V. Luke (2015). *Wireless substitution: Early release of estimates from the National Health Interview Survey, July–December 2014.* National Center for Health Statistics. Released June 2015. Available from http://www.cdc .gov/nchs/nhis.htm.)

Survey researchers have found that cell-phone-only users respond differently to many items, as compared to people whose households have landlines. **Figure 7.6** shows one example.[2] Had this national survey only sampled households with landlines, the results would have underestimated the percent of adults who reported having at least one day of heavy drinking (i.e., for men and women, respectively, consuming five or four alcoholic drinks in one day) during the prior year.

To obtain more representative samples of the populations being studied, survey researchers have had to supplement traditional, landline random digit dialing with additional samples of cell-phone-only users (Blumberg & Luke, 2015). However, as noted earlier, it is illegal in the United States to use automated dialers (i.e., with synthesized voices) to call cell phone users. Interviewers must personally make the calls, which raises survey costs. And regardless of whether automated dialing can be used, the probability sampling is tricky, because a landline typically covers a household, a cell phone typically covers one user, and many people have both. Therefore, if survey researchers develop two sampling frames—one for landline numbers and one for cell phone numbers—people who have landlines and cell phones may be randomly dialed via either list and thus have a greater probability of being selected for participation than people who only have landlines or cell phones. To avoid this, some survey organizations incur the extra expense of identifying cell-phone-only subscribers and then developing landline and cell phone sampling frames that do not overlap. The bottom line is that the explosion of cell phone and cell-phone-only use raises complex issues for survey researchers.

MAIL SURVEYS

Create your questionnaire, select your sample, and then let the postal service deliver it. If this sounds like a less expensive way to administer a survey than via in-person or telephone interviews, it typically is (Link et al., 2008). Mail surveys usually involve higher supply costs but lower labor costs as there are no interviewers to train and pay. Mail surveys also have other advantages. With a written questionnaire, people can look at each item for as long as they wish. A mail survey that asks you to rank order the importance of 10 global problems won't be affected by the working memory limitations that would occur if you could only hear the items over the phone. Some people may be more likely to answer highly personal questions in a mail survey than in an interview, particularly if they are assured that their responses will be anonymous.

---

[2] In Figure 7.6, the small I-shaped bar at the top of each big bar represents a "95% confidence interval." This relates to our discussion of margin of sampling error and confidence level. If the researchers conducted their sampling procedure 100 times, and did this repeatedly, on average we would expect that in 95 of 100 samples the result for this item would fall within the range of the I-shaped bar. See Statistics Modules 15.1 and 15.2 for more information about confidence intervals and error bars.

Despite these advantages, however, mail surveys have traditionally been regarded as less desirable than in-person or telephone interview surveys (Krosnick, 1999). People may start to fill out a mail survey but get interrupted or bored with the questions and never finish it. They may open the envelope the survey arrives in, glance at the survey, and then toss it in the garbage. Or, besieged by junk mail, they may just toss the survey before even opening its envelope. As a result of reactions like these, mail surveys generally have lower response rates than in-person or telephone surveys: Often, only 15% to 50% of a sample responds. This compares to response rates of 40% to 80% often reported for telephone surveys (Groves, 2006). To increase mail survey response rates, researchers may send reminder postcards and even mail a duplicate survey to people who initially fail to respond (Link et al., 2008).

Another problem with mail surveys is that, because no direct interaction with an interviewer occurs, participants are on their own when filling out the survey. There is no guarantee that people will read the questions carefully or complete the items in order. Despite the care that good survey researchers take to develop clear questionnaires, some participants may find certain questions to be ambiguous or difficult to follow. With mail surveys, no interviewer is present to help clarify those items.

ONLINE SURVEYS

As the Internet has become a popular vehicle for gathering survey data, it has created new opportunities and challenges for survey researchers (Dillman et al., 2014). One advantage is that labor and production costs are vastly reduced: There are no interviewers to be paid, no questionnaires to be printed and mailed. People input their own answers electronically, creating ready-made files for data analysis. Survey data can be gathered via the Internet more quickly than via other methods. Finally, online social networks (e.g., trauma support groups, product user groups) provide researchers with a means for accessing special samples of people (Birnbaum, 2004).

Many online surveys rely on convenience sampling. A survey goes up on the web, most people never see it, and among those who happen to come across it, some choose to respond. We discussed earlier that convenience sampling is used in, and is adequate for, most psychological research. Likewise, online convenience sampling can be adequate for some purposes, such as testing hypotheses about associations between variables. But, like other convenience samples, online convenience samples may be unrepresentative of the population of interest. They may even be unrepresentative of all web users within that population. With convenience sampling, it is not feasible to calculate a margin of sampling error and confidence level that would allow us to meaningfully estimate specific numerical values in a population (e.g., the percentage of people in a population that would respond a particular way).

Is it possible to create representative, probability-based samples for Internet surveys? The number of Internet users has been growing steadily for many years. Still, in terms of at least occasional personal use, roughly 16% of U.S. and Canadian adults are not Internet users (Perrin & Duggan, 2015; The Daily, 2013, October 28). Moreover, adult Internet users and nonusers differ from each other in important ways. For example, as Figure 7.7 shows, Internet users are younger (Perrin & Duggan, 2015). So, putting together a random sample of Internet users would not be an adequate way to obtain a nationally representative sample of the population. And, for those people who don't use the Internet, how can they possibly participate in an online survey?

Fortunately, there are solutions. For example, suppose we use random sampling to contact by telephone a nationally representative sample of people at home. We then ask them to participate in an online survey and give them the web address for the questionnaire. For people who don't have Internet access, we pay for it and also pay for any hardware they need. In fact,

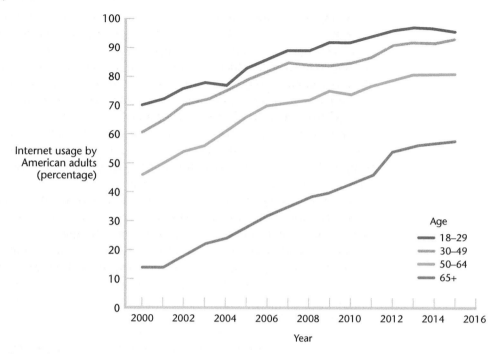

Figure 7.7 **Growth in Internet use among U.S. adults, 2000–2015.** (Information from Perrin & Duggan, 2015.)

we keep paying for their Internet access in the long term in exchange for their continued willingness to participate in other surveys from time to time. For people who already have web access, we offer other incentives for their future participation in surveys.

Using this procedure, one commercial company has developed a nationally representative sampling frame of about 55,000 adults who are available to participate in online surveys (GFK Knowledge Networks, 2013). Academic, governmental, and other organizations then contact this company and pay it a fee to obtain a nationally representative sample. For example, using this approach, social psychologist Linda Skitka and her colleagues conducted theory-testing surveys examining people's emotional reactions and political tolerance in the aftermath of the September 11, 2001, terrorist attacks (Skitka, Bauman, & Mullen, 2004). Academic researchers have been working with survey organizations to develop similar procedures for creating nationally representative online samples (Trei, 2006).

RESPONSE RATE AND NONRESPONSE BIAS

Ideally, every person in a randomly selected survey sample would complete the survey, but some people end up not participating for one of two general reasons. The first is *noncontact:* The researchers are unable to reach them. The second reason is *refusal* (also called *noncooperation*): People who are contacted may simply say, "No, thanks."

What happens, then, if there are important differences in demographic, psychological, or other characteristics of sampled people who end up taking part in the survey versus those who don't? Such differences could create a problem, called **nonresponse bias,** *which occurs when people who were selected but didn't participate in a survey would have provided significantly different answers (or other data) from those provided by participants.* Nonresponse bias introduces error into the values estimated for the population. To illustrate, in a national survey with a 50% response rate, if 44% of participants say they will vote for Candidate X, but only 32% of nonparticipants would have given this same response, then the conclusion that "44% of adults say they will vote for Candidate X, with a margin of error of +/−3%" would overestimate the support for Candidate X. Of course, if nonparticipants don't differ significantly from participants in how they would have responded, then nonresponse bias would not be a concern.

Common sense says that the lower the survey response rate, the greater the risk that the obtained sample will be nonrepresentative and thus nonresponse bias will distort the results. After all, if 100% of a sample participated, nonresponse bias wouldn't exist. For decades, this has been the conventional wisdom among survey researchers.

In some scientific studies of survey methodology, researchers have used several strategies to assess the degree of nonresponse bias in a survey. For example, they have used information from legally available records to directly compare certain characteristics of participants versus nonparticipants. Surprisingly, this research indicates that within the range of response rates typically found for surveys that use probability sampling, lower response rates are only weakly associated with greater nonresponse bias. Practically speaking, a survey's response rate is often a poor predictor of the degree of nonresponse bias (Groves, 2006; Groves & Peytcheva, 2008). It cannot be automatically assumed that a probability survey with a low response rate is less accurate in estimating the values of a population than a survey with a moderately high response rate.

Although the association between response rates and nonresponse bias may not be as strong as once thought, in general, survey researchers believe that the higher the response rate, the better. Therefore, they have become concerned with the decline in survey response rates that has occurred in recent decades. For example, in the late 1970s and early 1980s, response rates to the University of Michigan's Survey of Consumer Attitudes (a monthly, national telephone survey) were around 70%; by 2003 the response rate was down to 48% (Curtin, Presser, & Singer, 2005).

Declining response rates are partly due to phone interviewers having greater difficulty making contact with the people they call. The widespread adoption of technologies such as answering machines, voicemail, caller ID, and call blocking has increased people's ability to screen out phone calls from survey interviewers (Dillman, et al., 2014). And, among people with whom contact is made, refusal rates have increased (Curtin et al., 2005). Some researchers speculate that the boom in telemarketing calls may have contributed to declining survey participation. People today may be more annoyed by, or weary of, having their privacy invaded than they were in the past.

Survey researchers have tried several methods to combat declining response rates. Telephone interviewers may call someone dozens of times to try to make contact. If someone doesn't respond to a mail survey, a second survey may be mailed. Researchers also may send a pre-survey letter to people in the sample, sometimes including a prepaid monetary incentive, informing the recipients that they have been selected to participate and asking for their cooperation. Alternatively, an interviewer may offer a monetary incentive after making contact with someone, or only if the person initially declines to participate. In general, notification letters and monetary incentives have had mixed success in improving response rates (Singer, Hoewyk, & Maher, 2000).

✓ CONCEPT CHECK 7.4 ADMINISTERING THE SURVEY

Fill in each of the blanks below. In some cases, answer choices appear within parentheses. Answers appear on page 240.

1. _____ surveys (Face-to-face, Telephone, Mail, Internet) provide the best opportunity to establish rapport with respondents, but involve the highest costs.

2. Two major sources of interviewer effects are _____ and _____.

3. Overall, the growing number of cell-phone-only users has made it _____ (easier, harder) for survey researchers to conduct telephone surveys.

4. _____ occurs when the responses of people who didn't participate in a survey would have significantly differed from the participants' responses.

BEING A SMART SURVEY CONSUMER

Learning Objectives

After studying this section, you should be able to:

- Discuss several critical thinking questions that people should ask when reading about survey results.

- Explain "sugging," "frugging," and "push polling," and why they are unethical.

From one source or another—the Internet, TV, radio, newspapers, or magazines—you are likely to come across survey results throughout your life. You also may be asked to participate in surveys, including scientific surveys, commercial opinion polls, and marketing surveys. We'll conclude the chapter by briefly discussing these two aspects of being a survey research consumer.

THINKING CRITICALLY ABOUT SURVEY RESULTS

Findings from well-conducted surveys can keep you accurately informed, help you make good decisions (e.g., about a product to buy or a service to use), and enrich your life in various ways. In contrast, findings from poorly conducted surveys carry a significant risk of misleading you. I hope that the concepts covered in this chapter will help you better distinguish good from poor surveys. Moreover, as a critical thinker, here are some basic questions that you should keep in mind when you come across survey results.

First, *who conducted the survey, and for what purpose?* Was it conducted by an independent survey organization or research team? Was it conducted or sponsored by an organization that would have something to gain if the results were to turn out a particular way? Is the purpose of the survey basic or applied? Are claims being made that the survey is scientific, or is it acknowledged that the purpose was nonscientific?

Second, *was probability sampling used?* If yes, what are the margin of sampling error and confidence level? If not, was purposive sampling used and does the rationale for it seem reasonable? Or, did the survey use some type of convenience sampling? If so, do the authors acknowledge this and mention the drawbacks of convenience sampling?

Third, *what method was used to administer the survey?* Does the method seem appropriate? Does it introduce any special concerns that might decrease the validity of the findings? What was the response rate?

Fourth, *are the survey questions appropriate?* Do they represent a good measure of the variables of interest? Are they clearly written and unbiased? When a series of surveys have been used to study time trends, has the operational definition of any variables changed? Sometimes, to determine these answers, you may have to read the fine print. Take a look again at Figure 7.7. How would you define an "Internet user"? A footnote in the survey report clarifies that until January 2005, being an Internet user was measured by the item "Do you ever go online to access the Internet or World Wide Web or to send and receive email?" (Perrin & Duggan, 2015, p. 4). Since then, a two-part item has been used in the survey: "'Do you use the Internet, at least occasionally?' OR 'Do you send or receive email, at least occasionally?'" (p. 15). Someone who responds "yes" to either part is considered an Internet user.

Fifth, *are the results interpreted properly? Are the conclusions reasonable?* In particular, if a survey did not use probability sampling, are the results—such as statements about specific percentages—appropriately discussed as being applicable only to that sample? Or, are conclusions inappropriately being drawn about the broader population?

Unfortunately, in real life it may be impossible to get answers to all these questions. Often, an organization or media article fails to provide some key information about a survey. When reading claims based on surveys, be especially wary when no information is given about whether probability sampling was used, yet specific numerical projections are made about a population (e.g., 18% of Americans. . . ; 34% of college students. . .).

BEING AWARE OF BOGUS SURVEYS

Scientists and other legitimate survey researchers depend on people's willingness to participate in their studies. Conversely, in the long run, for people to continue to voluntarily participate, they must be able to trust that surveys are legitimate. So, consider the following situation in which a college student answers a phone call. The caller says, "Hello, we're conducting a brief student opinion survey about financial loans. It's only four questions and will take about one minute." Without pausing, the caller proceeds:

- Do you agree that financial loans can be helpful for college students?

- Do you agree that most students would put money from a loan to good use?

- Do you agree that most students are responsible and can manage a loan?

- I can tell you about our excellent loan services. If not now, what would be a good time to call back?

Although this example is fictitious (I created it), it illustrates a deceptive marketing technique, *sugging: selling under the guise of research*. The caller intended to sell a product, initially disguised that intent, and asked leading questions under the pretext of conducting a survey. A similar deceptive practice, *frugging*, involves *fund-raising under the guise of research*. Here, under the pretext of conducting a survey, a caller asks questions (e.g., often, leading questions emphasizing the virtues of a charitable cause, or of a political initiative or candidate) and then solicits a donation. Sugging and frugging are just two of several unethical practices involving bogus surveys. These practices also have been used in regular mail and Internet solicitations.

So-called push polls are another deceptive marketing technique. A *push poll* is an attempt to influence people's opinions under the guise of conducting a poll. Push polls often try to achieve this by embedding negative statements—about a candidate, organization, product, and so forth—within supposed survey questions. Such statements may be factual, untrue, or merely hypothetical comments designed to manipulate people's beliefs. For example, consider this question: "If you were to learn that Mayor Roberts, when she was chief executive at ABC Corporation, laid off 250 employees and had their jobs outsourced to foreign workers, would this make you less likely to vote for her as governor in the upcoming election?" Note that this item does not actually state that Mayor Roberts did these things. Instead, it is designed to plant the seed of such a past action in the respondent's mind. Push polling, like sugging and frugging, typically attempts to reach a wide audience in a short time; thus, the caller promises that the poll or survey contains "just a few items." Political scientist Kathy Frankovic (CBS News, 2000), a former director of surveys for CBS News, points out that legitimate political polls sometimes include questions containing negative facts or hypotheticals about an opposing candidate. But, she notes that unlike push polls, such surveys are longer and more detailed.

Deceptive Survey Practices

Major survey research, public opinion polling, and marketing organizations in North America and Europe condemn these practices and note how they can erode the public's trust in legitimate survey research. Still, such practices persist despite their illegality in some countries (Canadian Press, 2009, May 5). It's my hope that describing these deceptive practices will not dissuade you from participating in legitimate surveys, donating to charities based on legitimate requests, and so forth. If you receive a solicitation to participate in a survey, are inclined to participate, but have doubts about the solicitation's validity, ask questions. For example, ask for the names of the organizations who are conducting the survey and sponsoring it (they may differ), how you were selected to participate, the purpose and length of the survey, and whether it will involve any solicitation.

✓ **CONCEPT CHECK 7.5** BEING A SMART SURVEY CONSUMER

Fill in each of the blanks below. Answers appear on page 240.

1. When researchers report a time trend for a variable based on a series of surveys, it is important to know whether the _____ of that variable has remained the same throughout the series.

2. Using a bogus survey as a disguised telemarketing attempt to raise funds is called _____.

3. Using a bogus survey as a disguised telemarketing attempt to sell a product or service to people is called _____.

CHAPTER SUMMARY

- In survey research, questionnaires are usually administered to a sample of people to learn something about a broader population. Representative samples accurately reflect the important characteristics of the population.

- Survey data are commonly used to describe the characteristics of a population, describe and compare different populations or different groups within a population, and describe trends in a population over time. Survey data also are used to explore relations among variables, and to test hypotheses and theories.

- There are two general methods for selecting a sample. With probability sampling, each member of the population has a chance of being selected into the sample, and the probability of being selected can be determined. With nonprobability sampling, each member of the population either does not have a chance of being selected into the sample, the probability of being selected cannot be determined, or both.

- Simple random sampling, stratified random sampling, cluster sampling, and multistage sampling are types of probability sampling. Convenience sampling, quota sampling, and purposive sampling are types of nonprobability sampling. When probability sampling is selected, the results from a sample can be used to estimate the responses of

a population within a known margin of sampling error and confidence level.

- A questionnaire may contain many types of items. Open-ended questions allow people to respond in their own words. Closed-ended questions provide specific response options. Multiple-choice items, ranking scales, forced-choice items, and rating scales are examples of closed-ended questions.

- Good survey questions are simple, clear, and balanced. Leading questions, loaded questions, double-barreled questions, and questions that use double negatives should be avoided. Careful attention should be given to the ordering of the questions.

- Face-to-face interviews are the most expensive way to administer probability surveys, but generally have the highest response rates. Telephone interviews are the most common method for conducting probability surveys. Mail surveys cost less than face-to-face or telephone surveys, but typically have lower response rates. Most online surveys use convenience samples and thus should not be used to estimate the specific responses of a population.

- When people in a sample can't be reached or refuse to participate, this decreases a survey's response rate. Nonresponse bias occurs when sample members who didn't participate in a survey would have provided significantly different answers than those offered by participants. Probability surveys with lower response rates do not necessarily contain more nonresponse bias than surveys with higher response rates. Still, researchers generally take steps to maximize the response rates to their surveys.

- Because we often encounter survey results in everyday life, it's essential to consider whether the type of sampling used was appropriate to the purpose of the survey. It's also important to recognize that marketers sometimes use bogus surveys to sell products and fundraise, but don't let that dissuade you from participating in legitimate surveys.

KEY TERMS

closed-ended question (p. 223)
cluster sampling (p. 215)
confidence level (p. 221)
context effects (p. 227)
convenience (haphazard) sampling (p. 217)
double-barreled questions (p. 226)
double negatives (p. 226)
expert sampling (p. 219)
interrater reliability (p. 223)
interviewer effects (p. 230)
leading questions (p. 226)

Likert scale (p. 225)
loaded questions (p. 226)
margin of sampling error (p. 219)
multistage sampling (p. 215)
nonprobability sampling (p. 214)
nonrepresentative (biased) sample (p. 211)
nonresponse bias (p. 234)
open-ended question (p. 223)
population (p. 210)
probability sampling (p. 214)
purposive sampling (p. 218)
quota sampling (p. 217)

representative sample (p. 211)
response rate (p. 211)
sample (p. 210)
sampling frame (p. 210)
sampling variability (p. 219)
self-selection (p. 217)
simple random sampling (p. 214)
single-stage cluster sampling (p. 215)
social desirability bias (p. 213)
snowball sampling (p. 219)
stratified random sampling (p. 215)
survey (p. 210)

ASSESS YOUR KNOWLEDGE

1. Provide an example for each of the following concepts: population, sampling frame, sample, representative sample, nonrepresentative sample.

2. Describe five general reasons why scientists conduct surveys.

3. Explain some of the limitations of survey research.

4. What is probability sampling? Describe four types of probability sampling and their advantages.

5. What is nonprobability sampling? Describe four types of nonprobability sampling and explain why each type either does or does not have scientific value.

6. Explain the concepts of sampling variability, margin of sampling error, and confidence level.

7. How do population size, and the desired margin of sampling error and confidence level, influence the size of the sample we need to select?

8. If we wish to use survey data to estimate the scores of groups within a population, how does this affect the margin of sampling error and the needed sample size?

9. Discuss the major steps in developing a questionnaire.

10. Describe some advantages and disadvantages of open-ended and closed-ended questions. Provide examples of different types of closed-ended questions.

11. Identify common problems that contribute to the poor wording of questions.

12. Discuss some rules of thumb for deciding on the order of questions in a survey.

13. Explain some of the advantages and disadvantages of face-to-face, telephone, and mail surveys.

14. Describe the major problem with most online surveys. Explain how this problem can be overcome.

15. Discuss the concepts of response rate and nonresponse bias. How do survey researchers try to maximize response rates?

16. What are some questions that a critical thinker should ask when reading about the results of a survey?

ANSWERS TO CONCEPT CHECKS

7.1 Basic Characteristics of Surveys

1. population, sample, sampling frame
2. representative sample, nonrepresentative sample

7.2 Selecting a Sample

1. false   2. true   3. false   4. false

7.3 Constructing the Questionnaire

1. true   2. true   3. true   4. false

7.4 Administering the Survey

1. Face-to-face   2. interviewer bias, interviewer characteristics   3. harder   4. Nonresponse bias

7.5 Being a Smart Survey Consumer

1. operational definition (or measurement of)
2. frugging   3. sugging

THINKING CRITICALLY AND APPLYING YOUR KNOWLEDGE

EXERCISE 1   Would You Like a Sample?

Two surveys are briefly described below. For each, **(a)** identify whether probability or nonprobability sampling was used, **(b)** identify the specific type of probability or nonprobability sampling, and **(c)** decide whether the conclusion(s) drawn are appropriate or inappropriate, and explain why.

Survey 1: Sleep

Good Health Hospital of Toronto pays XYZ Consulting to conduct a sleep survey of adults with full-time jobs in Canada. XYZ develops an online questionnaire and purchases advertising space on several popular websites. The advertisements invite fully employed people over the age of 18 to "participate in an online sleep survey." Within two weeks, 150,000 people respond, with 70% reporting that "I feel tired during the work week because I don't get enough sleep," and 25% reporting that "I feel that I have a sleep disorder." When XYZ reports the results, it states that "based on our survey, it appears that 25% of today's fully employed adults feel they have a sleep disorder" and that "70% of fully employed adults who use the Internet say they are tired during the week due to insufficient sleep."

Survey 2: Future Trends for Colleges

The editors of *Cool Teen* magazine want to publish an article that discusses upcoming trends in liberal arts college education. Based on a 2016 *U.S. News & World Report* magazine article that ranked the top 178 American liberal arts colleges, *Cool Teen* editors contact the presidents of the top 25 schools. All 25 presidents agree to be interviewed for the survey. When asked to forecast trends for the next decade, 75% say they expect an increasing percentage of entering first-year students to take longer than 4 years to graduate.

Two months later, *Cool Teen* publishes the results of the survey in one of its monthly issues. The editors state that "most presidents of this year's top 25 American liberal arts colleges believe that over the next decade, a growing percentage of students will take more than 4 years to graduate."

EXERCISE 2   Are You Satisfied with Your Job?

Dr. Strauss is an industrial-organizational psychologist who conducts a job satisfaction survey for MacroHard, a computer hardware design and manufacturing company. MacroHard has 25,000 employees. Dr. Strauss randomly selects a sample of 1,100 employees, administers a job satisfaction questionnaire, and finds that 80% of the employees in the sample are satisfied with their jobs. (Assume, for simplicity, that all the employees selected for the sample completed the survey.)

(a) What type of sampling has Dr. Strauss used? Is this a form of probability or nonprobability sampling?

(b) Use Table 7.1 on page 221 to answer these questions. Based on the sizes of the population and the sample, if Dr. Strauss wants a 95% confidence level, then what would be the margin of sampling error in this survey? If instead, Dr. Strauss wants a 99% confidence level, what would be the margin of sampling error?

(c) Suppose that 55% of MacroHard's employees are male and 45% are female. What type of probability sampling should Dr. Strauss use to create a sample of 55% men and 45% women?

(d) Assume a total sample size of 1,100 employees, a sample composition of 55% men and 45% women, and a 95% confidence interval. If Dr. Strauss examines the job satisfaction of men and women separately, what would be the margin of sampling error in the "men's" analysis? For the "women's" analysis, is the sample size large enough to maintain this margin of sampling error?

EXERCISE 3 What Are You Asking? Critiquing Survey Items

Six survey questions appear below. Assume that each question is closed-ended. If a specific response format is included, then you should examine that as well. Decide whether each question is worded well or poorly. If poorly, explain why.

(a) Do you agree or disagree that poverty and hunger are among the most important problems in the world today?

(b) After you graduate from college, do you believe it likely or unlikely that you will not be able to find a good job?

(c) At present, people who are 21 years of age or older can drink legally in our state. The state government has proposed that a person must be at least 22 years old in order to drink legally. Do you support or oppose the proposal to raise the legal drinking age to 22 years?

(d) Do you agree that improving the quality of our public school system should be a higher priority?

(e) During the past few months, have you consumed 5 or more alcoholic drinks in a row?

(f) What is your current college grade point average?

    1. 4.0 to 3.0

    2. 3.0 to 2.0

    3. 2.0 to 1.0

    4. 1.0 or less

LaunchPad
macmillan learning

To practice key concepts from this chapter, visit the LaunchPad Solo for Research Methods at **launchpadworks.com.**

SINGLE-FACTOR EXPERIMENTAL DESIGNS

CHAPTER OUTLINE

C an you unscramble the following anagram to form a five-letter word?

NIDRK

Imagine you are participating in a laboratory experiment. The experimenter explains that your task is to solve 15 five-letter anagrams, similar to the one above (which, unscrambled, spells *drink*). After you complete a 5-minute practice anagram test, the experimenter hands you an envelope that contains the real test. Like the practice test, this test has a cover page followed by five pages, each containing three anagrams. Unlike the practice test, on the real test your answers will be scored and you'll receive feedback. Therefore, the experimenter asks you to make sure that your test contains a participant ID code number, which has been pre-assigned to you and is handwritten in the upper-right corner of each page. You check, and indeed the code is there.

The experimenter leaves and you begin the task. Five minutes later, the experimenter returns, scores the test, and tells you the score. Next, you complete a questionnaire, the experimenter debriefs you, and your session ends.

Social-personality psychologist Andrew Elliot and his colleagues conducted this experiment (Elliot, Maier, Moller, Friedman, & Meinhardt, 2007). There's just one important detail I haven't revealed to you: Based on random assignment, the pre-entered ID code that appeared on your pages was written in either red, green, or black ink. And as the researchers predicted, overall, participants who were assigned red ID codes performed more poorly on the task than participants assigned green or black codes.

Many experiments, conducted by diverse researchers, have shown that the color of objects can influence people's behavior and psychological functioning (see Elliot, 2015). Yet, how can something seemingly as trivial as the color of a code number influence people's cognitive performance? Maybe the result was a fluke? Well, Elliot's research team replicated the experiment several times (Elliot et al., 2007; Elliot, Payen, Brisswalter, Cury, & Thayer, 2011). They studied American, German, and French undergraduates, and German high school students. They always included the color red, but varied the other colors (green or blue, and black, gray, or white). Instead of an anagram test, they used numerical, analogy, or memory tasks taken from IQ tests. And rather than manipulating the color of code numbers in the test booklet, the researchers varied the color of the test's cover sheet. In every replication of the experiment, participants performed worse overall when they were exposed to the color red. **Figure 8.1** presents the results from two of Elliot et al.'s (2007) experiments: one (a) examining how red, green, and black code numbers affected U.S. undergraduates' anagram performance, the other (b) how very brief exposure to red, green, or white on a test booklet cover sheet affected German undergraduates' performance on analogy items from an IQ test.

Recall from prior chapters that in an **experiment,** *the researcher manipulates one or more variables, attempts to control extraneous factors, and then measures how the manipulated variables affect participants' responses.* Recall as well that the term **independent variable** *refers to the variable manipulated by the researcher,* and the term **dependent variable** *refers to the response that is measured, to determine whether an independent variable has produced an effect.*

This chapter examines experiments that contain a single independent variable. In Chapter 9, we'll explore experimental designs containing two or more independent variables. In Chapter 10, we'll focus on issues of validity that pertain to experiments and potential pitfalls that experimenters seek to avoid.

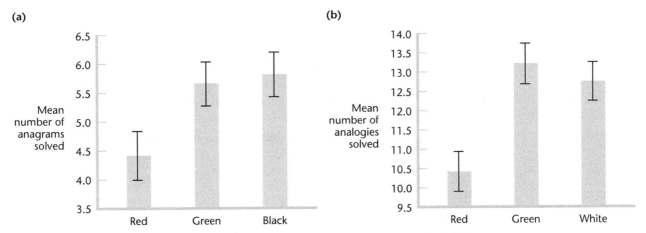

Figure 8.1 Effects of color on cognitive performance. (a) U.S. college students exposed to red ID codes correctly solved fewer anagrams than students exposed to green or black ID codes. **(b)** German undergraduates exposed to a partly red test booklet cover solved fewer analogy items than students exposed to a white or partly green cover. The thin I-shaped bars that straddle each large bar are called *error bars.* These particular error bars are called "95% confidence interval bars." They reflect the variability of scores within each condition. See Statistics Module 15 for more detail.

(Adapted with permission from the American Psychological Association from "Color and Psychological Functioning: The Effect of Red on Performance Attainment," by Elliot et al., 2007, *Journal of Experimental Psychology: General, 136*[1], p. 154.)

THE LOGIC OF EXPERIMENTATION

Learning Objectives

After studying this section, you should be able to:

- Describe the basic components of experimental control.
- Discuss how experimental control helps researchers to satisfy three key criteria for inferring cause and effect.

Psychologists conduct a dizzying array of experiments. One experimenter may disable a gene's functioning to determine whether it influences the feeding behavior of laboratory mice, while another may compare the effectiveness of different psychotherapies in treating depression. The goal of Andrew Elliot and his colleagues (2007, 2011) was to test the hypothesis that perceiving the color red would impair people's achievement on cognitive tasks. They based their hypothesis on learning theory: specifically, on classical conditioning principles (recall how Pavlov's dogs became conditioned to salivate to the sound of a tone). The researchers reasoned that, starting in childhood, the color red becomes associated with danger and poor achievement (e.g., red warning signs, teachers marking students' mistakes in red). Thus, the color red may become a conditioned stimulus that, without conscious awareness, increases people's sense of threat in achievement situations and thereby impairs their performance.

Regardless of the topic or whether a researcher's goal is to test a theory, all experiments share a common underlying method. You isolate a factor of interest (e.g., color), tinker around with it (e.g., expose people to different colors), try to keep other aspects of the situation constant, and then see what effects your tinkering produces. Although the experimental method has pitfalls and limitations, a well-crafted experiment is a scientific work of art: It is the best scientific tool available to draw clear conclusions about cause–effect relations. Let's examine why.

EXERCISING CONTROL OVER VARIABLES

In everyday life, one meaning of the word *control* reflects the ability to regulate or exercise direction over something. For scientists, the concept of **experimental control** *includes the ability to:*

1. *manipulate one or more independent variables;*
2. *choose the types of dependent variables that will be measured, and how and when they will be measured so that the effects of the independent variables can be assessed; and*
3. *regulate other aspects of the research environment, including the manner in which participants are exposed to the various conditions in the experiment.*

The goal of having such control is to enable researchers to conclude that the variable they manipulate—rather than other uncontrolled factors—is the cause of any obtained effects on behavior. For example, in their initial experiment, Elliot et al. (2007)

- manipulated the color of the ID code that was placed on the test;

- chose to measure cognitive performance via an anagram task, and controlled when the task was given;

- regulated other aspects of the research setting (e.g., task instructions were always the same), including how participants were exposed to the various colors (i.e., they were randomly assigned).

By carefully exercising these types of control, the researchers were able to conclude that the variation in ink color—rather than some other aspect of the situation—was the most plausible explanation for why participants' performance differed across the three color conditions.

CAUSAL INFERENCE AND EXPERIMENTAL CONTROL

How does experimental control enhance our ability to draw causal conclusions? Recall that three criteria need to be met in order to conclude that variable X has a causal influence on variable Y:

1. *Covariation of X and Y.* As X varies, Y varies.
2. *Temporal order.* The variation in X occurs before the variation in Y.
3. *Absence of plausible alternative explanations.*

In principle, if X is the only factor in a situation that varies prior to a change in Y, then the logical conclusion is that the variation in X must have caused the change in Y.

Now let's map the different components of experimental control onto these three causal criteria. The first causal criterion, the covariation of X and Y, is achieved by manipulating the independent variable—by creating two or more distinct conditions in an experiment—and measuring whether scores on the dependent variable differ among those conditions. Elliot et al. (2007) manipulated the independent variable, color, by creating red, green, and black ID code color conditions. They measured the dependent variable, cognitive performance, by determining the average number of anagrams solved by participants in each color condition. Their data analysis indicated that X and Y did covary: The number of anagrams solved differed significantly depending on the color condition.

The second causal criterion, temporal order, is achieved by exposing participants to the manipulated independent variable prior to any changes that may occur in the dependent variable. In the color experiment, participants were first exposed to one of three colors and then performed the anagram task. There is no way that Y (anagram performance) could have caused X (color exposure).

Researchers attempt to achieve the third causal criterion, the absence of plausible alternative explanations, by eliminating other factors that might systematically cause Y to vary. For example, there are many variables that might influence people's performance on an anagram task, such as how hot, humid, and noisy the room is while performing. Although some researchers might be interested in studying how these factors affect performance, Elliot et al. (2007) were not; they were interested in how color affects performance. Thus, to Elliot and his colleagues, each of these other factors represented an **extraneous variable:** *a factor that is not the focus of interest in a particular study, but that could influence the outcome of the study if left uncontrolled.* Therefore, in conducting their experiment, Elliot et al. would want to keep these extraneous environmental factors as constant as possible.

Let's consider two other extraneous variables. First, suppose that in the color experiment, the red ID code had been very large in size, whereas the green and black codes were small. In this case, perhaps it wasn't the code's red color that caused participants to perform more poorly, but its larger size; maybe a large-sized ID code of any color would have distracted participants. Second, suppose that the college students in the red, green, and black conditions participated in different weeks of the study (i.e., weeks 1, 2, and 3, respectively). Imagine that week 1 (when the red-condition students participated) was the week of midterms, and weeks 2 and 3 (the green-condition and black-condition participants) occurred after midterm week. Might it be reasonable to speculate that anxiety, distraction, or fatigue surrounding midterm exams caused the students in the red color condition to perform more poorly than the students in the other color conditions?

In these cases, the size of the ID code and the proximity to midterm exam week would represent extraneous factors that have now become confounding variables. A **confounding variable** *is a factor that covaries with the independent variable in such a way that we can no longer determine which one has caused the changes in the dependent variable.* **Table 8.1** illustrates how our hypothetical confounding variables covary with the independent variable of color.

Table 8.1 Potential Confounding of an Independent Variable

	Condition 1	Condition 2	Condition 3
Independent Variable Color (of ID code)	Red	Green	Black
Confounding Variable 1 Size of ID code on page	Large	Small	Small
Confounding Variable 2 Proximity to midterm exams	Midterm week	1 week after midterms	2 weeks after midterms

Good researchers acquire the ability to recognize ahead of time potential confounding variables that could ruin the interpretability of their studies. Researchers then design their studies to eliminate or at least minimize those confounding variables. In experiments, researchers typically reduce confounding variables by:

- keeping extraneous factors as constant as possible across the different conditions of the experiment; and

- balancing extraneous factors that, in principle, cannot be held constant.

Let's examine how these procedures are applied to potential confounding variables that arise from two sources: the research environment and characteristics of the research participants.

Potential Confounding Variables: Environmental Factors

Many extraneous environmental factors that might confound the results of an experiment can, in principle, be held constant or at least nearly so. All participants can perform the same anagram task in the same room and sit in the same chair. The room's temperature, humidity, and noise level can be kept reasonably steady.

There are other environmental factors that even in principle cannot be held constant, but that can be balanced across the different experimental conditions. These include the time of day, day of the week, and month of the year when each student participates. Thus, on any given day, as the researcher, I would try to "run" (i.e., conduct) the experiment with an equal number of participants from each condition in the morning and in the afternoon. This way, after the experiment is finished, you would not be able to say, "I think the reason that performance was worst in the red color condition was that those participants always performed the anagram task on Friday afternoon, at the end of the tiring school week, or early on Monday mornings while still recovering from a weekend of partying, whereas students in the other conditions always performed the task midweek." Over the entire experiment, these factors—time of day, day of week—will end up being as equivalent as possible across the three color conditions.

The experimenter who interacts with the participants also constitutes a part of the environment, and would be trained to behave in a standardized manner. However, the experimenter isn't a robot, and her or his behavior will fluctuate at least minimally. What researchers hope to avoid is a *systematic bias* in which the experimenter consistently alters her or his behavior toward participants based on the particular condition they are in.

Potential Confounding Variables: Participant Characteristics

No matter how successfully researchers have tamed potential environmental confounding factors, there is still one possible objection to the conclusion that, for example, the red color of the ID code caused poorer anagram performance. Perhaps the students in the red color condition would have performed the most poorly anyway, even if they had been shown a green or black ID code. Maybe, as a group, they simply had poorer anagram ability, less confidence, or lower levels of intelligence than the participants in the other color conditions. If so, their poorer performance might have had nothing to do with the color red.

Potential confounding variables due to participants' characteristics are addressed differently in two major approaches to designing experiments. With a **between-subjects design,** *different participants are assigned to each of the conditions in the experiment.* In this design, researchers typically minimize the potential confounding effects of subject characteristics by using **random assignment,** *a procedure in which each participant has an equal probability of being assigned to any one of the conditions in the experiment.* Random assignment distributes participants' individual differences across the experimental conditions in an unbiased, nonsystematic way. Thus, at the start of the color experiment, the three groups of participants are assumed to be equivalent to one another.

In a **within-subjects design,** *each participant engages in every condition of the experiment one or more times.* Because the same people participate in all the conditions, relatively stable factors such as participants' general anagram ability and intelligence essentially remain the same in each condition and cannot confound the results. However, factors such as boredom, fatigue, and experience with the task can change as each participant moves from one condition of the experiment to the next. If every participant engages in all the conditions in the same order with, say, the color red always being the last condition, we have no way of knowing whether the red color caused the poorer performance or whether participants might have been fatigued toward the end of the experiment. The solution to this problem is **counterbalancing,** *a procedure in which the order of conditions is varied so that no condition has an overall advantage relative to the other conditions.* Before we explore between- and within-subjects designs more closely, in the next section we'll discuss how independent variables can be manipulated.

 CONCEPT CHECK 8.1 THE LOGIC OF EXPERIMENTATION

Match each concept on the left with its correct description on the right. Answers appear at the end of the chapter on page 276.

1. between-subjects design
2. within-subjects design
3. experimental control
4. dependent variable
5. confounding variable
6. independent variable

(a) a factor manipulated by the experimenter
(b) examples are random assignment, counterbalancing
(c) each participant engages in only one condition
(d) each participant engages in all conditions
(e) provides an alternative explanation for the findings
(f) an outcome measured by the experimenter

MANIPULATING INDEPENDENT VARIABLES

Learning Objectives

After studying this section, you should be able to:

- Describe ways to manipulate an independent variable.
- Discuss factors that affect the number of conditions incorporated into an experiment.
- Explain the concepts of experimental and control groups.

In designing an experiment, we create an independent variable by forming two or more conditions that vary the amount or type of some factor. In other words, we can manipulate independent variables quantitatively and qualitatively.

VARYING THE AMOUNT OR TYPE OF A FACTOR

As people consume greater quantities of alcohol at a party, how does this affect their behavior? Does the size of a group influence the likelihood that a person will conform to the group's opinions? To study each question experimentally, we would manipulate the amount of alcohol we ask people to consume and the size of the group to which we expose people. These are quantitative manipulations and we could label these independent variables "alcohol dose" and "group size," respectively.

In contrast, consider two other questions. First, what type of psychotherapy most effectively treats moderate depression? Second, does our ability to accurately recognize emotions from facial expressions depend on the type of emotion? To study these questions experimentally, we would create different conditions, each of which represents a different type of psychotherapy or emotional expression. These are qualitative manipulations and would produce independent variables that we could label "type of therapy" and "type of emotion," respectively. In Elliot et al.'s (2007, 2011) color experiments, the independent variable was manipulated qualitatively: Participants were exposed to one of three colors.

As for the variety of factors that experimenters manipulate, here are some common approaches to creating independent variables (note that some may overlap):

- *altering the physical environment,* such as exposing people to different room temperatures, intensities or types of sounds, or schedules or types of reinforcement during a learning task;

- *altering the social environment,* such as leading participants to believe that a job applicant is female or male, exposing infants to familiar or unfamiliar voices, or varying the size of groups;

- *varying an intervention provided to people,* such as the type or amount of psychotherapy, counseling, or skills training;

- *varying the task that participants perform,* such as asking people to remember lists of words of varying lengths, or abstract versus concrete words;

- *varying the strategy that people are instructed to use when performing a task,* such as instructing people to learn material either by rote memorization or by using visual imagery;

- *manipulating an organism's characteristics,* such as in laboratory mice, disabling a particular gene or surgically lesioning a specific brain area to see how behavior is affected; or manipulating the type or intensity of people's mood by exposing them to pleasant or unpleasant stimuli, to determine how mood influences their subsequent task performance.

DETERMINING THE NUMBER OF CONDITIONS

In experiments, a **single-factor design** *has only one independent variable.* This independent variable must have at least two *conditions,* also called two *levels* of the independent variable. An experiment with one independent variable that has more than two levels is often called a *single-factor, multilevel design.* Table 8.2 provides examples of how independent variables can be manipulated so they have more than two levels.

The Research Question and Available Resources

What determines how many levels of an independent variable we should create? Essentially, the question about behavior that we ask, our personal preferences, and our assessment of

Table 8.2 Creating Independent Variables with Two or More Levels

Independent Variable	Design	
	Two-Level	Multilevel
Sleep deprivation	Total deprivation (8 hours) No deprivation (0 hours)	Total deprivation (8 hours) Partial deprivation (4 hours) No deprivation (0 hours)
Length of word list	15 words (long list) 3 words (short list)	15, 12, 9, 6, or 3 words
Monetary incentive	Low incentive High incentive	No incentive Low incentive Moderate incentive High incentive
Described sex of hypothetical job applicant	Female Male	Female Male No description (sex not mentioned)
Type of therapy	Psychodynamic therapy Cognitive therapy	No therapy Psychodynamic therapy Cognitive therapy Behavior therapy

available resources will be three key factors. If we are interested in age stereotyping, then we could ask participants to evaluate a job résumé, and vary whether we tell participants that the job applicant is 30 or 50 years old. If instead our research interest is ethnic stereotyping, then although we could limit the independent variable (i.e., ethnicity of job applicant) to two conditions, creating more conditions would yield more information. Thus, we could lead participants to believe that a 30-year-old female applicant, born in Chicago, is of African, Asian, Hispanic, White Northern European, or Native American descent.

As another example, if our research question is "How does fully depriving people of a night's sleep affect them psychologically?," then creating an experiment with two deprivation levels—8 hours (i.e., "total sleep deprivation") and 0 hours (i.e., "normal sleep control group")—may be sufficient. But, if we want to know how different degrees of sleep deprivation affect people, then we'll want to create more conditions. For example, one research team deprived people of 0 hours, 2 hours, 4 hours, or 8 hours of sleep and then measured how this affected participants' daytime sleepiness and cognitive performance (Roehrs, Burduvali, Bonahoom, Drake, & Roth, 2003).

Balanced against our desire to create more levels of an independent variable, we must consider practical issues, such as the resources available to us. Will enough participants be available? If they're to be paid or reimbursed for expenses, do we have sufficient funds? Is the sleep laboratory available for all the hours we need? Sometimes a researcher's first experiment on a topic may contain only one independent variable and just two or three conditions. Then, to further explore the topic, the researcher designs subsequent experiments that have more independent variables and/or more levels of an independent variable.

The Potential to Examine Nonlinear Effects

In Solomon Asch's (1955) classic experiments on conformity, groups of varying sizes performed a series of simple visual tasks: judging the length of lines. Only one member of each group was a real participant, and this participant was unaware that the other members were confederates who, according to plan, voiced clearly incorrect judgments on some of the trials. Asch manipulated group size by controlling the number of confederates in each group, and

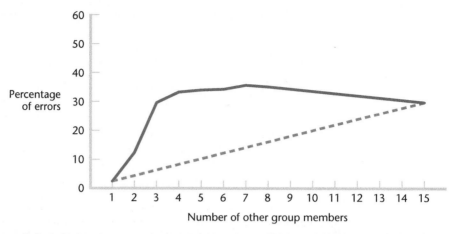

Figure 8.2 Relation between group size and conformity as determined by Solomon Asch. Asch found a nonlinear relation between group size and conformity to the group (see the solid line). Had he only included two group sizes in his experiment (see the dashed line), the nonlinear relation would not have been detected.

he measured the percentage of trials on which the real participants conformed to the group's erroneous opinion. As group size increased, would conformity increase in a linear fashion? As the solid line in **Figure 8.2** shows, Asch's finding was "no": Conformity rose as group size increased from about 1 to 4 other members, but after that, further increases in group size had little effect on conformity.

Looking at the dashed line in Figure 8.2, imagine that Asch (1955) had manipulated group size by creating only two conditions: groups with 1 other member, and with 15 other members. Would this straight line accurately portray the relation that Asch actually found? Of course not. If we quantitatively manipulate an independent variable by creating just two conditions, then any line graph of the data can only portray a straight line. Thus, there is no way to know whether this reflects an actual linear relation between the independent and dependent variables, or instead is merely an artifact imposed by the limitation of having only two data points in the graph. To examine whether a nonlinear relation exists—and to provide a more thorough test of a potential linear relation—we need to create an independent variable that has three or more levels.

As another example, the solid line in **Figure 8.3** illustrates a nonlinear relation between the amount of alcohol that young adults were administered in an experiment, and their perception of how much that alcohol impaired their cognitive task performance (Roehrs et al., 2003). Scores further below or above the y-axis point of 0 indicate greater amounts of perceived performance impairment and performance enhancement, respectively.

In this study, experimental-physiological psychologist Timothy Roehrs and his colleagues manipulated the dose of alcohol by having participants drink 0.0., 0.3, 0.6, or 0.9 grams of alcohol per kilogram of body weight (Roehrs et al., 2003). This produced, on average, breath alcohol concentrations of .00, .02, .04, and .09 a half hour after consumption. The graph shows that it was not until the highest dose of alcohol was administered that participants, overall, believed their performance was impaired. Had the researchers only used no alcohol and high dose conditions, as illustrated hypothetically by the dashed line, this would have masked the nonlinear relation.

What makes this multilevel design especially interesting is that Roehrs et al. (2003) also measured participants' daytime sleepiness and actual cognitive performance. Alcohol increased sleepiness and decreased performance in a linear fashion. Given these linear

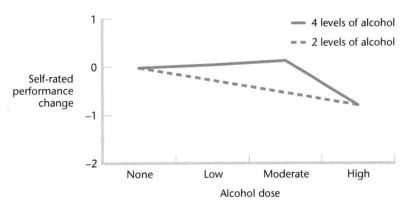

Figure 8.3 Self-perceived performance impairment as a function of alcohol dose. By manipulating four alcohol dosage levels, Timothy Roehrs and colleagues were able to examine whether the relation between alcohol dose and self-perceived performance impairment was nonlinear (solid line). Had only two dosage levels been manipulated (dashed line), the nonlinear relation would not have been detected. (Reprinted/adapted from Roehrs et al., *SLEEP* 2003; 26:981-5 with permission from Associated Professional Sleep Societies, LLC, Darien IL, 2016.)

relations, but the nonlinear relation between alcohol dose and perceived impairment, the researchers concluded that participants failed to recognize alcohol's impairing effects until they had consumed enough alcohol, on average, to be legally drunk in most jurisdictions.

EXPERIMENTAL AND CONTROL CONDITIONS

In many experiments, comparisons are made between experimental conditions and control conditions. An **experimental condition** (or **experimental group**) *involves exposing participants to a treatment or an "active" level of the independent variable*. In a **control condition** (or **control group**), *participants do not receive the treatment of interest or are exposed to a baseline level of an independent variable*. Depending on how an experiment is designed, different participants may be assigned to the experimental and control conditions, or the same participants may serve in both conditions.

One common way to create experimental and control conditions is to manipulate the *presence versus absence* of some factor. Suppose we want to examine whether exposure to traffic noise affects people's cognitive task performance. We expose an experimental group to an "active" level of the independent variable: Traffic noise will be present. The control group is not exposed to noise and this presents the baseline condition against which performance in the noise condition will be compared.

Instead of noise, to examine how high temperature affects performance, we can have participants in an experimental condition perform a task in a 100 °F (37.8 °C) room. This would represent the active level of the independent variable, but there's no such thing as creating a control condition in which an "absence" of temperature exists. Every room has a temperature, and exposing people to a frigid temperature of 0.0 °F (or 0.0 °C) would hardly be a "control"! So, we might create our control condition—our standard of comparison—by having a group perform the task at 72 °F (22.2 °C), a room temperature most people find comfortable.

There are also experiments in which the concept of a control group does not apply. Suppose we conduct an experiment to determine how accurately people can identify facial expressions of six emotions: anger, fear, joy, disgust, surprise, and sadness. Participants view a series of 60 photographs, created by having each of 10 actors portray the six emotions. In this study, each of the six emotions represents an experimental condition and there is no control condition per se (i.e., the design does not include a "no emotion" condition). However, if we were interested in examining the question "Do people recognize each of these emotional expressions more accurately than a neutral facial expression?," then we would need to add a control condition by including photos in which the same 10 actors each portray a neutral facial expression. Thus, whether we design our emotion recognition experiment to include a control group depends on the question we are examining.

Experiments sometimes call for special control groups to address potential confounding variables that a traditional "no treatment" or "baseline exposure level" control group cannot eliminate. We'll discuss these control groups in Chapter 10.

 CONCEPT CHECK 8.2 MANIPULATING INDEPENDENT VARIABLES

Decide whether each statement below is true or false. Answers appear on page 276.

1. Experimenters can only manipulate environmental factors; they cannot manipulate an organism's characteristics.
2. Independent variables must be quantitative; they cannot be qualitative.
3. A single-factor experimental design must include at least two conditions.
4. To examine nonlinear effects, researchers should use a multilevel design.
5. Some experiments do not include a control group.

BETWEEN-SUBJECTS DESIGNS

Learning Objectives

After studying this section, you should be able to:

- Explain the advantages and disadvantages of between-subjects designs.
- Describe several types of between-subjects designs.
- Discuss the differences between random assignment and random sampling.

Typically, in single-factor experiments, each participant either engages in only one condition, or engages in all the conditions. As noted earlier, these two approaches are called, respectively, a *between-subjects design* and a *within-subjects design*. Suppose we want to examine whether taking class notes longhand—as compared to taking class notes using a laptop computer—enhances, impairs, or has no significant influence on college students' learning of lecture content. The left side of **Figure 8.4** shows how we could investigate this issue by conducting an experiment that employs a basic between-subjects design. This design is basic in the sense that it only has two conditions, the minimum needed to conduct a between-subjects experiment. In one condition, students take longhand notes during a lecture, and in the other condition, students use a laptop to take notes during the same lecture. Each student in this experiment would participate in only one of these conditions.

For visual simplicity, the left half of Figure 8.4 shows a total of 20 participants in the experiment (in reality, we would want a larger sample size). Based on random assignment, 10 students are assigned to take longhand lecture notes and 10 others are assigned to use a laptop computer. To guarantee that each student is exposed to the same lecture content, delivery style by the lecturer, and note-taking environment, we could video-record a lecture and have each student view it in a laboratory, individually, so as not to be influenced by the presence and potential note-taking behavior of other students. Afterward, we would administer the same knowledge test (e.g., a multiple choice exam) to assess each student's understanding of the lecture material.

Pam Mueller and Daniel Oppenheimer (2014) compared the effectiveness of longhand versus laptop note-taking by conducting a series of experiments. Although their procedures varied from one experiment to the next, the key point is that they manipulated longhand versus laptop note-taking as a between-subjects independent variable in each experiment.

Infographic: **Figure 8.4**

BETWEEN-SUBJECTS AND WITHIN-SUBJECTS EXPERIMENTAL DESIGNS

Research Question: Compared to taking longhand lecture notes, does laptop note-taking enhance or impair students' learning?

Between-Subjects
Design
(Each participant engages in only one condition.)

Randomly assign students to take longhand or laptop notes. Individually expose students to the same prerecorded lecture.

Longhand Notes

measure student learning

Laptop Notes

measure student learning

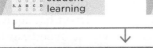

Compare learning in the longhand vs. laptop conditions

Within-Subjects
Design
(Each participant engages in every condition.)

Counterbalance order of note-taking conditions. Randomly assign students to Order 1 or Order 2. Individually expose students to the same prerecorded lectures.*

Order 1

Longhand Notes: first lecture

measure student learning

Laptop Notes: second lecture

measure student learning

Order 2

Laptop Notes: first lecture

measure student learning

Longhand Notes: second lecture

measure student learning

Compare learning in the longhand vs. laptop conditions

*In the within-subjects design, it would not make sense to expose students to the same lecture and knowledge test twice. So we need two lectures and must decide on their order of presentation. How would you do this? We will discuss this on pages 264–265.

 Using a similar between-subjects design, Mueller and Oppenheimer (2014) found that, compared to taking longhand notes, using laptops led students to take more notes, but also more verbatim notes, as opposed to writing notes in their own words. Laptop note-takers also showed poorer conceptual learning of the lecture content. The researchers concluded that laptop use promoted shallower, verbatim note-taking, which impaired students' learning of concepts.

Figure 8.4 describes their general findings and also illustrates how this experiment could be conducted using a within-subjects design, as we will discuss shortly.

ADVANTAGES OF BETWEEN-SUBJECTS DESIGNS

Between-subjects designs offer several advantages. First, because each participant only engages in one condition, effects caused by exposure to one condition (e.g., stress, fatigue) can't carry over to other conditions. Second, some scientific questions can only be examined using a between-subjects design. Consider a classic experiment by comparative psychologist Eckhard Hess (1959) on *imprinting*, a biologically primed form of attachment that occurs in some bird and mammalian species. If you've ever seen an adult duck or goose waddle or swim from one point to another, while being followed by a procession of its young, you've witnessed the end result of imprinting.

Hess (1959) hatched and raised mallard ducklings in a laboratory, isolating each one. He then manipulated the number of hours after hatching when each duckling was briefly removed from isolation and exposed to a realistic wooden model of an adult mallard duck. The wooden model was mechanically moved around a circular runway for 10 minutes, and the duckling could follow the model by waddling around a circular path (Figure 8.5). Later, Hess tested whether the duckling had imprinted on the model by measuring whether it followed either the original model or a different model duck it was seeing for the first time.

In his study, Hess (1959) found that imprinting was most likely to occur when a duckling was exposed to the model between 13 and 16 hours after hatching; by 32 hours, imprinting was successful for only a small percentage of the ducklings. Hess thus concluded that there was a "critical period" in imprinting, a particular age range during which exposure to the parent must occur or the capacity to imprint will be lost. In this experiment, a between-subjects design had to be used to manipulate the ducklings' age of initial exposure, because just as you only get one chance to make a first impression, there is only one opportunity to give each duckling its first exposure to the adult model.

A third advantage of between-subjects designs is that, even when it's possible to expose participants to every condition, doing so may require developing different but equivalent versions of the same task, and it also may tip off participants about the hypothesis being tested or true purpose of a study. This additional complexity may be avoided by using a between-subjects design. For example, in our between-subjects note-taking experiment, we can expose all students to the same lecture, and thus have to develop only one lecture to serve as the stimulus material. In contrast, using a within-subjects design, it would not make sense to have students view the same lecture twice and take the identical knowledge test, once when taking longhand notes and again when taking laptop notes. Instead, we would need to develop two equivalent lectures and knowledge tests, as we'll discuss more fully when covering within-subjects designs.

As another example, consider the color experiment by Elliot et al. (2007) described at the beginning of the chapter. Obviously, if each student were to participate in each of the three color conditions, we could not give them the same anagrams to solve each time! Thus, we would need to develop three sets of anagrams of equal difficulty. By using a between-subjects design, Elliot et al. were able to expose all participants to the same, single set of anagrams. In addition, if you were a participant, after first receiving an

Figure 8.5 Drawing of the imprinting apparatus used by comparative psychologist Eckhard Hess. (Hess, 1959.) (Reprinted with permission of *Science* from "Imprinting," by E. H. Hess, 1959, *Science*. Permission conveyed through Copyright Clearance Center, Inc.)

anagram packet with, say, a red ID code, and then one with a green code, and then a third one with a black code, might you begin to suspect that the experiment had something to do with color? And once this happened, you might alter your behavior. In a between-subjects design, participants are less likely to become sensitized to the hypothesis being tested because they are not exposed to—and therefore are unlikely to become aware of— the different manipulations of the independent variable that constitute the various conditions in the experiment. Based on discussions held with participants during debriefing sessions, Elliot et al. found that not a single participant in any of their experiments suspected the true purpose of the study.

Finally, there may be other reasons why it would be inadvisable to have each individual participate in all the conditions. For example, a task may be too time consuming, too fatiguing, or too stressful to either practically or ethically have people perform it in each condition of the experiment.

DISADVANTAGES OF BETWEEN-SUBJECTS DESIGNS

Of course, between-subjects designs have disadvantages as well as advantages. One disadvantage is that, although they usually are effective in creating equivalent groups across the various conditions of an experiment, they are less effective at this than are within-subjects designs. Simply put, in trying to keep extraneous factors such as participants' backgrounds, personality traits, and abilities as constant as possible across the various conditions of an experiment, what could be more equivalent than having the same participants engage in every condition?

With a between-subjects design, if we find a difference between how an experimental group and a control group have responded on the dependent variable, some portion of that difference may result not from the different levels of the independent variable itself, but from overall differences (even if small) between the groups in their preexisting personal characteristics. Therefore, in a between-subjects rather than a within-subjects design, the independent variable is essentially going to have to "work harder" (i.e., it will need to produce a bigger effect) to be noticed. Stated another way, if an independent variable truly has an influence on behavior, then overall, between-subjects designs will be less sensitive to detecting that effect than will within-subjects designs.

Another disadvantage of between-subjects designs is that the experimenter has to recruit and study more participants—often many more—in order to gather the same amount of information. Notice in Figure 8.4 that, using a between-subjects design, we end up with data from 10 students assigned to the longhand condition, and from 10 students assigned to the laptop condition. By employing a within-subjects design, we would end up with data from 20 students in each condition, because each student would participate in both conditions. The disadvantage of between-subjects designs in terms of recruiting participants becomes more prominent as the number of conditions in an experiment and the desired sample size per condition increase. For example, in an experiment with four conditions, if we want to gather data from 30 participants per condition, we'll need to recruit 120 participants in a between-subjects design, but only 30 using a within-subjects design.

TYPES OF BETWEEN-SUBJECTS DESIGNS

Now, let's examine two between-subjects experimental designs. We'll also discuss whether another common between-subjects design represents an experimental design.

Independent-Groups Design

In an **independent-groups design** (also called a **random-groups design**), *participants are randomly assigned to the various conditions of the experiment.* For example, in the color experiment, each participant was exposed to only one color—red or green or black—and that determination was made randomly. Random assignment means that each participant has an equal probability of being assigned to any particular condition.

Random assignment does not eliminate the fact that each research participant has a unique psychological and biological makeup, a unique set of experiences, and so forth. Nor does random assignment eliminate the reality that these individual differences may influence how people respond during the experiment. Rather, random assignment distributes these individual differences across the various conditions in an unbiased way. This enables researchers to assume with a high level of confidence that overall, prior to exposure to the independent variable, the groups of participants in the various conditions are equivalent to one another (1) on the attributes that will be assessed by the dependent measures, and (2) on other personal characteristics that might influence responses to the dependent measures.

Note that "equivalent" does not mean that the groups in the various conditions will be identical or perfectly matched on their personal characteristics at the outset of the experiment. Rather, it means that such preexisting differences will likely be too inconsequential to provide a plausible alternative explanation for any statistically significant findings that our experiment may obtain.

For example, in the color experiment, we can be highly confident in assuming that at the outset, participants in the red, green, and black conditions were equivalent, overall, in their ability to solve anagrams. Moreover, if factors such as intelligence and past experience with anagrams might influence current anagram performance, by using random assignment, we can be confident that the participants in the three color conditions were equivalent overall on these characteristics as well. Therefore, when participants performed most poorly after being exposed to the color red, we can confidently discard the alternative explanation that this was caused by poorer general anagram ability, lower intelligence, or less prior anagram experience.

You may have noticed that I've used terms such as *highly confident* rather than *absolutely sure*. Random assignment cannot guarantee the equivalence of groups with absolute certainty. There is always a possibility that purely by chance, participants will be distributed across the various conditions in a way that does create an important preexisting overall difference in their general anagram ability, intelligence, prior experience, and so forth. This can happen because, with chance, once in a while improbable outcomes do happen. To provide a rough analogy, if we flip a coin 10 times, the odds are less than 1 in a 1,000 that we'll get a Heads each time, but there is no guarantee that it won't happen.

This example brings up a related point: The greater the number of participants, the more likely random assignment will successfully create equivalent groups. Flip a coin only twice, and the odds of getting an extreme outcome of all Heads are fairly high: 25% (i.e., HH, HT, TH, TT). Flip it 20 times, and the odds of obtaining all Heads become infinitesimal, and the odds of getting any outcome with a large imbalance of Heads and Tails also drop dramatically. Likewise, as random assignment is used with a larger number of participants, the laws of chance have a greater opportunity to even things out. It becomes increasingly unlikely, for example, that most of the participants with poorer anagram ability would happen to end up in the "red condition."

Note that researchers typically don't flip coins or draw straws to randomly assign each participant. Rather, an experimenter would use a *random number table* (a table of randomly ordered sequences of digits) or a random number generator (a software program), many of which can be accessed online. Table 6 in Appendix C contains a portion of a random number table.

Block Randomization. If you flip a coin repeatedly, by chance you will get sequences of several Heads or several Tails in a row. Likewise, with basic random assignment, you will get sequences in which several participants in a row will be assigned to the same condition.

This is not ideal. Imagine, for example, that by chance several sequences result in too many participants being assigned to the red condition on a Friday afternoon or Monday morning. With random assignment, it's also likely that you'll end up with a slightly different number of participants in each condition (e.g., flip a coin 20 times, and the odds of getting precisely 10 Heads and 10 Tails are only 17.6%). Fortunately, there's a simple procedure that addresses both of these issues.

Using **block randomization,** *we conduct a single round of all the conditions, then another round, then another, for as many rounds as needed to complete the experiment. Within each round, the order of conditions is randomly determined.* Here's an example, based on Elliot et al.'s (2007) first color experiment. We have three conditions—red, green, and black—and we want 30 participants per condition. The experiment will begin next Monday, with three morning sessions and three afternoon sessions. Each session involves one participant. For Monday morning, we randomly order the three conditions, say, black–red–green. This constitutes the first "block" (i.e., "set" or "round") of conditions. Our 9 a.m. participant is assigned to receive the black ink code, the 10 a.m. participant the red ink code, and the 11 a.m. participant the green ink code.

For Monday afternoon, we randomly order the three conditions again, say, green–black–red. This is our second block of conditions. Respectively, the 1 p.m., 2 p.m., and 3 p.m. participants are assigned to the green, black, and red ink codes. We use this procedure each day, randomly ordering the three conditions for each new block. Because we want 30 participants per condition, we will conduct a total of 30 blocks. Following this approach, by the end of the experiment, each color condition ideally will have been conducted not only an equal total number of times, but also an equal number of times in the morning, in the afternoon, on each weekday, and during each week.

Matched-Groups Design

Instead of assigning participants on a purely random basis, let's now consider another approach to creating equivalent groups in a color-achievement experiment. We might try to match the groups in the three color conditions on their general anagram ability. Perhaps we could give all the participants an anagram test at an earlier point in time. Next, we would take the three participants with the highest anagram ability and randomly assign one of them to each color condition. Then we would take the next three best performers and randomly assign one of them to each condition. We would continue to do this until we reached the three poorest performers, and likewise, we'd randomly assign one of them to each color condition.

What we've done is to use anagram ability as a **matching variable,** *a characteristic on which we match sets of individuals as closely as possible.* Then, to create a **matched-groups design,** *each set of participants that has been matched on one or more attributes is randomly assigned to the various conditions of the experiment.* If our experiment had only two conditions—say, red and black—then we would match pairs of participants and randomly assign a member of each pair to each condition. This is often called a *matched-pairs design.*

It might seem that experimenters should always match their participants on the same attribute that will be assessed later by the dependent measure, but it is often impossible or impractical to do this. Moreover, in some cases, giving participants the same task or type of task that they will subsequently perform might tip them off about the purpose of the experiment.

Instead of matching participants on the same variable that constitutes the dependent measure, an alternative is to match them on some other variable that we are concerned about as a possible confounding factor. For example, if we know that intelligence and verbal aptitude are substantially correlated with anagram performance, then perhaps we would want to try using these as matching variables rather than leave the creation of equivalent groups to simple random assignment. This way, if the red color group performs worst, and if this group overall is matched with the other groups on IQ and verbal aptitude, then it's difficult to argue that IQ and verbal aptitude—rather than the red color—were responsible for our results.

To match the participants according to these criteria, we would either have to administer IQ and verbal aptitude measures to them, or try to obtain records of existing IQ or verbal aptitude scores. Sometimes, for reasons of confidentiality or other factors, it's not feasible to create correlated matching variables, but other times it is. For example, in an experiment in which two groups of elementary schoolchildren will be randomly assigned to receive one of two types of special tutoring programs, we might want to match the two groups on readily measurable characteristics such as gender and school grade.

Even when matching is feasible, however, the benefits need to be weighed against the cost of adding complexity to the experiment. By obtaining a sufficiently large number of participants for their experiments, many researchers choose to rely solely on random assignment to create equivalent groups and let chance "balance out" what otherwise might be too many potential matching variables to keep track of.

Natural-Groups Design

In many studies, researchers who are interested in examining a possible causal relation between variables X and Y create the different conditions of X not by manipulating an independent variable, but instead by selecting different groups of people based on their personal characteristics. Consider this question: Does self-esteem influence whether people are introverted or extraverted?

To answer this question, we design a study with high-self-esteem and low-self-esteem conditions. To create these conditions, we administer a psychological test that measures self-esteem to 200 college students. We identify the 40 students with the highest self-esteem, the 40 with the lowest self-esteem, and these groups operationally define our high- and low-self-esteem conditions. We then have each of these students individually come to our laboratory. In the lab, we expose the students to a situation in which they have the opportunity to interact with other people, and we record the degree to which their behavior is introverted or extraverted.

Subject Variables. People's natural level of self-esteem is a **subject variable:** *a personal characteristic on which individuals vary from one another.* What we have done in our self-esteem example is to develop a single-factor design by measuring (not manipulating) a subject variable and creating different conditions (i.e., groups) based on people's natural level of that variable. This research approach is called a **natural-groups design:** *A researcher measures a subject variable, forms different groups based on people's level of that variable, and then measures how the different groups respond on other variables.*

Similarly, depending on our research question, we can use other subject variables to create a natural-groups design. If we hypothesize that people's personality and values differ depending on their degree of morningness–eveningness (the tendency to be an "early bird" or "night owl"), then we could measure morningness–eveningness and create a natural-groups design with three conditions: morning types, intermediate types, and evening types (Vollmer & Randler, 2012). We would subsequently measure and compare the personality traits and values of the three groups. As another example, if we hypothesize that religiousness can have a positive influence on people's health, then we would measure people's religiousness (based on a particular operational definition) and use this to create a natural-groups design in which the different conditions reflect different degrees of religiousness (Lutgendorf et al., 2002). We would next measure and compare the health outcomes of the various groups. People's age, sex, and ethnicity are examples of subject variables frequently used to create natural groups (e.g., to study age, sex, and ethnic differences).

Is a Natural-Groups Design an Experiment? Two areas of disagreement arise concerning natural-groups designs. First, if a subject variable is the sole basis for creating different groups or conditions in a study, should we consider that subject variable to be an "independent variable"? Some researchers refer to such variables as *selected independent variables* or as *quasi-independent variables,* to distinguish them from *manipulated independent variables.* Others reserve the term *independent variable* only for variables that are manipulated. Personally, although I have no qualms about calling subject characteristics "independent variables" when discussing them conceptually, when discussing a single-factor natural-groups design operationally, I try to avoid doing so. But, many researchers do call them independent variables, and your course instructor may hold that view.

The second and more important issue is whether a single-factor natural-groups design constitutes an experiment. After all, it does seem as if the researcher is "tinkering around" with something by creating different groups. But in reality, a natural-groups design is a correlational study, not an experiment. As discussed in Chapter 5, in a correlational study the researcher measures variable X and variable Y, and then examines whether they are related statistically. Now reread the definition of a natural-groups design. They're the same, with one exception. To examine the relation between self-esteem and introversion–extraversion in a typical correlational study, we could give a self-esteem test to 200 students, and then correlate the actual self-esteem scores for all 200 students with their scores on a measure of introversion–extraversion. In a natural-groups design, we are not using each student's specific self-esteem score in the statistical analysis. Instead, we are using the score only to categorize the student into a low or high (or low, moderate, or high) self-esteem group. However, merely transforming the self-esteem data in this way does not transform the core methodology of a correlational study into an experiment. It doesn't change the fact that we measured people's naturally occurring self-esteem; we did not manipulate it.

It's important to understand that viewing a natural-groups design as a correlational study does not negate the importance of natural-groups designs. Correlational research has many important advantages and plays a vital role in advancing scientific knowledge. But, because a natural-groups design *is* correlational, its findings are open to the same two potential problems that limit the ability to draw clear causal conclusions from any correlational study: bidirectionality and the third-variable problem (see Chapter 5). For example, if we find that the low-self-esteem group, overall, is more introverted than the high-self-esteem group, the issue becomes: (1) Did lower self-esteem cause people to become more introverted, or did being introverted cause people to develop lower self-esteem (this is the bidirectionality problem); and (2) perhaps there is actually no causal relation between self-esteem and introversion; perhaps other personal or environmental factors either cause or are associated with lower self-esteem, and these other factors are the real causes of why people are more introverted (this is the third-variable problem). In sum, researchers need to be especially cautious when trying to draw causal conclusions from natural-groups designs.

RANDOM ASSIGNMENT VERSUS RANDOM SAMPLING

The ability to assign participants randomly to the different conditions of an experiment is a cornerstone of between-subjects experiments. Unfortunately, I've found that some students confuse random assignment with another important procedure, random sampling (discussed in detail in Chapter 7). Random assignment and random sampling do have some similarities: Both rely on the laws of probability and both are considered good scientific practice. But, they are used to achieve different goals. Here are some crucial differences:

- *Random sampling* is a procedure in which each member of a population has an equal probability of being selected into a sample chosen to participate in a study. In other words, random sampling is used to determine who will be asked to participate in a study. Surveys are a common example: From the population of adults in a nation, a random sample would be selected to participate in the survey.

- *The goal of random sampling* is to select a sample of people whose characteristics are representative of the broader population from which those people have been drawn.

- *Random assignment* of participants, within the context of experiments, is used to determine the specific condition to which each participant will be exposed. Using random assignment, each participant has an equal probability of being assigned to any particular condition. Random assignment is not used to identify and select the sample of people who will be asked to participate in the experiment. Rather, once someone has agreed or been chosen to participate, random assignment determines the particular condition into which that person is placed.

- *The goal of random assignment* in experiments is to take whatever sample of people you happen to put together and place them in different conditions in an unbiased way. By doing this, at the start of the study researchers can assume that the groups of participants in the various conditions are equivalent, overall, to one another.

Here's another way to think about it. To select who will be in an experiment, random sampling is rarely used. Instead, researchers may place notices in newspapers or on websites to announce that they are seeking participants for a study. In many experiments, the participants are college undergraduates (e.g., students taking introductory psychology) who are recruited using sign-up sheets that are posted online or in a psychology department building. Suppose, therefore, that in an introductory psychology class of 150 students, 40 students sign up to participate in an experiment on decision making. In this case,

- the participants are college students, and they cannot automatically be considered a representative sample of the overall adult population;

- the students on this campus may not be representative of college students in general;

- the students enrolled in introductory psychology may not be representative of the overall student body on this particular campus; and

- the students who sign up for this particular experiment may not be representative of the entire class of students enrolled in introductory psychology.

If you have already read Chapter 7, *Survey Research,* you may recognize that the type of sampling used to recruit participants in this (and most) human psychology experiments is

Table 8.3 Differences Between Random Sampling and Random Assignment

	Random Sampling	Random Assignment (in experiments)
Description	Each member of a population has an equal probability of being selected into a sample chosen to participate in a study.	People who have agreed to participate in a study are assigned to the various conditions of the study on a random basis. Each participant has an equal probability of being assigned to any particular condition.
Example	From a population of 240 million adults in a nation, a random sample of 1,000 people is selected and asked to participate in a survey.	After a college student signs up for an experiment (e.g., to receive extra course credit or meet a course requirement), random assignment is used to determine whether that student will participate in an experimental or control condition.
Goal	To select a sample of people whose characteristics (e.g., age, ethnicity, gender, annual income) are representative of the broader population from which those people have been drawn.	To take the sample of people you happen to get and place them into the conditions of the experiment in an unbiased way. Thus, prior to exposure to the independent variable, we assume that the groups of participants in the various conditions are equivalent to one another overall.

called *convenience sampling*. Selection into the study is not done randomly; rather, experimenters in most cases take whomever they can get. As discussed in Chapter 7, convenience sampling is usually an adequate method of recruiting participants for experiments. It doesn't negate an experiment's ability to examine cause–effect relations. But for now, the main point is that whatever the characteristics of this particular sample of students may be, the researcher will use *random assignment* to determine who is placed in the various conditions of the experiment. In this way, we can consider the participants in the different conditions to be equivalent to one another, overall, at the start of the study. This enables us to examine whether our independent variable causes these initially equivalent groups to behave in different ways. **Table 8.3** summarizes major differences between random sampling and random assignment.

✓ **CONCEPT CHECK 8.3** BETWEEN-SUBJECTS DESIGNS

Decide whether each statement below is true or false. Answers appear on page 276.

1. To study some topics, a between-subjects design, rather than within-subjects design, must be used.
2. Overall, between-subjects designs require more participants than within-subjects designs.
3. In experiments, the purpose of random assignment is to select a sample of participants that is representative of the overall population.
4. In matched-groups designs, the matching variable and dependent variable must measure different characteristics.
5. Overall, between-subjects designs are less sensitive than within-subjects designs.

WITHIN-SUBJECTS DESIGNS

Learning Objectives

After studying this section, you should be able to:

- Describe some advantages and disadvantages of within-subjects designs.
- Explain the goals of counterbalancing.
- Describe several types of within-subjects designs.

How good are you at recognizing people's emotions from their facial expressions? Are different emotions equally easy (or difficult) to judge from facial cues? To elaborate on a possible emotion recognition experiment described earlier, let's now contrast two approaches to designing such an experiment. In both approaches, the independent variable is the type of emotion expressed and we'll create nine conditions: nine facial photographs of the same person (an actor) portraying anger, fear, joy, disgust, interest, surprise, contempt, shame, and sadness. Using a between-subjects design, there will be 180 participants, 20 per condition. After providing instructions to each participant, we'll show the participant one photograph, and in a few seconds that participant will make a judgment as to which emotion is being portrayed. Next we'll debrief the participant, who can then leave.

This between-subjects design is a legitimate approach to conducting the experiment, although in practice we would not want to limit ourselves to only nine photographs of the same actor. Maybe some of this particular actor's facial expressions will be uniquely easy or hard to judge. It would be better to have a set of nine photos for each of, say, 10 different actors, so that our data will be based on a broader sample of faces. But now we have 90 photographs, and if we ask 20 participants to judge each one, we'll need to have 1,800 participants in our study, each making a single judgment that takes only a few seconds.

You may be thinking that this is an inefficient way to conduct the experiment. Instead of asking 1,800 participants to each make a single judgment, why not ask 20 participants to judge all 90 photographs? This probably will take no more than half an hour per participant. Using this approach, we have now entered into the realm of *within-subjects designs* (also called *repeated-measures designs*), in which each participant engages in every condition of the experiment one or more times.

ADVANTAGES OF WITHIN-SUBJECTS DESIGNS

As the preceding numbers make clear, a key advantage of within-subjects designs is that they need fewer participants to obtain the same amount of data per condition than do between-subjects designs. This can be especially important in experiments where there are many conditions, the desired number of participants per condition is large, or the experimenter must spend extensive time giving instructions or leading each participant through a lengthy or difficult set of practice trials. The need for fewer participants also is important when they come from special populations (e.g., people with uncommon abilities or disorders) or are otherwise difficult to obtain.

Consider an experiment by Gabriel Kreiman and his colleagues that attempted to find the individual neurons in regions of the human brain that fire most frequently in response to specific types of complex visual stimuli (Kreiman, Koch, & Fried, 2000). The researchers identified these "category-specific" neurons by implanting microelectrodes inside 427 individual neurons within the brains of 11 patients with epilepsy. The microelectrodes would help doctors determine the neural source of the patients' seizures, and possibly lead to surgery to better control their epilepsy.

For the scientists, the patients' informed consent provided a remarkable research opportunity. Kreiman et al. (2000) recorded the firing rate of each neuron as the patient was presented with visual images that represented nine categories of stimuli, such as household objects, animals, cars, and abstract patterns. Multiple pictures were used for each category (there were several faces, cars, animals, etc.) and they were presented to each patient several times, resulting in up to 600 stimulus presentations for some patients. Each trial lasted 1 second. Given the large number of trials, the brevity of each trial, the relatively small number of participants available, and the delicate microelectrode implantation procedure performed on each patient, a within-subjects research design clearly was the only feasible way to conduct this particular experiment.

Another advantage of a within-subjects design is that, rather than recruiting a smaller number of participants to obtain the same amount of data per condition as a between-subjects design, we can instead recruit the same number of participants and thus collect more data per condition. In Figure 8.4 on page 253, the between-subjects and within-subjects designs for the longhand versus laptop note-taking experiment each have a total sample of 20 participants. Using a between-subjects design, we end up with data from only 10 students in each condition. Using a within-subjects design, we obtain twice the amount of data because each of the 20 students engages in both conditions. And, for our emotion recognition experiment, if 180 participants are available, then whereas a between-subjects design (with nine photographs, one per emotion) would only have 20 participants per condition, a within-subjects design would yield data from all 180 participants in each condition.

There is an important methodological and statistical advantage to having more participants per condition: Any findings we obtain are, in a sense, more reliable (i.e., less open to unusual chance fluctuations) because they are based on a larger amount of data. Other things being equal, if an independent variable truly has an influence on a dependent variable, an experiment will be more likely to detect that influence as the number of participants increases.

A third advantage is that within-subjects designs are the only approach that can be used to answer certain types of questions. For example, to examine whether specific neurons *change* their rate of firing in response to different stimuli, we have to measure those same neurons repeatedly as we expose a given participant to the different stimuli in each condition in our experiment. Similarly, in the field of *psychophysics,* within-subjects designs are required to investigate questions such as, "What is the smallest amount of change in the intensity of a sound that an individual can reliably perceive?" The only way to establish these individual perceptual thresholds—called *just-noticeable differences* or *difference thresholds*— is to expose each participant to the same sound played at varying decibels.

Finally, compared to between-subjects designs, within-subjects designs do a better job of creating equivalent groups at the outset of the experiment. Nothing can be more equivalent than having the same participants in all the conditions!

DISADVANTAGES OF WITHIN-SUBJECTS DESIGNS

Within-subjects designs run the risk that exposing participants to all the conditions will make them aware of the experiment's purpose or hypothesis. Moreover, either logically or practically, some research questions do not lend themselves to within-subjects experiments. Hess's (1959) imprinting experiment provides one example: As we discussed earlier, a duckling's first exposure to an adult model duck can only occur at a particular number of hours after birth. The experimenter can control when the initial exposure occurs, but the duckling can't possibly engage in more than one "first exposure" condition. Research on whether visual deprivation after birth impairs normal visual development provides another example. In such visual deprivation studies, newborn animals are raised from birth either in a dark or light environment for varying lengths of time, and later their performance in running a visually complex maze is compared (Crabtree & Riesen, 1979). An animal can grow up either exposed or never exposed to light, but cannot possibly grow up from birth in both types of conditions. Likewise, in an experiment comparing the effectiveness of behavioral, cognitive, and psychodynamic therapy, we would need to assign each participant to receive only one type of treatment.

When within-subjects designs are feasible, they still present a potentially huge problem: **order effects** (also called **sequence effects**), *which occur when participants' responses are affected by the order of conditions to which they are exposed.* In an experiment with conditions A, B, and C, if participants respond differently in condition A depending on whether it is the first, second, or third condition to which they are exposed, then this would be an example of an order effect.

Some order effects, called **progressive effects,** *reflect changes in participants' responses that result from their cumulative exposure to prior conditions.* For example, in an experiment where participants perform the same task under different conditions, they gain increasing task practice with exposure to each successive condition. In an experiment that examines the effects of cell phone conversations on driving performance, suppose that each participant drives the same simulated route once while using a handheld phone, once while using a hands-free phone, and once while not talking on a cell phone. As participants move from one condition to the next, they become more familiar with the driving route. This can create a **practice effect,** *a performance improvement due to greater experience with a task.* Conversely, participants might experience a **fatigue effect,** *a performance decline that results from becoming tired, inattentive, or less motivated to perform well with repeated exposure to a task.* Thus, if all participants in the cell phone experiment engage in the three conditions in the same order, and driving performance differs across those conditions, practice and fatigue effects could provide alternative explanations for any findings we obtain.

Other order effects, called **carryover effects,** *occur when participants' responses in one condition are uniquely influenced by the particular condition or conditions that preceded it.* In an experiment asking you to judge the sweetness of different drinks, a particular drink may seem more or less sweet to you depending on whether the drink that immediately preceded it was the sweetest or least sweet drink of all. Similarly, imagine a within-subjects laboratory experiment in which each participant, on three separate nights, is allowed 0, 4, or 8 hours of sleep and then performs a series of tasks at noon. Unless the researcher spaces each person's three trials far apart, carryover effects from sleep deprivation could occur. For example, if participation occurred on consecutive nights, how well people perform after 4 hours of sleep may differ depending on whether they received no sleep or 8 hours of sleep on the preceding night. As in judging the sweetness of drinks, the way participants react in a particular condition may be altered by the specific condition that comes just before it.

Within-subjects designs also may produce another type of order effect, **sensitization,** *in which exposure to multiple conditions increases participants' awareness of, or sensitivity to, the variable that is being experimentally manipulated.* For example, as Greenwald (1976) notes, in a within-subjects experiment designed to examine how different levels of room illumination influence workers' performance, awareness of changes in how brightly the room is lit may cause workers to become more sensitized to illumination as a factor affecting their performance. This may even lead participants to form hypotheses about how room illumination should affect their performance, and these expectations, in turn, might influence their performance. This type of order effect differs from a contrast effect, in which the perception of a room's brightness or dimness might be affected by the illumination level in the immediately preceding condition. Rather, sensitization focuses on participants' greater readiness to perceive any changes in the independent variable due to their multiple exposures to it.

In some experiments, such as those where the goal is to examine people's maximum sensitivity to detect changes in a stimulus (e.g., light or sound intensity), sensitization may facilitate the researcher's goal (Greenwald, 1976). In other experiments, such as those where researchers want to prevent participants from identifying the independent variable or minimize their awareness of it, sensitization effects from using a within-subjects design would be an undesirable factor.

Lastly, depending on the topic being studied, another potential disadvantage of within-subjects designs concerns the need to develop multiple, equivalent sets of materials to which participants are exposed as they progress through the different conditions of the experiment. The longhand versus laptop note-taking experiment portrayed in Figure 8.4 (p. 253) provides an example. As noted earlier, it makes little sense to have students watch the same lecture twice and take the identical knowledge test twice, once when taking longhand notes and once while taking laptop notes.

Therefore, we would want to develop two lectures that are equivalent on key characteristics, such as length, the overall number and difficulty of key concepts covered, the enthusiasm and clarity with which the lecturer delivers them, and the degree to which students find the two lectures to be engaging. Likewise, we would want to develop two knowledge tests—one for each lecture—that have the same number and type of items (e.g., factual, conceptual), and that are similar in overall difficulty. Accomplishing this would involve a process of developing an initial pair of lectures and knowledge tests, and assessing their equivalence by gathering data from a sample of students. We would then revise the materials and reassess their equivalence one or more times, based on additional feedback from new samples of students, until we have developed two lectures and knowledge tests that are similar in their key features. We would then initiate the actual note-taking experiment with a new sample of students.

COUNTERBALANCING AND TEMPORAL SPACING

In a within-subjects experiment, if all participants engage in the various conditions in the same order, then any differences in the dependent measure might be due to the influence of the independent variable, or instead, to the particular order in which the conditions appeared. Consider the longhand versus laptop note-taking experiment portrayed in Figure 8.4. Imagine that all students first take longhand notes during a lecture, and then use a laptop to take notes during a second lecture. Suppose that we find students' learning is better when they take longhand notes. Is this result due to the fact that longhand note-taking is the better approach for promoting learning, or might it be due to the fact that, after taking longhand notes for the first lecture, participants became bored or fatigued while taking laptop notes for the second lecture?

As a second example, consider the cell phone driving experiment in which every participant drives the same route first while conversing on a handheld phone, next while talking on a hands-free phone, and last while not using a cell phone. We find that driving performance is worst in the handheld condition, better in the hands-free condition, and best in the no-phone condition. Can we conclude that talking on a cell phone, especially a handheld phone, impairs performance? Clearly not: An obvious alternative explanation is that as participants progressed from the handheld to the hands-free to the no-phone conditions, they performed progressively better because they gained familiarity with the route.

To rule out such plausible alternative explanations, we must design our within-subjects experiment to avoid confounding factors that could arise by having all participants engage in the same order of conditions. To accomplish this we need to counterbalance the order of the conditions so that no one condition has an advantage or disadvantage relative to any other condition. Counterbalancing will not change the fact that order effects are likely to occur. Participants may still become fatigued, bored, more experienced, and so forth, as they move on to each subsequent condition. What counterbalancing does, however, is just what it says: It balances the sequence of the positions so there is less likelihood that order effects will work against or in favor of any particular condition.

On page 253, the right side of Figure 8.4 illustrates how we would counterbalance the sequence of conditions in the longhand versus laptop note-taking experiment. We would create two orders. For Order 1, the longhand note-taking condition comes first, followed by the laptop note-taking condition. For Order 2, the laptop note-taking condition comes first, followed by the longhand note-taking condition. With a sample of 20 students, 10 students would be randomly assigned to Order 1, and 10 students would be assigned to Order 2.

Moreover, even though we have created two equivalent lectures and knowledge tests for this experiment, we would want to apply a simple counterbalancing procedure to the order in which students view the lectures. Let's say that one lecture is about economics and the other is about geography. For the 10 students assigned to Order 1, five of them would begin the experiment by taking longhand notes during the economics lecture, and then switch to taking laptop notes for the geography lecture. The other five students assigned to Order 1 would first take longhand notes during the geography lecture, and then switch to laptop notes for the economics lecture. Similarly, for the 10 students assigned to Order 2, five would begin by taking laptop notes during the economics lecture, and switch to longhand notes for the geography lecture. The other five students assigned to Order 2 would begin by taking laptop notes for the geography lecture, and then switch to longhand notes for the economics lecture. Applying counterbalancing in this way would make it implausible for someone to argue that any results we obtained—such as superior conceptual learning when taking longhand notes—was due to a confound in the order of note-taking conditions or sequence in which the lectures were viewed.

In addition to counterbalancing, in some experiments it may be feasible to reduce certain order effects by allowing sufficient time to pass in between participants' exposure to the various conditions of the experiment. Fatigue effects are one example. If the dependent variable in an experiment is the quality of task performance, and participants will perform the same task in each of two experimental conditions, researchers may choose to set exposure to the conditions far enough apart to allow participants time to physically recover. The rest interval might vary from merely seconds to weeks, depending on the task. This procedure could also be used if the experimental manipulation itself would be expected to produce a fatigue effect. For instance, although many college students attend consecutive lectures without a break due to their course schedules, in our longhand versus laptop note-taking experiment we might consider providing participants with a 15- to 30-minute rest period after viewing the first of the two lectures.

As an example of longer temporal spacing, one research team used a within-subjects experimental design to examine whether short-term sleep deprivation caused people to act more impulsively (Cedernaes et al., 2014). Each participant stayed overnight in a sleep lab on two separate occasions. In one session they were permitted a normal night's sleep, and in the other they were deprived of all sleep. The order of the conditions was counterbalanced such that, as determined randomly, some participants were first exposed to the sleep deprivation condition and others were first exposed to the sleep condition. Additionally, for each participant the two sessions were spaced at least four weeks apart. Impulsivity was assessed in the morning of each session by measuring participants' performance (e.g., reaction time, number of errors) at a decision-making task. Sleep deprivation was found to increase impulsivity.

TYPES OF WITHIN-SUBJECT DESIGNS

Within-subjects designs fall into two general categories: those in which each participant is exposed to every condition in the experiment (1) only once and (2) more than once. To illustrate specific designs within each category, we'll examine how the same research question would be handled by each design.

Our featured example involves a long-running, multi-billion-dollar battle between corporate giants who are fighting for your mind, heart, and primarily your cash: the cola wars (**Figure 8.6**). And, the weapon of choice is the seemingly simple taste preference test. In the 1970s, PepsiCo, the makers of Pepsi-Cola, launched the famous Take the Pepsi Challenge campaign, still continuing today in modified form. For years, advertisements appeared in newspapers and magazines, based on taste-test experiments that PepsiCo conducted in different cities.

Suppose we want to design an unbiased experiment to see which of four non-diet cola drinks people prefer the most: Pepsi, Coke, Royal Crown Cola (RC), and Shasta. (Sorry, Dr. Pepper lovers: Your drink is not advertised as a "cola.") On each trial, participants will taste a drink and then rate it. We need to address one of the major possible confounding factors in such an experiment: the order of the drinks.

Exposing Participants to Each Condition Once

We first examine three designs—*all possible orders,* the *Latin Square,* and *random selected orders*—in which every participant engages in all of the conditions one time.

Daniel Acker/Bloomberg via Getty Images

Figure 8.6 The Pepsi–Coke cola wars. In taste tests and in advertisements, the battle between the makers of Pepsi and Coke for consumers' hearts and wallets has spanned decades.

All-Possible-Orders Design (Complete Counterbalancing). In an experiment with n conditions (where n stands for the number of conditions), there are $n!$ ("n factorial") unique orders in which those conditions can be arranged. Thus, in our taste-test experiment, if we only had two drinks, Coke and Pepsi, there would be $2!$ (i.e., 2×1) = 2 possible orders: Coke–Pepsi and Pepsi–Coke. If we had three drinks (say, adding RC Cola), there would be $3!$ (i.e., $3 \times 2 \times 1$) = 6 possible orders:

Coke–Pepsi–RC	Pepsi–Coke–RC	RC–Coke–Pepsi
Coke–RC–Pepsi	Pepsi–RC–Coke	RC–Pepsi–Coke

And, if we have our full complement of four cola drinks (adding Shasta), we would have $4!$ ($4 \times 3 \times 2 \times 1$) = 24 possible orders, as shown in **Table 8.4**.

With an **all-possible-orders design** (also called **complete counterbalancing**), *the conditions of an independent variable are arranged in every possible sequence, and an equal number of participants are assigned to each sequence.* Thus, in our taste-test experiment with four drinks, we would need a minimum of 24 participants and assign one participant to each of the 24 taste-testing sequences. We could use one of several techniques for deciding which order each participant follows, with simple random assignment being the most straightforward. Thus, the first participant in our taste test might receive the order RC–Coke–Pepsi–Shasta, the second participant might get Pepsi–Shasta–RC–Coke, and so on. We could also use this design with any multiple of 24 participants: 48, 72, 96, and so forth, depending on where we want to balance the "more data" versus "fewer participants" benefit of using a within-subjects design. If we had 48 participants, for example, then for participants 25 through 48, we would run through the sequence of all 24 possible orders again, using new random assignments to determine which participants get which orders.

The strong advantage of this design is that, because every possible order is used an equal number of times, every possible confounding effect involving the sequence of conditions is completely counterbalanced. This is why the term *complete counterbalancing* is used along with or instead of *all possible orders* to describe this design. Specifically, this design accomplishes three counterbalancing goals:

Goal 1   Every condition of the independent variable appears equally often in each position (e.g., in our example, each of the four drinks appears equally often in the 1st, 2nd, 3rd, and 4th position).

Goal 2   Every condition appears equally often before and after every other condition (e.g., Coke occurs immediately before Pepsi equally as often as Pepsi occurs immediately before Coke; this will be the same for any combination of two drinks you examine).

Goal 3   Every condition appears with equal frequency before and after every other condition, *within each pair of positions in the overall sequence* (e.g., looking at the 1st vs. 2nd position in the order, Coke occurs immediately before Pepsi as often as Pepsi

Table 8.4 All Possible Orders for a Single-Factor Design with Four Conditions

Coke–Pepsi–RC–Shasta	Pepsi–Coke–RC–Shasta	RC–Pepsi–Coke–Shasta	Shasta–Pepsi–RC–Coke
Coke–Pepsi–Shasta–RC	Pepsi–Coke–Shasta–RC	RC–Pepsi–Shasta–Coke	Shasta–Pepsi–Coke–RC
Coke–RC–Pepsi–Shasta	Pepsi–RC–Coke–Shasta	RC–Coke–Pepsi–Shasta	Shasta–RC–Pepsi–Coke
Coke–RC–Shasta–Pepsi	Pepsi–RC–Shasta–Coke	RC–Coke–Shasta–Pepsi	Shasta–RC–Coke–Pepsi
Coke–Shasta–RC–Pepsi	Pepsi–Shasta–RC–Coke	RC–Shasta–Coke–Pepsi	Shasta–Coke–RC–Pepsi
Coke–Shasta–Pepsi–RC	Pepsi–Shasta–Coke–RC	RC–Shasta–Pepsi–Coke	Shasta–Coke–Pepsi–RC

There are a total of 24 orders: Six orders begin with Coke, six with Pepsi, six with RC, and six with Shasta. Therefore, we would need a minimum of 24 participants—one per order—to use this complete design.

occurs immediately before Coke; it's the same for the 2nd vs. 3rd position, and 3rd vs. 4th position, and this balancing will be the same for any pair of drinks you examine).

The biggest disadvantage of this design is that, as the number of conditions increases, the number of participants needed rises rapidly to exceed what the experimenter is likely to obtain. Adding a fifth condition (e.g., a fifth cola drink) to our taste test increases the number of possible orders to 120. With six conditions, we would need 720 participants, and with seven, 5,040 participants! Thus, depending on the number of participants available to the experimenter, this design is most commonly feasible with only two, three, or four conditions; maybe five if access is available to a huge subject pool.

Latin Square Design. Before defining this design, it will be best to consider an example. Look at the matrix in **Table 8.5**. Above the top row, we have the four possible positions, also called *trials,* in the series of drinks: 1st, 2nd, 3rd, and 4th position.

Inside the matrix there are four rows, with each row representing a different order (i.e., sequence) of drinks. If you look across the four rows and then down the four columns (for positions 1 through 4), you will see that each drink appears only once in each row and in each column. Welcome to the Latin Square, a sort of two-dimensional Rubik's cube. Any Latin Square—and there are many types—can be defined as follows. In a single-factor experiment where the number of conditions of the independent variable equals *n,* a **Latin Square** *is an* n *(number of positions in a series)* × n *(number of orders) matrix in which each condition will appear only once in each column and each row.* For example, if we had eight drinks, this would yield an 8 (positions) × 8 (orders) matrix.

For any given number of conditions (say, four drinks), there are multiple ways to design a Latin Square. The design in Table 8.5 is sometimes called a Williams Square, and its beauty is its remarkable efficiency. For an independent variable with four conditions, rather than using the 24 orders that would be required with an all-possible-orders design, the *Williams Latin Square* uses only four orders to accomplish the two most important counterbalancing goals achieved by the all-possible-orders design:

Goal 1   Every condition of the independent variable appears equally often in each position (e.g., in our example, each of the four drinks appears equally often in the 1st, 2nd, 3rd, and 4th position).

Goal 2   Every condition appears equally often before and after every other condition (e.g., Coke occurs immediately before Pepsi as often as Pepsi occurs immediately before Coke; this will be the same for any combination of two drinks you examine).

The only goal that the Williams Latin Square design does *not* accomplish is having each condition appear before and after every other condition between each pair of positions in the overall sequence. So, for example, Pepsi comes immediately before Shasta once, and vice versa, but the Pepsi–Shasta order occurs in the position-1-to-position-2 sequence (see row 1), whereas the Shasta–Pepsi order comes in the position-3-to-position-4 sequence (see row 3).

Table 8.5 Latin Square Using a Williams Design

Participant	Trial 1	Trial 2	Trial 3	Trial 4
Bria	Pepsi	Shasta	Coke	RC
Jinsoo	Shasta	RC	Pepsi	Coke
Beatriz	RC	Coke	Shasta	Pepsi
Tamara	Coke	Pepsi	RC	Shasta

Still, this often minor type of order imbalance is a small price to pay for the efficiency of the Williams Latin Square design.

The fact that our four-drink Latin Square has only four orders, one per participant, does not mean that we are restricted to only four participants in our study. We can have any multiple of four participants: 8, 12, 16, 40, 80, or more participants if we wish. Ideally, we would not use this specific Latin Square over and over for each set of four participants. Rather, if possible, we would use a different Williams Latin Square for each set of four participants to increase the variety of specific orders that will occur, overall, throughout our experiment.

The chief limitation of the Williams Latin Square is that when an independent variable has an odd rather than even number of conditions, you cannot construct a single Latin Square that will achieve counterbalancing Goal 2, described earlier. With a 5×5 matrix, each of the five drinks will appear equally often in the 1st, 2nd, 3rd, 4th, and 5th positions; but it is impossible, say, for Coke to immediately come before Pepsi 2½ times, and for Pepsi to immediately precede Coke 2½ times. The solution is to construct a pair of 5×5 Latin Squares that together will achieve counterbalancing Goal 2: In one matrix, Pepsi–Coke will occur more often than Coke–Pepsi, but in the other square this will be reversed. The use of two Latin Squares will require us to double the number of participants, if each participant is to be exposed to every condition only once.

Most Latin Square designs don't require this special doubling-up of matrices to accommodate an odd number of conditions. Table 8.6 shows a Latin Square created with a method called *random starting order with rotation*. In this method, we randomly select an order for the top row, and then rotate the position of each condition by one placement in each subsequent row. Thus, Coke moves from position 1 in row 1 to position 2 in row 2; Pepsi moves over to position 3; Shasta moves to position 4; and RC, which was last in row 1, swings over to the beginning of row 2. You can see that this approach continues as we move on to rows 3 and 4. With a fifth drink, we would simply have one more column (i.e., Trial 5) and one more row.

As with all Latin Squares, Goal 1 is achieved. Each drink appears only once in each position. But with a design based on a random starting order with rotation, counterbalancing Goal 2 and Goal 3 are not achieved. Coke, for example, immediately comes before Pepsi three times, but Pepsi never immediately precedes Coke. And without this, they can't possibly come immediately before and after each other within any pair of positions.

Random-Selected-Orders Design. Particularly when the number of conditions is large and thus the total number of possible orders greatly exceeds the number of participants available, another approach that some researchers use to counterbalance order effects is called a **random-selected-orders design:** *From the entire set of all possible orders, a subset of orders is randomly selected and each order is administered to one participant.* Realize that with this type of simple randomization, just as you are unlikely to get exactly 50 Heads in 100 flips of a coin, in our taste test it is unlikely that each of our four drinks will end up in the first position or any other position exactly 25% of the time, or will occur immediately before and after any other particular drink an equal number of times. Instead, the researcher is relying

Table 8.6 Latin Square Using a Random Starting Order with Rotation

Participant	Trial 1	Trial 2	Trial 3	Trial 4
Emaan	Coke	Pepsi	Shasta	RC
Brandon	RC	Coke	Pepsi	Shasta
Juan	Shasta	RC	Coke	Pepsi
David	Pepsi	Shasta	RC	Coke

on the laws of probability to create a set of orders that are unlikely to produce a statistically significant bias or advantage in favor of any particular condition relative to the others. Thus, by chance, Drink A may appear more often in position 1 than Drink C, but the magnitude of this difference is unlikely to be statistically significant. To be most effective, this counter-balancing approach should not be used when the number of participants is small; with only a few participants, there will not be enough random orders selected to let chance have a good opportunity to balance order effects.

Exposing Participants to Each Condition More Than Once

Before describing two designs of this type, perhaps you're wondering, "Why on earth would a researcher ever need or want to expose participants to each condition more than once?" There are at least three reasons why researchers would choose this approach:

- *For practical reasons.* In some cases, the experimenter may have access to only a small number of participants, too small to effectively use any of the counterbalancing designs we discussed earlier.

- *To examine the reliability (consistency) of participants' responses.* If the same participants taste the same set of four drinks again, would their ratings of the drinks be consistent with their earlier ratings? Would they again select the same drink as being the best? If we are interested in such questions, we will need to expose the same people to each condition multiple times.

- *To extend the generalizability of the results.* This involves representing each condition with multiple stimuli, rather than just one stimulus.

To illustrate this third reason, suppose we want to test whether people prefer, overall, the taste of cola drinks or that of clear "lemon-lime" soda drinks. We decide to use Pepsi and 7UP to represent each type of drink, and counterbalance the orders. If people prefer Pepsi to 7UP, have we really shown that they like cola drinks more than lemon-lime drinks? Perhaps if we had used Coke and Sprite, or Shasta and Sierra Mist, the results would have been different. To avoid this problem, we can choose several colas and several lemon-lime sodas. We expose each participant to the two conditions of our independent variable (cola vs. lemon-lime drink) several times, but each time the conditions involve different cola and lemon-lime drinks. Across the study, we counterbalance the order of drinks. Now, if people choose cola drinks more often, we are more confident in concluding that they generally prefer cola to lemon-lime drinks.

Block-Randomization Design. Imagine that the first participant, Teresa, shows up for our cola taste test. We administer each of the four colas to her one time, using a randomly selected order: RC–Shasta–Coke–Pepsi. This represents Block 1. Then we administer the four colas again, based on a fresh randomly selected order. So, for Block 2, suppose the order of drinks is Coke–Shasta–Pepsi–RC. Then (assuming that we have very nice, patient participants) we administer Block 3 to Teresa, once again randomly determining the order of drinks. We end with Block 4, which uses a freshly randomized order. When our second participant, Shih-Fen, arrives, she will also receive four blocks. And, for each of her blocks, the order of drinks will be randomized.

Earlier in the chapter, we discussed how block randomization is used in between-subjects designs to randomly assign different participants to the various conditions of an experiment (pp. 256–257). Here, as there, our entire set of conditions (in this case, the four types of cola drinks) is called a block, and the order of conditions in every block is randomly determined. However, block randomization is applied differently in within- versus between-subjects designs. In a between-subjects design, each participant only engages in a total of one condition within one particular block. In contrast, in the within-subjects design we are now discussing, each participant not only performs all the conditions within a block, but also is exposed to multiple blocks. More specifically, in a **block-randomization design,** *every participant is exposed to multiple blocks of trials, with each block for each participant containing a newly randomized order of all the conditions.* A portion of a block-randomization design appears in **Table 8.7**, with the four drinks abbreviated as C (Coke), P (Pepsi), S (Shasta), and R (RC).

Using this design, if the number of blocks must be small—due, for example, to the amount of time or effort that each participant must expend for each trial of the task—then a greater number of participants will be needed in order to give randomization the opportunity to counterbalance order effects over the entire experiment. But even with a small number of participants, if there are many blocks per participant, then block randomization can successfully counterbalance order effects across the entire experiment. With our taste-test experiment, we might be pushing participants' patience by having more than three or at most four blocks. However, in some block-randomized experiments, participants may engage in 15 or 20, or possibly more, blocks of trials.

Reverse-Counterbalancing Design. With a **reverse-counterbalancing design** (also called an **ABBA-counterbalancing design**), *each participant receives a random order of all the conditions, and then receives them again in the reverse order.* Even though an independent variable may have more than two conditions (condition A and condition B), the term *ABBA* is used to signify the mirror-image nature of this design. **Table 8.8** gives an example of an ABBA reversal design. Thus in our taste test, for our first participant, Zach, we randomly determine the order of the four colas (say, Pepsi–Shasta–Coke–RC) and then reverse the sequence so that Zach will receive the following overall sequence: Pepsi–Shasta–Coke–RC–RC–Coke–Shasta–Pepsi. We could stop there or have Zach go through another set, in which we start with a fresh random order and then reverse it. We could repeat this cycle more times if we

Table 8.7 Portion of a Within-Subjects, Block-Randomization Design

Participant	Block 1	Block 2	Block 3	Block 4	Block 5
Teresa	R S C P	C S P R	C P R S	S P R C	R P C S
Shih-Fen	C P R S	P R C S	R S C P	S R P C	P R S C
Rachel	S R P C	R S P C	R P S C	P R C S	R S P C
Averi	S C P R	C R P S	P C S R	R P C S	S C P R

Note: C = Coke; P = Pepsi; R = Royal Crown; S = Shasta.

Table 8.8 Portion of an ABBA Reversal Design

Participant	Trial															
	1	2	3	4	5	6	7	8	9	10	11	12	13	14	15	16
Zach	P	S	C	R	R	C	S	P	S	P	R	C	C	R	P	S
Miguel	R	S	P	C	C	P	S	R	P	R	C	S	S	C	R	P
Doug	C	P	R	S	S	R	P	C	C	S	R	P	P	R	S	C
Jon	R	C	S	P	P	S	C	R	R	S	C	P	P	C	S	R

Note: C = Coke; P = Pepsi; R = Royal Crown; S = Shasta.

wish, each time beginning with a new random order. For our next participant, Miguel, we use the same approach, each time starting with a new random order.

The logic behind reverse counterbalancing is that on average, for any ABBA sequence, each condition is guaranteed to end up with the same average position. So in our example, for Zach, in Trials 1 through 8, Pepsi is 1st and 8th, Shasta is 2nd and 7th, Coke is 3rd and 6th, and RC is 4th and 5th; thus, each drink has an average position of 4.5. This will be the same for every set of eight trials, for every participant. This is a rather different approach to counterbalancing, as opposed to trying to ensure that each drink appears equally often in each position. In Table 8.8, you can see that in three of the eight sets of trials shown, the first drink is RC Cola. You can see that Shasta comes in second in four of the eight sets. Now, if our experiment has considerably more participants or sets of trials per participant, then these types of imbalances become less likely to occur as randomization has a greater chance to operate. But as the number of sets per participant increases, this design—unlike pure block randomization—may enable participants to detect the ABBA pattern and thus start to anticipate the order of the conditions (at least in the last half of each series), or even to form hypotheses about the purpose of the experiment. Depending on the behavior being studied, such *anticipation effects* might alter the speed or nature of participants' responses and consequently begin to confound the results.

The notion that counterbalancing will be effective if the average position of the different conditions is kept equal is based on an assumption that the order effects which accrue with each trial add up in linear fashion. For example, in our taste test, with every drink tasted participants may get a touch more "fatigued" by the generally sweet taste of colas. Thus, a drink's advantage of being tasted first is balanced out by the disadvantage of being tasted last, to a similar degree that this balances out for drinks in positions 2-7, 3-6, and 4-5.

But suppose, analogous to our general discussion of nonlinear effects earlier in the chapter, that in a taste test the following happens for most people, as illustrated by Zach. For the first six tastes that Zach performs—Pepsi, Shasta, Coke, RC, RC, and Coke, everything is fine. Then, with just two drinks to go in the first set, Zach "hits the wall" and suddenly begins to find the sweet tastes of Shasta and Pepsi very bothersome, or sickeningly sweet. In this case, coming in position 7 and position 8 in the order takes on a substantially greater disadvantage that is not balanced out by whatever benefit might have accrued from being position 2 or position 1. In other words, if order effects build up in a nonlinear fashion, then the central assumption behind reverse counterbalancing doesn't work. This problem is called *nonlinear order effects*. There are several strategies for trying to minimize the confounding effect of nonlinear order effects in an ABBA design, but the researchers also might consider whether some other counterbalancing approach, such as the block-randomization design described above, would be more appropriate.

✓ CONCEPT CHECK 8.4 WITHIN-SUBJECTS DESIGNS

Fill in each of the blanks below. Answers appear on page 276.

1. Collectively, within-subjects designs are also called _____ designs.

2. In within-subjects designs, two common types of progressive order effects are _____ effects and _____ effects, and experimenters use _____ to minimize order effects as possible confounding variables.

3. It is not feasible to use an all-possible-orders design when an experiment has many _____.

4. In a within-subjects _____ design and _____ design, each participant engages in each condition more than once.

EXAMINING THE RESULTS: GENERAL CONCEPTS

To conclude this chapter, we'll briefly discuss the general approach that researchers use to examine the results from single-factor experiments. We'll focus on concepts and not on statistical formulas or computations.

Researchers use *descriptive statistics* to summarize their data. Reporting the mean scores of participants in the different conditions (as in Figures 8.1 and 8.7), and reporting the percentage of trials on which a particular response occurred (as in Figure 8.2), are examples of how researchers use descriptive statistics. Researchers then utilize *inferential statistical tests* to help them determine whether their findings are statistically significant, that is, unlikely to be due simply to chance. (See Statistics Module 1 for a further overview of descriptive and inferential statistics, and Module 9 for a discussion of statistical significance.)

In most experiments, researchers perform statistical tests designed for dependent variables that have been measured on an interval or ratio scale (as opposed to a nominal or ordinal scale). We'll focus on those tests here. The two most common statistical tests used to analyze interval- and ratio-scale data from experiments are the *t test* and the *analysis of variance*. A *t test* helps researchers determine whether the difference between the mean scores of two conditions is statistically significant. *Analysis of variance* (ANOVA) helps researchers determine whether the overall pattern of differences among the mean scores of the conditions is statistically significant. (See Statistics Modules 12 and 16 for more detail on the *t* test and ANOVA.)

When a single-factor experiment has only two conditions, either a *t* test or an ANOVA can be used. Moreover, when an experiment has only two conditions, there is only one step to perform: You directly compare the two conditions. The analysis will tell you the probability that the difference between the mean scores of the two conditions is due to chance. Traditionally, if less than a 5% probability exists that chance factors could be solely responsible for the results, then the finding is considered statistically significant.

When a single-factor experiment has three or more conditions, then the analysis may involve several steps. Typically, the first step is to perform an ANOVA to determine whether the overall pattern of findings is statistically significant. For example, **Figure 8.7** shows the

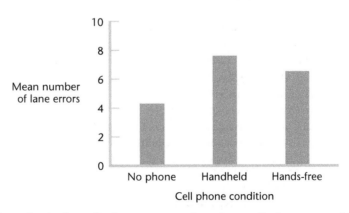

Figure 8.7 Hypothetical results from an experiment on cell phone use while driving.

results of a hypothetical experiment in which participants performed a driving simulator task while (1) not talking on a cell phone, (2) talking on a handheld cell phone, and (3) talking on a hands-free cell phone. The dependent variable is the number of lane errors: the number of times participants drove onto or across the white lane markers on either side of their lane. The ANOVA would determine whether, overall, the number of lane errors differs significantly depending on the phone condition.

Typically, if the ANOVA does not reveal a statistically significant overall pattern of findings, then the analysis stops. If the ANOVA is statistically significant, then researchers often proceed with tests that compare the means of specific conditions. Because these tests are performed after looking at the results and determining whether the overall pattern is significant, they are called *post-hoc tests* or *post-hoc comparisons*.

For example, if an ANOVA reveals that the overall pattern of results in Figure 8.7 is statistically significant, we can use a separate post-hoc comparison to determine whether there is a significant difference in the mean scores between (1) the no-phone versus handheld condition, (2) the no-phone versus hands-free condition, and (3) the handheld versus hands-free condition. Thus, our statistical analysis of a multilevel single-factor experiment has proceeded from an initial general analysis (ANOVA) to more specific comparisons between specific conditions (post-hoc tests). This is not the only data analysis approach that researchers can use, but it's a common one.

 CONCEPT CHECK 8.5 EXAMINING THE RESULTS: GENERAL CONCEPTS

Decide whether each statement below is true or false. Answers appear on page 276.

1. If an experimental finding is statistically significant, this means that it is unlikely the finding is due solely to chance.

2. To determine whether a finding is statistically significant, a researcher would use inferential statistics.

3. Usually, if an experiment has three or more conditions, the initial data analysis will examine whether the overall pattern of findings is significant, rather than examine differences in every possible pair of conditions.

CHAPTER SUMMARY

- Experiments provide the ability to manipulate an independent variable, to control how and when the dependent variable is measured, and to regulate extraneous factors. This control offers the best opportunity to examine how independent variables causally influence dependent variables.

- In between-subjects designs, potential confounding variables that can arise from differences in participants' characteristics are addressed by using random assignment to create equivalent groups at the start of the experiment. In within-subjects designs, such potential confounding variables are addressed by having the same people participate in every condition of the experiment and counterbalancing the order of conditions.

- In a single-factor design, the researcher manipulates one independent variable. An independent variable can have two levels, but more levels are needed to determine whether the relation between an independent and dependent variable is linear or nonlinear.

- An experimental group receives a treatment or an "active" level of the independent variable. A control group receives no treatment or a baseline level of an independent variable. In some experiments, the concept of a control group does not apply.

- Between-subjects designs have several advantages. There is no possibility of order effects and they are less likely than within-subjects designs to tip off participants about the hypothesis or underlying purpose of the experiment. However, they are less effective than within-subjects designs in creating equivalent groups and require more participants.

- In an independent-groups design, participants are randomly assigned to the various conditions. Block randomization ensures that the number of times each condition is conducted stays in lockstep with every other condition.

- Using a matched-groups design, sets of participants are matched on one or more variables before being randomly assigned to the various conditions of the experiment. The matching variable may be the same variable that constitutes the dependent measure, or it may be another variable that we are concerned about as a possible confounding factor.

- In a natural-groups design, the "conditions" are created by sorting people into different categories based on a naturally occurring subject variable. A natural-groups design is fundamentally a correlational study, not an experiment.

- Random assignment differs from random sampling. Random sampling is used to select the sample of individuals who will be asked to participate in a particular study. Random assignment is used in experiments to assign participants to one condition or another.

- Compared to between-subjects designs, within-subjects (repeated-measures) designs need fewer participants to obtain the same amount of data and do a better job of creating equivalent groups. They introduce the major potential confounding factor of order effects, which is addressed by counterbalancing the order of conditions.

- The all-possible-orders design, Williams Latin Square design, and random-selected-orders design are counterbalancing approaches that expose each participant to each condition just once. Block randomization and ABBA designs are counterbalancing approaches that expose each participant to each condition more than once.

- The *t* test and analysis of variance (ANOVA) are the most common statistical tests used to analyze data from single-factor designs. Either test can be used if the design only has two conditions. For multilevel designs, an ANOVA determines whether the overall pattern of differences among the mean scores is statistically significant. If it is significant, then post-hoc tests can be used to compare the means of specific conditions.

KEY TERMS

all-possible-orders design (complete counterbalancing) (p. 267)
between-subjects design (p. 247)
block randomization (p. 257)
block-randomization design (p. 271)
carryover effects (p. 264)
confounding variable (p. 245)
control condition (control group) (p. 251)
counterbalancing (p. 247)
dependent variable (p. 243)
experiment (p. 243)
experimental control (p. 244)

experimental condition (experimental group) (p. 251)
extraneous variable (p. 245)
fatigue effect (p. 263)
independent-groups design (random-groups design) (p. 255)
independent variable (p. 243)
Latin Square (p. 268)
matched-groups design (p. 257)
matching variable (p. 257)
natural-groups design (p. 258)
order effects (sequence effects) (p. 263)
practice effect (p. 263)

progressive effects (p. 263)
random assignment (p. 247)
random-selected-orders design (p. 269)
reverse-counterbalancing design (ABBA-counterbalancing design) (p. 271)
sensitization (p. 264)
single-factor design (p. 248)
subject variable (p. 258)
within-subjects design (p. 247)

ASSESS YOUR KNOWLEDGE

1. Describe the three key components of experimental control.
2. How do the components of experimental control enable experiments to satisfy the three key criteria for inferring cause and effect.
3. Identify and illustrate two general sources of potential confounding variables in experiments.
4. One way to create an independent variable is to manipulate some aspect of the physical

environment. Describe at least three other ways to create independent variables.

5. Provide some examples of quantitative and qualitative independent variables.

6. When deciding how many levels of an independent variable to create, what factors do researchers consider? How does the desire to examine nonlinear effects impact this decision?

7. What is a control group? Do all experiments have a control group? Explain.

8. How do between-subjects and within-subjects designs differ? What are some advantages of between-subjects designs?

9. How is block randomization used in an independent-groups design?

10. Explain the procedure for creating a matched-groups design, including two general ways to select a matching variable. What are some pros and cons of using matching versus an independent-groups design?

11. Explain some key differences between random assignment and random sampling.

12. What is a natural-groups design? Explain why a natural-groups design is or is not an experiment.

13. Describe some advantages and disadvantages of within-subjects designs.

14. Identify some specific types of order effects. What general approach is used in within-subjects designs to control for order effects?

15. Identify the names of five specific types of within-subjects designs.

16. Describe the procedure used in the all-possible-orders, Latin Square, and random-selected-orders designs.

17. Describe the procedure used in the block randomization and reverse counterbalancing within-subjects designs. As a group, what is the one key way in which these two designs differ from the all-possible-orders, Latin Square, and random-selected-orders designs?

18. Contrast the pros and cons of using within-subjects designs that expose each participant to each condition only once, versus more than once.

19. Discuss two general steps in analyzing the results of a single-factor design that has three or more conditions.

CONCEPT CHECKS: ANSWERS

8.1 The Logic of Experimentation

1. c   2. d   3. b   4. f   5. e   6. a

8.2 Manipulating Independent Variables

1. false   2. false   3. true   4. true   5. true

8.3 Between-Subjects Designs

1. true   2. true   3. false   4. false   5. true

8.4 Within-Subjects Designs

1. repeated measures 2. pratice; fatigue; counterbalancing 3. conditions 4. block randomization; reverse counterbalancing

8.5 Examining the Results: General Concepts

1. true   2. true   3. true

THINKING CRITICALLY AND APPLYING YOUR KNOWLEDGE

EXERCISE 1   Analyze the Experiment

The designs for two experiments are specified below. For each experiment, identify:

(a) the independent and dependent variable;

(b) whether the experiment represents a between- or within-subjects design;

(c) the specific type of between- or within-subjects design.

Bowl Me Over: The Original

Dr. Tindale recruits 30 women to participate in a laboratory experiment. None has ever bowled or played video bowling games. Using a Nintendo Wii U system, each woman bowls the virtual ball five times to get an idea of what the task involves. Then each woman bowls one complete game under each of two conditions: (1) alone (no audience is present) or (2) an audience of four men silently watches. Half the women bowl alone first, and then bowl with an audience watching. The other half bowls their first game with the audience watching, and their second game with no audience present. Dr. Tindale records how well participants perform (i.e., records their bowling scores) in each condition.

Bowl Me Over: The Sequel

Dr. Tindale conducts a second experiment, with the following changes. There are 60 new participants, each of whom bowls only one game either alone or in front of a four-person or an eight-person audience. The first three participants are randomly assigned, one to each of the three conditions. Then the next three participants are randomly assigned, such that each condition now has a total of two participants. This continues until there are 20 participants in each condition. Dr. Tindale records how well participants perform (i.e., records their bowling scores).

EXERCISE 2   To Be, or Not To Be—Manipulated

Three studies are described below. Answer the following questions for each one:

(a) Conceptually, what are the independent and dependent variables? How are they operationally defined?

(b) Is the independent variable manipulated or selected?

(c) Is the proposed study an experiment? Why or why not?

Place Your Bets

Dr. Hendricks uses a psychological test to identify 30 extraverted and 30 introverted college students. In a lab, students each receive $50 ($5 for each of 10 trials) to use in a gambling game, in which they choose the size of their bet on each trial. Students keep whatever money remains at the end of the experiment. To measure their degree of risk-taking, Dr. Hendricks records the size of each bet. She finds that, compared to introverts, extraverts make larger bets.

I Want to Eat

Dr. Denorfia conducts a hunger study. Participants (one per day) eat their normal breakfast at home between 8:30 a.m. and 9:00 a.m., and don't eat again until they come to the lab at 5 p.m. At the lab, the participants rate how hungry they feel and, based on

this, are classified into a low, moderate, or high hunger condition. They then are exposed to a buffet that offers 15 types of foods and are permitted to eat for 10 minutes. Dr. Denorfia records the total amount of food (i.e., measured by the weight of food) and number of different foods that each participant eats. He finds that as hunger increases, people eat more food but not a greater variety of food.

Seriously, I Want to Eat

Dr. Watanabe conducts a study on hunger. Each participant comes to the lab at 8:30 a.m. and is fed the same breakfast, ending at 9 a.m. Participants are randomly assigned to remain in the laboratory for either 3, 6, or 9 hours, during which time they are not permitted food. Based on this deprivation period, they are considered to represent low, moderate, and high hunger groups, respectively. At the end of the deprivation period, each participant is exposed to a buffet that consists of 15 different types of foods and is allowed to eat for 10 minutes. Dr. Watanabe records the amount of each food that each participant eats. She finds that as their level of hunger increases, people eat more food but not a greater variety of food.

EXERCISE 3   The Face of Emotion

Dr. Goodman studies people's brain activity in response to seeing facial expressions that signal different emotions. Each participant is shown different photographs of a person's face, with each photo portraying a different emotion:

Joy (J)   Anger (A)   Fear (F)   Sadness (S)

In the first and fourth experiments, three emotions are portrayed. In the other experiments, four emotions are portrayed. For each experiment, identify the specific type of within-subjects design that was used.

Experiment 1

	Trial		
	1	2	3
Participant 1	J	A	S
Participant 2	J	S	A
Participant 3	A	S	J
Participant 4	A	J	S
Participant 5	S	J	A
Participant 6	S	A	J

Experiment 2

	Trial			
	1	2	3	4
Participant 1	J	S	A	F
Participant 2	S	F	J	A
Participant 3	F	A	S	J
Participant 4	A	J	F	S

Experiment 3

	Trial			
	1	2	3	4
Participant 1	A	J	F	S
Participant 2	S	A	J	F
Participant 3	F	S	A	J
Participant 4	J	F	S	A

Experiment 4

	Trial					
	1	2	3	4	5	6
Participant 1	J	A	S	S	A	J
Participant 2	J	S	A	A	S	J
Participant 3	A	S	J	J	S	A
Participant 4	S	A	J	J	A	S
Participant 5	S	A	J	J	A	S
Participant 6	J	S	A	A	S	J

LaunchPad
macmillan learning

To practice key concepts from this chapter, visit the LaunchPad Solo for Research Methods at **launchpadworks.com.**

CHAPTER OUTLINE

imagine the following scenario. In the darkness of early morning, a man is killed in a knife fight. Several weeks later, the police place you in a lineup, during which four eyewitnesses identify you; three say you participated in the fight and one reports seeing you hide afterward. You deny ever having met the victim. What's more, you have an alibi: At the time of the fight, you were at home with your spouse and stepchildren. Nevertheless, the police arrest you.

The alleged murder weapon is recovered near the crime scene, and your DNA is not on it. Instead, the knife contains the blood of a person with a known violent past along with the victim's blood. This evidence might clear you, but the final police report sent to prosecutors fails to explicitly state that the victim's blood was on the knife. The prosecution then assumes that the knife was not the murder weapon. When your case goes to trial, eyewitness testimony provides the crucial evidence. Your lawyer doesn't call you or your family members to testify. The jury convicts you, the judge hands down a 30-year sentence, and years pass as you serve prison time.

This scenario describes the case of Maurice Patterson, arrested for murder in Chicago in 2002 (Innocence Project, n.d.; Warden, n.d.). Thanks to Patterson's persistence in trying to clear his name while imprisoned, the full DNA test results of the knife eventually became known. In October 2010, after years of wrongful incarceration, Patterson's conviction was overturned and he regained his freedom.

Inaccurate eyewitness testimony, a key factor in Patterson's case and many other known cases of wrongful arrest and conviction (Innocence Project, n.d.), has been a hot topic of psychological research in recent decades. In contrast, there is much less research on another common feature of criminal cases: the alibi. Patterson told the police he been at home with his family, but alibi witnesses (i.e., people who back up an alibi; also called "alibi providers") may be truthful or they may lie to protect the suspect. Police detectives' decisions about whether to further investigate or arrest a suspect, and jurors' beliefs about a defendant's guilt, hinge in part on whether they perceive alibi witnesses to be credible. For psychological scientists, this sparks the question: What factors influence people's willingness to believe an alibi witness?

In Chapter 8, you learned how between-subjects and within-subjects designs are used to study a single independent variable. This chapter discusses *factorial designs,* which researchers use to study two or more independent variables within a single experiment. Specifically, a **factorial design** *includes two or more independent variables and crosses (i.e., combines) every level of each independent variable with every level of all the other independent variables.* To provide an example and introduce basic aspects of factorial designs, let's discuss an experiment on criminal alibis.

BASIC CHARACTERISTICS OF FACTORIAL DESIGNS

Learning Objectives

After studying this section, you should be able to:

- Describe different types of factorial designs.
- Diagram a factorial design.
- Explain the advantages and limitations of factorial designs.

Cognitive psychologist Leora Dahl and legal psychologist Heather Price (2012) were interested in how two factors—the age of an alibi witness and the relationship between the alibi witness and crime suspect—influenced people's acceptance of an alibi. They studied this issue experimentally by simulating a police investigation during which they exposed participants to different alibi witnesses. Whereas prior experiments had studied people's perceptions of only adult alibi witnesses, Dahl and Price wanted to compare people's reactions to both child and adult alibi witnesses. Drawing on findings from research on child and adult eyewitness testimony, Dahl and Price predicted that people would be more likely to believe a child alibi witness than an adult alibi witness. They also wanted to examine how an alibi witness's age and relationship to a crime suspect jointly influenced people's willingness to believe an alibi.

Dahl and Price (2012) asked 134 Canadian undergraduates to assume the role of a police officer investigating a 50-year-old robbery suspect. Each participant received a simulated police file that contained details of the robbery and included an eyewitness account. The participant then searched a computer database of potential suspects with a history of prior arrests and decided whether to select one suspect for further investigation. Unknown to the participants, the database was constructed to create a good match between one particular suspect's profile and the information in the police file of the robbery. Only 10 participants failed to select this suspect, and for them the experiment was discontinued.

Participants were then randomly assigned to watch one of several videos showing the interview of a male Caucasian alibi witness. Dahl and Price (2012) used these videos to experimentally manipulate two independent variables. First, to manipulate the age of the alibi witness, some videos featured a 6-year-old alibi witness and other videos featured a 25-year-old alibi witness. Second, to manipulate the relationship between the alibi witness and crime suspect, in some videos the alibi witness said that he was the suspect's son, and in other videos he indicated that he was the suspect's neighbor. In the videos showing a child–neighbor alibi witness, the child stated that his grandmother had been sick and his mother was away that day caring for her, and this is why he had been under his neighbor's (i.e., the suspect's) care.

Table 9.1 Dahl and Price's 2 × 2 Factorial Design

Age of Alibi Witness (manipulated in video)	Relationship of Alibi Witness to Suspect (manipulated in video)	
	Son	Neighbor
Child (6-year-old)	Child son (Condition 1)	Child neighbor (Condition 2)
Adult (25-year-old)	Adult son (Condition 3)	Adult neighbor (Condition 4)

Source: Information from Dahl and Price (2012).

Beyond these differences, the actors who played the roles of alibi witness and interviewer in the videos all followed the same script.

Combining two independent variables, which have two levels each, creates an experimental design that has four conditions. This is the most basic factorial design possible, as illustrated in **Table 9.1**. The phrase "manipulated in video" appears beneath each independent variable to remind you that the alibi witness is an experimentally manipulated stimulus—an aspect of the social environment—to which participants were exposed. Each of the four conditions has an equal number of participants.

Dahl and Price (2012) measured several dependent variables. After watching the video, participants rated the degree to which they found the alibi witness and the alibi itself credible. Both before and after watching the alibi video, participants rated the probability that the suspect was guilty and indicated whether they would support his arrest. The results indicated that overall, participants gave low credibility ratings to the alibi and alibi witnesses. Dahl and Price noted that some prior studies had obtained a similar finding, possibly reflecting broad skepticism on the part of the public about alibis. Still, as the researchers expected, participants judged a child witness to be more credible than an adult witness.

Before watching the alibi witness video, on average, participants believed there was a 69% probability that the suspect had committed the robbery. Moreover, the average probability rating did not differ significantly across the four experimental conditions. But as **Figure 9.1**

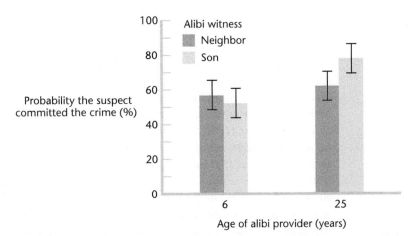

Figure 9.1 Mean probability ratings, post-alibi, that the suspect committed the crime. Each large bar in this graph portrays the result from one of the four conditions in this 2 (alibi provider age: 6 years old, 25 years old) × 2 (witness–suspect relationship: son, neighbor) factorial experiment. The thin I-shaped bars are called "error bars": These represent 95% confidence intervals (see Statistics Module 15). (Dahl & Price, 2012.)

shows, rating differences across conditions emerged after the participants viewed the alibi. Overall, those who viewed a child alibi witness decided it was significantly less likely that the suspect committed the crime (55% mean probability rating) than did participants who viewed an adult alibi witness (70% mean probability rating). Respectively, these percentages correspond to the average height of the two, leftmost large vertical bars in Figure 9.1 (the bars representing the two child–witness conditions) and the average height of the two, rightmost vertical bars (representing the two adult–witness conditions).

There was no statistically significant difference overall between the ratings of participants who were exposed to a son alibi witness (65% mean probability rating) and those exposed to a neighbor alibi witness (60% mean probability rating). In Figure 9.1, these percentages correspond to the average height of the two yellow vertical bars (representing the two son–witness conditions) and the average height of the two orange vertical bars (representing the two neighbor–witness conditions). But, this does not mean that the alibi witness's relationship to the suspect failed to influence participants' judgments: It did influence them, but its effect depended on whether the witness was a child or an adult.

When the alibi witness was 25 years old, participants were significantly more likely to judge the suspect as guilty if the witness was the suspect's son rather than a neighbor. This finding was consistent with the results of prior alibi experiments, which found that biological relatedness between an alibi witness and suspect decreases people's acceptance of an alibi. In contrast, when the alibi witness was 6 years old, the son–neighbor distinction did not, overall, significantly influence participants' judgments of the suspect's probable guilt. Prior experiments had not exposed participants to child alibi witnesses, so this finding adds new information to our understanding of how alibi witnesses may affect people's judgments.

We will return to Dahl and Price's (2012) experiment several times in the chapter, as we learn about different aspects of factorial designs. Before moving on, I should note that when participants made their final decision about whether to arrest the suspect, 41% stated they would, and this result did not differ significantly across the four conditions or from their overall arrest decisions before watching the alibi videos. At least in this study, the pattern of findings in Figure 9.1 concerning judgments of probable guilt did not carry over to participants' final yes/no decision on arresting the suspect.

DESCRIBING A FACTORIAL DESIGN

If you have experienced very hot weather, such as during a summer heat wave, you know how unpleasant it can feel if you are working outdoors or inside a room that is not air-conditioned. And if you have encountered hot weather in both humid and arid environments, you know that high relative humidity adds to the discomfort. Suppose, then, that we want to examine how room temperature and relative humidity influence people's performance on a cognitive task that requires rapid visual scanning and decision making. If you were a participant, you would look straight ahead at a computer monitor. A geometric shape, which we'll call a *target shape,* would appear at the top of the screen. For example, the target shape might be a three-quarters circle. Simultaneously, a set of 50 geometric shapes (e.g., a mix of circles, rectangles, and triangles) would be flashed on the main portion of the screen for 2 seconds. Your task would be to decide—yes or no—whether one of the 50 shapes matches the target shape. You would perform this task for a series of trials, say, 60 trials, with a rest interval of 2 seconds in between trials. The target shape would vary across trials, as would the shapes and arrangement of the other 50 objects.

To simplify this example, let's create two levels of room temperature, 68 °F and 95 °F (20 °C and 35 °C), and two levels of relative humidity, low versus high (operationally defined

Table 9.2 Effects of Room Temperature and Humidity on Cognitive Performance: A Hypothetical 2 × 2 Factorial Design

Humidity	Room Temperature	
	68 °F (20 °C)	**95 °F (35 °C)**
Low	68 °F (20 °C), low humidity (Condition 1)	95 °F (35 °C), low humidity (Condition 2)
High	68 °F (20 °C), high humidity (Condition 3)	95 °F (35 °C), high humidity (Condition 4)

as 20% vs. 70% relative humidity).[1] Our factorial design would yield four conditions, as diagrammed in Table 9.2.

This hypothetical experiment represents a 2 × 2 (i.e., "two by two") factorial design. The fact that two numbers are involved (i.e., first number × second number) tells us that there are two independent variables: in this case, temperature and humidity. The fact that the first number is a "2" tells us that temperature has two levels: 68 °F and 95 °F (20 °C and 35 °C). The fact that the second number is a "2" tells us that humidity has two levels: low and high humidity. Multiplying the number of levels of the two independent variables informs us that there are four conditions in the experiment, as shown in Table 9.2. Thus,

2	×	2	=	4
First independent variable (temperature: two levels)		Second independent variable (humidity: two levels)		Total number of conditions

Suppose, however, that our experiment has two temperature levels and four humidity levels (low, moderate, high, extreme). In Table 9.2, we would still have two columns for the two levels of temperature, but under the label "Humidity" there would now be four rows, labeled "Low," "Moderate," "High," and "Extreme," respectively. In this case, we would have a 2 × 4 factorial design. By multiplying the number of levels of the two independent variables, we see that there are eight conditions in the experiment. Thus,

2	×	4	=	8
First independent variable (temperature: two levels)		Second independent variable (humidity: four levels)		Total number of conditions

We also could describe this second experiment as having a 4 × 2 factorial design, so long as we correctly match the numbers of levels (4, 2) to the order of the independent variables (in this case, designating humidity as the first independent variable and temperature as the second).

For simplicity, most of this chapter will focus on factorial designs with only two independent variables. Keep in mind, however, that factorial designs can have more than two independent variables. To help you better understand the basics of how researchers describe factorial designs, imagine for a moment that in our temperature–humidity experiment, we add a third independent variable: noise intensity. We will have two levels of temperature, four levels of humidity, and to this we add three levels of noise (45, 60, and 75 decibels) that participants

---

[1] For those of you hardy souls who are thinking "that's not hot and humid; that's a piece of cake," the combination of 95 °F (35 °C) and 70% relative humidity produces a heat index of 123 °F (51 °C). Increasing either factor places the heat index in the "extreme danger" zone for prolonged exposure or strenuous exercise (National Weather Service, 2012). Although our hypothetical experiment involves only brief heat exposure and mental activity rather than physical exercise, it would require safety precautions and institutional ethics committee approval.

would hear while performing the visual scanning task. In this case, we would have a $2 \times 4 \times 3$ factorial design. The fact that there are three numbers (first number $\times$ second number $\times$ third number) tells us that there are three independent variables. The specific numbers ("2," "4," and "3") tell us that the first independent variable (temperature) has two levels, the second independent variable (humidity) has four levels, and the third independent variable (noise) has three levels. In total, our experiment would have $2 \times 4 \times 3 = 24$ conditions.

Describing Levels and Conditions

The individual cells of a factorial design are usually described by name, such as the "child–son condition" in Dahl and Price's (2012) experiment and the "95 °F (20 °C) high-humidity condition" (otherwise known as the "hot and humid condition") in our experiment. Conversing with a colleague, a researcher might say: "My experiment was a 2×4 factorial design with 20 participants randomly assigned to each of the eight conditions." When discussing factorial designs in general, the individual cells may be labeled by a number or letter, such as Condition 1, Condition 2, and so forth, as in the 2×2 diagrams shown in Table 9.1 (p. 281) and Table 9.2 (p. 283). Another approach is to designate each independent variable by a different letter, such as A and B in a 2×2 design. The two levels of variable A are designated A_1 and A_2, the two levels of B are designated B_1 and B_2, and the four cells are labeled as shown in **Table 9.3**.

If we had a 2×3 design, the third level of independent variable B would be identified as B_3, and the diagram would contain a third column on the far right with two new cells below it, labeled A_1B_3 and A_2B_3, respectively. As you can see, this system is straightforward. You can also choose to place variable A along the top and variable B along the side.

Notice that in Table 9.3, I have used the term *level* rather than *condition* to label the rows and columns of each independent variable. In this chapter, to avoid confusion, I will use the term *condition* to refer to the individual cells (e.g., A_1B_1) within a factorial design, as already illustrated in Table 9.1 and Table 9.2. Just be aware that, in practice, researchers often use the term *condition* to refer not only to individual cells within a factorial design, but also to the overall levels of independent variables (e.g., "The experiment had two humidity conditions: a low-humidity condition and high-humidity condition").

Describing Assignment to Conditions

When researchers describe a factorial design, they often use terminology that succinctly informs the reader about whether the independent variables were studied using a between-subjects design, within-subjects design, or mixture of approaches. For example, in our 2×2 temperature–humidity experiment, we could randomly assign different participants to each of the four specific conditions. This would represent a **between-subjects factorial design:** *a factorial design in which each subject engages in only one condition.* Alternatively, we could have each participant perform the visual scanning task in all four conditions, inserting a rest break between conditions and using counterbalancing to control for order effects. This would represent a **within-subjects factorial design:** *a factorial design in which each subject engages in every condition.*

Table 9.3 One Approach to Labeling the Components of a 2 × 2 Factorial Design

Independent Variable A	Independent Variable B	
	Level B_1	Level B_2
Level A_1	A_1B_1	A_1B_2
Level A_2	A_2B_1	A_2B_2

A third approach would be to treat one independent variable—say, temperature—as a between-subjects factor and the other independent variable as a within-subjects factor. Using random assignment, we would set the room temperature at 68 °F (20 °C) for half of the participants, and at 95 °F (35 °C) for the other half. Within each of these room temperature groups, every participant would perform the task once when the humidity is low and again when the humidity is high, allowing a rest break and counterbalancing the order of humidity exposure. This approach is called a **mixed-factorial design:** *a factorial design that includes at least one between-subjects variable and at least one within-subjects variable.*

Thus, if researchers describe their experiment as a 4×3 between-subjects factorial design, this lets you know that (1) their experiment had two independent variables, one with four levels and one with three levels, (2) there were a total of 12 conditions in the experiment, and (3) each participant engaged in only one of those 12 conditions. Applying these concepts to the alibi witness experiment, Dahl and Price (2012) described their study as employing a 2 (alibi witness age: 6 years old, 25 years old) $\times$ 2 (witness–suspect relationship: son, neighbor) between-subjects factorial design.

ADVANTAGES OF FACTORIAL DESIGNS

In everyday life, multiple factors often operate simultaneously to influence our behavior at any given moment. Factorial designs are better able to capture this real-life causal complexity than are designs that manipulate only one independent variable.

Examining the Overall Effects of Multiple Independent Variables

In conducting our temperature–humidity factorial experiment, one question that we can ask is "Overall, does a room's temperature affect people's visual scanning performance?" We can also ask a second question: "Overall, does humidity affect people's visual scanning performance?" Each of these questions asks whether a variable has a **main effect,** *which occurs when an independent variable has an overall effect on a dependent variable.* A main effect for room temperature would mean that overall, as room temperature changes, this influences task performance. A main effect for humidity would mean that overall, as humidity changes, this influences task performance.

Later in the chapter, we will work through several examples to explore the concept of a main effect in depth and give you practice in identifying main effects from simple sets of data. For now, to gain an initial idea of what a main effect represents, let's examine **Figure 9.2**. We will assume that the number of participants in each of the four conditions is the same. With regard to room temperature, we can see that overall, participants made more errors when the room temperature was higher than when it was lower. At the higher room temperature, by averaging the two data points (20 errors and 15 errors, respectively), we see that participants made 17.5 errors overall. At the lower room temperature, by averaging the two data points (10 errors and 5 errors, respectively), we see that participants only made 7.5 errors overall. Thus, room temperature had a main effect: Overall, the change from 68 °F (20 °C) to 95 °F (35 °C) increased the number of errors made by participants.

Turning to humidity, in Figure 9.2 we can see that overall, participants made more errors when the humidity was higher than when it was

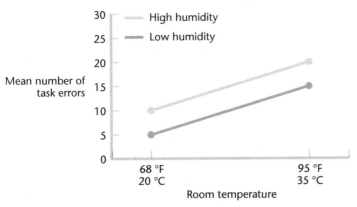

Figure 9.2 Outcome of a hypothetical 2 × 2 factorial design experiment. In this design, there are two levels of temperature (68 °F, 95 °F [20 °C, 35 °C]) and two levels of humidity (low, high).

lower. Here, the yellow line represents performance when humidity was high. Under high humidity, participants averaged 20 errors when the temperature was 95 °F (35 °C), and 10 errors when the temperature was 68 °F (20 °C). Taking the average of these two data points, which is equivalent to determining the midpoint of the yellow line, informs us that overall, participants made a mean number of 15 errors when exposed to high humidity. In Figure 9.2, the orange line represents performance when humidity was low, and here we see that participants averaged 15 errors when the temperature was higher and five errors when the temperature was lower. Taking the average of these two data points, which is equivalent to determining the midpoint of the orange line, indicates that overall, participants made a mean number of 10 errors when humidity was low. Thus, humidity had a main effect: Overall, the change from low humidity to high humidity increased the number of errors made by participants.

Of course, we could examine whether room temperature and humidity influence visual scanning performance by conducting one experiment on room temperature and a separate experiment on room humidity. But here's another question that we can best answer by simultaneously manipulating room temperature and humidity within a single experiment: "How do these two variables jointly affect behavior?" For example, if room temperature influences behavior, does it have the same effect on behavior when humidity is low as when humidity is high? Or conversely, if humidity affects behavior, does higher humidity have the same effect when the room temperature is 68 °F (20 °C) as when the room is 95 °F (35 °C)? This brings us to a key advantage of factorial designs: the ability to examine interactions between independent variables.

Examining Interactions Between Independent Variables

Studying two independent variables in the same experiment allows us to determine whether the way one independent variable influences behavior differs, depending on the level of the second independent variable. Here's an analogy. You probably have heard of the fact that, in terms of taking medical drugs, it is possible for a person to use Drug A and not suffer any side effects. Similarly, that same person, only using Drug B, might not suffer any side effects either. However, if the person is using both Drug A and Drug B, the unique combination of the two drugs could potentially produce severe side effects. This situation is known as a drug interaction: The effect of one drug differs, depending on whether a second drug is also being used.

Likewise, in behavioral research, an **interaction** (or **interaction effect**) *occurs when the way in which an independent variable influences a dependent variable differs, depending on the level of another independent variable.* Interaction effects are common in psychological research. The most important advantage of factorial designs is the ability to test whether unique combinations of two or more independent variables affect our behavior in ways that cannot be predicted simply by knowing how each variable individually affects behavior.

Figure 9.3 illustrates the concept of an interaction based on hypothetical findings from our temperature–humidity experiment. The figure provides three examples, each portraying one of three general ways in which an interaction can occur between two independent variables in a 2 × 2 factorial design. In describing these general patterns, let's label the two independent variables "#1" and "#2." Thus, in our example, we could label room temperature as independent variable #1 or as independent variable #2. It doesn't matter: If an interaction is present, it will show up regardless of which independent variable is labeled #1 or #2.

- Independent variable #1 has opposite effects on a dependent variable, depending on the level of independent variable #2.

- Independent variable #1 influences a dependent variable only at one level of independent variable #2; it does not influence the dependent variable at the other level of independent variable #2.

Infographic: **Figure 9.3**

UNDERSTANDING INTERACTIONS: 2 X 2 FACTORIAL DESIGNS

What is an interaction? The effect of an independent variable (i.v.) on a dependent variable (d.v.) differs, depending on the level of another independent variable. For example, the effect of room temperature on rapid visual scanning performance differs, depending on the level of relative humidity.

Does this shape ◖ appear below? Target and array shapes vary per trial. Each full array has 50 objects.

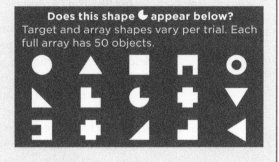

Experiment: 2 x 2 between-subjects factorial design	
I.V.₁	room temperature (68°/95° F; 20°/35° C)
I.V.₂	relative humidity (low, high)
D.V.	visual scanning performance (number of errors on sixty 2-second trials of a visual scanning task)

DEPENDING ON THE LEVEL OF I.V.₂, I.V.₁ PRODUCES:

EXAMPLE 1: Opposite Effects

Humidity:
● high ● low

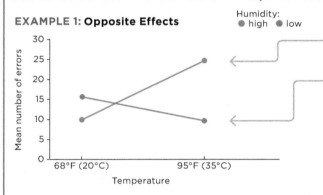

When humidity is high, the increase in room temperature produces more task errors.

When humidity is low, the increase in room temperature produces fewer task errors.

Thus, room temperature influences performance in opposite directions, depending on whether humidity is high or low.

EXAMPLE 2: An Effect at Only One Level of I.V.₂

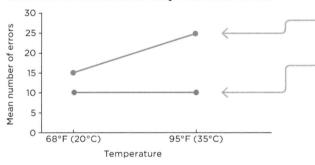

When humidity is high, the increase in room temperature produces more task errors.

When humidity is low, the increase in room temperature does not change the mean number of task errors.

Thus, room temperature influences performance at one level, but not at the other level, of humidity.

EXAMPLE 3: Effects in the Same Direction that Differ in Strength

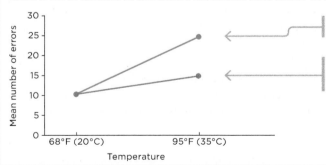

When humidity is high, the increase in room temperature produces an increase in errors.

When humidity is low, although the increase in room temperature produces more task errors, this effect is not as strong as when humidity is high.

Thus, the influence of room temperature on performance is in the same direction, but differs in strength, depending on the level of humidity.

TIP: In each graph, you can see that the data lines are not parallel. Nonparallel lines indicate an interaction may be present. Parallel lines indicate that there is no interaction. Before concluding that two variables interact, researchers perform analyses to assess whether that result is statistically significant.

- Independent variable #1 influences a dependent variable in the same direction at both levels of independent variable #2. However, the strength of this influence differs, depending on the level of independent variable #2.

In all three of the examples in Figure 9.3, the common ingredient is that the relation between temperature and performance differs, depending on the humidity level. We can also describe the interaction in each of these graphs from the viewpoint of how humidity affects performance. For example, in the top graph in Figure 9.3, we can see that at 68 °F (20 °C), fewer errors occurred when the humidity was high rather than low. In contrast, at 95 °F (35 °C), more errors occurred when the humidity was high rather than low. Thus, the effect of high versus low humidity on performance differs, depending on room temperature.[2]

Recall that after Dahl and Price's (2012) participants watched the alibi witness video, they judged how likely it was that the suspect committed the crime. Figure 9.1 illustrated those findings; it revealed a significant interaction between the age of the alibi witness and witness–suspect relationship. As noted earlier, Dahl and Price found that when the alibi witness was an adult son, participants' guilt-probability ratings were higher (on average) than when the witness was an adult neighbor. In contrast, participants' ratings in the child–son and child–neighbor conditions did not differ significantly. Thus, the effect of the witness–suspect relationship on participants' judgments differed, depending on whether the witness was a child or adult.

There are many theories in psychology that predict interactions among causal factors, and thus factorial designs provide scientists with a way to test the validity of such theories. Researchers also use factorial designs to test hypotheses about interactions that are not based on theory. And finally, there are times when researchers have no formal hypothesis in mind and use factorial designs simply to explore whether independent variables interact. Regardless of the scientific motivation, interaction effects can readily be examined in an experiment that has two or more independent variables.

Together, Figure 9.1 and Figure 9.3 provide four examples of an interaction, but how can we tell when there is no interaction between independent variables? What might that look like? To see one example, let's briefly return to Figure 9.2 on page 285. Notice that the increase in room temperature led to more errors when humidity was high, and also led to more errors when humidity was low. Moreover, as room temperature increased, the number of errors jumped by the same amount when humidity was high (an increase of 10 errors) as when humidity was low (an increase of 10 errors). Thus, regardless of the level of humidity, the change from a lower to higher room temperature produced the same effect on performance—both in direction and in strength (i.e., an increase of 10 errors). Stated differently, the effect of room temperature on performance *did not differ,* depending on the level of humidity. This is reflected in the fact that the data lines in Figure 9.2 are parallel. In a line graph, the presence of parallel lines informs us that there is no interaction between the independent variables.

Contrast the graph in Figure 9.2 with the three line graphs in Figure 9.3, each of which illustrates an interaction portrayed by nonparallel lines. In this chapter, for the purposes of gaining a basic understanding of these concepts, nonparallel data lines in a graph will indicate the presence of an interaction. In actual research and data analysis, before we would conclude that two independent variables interact, we would perform statistical tests to determine whether that finding is statistically significant (i.e., unlikely to be due solely to chance). If the finding is not statistically significant, then we would refrain from concluding that an interaction occurred.

---

[2] Although Figure 9.3 focuses on interactions, statistical analyses would also indicate whether main effects for temperature and humidity occur in each set of findings. After you gain practice in examining the results of 2 × 2 factorial experiments later in the chapter, you can return to this figure for additional practice and determine whether each graph reveals main effects. You'll find answers on page 308, in the first paragraph of Exercise 3, within the section "Thinking Critically and Applying Your Knowledge."

Examining Moderator Variables

As discussed in Chapter 4, a *moderator variable* is a variable that alters the strength or direction of the relation between an independent and dependent variable. In other words, the effect of the independent variable on behavior *depends on* the level of the moderator variable, and this is precisely what an interaction involves. Thus, one of the most common strategies for testing a hypothesized moderator variable, or for exploring whether a variable might be a moderator, is to incorporate it into a factorial design and examine whether it produces an interaction effect (Baron & Kenny, 1986).

For example, suppose we hypothesize that talking on a cell phone will have a stronger negative effect on driving performance when traffic density is high than when traffic density is low. To test this hypothesis, we create a 2 (cell phone use–no use) × 2 (high–low traffic density) within-subjects factorial design. For 40 minutes (divided into four 10-minute segments), each participant will drive the same route in a realistic driving simulator while conversing on a hands-free cell phone with a research assistant during two segments and having no cell phone conversation during the other two segments. We'll program the driving simulator so that for each participant, traffic density will be low during one cell phone segment and one no-phone segment, and high during the other segments. Thus, a particular participant might be exposed to the following order of conditions: (1) cell phone–high density, (2) no phone–low density, (3) no phone–high density, (4) cell phone–low density. Other participants will be exposed to other orders of conditions. The key point is that, overall, across the entire sample of participants in the experiment, the order of conditions will be counterbalanced so that each of the four driving conditions will occur equally often in each route segment.

Using this design, we can examine whether traffic density has an overall effect (i.e., main effect) on driving performance, and whether cell phone use has an overall effect (i.e., main effect) on driving performance. Our primary interest, however, is determining whether an interaction occurs: Will the effects of using a cell phone on driving performance differ, depending on the level of traffic density? If the findings reveal a statistically significant interaction, this means that traffic density moderates the effects of cell phone use on driving performance. Note that in our hypothesis, we're conceptualizing traffic density as a moderator variable. Operationally, however, it is being incorporated into our 2 × 2 design as an independent variable that we manipulate.

Other Advantages

Factorial designs have additional advantages. They often are more efficient to conduct, as compared to conducting a series of separate experiments, each of which examines only one independent variable. Rather than setting up equipment and initiating procedures for recruiting and scheduling participants for each individual experiment, all these administrative and procedural aspects of conducting an experiment can be done just once when a factorial design is used. Second, researchers frequently wish to examine whether situational factors have different effects on different types of people. For example, would the effects of room temperature and humidity on task performance be the same for women and men, or older versus younger adults? In an experiment comparing the effectiveness of two psychotherapeutic approaches to treating depression, does the answer to the question "Which therapy is best?" depend on whether a patient's depression is mild, moderate, or severe? Factorial designs easily lend themselves to examining these types of questions, as we'll discuss shortly.

LIMITATIONS OF FACTORIAL DESIGNS

The key limitation of using factorial designs is imposed by the fact that as the number of independent variables increases, and as the number of levels within each independent variable increases, the total number of conditions in an experiment can rapidly increase beyond manageable proportions. As the total number of conditions increases, practical issues such as the number of participants that need to be recruited and/or the amount of time that each participant must devote to the experiment, as well as the amount of time and effort that the researchers need to expend, may make it difficult if not practically impossible to conduct the experiment.

For example, if we want to include five temperature levels and five humidity levels in a factorial design, this would produce 25 experimental conditions. Manipulating our variables between subjects, we would now have to recruit many more participants. Manipulating our variables within subjects, each participant would then have to perform the task over and over many times under different temperature–humidity combinations. Suppose we scale back to our original two levels of temperature and two levels of humidity, but want to add three more independent variables: noise intensity (low, high); noise pattern (constant, periodic); and noise type (traffic noise, people talking). Our $2 \times 2 \times 2 \times 2 \times 2$ design would have 32 conditions, and if we prefer to have 3 or 4 levels of some independent variables, we could easily approach or exceed 100 conditions! As the number of independent variables and conditions increases, interpreting the results often becomes more difficult and mentally taxing because of all the possible outcomes that can occur.

> ✓ **CONCEPT CHECK 9.1** BASIC CHARACTERISTICS OF FACTORIAL DESIGNS
>
> Fill in each of the blanks below. Some answers may require two or more words, such as a phrase. Answers appear on page 308 at the end of the chapter.
>
> 1. In a factorial design with two independent variables, A and B, every level of A is _____ with every level of B. If A is manipulated between subjects and B is manipulated within subjects, then this would be a _____ design. Factorial designs have at least _____ conditions [fill in a number].
> 2. In a $4 \times 2 \times 3$ factorial design, the "4," "2," and "3" represent, respectively, _____, _____ , and _____ .
> 3. Compared to single-factor designs, factorial designs are better able to capture the _____ of real life. The key limitation of factorial designs is that _____.
> 4. When the effect of one independent variable on behavior differs, depending on the level of a second independent variable, this is called _____.

UNDERSTANDING MAIN EFFECTS AND INTERACTIONS

Learning Objectives

After studying this section, you should be able to:

- Describe different types of outcomes that can occur in a factorial design that has two independent variables.
- Examine relatively simple sets of findings from factorial designs and identify whether main effects and interactions are likely to be present.

To gain a deeper understanding of main effects and interactions, let's work through some examples of simplified findings from a hypothetical 2×2 experiment. Suppose we are interested in how the number of alibi witnesses and their relationship to a crime suspect affect people's probability judgments about whether a crime suspect is guilty. In some instances, crime suspects (such as Maurice Patterson, the wrongfully convicted man mentioned in the chapter opening) assert that at the time of the crime they were with several family members or friends, or that more than one neighbor saw them. It would be interesting to create several levels of the number-of-witnesses variable (e.g., one, two, three, four), but for simplicity we'll use just two levels: one witness and three witnesses. We'll follow the general procedure used by Dahl and Price (2012). The 50-year-old male suspect's supported alibi will be that either he was with one or three of his young adult daughters, or he was seen repeatedly by one or three young adult female neighbors while working outside near their homes.

As we work through each example, the same set of data will be presented in a table, line graph, and bar graph, to familiarize you with how the same main effects and interactions would look when displayed in different formats. In the graphs, number of witnesses will be the *x*-axis independent variable. Keep in mind that, although this is a quantitative variable, it is discrete rather than continuous. You can't have 1.4 or 2.7 witnesses. As discussed in Chapter 4, line graphs typically are used when, at a conceptual level, the *x*-axis represents a quantitative variable that is continuous (or, if discrete, when there are so many *x*-axis values that a line graph provides a clearer visual presentation than a bar graph). Thus, although line graphs are included here for instructional purposes, if we were writing a research report based on our hypothetical study, we would present the data in a table or bar graph because number of witnesses is a discrete variable with only two values.

POSSIBLE OUTCOMES IN A 2 × 2 DESIGN

In a factorial design that has two independent variables, there are eight possible combinations of outcomes that can occur. For variable A, there either will or will not be a main effect. Likewise, for variable B, there either will or will not be a main effect. Finally, there either will be or will not be an A × B interaction. Multiplying these possibilities yields eight potential combinations. We'll cover four of these combinations in this section and use the others as an exercise for you to check your understanding. For each example, we will assume that there are 45 participants in each of the four conditions.

In the tables that follow, the statistic in each cell—called a *cell mean*—represents participants' mean rating of the probability (expressed as a percent) that the suspect committed the crime. For simplicity, in all of the practice examples in this chapter, we'll work with whole numbers in the cell means and assume that the number of observations (i.e., number of participants) is the same in each cell. In the margins, the statistic to the right of each row and below each column—called a *marginal mean*—is the average of the cell means for that particular row or column. Thus, in the table below the marginal mean of 60% at the bottom of the left column represents the average of the cell means in Condition 1 (70%) and Condition 3 (50%).

One strong recommendation: As we cover these examples, do not try to memorize specific sets of data, because there are countless examples that you might encounter. Rather, focus on understanding the underlying concepts of a "main effect" and an "interaction." Once you grasp these concepts, you should be able to successfully apply your understanding to many potential examples.

Example 1. In this example, we'll spell out each step in the analysis as we answer three questions: Is there a main effect of number of witnesses, a main effect of witness–suspect relationship, and an interaction?

	Number of Alibi Witnesses		
Relationship to Suspect	One	Three	*Marginal Mean*
Daughter	70% (Condition 1)	70% (Condition 2)	*70%*
Neighbor	50% (Condition 3)	50% (Condition 4)	*50%*
Marginal Mean	*60%*	*60%*	

Note: The data represent participants' mean ratings of the probability the suspect is guilty.

(a) *Is there a main effect of number of witnesses?* In other words, if we compare the average rating of the 90 participants exposed to three witnesses to the average rating of the 90 participants exposed to one witness, did an overall difference occur? To answer this question, we examine the marginal means at the bottom of each column. For the moment, we combine the results from Condition 1 and Condition 3; together, these are the "one witness" results. The marginal mean beneath the left column indicates that, on average, participants exposed to one alibi witness believed there was a 60% chance that the suspect committed the crime. Similarly, we combine the results from Condition 2 and Condition 4; together, these are the "three witnesses" results. The marginal mean beneath the right column is the same (60%) as that beneath the left column. Therefore, ignoring for the moment that there is another independent variable (witness–suspect relationship) and just focusing on the one-versus three-witness conditions, no overall difference in their ratings occurs. There is no main effect of number of witnesses.

(b) *Is there a main effect of witness–suspect relationship?* To answer this question, we compare the average rating of the 90 participants exposed to daughter witnesses to the average rating of the 90 participants exposed to neighbor witnesses. Thus, we compare the marginal means at the end of the rows. When the alibi witnesses are daughters (the combination of Condition 1 and Condition 2), the average probability rating is 70%. But, when the alibi witnesses are neighbors (the combination of Condition 3 and Condition 4), the average rating is 50%. For simplicity, in all the examples in this chapter, we will treat any differences between the marginal means in the rows, as well as any differences between the marginal means in the columns, as statistically significant. Thus, the witness–suspect relationship produces a significant main effect: Overall, participants' ratings were influenced by whether a witness was a daughter or neighbor.

(c) *Is there a Number of Witnesses × Witness–Suspect Relationship interaction?* Does the effect of the witness–suspect relationship (daughter vs. neighbor) on participants' judgments differ, depending on the number of witnesses? We also could phrase this as follows: Does the effect of number of witnesses differ, depending on whether witnesses are daughters or neighbors? To answer this question, we ignore the marginal means and examine the pattern of means across the four individual cells (each of which has 45 participants). Alibis provided by daughters rather than neighbors led to a 20% higher average guilt rating (70% − 50%) when there was one witness, and a 20% higher average guilt rating (70% − 50%) when there were three witnesses. Thus, the influence of having daughter versus neighbor witnesses was the same, regardless of the number of witnesses. No interaction exists between the two independent variables.

Finally, **Figure 9.4** displays these same findings in a line graph (a) and a bar graph (b). In the line graph, if you determine the vertical midpoint between the yellow line and orange line when there is one witness, and do the same when there are three witnesses, those midpoints are the same. Thus, there is no overall main effect of number of witnesses. In contrast, the midpoint of the yellow line (daughters) clearly is above the midpoint of the orange line (neighbors). This represents the main effect of the witness–suspect relationship. The fact that the two lines are parallel says there is no interaction: The flat slope of both lines indicates that the number of witnesses had no effect on the mean ratings, regardless of the witness–suspect relationship.

For the bar graph, the average height of the two bars when there is one witness is the same as the average height of the two bars when there are three witnesses. This indicates the absence of a main effect for number of witnesses. In contrast, the average height of the two yellow bars differs from the average height of the two orange bars, indicating a main effect for the daughter–neighbor manipulation. Finally, in the bar graph, we can see that the difference in height between the yellow and orange bars when there is one witness is the same as the height

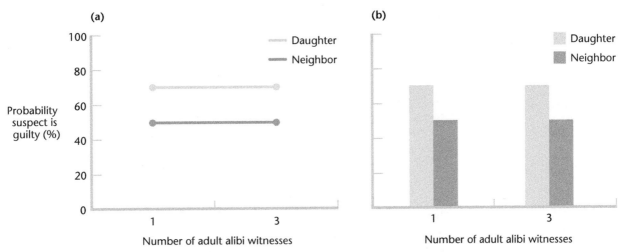

Figure 9.4 Example 1: Main effect without an interaction. Both graphs **(a)** and **(b)** portray a witness–suspect relationship (i.e., daughter–neighbor) main effect, no main effect of number of witnesses, and no interaction.

difference between the yellow and orange bars when there are three witnesses, indicating the lack of an interaction. In other words, the degree of difference in guilt probability ratings when the alibi witness is a daughter versus a neighbor does not depend on the number of witnesses: It is the same (a 20% difference) regardless of the number of witnesses.

Example 2. Here is a second data set, and once again, we ask three key questions: (a) Is there a main effect of number of witnesses? (b) Is there a main effect of witness–suspect relationship? (c) Is there a Number of Witnesses × Witness–Suspect Relationship interaction?

	Number of Alibi Witnesses		
Relationship to Suspect	**One**	**Three**	*Marginal Mean*
Daughter	80% (Condition 1)	60% (Condition 2)	*70%*
Neighbor	50% (Condition 3)	30% (Condition 4)	*40%*
Marginal Mean	*65%*	*45%*	

In this data set, we see two main effects and no interaction. First, we compare the marginal means beneath the two columns to determine if number of witnesses produced a main effect. On average, participants gave higher guilt probability ratings when there was one witness (65%) than when there were three witnesses (45%). This difference indicates that indeed there is a main effect for number of witnesses. Note that if the difference had occurred in the other direction—a higher average rating in the three-witness condition compared to the one-witness condition—this also would reflect a main effect. The key is that there is an overall difference (regardless of direction) between the one- versus three-witness conditions.

The marginal means at the end of the rows indicate that the witness–suspect relationship also produced a main effect. The average guilt probability rating was higher among the participants exposed to a daughter witness (70%) rather than a neighbor witness (40%). Overall, participants were more skeptical about alibis provided by daughters rather than neighbors. In addition, there is no Number of Witnesses × Witness–Suspect Relationship interaction. The difference in ratings when the witness was a daughter versus a neighbor was the same regardless of whether there was one witness (80% − 50%) or three witnesses (60% − 30%).

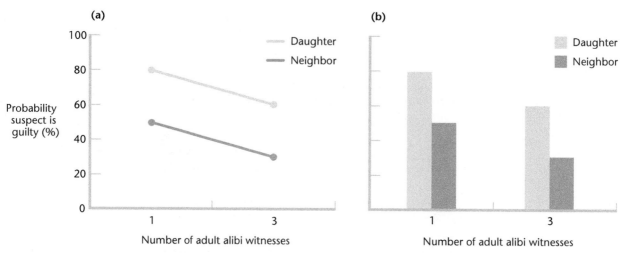

Figure 9.5 Example 2: Two main effects without an interaction. Both graphs **(a)** and **(b)** portray a witness-suspect relationship main effect, a main effect of number of witnesses, and no interaction.

Figure 9.5 displays these results in graphs. In the line graph (a), the midpoint between the yellow and orange lines when there is one witness is higher than the midpoint between the yellow and orange lines when there are three witnesses. This is the main effect of number of witnesses. The main effect of the witness–suspect relationship is the fact that, as seen in the graph, the orange line is always beneath the yellow line (and thus, the midpoints of these lines differ). Finally, the lines are parallel, indicating that no interaction occurs.

In the bar graph (b), the average height of the two bars in the one-witness condition differs from the average height of the two bars in the three-witness condition. This represents the main effect of number of witnesses. Similarly, the average height of the two yellow bars differs from the average height of the two orange bars, illustrating the main effect of the witness–suspect relationship. Finally, the difference in height between the yellow and orange bars when there is one witness is the same as the difference in height between the yellow and orange bars when there are three witnesses, indicating that no interaction occurs.

Example 3. Here is a third data set.

Relationship to Suspect	Number of Alibi Witnesses		*Marginal Mean*
	One	**Three**	
Daughter	50% (Condition 1)	50% (Condition 2)	*50%*
Neighbor	70% (Condition 3)	30% (Condition 4)	*50%*
Marginal Mean	*60%*	*40%*	

The marginal means beneath the columns differ, indicating that there is a main effect for number of witnesses. Overall, participants believed it was more likely that the suspect was guilty when there was only one alibi witness (60% probability) rather than three (40% probability). Both row marginal means are 50%, indicating that there is no main effect of witness–suspect relationship. Examination of the four cell means reveals an interaction.

Why is there an interaction? When there was only one witness, participants were less likely to think the suspect guilty if that witness was a daughter rather than a neighbor (50% – 70% = a difference of –20%; be mindful of the minus sign), but the opposite occurred when there were three witnesses: Participants were more likely to think the suspect guilty if the witnesses were daughters rather than neighbors (50% − 30% = a difference of 20%). In other words, the influence of the witness–suspect relationship on guilt probability ratings differed, depending on the number of alibi witnesses present.

We can also understand how these data reveal an interaction by interpreting the findings from the other way around; that is, by examining how the influence of number of alibi witnesses on guilt probability ratings differs, depending on the witness–suspect relationship. Overall, when the witnesses were daughters, participants' guilt probability ratings were the same regardless of whether there were one or three witnesses (50% − 50% = 0). Yet, when the alibi witnesses were neighbors, guilt probability ratings were substantially higher when there was only one witness rather than three witnesses (70% − 30% = 40%). Thus, the number of witnesses had no influence on the believability of daughters, but it did influence the believability of neighbors: Participants were more likely to accept the alibi of a neighbor when three neighbors, rather than only one, supported it.

To determine whether an interaction is present, what we have just done is examine whether there is a "difference between the differences" in the results of certain pairs of conditions. Does the effect of daughter-witness versus neighbor-witness on participants' ratings differ, depending on whether there are one versus three witnesses? If the results in

(Condition 1 − Condition 3) versus (Condition 2 − Condition 4)
(50% − 70% = −20%) versus (50% − 30% = 20%)

had been equal, then there would be no interaction. But we can see in this case that the results (−20% versus 20%) are not equal, which indicates that an interaction is present.

Alternatively, we can ask whether the effect of one versus three witnesses depends on whether those witnesses are daughters or neighbors. Thus, we are comparing the differences between conditions as follows:

(Condition 1 − Condition 2) versus (Condition 3 − Condition 4)
(50% − 50% = 0) versus (70% − 30% = 40%)

No matter which of these two ways we calculate it—focusing on the daughter–neighbor manipulation as independent variable #1 or independent variable #2—if we obtain evidence of an interaction using one formula, the other formula also will reveal the interaction.

You might wonder how number of witnesses can have a main effect if this variable had no influence on the ratings when the alibi witnesses were daughters. The answer is that in determining whether a main effect exists, we only examine marginal means. In this case, the column marginal means tell us that, statistically, there is a main effect of number of witnesses. However, it's clear that this main effect has resulted entirely from the results that occurred in the one-neighbor (Condition 3) versus three-neighbor (Condition 4) conditions. It would be misleading, in a sense, to describe these results to someone and let that person walk away with the impression that "in general, having more witnesses causes lower ratings of suspect guilt." The key issue is that the interaction overrides or "qualifies" the main effect of number of witnesses. In our experiment, "having more witnesses causes lower ratings of suspect guilt" *only when* the witnesses are neighbors, not when they are the suspect's daughters. The essential point to remember is that whenever main effects occur along with an interaction, the interaction requires us to carefully inspect the findings in each of the four conditions. We perform this inspection to determine how the interaction qualifies the conclusions we draw based on the main effects.

Figure 9.6 shows a line graph (a) and a bar graph (b) of these data. The line graph reveals that the two lines are not parallel, which indicates that an interaction does occur. Keep in mind that with real data, nonparallel lines suggest the possibility of an interaction, and we would perform statistical tests to determine whether the interaction is statistically significant.

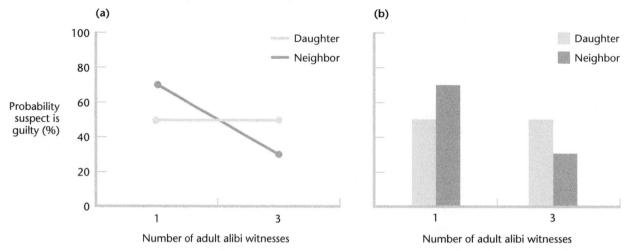

Figure 9.6 Example 3: Interaction with a main effect. Both graphs **(a)** and **(b)** portray a main effect of number of witnesses, no main effect of witness–suspect relationship, and a Number of Witnesses × Witness–Suspect Relationship interaction.

This type of interaction is called a *disordinal* (or *crossover*) interaction. At one end of the lines, the mean score for the daughter condition is above the mean for the neighbor condition, whereas at the other end, the opposite "above/below" order occurs. Both graphs also make it clear how the interaction qualifies the main effect of number of witnesses. In the line graph, for example, the slope of the yellow line is flat, indicating that when the witnesses were daughters, the number of witnesses had no effect on participants' ratings. The slope of the orange line illustrates that the number of witnesses did affect participants' ratings when the witnesses were neighbors. Analogously, in the bar graph, the height of the bars is the same in the two conditions that represent daughters, but differs considerably in the two conditions that represent neighbors. This indicates that the number of witnesses affected the ratings only when the witnesses were neighbors.

Example 4. This final example illustrates two important points about interactions and main effects. We'll address them as we interpret these data.

Relationship to Suspect	Number of Alibi Witnesses		*Marginal Mean*
	One	**Three**	
Daughter	70% (Condition 1)	50% (Condition 2)	*60%*
Neighbor	60% (Condition 3)	10% (Condition 4)	*35%*
Marginal Mean	*65%*	*30%*	

The marginal means indicate that we have two main effects. Overall, participants were less likely to judge the suspect as guilty when there were three witnesses rather than one, and when the witnesses were neighbors rather than the suspect's daughters. Looking at the four individual cells reveals an interaction. When the witnesses were daughters, having more witnesses decreased the probability ratings from 70% (one witness) to 50% (three witnesses). When the witnesses were neighbors, having more witnesses decreased the probability ratings from 60% (one witness) to 10% (three witnesses). Thus, the effect of number of witnesses on participants' ratings was in the same direction regardless of whether the witnesses were neighbors or daughters, but the effect was much stronger when the witnesses were neighbors.

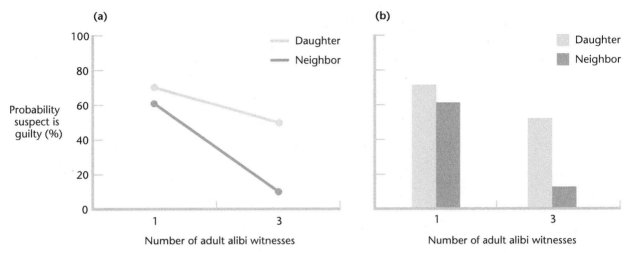

Figure 9.7 Example 4: Interaction with two main effects. Both graphs **(a)** and **(b)** portray a main effect of number of witnesses, a witness–suspect relationship main effect, and a Number of Witnesses × Witness–Suspect Relationship interaction.

The line graph (a) and bar graph (b) in **Figure 9.7** visually portray that in this data set, we have an *ordinal interaction:* At each level of number of witnesses, the mean probability rating in the daughter condition is higher than the rating in the corresponding neighbor condition, but the size of this difference is much greater when there are three witnesses.

Note that, as most easily seen in the line graph in Figure 9.7, the interaction in this example does not negate the truthfulness of the conclusions based on the main effects. It is accurate to say that, overall, the presence of three alibi witnesses led to lower ratings of the suspect's guilt than did the presence of one witness. However, the presence of an interaction requires us to add the following: "but the number of witnesses had a stronger impact when the witnesses were neighbors rather than daughters." Likewise, it is accurate to say that overall, participants were less likely to judge the suspect to be guilty when the alibi was supported by neighbors rather than daughters. However, the presence of an interaction requires us to add this: "but the degree to which neighbors were more believable than daughters as alibi witnesses was much greater when there were three witnesses, rather than just one."

Figure 9.8 presents four more hypothetical sets of data in various formats (a–d) so that you can check your understanding of main effects and interactions. These examples represent the four outcomes of 2 × 2 designs that we have not discussed, but that you should be able to identify at this point. For each example, determine (yes/no) whether there is a main effect for each independent variable, and whether an interaction exists. Answers appear in the first paragraph of "Exercise 3: Identify the Main Effects and Interactions," at the end of this chapter.

INTERACTIONS AND EXTERNAL VALIDITY

Suppose that when we conduct our 2 (number of witnesses) × 2 (witness–suspect relationship) experiment the results come out as portrayed in Example 2 on pages 293–294: two main effects and no interaction. These findings indicate that, at least in our experiment, increasing the number of witnesses decreased participants' judgments about the suspect's guilt to the same degree for both types of alibi witnesses. Compared to a single-factor experiment that only manipulates the number of witnesses, we provided a stronger basis for the external validity of our findings.

To understand how we've accomplished this, imagine that we had only conducted a single-factor experiment in which the independent variable was the number of witnesses,

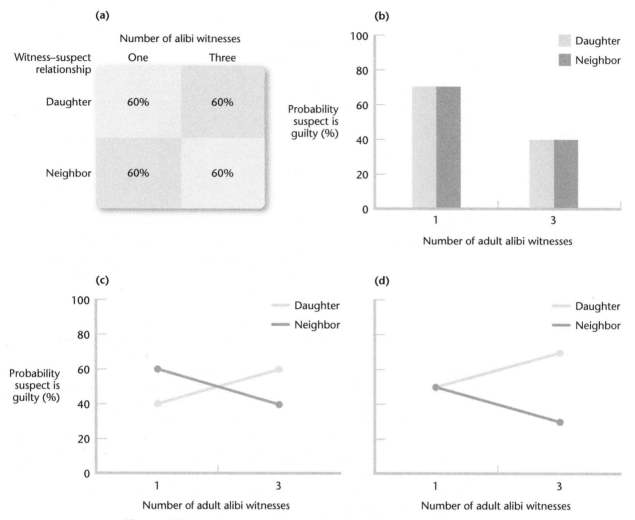

Figure 9.8 **Practice examples (a–d): Main effects and interactions.**

represented by two levels: one witness and three witnesses. In this experiment, the alibi witnesses were always neighbors. When we report our finding that increasing the number of witnesses increased people's willingness to accept the alibi (as indicated by the lower guilt probability ratings), someone might say, "Well, OK, but maybe this only holds true for witnesses who are neighbors." In our 2 × 2 experiment, we've already countered this objection by incorporating two types of witnesses (neighbors and daughters) as a second independent variable. We found that increasing the number of witnesses increased acceptance of the alibi both when the witnesses were neighbors and when the witnesses were daughters.

Suppose, however, that we do find a Number of Witnesses × Witness–Suspect Relationship interaction like the one in Example 3 (pp. 294–296). Despite the main effect of number of witnesses, the interaction indicated that the change from one to three witnesses only affected participants' ratings when the alibi witnesses were neighbors. Thus, if our goal had been to establish a general psychological conclusion that "increasing the number of alibi witnesses will increase people's acceptance of an alibi," then our findings limit the external validity of such a conclusion. In sum, to repeat an earlier point, interactions always must be examined carefully for the way in which they qualify any general conclusions that otherwise would be implied by statistically significant main effects. This leads us to a general, brief discussion of how data from factorial designs are analyzed.

ANALYZING THE RESULTS: GENERAL CONCEPTS

There are different ways to statistically analyze the data from factorial experiments. We'll discuss one common approach, in which the first step is to determine whether any main effects and interactions are statistically significant. Depending on the results, the researcher may then conduct follow-up tests to examine the findings more closely.

When dependent variables have been measured on an interval or ratio scale, analysis of variance (ANOVA) is a widely used statistical procedure for determining whether the main effects and interactions in factorial designs are statistically significant. The basic logic of the ANOVA procedure is the same as we discussed in Chapter 8. However, whereas in an experiment with one independent variable the ANOVA yields a single test of statistical significance, with a factorial design that has two independent variables the ANOVA involves three tests of statistical significance. There is one test for the main effect of independent variable A, one for the main effect of independent variable B, and one for the A × B interaction.

Let's consider one example, for which the findings from a hypothetical 3 (room temperature) × 2 (humidity) between-subjects factorial design portrayed in **Figure 9.9** will best serve our purpose. Assume that there are equal numbers of participants in all six conditions.

Suppose that an ANOVA reveals a statistically significant main effect of room temperature. On average, across the three increasing levels of room temperature, 13, 14, and 16 errors occurred, respectively. A statistically significant main effect of humidity also is found: On average, 12 errors occurred when humidity was low, and 16 errors occurred when humidity was high. In addition, suppose the Temperature × Humidity interaction is statistically significant.

Viewing the graph reveals how this interaction qualifies the main effects. First, although the average number of errors increased as temperature increased, this main effect of temperature was entirely due to the fact that the number of task errors increased substantially when humidity was high. When humidity was low, the increases in room temperature produced a decrease in task errors. Thus, the effect of temperature on performance differed, depending on humidity.

As for the humidity main effect, although more errors occurred overall when humidity was high, the interaction indicates that this was not the case at the lowest room temperature, where this outcome is reversed: Here, participants exposed to high humidity made fewer errors than those exposed to low humidity. Thus, the relation between humidity and performance differed, depending on the room temperature.

Our goal now is to dig deeper into the nature of the interaction by performing follow-up statistical analyses. One approach we can take is to break down the interaction into what are called *simple main effects*. A **simple main effect** *represents the effect of one independent variable at a particular level of another independent variable.* So, for the variable of humidity, there would be three simple main effects we could examine, one at each of the three levels of room temperature. Was there a statistically significant difference in performance under exposure to low versus high humidity when the room temperature was 68 °F (20 °C), when it was 77 °F (25 °C), and when it was 86 °F (30 °C)? To answer this question, we would perform a separate statistical test of each of these three simple main effects. We may find that all, none, or just one or two of these simple main effects are statistically significant. For example, we might find that the difference in performance when exposed to low versus high humidity is statistically significant only at the highest temperature level.

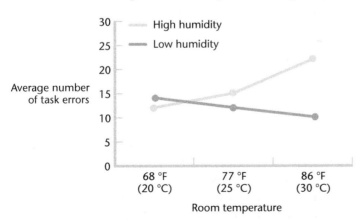

Figure 9.9 **Hypothetical results from a 3 (temperature) × 2 (humidity) factorial design.**

For our independent variable of room temperature, there would be two simple main effects to examine, one at each level of humidity: (1) Overall, did temperature influence performance when humidity was low? (2) Overall, did temperature influence performance when humidity was high? If we statistically test each of these simple main effects, we may find that temperature significantly influenced performance when humidity was low and also when humidity was high. Or, perhaps we'll find that, when humidity was low, the differences in errors across the three levels of room temperature were not statistically significant. It's even possible that neither simple main effect will be significant: As room temperature increases, neither the increase in errors when humidity was high nor the decrease in errors when humidity was low may be large enough to be statistically significant. This would tell us that as temperature increased, the net effect of performance spreading farther apart when exposed to low versus high humidity represented a statistically significant interaction, even though, individually, neither component of the interaction (i.e., neither simple main effect of temperature) was statistically significant.

Let's assume, however, that temperature did significantly influence performance when humidity was high, but not when humidity was low. Because the simple main effect of temperature was statistically significant only when humidity was high, we now focus on the participants who were exposed to high humidity. We perform a final series of statistical tests comparing their performance between different pairs of temperatures. These comparisons of specific pairs of means are called *simple contrasts*. For example, these tests might reveal that when humidity was high, participants averaged significantly more errors at 86 °F (30 °C) than at 68 °F (20 °C), but that neither of these means differs significantly from the mean score at 77 °F (25 °C). Note that these simple contrasts represent *post-hoc comparisons* (also called *post-hoc tests*), because we decided to conduct them after the fact: after we saw the pattern of our findings and obtained the ANOVA results. In sum, using this data analysis approach of

$$\text{ANOVA} \rightarrow \text{tests of simple main effects} \rightarrow \text{post-hoc comparisons}$$

we have progressively moved from more general to more specific tests of statistical significance.

In contrast to this multistep analysis approach, researchers sometimes plan—prior to gathering their data—to bypass an ANOVA and instead perform a small number of tests that will determine whether the differences between certain pairs or combinations of means will be statistically significant. For example, a study may test a theory or hypothesis that predicts the mean scores in two particular conditions will differ significantly. Such tests are called *planned comparisons*. The reward for using planned rather than post-hoc comparisons is that, statistically (other things being equal), differences between means do not have to be as large in order to be found statistically significant. The drawback is that planned comparisons should be limited in number, and therefore in a factorial design that involves many means, unexpected or other potentially important findings that are not within the scope of the planned comparisons go untested.

✓ CONCEPT CHECK 9.2 UNDERSTANDING MAIN EFFECTS AND INTERACTIONS

Suppose we have a factorial design with two independent variables: A and B. Decide whether each statement below is true or false. Answers appear on page 308.

1. If A has a main effect, then B cannot also have a main effect.
2. If there is an A × B interaction, then neither A nor B can have a main effect.
3. A disordinal interaction is also known as a "crossover" interaction.
4. An interaction may limit our ability to draw a general conclusion that is suggested by the presence of a main effect.

DESIGNING A FACTORIAL EXPERIMENT

Learning Objectives

After studying this section, you should be able to:

- Discuss how factorial designs can be used to identify nonlinear effects.

- Describe why and how subject variables are often included in factorial designs, and why caution is needed in interpreting findings that involve subject variables.

- Discuss how factorial designs can be used to examine changes in behavior over time.

Thus far, we have mainly focused on the simplest of factorial designs—the 2 × 2 design—in which each independent variable has been manipulated by the researcher. Here and in the final section of the chapter, we'll explore a greater diversity of designs and issues that researchers consider when creating a factorial design.

DETERMINING THE NUMBER OF CONDITIONS

The research question that scientists are investigating and practical limitations in the resources available to them are key factors in determining (1) the number of independent variables, (2) the number of levels of each independent variable, and therefore (3) the total number of conditions that they will incorporate into a factorial design. With regard to the number of independent variables, recall that Dahl and Price (2012) examined how alibi witness age and witness–suspect relationship affected people's judgments of a suspect's guilt. In all cases, there was one alibi witness. Would their pattern of results, shown in Figure 9.1 (p. 281), have been different if there were three alibi witnesses rather than one? One way to address this question would be to incorporate number of witnesses as a third independent variable in the factorial design, creating a Witness Age × Witness–Suspect Relationship × Number of Witnesses design. Similarly, if we wish to examine how cognitive performance is affected not just by room temperature and humidity, but by the joint effects of temperature, humidity, and background noise, we can design a factorial experiment that incorporates all three of these independent variables.

As for determining the number of conditions of each independent variable, let's consider a situation in which you would want an independent variable to have more than two levels. As we noted in Chapter 8, when a researcher seeks to determine whether an independent variable has a nonlinear influence on behavior, that variable must be designed to have three or more levels. Suppose we hypothesize that as room temperature increases from 68 °F to 95 °F (20 °C to 35 °C), this will have a nonlinear effect on people's task performance. We want to determine whether this nonlinear effect will differ, depending on the level of humidity. Imagine that we create four temperature levels and the findings turn out like those in **Figure 9.10**. It's immediately apparent that the two data lines are not parallel, and this lack of parallelism suggests the presence of an interaction. Overall, as room temperature rises, errors increase both when humidity is low and when humidity is high, but the temperature change has a larger effect when humidity is high.

Moreover, Figure 9.10 reveals the nonlinear effects of temperature at both levels of humidity. Regardless of the humidity level, the increase in room temperature from 68 °F to 77 °F (20 °C to 25 °C) has little effect on performance. Beyond that point, errors increase more rapidly at progressively higher temperatures when humidity is low, and even more so when

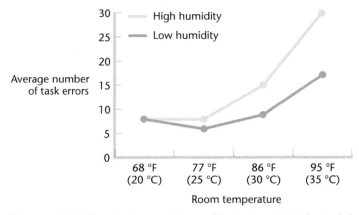

Figure 9.10 Examining nonlinear effects in a 4 × 2 factorial design experiment. To examine whether an independent variable has nonlinear effects on a dependent variable, three or more levels of that independent variable must be incorporated into the factorial design.

humidity is high. Had we only incorporated two temperature levels into our experiment—say, the lowest and highest temperature levels—we could not have detected these nonlinear relations.

INCORPORATING SUBJECT VARIABLES

In the examples of factorial designs discussed so far, all the independent variables within each experiment have been situational factors—aspects of the social or physical environment—that the experimenter manipulated. We've discussed manipulating and then exposing participants to different alibi witnesses, different room temperatures and humidity levels, and different driving situations. Now let's add a new and important ingredient to the mix: *subject variables,* which (as we discussed in Chapter 8) represent characteristics of the people or nonhuman animals who are being studied.

The scientific and often practical question is this: How do different types of individuals respond to the same situational factors? Or, we can rephrase the question this way: Does the effect of a situational factor on behavior differ, depending on the type of individual? As you may recognize, these questions ask whether a subject characteristic interacts with a situational factor. Here are some examples. Do success and failure outcomes have the same psychological impact on people who have high versus low self-esteem? Does the way in which people respond to consuming various doses of alcohol depend on their expectations of how alcohol will affect them? Are the effects of room temperature and humidity on cognitive performance the same for younger adults as for older adults?

The Person × Situation Factorial Design

In designing an experiment to address such questions, the most common approach is to create a **person × situation** (also called **person × environment**) **factorial design:** *an experimental design that incorporates at least one subject variable along with at least one manipulated situational variable.* The word *person* is used liberally here (*organism* would be more inclusive), because experiments with nonhuman animals may also combine subject variables (e.g., the animal's age or sex) with manipulated situational variables. Also note that although the word *person* appears first in the term *person × situation,* when researchers describe the design of their study, they may list subject variables before or after situational variables, as we'll see below.

In the simplest possible case, we would have one subject variable with two levels and one manipulated independent variable with two levels. For example, in an experiment examining the effects of cell phone use on driving performance, we would have our original manipulated independent variable (cell phone use–no phone use) and then add a subject variable, such as driver experience (experienced–inexperienced). This would produce a 2 × 2 design with four conditions: (1) cell phone use by experienced drivers; (2) cell phone use by inexperienced drivers; (3) no cell phone use by experienced drivers; (4) no cell phone use by inexperienced drivers.

Of course, many subject variables can have more than two levels. In our cell phone experiment, we could measure the driving experience of a sample of people and then select participants for placement into one of three levels: inexperienced, moderately experienced, and highly experienced. We also can examine more than one subject variable in a factorial design. For example, we could manipulate cell phone use (yes, no) and include driver experience (experienced, inexperienced) and sex (male, female drivers) as subject variables. This would yield a 2 × 2 × 2 factorial design.

Thinking Critically About Subject Variables

In describing the design of a person × situation experiment, each subject variable is considered an independent variable. Thus, we would say that our 2 (cell phone) × 2 (driver experience) design has two independent variables. But when interpreting the results, we must keep in mind that there is an important distinction between independent variables that are manipulated and those that are created by measuring subjects' natural characteristics. For example, in our experiment, we are manipulating the situational factor of cell phone use. Either through counterbalancing (in a within-subjects design) or random assignment (in a between-subjects design), we are the ones who control whether a participant will use a phone during any particular time segment of the simulated driving route. In contrast, we have not manipulated people's driving experience. Rather, we have created an independent variable by forming two levels (experienced/inexperienced) based on participants' preexisting amount of driving experience. Through a questionnaire or interview item, for example, we have measured how much driving experience people have naturally accumulated and then used this information to categorize them as either experienced and inexperienced drivers. As we discussed in Chapter 8, many researchers refer to such subject variables as *selected independent variables* or *quasi-independent variables,* to distinguish them from manipulated independent variables.

When subject variables produce a main effect or interaction in a factorial experiment, we need to be especially cautious about drawing conclusions concerning their causal influence. The reason for this is that any particular subject variable is likely to be correlated with other subject characteristics. For example, if cell phone use impairs the performance of inexperienced but not experienced drivers, is it really the level of driving *experience* that has caused this interaction? Experienced drivers are likely to be older, and perhaps some personal characteristic associated with age (e.g., greater cautiousness or vigilance) was the real factor that enabled experienced drivers to cope with the potentially distracting effects of talking on a cell phone.

Anticipating this, the experimenter could try to match the inexperienced and experienced drivers on the variable of age, or at least measure their age and see whether age correlates with driving simulator performance. If it does, there are statistical procedures that can be used to filter out the correlation with age from the analysis of main effects and the interaction. Still, it is unlikely that the experimenter could match participants on, or even measure, every relevant personal characteristic associated with driver experience. In sum, always keep in mind the distinction between manipulated and nonmanipulated independent variables.

EXAMINING CHANGES IN A DEPENDENT VARIABLE OVER TIME

Psychologists often want to know how exposing people or nonhuman animals to an independent variable changes subjects' behavior or other characteristics over time. To examine this, the researcher measures the dependent variable on at least two occasions. For example, in their alibi witness experiment, Dahl and Price (2012) measured participants' beliefs about whether the suspect was guilty both before and after the participants watched an alibi witness video. An experimental psychologist who studies topics such as learning, memory, and sleep may measure a dependent variable (e.g., task performance) over many task trials to assess short-term and long-term effects of independent variables such as different schedules of reinforcement, different memory strategies, or different amounts of sleep deprivation. In experiments that examine psychotherapy's effectiveness, clinical psychologists may measure dependent variables (e.g., scores on psychological tests of depression, posttraumatic stress symptoms) not only soon before and after treatment, but also on a regular basis during treatment and in long-term follow-ups (Resick et al., 2008).

When researchers measure a dependent variable multiple times, one option for analyzing the change in the dependent variable over time is to treat the multiple measurement periods as levels of an additional independent variable. In such cases, this factor is often labeled as "Time," "Trial," "Testing Session," or something similar. In the simplest case, the dependent variable is measured only twice: once before and once after exposure to the independent variable. Dahl and Price used this approach in some of their analyses. Thus, although their basic experimental design was a 2 × 2 factorial (Figure 9.1), to examine how exposure to the alibi witness video changed participants' judgments about the suspect, they conducted a 2 (age: child, adult) × 2 (relationship: son, neighbor) × 2 (time of measurement: pre-alibi, post-alibi) analysis of participants' probability ratings. They found, for example, that compared to judgments made before watching the video, participants became less likely to believe the suspect was guilty after observing either the child–neighbor or child–son alibi witness. In contrast, exposure to the adult alibi witnesses did not decrease participants' guilt judgments. The bottom line is this: When you read about an experiment or other study that examines how participants change over time, time of measurement may be labeled as an independent variable in the research design or statistical analyses.

 CONCEPT CHECK 9.3 DESIGNING A FACTORIAL EXPERIMENT

Decide whether each statement below is true or false. Answers appear on page 308.

1. With two independent variables A and B, if A has four levels and B has two levels, you can examine the potential nonlinear effects of A, but you cannot examine the nonlinear effects of B.

2. In a person × situation factorial design, both independent variables are manipulated.

3. Manipulated independent variables permit clearer causal conclusions than selected independent variables.

EXPERIMENTS WITH MORE THAN TWO INDEPENDENT VARIABLES

Learning Objectives

After studying this section, you should be able to:

- Describe the main effects that are possible in an experiment with three independent variables.

- Identify the total number of interactions possible in an experiment with three independent variables, and define the concept of a three-way interaction.

By examining more than two independent variables, factorial experiments can better capture the complexity of real life. But as noted earlier, as the number of independent variables increases, the number of conditions may rapidly increase beyond what is practical for the researcher to study. To end the chapter, we'll discuss some basic points about the simplest possible factorial design with three independent variables: a 2 × 2 × 2 design.

Suppose we want to examine whether the effects of room temperature and humidity on cognitive performance differ, depending on participants' age. Room temperature is a manipulated independent variable with two levels: 68 °F (20 °C) and 95 °F (35 °C). Likewise, humidity is manipulated and has two levels: low, high. Age is a selected independent variable with two levels: younger adults (25- to 35-year-old participants) and older adults (55- to 65-year-old participants). To simplify the discussion, we'll label each of the eight conditions with a number and assume that we have a completely between-subjects design, with 20 participants in each condition. Table 9.4 illustrates the design of our experiment.

Just as with the 2 × 2 design with which you're already familiar, in a 2 × 2 × 2 design the main effect of temperature is determined by comparing the average performance of all participants exposed to one room temperature to the average performance of all participants

Table 9.4 2 (Temperature) × 2 (Humidity) × 2 (Age) Factorial Design

Humidity	Age			
	Younger Adults		Older Adults	
	Room Temperature		Room Temperature	
	68 °F (20 °C)	95 °F (35 °C)	68 °F (20 °C)	95 °F (35 °C)
Low	(Condition 1)	(Condition 2)	(Condition 5)	(Condition 6)
High	(Condition 3)	(Condition 4)	(Condition 7)	(Condition 8)

exposed to the other temperature. To make this concrete, we are simply asking whether, overall, the 80 participants who performed the task at 68 °F (20 °C)—the participants in Conditions 1, 3, 5, 7—did better or worse, on average, than the 80 participants who performed the task at 95 °F (35 °C)—the participants in Conditions 2, 4, 6, 8.

Similarly, to examine the main effect of humidity, we would determine whether, on average, the 80 participants exposed to low humidity (Conditions 1, 2, 5, 6) performed better or worse than the 80 participants exposed to high humidity (Conditions 3, 4, 7, 8). And, to examine the main effect of age, we would compare the average performance of the 80 younger adults (Conditions 1, 2, 3, 4) to the average performance of the 80 older adults (Conditions 5, 6, 7, 8).

Turning to interaction effects, we've seen that in a 2 (variable A) × 2 (variable B) factorial design, there is one possible interaction: A × B. In a factorial design with three independent variables, A and B and C, the number of possible interactions jumps to four. Consider first that A might interact with B, A might also interact with C, and B and C might interact. These are called **two-way interactions:** *Among two independent variables, the way that one independent variable influences a dependent variable depends on the level of the second independent variable.* This is the type of interaction that we have discussed throughout the chapter. For example, a Room Temperature × Humidity interaction ignores age as a variable and only involves the pattern of results among the four possible combinations of temperature and humidity. In this case, the performance scores of the 20 younger adults in Condition 1 and the 20 older adults in Condition 5 would be combined and then averaged. For the moment, we ignore age and treat these scores as coming from 40 participants who were all exposed to the 68 °F (20 °C), low-humidity environment. Similarly, ignoring age, we would determine the mean scores for the 40 participants exposed to the 68 °F (20 °C), high-humidity environment (i.e., Conditions 3 and 7), the 40 participants exposed to the 95 °F (35 °C), low-humidity environment (Conditions 2 and 6), and the 40 participants exposed to the 95 °F (35 °C), high-humidity environment (Conditions 4 and 8). This would generate four means, from which we could create a 2 × 2 table or graph and examine whether a two-way interaction between temperature and humidity might be present.

In addition to the three possible two-way interactions, the fourth possible interaction is A × B × C. This is called a **three-way interaction:** *The interaction of two independent variables depends on the level of a third independent variable.* For example, on the next page, part (a) of Figure 9.11 shows a Temperature × Humidity interaction for the younger adults' performance scores. Now, if you look at part (b) of Figure 9.11, you'll see that among older adults, the Temperature × Humidity interaction takes on a different form. Assuming that this pattern of differences is statistically significant, then our finding is this: The nature of the interaction between room temperature and humidity depends on participants' age. Thus, when a third independent variable is added to our factorial design, the findings may become much more complex. But, potentially, we stand to learn a great deal more about the variables of interest.

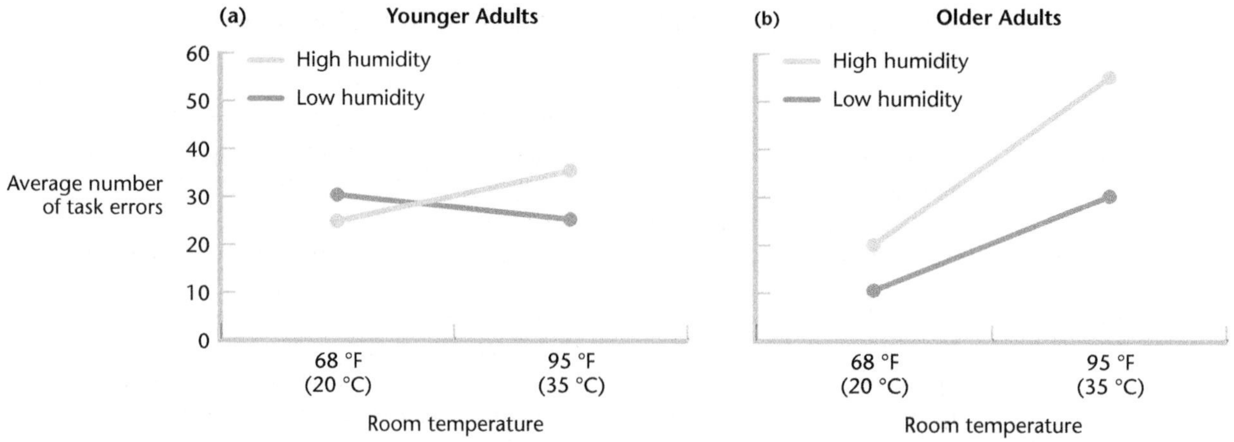

(a) **Younger Adults**

(b) **Older Adults**

Figure 9.11 A three-way interaction. In this 2 (temperature) × 2 (humidity) × 2 (age) design, the pattern of the Temperature × Humidity interaction differs, depending on whether participants are younger adults **(a)** or older adults **(b)**. This yields a three-way interaction.

✓ CONCEPT CHECK 9.4 EXPERIMENTS WITH MORE THAN TWO INDEPENDENT VARIABLES

Fill in each of the blanks below. Answers appear on page 308.

1. In a 3 × 3 × 2 factorial design, there are _____ independent variables and a total of _____ conditions (i.e., cells).

2. If a factorial design has three independent variables, then the maximum number of possible main effects is _____ [enter a number], and the maximum number of possible interactions is _____ [enter a number].

3. If the way that two independent variables interact is different, depending on the level of a third independent variable, then this represents a _____ interaction.

CHAPTER SUMMARY

- In an experiment that uses a factorial design, every level of each independent variable is combined with every level of all the other independent variables. Factorial designs are described numerically as, for example, a 2 × 4 × 3 design. The fact that there are three numbers indicates that there are three independent variables. The "2" tells us that the first independent variable has two levels. The "4" and "3" tell us, respectively, that the second independent variable has four levels and the third independent variable has three levels.

- In a between-subjects factorial design, each participant engages in only one condition of the experiment. In a within-subjects factorial design, each participant engages in all the conditions. When a factorial design includes at least one between-subjects variable and at least one within-subjects variable, it is called a mixed-factorial design.

- Factorial designs are better able to capture the causal complexity of real life than are designs that include only one independent variable. Each independent variable incorporated into a factorial design can, potentially, have a main effect. A main effect occurs when an independent variable has an overall effect on a dependent variable. In addition, the different independent variables in a factorial design can interact with one another. An interaction occurs when the way in which one independent variable influences a dependent variable differs, depending on the level of another independent variable.

- Factorial designs can examine interactions, whereas single-factor designs cannot. Factorial designs are also used to examine whether a variable acts as a moderator. The variable is incorporated into the factorial design, operationally, as an additional independent variable.

If that variable produces an interaction, then it is a moderator. In addition, a factorial experiment is often more efficient to conduct than multiple single-factor experiments.

- The main limitation of factorial designs is that as the numbers of independent variables and levels of independent variables increase, the total number of conditions in the experiment rises rapidly and may exceed the resources available to conduct the experiment.

- In a factorial experiment with two independent variables (A and B), eight outcomes are possible. When there is no A × B interaction, four outcomes are possible: (1) No main effects exist; (2) A, but not B, has a main effect; (3) B, but not A, has a main effect; and (4) both main effects occur. Likewise, when there is an A × B interaction, you can get the same four possible outcomes regarding the main effects.

- When an interaction occurs, any main effects need to be interpreted carefully because the interaction may limit the general conclusion that would be drawn solely from a main effect.

- Often, data from a factorial experiment are initially analyzed to determine whether there are any main effects or interactions. If an interaction occurs, then simple main effects are analyzed. A simple main effect represents the effect of one independent variable at a specific level of another independent variable. If a simple main effect is statistically significant, then the researcher can use post-hoc tests to compare the findings between specific pairs of conditions.

- The particular question that a researcher wants to examine, and practical limitations in the resources available to the researcher, are key factors in determining the number of independent variables, and the number of levels of each independent variable, that will be incorporated into a factorial design.

- Subject variables are often incorporated into factorial designs that also include at least one manipulated variable. This creates a person × situation factorial design. Because subject variables are measured, not manipulated, findings that appear to be caused by a subject variable may, in fact, be caused by other factors that are correlated with the subject variable.

- In a factorial experiment with independent variables A, B, and C, each variable potentially has a main effect. There may also be an A × B interaction, an A × C interaction, a B × C interaction, and a three-way A × B × C interaction.

KEY TERMS

between-subjects factorial design (p. 284)
factorial design (p. 280)
interaction (interaction effect) (p. 286)

main effect (p. 285)
mixed-factorial design (p. 285)
person × situation (person × environment) factorial design (p. 302)

simple main effect (p. 299)
three-way interaction (p. 305)
two-way interaction (p. 305)
within-subjects factorial design (p. 284)

ASSESS YOUR KNOWLEDGE

1. Describe the defining characteristics of a factorial design and mixed-factorial design.

2. When an experimental design is described as a "3 × 2 × 4," what information does this convey about the design?

3. Describe the key advantages and limitations of factorial designs.

4. In a factorial design, what does it mean to say that an independent variable has a main effect on a dependent variable? What does it mean to say that two independent variables interact?

5. Identify the eight possible types of outcomes that can occur in a 2 × 2 factorial design.

6. How can the presence or absence of an interaction influence the generalizability of the findings obtained from a factorial experiment?

7. Describe one general approach—the sequence of steps—used to statistically analyze the results of a factorial design.

8. If you want to examine the potential nonlinear effects of an independent variable, how does this affect the way you create a factorial design?

9. Why do researchers incorporate subject variables into factorial designs?

10. When a factorial design includes one or more subject variables, what cautions does this raise?

11. In a factorial experiment with three independent variables, how many main effects and interactions can occur?

12. Explain the concept of a three-way interaction.

CONCEPT CHECKS: ANSWERS

9.1 Basic Characteristics of Factorial Designs

1. crossed (or "combined"); mixed factorial; four
2. four levels of independent variable A, two levels of independent variable B, three levels of independent variable C 3. complexity; as more independent variables and more levels of each variable are added to the design, the total number of conditions grows rapidly and may be difficult to manage. 4. an interaction

9.2 Understanding Main Effects and Interactions

1. false   2. false   3. true   4. true

9.3 Designing a Factorial Experiment

1. true   2. false   3. true

9.4 Experiments With More Than Two Independent Variables

1. three, eighteen   2. three, four   3. three-way

THINKING CRITICALLY AND APPLYING YOUR KNOWLEDGE

EXERCISE 1   Describe the Factorial Design

Four factorial designs are listed below. For each, identify the number of (a) independent variables; (b) levels of each independent variable; and (c) individual conditions (i.e., cells) in the experiment.
Experiment 1: 2×6 design
Experiment 2: $3 \times 3 \times 2$ design
Experiment 3: $3 \times 2 \times 2 \times 2$ design
Experiment 4: $2 \times 2 \times 4$ design

EXERCISE 2   Identify the Factorial Design

For each of the two experiments described below, identify the design (e.g., 2×6; $3 \times 3 \times 2$) and indicate whether it is a between-subjects, within-subjects, or mixed-factorial design.

Experiment 1: Words to Remember
Dr. Rousseau examines how the amount, meaningfulness, and rate of information influence working (i.e., short-term) memory. Each participant is exposed to eight lists of words: Four lists each contain 15 words, and four each contain 7 words. For each list length, half of the lists contain meaningless nonsense syllables (e.g., GIR, TOX) and half contain meaningful words (e.g., MAP, BIN). Finally, for each combination of list length and list meaningfulness, half of the lists are presented at a rate of one word per second, and half are presented at a rate of two words per second. After

each list is presented, the participant will be asked to immediately recall as many words in the list as possible.

Experiment 2: May I Sleep?
Dr. Klein conducts a laboratory experiment that examines how sleep deprivation affects physical performance. Half of the participants will be younger adults, and half will be older adults. For each age group, half of the participants will be "short sleepers" (i.e., those who normally need 4 to 6 hours of nightly sleep), and half will be "long sleepers" (i.e., those who normally need 7 to 9 hours of nightly sleep). For each of these four groups, participants are randomly assigned to one of three levels of sleep deprivation: (a) no sleep deprivation, (b) REM-only deprivation (participants will be awakened every time their body attempts to go into REM sleep, but are allowed to sleep through other sleep stages), and (c) total sleep deprivation. After experiencing either no, REM-sleep, or total sleep deprivation, each participant's performance on a physical task is measured.

EXERCISE 3   Identify the Main Effects and Interactions

First, with regard to whether the graphs in Figure 9.3 on page 287 reveal main effects, for each graph, there is a main effect for temperature and a main effect for humidity. This assumes, as we have for simplicity throughout the chapter, than any differences in the overall means between levels of an independent variable are statistically significant. Second, here are the answers for the four examples of 2 × 2 designs in Figure 9.8 on page 298: **(a)** no main effects and no interaction; **(b)** main effect of number of witnesses, no main effect of witness–suspect relationship, no interaction; **(c)** no main effects, an interaction; **(d)** main effect of witness–suspect relationship, no main effect of number of witnesses, an interaction. Now let's proceed to a new exercise.

After conducting the experiment described in Exercise 2, Dr. Klein conducts another sleep experiment. This time, all participants are people who typically sleep 8 hours per night. In a sleep laboratory, Dr. Klein manipulates the number of consecutive hours of sleep that participants are allowed to have—2 hours, 4 hours, 6 hours, or 8 hours—before being awakened. Participants' age—younger (25 to 35 years) or older

(55 to 65 years) adults—is a selected independent variable. After being awakened, participants' performance (number of errors) on a physical task is measured.

Two hypothetical sets of results—one portrayed in a line graph (a) and one in a bar graph (b)—are presented below. This 4 × 2 design is intended to stretch your thinking, as compared to just going over more 2 × 2 designs. However, if you understand the concepts of "main effect" and "interaction," you should be able to quickly complete this exercise.

For each graph, answer the following three questions *and treat any overall differences in the data between levels of a variable as statistically significant*:

(a) Does sleep length have a main effect?
(b) Does participant age have a main effect?
(c) Is there an Age of Participant × Sleep Length interaction?

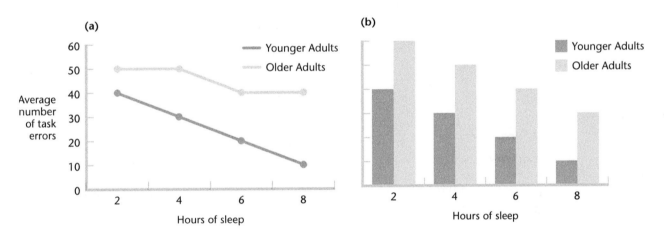

To practice key concepts from this chapter, visit the LaunchPad Solo for Research Methods at **launchpadworks.com.**

CHAPTER OUTLINE

ntelligence is determined by heredity, and I'm going to prove it to you. First, I'm going to obtain a large number of laboratory rats from over 30 different litters that do not share common ancestry (at least, going back for many generations). Therefore, the initial sample of rats will be genetically diverse.

When the rats reach adulthood, I will expose them to a large, complex maze. They must learn the layout to receive a food reward at the end of the maze. As a rat moves through the corridor, it reaches a fork in the maze: Turning in one direction leads to a dead end; turning in the other direction eventually leads to the reward. The maze involves 17 such forks, and each time the rat enters the dead-end corridor of a fork, this will constitute an "error." Each rat will perform the maze 19 times. Overall, they will make fewer errors as they perform more trials and learn the layout of the maze, but more intelligent rats should learn the maze more quickly than less intelligent rats. Therefore, the total number of errors made by each rat over the 19 trials will operationally define its intelligence: Fewer errors represent greater intelligence.

After measuring the rats' intelligence with this 19-trial maze task, I will select the rats who made the fewest maze errors and those who made the most. Respectively, I'll label them "maze-bright" and "maze-dull" rats. Next, I'll begin to develop separate genetic strains of rats by mating maze-bright males with maze-bright females, and maze-dull males with maze-dull females. These rats will represent generation P ("P" stands for parents). Their offspring will be generation F_1 ("Filial-One," the first generation of offspring). When the F_1 rats reach adulthood, I'll repeat the maze learning and selective breeding procedures, mating the brightest F_1 rats with one another and the dullest F_1 rats with one another. Their offspring will be generation F_2, and I will repeat this experimental procedure for 21 generations.

For each generation, I compare the intelligence of the bright versus dull rats, as reflected by their maze performance. **Figure 10.1** shows the findings. In this graph, the initial reference point (the orange dot within the blue circle) represents the performance of the original sample of rats (labeled "0" on the x-axis) from which the maze-bright and maze-dull P generations were selected. The data points for the ensuing F generations (values "1" through "21" along the x-axis) indicate that by F_2, on average, the maze-bright offspring have made fewer errors than the maze-dull offspring. The overall difference in intelligence between the bright and dull rats continues to spread apart over the next few generations, and then stabilizes. In sum, due to their heredity, which I have manipulated, the mentally bright strain has gotten brighter and the mentally dull strain has become duller. Should we conclude that intelligence is genetically determined?

If you're skeptical about the validity of my claim that this experiment proves heredity determines intelligence, that's good: You should be. For one thing, recall that scientists typically avoid claims of absolute proof when discussing research results. For another, claiming that heredity "determines" intelligence seems to close the door on other factors that play a role. Thus, a claim that "heredity influences intelligence" (more precisely, that it partly accounts for individual differences in intelligence) would be more appropriate. Still, would it be valid, based on this experiment?

In Chapters 8 and 9, we examined how scientists use single-factor and factorial designs to identify the causal influence of independent variables on dependent variables. In this chapter, we will explore factors outside the experimental situation, as well as aspects within it, that influence scientists' ability to draw valid conclusions from their research. Some concepts that we will cover (e.g., internal, external, and construct validity; confounding) are already familiar to you from earlier chapters. Here, as part of our ongoing focus on learning to critically

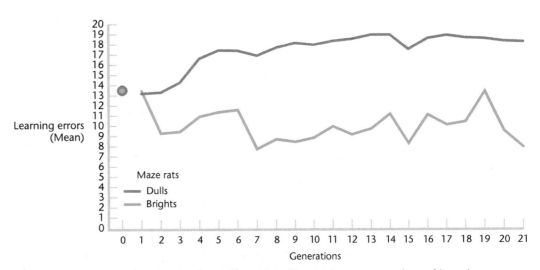

Figure 10.1 Tryon's selective breeding experiment. Average number of learning errors by maze-bright and maze-dull rats over 21 generations in Tryon's experiment.
(Data from McClearn, 1962.)

evaluate the validity of scientific claims, we'll explore these concepts in more depth. Although we'll focus on validity as it applies to experiments, the concepts we'll cover also are relevant to other types of research and claims made in everyday life.

CRITICAL THINKING, INFERENCE, AND VALIDITY

Learning Objective

After studying this section, you should be able to:

• Describe four categories of scientific inferences.

Conducting research is a grand exercise in critical thinking. Difficult decisions often have to be made at many points along the way: what variables to study, how to operationalize them, how to best analyze the data, what conclusions to draw, and so forth. The critical thinking at each juncture often centers on issues of valid inference. Given the feasible options available to us as we plan and conduct our study, which ones will maximize our ability to make valid claims when we report the findings?

Concerns about valid inference also go to the heart of evaluating claims encountered in everyday life: scientific claims made in media reports, pseudoscientific and advertising claims found on the web and TV, and so on. This chapter highlights the already familiar theme of thinking about "plausible alternative explanations," a theme that I hope you'll apply as an aid to critical thinking in other courses, your career, and everyday events.

CATEGORIES OF INFERENCE

Concerns about validity apply to different kinds of inferences that scientists make (Shadish, Cook, & Campbell, 2002). For example, my conclusion that "heredity influences intelligence" hinges on the validity of several specific inferences:

• *Inferences about constructs.* I've assumed that selective breeding altered the rats' heredity and that maze performance measured their intelligence. If valid, this allows me to talk about my research using the constructs "heredity" and "intelligence."

• *Statistical inferences.* I've inferred from my data analysis that the maze performance difference between the bright and dull strains of rats is unlikely to be the result of mere chance (i.e., it reflects more than mere random variation in performance). If valid, this allows me to claim that my two strains of rats genuinely differed in their maze performance.

• *Causal inferences.* I've inferred that my experimental manipulation (selective breeding)— not some other factor—caused the between-group maze performance differences. If valid, this enables me to claim that a *causal* relation existed between selective breeding and maze performance. If my construct, statistical, and causal inferences are all valid, then I can claim my experiment demonstrated that heredity influenced these rats' intelligence.

• *Inferences about generalizability.* By claiming that heredity influences intelligence, I am inferring that the relation between variables found in my research is generalizable: that it applies not just to this sample of rats and the specific learning task they performed, but to rats and learning tasks more generally. Beyond that, the claim's breadth infers that this relation occurs in other species, such as humans. If this inference about generalizability is valid, then combined with the three other inferences, the causal conclusion drawn from the experiment will not need to be restricted to "selective breeding influenced these particular rats' intelligence as measured using this particular maze."

The types of validity that we'll discuss address these four categories of inference. Following common scientific shorthand, I'll often use phrases such as "validity of an experiment" or "validity of the findings." But strictly speaking, validity applies to *inferences* about studies and findings; not to the studies or findings themselves (Brewer, 2000).

We'll use the selective breeding experiment as an example. As you'll learn momentarily, this experiment was actually performed. As a second example, we'll discuss a human experiment: research by social psychologist Andrew Elliot and his colleagues (2007), in which exposing college and high school students to the color red impaired their achievement performance. If you need to refresh your memory of that experiment or haven't covered it yet, take a minute to read the opening of Chapter 8 (pp. 242–243).

INFERENCE IN TRYON'S SELECTIVE BREEDING PROJECT

Experimental comparative psychologist Robert Tryon initiated a famous, decade-long selective breeding project in 1927, when he was finishing graduate school at the University of California, Berkeley (Tryon, 1930, 1940). Tryon's goal was to demonstrate experimentally that individual differences in psychological qualities, such as learning ability, had a hereditary basis. This research helped to establish a new field of study, initially called "psychogenetics" and subsequently named *behavior genetics,* the term still used today (Hirsch & Tryon, 1956). The following quote helps to place this research in historical context:

> At the time of his work, the nature–nurture issue was being heatedly contested in psychology, and with the ascendancy of behaviorism the exclusively environmental interpretation of the determinants of behavior became near dogma. Tryon's study, elegant and precise, constituted the principal contrary evidence, and almost alone, preserved hereditary concepts from complete obliteration within the psychology of learning. (Krech, Crutchfield, & Ghiselli, 1969, p. 51)

I should emphasize that Tryon did *not* claim in his research reports that he was examining the genetic basis of intelligence. My use of the word *intelligence* in the chapter opening story was intended to stimulate your critical thinking. There has been a hot scientific debate—both then and now—concerning whether intelligence represents a single, general mental capacity (Spearman, 1923), or a collection of fundamental mental abilities such as reasoning, rote memory, and perceptual speed (Thurstone, 1938). Tryon was in the latter camp, believing that there was an "extensive universe" of more specific behavioral competencies (1940, p. 324). He used terms such as "maze-learning ability" and "learning ability" rather than "intelligence," but also believed that maze learning involved mental skill. Tryon concluded that his bright and dull rats differed in cognitive ability as a function of their experimentally controlled heredity.

✓ **CONCEPT CHECK 10.1** CRITICAL THINKING, INFERENCE, AND VALIDITY

In an experiment, college students exhibit higher blood pressure measurements after viewing a crime video than a comedy video. Fill in each of the blanks below. Answers appear on page 343 at the end of the chapter.

1. The statement "the difference in blood pressure measurements between the two conditions is beyond what we would expect simply by chance" is a(n) _____ inference.

2. Based on blood pressure measurements, the statement that participants had higher anxiety after viewing the crime video rather than the comedy video is an inference about _____.

3. The statement "watching the videos influenced participants' blood pressure measurements" is a(n) _____ inference.

4. The statement "in this experiment, participants watched a high-threat (crime video) or low-threat (comedy video) stimulus" is an inference about _____.

TYPES OF VALIDITY

Learning Objectives

After studying this section, you should be able to:

• Explain the concepts of construct validity, statistical conclusion validity, internal validity, and external validity.

• Provide an example to illustrate these types of validity.

Four types of validity—construct, statistical conclusion, internal, and external—are of central concern when conducting experiments (Campbell & Stanley, 1966; Shadish et al., 2002). Chapter 2 introduced the concepts of internal and external validity, and Chapter 4 discussed construct validity. Let's examine how these concepts and statistical conclusion validity apply to Tryon's (1940) and Elliot et al.'s (2007) research.

CONSTRUCT VALIDITY

In the context of experimentation, construct validity applies to both measuring and manipulating variables. Specifically, **construct validity** *concerns the issue of whether the constructs (the conceptual variables) that researchers claim to be studying are, in fact, the constructs that they truly are manipulating and measuring.* To consider an extreme example, if we're examining whether fear increases people's tendency to affiliate with other people, but our experimental conditions only influence how bored participants are—not how afraid they are—then an inference like "We found that fear increased affiliation" is going to be invalid. Something may have influenced affiliation, but it wasn't fear, because we failed to manipulate fear properly.

Construct validity, therefore, is affected by how faithfully the operational definitions of the independent and dependent variables represent the constructs that the researchers intend to study. As Shadish et al. (2002) note, "The operations in an experiment are rarely pure representations of constructs" (p. 75). The question then becomes, do the experimental operations reasonably capture the intended constructs, or are they compromised to a significant degree? Let's look at some examples.

Example 1: Heredity and Learning Ability It's one thing to claim that "selective breeding produced differences in maze performance errors between two strains of rats." It's quite another to claim that heredity (genetics) produced differences in the rats' cognitive ability. The first statement is a causal inference at an operational level; the second, a causal inference at a conceptual level. Construct validity concerns the validity of the leap from the operational to the conceptual level.

Does selectively breeding generations of rats constitute a valid operational definition of the construct we call "heredity"? Does it really alter organisms' genetic makeup? Clearly, the answer is yes (Hedrich, 2006). What then about Tryon's dependent variable: performance errors? Tryon considered several operational definitions of "maze learning ability": number of errors, amount of time to reach the end of the maze, number of trials needed to run the maze without making any errors, and an overall score combining all three factors. He examined the properties of each measure and decided that "number of errors" was the most valid one.

Because Tryon also used maze performance to infer cognitive ability, we must consider the construct validity of this inference as well. Tryon's labels of "bright" and "dull" go to the heart of the matter. Consider whether any of the following terms might be just as appropriate for labeling the best- and worst-performing rats:

- "inquisitive" versus "uninquisitive" (rats who make more errors do so because they are more inquisitive about exploring the maze);

- "keen-vision/olfaction" versus "dull-vision/olfaction" (rats who make more errors do so because they have poorer vision or a less keen sense of smell);

- "motivated" versus "unmotivated" (rats who make more errors do so because they are less strongly motivated by the food reward);

- "fearful" versus "not fearful" (rats who make more errors do so because they are more fearful in new environments, and their fear interferes with learning).

You can see that the question of construct validity concerning Tryon's dependent variable boils down to the following: "What underlying attribute(s) did maze performance really measure?" Did heredity influence the rats' cognitive ability, or did it instead influence their sensory capabilities, motivational traits, or emotionality?

Tryon conducted a great deal of painstaking research to answer this question. He noted:

> Our experiments . . . indicate that the difference is not one of sense acuity . . . but rather the capacity to develop abstract spatial orientations as defined by the maze path. In addition to this cognitive difference . . . [b]right rats appear to be more emotionally disturbed in non-maze situations, whereas the dulls show more disturbance in the maze proper. . . . [B]rightness and dullness turns out dynamically to be an exceedingly complex affair. (Tryon, 1942, p. 358)

Tryon (1940) concluded that the main difference between the bright and dull rats lay in a specific cognitive ability to form spatial orientations. Controversy continued, however, over whether Tryon's rat strains primarily differed in cognitive or noncognitive attributes, and whether he had assessed a highly specific or more general maze-learning ability (Rosenzweig, 2007). In any case, his rigorous research program provided some of the first sound scientific evidence that heredity influenced a species' psychological characteristics. It is worth noting that descendants of Tryon's rat strains were used in research for decades. Among the findings: It appears that the maze-bright rats have a stronger liking for alcohol than do maze-dull rats (Amit & Smith, 1992). Do not, however, take this as evidence supporting the sorely mistaken belief that drinking makes you smarter!

Example 2: Color and Achievement Performance Turning briefly to Elliot et al.'s (2007) color–achievement performance experiments, construct validity would involve asking two questions: (1) Is exposing students to a large red, green, or black code number on a booklet a valid manipulation of "color"? (2) Are scores on anagram and arithmetic tasks a valid measure of "achievement performance"? In some experiments, Elliot et al. also tested the hypothesis that exposure to red would arouse more avoidance motivation (i.e., fear of failure) than would other colors. They measured the construct of avoidance motivation by recording students' physiological responses and giving them a choice to work on an easy or moderately difficult task. Selection of the easy task was taken as evidence of avoidance motivation. Are these valid measures? Fortunately, prior research had already established the construct validity of these measures. This is one example of how researchers build on the work of scientists who came before them.

STATISTICAL CONCLUSION VALIDITY

Statistical conclusion validity *concerns the proper statistical treatment of data and the soundness of the researchers' statistical conclusions.* The key question boils down to this: When the researchers concluded that there was or was not a statistically significant (i.e., nonchance) relation between the independent and dependent variables, was this conclusion based on appropriate statistical analyses?

Scientists rely on their experience and knowledge of accepted practices in their field to guide their approach to statistical analysis, and they may consult with expert statisticians. When scientists submit research reports to peer-reviewed journals, the reviewers' judgments about statistical conclusion validity will factor heavily into the decision over whether the report should be accepted for publication. If reviewers believe the statistical analyses were inadequate, but that in other respects the study has scientific merit, they may recommend that the researchers revise or perform additional statistical analyses and resubmit the report for publication.

Examples: Heredity–Learning and Color–Achievement

Tryon (1940, 1942) rigorously analyzed his data on rats' maze performance. He had a keen interest in statistical issues and wrote articles and books on advanced statistical techniques. Yet, one the most compelling presentations of his findings was elegantly simple. As mentioned earlier, the data in Figure 10.1 represent the average performance of each generation of maze-bright and maze-dull rats.

But perhaps many bright and dull rats did not differ significantly from each other in maze performance, and the average difference between the two groups of each generation resulted from the extremely good or extremely poor performance of only a small number of rats. To investigate this possibility, Tryon examined the distribution of all the performance scores for each generation. He found that by the seventh generation, the vast majority of maze-bright rats were performing better than even the top performers in the dull group.

We can see a different example of careful data analysis in Elliot et al.'s (2007) research, which included several advanced features that enhanced statistical conclusion validity. Because Elliot and his co-workers randomly assigned participants in their first experiment on anagram performance to the red, green, and black conditions, we can assume that these three groups were equivalent overall in their anagram ability at the outset of the experiment. But rather than rest on this assumption, the researchers obtained a premeasure of participants' anagram ability, as well as their self-reported SAT scores (as a general measure of academic ability) and used these variables as statistical controls in the analysis. Thus, even after random assignment, to whatever extent participants in the three color conditions differed overall in their premeasure anagram performance or SAT scores, the statistical analysis would have adjusted for those differences.

Statistical Issues

Although the statistical treatment of data may seem like a cut-and-dried topic, it's anything but. *Quantitative psychology* is a subfield that specializes in issues concerning research design, the measurement of variables, statistical analysis, and mathematical models of behavior. Lively (and highly technical) debates abound among quantitative and other psychologists about optimal ways to analyze various types of data.

Inferential statistical tests for determining statistical significance typically require that certain assumptions be met in order for a particular test to be used in a valid manner. For example, the proper use of some statistical tests assumes that there is a certain minimum number of observations in each cell of a research design. Another assumption involves the scale of measurement. Some statistical tests are designed for use with variables that have been measured on an interval or ratio scale, other tests can be used for variables measured on an ordinal scale, and still others are needed when the measurement scale is nominal.

A third assumption for some statistical tests involves the pattern—the distribution—of scores in a data set. For example, you probably have heard of the term "bell curve." More formally, this is a mathematical concept called a *normal distribution,* which portrays a hypothetical distribution for a population of scores. The mean, median, and mode are identical and 50% of the cases fall on either side of the mean. As scale values move further away from the mean, the frequency of cases becomes progressively smaller. This produces a symmetric curve that peaks in the middle. You can see an example on page 429 in Statistics Module 6. Some inferential statistical tests, such as analysis of variance discussed in Chapters 8 and 9, assume that the data being analyzed take the form of (or at least approximate) a normal distribution.

If a researcher uses a statistical test when the requisite statistical assumptions are violated, statistical conclusion validity will be compromised. The question is, by how much? There is a longstanding debate among statistical experts about whether some frequently used statistical tests are "robust" to certain types of violations (Rasch & Guiard, 2004). "Robust" means that a statistical test can yield accurate results (or that the amount of error will only be slight) even if a data set violates the test's statistical assumptions. However, even if one sides with experts who argue that some tests are robust to certain violations, violating other assumptions of these tests can severely compromise statistical conclusion validity (Erceg-Hurn & Mirosevich, 2008).

INTERNAL VALIDITY

Statistical conclusion validity allows us to claim that there is an association between the independent and dependent variables, and that it's unlikely this relation is due merely to chance (i.e., to random variations in behavior). But, statistical conclusion validity alone does not enable us to conclude that the relation is *causal*. To conclude that the independent variable was responsible for producing the changes in the dependent variable, we need to be confident that other factors were not responsible.

Internal validity *concerns the degree to which we can be confident that a study demonstrated that one variable had a causal effect on another variable.* In other words, in an experiment, can we conclude that it truly was exposure to the different conditions of the independent variable—rather than some other factor—that caused the differences in the dependent variable? Inferences about causality have internal validity when the research design and experimental procedures are sound and thus enable us to rule out plausible alternative explanations for the findings. Poor internal validity results from the presence of confounding variables that provide a reasonable alternative explanation for why participants' responses differed, overall, across the various conditions of the experiment.

Examples: Heredity–Learning and Color–Achievement

In Tryon's (1940) experiments, was it really the selective breeding manipulation that caused the two strains of rats to differ in their overall maze performance? Or could other factors have been responsible? He knew that the bright and dull strains had to live, and be tested, under equivalent environmental conditions. Otherwise, critics could argue that environmental factors—not selective breeding—caused the maze-bright rats to perform better.

Tryon housed maze-bright and maze-dull rats together in the same cages until they were tested, fed them the same food, and gave them equivalent care. Once testing began, the rats were housed in individual cages under equivalent, automated conditions. General handling by humans was kept to a minimum, and to completely avoid handling immediately before and after running the maze, a mechanical system was invented to deliver the rats to the maze and retrieve them from it. The two strains of rats performed the same maze under equivalent illumination and were given the same food reward at the end. These are just some of the extensive environmental controls Tryon used. By rigorously controlling for key potential confounding variables, Tryon greatly enhanced the internal validity of his causal conclusions.

In similar fashion, researchers conducting human experiments strive to anticipate potential confounding factors and design experiments to eliminate or minimize them. Elliot et al.

(2007) tried to ensure that their independent variable—exposure to red or green or an achromatic color—was the only situational variable that differed systematically across the various conditions in the experiment. For example, it would have been poor procedure to require each red-condition participant to perform the task in one room and the other participants to perform in a more pleasant room. If the "red" room was smaller, had less comfortable chairs or distracting artwork on the wall, had poorer ventilation or temperature control, or was noisier because it happened to be located next to another lab where construction was ongoing, then it would be plausible to argue that any of these differences—not the color red—caused the students' poorer performance.

EXTERNAL VALIDITY

External validity *concerns the generalizability of the findings beyond the present study.* Here are some examples of questions that pertain to external validity:

- *Generalization across populations.* Does exposure to red impair intellectual performance among schoolchildren, among adults who aren't students, and among people who live in cultures where red isn't artificially associated with stimuli that signal threat (e.g., stop signs, red ink from teachers' grading)? If research shows that cognitive-behavioral therapy reduces severe depression among Hispanic American women, will the therapy be effective in treating depression among men and adolescents; among African, Asian, and Caucasian Americans; and among people who are moderately or mildly depressed?

- *Generalization across settings.* Does exposure to red impair performance at other intellectual tasks, at physical strength tasks, and at tasks requiring fine perceptual-motor coordination? Does red impair performance during actual classroom exams? If a laboratory experiment reveals a serial position effect (enhanced recall for the first and last few items in a list) when people are shown a list of 15 words and immediately recall the words, will the serial position effect occur when the stimuli are photos of faces, or when people are asked to recall the items after a time delay? Would the serial position effect occur when trying to recall lists of items in real-life settings, such as at the supermarket, when you can't access a grocery list because your cell phone ran out of power?

Although we might consider this an aspect of generalization across populations, for nonhuman animal research a specific concern is:

- *Generalization across species.* Does Tryon's finding that heredity influences rats' cognitive ability generalize to humans? Do findings on brain functioning, hormonal influences, drug effects, schedules of reinforcement, and developmental processes obtained in nonhuman animal experiments generalize to humans?

Ecological Validity and the Realism of Experiments

Imagine 10 research teams around the globe conduct laboratory experiments that find, as Elliot et al. (2007) did, that exposure to the color red impairs performance on intellectual tasks. Even if every experiment studied college students and used the same task (e.g., anagrams), these findings would support the external validity of Elliot and co-workers's original conclusion; that is, they demonstrate the same color–performance relation among participants from different cultures and geographic regions. If some experiments studied children, others adolescents, and others young adults and older adults, this would further broaden the external validity of the original conclusion by establishing a relation between color exposure and intellectual performance across diverse age groups.

Still, an important question remains: "Do people behave in real life as they do in our experimental laboratories?" (Bem & Lord, 1979, p. 833). Does the color–performance relation established in all these laboratory experiments generalize to real-life settings, such as classrooms and the workplace, where people perform intellectual tasks? The concept of *ecological validity* encompasses this question. **Ecological validity** *concerns the degree to which responses obtained in a research context generalize to behavior in natural settings* (Schmuckler, 2001). Some psychologists view ecological validity as a subset of external validity (Brewer, 2000). That is, the question of external validity asks whether research conclusions are generalizable to other settings, and this includes both other laboratory and real-life settings. Thus, if a field experiment conducted in high schools finds that exposure to red impairs performance on classroom assignments, this would help establish the ecological validity—and also the broader external validity—of the inference that the color red impairs intellectual performance.

Ecological validity is also often discussed in reference to how well the research setting and methods—such as the tasks, stimuli, and procedures used in a laboratory experiment—correspond to what people encounter in daily life (Schmuckler, 2001). Some experimenters believe it is important to use tasks and procedures that are as ecologically valid as possible, because this will increase the likelihood that research findings will generalize to settings in the real world. Others emphasize that using ecologically valid tasks in the laboratory hardly guarantees that research findings will generalize to real-life situations, and note that many important psychological principles have resulted from laboratory experiments that employed tasks dissimilar to those encountered in everyday life (Banaji & Crowder, 1989).

Similarly, social psychologist Elliot Aronson and his colleagues (Aronson, Wilson, & Brewer, 1968) argue that at least in terms of uncovering principles of human social behavior, *mundane realism*—the surface similarity between the experimental environment and real-world settings—is less important than psychological realism. *Psychological realism* represents the degree to which the experimental setting is made psychologically involving for participants, thereby increasing the likelihood that they will behave naturally rather than self-monitor and possibly distort their responses.

Establishing Generalizability

Evidence for or against external validity accrues over time as scientists replicate (i.e., repeat) and build on the original research. **Replication** *refers to the process of repeating a study in order to determine whether the original findings will be upheld.* Because replication is so central to science, we'll explore different replication strategies in a separate section at the end of the chapter.

Once researchers choose to investigate a topic, they have to start somewhere in terms of deciding whom to study, what tasks to use, what the general setting will be, and so forth. No single study will be able to satisfy all questions about external validity, but even in their initial research on a topic, experimenters can take some steps to increase confidence in the external validity of their findings.

For example, scientists can replicate their own studies within their initial research project. This is the approach Elliot et al. (2007) took in their color–achievement performance research. Their journal article reported findings from six experiments, four of which focused on the effects of color on achievement performance. Each experiment employed only one participant population, task, setting, mode of presenting the color, and set of control condition colors. But across the four experiments, Elliot et al. varied these factors. Thus, their research report provided some initial evidence for the external validity of their color–performance finding across different populations (American college students, German college students, German high school students); tasks (anagrams, analogies, and numerical problems); settings (laboratory, classroom); mode of presenting the color (colored ID code, partly colored cover sheet on test booklet); and control condition colors (green, and either black, gray, or white).

Before we examine several threats to validity in depth, let's explore one more example of these four types of validity. In this example, the claim is that eating chocolate temporarily boosts people's happiness, and two researchers have tested this claim by conducting a single-factor between-subjects experiment with two conditions: one in which randomly assigned participants consume a large bar of chocolate, and another in which randomly assigned participants do not eat anything. Five minutes later, participants complete a questionnaire, and the key item (for the researcher's analysis) is one in which participants rate their happiness on a 5-point scale. The results indicate that the mean happiness rating is higher in the chocolate condition than in the no-chocolate condition, and the researchers conclude that their hypothesis is supported: Eating chocolate temporarily boosts people's happiness. Figure 10.2 illustrates how the concepts of construct, internal, statistical conclusion, and external validity can be used to generate questions that help us evaluate the truthfulness of the researchers' conclusion.

 CONCEPT CHECK 10.2 TYPES OF VALIDITY

Dr. Choi tests the hypothesis that providing people with high rather than low social support will reduce their stress. Results support the hypothesis. Match each concept on the left to the proper item on the right. Answers appear on page 343.

1. Internal validity

    (a) Do the findings generalize to other populations and settings?

2. Construct validity

    (b) Was the data analysis appropriate and properly conducted?

3. External validity

    (c) Did the experimental manipulation truly create high and low social support, and not something else? Did the measurement techniques truly assess stress?

4. Statistical conclusion validity

    (d) Was it exposure to the independent variable that truly caused the changes to the dependent variable?

BASIC THREATS TO INTERNAL VALIDITY

Learning Objectives

After studying this section, you should be able to:

- Define and illustrate seven basic threats to internal validity.
- Identify the threats that properly conducted experiments control, and explain why they are controlled.

Because the goal of experimentation is to investigate causal relations, we'll now focus on several types of confounding variables that can threaten a study's internal validity (Campbell & Stanley, 1966; Shadish et al., 2002). To illustrate them most easily, we'll first cover a study that exposes participants to a treatment, but lacks some key aspects of experimental control. Then we'll examine how more highly controlled experiments attempt to address these validity threats.

SEVEN SOURCES OF THREAT

Suppose Dr. Rodriguez wants to assess the effectiveness of a new form of psychotherapy for severe depression among adults who are not taking antidepressant medication. Fifty-four depressed adults apply to participate. To measure their depression, Dr. Rodriguez interviews them and administers a psychological inventory. She selects the 20 most severely depressed adults. Before therapy begins, another clinical psychologist observes video recordings of the interviews and rates each participant's level of depression. Therapy lasts for 14 weeks.

APPLYING FOUR TYPES OF VALIDITY TO QUESTION A CAUSAL CLAIM

Based on the results of a laboratory experiment in which college students either eat 1.5 ounces (42.5 grams) of a dark chocolate bar or don't eat anything, two researchers conclude that the findings support their hypothesis: Consuming chocolate temporarily increases happiness. What questions should we ask to evaluate whether this causal claim is valid?

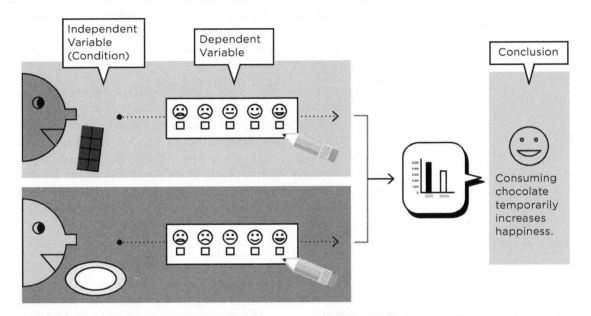

Construct Validity

Did the researchers truly manipulate and measure the constructs they claimed to be studying?

- Was the operational definition of *chocolate consumption* reasonable, including the quantity, type, and form of chocolate used? Did this two-condition design only manipulate chocolate consumption, or did it also manipulate other constructs (e.g., food consumption)? Were more comparison conditions or different procedures needed to better isolate the construct of chocolate consumption?

- Was the self-report rating scale a valid measure of happiness? Should other measures (e.g., facial expressions) have been used or added? If so, what evidence supports their validity?

- Were the research design and number of measurements adequate to capture the construct of a temporary change in happiness?

Statistical Conclusion Validity

Are the differences in scale ratings between the chocolate and no chocolate conditions unlikely to be due solely to chance?

- Were the statistical tests appropriate for the types of data collected?

- Were the results of the statistical analyses interpreted properly?

Internal Validity

Was it the manipulation of the independent variable—rather than another factor—that caused any differences between conditions on the dependent variable?

- Were participants in the experimental versus control conditions differentially exposed to other situational factors that might plausibly account for the results? Or, did the research design and procedures control for exposure to such factors?

- Can preexisting differences in participants' characteristics plausibly account for the results, or did the research design and procedures (e.g., random assignment) control for this?

- If attrition (i.e., a loss of participants) occurred, can differences between conditions in attrition rates or reasons for attrition plausibly account for the results?

External Validity

Is it valid to infer that the findings generalize to other stimuli, populations, and settings? Do the findings reproduce when the study is replicated:

- using different amounts and types of chocolate, and types of chocolate products?

- across different age groups, cultures, and other population characteristics?

- in different settings (at home alone, at parties)?

Dr. Rodriguez then re-administers the psychological inventory and the other psychologist observes and rates each participant again. Notice that in designing her study this way, Dr. Rodriguez exposes all participants to the same treatment; there is no control condition (e.g., no comparison group that does not receive the treatment). Dr. Rodriguez analyzes the scores taken prior to (pretest) and after (posttest) treatment and finds that, on average, after treatment participants are only mildly depressed. She concludes that her treatment reduces depression. Let's now examine several factors that potentially threaten the validity of this conclusion.

History

History *refers to events that occur while a study is being conducted, and that are not a part of the experimental manipulation or treatment.* For example, during Dr. Rodriguez's 14-week study, perhaps the national or local economy improved, reducing participants' financial stress and fears about losing their jobs. Perhaps therapy began in the gloom of winter and ended in the spring, substantially reducing a few participants' depression. Of course, neither these nor other confounding external events might have occurred, but Dr. Rodriguez's research design doesn't rule out history as a potential confounding variable. Whether history rises to the status of a plausible confounding variable will depend on the events that took place during this period.

Maturation

Maturation *refers to ways that people naturally change over time, independent of their participation in a study.* This includes changes in cognitive and physical capabilities that occur with aging, fluctuations in alertness and fatigue that accompany biological rhythms, and normal recovery from physical illness or psychological disorders. Maturation also includes the general accrual of knowledge and skills as we gain more experience over time.

In Dr. Rodriguez's study, maturation is a plausible confound because many people who suffer from major depression experience full or partial recovery over time, even without treatment. This type of recovery is called *spontaneous remission,* and it occurs with many disorders and illnesses. For example, based on a meta-analysis of 19 studies, Whiteford et al. (2013) estimated that among adults whose major depression is not treated, 23% will no longer be depressed within 3 months, and 53% will experience remission within a year.

Testing

Testing *concerns whether the act of measuring participants' responses affects how they respond on subsequent measures.* For example, Dr. Rodriguez's participants took the same depression inventory twice, and we don't know whether their pretest experience affected their posttest scores. The second time around, people are more familiar with the testing format and environment, they may be more or less anxious due to their prior testing, and so forth. Thus, we can't rule out the possibility of a testing confound. Changes in motivation or practice habits that occur in response to taking a performance pretest also illustrate testing effects (Shadish et al., 2002).

Instrumentation

Instrumentation *refers to changes that occur in a measuring instrument during the course of data collection.* Suppose you buy a cheap scale and weigh yourself weekly for a year. You believe you've lost 8 pounds, but actually the scale's cheap springs have worn so that by now it consistently underestimates your weight by 3 pounds. This would be an example of an instrumentation confound.

Dr. Rodriguez used the identical psychological inventory for the pretest and posttest, so there's no instrumentation confound with that measure. But, there's another measuring instrument: the clinical psychologist who provided pretest and posttest ratings after observing each participant. When observers measure behavior, systematic changes in their performance during a study represent instrumentation effects. Such effects could result from factors such as observer illness or fatigue, gaining experience with a rating or coding system, and nonconsciously adopting different criteria when deciding how to rate or categorize a response. In Dr. Rodriguez's study, there's no way to know whether the observer's measurement approach remained consistent from start to finish.

Regression to the Mean

Regression to the mean *is the statistical concept that when two variables are not perfectly correlated, more extreme scores on one variable will be associated overall with less extreme scores on the other variable.* Imagine that 2,000 students each flip a coin 10 times (variable A) and repeat this (variable B). On variable A, some students obtain scores of 9 or 10 Heads, and others 1 or 0 Heads. Take these high- and low-scoring groups: On average, their scores on variable B (i.e., the number of Heads on the second round of 10 flips) will regress toward—be closer to—a mean of around 5 Heads in 10 flips. Regression to the mean also would occur if you were to identify the students who had an extremely high or low number of Heads on the second round: Extreme scores on variable B will be associated, overall, with less extreme scores on variable A.

Dr. Rodriguez selected participants based on their very high pretest depression scores (relative to the adult population). Applying the concept of statistical regression, we would expect that even if participants' degree of actual depression did not change, on average, participants' depression scores will be somewhat lower on a posttest. Because the study involved only one condition (treatment), a problem in interpreting the findings arises. What appears to be a pretest to posttest decrease in depression caused by therapy may, at least in part, reflect statistical regression to the mean.

Attrition

In research, **attrition** (also called **subject loss**) *occurs when participants fail to complete a study.* Attrition can occur for many reasons. In a laboratory, a piece of equipment may malfunction or a participant may feel uncomfortable and not wish to continue. In longitudinal research, some participants may move away, lose interest, become too ill to continue, or die before the study is completed. Attrition is always undesirable, and it poses the greatest threat to internal validity when participants who discontinue differ from those who complete the study in some attribute that could account for the changes obtained on the dependent variable.

Suppose that six of Dr. Rodriguez's 20 participants drop out before the study ends. She examines their pretest depression scores and finds that, overall, these six participants were neither more nor less depressed than the 14 participants who have continued. She contacts the six who discontinued and learns that they dropped out because they perceived (perhaps accurately) they weren't benefitting from the treatment and that further involvement would be a waste of time. We now have a situation in which attrition may have changed the psychological makeup of the research sample: The remaining group of 14 participants now excludes a sizable number of participants who weren't benefitting (or at least felt they weren't benefitting) from the treatment. Perhaps the 14 who remain are less pessimistic, more insightful, or more motivated than the six who dropped out. Whereas comparing the pretest versus posttest scores of the 14 final participants shows a reduction in depression, it's possible that had the six dropouts remained in the study, the pretest–posttest difference in depression might have been smaller or nonexistent.

Table 10.1 Some Potential Threats to Internal Validity

Source	Potential Threat
History	Events to which people are exposed while participating in a study, but that are not part of the experimental manipulation (e.g., the treatment or intervention) being examined.
Maturation	Ways in which people naturally change over time, independent of their participation in a study.
Testing	The act of measuring individuals' responses may affect their responses on subsequent measures.
Instrumentation	Changes that occur in a measuring instrument during the course of data collection.
Regression to the mean	The statistical concept that when two variables are not perfectly correlated more extreme scores on one variable will be associated, overall, with less extreme scores on the other variable. When people selected for a treatment have an extreme pretest mean score and a less extreme posttest mean score (e.g., overall, high depression scores decrease; low performance scores increase), this may partly or fully reflect statistical regression.
Attrition	Also called subject loss; occurs when participants fail to complete a study.
Selection	Refers to the fact that, at the start of a study, participants in the various conditions already differ on a characteristic that can partly or fully account for the eventual results.

Selection

Selection *refers to situations in which, at the start of a study, participants in the various conditions already differ on a characteristic that can partly or fully account for the eventual results.* Dr. Rodriguez's study only included one condition (i.e., therapy), so selection differences would not be a potential confounding variable. **Table 10.1** summarizes the seven sources of threat that we have discussed.

HOW EXPERIMENTS ADDRESS THESE THREATS

To examine how experimenters address these potential threats to internal validity, we'll consider two diverse experiments. The first is Elliot et al.'s (2007) initial color–achievement performance experiment. The second is a redesign of Dr. Rodriguez's therapy effectiveness study.

Example 1: Color and Achievement Performance Elliot and co-workers (2007) exposed college students to the color red, green, or black during one laboratory session per participant. Those exposed to red subsequently performed most poorly on an anagram task.

History. The highly controlled laboratory environment and short duration of each experimental session minimized each student's' exposure to extraneous external events while being studied. More broadly, suppose that during part of the entire time period in which the experiment was conducted, one or more history effects occurred that plausibly might have influenced students' anagram performance (e.g., national or school-related events that might have had an effect on some students' general motivation or concentration). By using a procedure such as block randomization to assign participants to the various conditions, the potential influence of such history effects should be distributed equivalently across those conditions.

History can be a problem if an experiment is poorly executed. For example, if all green-condition participants are studied at the start of a semester and all red-condition participants are studied just before or during the midterm exam period, then history effects related to the time of the semester might confound the results. Block randomization will render this and other history effects (e.g., time of day, day of the week) implausible as confounding variables.

Maturation. Experiments don't prevent maturation, but by randomly assigning participants to conditions, Elliot et al. (2007) could assume that any maturation effects would be equivalent across the various conditions. Therefore, maturation is not a plausible confounding variable.

Testing. Many experiments do not include a pretest because due to random assignment, the participants in the various conditions are, overall, assumed to be equivalent at the start of the experiment. This eliminates the possibility of a testing confound. Elliot et al.'s experiment did involve a pretest, but because all participants took it, testing effects should be equivalent in all the conditions and therefore won't be a confounding variable.

Instrumentation. As long as random assignment (combined with block randomization) or proper counterbalancing procedures are used, then any instrumentation effects that might occur over the course of an experiment should, overall, affect participants in all conditions to an equivalent degree. Instrumentation is unlikely to be a confounding variable.

Regression to the mean. Elliot et al. (2007) did not select participants based on extreme scores. Even if they had, the degree of regression to the mean should be equivalent across conditions as long as participants are randomly assigned. This eliminates regression to the mean as a plausible confounding variable.

Attrition. Attrition can threaten the internal validity of a well-designed experiment. **Differential attrition** *occurs when significantly different attrition rates or reasons for discontinuing exist, overall, across the various conditions.* It suggests that something intrinsic to certain conditions caused attrition and may bias the results. Although we were able to assume that random assignment created equivalent groups at the beginning of our experiment, differential attrition can result in nonequivalent groups by the end of the experiment (Shadish & Cook, 2009). Experimenters should determine why participants discontinue and examine any available pretest scores to determine whether continuing versus discontinuing participants differ, overall, in ways that could plausibly account for the findings. Realize that in many laboratory experiments, attrition may be minimal or nonexistent.

Selection. Experiments involve multiple conditions, and when between-subjects designs are used, the key to preventing a selection confound is to create equivalent groups at the start. This is achieved by randomly assigning participants to conditions, as Elliot et al. (2007) did.

Example 2: Psychotherapy for Depression Suppose that Dr. Rodriguez redesigns her therapy effectiveness study so that it represents a **randomized controlled trial** (also called **randomized clinical trial**): *an experiment in which participants are randomly assigned to different conditions for the purpose of examining the effectiveness of an intervention.* Randomized controlled trials are conducted in fields such as clinical, counseling, health, and educational psychology; and in psychopharmacology, medicine, and nursing.

Pretest depression scores are used to identify severely depressed adults, who are then randomly assigned to therapy or control conditions. Different types of control conditions could be used, and Dr. Rodriguez might include several of them. For simplicity, let's say that she creates a **wait-list control group:** *a group of randomly selected participants who do not receive a treatment, but expect to and do receive it after treatment of the experimental group(s) ends.* The findings indicate that, overall, participants in the two conditions do not differ significantly in level of depression on the pretest, but on the posttest those who received therapy were significantly less depressed than the control group participants.

History. General history effects cannot explain the findings. If the economy improved, if seasons changed, if world peace broke out during the study, all participants would be exposed to those events. Moreover, because participants were randomly assigned, in principle, there is no reason to assume that significant overall history differences will exist regarding personal events (e.g., vacations, job changes, family births).

Maturation, regression, and testing. These are not plausible confounding variables. Participants came from the same population (severely depressed adults) and were randomly assigned. Overall, the participants in the therapy and control conditions should experience equivalent maturation (e.g., spontaneous remission). On average, changes in pretest to posttest depression scores in the two conditions should reflect an equivalent degree of statistical regression. As for testing, all participants took the psychological inventory twice and overall should experience equivalent testing effects.

Instrumentation. Because the same psychological inventory was used for the pretest and posttest, instrumentation is not a plausible confound regarding that measure. As for the psychologist who observed and rated the participants, pretest to posttest differences in experience, fatigue, and rating criteria could cause instrumentation effects. However, if proper procedures are used (e.g., observations of control group and therapy group participants are randomly alternated; the observer is kept unaware of who is in each group), instrumentation effects should be equivalent in both conditions.

Attrition. No matter how well a study is designed, attrition remains a concern. If attrition is high or if differential attrition occurs, Dr. Rodriguez should try to assess whether participants in the two conditions discontinued for different reasons, and decide whether attrition is a plausible alternative explanation for the results.

Selection. Because participants were randomly assigned to conditions, the therapy and control groups are assumed to be equivalent, overall, at the start of the experiment.

 CONCEPT CHECK 10.3 BASIC THREATS TO INTERNAL VALIDITY

Decide whether each statement below is true or false. Answers appear on page 343.

1. Simply by taking the same test twice (e.g., the SAT), participants' mean score improves. This is an instrumentation effect.

2. Outside events cause participants' responses (the dependent variable) to change during a study. This is a history effect.

3. Highly aggressive children are randomly assigned to a behavior therapy or control condition. Mean pretest aggression scores in the two conditions are equivalent. The therapy group shows a larger pre- to posttest aggression score decrease than the control group. Statistical regression is a major confounding variable.

4. Even in a randomized experiment, the potential for attrition remains a concern.

OTHER ISSUES CONCERNING EXPERIMENTAL CONTROL

Learning Objectives

After studying this section, you should be able to:

- Describe how demand characteristics, experimenter expectancy effects, and placebo effects can distort research results, and how these problems can be reduced.

- Explain and illustrate the purpose of yoked control groups.

- Discuss how researchers use pilot studies, manipulation checks, and debriefing to improve the validity of an experiment.

Beyond designing their research to minimize the aforementioned threats to internal validity, behavioral scientists must also anticipate other potential problems that, if left uncontrolled, could become confounding variables. The first five topics in this section, though by no means exhaustive, describe some of the additional control problems that experimenters often face. We'll explore these problems and then discuss ways in which experimenters attempt to address such problems.

DEMAND CHARACTERISTICS

Martin Orne, a psychologist and psychiatrist who studied diverse topics related to psychotherapy (e.g., hypnosis, memory), proposed that when people consent to participate in an experiment, they are entering a social setting that involves its own *implicit norms*—unwritten rules—about how research participants ought to behave (Orne, 1962; Orne & Whitehouse, 2000). One norm calls for participants to assume the *good subject role,* which involves providing responses that help to support the perceived hypothesis of the study. This norm partly arises from people's hope that their responses will contribute to science and the study's success. Orne (1962) suggested that this response distortion typically occurs nonconsciously, just as social norms often shape our daily behavior without our conscious awareness. Although some participants may assume a defiant-subject role and act in ways that will disconfirm the perceived hypothesis, in general, the good-subject role seems to prevail (Nichols & Maner, 2008).

To minimize this response bias, experimenters typically conceal the hypothesis and study's specific purpose from participants until the debriefing session. But, Orne (1962) noted that many participants will still assume the experimenter is "looking for something" and form beliefs about the hypothesis. Research settings provide cues that may shape participants' guesses about the hypothesis. These cues can include the experimenter's behavior, a laboratory's layout, and the nature of the experimental tasks. Orne coined the term **demand characteristics** *to refer to cues that influence participants' beliefs about the hypothesis being tested and the behaviors expected of them.* If demand characteristics lead participants to guess the hypothesis accurately, this may create a plausible alternative explanation if the hypothesis is supported: Were participants' responses influenced by the intended manipulation of the independent variable, by demand characteristics, or by both? (See **Figure 10.3**.)

An Example of Demand Characteristics

Experiments in the 1950s found that depriving people of normal sensory stimulation for hours often produced discomfort and temporarily impaired cognitive performance. Deprivation was achieved in various ways, such as having people lie on a bed in a sound-proofed room, with translucent goggles covering their eyes and pads on their arms and hands to reduce tactile stimulation. Orne and Scheibe (1964) hypothesized that participants' responses might have resulted from demand characteristics. To test this idea, they conducted an experiment that did not involve sensory deprivation but did expose college students to demand characteristics typical of deprivation experiments.

Imagine that you're a participant in such a study, and that you are assigned to the experimental condition. You're told that you will be placed in an "isolation chamber" for 4 hours to examine the effects of sensory deprivation. The room is in a mental health center. The experimenter has a serious demeanor, wears a white lab coat, and asks about your medical history. Nearby is a tray labeled "Emergency Tray" that contains medical items. The experimenter tells you that during the procedure you should speak into a microphone to report any disorientation, hallucinations, or discomfort, because such reactions are "not unusual" (Orne & Scheibe, 1964, p. 5). There's also a

"What it comes down to is you have to find out what reaction they're looking for, and you give them that reaction."

Figure 10.3 Demand characteristics and the good-subject role.

button labeled "Emergency Alarm"; you can push it at any time to end the experiment. You are asked to sign a form releasing the health center and experimenter from legal responsibility for any outcomes.

If instead you are assigned to the control condition, you're told that you are in a control group for a sensory deprivation experiment. You are placed in the same room as the one used in the experimental condition, but the experimenter wears a business suit and acts warmer. There's no "Emergency Tray," no "Emergency Alarm," and you're simply told to report any feelings that you experience. If you want to end the experiment, you can just knock on the window. As in the experimental condition, the room is well lit and relatively quiet (outdoor sounds can be heard), there are comfortable chairs, and food and water. Your eyes aren't covered, and you can move about, as could the "sensory deprivation condition" participants. The room is definitely not an isolation chamber. As Orne and Scheibe (1964) predicted, students exposed to the bountiful demand characteristics reported significantly more "deprivation symptoms" (e.g., perceptual disturbances). Afterward, they performed more poorly than control group participants on many cognitive tasks that had been used in actual deprivation experiments.

Addressing Demand Characteristics

Suspicion probes—conversational strategies conducted during debriefing in which experimenters explore participants' beliefs about the study and its hypothesis—are probably the most common approach to addressing whether demand characteristics influenced participants' behavior. As Orne (1962) and other experienced researchers emphasize, for suspicion probes to be effective, the experimenter first needs to establish rapport with participants during debriefing, introduce the probes gradually, begin probing prior to revealing the true hypothesis, and progressively pursue the participants' beliefs in greater depth if they initially claim that they weren't aware of the hypothesis. Particularly before rapport is established, abruptly asking participants direct questions such as "What do you think the purpose of the study was?" or "Our hypothesis was X. Were you aware that this is what we were testing?" may elicit untruthful answers from many participants who did, in fact, know or figure out the hypothesis (Nichols & Maner, 2008; Orne, 1962).

Other approaches to addressing demand characteristics include:

- increasing the psychological realism of the experiment so that participants will be more involved in the situation and thus more likely to behave spontaneously;

- pilot testing the experiment to help identify potential demand characteristics ahead of time;

- using dependent measures that are unobtrusive or more difficult for participants to distort (such as measures of nonverbal behaviors or certain physiological responses);

- avoiding within-subjects designs when participants' exposure to all the conditions will likely increase their awareness of the hypothesis (e.g., in a color–achievement experiment, receiving materials with green markings in one condition and red and gray markings in other conditions may cue participants that the hypothesis deals with color);

- identifying participants who do claim versus those who don't claim to have been aware of the hypothesis, and analyzing their results separately to gain insight into whether this knowledge affected their responses;

- manipulating participants' knowledge of the hypothesis (e.g., tell some the hypothesis, tell others the opposite hypothesis, and don't inform others) to determine whether this affects their responses on the dependent variables (Allen & Smith, 2012).

Finally, there's the so-called *red herring technique* (Laney et al., 2008). The phrase "red herring" refers to diverting people's attention from a real issue by raising an irrelevant issue. In this approach, researchers tell participants a fictitious story about the experiment's purpose and also create misleading demand characteristics to divert the attention of any participants who may still be trying to figure out what the experiment "is really about." This procedure can be effective, but has the ethical drawback of adding another layer of deception.

EXPERIMENTER EXPECTANCY EFFECTS

Participants aren't the only ones whose behavior in an experiment can be influenced by beliefs about the study's purpose. Experimenters' knowledge of the hypothesis or nature of the study can bias their behavior as well. Imagine that you are a student in an advanced psychology class on learning and conditioning. As part of a class project on operant conditioning, you and your classmates will be the experimenters for a study of maze learning in laboratory rats. You will care for the rats, train them, and measure their maze performance. Your rats, by the way, are "maze-bright": They have been selectively bred for superior maze learning ability. Some of your classmates also have maze-bright rats, while others have "maze-dull" rats bred for poor maze learning ability. Not surprisingly, after the data are collected and analyzed, the results indicate that the maze-bright rats' performance was indeed superior to the maze-dull rats' performance. There's just one problem: The rats actually came from standard litters that had not been bred for superior or inferior maze learning ability. Based on random assignment, you and your classmates were told that your rats were maze-bright or maze-dull in order to manipulate your expectations about the rats' learning ability. Somehow, as experimenters, your expectations translated into performance score differences by the rats.

In 1963, social-clinical psychologists Robert Rosenthal and Kermit Fode published a report of the experiment described above. For Rosenthal, this was one of several studies in which he manipulated experimenters' expectations about how their human or nonhuman research subjects would perform, and found that these expectations influenced the subjects' performance. Rosenthal concluded that the experimenters were not falsifying data or consciously acting in a biased manner. Rather, they seemed to be influencing their participants in subtler ways. This type of bias is called **experimenter expectancy effects,** *unintentional ways in which researchers influence their participants to respond in a manner consistent with the researchers' hypothesis.*

Experimenter Expectancy Effects and Experimenter Behavior

Mental imagery research by cognitive psychologist Margaret Intons-Peterson (1983) suggests one way in which experimenters' expectancies can bias their behavior and, in turn, influence participants' performance. In one study, four advanced undergraduates served as experimenters. Participants performed a reaction time task in which, on each trial, an image of a hand was flashed on a monitor. They had to decide as quickly as possible whether it was a left or right hand and then press a button marked "L" or another marked "R." Immediately before each reaction time trial, participants were "primed" (i.e., psychologically readied) for that trial in one of two ways:

1. A signal on the monitor instructed the participant to form a mental image of a hand (this condition was called *imaginal priming*), or
2. The monitor flashed a drawing of an outline of a hand and the participant merely had to look at it (this condition was called *perceptual priming*).

Intons-Peterson (1983) led two experimenters to expect that imaginal priming would lead to faster reaction times, and the other two to expect that perceptual priming would produce faster reaction times. The experimenters were trained in reading a set of typewritten,

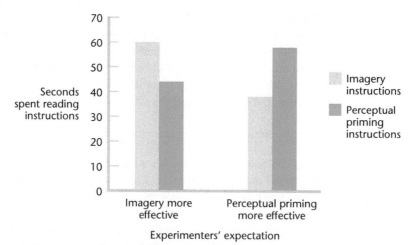

Figure 10.4 Experimenter expectancy effects. Experimenters led to believe that mental imagery would produce faster reaction times spent more time reading imagery instructions to participants. Experimenters led to believe that perceptual priming would produce faster reaction times spent more time reading those instructions. (Adapted from Intons-Peterson, 1983.)

standardized instructions to each participant. During the reaction time task, the experimenter and participant were in different rooms; the entire procedure and data collection were automated. The findings revealed that imaginal priming produced faster reaction times than perceptual priming, but only for the experimenters who had been led to expect such an outcome.

How could this have happened when so much of the procedure had been automated? Intons-Peterson (1983) had video-recorded experimenters' behavior. The video analysis revealed that when the experimenters read the task instructions to their participants, experimenters who had been led to expect faster times with imaginal priming read the mental imagery portion of the instructions more slowly than the perceptual priming portion. The opposite pattern emerged for the experimenters who had been led to expect that perceptual priming would produce faster reaction times (**Figure 10.4**). In short, the experimenters gave more emphasis to the portion of the task instructions that fit with their expectations. This may have biased how well participants understood the different portions of the tasks, or it may have provided a cue—a demand characteristic—that participants noticed and that subsequently influenced their task behavior.

Addressing Experimenter Expectancy Effects

Although research on experimenter expectancy effects has had its share of controversy, behavioral scientists widely acknowledge the potential for experimenters' expectations to influence participants' responses (Brown, 2007). Rigorously training experimenters to follow a well-scripted research protocol is a starting point in attempting to minimize experimenter expectancy effects. Whether dealing with how experimenters care for and test nonhuman animal subjects, or emit verbal and facial cues that express a warm or cool demeanor to human participants, it's important for researchers to standardize the experimenters' behavior as much as possible (Schellinck, Cyr, & Brown, 2010).

A second approach is to carry standardization further by automating participants' instructions and the procedures for presenting tasks and collecting data. In his selective breeding experiments, Tryon (1940) used a maze that was highly advanced for its time: It employed mechanical sensors tied to an electrical scoring system to record the rats' errors. Of course, as we saw earlier in the research using left- and right-hand images by Intons-Peterson (1983), even with automation, experimenter expectancy effects can occur (although she did not automate the task instructions). Experimenters still greet participants, answer questions, and clarify procedures, opening up opportunities for expectancy effects to operate.

A third approach is to use **masking** (also called **blinding**), *a procedure in which the parties involved in an experiment are kept unaware of:*

- *the hypothesis being tested, and/or*

- *the condition to which each participant has been assigned.*

Keeping an experimenter blind to the hypothesis being tested is accomplished by assigning the role of experimenter to someone other than the researchers who have designed the study. In an academic setting, advanced undergraduates may join a research team, serve as experimenters, and be masked to the hypothesis until the experiment ends.

Masking an experimenter to a participant's assigned condition is a common procedure. In Elliot et al.'s (2007) color–achievement performance experiments, the experimenters were (1) not told the hypothesis and (2) prevented from seeing whether each participant had red or green or achromatic stimulus materials. With these procedural controls, experimenter expectations are not a plausible alternative explanation for the findings. In fact, even if experimenters know the hypothesis, masking them to each participant's condition is an effective approach for controlling experimenter expectancy effects.

In some studies, keeping the experimenter masked may require the use of multiple experimenters. Suppose we compare two reading strategies and hypothesize that strategy A will produce better performance on easy material, but strategy B will yield better performance on difficult material. Experimenter 1 trains each participant to use strategy A or B, based on random assignment. However, using masking, Experimenter 1 does not know whether the participant will perform the easy or difficult reading task. Experimenter 2 interacts with each participant during the reading task, but does not know whether the participant was taught strategy A or B by Experimenter 1. In this manner, even if both experimenters know the hypothesis, it is difficult to argue that their expectations systematically biased the results.

PLACEBO EFFECTS AND PLACEBO CONTROL GROUPS

Suppose that we want to test whether a new drug reduces pain among chronic pain patients. Half of the patients are randomly assigned to receive the drug and the control condition patients don't receive any substance. If the experimental group subsequently experiences less pain than the control group, we can't be sure that the drug's chemical properties produced this result. Perhaps the patients' mere expectation that the drug would help them partly or fully produced their pain reduction. This phenomenon is called a **placebo effect:** *People's expectations about how a treatment will affect them influence their responses (on the dependent variable) to that treatment.*

The Scope of Placebo Effects

Although placebo effects don't always occur, they have been found to influence a wide range of responses, such as immune system and hormonal functioning, sexual arousal, social behaviors, pain, and symptoms of Parkinson's disease (Buhle, Stevens, Friedman, & Wager, 2012). The importance of controlling for placebo effects extends well beyond psychological research on drugs. For example, in clinical research examining the effectiveness of various psychotherapies, and in health psychology research examining whether various interventions (physical exercise, biofeedback, meditation) reduce stress and pain, the possibility exists that changes in participants' mental and physical health may be caused by their expectations that the intervention will be beneficial (Buhle et al., 2012).

Controlling Versus Assessing Placebo Effects

To gain clearer causal information in our chronic pain experiment, we can add a **placebo control group** *in which participants do not receive the core treatment, but are led to believe that they are (or may be) receiving it.* For example, we could inform placebo control patients that they are receiving the drug, but instead administer a *placebo* (e.g., a presumed inert substance such as a starch pill or saline injection) that merely simulates the actual treatment. If the experimental, placebo control, and standard control groups, respectively, experience an overall reduction in pain intensity of 36%, 33%, and 7%, this suggests that the improvement was primarily due to a placebo effect. Conversely, if the respective results reveal a 36%, 11%, and 7% pain intensity reduction, this suggests that the drug's chemical properties produced a large benefit over and beyond a patient's mere expectations.

Double-Blind and Single-Blind Procedures

Experimenters often use masking in conjunction with a placebo control design to produce a **double-blind procedure** *in which neither the participants nor the experimenters are aware of who is receiving the actual treatment and who is receiving a placebo.* This procedure controls for participants' expectations and prevents experimenter expectancy effects. Experimental and placebo control participants are told that they will receive either the real treatment or a placebo, but which one they get is not identified. Experimenters who interact with participants and record their behavior are masked to the participants' condition. Other personnel must diligently keep track of which participants are in each condition (**Figure 10.5**). In a **single-blind procedure,** *either the participants or experimenters, but not both, are masked to the participants' condition.*

Placebo control groups usually are incorporated in a between-subjects design. In some experiments, however, within-subjects designs are used and participants serve as their own placebo control group. For example, health psychologist Jack James (1998) examined the effects of caffeine consumption and withdrawal on people's moods, sleep, cognitive task performance, and headache frequency by having participants take gelatin capsules containing caffeine or a placebo on different occasions over 4 weeks. Each participant engaged in both conditions.

"It was more of a 'triple blind' test. The patients didn't know which ones were getting the real drug, the doctors didn't know, and, I'm afraid nobody knew."

Figure 10.5 When double-blind designs go wrong.

YOKED CONTROL GROUPS

This design is best explained by example, so consider an experiment on REM (rapid eye movement) sleep. During REM sleep, the body is highly aroused and dreaming is most frequent. Different theories exist as to the functions of REM sleep and other sleep stages, and researchers often test these theories by conducting sleep-deprivation experiments.

A night without any sleep increases daytime sleepiness, but does REM sleep deprivation—by itself—increase sleepiness? In a sleep laboratory, we monitor participants during their nightly sleep, and every time a participant enters a REM sleep stage, we awaken the person and keep her or him awake for 15 minutes to minimize the odds that the participant will fall right back into REM sleep. Before and after the deprivation procedure, we measure participants' daytime sleepiness by using a multiple sleep latency test, in which participants nap at five specified times during the day; falling asleep more quickly during the naps indicates greater daytime sleepiness.

We also have a standard control group that sleeps through the night and therefore gets their normal amount of REM sleep. The results indicate that REM-deprived participants are sleepier during the day than the control group. Should we conclude that loss of REM periods causes greater daytime sleepiness? Can you think of at least two confounding variables that provide plausible alternative explanations? Put yourself in the shoes of a REM-deprivation participant. Perhaps your daytime sleepiness has nothing to do with a loss of REM sleep, per se, but instead was caused by (1) having your sleep interrupted multiple times during the night, and/or (2) a loss of total sleep time (i.e., losing 15 minutes of sleep each time the experimenters awakened you). Therefore, we need an additional control group that addresses these confounding factors.

Our best option would be to include a **yoked control group,** *in which each control group member is procedurally linked (i.e., yoked) to a particular experimental group member, whose behavior will determine how both of them are treated.* Typically, yoking is done via random assignment or matching. Let's say Terry is the control group participant who has been yoked to you. Each time you go into REM sleep that night, when I awaken you, my assistant will awaken Terry. If Terry is also in REM sleep at that moment, we'll have to delay the awakening until a non-REM (i.e., NREM) stage. In any case, for each sleep interruption, you and Terry will each be kept up for 15 minutes. By morning, ideally, you and Terry will each have been awakened the same number of times (say, 9 times) and will have lost a similar total amount of sleep. Likewise, if I have to awaken Lavonne and Roberto from REM sleep 12 and 17 times, respectively, then my assistant will awaken Tina (yoked to Lavonne) and Scott (yoked to Roberto) 12 and 17 times from NREM sleep, respectively.

By yoking one control group member to each experimental group member, upon completion of the experiment, the two groups should, overall, have been interrupted from sleep a similar number of times and been kept awake by the researchers for an equivalent total amount of time. Any resulting differences in daytime sleepiness between the two groups cannot be attributed plausibly to confounding created by differences in the number of sleep interruptions or the amount of total sleep lost. Using a similar yoking procedure, Keith Nykamp and his colleagues found that depriving people of REM sleep for 2 days did not affect the participants' daytime sleepiness (Nykamp et al., 1998). In contrast, yoked control participants were sleepier during the day after having their NREM sleep interrupted, a finding consistent with theories proposing that certain NREM stages play the key role in helping the body recover from sleepiness.

Yoked control group designs are used when the procedures applied to each experimental group member—the number of forced sleep awakenings, the amount of reinforcement given for responding correctly—vary because they depend on the participant's own responses (e.g., the number of REM episodes, the amount of correct performance). Adding a yoked control group makes the overall treatment of the experimental and control groups as similar as possible on factors other than the intended manipulation of the independent variable. Psychologists have used yoked control group designs in human and nonhuman animal experiments on a variety of topics, such as learning, memory, and addictive behavior (Nic Dhonnchadha et al., 2012).

CEILING AND FLOOR EFFECTS

To demonstrate that an independent variable influences a dependent variable, there must be room for scores on the dependent variable to differ—to be able to vary—from one condition to another. If we want to examine whether a healthy versus unhealthy school lunch diet influences fifth graders' physical strength, we wouldn't measure arm strength by asking them to lift a feather or a 600-pound weight. Regardless of diet and how we measure arm strength (e.g., how quickly the object is lifted), virtually all fifth graders would lift the feather easily, and virtually none would be able to lift the 600-pound weight. A **ceiling effect** *occurs when scores on a dependent variable bunch up at the maximum score level* (e.g., all students attain the maximum score for lifting the feather). A **floor effect** *occurs when scores on a dependent variable bunch up at the minimum score level* (e.g., all the scores for lifting the 600-pound weight are zero). Ceiling and floor effects are problematic because they can lead us to the false conclusion that an independent variable doesn't influence behavior, when in fact it does.

Let's consider a psychological example. Suppose that in Elliot et al.'s (2007) experiments on the color red, the researchers had used very easy anagrams to measure participants' cognitive performance. And, imagine that the results revealed no statistically significant performance differences: In the red, green, and black conditions, participants solved all or almost all of the anagrams. The findings fail to support the researchers' hypothesis that red impairs performance on cognitive achievement tasks—but is the hypothesis truly incorrect?

On the one hand, in the real world it may be that exposure to red doesn't impair cognitive performance. On the other hand, perhaps in the real world exposure to red truly does impair cognitive performance, but this experiment failed to detect that relationship because of a ceiling effect: The anagram task was so easy that people could have solved it under any circumstance. Conversely, very difficult anagrams could produce a floor effect, resulting in extremely low performance scores in the red, green, and black color conditions. In such a case, it would be difficult to demonstrate that the color red impairs performance because performance already is at such a low level for everyone.

Ceiling and floor effects are examples of *range restriction*—reduced variability in the scores on a dependent measure—a problem that can affect correlational studies as well as experiments (see Chapter 5). Moreover, ceiling and floor effects are not limited to performance tasks. For example, suppose we want to assess whether exposure to violent-crime content in TV dramas and news (as opposed to nonviolent content) increases people's support for tougher crime-control laws. If we use a 5-point rating format (1 = disagree, 5 = agree) to measure people's attitudes and beliefs, but choose items with which virtually anyone would agree (e.g., "Crime is harmful to society"), then a ceiling effect will leave little room to demonstrate that viewing media crime violence can further strengthen such attitudes.

Elliot et al. (2007) reduced the chances that a ceiling or floor effect would occur by pretesting the difficulty of many anagrams and then only selecting items that were moderately difficult. Thus, the researchers developed a dependent measure (the number of anagrams correctly solved) that was sensitive to the potential influence of exposing students to various colors. **Sensitivity** *refers to the ability to detect an effect that actually is present*. A sensitive measure is one that can detect differences or changes that actually occur in a response, even when they are small. Sensitivity also is a term applied to the overall design of an experiment. A sensitive experiment is one that is likely to detect the influence of an independent variable on a dependent variable if indeed, in the true state of the natural world, such an effect exists. Developing sensitive dependent measures, creating strong manipulations of the independent variable, and controlling extraneous variables are all ways to increase the sensitivity of an experiment.

PILOT STUDIES, MANIPULATION CHECKS, AND DEBRIEFING

A **pilot study** *is a trial run, usually conducted with a smaller number of participants, prior to initiating the actual experiment*. It's similar to a shakedown cruise for a ship; it allows the experimenters to practice the procedures, verify that equipment is working properly, and identify potential problems in the way independent variables are manipulated and dependent variables are assessed.

A key difference often found between pilot studies and actual experiments is that, in pilot studies, researchers may debrief participants more extensively at the end of the procedure.

In particular, they seek to gather information about how the participants perceived their experience. What hypothesis, if any, did participants believe was being tested? Were the task instructions clear? If rating scales were used to measure dependent variables, were they easy to understand? Information gained from a pilot study can lead to minor or major adjustments to the procedures, and further pilot testing may be conducted to ensure that problems were corrected. Data collected from a pilot study are not a part of the actual experiment, and should not be combined with the responses that are recorded once the full experiment begins.

In pilot studies and experiments, researchers often include **manipulation checks,** *measures to assess whether the procedures used to manipulate an independent variable successfully captured the construct that was intended.* For example, if the experimental condition task is supposed to be arousing, and the control condition task is designed to be boring, do the two tasks actually create these different reactions in participants? In a pilot study, if manipulation checks (e.g., self-report ratings of arousal, boredom) reveal that the independent variable manipulation is not functioning as intended, then the procedures can be redesigned and retested prior to conducting the actual experiment.

After each participant completes the research procedures, the experimenter conducts a **debriefing,** *a conversation with the participant that conveys additional information about the study.* Because debriefing is discussed in Chapter 3, I'll just reiterate that debriefing provides the experimenter with opportunities to more fully explain the purpose of the study to participants, and also to gather information about how participants perceived their research experience. During debriefing, the experimenter may further probe whether the manipulation of the independent variable produced its intended effect, and whether participants became clued in to the true purpose of the experiment (if this information was indeed concealed).

✓ **CONCEPT CHECK 10.4** OTHER ISSUES CONCERNING EXPERIMENTAL CONTROL

Fill in each of the blanks below. Answers appear on page 343.

1. If an experimental task is so easy that participants in all conditions perform very well, this is called a _____ effect. If a task is so difficult that everyone performs very poorly, this represents a _____ effect.

2. A cue that influences participants' beliefs about the hypothesis being tested and about how they should behave is called a(n) _____.

3. The purpose of the double-blind procedure is to control for _____ effects and _____ effects.

4. In a _____ control group design, the responses of each experimental group member determine how she or he and a corresponding control group member will be treated.

STRATEGIES FOR REPLICATING RESEARCH

Learning Objectives

After studying this section, you should be able to:

- Identify and illustrate different types of replications.
- Explain the importance of conceptual replications and the strategy of replication and extension.
- Describe why factorial designs are well suited to examining external validity.

As discussed in earlier chapters, self-correction is a basic characteristic of science. The inferences that scientists draw based on their research may be in error for several reasons, including possible flaws in the research design or procedures. In experiments, this may lead to the false conclusion that an independent variable, rather than some confounding factor, influenced the dependent variable. And even in well-executed studies, when data analyses reveal that a finding is statistically significant, this indicates that it is unlikely the results were due solely to chance, but it does not provide an absolute guarantee against this possibility. There is always some risk of sounding a false alarm—of committing a Type I error—when inferential statistical tests lead researchers to conclude that their findings are statistically significant. Thus, the ability to verify scientific findings by replicating the research on which they are based is one of the cornerstones of science. We'll now examine some different approaches to conducting replications. Collectively, they provide a key source of evidence in establishing the internal and external validity of scientific claims.

WHO CONDUCTS THE REPLICATION?

Studies may be replicated by the scientists who conducted the original research or by other scientists. When scientists replicate their own studies, this represents a non-independent replication. One approach to non-independent replication, which Kunert (2016) calls **internal replication,** *occurs when researchers follow up their initial study with one or more replications and present this series of studies in a single research report.* Compared to several decades ago, when the overriding norm was to publish reports of single experiments, internal replications are now more common. As mentioned earlier, Elliot et al. (2007) used this approach in their color–achievement performance research. They replicated their initial experiment three times by testing the same principle with different types of participants, tasks, and methods of manipulating exposure to color. This series of four experiments and two others were presented in a single journal report. Successful internal replication helps researchers' make the case that their initial finding was not a fluke.

In contrast, an **independent replication** *is a replication conducted by researchers who were not part of the original research group.* Two large-scale replication projects in psychology, the Reproducibility Project (Open Science Collaboration, 2015) and the Many Labs Replication Project (Klein et al., 2014), involved independent replications. The scientists in these projects, which we will discuss later in this section, were not part of the original research teams. In general, independent replications are considered to be a stronger source of evidence for reproducibility than non-independent replications.

COMPLETE AND PARTIAL REPLICATION

A **complete replication** (also called **full replication**) *includes all the conditions of the original study;* a **partial replication** *only includes some of the original conditions.* For example, suppose Dr. Nguyen creates low-, moderate-, and high-stress conditions to examine whether stress increases people's food consumption. To fully replicate Dr. Nguyen's experiment, we would include all three stress conditions. If we're only interested in comparing low versus high stress conditions, this would be a partial replication. Similarly, in a recent large-scale project, researchers identified 13 key findings drawn from 12 prior studies and set out to replicate these studies (Klein et al., 2014). For practical reasons, they selected simple studies to replicate: those that typically had only two conditions. But in one case, the original study involved three conditions in which people made judgments about outcomes in gambling events. To get this replication to conform to the two-condition designs of the other replications, they eliminated one condition. Thus, this was a partial rather than a complete replication.

DIRECT REPLICATION

In a **direct** replication (or **exact replication**), *the researchers follow the procedures used in the original study as closely as possible* (Sidman, 1960). Most importantly, they operationalize the independent and dependent variables in the same way as in the original experiment. Thus, to directly replicate Elliot et al.'s (2007) first color–achievement performance experiment, we would use their manipulation of the independent variable (i.e., red, green, and black ID codes) and the same dependent measure (anagram test performance, ideally using their 15 anagrams). We would also replicate other procedural aspects of their study, such as giving participants the same task instructions and testing participants one at a time.

Although this approach is sometimes called "exact replication," there always will be some differences between our experiment and theirs: At a minimum, the participants and/or time period will differ. Elliot et al.'s (2007) participants attended college in upstate New York. If we study college students, ours may attend college in a different geographic region and our sample may differ from theirs in gender and ethnic composition. Moreover, we might decide to directly replicate their procedures, but study a different population, such as schoolchildren or business managers.

If our direct replication reveals that exposure to red impairs performance, this provides evidence that Elliot et al.'s (2007) findings were not a fluke and helps to establish external validity across different types of participants. Conversely, if our findings don't replicate theirs, this raises scientific uncertainty. Were the original results a fluke? Are ours? Or, despite the intended procedural similarity of the two experiments, was there a procedural difference that might account for the disparate results?

Traditionally, at least in many fields within the behavioral and social sciences, direct replications have not been viewed as a prestigious form of research. The reward system for career advancement in science and opportunities for getting one's work published favors research that contributes new ideas (Open Science Collaboration, 2015). But as Anderson and Maxwell (2015) note, "While direct replications were once avoided for lack of originality, historically, authors have recently urged the field to take note of the benefits and importance of direct replication" (p. 3). Two recent and massive replication projects, which we'll discuss shortly, reflect this renewed emphasis on conducting direct replications.

CONCEPTUAL REPLICATION

Especially when the goal of research is to uncover general scientific principles, direct replications leave important questions about external validity unanswered. For example, if every replication of Elliot et al.'s (2007) color experiment used the same operational definitions of "color" and "performance" and confirmed the original findings, then the general inference that "red impairs performance" would rest entirely on the finding that "exposure to a red colored ID code impairs anagram performance." This conclusion might interest hobbyists who enjoy solving "word jumble" games, but would leave scientists wanting more.

What we really want to know is whether the original experiment truly uncovered a general principle that "exposure to the color red impairs achievement performance." To assess this, we must replicate the original experiment with different operational definitions of the constructs "exposure to red" and "achievement performance." This type of study, called **conceptual replication,** *examines the same question investigated in the original study, but operationalizes the constructs differently.* Typically, a conceptual replication operationalizes the independent variable, dependent variable, or both variables in a new way.

Elliot et al. (2007) conceptually replicated their own initial color-anagram experiment. Their color manipulation always included red and green, but the replications used different neutral colors (black, white, gray) and a different method of presenting the color (a colored cover sheet instead of an ID code). Performance was operationalized using different tasks (anagram, analogy, or arithmetic tasks). Because their hypothesis was supported across these various manipulations and tasks, we gain more confidence in the external validity of the principle that "exposure to the color red impairs achievement performance" than would be the case if each experiment had been a direct replication of the first experiment.

REPLICATION AND EXTENSION

A **replication and extension** (also called **replication with extension**) *is a replication that adds a new design element to the original study.* The replication can be full or partial, and direct or conceptual. In experiments, the new design element often involves one or more of the following:

- adding new conditions to an original independent variable;
- adding a new independent variable;
- adding new dependent variables.

Researchers can extend previous studies in other ways, such as by changing the time period over which behavior is measured. In controlled clinical, industrial-organizational, or educational psychology experiments, for example, a long-term follow-up assessment can be added to determine whether the effects of an intervention persist over time (Bolton et al., 2011).

Extending Independent Variables

Adding a new independent variable or new conditions to an existing independent variable is an excellent strategy for assessing external validity. For example, one reason why we might want to add new conditions to an existing quantitative independent variable is to better analyze whether it has nonlinear effects on the dependent variable. Suppose that Dr. Nguyen's original experiment to examine whether stress influences people's food consumption had only included two conditions: low stress and high stress. In our replication and extension, we could add a moderate stress condition. This would enable us to determine whether any effects of high stress that Dr. Nguyen found (e.g., increasing food consumption) would generalize to an intermediate stress level. It would also enable us to examine whether, as stress increases across these three levels, its effect on food consumption is linear or nonlinear.

Researchers add new conditions to qualitative independent variables for many reasons. As an example, suppose a randomized clinical trial reveals that severely depressed adult women who receive cognitive-behavioral therapy (CBT) show greater improvement than severely depressed adult women in a wait-list control condition. We replicate that experiment, but add a third condition: brief psychodynamic therapy. This enables us to determine not only whether the original findings hold up, but also whether psychodynamic therapy is (1) more effective than no therapy, and (2) more or less effective than CBT.[1]

Adding new independent variables allows us to directly examine external validity across populations and settings. For example, in a replication and extension of Dr. Nguyen's stress-food consumption experiment, we could manipulate a second independent variable—the type of food available to people (e.g., high fat content, low fat content)—to examine whether the effects of stress on food consumption generalize across different types of foods. In the therapy effectiveness experiment, we could add a selected independent variable—age, gender, or severity of depression—to examine whether the benefits of CBT generalize across adults and adolescents, women and men, and moderate as well as severe depression.

---

[1] Classic psychodynamic therapy, such as Freudian psychoanalytic therapy, can last for years. Brief psychodynamic therapies would be more comparable in length to CBT. We would not want to confound type of therapy with length of therapy. Also note that wait-list control groups raise ethical issues about delaying participants' treatment. Depending on the length of delay, disorder being treated, and other factors, a researcher may need to use a different type of control condition, such as one that provides a treatment that is standard at the time.

Advantages of Replication and Extension

You might wonder, if our goal is to determine whether CBT is effective in treating, say, adolescents, why we bother to replicate the therapy condition with adults. After all, the original experiment already established that CBT was effective for them. Why not just repeat that experiment, but with adolescents? This approach is common, and it represents one way that scientists build knowledge about external validity. There are two key advantages, however, to studying both the original age group (adults) and a second age group (adolescents) within the same experiment.

First, in order to examine interaction effects, we need to have more than one independent variable. By creating a 2 (CBT/wait-list control) × 2 (adults/adolescents) factorial design, we can now examine whether there is a main effect of therapy, a main effect of age group, and also whether a Therapy × Age interaction occurs. Perhaps we'll find that CBT is effective for both age groups, but significantly more effective for adults.

Second, suppose our replication only includes adolescents. We find that CBT is not effective. Is it valid to conclude that CBT works with adults (original experiment) and not with adolescents (our experiment)? There may be plausible alternative explanations. What if, compared to the original experiment, our therapists weren't as experienced in CBT or our CBT treatment involved fewer sessions? By including both age groups in our experiment, we can expose them to the same therapists and number of sessions. If we replicate the original finding that CBT is effective with adults, then our new finding that CBT didn't benefit adolescents cannot be attributed plausibly to factors such as general therapist experience or the length of therapy.

TWO APPROACHES TO "BIG REPLICATION"

Psychological science took a very public and unflattering hit on August 27, 2015, when news organizations and other media outlets worldwide carried headlines such as "Many Psychology Findings Not as Strong as Claimed, Study Says" (*New York Times*; Carey, 2015, August 27), "Many Psychology Studies Fail Reproducibility Test" (CBC News; Associated Press, 2015, August 27), and "Scientists Replicated 100 Psychology Studies, and Fewer Than Half Got the Same Results" (*Smithsonian Magazine*; Handwerk, 2015, August 27). Even online tech sites (e.g., CNET) covered the story. These reports described the findings of one of the largest research projects ever conducted in psychology: the Reproducibility Project (Open Science Collaboration, 2015).

This project involved 270 scientists across the globe who, in total, performed independent direct replications of 100 recent cognitive and social psychology studies that had been published in major psychology journals. Some studies were experiments, others were correlational, and each of the 100 studies was replicated once. Each replication focused on one key finding from one of the original studies. Overall, only 36% to 47% of these findings were successfully reproduced, depending on the criteria used to judge success.

Yet, only a year earlier, a large-scale Many Labs Replication Project (Klein et al., 2014) offered more optimistic results about the reproducibility of psychological findings. Seventy researchers from around the globe conducted a total of 36 new studies, each of which involved the same set of 13 replications of key findings from classic and recent social psychology studies. Ten findings (77%) were consistently reproduced across the individual studies, and 11 findings (85%) were upheld when the data from all 6,344 participants were analyzed collectively (Klein et al., 2014).

It's not clear why the proportions of successful replication in these two projects were so different. Some critics argue that the disappointing results of the Reproducibility Project were due to flaws in the design, procedures, and analyses (Gilbert, King, Pettigrew, & Wilson, 2016), but the authors of that project have defended their approach (Anderson et al., 2016).

Perhaps the Many Labs Project had more replication success because only studies with relatively simple designs and procedures (e.g., most had only two conditions) were selected for replication. Moreover, for the sake of ensuring diversity, some studies were selected because they had already been successfully replicated by other researchers, and some because their reproducibility had not yet been established.

Most importantly, these two projects serve as a reminder of the importance of conducting replications, and offer two models for doing so. Both illustrate what science journalist Ed Yong (2013) has called "the era of big replication" (p. 1): an independent replication approach in which many research teams at different sites collaborate to assess the reproducibility of prior findings. In the Reproducibility Project, key findings from many prior studies (100) were each subjected to one replication attempt. In the Many Labs Replication Project, a smaller number of prior research findings (13) were each scrutinized in a large number of replications (36). Of course, other approaches to big replication are also possible, such as having many independent research teams focus their replications on the same, single prior study. Whether big replication approaches become more common in the sciences remains to be seen, but at least one massive replication project is currently under way in the field of cancer biology (Center for Open Science, n.d.).

REPLICATION, FACTORIAL DESIGNS, AND EXTERNAL VALIDITY

In conducting replications, factorial designs are ideal for assessing the external validity of previous research findings. Different populations, tasks, stimuli, or other aspects of the setting can be added as a new independent variable and factorially combined with the original independent variables. The conclusions drawn about external validity will depend on the nature of main effects and interactions obtained.

To illustrate, suppose we examine the external validity of Elliot et al.'s (2007) finding that exposure to red impaired achievement performance. They used intellectual tasks. We'll use an intellectual task (solving anagrams) and a physical task (e.g., throwing a ball into a target basket), and will pretest them so that under standard conditions the success rate for each is approximately 50%. We will use a task instruction sheet to manipulate exposure to the color red, green, or gray. Suppose that our 3 (color) × 2 (type of task) experiment yields one of the following results:

1. Red impairs performance on both tasks (main effect, no interaction).
2. Red impairs performance on both tasks, but especially on the intellectual task (main effect plus interaction).

Either finding would support the external validity of the principle that red impairs achievement performance. The second finding tells us that the strength of this effect depends on the type of task.

But imagine that, instead, we find an interaction such that:

3. Red impairs intellectual task performance, but either enhances or does not significantly influence physical performance.

These results offer mixed support for the external validity of the original research findings. On the one hand, we've replicated the finding that red impairs intellectual performance with a different population—say, college students from a different region. On the other hand, we've tentatively established that the principle "red impairs performance" does not generalize to physical tasks. In other words, type of task appears to be a moderator variable. Further research will be needed to replicate this finding and assess how red affects performance at other types of tasks, with different populations, and in real-world settings.

CONCEPT CHECK 10.5 STRATEGIES FOR REPLICATING RESEARCH

Match each numbered concept on the left to the proper description on the right. Answers appear on page 343.

1. direct replication   **(a)** includes all the conditions of the original study; the procedures may or may not differ from the original ones

2. conceptual replication   **(b)** adds new design elements to the original study

3. full replication   **(c)** examines the same variables as the original study, but operationalizes them differently

4. replication and extension   **(d)** attempts to follow the original study's procedures as closely as possible

CHAPTER SUMMARY

- Research involves inferences about constructs, statistical inferences, causal inferences, and inferences about generalizability. Construct validity concerns the issue of whether the constructs (the conceptual variables) that scientists claim to be studying are, in fact, the constructs that they truly are manipulating and measuring in their research. Researchers increase construct validity when they employ operational definitions and other procedures that capture the constructs they intend to study.

- Statistical conclusion validity concerns the proper statistical treatment of data and soundness of statistical conclusions. It allows researchers to claim that associations between independent and dependent variables are genuine and unlikely to be the result of mere chance, but it does not address whether those associations are causal.

- Internal validity allows researchers to conclude that there is a causal relation between the independent and dependent variables. To establish internal validity, the research design and procedures must rule out plausible alternative causal explanations for the findings.

- External validity addresses whether the findings of a study generalize to other populations and situations. Scientists assess external validity by replicating research, using different types of participants and settings.

- Many extraneous variables can threaten a study's internal validity. *History* refers to other events that occur while a study is being conducted. *Maturation* refers to ways that people naturally change with the passage of time, independent of their participation in a study. *Testing* refers to how the act of measuring responses can alter responses on subsequent measures. *Instrumentation* refers to changes that

occur in a measuring instrument during the course of a study. *Regression to the mean* creates ambiguity when groups selected for a treatment have an extreme pretest mean and a less extreme posttest mean. This may reflect statistical regression rather than a true change in the attribute being measured. *Attrition* occurs when participants don't complete a study, and *selection* occurs when participants in various conditions, overall, already differ on a relevant characteristic before the study even begins.

- Properly conducted experiments that use randomized between-subjects designs or counterbalanced within-subjects designs generally control for all these threats, except for attrition. Differential attrition can be an especially serious concern.

- Demand characteristics, experimenter expectancies, and placebo effects can influence participants' behavior. Conducting suspicion probes during debriefing is the most common approach to identifying demand characteristics. Masking procedures and placebo control groups are commonly used to control for experimenter expectancies and placebo effects.

- In some experiments, the procedures applied to each experimental group participant will partly depend on that participant's own behavior. Such experiments often include a yoked control group, in which each control group member is procedurally linked to a particular experimental group member, whose behavior then determines how both of them are treated.

- Ceiling effects and floor effects restrict the range of scores on the dependent variable. They can mask the true effect of an independent variable. A good dependent measure will be sensitive to the potential effects of an independent variable.

- Before conducting an experiment, researchers often perform pilot studies. Manipulation checks determine whether the manipulation of the independent variable is functioning as intended, and postsession debriefing enables experimenters to learn how participants perceived their experience.
- There are distinct strategies for replicating a study. In a direct replication, the procedures used in the original study are followed as closely as possible.

Conceptual replications examine the same question investigated in the original study, but operationalize the constructs differently. In a replication and extension, the original study is fully or partly replicated, but the researcher adds new conditions to the original independent variables or adds new independent variables to the design. In the big replication approach, many research teams at different sites collaborate to assess the reproducibility of prior findings.

KEY TERMS

attrition (subject loss) (p. 323)
ceiling effect (p. 334)
complete replication (full replication) (p. 336)
conceptual replication (p. 337)
construct validity (p. 314)
debriefing (p. 335)
demand characteristics (p. 327)
differential attrition (p. 325)
direct replication (exact replication) (p. 336)
double-blind procedure (p. 332)
ecological validity (p. 319)
experimenter expectancy effects (p. 329)

external validity (p. 318)
floor effect (p. 334)
history (p. 322)
independent replication (p. 336)
instrumentation (p. 322)
internal replication (p. 336)
internal validity (p. 317)
manipulation check (p. 335)
masking (blinding) (p. 331)
maturation (p. 322)
partial replication (p. 336)
pilot study (p. 334)
placebo control group (p. 332)
placebo effect (p. 331)

randomized controlled trial (randomized clinical trial) (p. 325)
regression to the mean (p. 323)
replication (p. 319)
replication and extension (replication with extension) (p. 338)
selection (p. 324)
sensitivity (p. 334)
single-blind procedure (p. 332)
statistical conclusion validity (p. 315)
testing (p. 322)
wait-list control group (p. 325)
yoked control group (p. 333)

ASSESS YOUR KNOWLEDGE

1. Identify four categories of inference and the type of validity most germane to each one.

2. In the context of experiments, what is construct validity? Provide an example.

3. If internal validity is high, what conclusion can be drawn about the independent and dependent variable? In general, what decreases an experiment's internal validity?

4. What is external validity? How do researchers assess whether findings are externally valid?

5. Explain how history and maturation can threaten internal validity. Provide an example of each threat.

6. How does a testing confound differ from an instrumentation confound?

7. Describe the concept of statistical regression to the mean. When would a researcher not have to worry about a potential regression confound?

8. How can attrition and selection threaten internal validity? Give an example of an attrition confound.

9. Illustrate how a properly conducted, randomized between-subjects experimental design controls for most threats to internal validity.

10. Explain the concept of demand characteristics and the ways in which researchers attend to them.

11. Provide an example of experimenter expectancy effects and explain how researchers try to control for such effects.

12. Identify and describe two types of biases that a double-blind procedure attempts to control.

13. Describe why yoked control groups are used and how they are created.

14. Explain the key difference between a direct replication and a conceptual replication. Describe the advantages of the replication and extension strategy.

CONCEPT CHECKS: ANSWERS

10.1 Critical Thinking, Inference, and Validity

1. statistical   **2.** a construct   **3.** causal   **4.** a construct [For item 2, the inference is that blood pressure is a valid measure of the construct of "anxiety." For item 4, the inference is that exposing people to a crime or comedy video is a valid method of manipulating the construct of "threat"—that is, creating high versus low threat conditions.]

10.2 Types of Validity

1. d   **2.** c   **3.** a   **4.** b

10.3 Basic Threats to Internal Validity

1. false   **2.** true   **3.** false   **4.** true

10.4 Other Issues Concerning Experimental Control

1. ceiling; floor   **2.** demand characteristic
3. experimenter expectancy; placebo   **4.** yoked

10.5 Strategies for Replicating Research

1. d   **2.** c   **3.** a   **4.** b

THINKING CRITICALLY AND APPLYING YOUR KNOWLEDGE

EXERCISE 1   Let's Get Physical

Dr. Adams conducts a study to examine whether exposing people to regular exercise and thus improving their physical fitness will enhance their self-esteem. He places ads in local newspapers to recruit 35- to 40-year-old participants who have no major medical problems and haven't exercised regularly for the past 3 years (no regular jogging, biking, exercise walking, health club participation, etc.). A total of 73 qualified men and 68 qualified women apply. Dr. Adams administers a validated psychological test of self-esteem to each applicant. He selects the 15 men and 15 women who have the lowest scores on the self-esteem test. Three times a week, for 10 weeks, the participants meet with exercise trainers from 5:30 p.m. to 7:30 p.m. at a fitness club and engage in stretching, exercising on bicycle machines or treadmills, and lifting weights. Each session ends with 20 minutes of group recreational sports (e.g., volleyball, basketball). The intensity of exercise is increased gradually over the 10 weeks. Dr. Adams re-administers the self-esteem test at the end of the program. He analyzes the data (we'll assume he used appropriate statistical tests) and finds that, on average, participants' physical fitness increased and self-esteem also increased for the women and men. He concludes that increasing people's physical fitness improves their self-esteem.

(a) Evaluate the internal validity of Dr. Adams's conclusion in terms of the seven basic threats to internal validity discussed in this chapter.

(b) Are there other experimental control problems that affect the validity of Dr. Adams's conclusion? If so, describe them.

(c) Redesign Dr. Adams's study to achieve better experimental control, given the realistic constraints of this field setting.

EXERCISE 2   Seeing Red

Elliot et al. (2007) found that exposure to the color red impaired college and high school students' performance on intellectual achievement tasks. On page 340, I describe three possible outcomes of a replication and extension—a 3 (color) × 2 (type of task) factorial experiment—to examine the external validity of their findings.

(a) For each of the three outcomes I described, draw a bar graph that portrays the results. For your first chart, be sure to carefully label your *x*- and *y*-axes and draw the bars. Include a legend to indicate the conditions represented by the bars, and also include a specific scale of values for the *y*-axis. For the remaining two graphs, you can assume that the same features (legend, labels, scale values) are present and just draw the bars. If you find this task difficult, refer to the graphs in Chapter 9 that illustrate main effects and interactions.

(b) Develop a different replication and extension by creating a new factorial design. Assume that one independent variable is "color" (red, green, gray) and think about a second independent variable that would represent an important factor for establishing the external validity of the color–performance relationship. *To make this more challenging, your second independent variable should be a manipulated independent variable, not a subject variable.* Thus, don't choose something like age, gender, or ethnicity as your second independent variable.

EXERCISE 3   A Dirty Sales Pitch

There may be fewer door-to-door vacuum cleaner salespeople today than decades ago, but it's still an occupation that generates huge nationwide sales. So, imagine an at-home sales pitch that goes something like this:

"Yes, our Mega-Suck vacuum cleaner is pricey, but I'm going to prove to you that it does a much better job of cleaning carpets than your vacuum cleaner. Let's do a scientific test. I'm going to pour some dirt onto this small area of your carpet. Why don't you suck up all the dirt you can with your machine. OK, finished? Now I'll take the Mega-Suck and go over the same part of the carpet. OK, I'm done. Let's open the Mega-Suck and check inside. See all the dirt that your machine didn't pick up but the Mega-Suck did! I know $1,800 is a lot to pay, but can you really accept living in a house with all that hidden dirt?"

(a) Assess the quality of this "scientific test" and the validity of the inference that the Mega-Suck is the better machine. Identify and describe any confounding variables that exist.

(b) Design a more valid test to compare the two machines.

 **LaunchPad**
macmillan learning

To practice key concepts from this chapter, visit the LaunchPad Solo for Research Methods at **launchpadworks.com.**

QUASI-EXPERIMENTAL DESIGNS

CHAPTER OUTLINE

To begin this chapter, consider two vastly different research issues. First, after a workplace survey reveals that employees in a government department are overly stressed, two psychologists are asked to design a stress-reduction intervention. Guided by psychological theory, they hypothesize that providing employees with greater control over their job assignments, communication procedures, and opportunities for feedback will reduce the workers' stress. To enhance employees' control, the psychologists develop a program that reorganizes workplace policies. They assess its effectiveness by studying six groups of employees who work in the same departmental division. Three work groups receive the program (treatment condition), and three other groups do not (control condition). Data collected before the program and 13 months later indicate that employees in the treatment condition feel greater job control, report better mental health, and have had fewer absences during the past year due to illness (Bond & Bunce, 2001).

Second, can people psychologically postpone death—hold onto life—long enough to reach major ceremonial events such as birthdays or important holidays? A so-called death-dip hypothesis predicts a dip in death rates prior to such events. There's also a death-rise hypothesis, which predicts that mortality rates rise above average after major ceremonial events because people who have postponed death can now "let go." The initial study on this topic, which focused almost entirely on samples from the United States, found a death dip prior to birthdays, U.S. presidential elections, and a major religious holiday (Phillips & Feldman, 1973). But, roughly a dozen subsequent studies, some based on census data involving up to nearly 30 million deaths, have yielded a mixture of supportive and unsupportive results for the concept of death postponement (Peña, 2015; Shimizu & Pelham, 2008).

The scientists who conducted the studies on these diverse issues shared a common purpose and faced a common problem. Examining causality was the shared purpose: Will enhancing employees' job control reduce their work stress? Does the approach of major ceremonial events cause mortality rates to dip temporarily and rise afterward, presumably mediated by people's motivation to "make it" to that date? Confronted with studying these questions in real-life settings, the researchers' common problem was an inability to explore these research questions by means of highly controlled experiments. In this chapter, we'll explore *quasi-experimental research designs,* which behavioral scientists often use in real-life settings when between- and within-subjects experimental designs that have a high degree of control are not feasible.

WHAT IS A QUASI-EXPERIMENT?

Learning Objectives

After studying this section, you should be able to:

- Describe how quasi-experiments differ from true experiments.
- Discuss the advantages and disadvantages of quasi-experimental designs.

Control is the defining feature of any experiment. As you learned in Chapter 8, experimenters control the independent variable by manipulating it. They control dependent variables by determining what behaviors to measure, and how and when to measure them. They control extraneous environmental factors by attempting to keep them constant or balanced across the different experimental conditions. And, they attempt to control for possible confounding participant characteristics by randomly assigning participants to conditions or by having the same participants engage in a counterbalanced order of conditions.

QUASI-EXPERIMENTS AND EXPERIMENTAL CONTROL

Experiments that have a high degree of control are sometimes referred to as "true" experiments (Campbell & Stanley, 1966). In contrast, a **quasi-experiment** *has some features of an experiment, but lacks key aspects of experimental control.* Like true experiments, quasi-experiments examine the effects of treatments. Participants are exposed to a treatment and dependent variables are measured. Remember, "treatment" refers to an intervention, event, task, or stimulus to which participants are exposed. In this context, job reorganizations to reduce worker stress, anti-bullying and HIV/AIDS prevention programs, major holidays and birthdays, psychotherapy, and word lists of different lengths (as in a memory experiment) all represent treatments.

Here are major ways in which quasi-experiments may lack true experimental control:

- *Independent variables.* The experimenter may not have control over the content or design of the treatment, when it occurs, or whom it affects. These factors may be determined by other people (e.g., school, business, or government officials) or natural forces (e.g., earthquakes).

- *Dependent variables.* The experimenter may not have control over the choice of dependent variables, or how, when, and for whom they are measured.

- *Extraneous environmental variables.* Experimenters typically have little if any control over extraneous environmental events during the study.

- *Participant characteristics.* In quasi-experiments, treatment and control groups cannot be assumed to be equivalent at the start of the study because random assignment either is not used or is inadequate. Moreover, in some quasi-experiments there is only a treatment group, and participants' behavior is measured before and after the treatment. If their behavior changes, is this due to the treatment or does it reflect natural changes in participants' characteristics that would have occurred anyway, over time?

The degree to which quasi-experiments fall short of full experimental control depends on the design and circumstances of the study. For example, in some quasi-experiments researchers control the independent and dependent variables; in others they don't.

For some experts, the inability to randomly assign individual participants to treatment and control conditions is the key factor that distinguishes quasi-experiments from true between-subjects experiments (Shadish, Cook, & Campbell, 2002). In many quasi-experiments, practical limitations make it impossible to use random assignment at all. In other quasi-experiments, researchers do use random assignment, but it is inadequate to create equivalent groups at the start of the experiment. For example, suppose that four high schools participate in a quasi-experiment. They are randomly assigned to treatment and control conditions. Although each high school has many students, the unit of random assignment is the high school, not the individual student. Overall, even before the treatment begins, the student bodies at the two treatment schools may differ in important ways from their peers at the two control schools. There are simply too few schools for randomization to work properly (Lipsey & Cordray, 2000).

Similarly, when Frank Bond and David Bunce (2001) conducted their study to assess whether providing employees with more job control would reduce workplace stress, the researchers were not able to individually randomly assign each of the 97 participants to the treatment or control condition. Rather, each participant was a member of one of six distinct work groups, with each group performing a particular task (e.g., related to financial planning, auditing, or business strategy) within the same administrative division of a government department. Practical limitations in the workplace made it necessary for Bond and Bunce to randomly assign entire groups to either the treatment or control conditions. With a small sample size of only six work groups, we cannot assume that random assignment was adequate to balance participants' characteristics across the treatment and control conditions at the outset of the study. Thus, even though Bond and Bunce had control over the manipulation and measurement of key variables, limitations related to random assignment were among the reasons why they considered their study to be a quasi-experiment.

ADVANTAGES AND DISADVANTAGES

Quasi-experiments are frequently used to examine the effects of *social programs,* which are interventions designed to improve social conditions and people's well-being. A workplace stress management program, such as the one described at the beginning of the chapter, is an example. Similarly, governments sponsor numerous social programs that provide mental health care, financial aid for college students, early education for children, incentives for energy conservation, and so forth. Governments also pass laws that, in effect, represent sweeping social interventions designed to modify people's behavior. Examples are laws that mandate the use of seat belts in cars, require public schools to desegregate, impose penalties for committing a crime, and ban various types of workplace discrimination. When randomized experiments cannot be used to evaluate social programs, quasi-experimental designs provide a viable option.

The main limitation of quasi-experimental designs is that they are more vulnerable to internal validity threats than true experiments. As you will see, quasi-experimental designs vary greatly in their ability to rule out threats to internal validity. If the best designs are used, reasonably strong causal inferences can be drawn when certain data patterns occur. If weak designs are used, clear causal conclusions can't be drawn. Why not always use the best quasi-experimental designs? Once again, situational constraints may not allow this.

Although much quasi-experimental research is applied, these designs are also used in basic research. Research on the death-dip and death-rise hypotheses is one example. Interest in this topic is primarily driven by curiosity and a desire for knowledge about relations between psychological factors, people's social connectedness, and physical health, rather than by applied concerns. By gathering archival records of birth and death dates, and using quasi-experimental designs that examine trends over time, researchers have been able to examine death-postponement hypotheses.

For example, the findings in **Figure 11.1** are based on government records for almost 30 million deaths that occurred in the United States between 1990 and 2003. Social psychologists Mitsuru Shimizu and Brent Pelham (2008) found that deaths were least frequent in the month prior to people's birth month and peaked during the birth month. Interpreting the birth month peak is difficult, because deaths within a birth month that occur prior to people's specific birth date (e.g., a person dies on June 2, but her birthday is June 25) would run counter to the notion that people can postpone death until after they reach a major event (Schulz & Bazerman, 1980). The peak also represents less than a 1% increase in the number of deaths compared to the month before. Still, consistent with the idea of death postponement, Figure 11.1 indicates that fewer deaths occurred in the months prior to people's birth month than in the few months afterward.

In other analyses covering a similar historical period, Shimizu and Pelham (2008) examined deaths that occurred 2 days before through 2 days after birthdays, Thanksgiving, Christmas, and New Year's Day. They concluded that, overall, death was more likely to occur

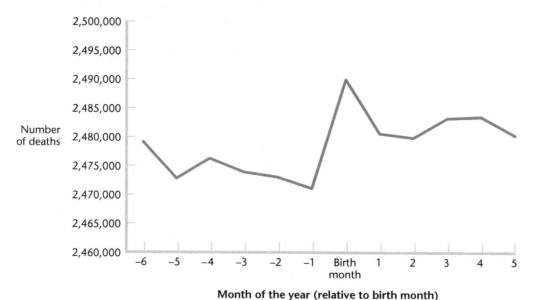

Month of the year (relative to birth month)

Figure 11.1 Examining the death-postponement hypothesis. These archival data, based on government records, encompass almost 30,000,000 deaths (age 2 through adulthood) in the United States between 1990 and 2003. (Copyright 2008. From "Postponing a Date With the Grim Reaper: Ceremonial Events and Mortality," by M. Shimizu and B. W. Pelham, 2008, *Basic and Applied Social Psychology, 30*, p. 42. Reproduced by permission of Taylor & Francis LLC [http://www.tandfonline.com].)

after, rather than before, people reached major ceremonial events. They examined and rejected possible confounding factors such as seasonal changes in death rates and travel (i.e., differences in death rates due to travel accidents before and after major holidays). Nevertheless, controlled experiments on this topic are not possible. The available archival data, for example, did not permit an examination of other possible confounding factors (e.g., pre-event vs. post-event differences in types or amounts of activities, and in eating, drinking, and sleep habits).

DIAGRAMMING QUASI-EXPERIMENTAL DESIGNS

There is a system for diagramming quasi-experimental designs (Campbell & Stanley, 1966). In this system:

- X = the treatment;
- O = an observation (i.e., measurement period); and
- temporal order proceeds from left to right.

For example, if the reading ability of children at School A is measured once before and once after they participate in a special reading training program, this would be represented by the top line in the following design:

$$O_1 \quad X \quad O_2$$
$$-------$$
$$O_1 \quad\quad O_2$$

The subscripts 1 and 2 represent the first and second observation periods. The procedure for control group children at School B who take the pretest and posttest but don't receive the treatment appears below the dashed line. The dashed line indicates that it is a nonequivalent control group.[1]

The symbol "O" refers to a distinct measurement period. It could represent the single administration of a test to participants on one day. However, the measurement period can be longer, as when a researcher observes pedestrians' behavior at a traffic intersection for a week. If the researcher treats that entire week as a single observation period (e.g., "overall weekly jaywalking") rather than as seven independent daily observation periods, this is considered a single "O" in the design.

✓ **CONCEPT CHECK 11.1** WHAT IS A QUASI-EXPERIMENT?

Decide whether each statement below is true or false. Answers appear at the end of the chapter on page 377.

1. The inability to randomly assign individual participants to conditions is a common feature separating quasi-experiments from true experiments.
2. In some quasi-experiments, the researcher has no control over how the independent variable is created or manipulated.
3. Quasi-experiments are only used in applied research; they are not suitable for basic research.
4. Some types of quasi-experimental designs allow reasonably clear causal conclusions to be drawn.

---

[1] As noted earlier, treatment and control groups may be nonequivalent because assignment to conditions is nonrandom (NR) or random (R) but insufficient (e.g., based on a small number of intact units, such as work groups) to permit an assumption of equivalency. Diagrams of quasi-experimental designs sometimes display the letters NR or R to the left of both groups, to indicate whether assignment is nonrandom or random (Shadish et al., 2002).

DESIGNS WITHOUT A CONTROL GROUP

Learning Objectives

After studying this section, you should be able to:

- Describe the basic features of one-group posttest-only, one-group pretest-posttest, and simple interrupted time-series designs.

- Discuss key threats to the internal validity of each of these three designs.

In this section, we'll examine quasi-experimental designs that only have a treatment group; they lack an independent control group. In the next section, we'll consider designs with control groups. The reason for this sequence is that the same general set of potential confounding variables applies to all the one-group designs, whereas a related set of confounding variables applies to designs that have two or more groups.

BASIC THREATS TO INTERNAL VALIDITY

In Chapter 10, you learned about seven basic threats to the internal validity of experiments. We'll now consider six of those threats. The seventh threat, *selection* (preexisting differences between participants in different conditions), will come up when we discuss two-group designs. To refresh your memory, here are the six threats:

- **History.** *Events that occur while a study is being conducted, and that are not a part of the experimental manipulation or treatment.*

- **Maturation.** *Ways in which people naturally change over time, independent of their participation in a study.*

- **Testing.** *Concerns whether the act of measuring participants' responses affects how they respond on subsequent measures.*

- **Instrumentation.** *Changes that occur in a measuring instrument during the course of data collection.*

- **Regression to the mean.** *The statistical concept that when two variables are not perfectly correlated* (e.g., scores on a pretest and posttest), *more extreme scores on one variable will be associated, overall, with less extreme scores on the other variable.*

- **Attrition.** *A loss of participants from the study.*

As we discuss the designs in this section, we'll consider major threats that apply to each one.

ONE-GROUP POSTTEST-ONLY DESIGN

In a **one-group posttest-only design,** *a treatment occurs and afterward the dependent variable is measured once.* This is the weakest quasi-experimental design and is diagrammed as

$$X \qquad O_1$$

To revive and modify an example from the last chapter, suppose that in a depression therapy study by Dr. Rodriguez, 54 people respond to newspaper advertisements soliciting adult volunteers who are severely depressed and not taking antidepressant medication. Dr. Rodriguez selects 20 participants based on their time availability: There's no pretest measure of depression with this design. Therapy lasts for 14 weeks. Dr. Rodriguez then administers a validated psychological inventory that measures depression and also asks another clinical psychologist to observe and rate each participant's level of depression, based on a video recording of a posttherapy interview. Dr. Rodriguez finds that, on average, participants are only moderately depressed. Can she conclude that her treatment reduces depression?

You can readily see why such a conclusion would be invalid. First and foremost, we have nothing formal with which to compare participants' posttreatment depression scores. Without a pretest, we don't know how depressed participants were before therapy. Did their depression really decrease? If so, by how much, and was the decrease statistically significant? The absence of a pretest doesn't negate the *possibility* that participants improved during therapy. But even so, such improvement could result from confounding factors, most notably a history confound (e.g., events outside therapy) and a maturation confound (e.g., spontaneous remission). There's also no way to rule out other possible control problems, such as a placebo effect. Perhaps the improvement was produced by participants' expectation that the treatment would be helpful, rather than anything unique to Dr. Rodriguez's therapy approach.

One-group posttest-only designs are sometimes used in studies where participants receive a special skill training program and then, after completing the program, their performance of that skill is measured. Roh and Issenberg (2014) assessed the skill level of 124 second-year nursing students in performing five trials of CPR (cardiopulmonary resuscitation) immediately after those students had completed a 2-hour CPR training session. Six specific skills were assessed. For example, posttraining, 76% of the students displayed correct hand placement and 58% performed the chest compressions at the proper rate. Unfortunately, we have no way to know what percentage of students would have correctly displayed such skills prior to training. The researchers gave participants a multiple-choice knowledge test about CPR before the training, but did not obtain behavioral skill measures against which to compare posttest results. Nevertheless, despite the weak posttest-only design, the finding that only one student performed all skills on all five trials of CPR correctly was surely of benefit to the researchers in gauging the program's success (or lack thereof)!

One-group posttest-only designs are also used in studies where participants, after exposure to an intervention, are asked to report whether they believe it has benefited them (Kushner, Kessler, & McGaghie, 2011). For example, in one study single mothers living on low incomes participated in an 8-week life skills training program. Subsequently, they reported that their parenting, assertiveness, and problem-solving skills had improved (Whittington, 1986). The researcher appropriately cautioned that these findings were based on a posttest-only design involving self-reports.

In such studies, people may believe that their behavior has changed when, in fact, it has not. Their responses also may reflect a placebo effect or demand characteristics that call for positively evaluating the intervention. Such factors, coupled with the basic threats to internal validity described above, make it impossible to draw clear causal conclusions. If someone offers you "proof" that a program or product works based solely on one-group posttest self-reports, beware.

ONE-GROUP PRETEST-POSTTEST DESIGN

In a **one-group pretest-posttest design,** *a dependent variable is measured once before and once after a treatment occurs:*

$$O_1 \qquad X \qquad O_2$$

Adding a pretest to the previous design makes it possible to assess the amount of change in the dependent variable. Nevertheless, it often remains difficult to draw a valid conclusion that the treatment was responsible for this change. In Dr. Rodriguez's therapy depression study, plausible alternative explanations might include:

- History (e.g., improved economic, employment, or job conditions)

- Maturation (e.g., spontaneous remission)

- Testing (i.e., taking the depression pretest may have affected scores on the posttest)
- Instrumentation (e.g., pretest to posttest changes in the observer's criteria for rating depression)
- Regression to the mean (if participants' pretest depression scores were high, then, on average, regression to the mean in their posttest scores would be expected)
- Attrition (if participants dropped out, they may have done so because they believed the therapy wasn't helping; this creates a biased sample among those who remain)

The degree to which these factors confound the results will depend on the actual circumstances of the study. If all participants complete the study, we can rule out attrition. If Dr. Rodriguez had only used the psychological inventory for the pretest and posttest measure (i.e., no observer ratings), then we can rule out changes in instrumentation as a confounding variable. In a study where participants are not selected because they are above or below average on some attribute, regression to the mean is less likely to be a plausible alternative explanation for its results. A researcher can try to determine whether outside events occurred that might plausibly confound the results. Perhaps during Dr. Rodriguez's study the local and national economies were stable, and there was no overall change in participants' employment (or unemployment) conditions. This would make an economic history confound less plausible. In sum, the plausibility of a confounding variable has to be assessed on an individual basis for each study.

Adding Follow-Up Observations: A Hospital Hygiene Intervention

Researchers often modify pretest-posttest designs to suit their goals by adding follow-up observations. Let's consider an example. Perhaps you've heard people say that a hospital is the last place you want to be when you're ill. Though tongue-in-cheek, the statement focuses on the problem of *hospital-acquired infections:* patients contracting other infections that can spread within a hospital environment. To reduce such infections, researchers implemented a hand hygiene program in the neonatal intensive-care unit of a university hospital in Thailand (Picheansathian, Pearson, & Suchaxaya, 2008). The program had several components, including a hand hygiene training session and performance feedback. Nurses were observed unobtrusively for one measurement period of 8 weeks before the program began and for seven monthly measurement periods afterward. Instances in which the nurses fully complied, partially complied, and completely failed to comply with the hospital's official hand-washing protocols were recorded. **Figure 11.2** shows that full compliance increased dramatically in the 2 months following the intervention and remained at a high level thereafter. Unfortunately, though, the rate of hospital-acquired infections among patients did not decline. The researchers speculated that this finding may relate to the fact that the program did not target other personnel (e.g., doctors, medical and nursing students) who came into contact with patients.

Advantages and Limitations

Adding follow-up observation periods to a one-group pretest-posttest design has two main benefits. First, it allows researchers to examine whether any immediate posttreatment changes persist over time. Second, an intervention may have delayed effects that would not be detected by using only one posttest. In the hospital study, full compliance with hand-washing protocols almost doubled between the first and second posttests.

Unfortunately, adding more posttests does not, by itself, help us rule out basic threats to internal validity and other control problems. For example, initial changes between the pretest and first posttest may still be due to a history confound, and further posttreatment

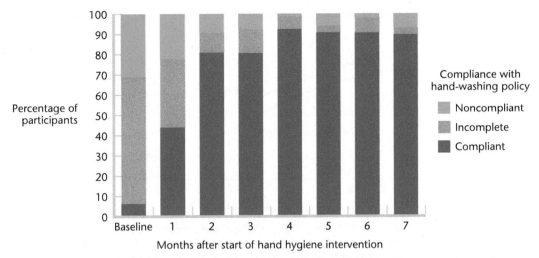

Figure 11.2 A pretest-posttest design with multiple posttests. The percentage of neonatal intensive-care unit nurses adhering to official hospital hand-washing protocols before and after a hygiene promotion program. (Information from "The Effectiveness of a Promotion Programme on Hand Hygiene Compliance and Nosocomial Infections in a Neonatal Intensive Care Unit," by W. Picheansathian, A. Pearson, and P. Suchaxaya, 2008, *International Journal of Nursing Practice, 14*, p. 317.)

changes may likewise result from outside events that occur during the follow-up period, not the delayed effects of a treatment. In the hospital study, a highly publicized case or news story about hospital-acquired infection could create such a history effect. As we'll now see, including multiple posttests *and* multiple pretests can help rule out some potential confounding variables.

SIMPLE INTERRUPTED TIME-SERIES DESIGN

In a **simple interrupted time-series design,** *a dependent variable is repeatedly measured at periodic intervals before and after a treatment.* The key is to have enough observations to establish both pretreatment and posttreatment trends in the dependent variable. Shadish et al. (2002) suggest including about 100 observation periods, but note that even a "short time series" can improve internal validity. Campbell and Stanley (1966) diagrammed this design as

$$O_1 \qquad O_2 \qquad O_3 \qquad O_4 \ X \ O_5 \qquad O_6 \qquad O_7 \qquad O_8$$

Although in practice it's unlikely that Dr. Rodriguez would delay therapy until multiple depression pretests were collected, let's imagine that she measures her participants' depression at 4-week intervals over a span of 28 weeks, with therapy commencing midway. Therapy lasts for 14 weeks, so the last posttest coincides with the end of therapy. **Figure 11.3** illustrates three possible outcomes. For simplicity, assume that scores on the depression inventory can range from 0 to 10, with higher scores indicating greater severity of depression. Looking first at line A in the leftmost graph, we can see that depression was steadily decreasing even before therapy began. Exposure to therapy didn't change such a trend one bit, so the most plausible conclusion is that therapy had no effect. The situation is the same for line B in the leftmost graph, except that depression decreases in a nonlinear fashion before treatment onset (the decrease becomes progressively larger between each pair of measurements). That identical progressive trend continues during therapy, so again, the most logical conclusion is therapy had no effect.

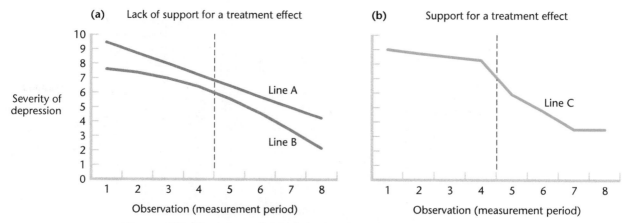

Figure 11.3 Three hypothetical outcomes in a simple interrupted time-series design. In both graphs, the vertical dashed line represents the start of psychotherapy to treat the participants' depression. In graph **(a)**, neither line A nor line B provides evidence of a treatment effect. In graph **(b)**, the data reveal an immediate change in the trend line after treatment began.

Turning to line C, shown separately in the rightmost graph in Figure 11.3, although we see that depression decreased prior to therapy, two changes emerge after therapy starts. First, there is a large decrease in the level of depression from O_4 to O_5. Second, between O_4 and O_7, the rate at which depression continues to decrease (i.e., the slope of the trend line) is greater than it was before treatment.

Advantages and Limitations

These findings from line C suggest that therapy influenced depression. But, as always, the key question is whether the therapy or confounding variables were responsible. Compared to a one-group pretest-posttest design, the time-series design strengthens the argument that therapy was the cause. First, confounding variables would have to account not only for the large O_4 to O_5 decrease in depression once therapy began, but also for the change in rate of improvement while therapy continued.

Second, time-series designs help us determine whether maturation, testing, and regression are potential confounding variables. If participants' depression scores decrease due to spontaneous remission or taking the depression inventory multiple times, or if this reflects statistical regression, then in combination the presence of these confounding variables will show up in the pretreatment trend line. Now, if the trend line changes in level and/or rate during therapy (as illustrated by line C), we assume that these changes are over and beyond what would have been expected solely from maturation, testing, and regression. Of course, other basic threats to internal validity (history, instrumentation, attrition) and other control problems (e.g., placebo effects) still must be considered as they pertain to each study.

Example: A Law to Reduce Drinking and Driving Figure 11.4 shows the findings from a simple interrupted time-series design that examined the effects of stricter drunk-driving legislation on drivers' behavior. Like many other U.S. states and Canadian provinces, in 1997 the state of Illinois lowered the legal drinking limit for drivers, making it illegal to drive with a blood alcohol concentration (BAC) of .08% or higher. The National Highway Traffic Safety Administration (2001) analyzed fatal traffic accidents that occurred in Illinois for each month from 1988 to 1999. The dependent variable was the percentage of all drivers involved in these

Figure 11.4 Drinking and driving: A simple interrupted time-series design. Monthly percentage of all drivers in fatal automobile crashes in Illinois who tested positive for blood alcohol concentrations, before and after implementation of a law mandating a .08% BAC limit. For 1997–1999, the projected findings are based on a mathematical model and indicate the data that would have been expected if the .08 BAC limit law had not been in force. (Information from National Highway Traffic Safety Administration/U.S. Department of Transportation, 2001.)

crashes who had a BAC greater than 0.00. This does not imply that these drivers caused all the accidents or that they were drunk. Rather, it's a broad measure of whether people involved in fatal accidents drove after having consumed alcohol.

The graph shows that in the years before the legislation, the percentage of drinking drivers decreased substantially in the early 1990s, and then rose again starting in 1995. The factors that caused these trends aren't known, nor are they the focus of the analysis. The key finding is that in 1997, there was an immediate drop in the percentage of drinking drivers when the new law was implemented. The percentage rises after that, but remains at a lower overall level than was projected to occur, based on the rising trend that was occurring prior to the legislation. The expected percentages were calculated using a mathematical model.

History is often the main potential threat to the internal validity of time-series designs. The researchers propose that this threat was minimized because they examined the percentage of drinking drivers (i.e., drinking drivers/[drinking + nondrinking drivers]), rather than the absolute number of drinking drivers. In other words, history confounds related to changes in weather, highway conditions, gasoline prices, and the like would have affected all drivers, whether they had been drinking or not.

✓ **CONCEPT CHECK 11.2** DESIGNS WITHOUT A CONTROL GROUP

Fill in each of the blanks below. Answers appear on page 377.

1. In a one-group posttest-only design, _____ is the most basic problem created by the absence of a pretest.

2. Regression to the mean is most likely to threaten the internal validity of a one-group pretest-posttest design when participants are chosen due to their _____.

3. Compared to a one-group pretest-posttest design, the simple interrupted time-series design allows researchers to better rule out the possible confounding variables of _____, _____, and _____.

DESIGNS WITH A NONEQUIVALENT CONTROL GROUP

Learning Objectives

After studying this section, you should be able to:

- Describe the features and threats to the internal validity of posttest only, pretest-posttest, and time-series designs that have nonequivalent control groups.

- Explain why switching replication designs are generally considered to be strong quasi-experimental designs.

Let's turn to several quasi-experimental designs that include a nonequivalent control group. Treatment and control groups are considered nonequivalent when (1) it isn't possible to randomly assign participants to conditions, or (2) random assignment is used in a way—such as with a small number of intact groups (e.g., schools, business units)—that cannot be assumed confidently to create equivalent groups at the start of a study.

BASIC THREATS TO INTERNAL VALIDITY

The presence of two or more groups means that we now consider *selection* and other factors related to selection as possible threats to internal validity. Recall that **selection** *refers to situations in which, at the start of a study, participants in the various conditions already differ on a characteristic that can partly or fully account for the eventual results.* In a randomized experiment, we typically rule out selection because random assignment is assumed to create equivalent groups. In a quasi-experiment, because the treatment and control groups are nonequivalent, selection is a greater potential threat.

Selection may also interact with the other types of threats that you've already learned about. For example, suppose that in her therapy study Dr. Rodriguez is not able to obtain a large enough sample of severely depressed people to assign half of them to a treatment group and the other half to a waiting list control group. Instead, because she is most interested in knowing whether her therapy effectively treats severe depression, she uses pretest depression scores to assign severely depressed individuals to the treatment condition and moderately depressed individuals to the control group. In this event, we would expect that although a decrease in the average pretest to average posttest scores of both groups would reflect some regression to the mean, the degree of regression will likely be greater for the treatment group because their pretest depression scores were more extreme than the pretest scores of the control group. This represents an interaction of selection with regression, called *selection × regression* or, alternatively, *differential regression,* that may plausibly explain part or all of the findings. In addition, the rates of spontaneous recovery may differ for the severe versus moderately depressed participants, which would create a *selection × maturation* confound (pronounced, "selection by maturation" confound). We'll call this entire category of potential threats **selection interactions:** *the interaction of selection with another threat to internal validity.* These are spelled out as follows:

- *Selection × history (differential history).* Participants in one group experience outside events that the other group does not.

- *Selection × maturation (differential maturation).* Overall, the two groups have different maturation rates.

- *Selection × testing (differential testing).* One group experiences testing effects that the other group does not.

- *Selection × instrumentation (differential instrumentation).* Changes occur in a measuring instrument that affect how one group's behavior is recorded but do not affect, or have a different effect on, recording in the other group.

- *Selection × regression (differential regression).* When one group is selected on the basis of more extreme scores (e.g., on a pretest or a related measure) than another group, it is likely that the groups' average posttest scores will reflect different degrees of regression to the mean.

- *Selection × attrition (differential attrition).* The rate of attrition, or the reasons for attrition, differ between two groups.

POSTTEST-ONLY DESIGN WITH A NONEQUIVALENT CONTROL GROUP

In a **posttest-only design with a nonequivalent control group,** *participants in one condition are exposed to a treatment, a nonequivalent group is not exposed to the treatment, and scores from both groups are obtained after the treatment ends.* This design is diagrammed as follows:

$$X \quad O_1$$
$$\overline{}$$
$$O_1$$

This is the weakest of the quasi-experimental designs with a control group, but there are times when a researcher may not have the opportunity to gather pretest data. Compared to a one-group posttest-only design, which provides absolutely no basis for comparison, the addition of the nonequivalent control group may enhance the study's internal validity, or it may do nothing to reduce potential confounding variables. It all depends on the degree of similarity between the treatment and control groups.

Suppose that Dr. Rodriguez had to use this design in her depression therapy study. Who would constitute the nonequivalent control group? A sample of 20 introductory psychology students would be a poor, highly dissimilar choice. Imagine instead that when 54 people responded to Dr. Rodriguez's recruiting advertisement seeking "people with severe depression," the final group of 20 had been selected not on the basis of pretest depression scores (in this example, there aren't any), but rather on their ability to fit into the time slots available for weekly therapy. Perhaps the respondents who weren't selected for treatment (because of schedule conflicts) could be the nonequivalent control group and the depression inventory could be administered to them at the end of the study.

Unfortunately, without pretests, we still face serious difficulties in interpreting any results. If the posttests reveal that the treatment group is less depressed than the control group, perhaps they were already less depressed at the start of the study. Without random assignment or a pretest, we can't assume that the two groups had similar depression levels before therapy began. In fact, perhaps both groups are just as depressed now as they were 14 weeks ago, and all we're seeing in the posttest data is the preexisting difference in depression! Even if their pretest depression levels had been equivalent, the two groups may differ in other ways that might have influenced the results. For example, perhaps the reason the treatment participants could better fit into the therapy session schedule is that they have more flexible hours stemming from different types of jobs. Perhaps more people in the treatment group are self-employed, or part-time workers, or unemployed, and these different types of work experiences would create a differential history confound for the two groups over the course of the study. Dr. Rodriguez could gather demographic data to assess participants' job status; a lack of statistically significant differences between the groups might strengthen the argument that they are reasonably equivalent. Still, they might differ in other ways that Dr. Rodriguez didn't assess. Perhaps the two groups had similar jobs and equally rigid job schedules, but the selected participants were more willing to adjust their daily schedules because they were more motivated to get better.

Example: Studying an Unpredictable Event In October 1989 the greater San Francisco Bay area was devastated by the most powerful earthquake (7.1 on the Richter scale) to strike an American city in over 80 years. The quake caused billions of dollars of property damage and killed 62 people. Clinical psychologist James Wood and his colleagues at the University of Arizona and Stanford University teamed up to study how exposure to this natural disaster affected people's nightmares (Wood, Bootzin, Rosenhan, Nolen-Hoeksema, & Jourden, 1992). This was basic research: Their goal was to obtain general knowledge about how trauma affects nightmares.

Forty students from San José State University and 90 students from Stanford—both located in the greater San Francisco Bay area—participated. Each morning for 3 weeks, they recorded whether they had experienced any nightmares the previous night and, if so, how many, their intensity, and whether the nightmare was about an earthquake. Obviously, there were no pre-earthquake measures because the earthquake's timing had been unpredictable. For a control group, the researchers obtained dream logs over a similar 3-week period from 107 University of Arizona students who had not been exposed to the earthquake. As **Figures 11.5a** and **11.5b** show, compared to University of Arizona students, students from the Bay area experienced more nightmares and a greater percent of them had nightmares about earthquakes, respectively. On average, nightmare intensity did not differ significantly across the groups.

The researchers also examined one dependent variable, the percentage of students who reported having any type of nightmare, on a nightly basis for 3 weeks. Thus, for this variable, the analysis reflected a *posttest-only design with multiple posttests and a nonequivalent control group*. The percentage of students in the Bay area who had a nightmare on any given night was consistently greater over time than the percentage of students in Arizona.

As always, internal validity is a key question: Were the between-group nightmare differences caused by the earthquake, or by other factors? Without pre-earthquake data, selection is clearly the largest threat. Even if this earthquake had not occurred, perhaps people living in a highly earthquake-prone region normally experience more nightmares, and nightmares about earthquakes, than people living elsewhere. Perhaps compared to students in Arizona, the Bay area students differed in other personal attributes that contributed to more frequent nightmares. The researchers also pointed out that being asked to keep a dream log—needing to report each day whether they had experienced any earthquake nightmares—might have triggered more frequent nightmares among the Bay area students. This would be a type of

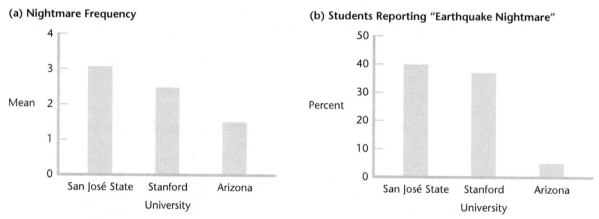

Figure 11.5 Posttest-only design with a nonequivalent control group. Nightmare frequency **(a)** and earthquake-related nightmares **(b)** among students at three universities after a powerful 7.1 quake near San Francisco. (Adapted with permission of the American Psychological Association from "Effects of the 1989 San Francisco Earthquake on Frequency and Content of Nightmares," by J. M. Wood, R. R. Bootzin, D. Rosenhan, S. Nolen-Hoeksema, and F. Jourden, 1992, *Journal of Abnormal Psychology, 101*, p. 219.)

differential testing confound (e.g., testing influences one group but not another). The researchers examined several potential confounding factors and made compelling arguments for why these factors were not plausible explanations for the results. They concluded that "the probability appears small that California residents normally have as many earthquake nightmares as were observed" (Wood et al., 1992, p. 222).

PRETEST-POSTTEST DESIGN WITH A NONEQUIVALENT CONTROL GROUP

In a **pretest-posttest design with a nonequivalent control group,** *pre- and posttreatment scores are obtained for a treatment group and a nonequivalent control group.* This design is diagrammed as follows:

$$O_1 \quad X \quad O_2$$
$$\overline{}$$
$$O_1 \qquad O_2$$

Advantages and Limitations

Adding a pretest to the previous posttest-only design creates several benefits (Shadish et al., 2002). First, it provides information about the extent to which the treatment and control groups were nonequivalent on the dependent variable prior to the treatment. In Dr. Rodriguez's therapy study, if the nonequivalent control group comprised those applicants whose schedules couldn't accommodate the therapy sessions, we would hope that the control and therapy groups would have similar mean pretest depression scores.

Second, the pretest lets us gauge how much the dependent variable changed during the study for each group. Imagine that the posttest means for the treatment and control groups are 5.0 and 6.5, respectively (on a 0 to 10 scale, with higher scores indicating greater depression). If the pretest means for the two groups were also 5.0 and 6.5, then overall, depression scores didn't change over time and apparently the therapy had no effect. If the respective pretest means were 6.0 and 7.5, then we've learned that depression scores decreased in both groups, but to the same degree. Again, the therapy apparently had no effect. But, if both groups had a pretest mean of 8.0, then this establishes that the treatment group experienced a larger decrease in depression scores.

Finally, the pretest scores may give us some clues about possible threats to internal validity, most notably, statistical regression and attrition. For example, if the treatment group has more extreme pretest depression scores than the control group, this indicates that differential regression is likely to occur. If differential attrition occurs over the course of the study, we can at least look at the pretest scores to determine whether within each group, pretest levels of depression differed between participants who dropped out versus those who did not.

Let's imagine that the mean pretest depression scores of Dr. Rodriguez's treatment and control groups are similar and that the posttest reveals the therapy group experienced a significantly larger decrease in depression. Differential regression, differential maturation, and differential testing are implausible alternative explanations. Because the two groups were, overall, similarly depressed at the pretest, the degree of statistical regression should be equivalent and there's no reason to expect that the groups will have different maturation (i.e., spontaneous recovery) rates. Differential testing is unlikely because both groups took the depression inventory twice. We can likely rule out differential instrumentation: Even if the clinical psychologist who observes and rates the participants' depression becomes more stringent, fatigued, or experienced from pretest to posttest, those instrumentation changes should affect both groups' scores comparably. If there was little or no attrition, or if it occurred for similar reasons in the two conditions, we can rule out differential attrition as a plausible confounding variable.

With this design, selection and differential history usually are the primary confounding variables to consider. Although their pretest depression scores were similar, did the participants in the two groups differ in other important ways at the start of the study (e.g., demographic factors, psychological qualities such as motivation) that plausibly explain the results? And, did one group experience certain outside events that the other group did not, and which might account for the results? The researchers' task is to collect information that will help determine the presence or absence of such confounding variables.

Example: Job Control and Employee Mental Health Many quasi-experiments employ a pretest-posttest design with a nonequivalent control group. The workplace stress management study by Bond and Bunce (2001) discussed at the beginning of the chapter provides an example. As we saw earlier, employees from six work groups participated. Three groups were randomly assigned to receive the stress intervention and the other groups were assigned to the control condition. Despite this random assignment, because there were only six groups (and especially because the groups performed different tasks from one another), this would be considered a nonequivalent control group design. Still, to create treatment and control groups that were as similar as possible, Bond and Bunce (2001) chose work units that were part of the same government division and, despite their different tasks, experienced similar workload and time pressures. Moreover, the employees in the various units were similar in their age distribution, gender composition, educational level, and job ranks. Analysis of demographic variables on the pretest revealed no significant overall differences between the treatment and control groups. Finally, because the work groups varied considerably in size, Bond and Bunce used a matching procedure prior to random assignment. The two smallest groups (nine or fewer members) were matched, as were the two medium-sized (10 to 20 members) groups and the two largest (25 to 40 members) groups, and then one group of each size was randomly assigned to either the treatment or control condition.

Figure 11.6 shows that prior to the stress intervention, the treatment and control groups had a similar degree of perceived control over their jobs (a) and a similar rate of absenteeism for the prior year (b). Analyses of the posttest data, which were recorded 13 months later, indicated that the employees whose work units were reorganized to enhance job control did, in fact, perceive that they had more control over their jobs and accrued fewer yearly absences than the employees who didn't receive the intervention. On average, the intervention also seemed to improve employees' mental health (e.g., reduced stress), whereas the mental health of employees in the control group showed no overall improvement. Discussing the

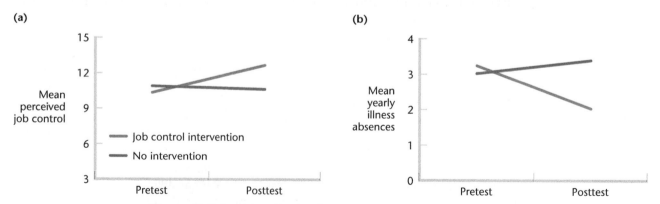

Figure 11.6 Pretest-posttest design with a nonequivalent control group. Effects of an employee stress management intervention on perceived job control **(a)** and absenteeism due to illness **(b)**. (Adapted with permission from American Psychological Association from "Job Control Mediates Change in a Work Reorganization Intervention for Stress Reduction," by F. W. Bond and D. Bunce, 2001, *Journal of Occupational Health Psychology, 6,* p. 290.)

methodological limitations of their study, the researchers identified differential attrition as the main potential threat to internal validity. The intervention (56%) and control (53%) groups experienced similar but high attrition rates over the year, raising the concern that the reasons for attrition may have differed between the groups and substantially confounded the results. So, the researchers gathered additional data that plausibly ruled out an attrition confound.

INTERRUPTED TIME-SERIES DESIGN WITH A NONEQUIVALENT CONTROL GROUP

In an **interrupted time-series design with a nonequivalent control group,** *a series of pre- and posttreatment scores are obtained for a treatment group and a nonequivalent control group.* This design is diagrammed as follows:

$$O_1 \quad O_2 \quad O_3 \quad O_4 \ X \ O_5 \quad O_6 \quad O_7 \quad O_8$$
$$\text{-----------------------------}$$
$$O_1 \quad O_2 \quad O_3 \quad O_4 \quad O_5 \quad O_6 \quad O_7 \quad O_8$$

Advantages and Limitations

This design allows us to examine how nonequivalent the two groups are prior to the intervention on the dependent variables and other variables (e.g., demographic factors, personality traits) for which pretests exist. Further, the advantages of a time-series design are now applied to both groups. In Dr. Rodriguez's therapy study, if extraneous variables such as maturation and testing influence participants' depression scores, or if statistical regression occurs, this should start to show up for each group in the pretest series. This means that even if the two groups are substantially nonequivalent at the outset (i.e., a significant selection confound), the combined effects of any differential maturation, differential regression, and differential testing will start to be evident in comparing the pretest trend lines for the two groups. Moreover, both groups would be exposed to the same general history effects (e.g., overall changes in the economy) and general instrumentation changes (e.g., gradually changing criteria employed by the clinical observer). If differential attrition occurs, its effect on the pretreatment trend lines can be examined.

In **Figure 11.7**, the green line labeled "Treatment" in both graphs below presents the same data from the treatment group shown earlier in Figure 11.3 (p. 354), when we discussed a simple interrupted time-series design (in that graph, it is Line C). Now let's add hypothetical data from a control group, first in the leftmost graph of Figure 11.7. Had we only used a simple

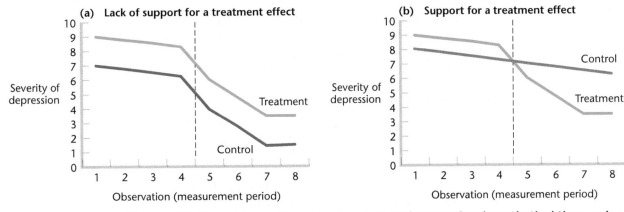

Figure 11.7 Comparison of treatment and control groups in a hypothetical time-series design with a nonequivalent control group.

interrupted time-series design with the treatment group, it is likely that we would be feeling reasonably confident the therapy was responsible for lower depression scores on measurements O_5 through O_8. The line portraying the findings for the control group, however, leads us to conclude that the therapy had no effect. The depression scores for the control group are consistently lower than those for the treatment group and, most critically, follow the same pattern of change. The sudden, large drop in depression that occurs for the treatment group between Observation 4 and Observation 5 (when the treatment is introduced) and that continues over the next few observations is paralleled by the decrease in depression for the control group. This suggests that some factor other than the introduction and continuation of the treatment produced this decrease in depression.

In contrast, if the data from our control group resembled those displayed in the rightmost graph, this would radically change our interpretation of the results. For the control group, the decrease in depression remains slow and steady for the entire period of the study, and does not parallel the larger decreases in depression that occurs in the treatment group once that group begins to receive therapy. Here, the addition of the control group strengthens the argument that the treatment group's large decline after measure O_4 was caused by the therapy. The primary potential confounding variable that we need to consider is differential history: Did the treatment group experience certain outside events (often called *local history*) that the control group did not? But, for this to be a plausible confound, those local history effects would have had to begin precisely during the O_4 to O_5 measurement period.

In short, adding time-series data from a control group helps us determine whether the treatment produced an effect. However, the control group time-series data do not address other control problems like demand characteristics, experimenter expectancy effects, and placebo effects. The researcher will have to minimize these potential confounding factors by using the procedural controls discussed in Chapter 10.

Example: Examining the Effects of a Child Car Seat Law If you are under 30 years of age and grew up in the United States, odds are that when you rode in a car as an infant, you were placed in a protective child car seat. By the mid-1980s almost every U.S. state had enacted some type of child passenger safety law. Developmental psychologist Diana Guerin and quantitative psychologist David MacKinnon (1985) used an interrupted time-series design with a nonequivalent control group to assess the effectiveness of a child car seat safety law that took effect in California on January 1, 1983. The law required that all infants and children through the age of 3 years ride in approved safety seats. The researchers obtained monthly child passenger injury data from the California Highway Patrol for the years 1979 through 1983. Because the law did not affect older children, Guerin and MacKinnon obtained injury data for 4- to 7-year-olds, who represented the nonequivalent control group. In addition, the researchers obtained injury data for the younger age group for the same time period from the state of Texas, which did not enact a child passenger safety law.

Figure 11.8 shows the data from California (the Texas data are not graphed). You can see that prior to 1983, the injury data for the two age groups show a similar pattern, with a lot of variability across some months. After the safety law took effect, the number of injuries initially decreased for both groups, but more so for the younger children. Both age groups then exhibited an increasing trend after that point—possibly due to people driving more often, overall. The key finding is that the data lines for the two age groups separate, with fewer injuries occurring yearly in the younger age group. Analyses revealed that after the law was enacted, the number of injuries decreased significantly only in the younger age group. Moreover, data from Texas indicated that for this time period, during which no child safety law was in effect, the number of injuries among infants and children age 3 and younger did not change significantly (there was a nonsignificant increase, just as there was for the older California age group).

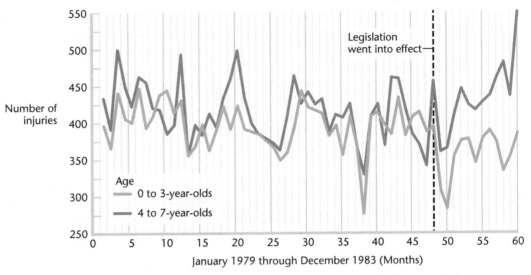

Figure 11.8 An interrupted time-series design with a nonequivalent control group. Number of child passenger injuries before and after implementation of a California child seat restraint law. (Information from "An Assessment of the California Child Passenger Restraint Requirement," by D. Guerin and D. P. MacKinnon, 1985, *American Journal of Public Health, 75*, 142–144 [Figure 1, p. 143]. Published by the American Public Health Association (APHA); used by permission of Sheridan Content Services.)

Guerin and MacKinnon's (1985) time-series design with two nonequivalent control groups makes it difficult to argue that other factors caused the decrease in injuries among the younger children. Possible pre-to-post general history effects such as manufacturing improvements in automobile safety, fluctuations in weather, and changes in the number of monthly automobile trips due to gas prices would all be controlled for by either one or both control groups. Further, to examine the possibility that fewer young children were injured in 1983 because of decreased California birthrates for that age group, Guerin and MacKinnon examined birthrate data and found that the number of children age 3 or under actually was greater in 1983 than in prior years.

Note that in quasi-experiments involving archival data collected by outside agencies (e.g., governmental, business, or school statistics), researchers need to be on guard for a possible differential instrumentation confound. The reason is that from time to time agencies may change their methods for reporting statistics or alter their definitions of what constitutes a particular outcome (e.g., unemployment, absenteeism). For example, during the time period of Guerin and MacKinnon's study, if the state of California had adopted a stricter definition of what constitutes a child automobile injury in 1983, while the state of Texas enacted no such change, this could explain why the number of recorded injuries for the youngest children decreased in California but not Texas. There was, however, no evidence for such a confounding variable in this study.

Before we move on to the next section of the chapter, which examines an additional way to enhance the quality of quasi-experimental designs, take a look at **Figure 11.9**. This figure summarizes the quasi-experimental designs covered thus far. It shows two paths for improving the very weak one-group posttest-only design that was our starting point. The path on the left involves the addition of a nonequivalent control group and, subsequently, a pretest measurement period for each group. The path on the right where only one group is available to study, involves the addition of a pretest and, subsequently, multiple pretest and posttest

HOW TO BUILD A STRONGER QUASI-EXPERIMENTAL DESIGN

One-Group Posttest-Only Design

$$X \ O_1$$

The weakest quasi-experimental design: There are no corresponding measures with which to compare the posttreatment results.

➕ Add a nonequivalent comparison group

➕ Add a pretest

Posttest-Only Design with a Nonequivalent Control Group

$$X \ O_1$$
$$---------$$
$$O_1$$

A relatively weak design, especially as nonequivalence of the groups increases: If the treatment and control groups differ on the dependent variable, we can't determine whether this difference existed even prior to treatment. There are also many potential threats to internal validity.

One-Group Pretest-Posttest Design

$$O_1 \ X \ O_2$$

A relatively weak design: If scores on the dependent variable change significantly from pre- to posttest, there are many potential threats to internal validity.

➕ Add a pretest

➕ Add multiple pre- and posttest measurement periods

Pretest-Posttest Design with a Nonequivalent Control Group

$$O_1 \ X \ O_2$$
$$-------------$$
$$O_1 \quad\quad O_2$$

A better design: Preexisting differences between the treatment and control groups can be assessed, although many potential threats to internal validity remain.

Simple Interrupted Time-Series Design

$$O_1 \quad O_2 \quad O_3 \quad O_4 \quad X \quad O_5 \quad O_6 \quad O_7 \quad O_8$$

A better design: There should be enough measurement periods to establish meaningful pre- and posttreatment data trends. This may help rule out threats to internal validity such as maturation, testing, and regression to the mean.

➕ Combine multiple pretest and posttest measurements with the inclusion of a nonequivalent comparison group

Interrupted Time-Series Design with a Nonequivalent Control Group

$$O_1 \quad O_2 \quad O_3 \quad O_4 \ X \ O_5 \quad O_6 \quad O_7 \quad O_8$$
$$-----------------------------------$$
$$O_1 \quad O_2 \quad O_3 \quad O_4 \quad\quad O_5 \quad O_6 \quad O_7 \quad O_8$$

A strong quasi-experimental design: We can examine whether the introduction of the treatment produces a change in the slope or absolute level of the trend line, relative to the trend line for the control group. Differential history is often the main potential confounding variable to consider.

measurements. The final design we discussed in this section, the interrupted time-series design with a nonequivalent control group, can be viewed as the convergence of these two paths, yielding the strongest quasi-experimental design we have discussed thus far.

 CONCEPT CHECK 11.3 DESIGNS WITH A NONEQUIVALENT CONTROL GROUP

Dr. Jones conducts a 6-month quasi-experiment at two elementary schools, A and B. School A, but not B, uses a new math instructional method. Identify the major internal validity threat created by each situation. Answers appear on page 377.

1. During the 6-month period, School A—but not School B—also begins a new high-nutrition lunch program.

2. Students at School A have their math achievement measured each month with a standardized test. To save money, only a pretest and posttest are used at School B.

3. School A is selected because its students have the poorest math scores in the city. Overall, School B's students are average in math performance.

SWITCHING REPLICATION DESIGNS

Learning Objectives

After studying this section, you should be able to:

- Describe two types of switching replication designs.
- Explain how a switching replication design can enhance the internal validity of a quasi-experiment.

In a **switching replication design,** *one group receives a treatment, and a nonequivalent group initially does not receive the treatment but is then exposed (i.e., switched) to it at a later point in time.* In a standard switching replication design, the initial treatment group continues to receive the treatment throughout the study.

Switching replications can be used with pretest-posttest and time-series designs. Here, we'll examine two variations of a pretest-posttest switching replication design.

PRETEST-POSTTEST DESIGN WITH SWITCHING REPLICATION

With the simplest pretest-posttest design, a switching replication procedure would look like this:

$$O_1 \quad X \quad O_2 \qquad\qquad O_3$$
$$\text{-----------------------}$$
$$O_1 \qquad\quad O_2 \quad X \quad O_3$$

The switching replication component of this design has two purposes. First, if the results for the delayed treatment group parallel those of the initial treatment group, we have initial support for the replicability of the findings. Second, it provides additional information about possible threats to internal validity. For example, if the treatment group's behavior improves upon receiving the intervention, and if the nonequivalent control group's behavior doesn't improve until later, when it receives the treatment, this makes it less plausible that confounding variables such as differential history could explain the results. Why? Because you would have to identify both a history effect that caused improvement only in the initial treatment group between times O_1 and O_2, and another history effect that caused improvement only in the initial control group (the delayed treatment group) between times O_2 and O_3. Although this pattern could happen, it's more difficult to make a plausible case for such a pattern in a switching replication design than it would be if only a pretest-posttest design had been used. The same goes for other confounds such as differential maturation and differential instrumentation.

Of course, to the extent that other control problems such as demand characteristics, experimenter expectancies, and placebo effects caused the improvement in the initial treatment group, those same factors would operate upon the switched control group and could plausibly explain the pattern of results. Again, this is where researchers need to be sensitive to these additional control problems and do their best to eliminate or minimize them.

Example: HIV/AIDS Prevention in Tanzania Peter Vaughan and his colleagues used this design in a 4-year, nationwide HIV/AIDS prevention study in Tanzania (Vaughan, Rogers, Singhal, & Swalehe, 2000). One difference from the diagram on page p. 365 is that they included a total of five measurement periods rather than three. The study began in 1993, at which time Tanzania had one of the highest rates of HIV/AIDS in the world. The researchers and Tanzanian government collaborated on the project. The intervention, which was based on several psychological theories of behavior change, involved an entertaining radio soap opera series. The soap opera's characters educated listeners about HIV/AIDS and modeled behaviors (most notably, marital fidelity and refraining from sex with multiple partners) intended to reduce the risk of HIV infection. Once per year during the study, several types of HIV/AIDS risk behaviors (e.g., self-reported number of sexual partners and condom use) were measured as part of an ongoing national survey conducted by the government.

To create the treatment and control groups, Tanzania was divided into two geographic regions, A and B. The soap opera was broadcast twice weekly throughout Region A (comprising most of Tanzania); Region B initially received no broadcasts. Pretest data were collected from both regions in 1993. Later that year, the treatment region began receiving the radio broadcast and continued to receive it until the study ended in 1997. The control region began receiving the broadcast after the third (1995) measurement period was completed, and continued to receive it through 1997. The design is diagrammed as follows:

1993		1994	1995	1996	1997
O_1	X	O_2	O_3	O_4	O_5
O_1		O_2	O_3 X	O_4	O_5

Note that although this study took years to conduct, it does not represent a time-series design because there are too few measurement periods. If behavior had been measured monthly for each year, yielding a total of 60 observation periods, then time trends could be examined easily. But, five observation periods are not sufficient to do this, particularly when the treatment group only has one pretest measurement period.

As you can imagine, conducting a nationwide study over 4 years involves giving up a considerable amount of control over external factors that can influence participants' lives. The researchers carefully examined many potential confounding variables and presented arguments for why these variables were unlikely to account for the results. What we'll focus on here is solely the logic behind the interpretation of the pattern of results, using one dependent variable: reported condom use among participants with more than one sexual partner. **Figure 11.10** shows the findings.

You can see that condom use increased sharply in Region A, the initial treatment group (blue line), for the first 2 years after the intervention began. In contrast, condom use in Region B, the control group, decreased steadily for those 2 years and then increased for 2 years only after Region B received the broadcast. The one finding that is difficult to interpret is the decrease in condom use in Region A from 1995 to 1996. Still, this drop does not alter the fact that both regions showed an immediate increase in condom use the particular year they began to receive the radio broadcast. Nor does the drop change the fact that condom use increased in 3 of the 4 years that Region A was exposed to the broadcast, and in both years that Region B received the broadcast.

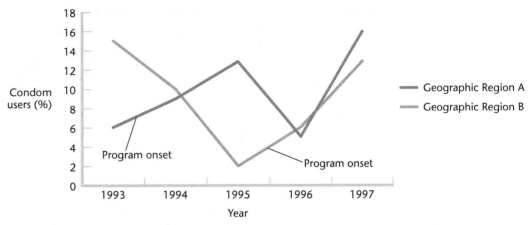

Figure 11.10 A switching replication design. A nationwide HIV/AIDS prevention program in Tanzania: percent of condom users measured once yearly. (Copyright 2000. From "Entertainment-Education and HIV/AIDS Prevention: A Field Experiment in Tanzania," by P. W. Vaughan, E. M. Rogers, A. Singhal, and R. M. Swalehe, 2000, *Journal of Health Communication*, 5 (Supplement 1), p. 95. Reproduced by permission of Taylor & Francis LLC [http://www.tandfonline.com].)

Although the 1996 data for Region A complicate the task of drawing causal conclusions, the key point is that even with this pattern, the addition of the switching replication group strengthened the argument that the intervention produced an effect. Based on their statistical analysis and examination of potential confounding factors, the researchers concluded that, overall, the prevention program increased participants' condom use and reduced the number of sexual partners per year.

SWITCHING REPLICATION WITH TREATMENT REMOVAL

In a basic switching replication design, the initial treatment group continues to receive the treatment while the control group receives delayed treatment. In a variation of this procedure, the initial treatment group no longer receives the treatment after the control group is switched. In its simplest form, this design would be diagrammed as follows, with the line through the "X" (i.e., $\bar{X}$) indicating that the treatment has been removed:

$$
\begin{array}{ccccc}
O_1 & X & O_2 & \bar{X} & O_3 \\
\hline
O_1 & & O_2 & X & O_3
\end{array}
$$

For example, in Dr. Rodriguez's therapy study, the initial treatment and control groups would be given a pretest (O_1), and 14 weeks later when the treatment group has completed therapy (O_2), a posttest is administered to both groups. At this time, the original control group begins their 14 weeks of therapy, while the original treatment group is, of course, no longer receiving therapy. At the end of these 14 weeks, the final posttest is given (O_3). This posttest allows Dr. Rodriguez to assess not only how the control group has changed in response to receiving their delayed therapy, but also whether the initial therapy group maintained their improvement after therapy ended.

Example: Teaching Students with Math Learning Disabilities Special education researcher Brian Bottge and his colleagues examined the effectiveness of an instructional technique called Enhanced Anchored Instruction (EAI) to teach math skills to middle school students who had been identified as students with math learning disabilities (Bottge, Rueda, LaRoque, Serlin, & Kwon, 2007). EAI uses educational software and multimedia to present students with mathematical problems of varying degrees of difficulty, carefully adjusted to each student's level of performance. Students also do some problem-solving work in small groups.

The 100 students came from three schools and currently received all their instruction in special education classes, taught by a total of four special education teachers. For the roughly 4-week period of this study, two teachers were randomly assigned to use an instructional sequence in which they first taught math according to the EAI approach and then returned to their typical instructional methods. The other two teachers maintained their typical methods for the first 2 weeks and then switched to EAI instruction. Therefore, this was a switching replication with a treatment removal design, diagrammed exactly as shown on page 367.

Math performance was measured using several subscales from nationally standardized math tests and a separate math test previously developed to assess learning of the particular skills taught in the EAI instructional module. **Figure 11.11** displays one set of findings. You can see that each group of students showed greater improvement in math performance when they received the EAI instruction (orange line) rather than their typical instruction (green line). Whether these improvements are long lasting is not clear, particularly given what appears to be a decline for the Sequence A group when they reverted back to typical instruction methods. But ironically, the fact that the initial EAI group did not continue to improve after EAI instruction was removed strengthens the claim that exposure to EAI instruction caused their initial O_1 to O_2 improvement. Overall, it would be difficult to come up with a plausible argument that potential confounding factors such as differential history, differential maturation, differential testing, and so forth produced this pattern of results.

Whether it truly was the unique content and techniques of the EAI that were responsible for the improved learning is, however, another matter. Perhaps expectancy effects played a role; perhaps simply breaking up the teachers' and students' normal instructional routine with anything new played a role.

The design of this study would have been improved by adding two placebo control groups that "tried something different"—something other than EAI but which in theory would not be expected to enhance students' typical rate of learning (although teachers and students would be masked to the fact that this was a placebo intervention). In such a redesign, a Sequence C group would receive this placebo instructional technique for 2 weeks and then revert back to their typical instructional method. A Sequence D group would start off with their typical method and switch to the placebo treatment for the last 2 weeks. If the results for these two

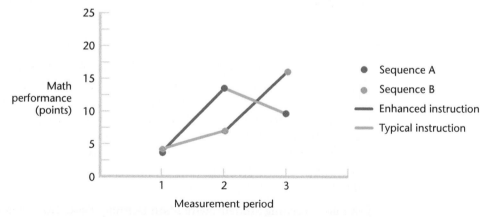

Figure 11.11 A switching replication with treatment removal. In both the initial treatment group (Sequence A) and delayed treatment group (Sequence B), students with math learning disabilities exhibited more math improvement when they received enhanced rather than typical instruction. (Information from "Integrating reform-oriented math instruction in special education settings," by B. A. Bottge, E. Rueda, P. T. LaRoque, R. C. Serlin, and J. Kwon, 2007, *Learning Disabilities Research & Practice, 22*, 96–109 [Figure 4, p. 104]. Copyright © 2007, John Wiley and Sons. Used with permission.)

groups look like those shown in Figure 11.11, then we would conclude that it was not the content or method of EAI instruction per se that caused the change; instead, anything new seemed to produce the change. But if the students' learning was not enhanced by the placebo treatment, this would support the conclusion that something unique to the EAI method enhanced the students' math performance.

 CONCEPT CHECK 11.4 SWITCHING REPLICATION DESIGNS

Decide whether each item is true or false. Answers appear on page 377.

In switching replication designs with two groups:

1. participants are randomly assigned, individually, to the two groups.
2. the initial control group receives the treatment, but on a delayed basis.
3. when the initial control group begins treatment, treatment for the other group may either continue or be terminated.
4. threats to internal validity are, in general, better controlled than in nonequivalent control group designs that don't include switching replications.

PROGRAM EVALUATION

Learning Objectives

After studying this section, you should be able to:

- Discuss the benefits and risks of conducting program evaluations.
- Describe five types of program evaluation.
- Identify four phases of program diffusion and factors that contribute to successful diffusion.

In this chapter, we've covered several examples in which researchers used quasi-experimental designs to assess the effectiveness of a social program. Presumably, social programs arise from a perceived need and, like any other treatment, their effectiveness can and should be empirically assessed. In the behavioral and social sciences, **program evaluation** *involves the use of research methods to assess the need for, and the design, implementation, and effectiveness of, a social intervention* (Kaufman et al., 2006).

BENEFITS AND CONSTRAINTS OF PROGRAM EVALUATION

You probably don't have to look far to come up with examples of social programs implemented in your community: Drug prevention and treatment programs, violence prevention and special education programs in schools, suicide and counseling hotlines, and youth programs are all possible examples. Why do these programs exist? How many people actually use them? Do they work, and can they be improved? Beyond their practical applications, do they contribute to our understanding of behavior?

Benefits

Program evaluations gather information that serves many purposes. Chief among them are:

- to help organizations, governments, other agencies, and local communities determine whether there is a need for a program;
- to identify whether a program is effective (i.e., producing the intended outcomes) and efficiently run, and thus whether it should be continued, expanded, reduced, or terminated;

- to help administrators, planners, and funding agencies improve a current program;

- to add to scientific knowledge by (1) assessing whether theories and other principles generated from basic research can guide the development of successful, real-world applications, and (2) uncovering new findings and possible causal relations in real-world settings that are then examined under more controlled conditions in basic research (Rossi, Lipsey, & Freeman, 2004).

Ultimately, good-quality program evaluation research has a major impact on people's lives. It helps agencies direct appropriate services to people who need them and contributes to the wise use of funds and other resources. Today, there is considerable societal emphasis on developing *evidence-based programs and public policies.* Scientifically sound program evaluations play an important role in shaping decisions about those programs and policies.

Constraints

Program evaluations are usually commissioned by government agencies, business organizations, or other groups with a vested interest in developing a new program to solve an applied problem, or assessing the effectiveness of a current program. Sponsoring agencies or individuals are called *evaluation sponsors.* For example, if the board of directors of a university or a business initiates a program evaluation, they would be the evaluation sponsors. There will likely be other individuals, called *stakeholders,* who also have a vested interest in the results of the evaluation: administrators, faculty, staff, and students at a university; administrators, employees, and possibly customers in a business setting; members of the community or of various groups within the community; and so on.

One challenge for program evaluation researchers is the need to carry out their work in a context that can be highly politically charged. There may be conflicting interests between sponsors on the one hand and stakeholders on the other, or among different evaluation sponsors or different groups of stakeholders. Although the scientific goal is to obtain the most objective information possible, conflicting agendas held by various groups can influence the degree to which program administrators, service providers, users, and nonusers will be willing to participate or provide honest answers.

Program evaluation researchers often face other constraints. Unless they are evaluating programs that they have developed themselves, the researchers may not get to choose the objectives of the evaluation. They may be able to help determine the dependent variables to be studied and how they will be measured, or may have no choice in such matters. Time and funding constraints may require the researchers to collect data for a shorter period of time than they desire, as when a time-series design would yield better internal validity but only a pretest-posttest design can be used.

Ethical issues are central to all research, but in program evaluation serious complications may arise if the confidentiality of participants' responses is breached. For example, employees may be asked to discuss or rate the leadership ability and other attributes of people who hold direct power over them: their supervisors, managers, and vice presidents, for example. Negative comments by employees about their leaders, although presumably solicited by the researcher for the purpose of improving a program, risk triggering retaliation by those in charge. Researchers therefore need to take every reasonable precaution to safeguard confidentiality.

COMPONENTS OF PROGRAM EVALUATION

From the researchers' standpoint, one of the first steps in conducting a program evaluation is to meet with the evaluation sponsors and key stakeholders to determine why the evaluation has been requested. What are the perceived issues, goals, specific objectives, resources, and time frame? Using this and other information, the researchers will need to develop an overall plan for conducting the evaluation that is tailored to the situation.

Because program evaluation may occur over a long time period, different questions assume the greatest importance at various stages along the way. In general, we can think of a comprehensive program evaluation as having five major components, each of which focuses on a different set of questions. The components are: *needs assessment, program theory and design assessment, process evaluation, outcome evaluation,* and *efficiency assessment* (Rossi et al., 2004). Often, these components are simply viewed as different types of program evaluation, because in most instances a researcher does not conduct all of them. For example, after a program is already up and running, a research team may be called in only to evaluate whether the program is effective. In this case, they would conduct a program outcome evaluation. In another setting, before a program is developed, a researcher might be brought in only to determine if a need for the program exists. This researcher would conduct a needs assessment.

Figure 11.12 diagrams one sequence in which program evaluation occurs, often as a set of independent evaluations rather than as part of a single, comprehensive evaluation. It's not the only possible sequence. For example, an organization may want to know whether a new program is likely to be cost-effective before committing funds to it. This assessment would examine the projected efficiency of the program. Another efficiency analysis may be conducted after the program is operating. Figure 11.12 also shows the relationship between program evaluation and another issue called program diffusion, which we'll cover shortly.

Needs Assessment

A **needs assessment** *determines whether there is a need for a social program and the general steps required to meet that need.* Just because a politician, community leader, or investigative news reporter claims that a problem exists, or denies its existence, does not make it so. Therefore, researchers who conduct a needs assessment must first identify whether a significant problem actually exists. They will need to clearly define the problem, examine the objectives and standards that evaluation sponsors and stakeholders want to achieve (e.g., the types of reading skills that students "should possess" by Grade 9), and determine whether those objectives are currently being met.

Often, different sponsors and stakeholders view a problem differently (e.g., executive-level mental health clinic administrators citing a lack of staff commitment; staff members citing poor leadership and support from top administrators). Therefore, to reach a good-quality, independent decision about the need for a program, researchers typically attempt to gather data from multiple sources, including not only staff and administrators, but also members of the intended target population. This allows researchers to identify the population's perceived needs as well as important characteristics that may facilitate or impede the eventual success of

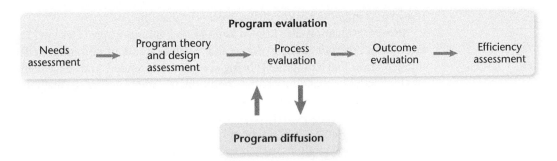

Figure 11.12 One possible sequence of program evaluation, followed by program diffusion.

the program. As part of the needs analysis, the researcher also identifies the types of services that are available or could be developed to address the problem. As Rossi et al. (2004) note: "Needs assessment is fundamental because a program cannot be effective at ameliorating a social problem if there is no problem to begin with or if the program services do not actually relate to the problem" (p. 102).

Program Theory and Design Assessment

A **program theory and design assessment** *evaluates the rationale for why a program has been, or will be, designed in a particular way.* What components or services should the program include? How should those services be delivered? What's the logic justifying those choices?

Presumably, the components that end up being included in the program will each have a valid purpose. There should be a theoretical or empirical justification for expecting that the specific services will contribute to solving the problem at hand, and in combination the services should address the array of key issues identified in the needs analysis. Suppose a program is being designed to improve the social conditions of people who are homeless, and a component of that program is designed to teach them self-defense skills. This component would have little validity if the intended recipients don't perceive those skills as important, if they say they wouldn't use the training, or if the specific training procedures have been demonstrated in prior studies to be ineffective in actually enhancing people's self-defense skills.

The logic of including self-defense skills training would also be suspect if the program design fails to address other issues that are identified in the needs assessments as more important (e.g., training in strategies for finding a place to live). On the other hand, if the researchers have gathered extensive data demonstrating that enough homeless individuals perceive a need for improving their self-defense skills (as was found to be the case among 30% of homeless women in one large-scale needs assessment) and have directly tied their selection of program components to these and other identified needs, then there is a sound rationale for the program's design (Herman, Struening, & Barrow, 1994; Rossi et al., 2004).

Process Evaluation

A **process evaluation** *determines whether a program is being implemented as intended.* Key issues include whether the program's services are being delivered (1) in the form that they were intended, (2) by the personnel who are supposed to deliver them, (3) to members of the intended target population, and (4) to the number of recipients that had been projected. A process evaluation can determine whether administrative goals and guidelines are being met and whether the program is failing to reach people who need it (Rossi et al., 2004). Direct behavioral observations, surveys, formal and informal interviews, and analyses of appropriate archival records (e.g., program attendance or usage statistics) are among the techniques that researchers might use to conduct a process evaluation.

Process evaluation, also known as *program monitoring,* provides vital knowledge that will facilitate or limit our ability to draw valid conclusions about a program's effectiveness. It's one thing to know that a program is being executed as intended, and subsequently find out that it was ineffective in changing a social condition. It's quite another to conclude that a program is ineffective when, in fact, it was never delivered as intended.

For example, suppose that based on initially positive research findings from a few schools (Bottge et al., 2007), school board administrators decide to implement computerized instructional modules in their special education classes program within an entire school district. The program design calls for the modules to be delivered only by special education teachers, and also stipulates that the student-to-teacher ratio should be low. Unfortunately, due to budget cuts or a shortage of special education teachers, when the program is executed, the student-to-teacher ratio is far higher than mandated. If a subsequent outcome evaluation determines that the program produced no benefits beyond typical instructional techniques, was that because the program was inherently ineffective, or because its implementation was ineffective?

Similarly, imagine that most members of a target population aren't aware that a program is available to them at no cost, or even that it exists. If an outcome evaluation indicates little overall change in the dependent variable, administrators might erroneously conclude that the treatment components of the program were ineffective when, in fact, the treatments hadn't been given a fair test. Performing a process evaluation first will inform administrators about whether the program is successfully reaching its intended audience. If it isn't, steps can be taken to increase people's awareness of it—or correct other implementation problems—before an official evaluation of the program's effectiveness takes place.

Outcome Evaluation

An **outcome evaluation** *assesses a program's effectiveness.* Researchers must design and execute a study that meets ethical standards, operationalize variables in valid ways, gather and analyze data, and draw conclusions about whether a program had its intended effects. Data may be gathered using questionnaires, interviews, behavioral observation, performance tests, psychological inventories, unobtrusive and archival measures, and other techniques discussed throughout this book. Because outcome evaluation focuses on issues of causation, experimental designs are ideally suited to this phase of program evaluation. Depending on real-world constraints and the type of social program that researchers are evaluating, they may be able to design and conduct a randomized controlled trial. Otherwise, researchers typically turn to quasi-experimental designs or some of the "single-case" experimental designs that you'll learn about in the next chapter.

As you've seen, quasi-experimental designs vary greatly in the degree to which they allow researchers to rule out various threats to internal validity, and researchers seek to use the strongest quasi-experimental design possible in their given situation. The quality of the research design will influence the credibility of the evaluation report. As Kaufman et al. (2006) emphasize, "Evaluations are most likely to be utilized if they are theory driven, emphasize stake holder participation, employ multiple methods and have scientific rigor" (p. 191).

In determining whether a program is effective, one further potential problem deserves mention: **contamination,** *which occurs when knowledge, services, or other experiences intended for one group are unintentionally received by another group.* In experiments, a particularly worrisome form of contamination occurs when participants in a control condition acquire information, skills, or services that were intended only for the treatment group. If the treatment actually is effective, this unintended exposure will influence the control group's behavior. In turn, this will shrink the size of, or completely eliminate, posttreatment differences between the control group's and treatment group's scores on the dependent variables. Thus, it may seem that the treatment had no effect, when, in fact, it affected the behavior of both groups.

It's important therefore, either as part of the outcome evaluation or preferably during a process evaluation, to determine whether contamination exists. For example, in Vaughan et al.'s (2000) 4-year, nationwide HIV/AIDS intervention study in Tanzania, contamination could occur if many people in the geographic region that didn't receive the radio broadcast traveled to other regions and heard the program there, or heard a lot about the program from visitors coming from the treatment regions. The researchers, however, expected contamination to be low because travel was difficult and limited due to people's low incomes, and this was confirmed by additional data collected during the study.

Efficiency Assessment

An **efficiency assessment** *weighs the program's benefits and effectiveness in relation to its costs, to determine whether it is an efficient method for addressing the problem.* You've probably heard the term *cost–benefit analysis*, which represents one common type of efficiency assessment. In a cost–benefit analysis, the researcher assesses the financial cost of the program and tries to determine the cost savings (financial benefits) that the program yields.

Rossi et al. (2004) describe the case of a large bank that opened an on-site daycare center at one of its operations locations. The daycare center was funded and built only after an initial cost–benefit analysis determined that the center's projected monetary benefits would outweigh its projected costs. A second cost–benefit analysis was conducted after the daycare center had operated for a year. An outside consultant analyzed turnover and absenteeism rates for all bank employees, for employees who used the center, and for employees who used other daycare centers. She also examined the length of employees' maternity leaves. The findings suggested that use of the on-site daycare center lowered turnover and absenteeism, and shortened maternity leaves by about a week. Dollar savings were estimated for each of these effects, and also for free mass media publicity about the company generated by the on-site center. Overall, the consultant estimated that the daycare center saved the bank up to $232,000 for the year.

PROGRAM DIFFUSION

Clinical psychologists Joseph Durlak and Emily DuPre (2008) note that if social scientists' goal is to have the broadest possible impact on peoples' well-being, then demonstrating the effectiveness of a program is only an initial step. From that point, it becomes important to extend the program to other appropriate groups and settings, and then maintain the program for as long as it is needed. This process is called **program diffusion:** *implementing and maintaining effective programs in other settings or with other groups.* Building on earlier theoretical work (Rogers, 2003), Durlak and DuPre identify several phases of program diffusion:

* *dissemination,* which focuses on informing target groups and organizations that a program exists, has been demonstrated to be effective, and can be of value to them;

* *adoption,* which occurs when a new group or organization agrees to implement the program;

* *implementation,* which involves initiating the program in the new setting and executing it properly during a trial period;

* *sustainability,* which concerns maintaining the program over time.

Psychologists and other behavioral scientists may be called on to conduct applied research that helps administrators design effective strategies for program diffusion, or that seeks to determine why an initially effective program subsequently failed to diffuse. An awareness of common roadblocks that occur at each phase of the diffusion process can help researchers achieve such goals. Many of these roadblocks converge on a major theme promoted in the field of *community psychology:* the importance of collaboration and shared decision making between program developers and community members.

Durlak and DuPre (2008) note that poor dissemination of information often leaves other communities and potential sponsors unaware of a program's existence. If dissemination is inadequate, no leaders may emerge to spearhead the program's adoption, or potential sponsors may resist changing their current ways of doing things. If a program is adopted, unforeseen budgetary, personnel, or legal issues may delay or block its implementation in a particular community. If a program is implemented, that implementation may be of poor quality or too limited in scope. It is unrealistic to expect that a program will be implemented perfectly with all groups, and the more realistic question is whether the implementation is faithful enough to the intended design to achieve positive outcomes for program users. Poor or limited implementation reduces the chances of program success and jeopardizes program sustainability. Even effective programs may not be sustained over time due to budgetary cuts or revised funding priorities, personnel turnover, diminished community interest and changes in communities' needs, and the development of more efficient programs.

 CONCEPT CHECK 11.5 PROGRAM EVALUATION

Match each program evaluation stage on the left to the item on the right with which it is most strongly associated. Answers appear on page 377.

1. outcome evaluation

2. theory/design assessment

3. needs assessment

4. efficiency assessment

5. process evaluation

a. program monitoring. Is the program operating as intended?

b. Is there a valid rationale for each program component?

c. cost–benefit analysis

d. quasi-experimental or other experimental research

e. initial meetings with stakeholders, staff, target population

CHAPTER SUMMARY

- A quasi-experiment has some features of an experiment but lacks key aspects of experimental control. Individual participants in quasi-experiments are not randomly assigned to different conditions or, if there is only one group, no counterbalanced exposure to different conditions occurs. Quasi-experiments are often used to examine the effectiveness of treatments in real-world settings. They are more vulnerable to basic internal validity threats than true experiments.

- In a one-group posttest-only design, a treatment occurs and afterward the dependent variable is measured once. This is the weakest possible quasi-experimental design because there are no data with which the treatment group's posttest scores can be compared. Many confounding factors can produce the posttest scores. In a basic one-group pretest-posttest design, a dependent variable is measured once before and once after a treatment occurs. The degree to which a treatment group has changed can be assessed, but history, maturation, testing, instrumentation, regression, and attrition may be plausible confounding variables.

- In a simple interrupted time-series design, a dependent variable is repeatedly measured at periodic intervals before and after a treatment occurs. Typically, this design helps to examine maturation,

testing, and regression as potential confounds, as their effects will start to show up before treatment begins.

- In quasi-experiments with two or more groups, selection is a potential confounding variable, and selection also may interact with history, maturation, testing, instrumentation, regression, and attrition. In a posttest-only design with a nonequivalent control group, participants in one condition are exposed to a treatment, a nonequivalent group is not exposed, and scores from both groups are obtained after treatment ends. This is the weakest of the two-group designs: We can't be sure that any posttest differences weren't already present before the treatment began.

- In a pretest-posttest design with a nonequivalent control group, pre- and posttreatment scores are obtained for a treatment group and nonequivalent control group. Differential history is a major potential confound. If the treatment group has been chosen based on extreme pretest scores but the control group has not, differential regression will be a confounding variable. Other confounding variables also must be considered.

- In an interrupted time-series design with a nonequivalent control group, a series of pre- and posttreatment scores are obtained for a treatment group and nonequivalent control group. This is a strong quasi-experimental design. Differential history at the time of treatment exposure often is the major potential confound to consider.

- In a switching replication design, after a treatment group receives an intervention, the intervention is then administered on a delayed basis to the nonequivalent control group. Switching replications are considered strong quasi-experimental designs that can rule out most basic threats to internal validity.
- Different components of a comprehensive program evaluation have different functions. A needs assessment determines whether a need exists for a social program. A program theory

and design assessment evaluates the rationale for why a program is designed in a particular way. A process evaluation determines whether a program is being implemented as intended, and an outcome evaluation assesses whether a program is effective. Lastly, an efficiency assessment weighs the program's benefits and effectiveness in relation to its costs, to determine whether it is an efficient method for addressing the social problem at hand. Program diffusion is the process by which effective programs are implemented and maintained with different populations and in other settings. Dissemination, adoption, implementation, and sustainability are four stages of program diffusion.

KEY TERMS

attrition (p. 350)
contamination (p. 373)
efficiency assessment (p. 374)
history (p. 350)
instrumentation (p. 350)
interrupted time-series design with a nonequivalent control group (p. 361)
maturation (p. 350)
needs assessment (p. 371)
one-group posttest-only design (p. 350)

one-group pretest-posttest design (p. 351)
outcome evaluation (p. 373)
posttest-only design with a nonequivalent control group (p. 357)
pretest-posttest design with a nonequivalent control group (p. 359)
process evaluation (p. 372)
program diffusion (p. 374)
program evaluation (p. 369)

program theory and design assessment (p. 372)
quasi-experiment (p. 346)
regression to the mean (p. 350)
selection (p. 356)
selection interactions (p. 356)
simple interrupted time-series design (p. 353)
switching replication design (p. 365)
testing (p. 350)

ASSESS YOUR KNOWLEDGE

1. Describe how quasi-experimental designs differ, overall, from true experimental designs. What makes a control group "nonequivalent"?

2. What are some basic threats to internal validity when a quasi-experimental design has only a treatment group?

3. Describe why it's difficult to draw clear causal inferences from one-group posttest-only designs and one-group pretest-posttest designs.

4. Diagram a basic one-group pretest-posttest design and a simple interrupted time-series design. Describe how the time-series design improves on the internal validity of the one-group pretest-posttest design.

5. Overall, what basic threats to internal validity must be considered when a quasi-experimental design has a treatment group and a nonequivalent control group?

6. Explain the disadvantages of using a posttest-only design with a nonequivalent control group. Why do researchers sometimes have to use this design? Describe an example.

7. Diagram a pretest-posttest design with a nonequivalent control group, and explain the major internal validity threats to this design. Provide a research example.

8. Discuss why adding a nonequivalent control group usually improves the internal validity of a time-series design. Also describe why adding a time-series component improves the validity of a basic pretest-posttest design with a nonequivalent control group. Illustrate your points by describing an example.

9. What is a switching replication design? Diagram and discuss an example of a hypothetical or actual study.

10. Describe an example of a switching replication design with treatment removal. Explain how switching replication designs help to rule out several basic threats to internal validity.

11. Discuss some of the purposes and risks of conducting a program evaluation.

12. Name and describe five main components of a program evaluation, and their possible sequence within a single comprehensive program evaluation.

13. What are the four general phases of program diffusion? Illustrate how problems at each stage can prevent the diffusion of an effective treatment.

CONCEPT CHECKS

11.1 What Is a Quasi-Experiment?

1. true   **2.** true   **3.** false   **4.** true

11.2 Designs Without a Control Group

1. the absence of any data (e.g., mean scores, percentages) against which to compare the posttest scores   **2.** extreme scores on a measure (i.e., on the dependent variable or a characteristic related to the dependent variable)   **3.** maturation, testing, and regression to the mean

11.3 Designs With a Nonequivalent Control Group

1. selection × history [Arguably, the high nutrition program might affect the children's maturational

processes, also creating a selection × maturation confound. However, selection × history is the most direct answer.]   **2.** selection × testing   **3.** selection × regression to the mean

11.4 Switching Replication Designs

1. false   **2.** true   **3.** true   **4.** true

11.5 Program Evaluation

1. d   **2.** b   **3.** e   **4.** c   **5.** a

THINKING CRITICALLY AND APPLYING YOUR KNOWLEDGE

EXERCISE 1   Identify the Quasi-Experimental Design

Three quasi-experimental studies are briefly described below. For each study: **(a)** explain the characteristics that make its design quasi-experimental, **(b)** identify the specific type of quasi-experimental design that was used.

Study 1

Two college professors, one in southern Florida and one in Ohio, are interested in dream research and collaborate on a study. Both professors survey their introductory psychology students during one lecture. Students are asked how many nights (0 to 7) during the past week they experienced a nightmare. Unexpectedly, a month later, a devastating hurricane sweeps across southern Florida. A week later, after classes resume, both professors direct their students to fill out a second survey. Students are asked, again, to report the number of nights during the past week that they experienced a nightmare. The professors compare the frequency of nightmares for the two study periods for the two campuses.

Study 2

In 2005 a computer firm donated 50 new computers to Honeybee Elementary School. Located in a poor rural

area, the school previously had no computers for daily student use. The company's goal was to help improve the students' academic achievement. Honeybee uses the computers to create computer laboratories that sixth-grade students can utilize every day. Students in other grades don't use the computers. A researcher plots the standardized achievement test scores of Honeybee sixth-grade students for the years 1995 to 2014, which represent the 10 years before and 10 years after the computers were introduced. She also plots the scores of Honeybee fifth-graders for the same 20-year period. The researcher then examines the changes in the fifth- and sixth-graders' test score performance over this 20-year period.

Study 3

For 1 year, a physician monitors the weight of her patients who are on a special low-fat diet. She weighs each such patient once weekly. After the first year of the diet, the physician asks her patients to continue the diet and also take a "Wonder-Weight Loss" diet supplement. All weight-loss patients agree to take it over the next year. The physician continues to weigh her patients weekly for the next year and then compares the data from the diet-only period with the data from the diet + supplement period.

EXERCISE 2   **Daycare and Employee Absenteeism**

Industrial-organizational psychologist Michael Aamodt (1991) describes a case in which a large company decided to open an on-site daycare facility for its employees. Company officials hoped that this action would help reduce employee absenteeism, which usually was above 4% per month and was costly. Aamodt presents the findings from a time-series design that was used to evaluate whether opening the daycare center reduced absenteeism. Monthly absenteeism data for the company were gathered for the year before and year after the daycare center opened. The overall absenteeism rates were, respectively, 5.1% and 3.0% during the pretest and posttest periods. This 2% absolute reduction represents a 40% relative reduction in absenteeism, which is very significant for a large company. **Figure 11.13** shows the monthly data.

Imagine that you are an industrial-organizational psychologist and have been brought in on this project as a consultant. Here are your tasks for this exercise:

(a) Based on the data in Figure 11.13, what conclusion do you draw about whether the daycare center reduced employee absenteeism?

(b) Assume that the company had very low employee turnover (i.e., low attrition) during these 2 years. To what degree do you believe each of the following extraneous variables—history, maturation, testing, instrumentation, and regression to the mean— threaten the internal validity of a conclusion that the daycare center reduced absenteeism? Think

carefully about events outside the company, and also inside the company, that might affect absenteeism. What local, regional, or national factors might be responsible for some of the monthly fluctuations in absenteeism rates shown in Figure 11.13? What other types of changes in company policies or programs might affect absenteeism? How might differences in these factors before versus after the daycare center opened provide an alternative explanation for the results (i.e., a history confound)?

(c) This section contains a brief description of actual extraneous variables that occurred during the 2 years of data collection, and a follow-up question for you to answer. Don't read further until after you have completed parts **(a)** and **(b)** of this exercise. Based on the information provided in the next two paragraphs, what conclusion do you now draw about whether the daycare center reduced absenteeism? Explain your answer.

1985 (pretreatment): March, the local unemployment rate is 4.1%; June, the main highway to the workplace closes and then reopens in August; November, there is a major snowstorm.

1986 (posttreatment): March, a more flexible work schedule is introduced (e.g., instead of working from 8 a.m. to 5 p.m. each day, a worker can arrive and leave an hour earlier or later, to take care of personal business); April, the local unemployment rate is 9.3%; July, the company starts a wellness (i.e., mental/physical fitness) program for its employees; November and December, the weather is mild.

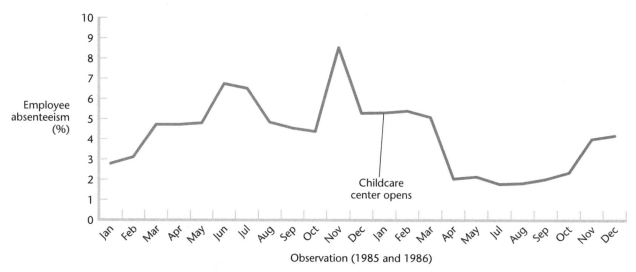

Figure 11.13 Monthly absenteeism before and after the opening of an on-site employee daycare center. Note that data from June 1986 are missing from the original data set. (Republished with permission of Cengage Learning SO, from "Monthly absenteeism before and after the opening of an on-site employee daycare center." *Applied Industrial/Organizational Psychology*, Aamodt, 1991. Permission conveyed through Copyright Clearance Center, Inc.)

(d) Suppose that we were going to add a nonequivalent control group to this design. Name one good option for the nonequivalent group: Who might they be?

EXERCISE 3 Big Brother Is Watching

In a large city, traffic safety officials notice that over the past 2 months, four major intersections have experienced a sharp spike in the number of automobile accidents. Most major intersections in the city have an average of 1 to 2 accidents per month. Over the past year, the average accident rate for these intersections was 2 per month, for the first 10 months. But the last 2 months, these same intersections have averaged 6 accidents per month.

Police reports suggest that many of the accidents were caused by drivers running red lights (i.e., drivers speed up to make it through the intersection before the light turns red). So, with great speed and efficiency, traffic engineers install red light cameras at each of those intersections in less than a week. If a car runs the red light, the camera takes a photo of the car and a ticket is sent to the driver. (My city already has such cameras, and if yours doesn't, just wait.) Signs are posted to warn drivers that the intersections are being monitored by cameras and that costly tickets will be issued for running red lights.

That month and the next, the overall number of accidents at those intersections returns to a near-normal rate. Here are the data (number of accidents) for the 2 months before and 2 months after the cameras are installed:

Intersection A: 6, 5, 2, 2
Intersection B: 8, 6, 1, 2
Intersection C: 7, 4, 1, 2
Intersection D: 7, 5, 3, 1

City officials conclude that, at least based on the short-term data, the red light cameras appear to have worked in reducing traffic accidents. Citizen groups, however, aren't so sure that the money to install the cameras was wisely spent during tough economic times.

(a) Identify at least two basic threats to internal validity that could explain, in part, why the number of accidents decreased at these intersections after the red light cameras were installed.

(b) Assume that the city budget will not permit more than four intersections to be outfitted with red light cameras. Choose another research design that would be realistic to use and might yield better-quality information about the effectiveness of the red light cameras.

LaunchPad
macmillan learning

To practice key concepts from this chapter, visit the LaunchPad Solo for Research Methods at **launchpadworks.com.**

12

SINGLE-CASE EXPERIMENTAL DESIGNS

CHAPTER OUTLINE

Some people diagnosed with autism or other developmental disorders engage in repetitive behaviors that inflict self-injury: actions such as banging their heads against objects, striking their heads with their fists, and biting themselves (MacLean & Dornbush, 2012). Travis, diagnosed as having severe autism, began to engage in frequent self-injurious behavior when he was 11 to 12 years old (Banda, McAfee, & Hart, 2009, 2012). On average, he struck his head with powerful closed-fist blows several times a minute. To reduce the risk of injury, he was forced to wear lightweight boxing gloves and a padded boxing helmet at school and at home.

Travis's special education teachers worried about his potential for injury and his social rejection by classmates, who feared him. The teachers contacted members of an educational psychology department who had expertise in special education and in developing interventions to reduce behavioral problems. Led by Devender Banda, the researchers used operant conditioning principles (e.g., positive reinforcement) to reduce Travis's self-injurious behavior, but the beneficial effects didn't last (Banda et al., 2009).

When Travis was 14 years old, the researchers devised a second treatment (Banda et al., 2012). On his own, Travis "had recently begun wrapping his hands tightly in one or more large blankets, covering his head with a blanket, or placing one or more blankets in his lap at various times" (p. 166). Travis hit himself less often while using the blankets, but he couldn't use them all the time (e.g., at mealtimes). His parents and teachers also believed that the blanket use would lead to continued peer social rejection.

Banda et al. (2012) sought to reduce Travis's self-injurious behavior and reliance on the blankets. During their study's initial stage, called a *baseline phase,* they conducted seven 5-minute sessions at school in which a teaching assistant presented Travis with various activities (e.g., puzzles). No blankets were allowed, and Travis wore his helmet and gloves. If Travis started to hit himself, the assistant followed standard school procedure: She verbally reprimanded him (e.g., "Don't hit") and attempted to block his further attempts. The researchers measured how many times Travis hit himself during each session.

Next, during an initial *intervention phase,* the researchers held 13 task sessions in which (1) Travis could hold a large blanket in his hands, (2) the assistant verbally reinforced Travis (e.g., "Good job") every 10 seconds after he refrained from hitting himself, and (3) the assistant withdrew attention by looking away and not speaking to Travis for 10 seconds each time he hit himself. Figure 12.1 shows that Travis's self-blows decreased markedly from the initial baseline to the initial intervention phases.

For the next two sessions—a second baseline phase—the researchers reinstated the procedures from the first baseline phase (e.g., no blanket, standard school procedure). During this phase, Travis frequently hit himself. Then, in a second intervention phase, the researchers reinstated the intervention treatment for four sessions; Travis only hit himself once during this phase. The pattern of findings over these first four phases supported the conclusion that the intervention caused the change in Travis's behavior.

In the next two phases, the researchers faded (i.e., gradually reduced) the blanket's size by almost 90% and then removed it entirely. This procedure successfully maintained Travis's low rate of self-injurious behavior. Finally, the researchers conducted follow-up observations 5 and 6 months later. Figure 12.1 shows that the beneficial treatment effect persisted. Travis's teachers and mother also reported that his self-injurious behavior had decreased at school and home, and only occasionally did he seek out a blanket or small towel to help prevent himself from striking his head.

Banda et al.'s (2012) study illustrates an important category of research designs called **single-case experimental designs,** *which allow researchers to systematically examine how an independent variable influences the behavior of an individual case.* For example, Banda and coworkers manipulated an independent variable by creating four phases of the study in

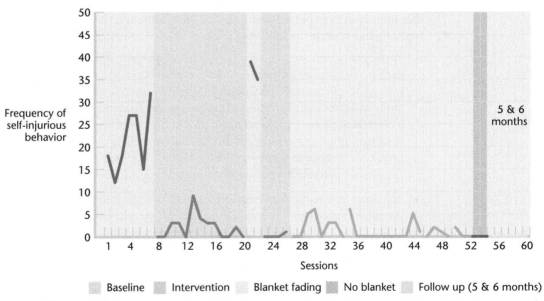

Figure 12.1 Frequency of self-injurious behavior in a 14-year-old boy. This single-case experimental design has seven phases: baseline, intervention, (return to) baseline, (return to) intervention, fading (gradual reduction of the intervention), no blanket, and follow-up observations recorded 5 and 6 months later. (Data from Banda et al., 2012.)

which a treatment was either present or absent, and a fifth phase in which they slowly faded the treatment. The researchers monitored Travis's self-injurious behavior (the dependent variable) throughout each phase and exposed him to these phases in a particular sequence that would permit plausible conclusions to be drawn about the treatment's effectiveness.

A SINGLE-CASE APPROACH TO EXPERIMENTATION

Learning Objectives

After studying this section, you should be able to:

- Describe key features of single-case experimentation and its advantages.
- Discuss the use of single-case designs in basic and applied research.

There are many types of single-case experimental designs. Collectively, researchers refer to them by different, interchangeable names: *single-case experimental designs, single-case designs, single-subject* or *single-participant designs, N = 1 designs,* and *small N designs.* Let's discuss some key characteristics of these designs.

KEY FEATURES

Single-case experiments often involve only one participant, but they do not limit a researcher to studying just one individual. A research design similar to the one portrayed in Figure 12.1, involving a sequence of baseline and intervention phases, can be applied to several individuals within one study. Using a single-case approach, we would examine the results individually for each participant.

What makes a design a *single-case* design is not that only one participant is studied. In fact, some single-case experimental designs require two or more participants, and single-case designs are also used in experiments where the "case" is a group, a community, or some other social unit that comprises many people. Rather, these designs are called "single-case" because they enable researchers to draw causal conclusions about how an independent variable influences each participant or social unit. Although there are exceptions, these designs typically incorporate the following features (Barlow, Nock, & Hersen, 2009).

- *Participants serve as their own control or comparison.* This is accomplished by exposing each participant, at least once, to an experimental and a control condition, or to multiple experimental conditions. In applied research, such as Banda et al.'s (2012) study of Travis's self-injurious behavior, the experimental condition is referred to as a **treatment phase** (or **intervention phase**) *that involves the presentation of a specific treatment or other intervention.* In the control condition, commonly called a **baseline phase**, *the treatment is not presented.* Single-case experiments often begin with a control condition to establish a participant's initial baseline behavior.

- *The dependent variable is measured across multiple trials or sessions within each condition of the experiment,* to gain a more reliable assessment of the participant's behavior.

- *The research design includes built-in replications,* allowing the researcher to assess whether the effects of an independent variable on individual behavior are reliable. One design strategy, for example, is to alternate a participant's exposure to the control and experimental conditions for at least two cycles, to see whether a similar pattern of results emerges for each cycle.

- *The data are examined separately for each participant,* because the researcher seeks to determine how each individual responded to the independent variable. This approach differs from the typical data analysis conducted in *group experimental designs* (i.e., between- and within-subjects designs) described in Chapters 8 and 9. In group designs, the influence of an independent variable is typically determined by aggregating the data collected from multiple participants within each condition. For example, a researcher would statistically test whether the mean score for all participants in a treatment group differs significantly from the mean score for all participants in a control group or another treatment group. Note that single-case experimenters may choose to supplement their analysis of individual participants' responses with overall group analyses.

- *A visual analysis of the data may be the sole basis for judging whether the independent variable produced an effect.* Data gathered in single-case experiments are typically analyzed by graphing or otherwise visually inspecting each participant's pattern of results (Smith, 2012). Especially in applied research examining the effectiveness of interventions, many single-case experimenters believe that when visual inspection reveals an obvious and consistent difference in behavior between the experimental and control conditions, it is not necessary to use inferential statistical tests to determine whether an effect is statistically significant. Other single-case researchers employ statistical tests, an approach that has been increasingly advocated in recent decades (Shadish, Hedges, & Pustejovsky, 2014).

ADVANTAGES

When investigating some issues, an experimenter may have access to only a relatively small number of potential participants. This situation might arise, for example, when studying a rare psychological disorder or medical condition, or conversely, an extraordinary but rare ability, such as musical genius. To illustrate, in the 1960s and 1970s, groundbreaking cognitive neuroscience research by psychobiologist Roger Sperry, psychologist Michael Gazzaniga, and their colleagues analyzed how the left and right cerebral hemispheres of the human brain respond independently to various experimental tasks (Gazzaniga, Bogen, & Sperry, 1965).

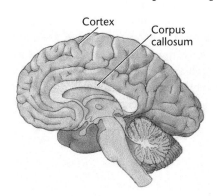

The participants in these studies were medical patients who, in order to control their severe epileptic seizures, had undergone a rare operation that severed their corpus callosum, the major neural connection between the brain's left and right hemispheres (**Figure 12.2**). These individuals became known as "split-brain patients," and there weren't many of them. Both then and now, split-brain experiments often take place with just one, two, or a few more patients (Mooshagian, Iacoboni, & Zaidel, 2009). Split-brain research led to major discoveries about the relative specialization of the left and right hemispheres of the human brain.

It would be a mistake, however, to view single-case experiments as merely a "last resort" option that researchers use only when they can't gain access to enough participants to use traditional between-subjects or within-subjects designs. In many instances, a researcher's interest lies solely or primarily in examining whether an intervention has influenced a single person's, or each of several people's, behavior (Barlow & Nock, 2009). A therapist may want to assess whether a treatment alters a patient's behavior, or an educator may seek to determine whether teaching a new reading strategy to two developmentally delayed children will improve each child's reading performance.

Clinical researchers who use single-case designs point out another advantage of this approach: flexibility (Tate et al., 2008). Treatments can be customized for particular individuals and settings, and then assessed.

Figure 12.2 Single-case experiments with split-brain patients. The corpus callosum is a band of about 200 million neuronal axons that provides the main neural connection between the left and right cerebral hemispheres. In split-brain patients, this connection has been cut as a means to control their epilepsy. (Data from Kolb & Whishaw, 2006.)

If a treatment doesn't appear to be producing meaningful change in a participant's behavior, researchers need not discontinue the experiment and start over from scratch. Rather, they can tweak the treatment—or introduce an entirely new treatment—and then continue to record data as they introduce the revised treatment in a new phase of the experiment. If the revised treatment appears to produce a change in behavior, the researchers can then introduce additional baseline and treatment phases to examine whether these behavior changes are replicable.

Many advocates of single-case experimentation also argue that this approach avoids what they see as a key drawback to traditional group experimental designs: the potential for averaged results to mask important individual differences (Barlow et al., 2009). Using a within-subjects experimental design, for example, suppose a cognitive psychologist exposes 40 participants to the same word lists. Half the lists contain concrete words (e.g., *dish, map, wrist*) and half contain abstract words (*just, see, think*). Examining the mean number of words recalled for each type of list, the researcher finds a statistically significant difference such that, overall, participants remembered more concrete words than abstract words, a principle called the *concrete word effect*. This overall finding does not mean, however, that the effect occurred with each participant in the experiment. Rather, some participants may have recalled more abstract words than concrete words, and for others the type of word may have made no difference.

Similarly, suppose that a clinical psychologist uses a matched-groups waiting list control design to evaluate the effectiveness of a new psychotherapy treatment for depression. The results indicate that, overall, participants who received this new treatment experienced a significantly greater reduction in depression than did participants assigned to the waiting list or to a more traditional form of psychotherapy. This "averaged" finding does not mean that every patient benefited from the new psychotherapy: Some may have shown no improvement, and some may have even become more depressed.

Lest you begin to doubt the value of traditional between- and within-subjects designs, let me emphasize that the group-design approach of examining averaged responses is not a flaw: It's simply an important part of "doing business" when it comes to studying human and nonhuman behavior. Organisms vary within a given species; such variability increases the challenge of uncovering principles of behavior. Moreover, person × situation factorial designs can lead to important discoveries about the *types* of people (or nonhumans) who respond one way, the opposite way, or not at all, to a particular independent variable. Group designs represent one major approach to basic and applied experimental research, and single-case designs bring another approach to the scientific table. Each has its own advantages and disadvantages.

USE IN BASIC AND APPLIED RESEARCH

Single-case experimentation was a common basic research strategy in psychology's early years. In the mid- to late 1800s, pioneering German experimental psychologists such as Gustav Fechner (1801–1887) and Wilhelm Wundt (1832–1920) studied human sensation and perception by repeatedly exposing small numbers of participants to various stimuli (e.g., lights, sounds). Fechner founded a subfield called **psychophysics**, *which examines the relation between physical properties of stimuli (such as their intensity) and sensory-perceptual responses.* For example, to determine a person's *absolute threshold* for hearing a sound (e.g., "What is the faintest level of a particular sound that a person can reliably hear?"), Fechner systematically varied the loudness of a sound over many trials and asked participants to report whether they detected the sound for each trial. Data collected from each participant were analyzed at the individual level.

Alan Kazdin (1982), a leading proponent of single-case research, noted that

> analyses of publications in psychological journals have shown that from the beginning of the 1900s through the 1920s and 30s research with very small samples (e.g., one to five subjects) was the rule rather than the exception (Robinson & Foster, 1979). Research typically excluded the characteristics currently viewed as essential to experiments, such as large sample sizes, control groups, and the evaluation of data by statistical analysis. (p. 6)

Over time, a shift occurred in experimental methodology toward the types of between-, within-, and factorial experimental designs described in Chapters 8 and 9: designs in which larger samples typically are included and the conclusions are based on comparing how people respond, *on average*, in the various conditions of the experiment. The development of statistical techniques for analyzing such aggregated data facilitated this methodological shift. Thus, single-case experimentation joins its nonexperimental cousin—the case study—in providing a methodological and philosophical alternative to the "group methodological approach" that predominates in contemporary psychological science.

The Experimental Analysis of Behavior

Within psychology, behaviorist B. F. Skinner's highly influential research on operant conditioning rested heavily on single-case experimentation (Skinner, 1938). Operant conditioning is a form of learning in which behavior is influenced by its consequences—consequences such as positive reinforcement, negative reinforcement, and punishment. Skinner sought to discover general laws of learning by using a scientific approach that he called the **experimental analysis of behavior**, *the intensive study, under controlled conditions, of how environmental stimuli and consequences regulate an individual organism's behavior.*

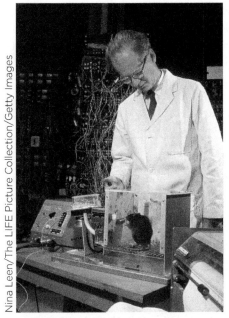

Skinner's basic research took place in the laboratory, most often with rats or pigeons as subjects (**Figure 12.3**). Relying on visual rather than statistical analysis, Skinner examined changes that occurred in each organism's observable behavior (e.g., pressing a lever) in response to environmental changes that he manipulated as the independent variable. Skinner's approach emphasized studying many responses—often thousands of responses—from a single or small number of subjects, rather than a few responses from many subjects. The experimental analysis of behavior eventually emerged as its own psychological subfield and became strongly associated with use of single-case experimental designs (Kazdin, 1982).

Applied Behavior Analysis and Other Fields

Over time, behavioral researchers developed a growing interest in applying operant conditioning principles to enhance human welfare. Additionally, clinical psychologists and other practitioners who used newly emerging behavioral therapies wanted to empirically demonstrate the effectiveness of their treatments for the individual cases they treated, and do so with greater scientific control than was common in typical case study reports (Hersen, Michelson, & Bellack, 1984). Single-case experimental designs provided just the ticket.

Eventually, this field of clinical research became known as **applied behavior analysis**, *the application "of the experimental analysis of behavior to problems of social importance"* (Society for the Experimental Analysis of Behavior, 2012, para 1). Banda et al.'s (2012) study to reduce

Figure 12.3 Behaviorist B. F. Skinner. Skinner used a single-case experimental approach to discover many principles of operant conditioning.

Nina Leen/The LIFE Picture Collection/Getty Images

Travis' self-injurious behavior, discussed at the start of the chapter (see Figure 12.1), illustrates applied behavior analysis. In the past 50 years, single-case experimental designs have evolved in number and complexity. Much of this impetus has come from researchers working in applied behavior analysis, other applied clinical fields, and the experimental analysis of behavior (e.g., Kazdin, 1982; Barlow et al., 2009).

In other fields, psychologists who study psychophysics and other sensory-perceptual processes continue to conduct single-case experiments, often performing individual and group analyses (Meddis & Lecluyse, 2011). In *cognitive neuroscience*, psychologists and other scientists have conducted single-case experiments (again, often in combination with group analyses) to examine brain processes that underlie memory, perception, language, and consciousness (Herbert & Kübler, 2011).

On the applied front, in *clinical neuropsychology* (the psychological assessment and treatment of people with brain injuries) and other fields, single-case experiments are among the research approaches used to evaluate treatment effectiveness (Baldwin & Powell, 2015). Researchers in *psychopharmacology* (the study of how drugs affect psychological functioning) sometimes use single-case experiments to assess whether individual patients benefit from specific medical drugs.

✓ **CONCEPT CHECK 12.1** **A SINGLE-CASE APPROACH TO EXPERIMENTATION**

Decide whether each statement below is true or false. Answers appear on page 407 at the end of the chapter.

1. An experiment using a single-case design must have only one participant.
2. Typically, in single-case designs, the participant's behavior is measured several times in each condition.
3. A century ago, psychological experiments often involved few participants and the individual analysis of each participant's responses.
4. Experimenters should use single-case designs only when they cannot recruit enough participants to use a traditional between- or within-subjects design.
5. Applied behavior analysis is the only field that currently uses single-case designs.

TYPES OF SINGLE-CASE DESIGNS

Learning Objectives

After studying this section, you should be able to:

- Describe the key features of ABAB, multiple-baseline, and changing-criterion designs.
- Explain how each design attempts to rule out alternative causal explanations.
- Identify strengths and limitations of each design.

In recent decades, the most extensive and comprehensive discussions of single-case designs as a distinct experimental methodology have focused on clinical and other applied contexts (Barlow et al., 2009). Therefore, we'll focus on how several types of single-case experimental designs are used to draw causal conclusions about the effectiveness of interventions.

ABAB (WITHDRAWAL/REVERSAL) DESIGNS

ABAB designs *typically involve a sequence of phases in which a treatment is either absent or present.* They are the most basic of all single-case experimental designs. Most often, an "A" phase represents a period of baseline observation in which the treatment is absent, and "B" represents a phase in which the participant is exposed to a treatment. The temporal sequence of phases is indicated by reading from left to right. An ABAB design, for example, involves an initial baseline phase, first treatment phase, second baseline phase, and second treatment phase. Note that in the plural form, the term *ABAB designs* often refers to a general category of single-case designs. Thus, specific designs such as ABA, ABAB, ABABA, and ABABAB all fall under the general label of ABAB designs (Kazdin, 1982).

ABAB designs are also commonly called **withdrawal designs** (or **reversal designs**), *because after the initial A phase the subsequent A phases involve a "withdrawal" of the treatment or a "reversal" of the procedures.* Thus, in an ABAB design, the second A phase might be referred to as a "second baseline phase," a "withdrawal phase," or a "reversal phase." Banda et al.'s (2012) experiment in which they reduced Travis's self-injurious behavior was, at its core, an ABAB design to which extras phases were added to reduce the size of Travis's blanket, remove the blanket, and obtain follow-up assessments.

Although the "A" phase in most applied withdrawal designs represents a period in which the treatment is not present—namely, an initial baseline phase—in some experiments the A phase represents one treatment and the B phase represents another. For example, in one study, neuropsychologists used an ABAB design to directly compare the effectiveness of two treatments, treatment A and treatment B, in improving the ability of a man with a brain injury to remember to perform daily tasks (McKerracher, Powell, & Oyebode, 2005).

An ABAB Experiment

A classic study designed by experimental psychologist Montrose Wolf, a laboratory animal researcher who became a pioneer of applied behavior analysis, nicely illustrates the key features of an ABAB design. In contrast to Banda et al.'s (2012) intervention, which reduced the frequency of undesirable responses (i.e., self-injurious behaviors), this study by Margaret Johnston, Montrose Wolf, and their colleagues increased the frequency of a desired behavior (Johnston, Kelley, Harris, & Wolf, 1966).

The participant was a 3½-year-old named Mark, who at preschool was physically sedentary and spent little time playing with other children. The researchers devised a treatment that used social reinforcement to increase Mark's level of physical activity. His teachers had observed that Mark spent little time playing on outdoor climbing equipment and especially avoided a large "climbing frame" (otherwise known as "monkey bars"). Thus, Johnston and her colleagues initially focused on the goal of increasing the amount of time that Mark used the climbing frame, which in the terminology of applied behavior analysis represented the **target behavior**: *the behavior that a treatment is designed to change.* In broader methodological terms, the target behavior was a dependent variable and the presence or absence of the treatment constituted the independent variable.

Figure 12.4 shows the study's design and results. The first baseline phase took place during outdoor play periods for 9 days, during which Mark's two teachers interacted with him as they normally did. Mark spent little time using any climbing equipment. On Day 7 he touched the climbing frame once; this represented his total contact with the climbing frame during the baseline period. During this phase, Mark spent most of his time by himself in the sandbox.

Next, the researchers introduced a treatment phase that they called the first reinforcement phase. Mark received continuous social reinforcement from one of his teachers whenever he used the climbing frame. The teacher paid attention to him, smiled, spoke to him, and so on. He did not receive the teacher's social attention during outdoor play when he engaged in other behaviors (e.g., standing around or sitting in the sandbox). Because Mark rarely used the climbing apparatus to begin with, a procedure called *shaping* was initially used to get him to the climbing frame so that continuous social reinforcement could be applied. At first, the

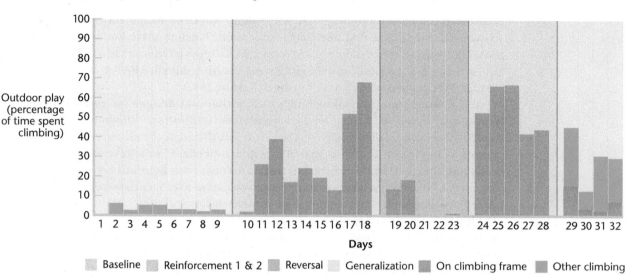

Figure 12.4 An ABAB design with a generalization phase. Along the *x*-axis, baseline and reversal (i.e., return to baseline) represent the two "A" phases; Reinforcement 1 and Reinforcement 2 are the two "B" phases (i.e., treatment phases). A generalization phase was added to the basic ABAB design. (Data from Johnston et al., 1966.)

teacher provided social reinforcement if Mark merely approached the climbing frame. Then reinforcement was given only when he came closer to it, then closer still, and finally only when he touched or climbed on the frame. It didn't take long for Mark to start playing on the frame. Figure 12.4 shows that compared to his baseline, Mark's time spent on the climbing frame increased substantially during the 9 days of treatment.

Next, a reversal (i.e., second baseline) phase was instituted for 5 days. The teacher stopped providing Mark with praise and attention when he used the climbing frame, but did provide social reinforcement to him at other times. Mark's climbing frame behavior quickly decreased and by the end of this reversal phase he was hardly spending any time on the frame. Had the study ended at this point, it would have represented an ABA design. However, Johnston et al. (1966) reinstated the treatment, which they called Reinforcement Phase 2. This constituted the second B phase, converting the design into ABAB. During this phase, the percent of out-door time that Mark spent on the bars jumped dramatically and remained high.

Figure 12.4 shows that beyond the standard ABAB phases, Johnston et al. (1966) added a fifth stage to the study. During this *generalization phase,* the amount of social reinforcement that Mark received while on the climbing frame was reduced gradually. Mark's teachers also began to periodically reinforce Mark when he engaged in other forms of physical activity, including climbing on other playground equipment. Ultimately, the teachers provided social reinforcement to Mark at a level similar to that provided to the other preschool children. Mark's physical activity level during the generalization stage remained well above his initial baseline levels, and when the researchers conducted follow-up observations of Mark the next autumn, he was still physically active.

Drawing Causal Inferences

If the researchers' goal was to demonstrate that social reinforcement could be successfully applied to increase Mark's physical activity, then why not just have two stages: baseline (A) and treatment (B)? Mark's climbing behavior increased substantially during stage B, and it seems obvious, doesn't it, that the new social reinforcement procedures caused this change in his behavior? Although some people might accept such a conclusion as fact, as a student of research methods, you're probably not one of them, because you know that we need to think critically about potential confounding variables that might threaten the internal validity of this AB design.

In Mark's case, for example, *history* would be one confounding variable that we need to consider. A history confound would occur in an AB design if the change in the target behavior from Phase A to Phase B resulted not from the treatment, but from other environmental factors that may have differed between these two time periods. Perhaps during the baseline phase, it just so happened that the weather was cool and gloomy, or Mark's parents experienced a spike in marital problems and often argued in front of him. And perhaps as the treatment phase began and then continued, the weather became warm and sunny, or his parents' marital conflict lessened. These factors might have affected Mark's general energy level and mood, and partly or fully accounted for his greater level of physical activity during the treatment phase. We would also need to consider whether Mark, after being relatively inactive and solitary for so long, might have finally been ready on his own to branch out and try something new (i.e., playing on the climbing frame) even without the treatment. This would represent a *maturation* confound: a change in behavior resulting from normal biological maturation or an accumulation of personal experiences, rather than from a treatment.

Because it fails to rule out many potential confounding variables, the AB design represents a "pre-experimental" design rather than a true single-case experimental design (Barlow et al., 2009). Converting an AB design into an ABA design lets us examine whether behavior reverts to its initial levels—or at least moves in that direction—when the treatment is withdrawn. If it does, this boosts our confidence that the treatment was the most plausible cause of the change in the target behavior. In Mark's case, the amount of time he spent on the climbing frame decreased substantially in the first two days after treatment was withdrawn, and then dropped close to baseline levels. What plausible alternative explanations exist? Just when the treatment was withdrawn, his parents coincidentally happened to start fighting again? The weather just happened to change for the worse again? It's possible, but unlikely.

Adding a second treatment stage, which converts an ABA design to an ABAB design, has two benefits. First, if the target behavior changes in a way similar to how it changed during the first treatment stage, this strengthens the internal validity of the experiment. In essence, we will have conducted an AB design twice (i.e., $A_1B_1 \ldots A_2B_2$) and replicated our initial results. To offer an alternative causal explanation, we would now have to identify a confounding factor that varied between A_1 and B_1, between B_1 and A_2, and between A_2 and B_2, in such a way that could plausibly account for the changes in the target behavior. A second benefit of adding a second "B" stage is that, if the treatment is in fact successful, then the desired behavior change will be in effect when the study ends. In Mark's case, had Johnston et al. (1966) used an ABA design, the study would have ended where it began during the initial baseline phase: with a physically inactive child who also spent little time playing with other children.

Special Concerns

ABAB designs have two potential drawbacks: one ethical and one logical. The ethical concern arises in treatment effectiveness research. Suppose that after an initial baseline phase, the first treatment phase produces the intended change in behavior (e.g., Travis strikes his head less often; Mark is more physically active). To rule out potential confounding variables and increase the internal validity of the experiment, the treatment must now be removed—at least temporarily—to assess whether the target behavior reverts to baseline levels. This withdrawal phase also has practical value. If the treatment isn't the true cause of the behavior change, then continuing it would waste resources, and efforts could be better spent finding another treatment that truly benefits the participant. But, is it ethical to remove a treatment that initially seems to be effective and thus risk that a participant's problem behavior (e.g., striking one's head, being physically sedentary) will increase? Applied researchers who are considering ABAB designs need to take into account potential physical, psychological, and social risks that may result from exposing the participant to a treatment withdrawal phase.

The second drawback to ABAB designs involves a difficulty in drawing conclusions if the target behavior (or any dependent variable) *does not* revert toward baseline levels during a withdrawal phase. Suppose that during the second baseline phase in Johnston et al.'s (1966) experiment, Mark's time playing on the climbing frame did not decline (i.e., there was no clear decrease toward baseline levels). **Figure 12.5** illustrates this hypothetical pattern of results. What can we conclude?

If your first thought is, "Well, this means that the social reinforcement wasn't the real cause of why Mark's behavior changed from Baseline Phase 1 to Treatment Phase 1," you might be correct; but you might just as likely be wrong. The problem is that it's not clear what we can infer from the pattern of data in Figure 12.5. It is possible, for example, that during the first treatment phase the teachers' social reinforcement was indeed responsible for increasing the time Mark spent on the climbing frame, but once he began to play regularly on the frame, other consequences acted as reinforcers and maintained his behavior after the treatment was withdrawn. Perhaps he received attention from other children on the climbing frame. Perhaps, to his surprise and delight, he found that he actually enjoyed scampering around the climbing frame. In other words, the reinforcement Mark received from a teacher during the treatment phase may no longer have been needed to maintain Mark's behavior of playing on the climbing frame, but it still may have been the causal factor responsible for getting him to play on the climbing frame in the first place.

If we wish to conduct a single-case experiment but believe that a target behavior will not likely revert to baseline levels during a withdrawal phase, then we should avoid using an ABAB design. For example, suppose the treatment is designed to enhance an academic, athletic, social, or job skill. We might expect that if the participant's skill improves during the

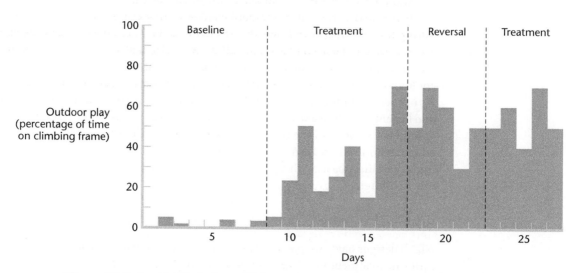

Figure 12.5 An ABAB design with hypothetical results demonstrating a lack of target behavior reversal during the reversal phase. For the baseline and two treatment (i.e., reinforcement) phases, these hypothetical results are similar to those shown in Figure 12.4. However, in this figure, during the reversal phase Mark continued to spend considerable time playing outdoors on the climbing apparatus. This pattern of findings would make it more difficult to draw clear conclusions about the treatment's effectiveness.

initial treatment phase, then once this learning has occurred, the participant's skill will not diminish just because the treatment is withdrawn. In this event, to demonstrate the causal effect of a treatment, we could turn to another category of single-case designs: multiple-baseline designs.

MULTIPLE-BASELINE DESIGNS

Like ABAB designs, multiple-baseline designs incorporate initial A and B phases, but they take a different approach to replicating those phases so that the potential effects of confounding factors can be ruled out. In a **multiple-baseline design**:

- *behavior is repeatedly measured first during a baseline period and then during a treatment period;*
- *this procedure is replicated using at least one other person, behavior, or setting;*
- *the time at which the treatment is introduced (and thus, typically, the length of the baseline period) varies across the different people, behaviors, or settings.*

Remember that the term "treatment" is used broadly here: It refers to any type of intervention or different condition of an independent variable that the researcher manipulates.

There are three major types of multiple-baseline designs: across subjects, across behaviors, and across settings. They share a simple underlying logic on which the ability to draw causal inferences is based. To begin, a baseline phase is initiated for each person, behavior, or setting being studied, which creates multiple baselines. Second, the baseline phase is switched to a treatment phase only for the first person, behavior, or setting. In this phase, the researcher hopes to see a clear, immediate change in scores on the dependent variable—but only for that person, behavior, or setting. Meanwhile, all the other baseline phases remain in effect and no change in the dependent variable scores is expected because there is no exposure to the treatment. Later, the baseline phase for the second person, behavior, or setting is switched to a treatment phase, and then on a staggered schedule this same procedure is followed for each remaining person, behavior, or setting.

If scores on the dependent variable reliably change only when each particular person, behavior, or setting is exposed to the intervention, this suggests that the treatment was responsible for those changes. Any alternative explanation for the results would have to explain not only why scores on the dependent variable differed between the baseline and treatment phases, but also why the scores changed only at the unique time when the treatment was introduced for each person, behavior, or setting. Thus, the temporal pattern created by using baselines of different lengths helps to rule out what otherwise might be many plausible alternative explanations. Let's make this logic more concrete by looking at some examples.

Multiple-Baseline Design Across Subjects

In a **multiple-baseline design across subjects**, *two or more participants are exposed to the same treatment and the switch from baseline to treatment periods is staggered across participants.* Although this design requires at least two participants, it typically involves more. To illustrate, consider the following study, one that you might relate to if you've ever suffered physical strain or injury while working at a part-time or full-time job. Work-related injuries are a serious concern. Overall, almost 3.5 million workers in the United States experience nonfatal on-the-job injuries in a given year, and in about half of those cases, the injury causes the worker to miss days from work, to experience restricted job duties, or to transfer to a different job (U. S. Department of Labor, Bureau of Labor Statistics, 2015).

Megan Scherrer and David Wilder (2008) used a multiple-baseline design across subjects to examine the effectiveness of a job safety training program. The three voluntary participants, Sara, Mike, and Tanya, were young adults employed as full-time cocktail servers in a large bar located in a southeastern American city. For hours during each shift, they and the other cocktail servers at this bar carried drinks to customers on cocktail trays that could weigh as much as 20 pounds when fully loaded. Especially when the bar was packed with customers, this repetitive carrying of heavy loads caused some cocktail servers to experience sore muscles and aching joints, and they had complained to their managers about it. The servers and managers wanted to alleviate these symptoms and prevent them from developing into disabling musculoskeletal disorders, which involve injuries to muscles, joints, and nerves. If you've heard of carpal tunnel syndrome, then you're familiar with one example.

The researchers developed a safety checklist of eight behavioral guidelines that specified the proper way to carry cocktail trays so as to minimize the risk of injury. For example, two items on the checklist were "Safe wrist position: Wrist is straight and tray is resting on (i.e., touching) forearm" and "Safe tray height from the body: Tray is held near body, not above shoulder height." The training program was implemented individually for each participant in the same way, but at a different time. For each of the eight carrying techniques, the trainer first explained the technique and then demonstrated it. Next, each participant was asked to describe and demonstrate the correct technique, with the trainer providing verbal feedback. The researchers then conducted test trials in which the participants, carrying trays of varying loads, had to demonstrate the proper carrying technique on four out of five trials. Once the participants met this criterion, they were considered to be trained.

Scherrer and Wilder (2008) also trained research assistants to observe the participants' behavior. The observers used the eight-item safety checklist to record the frequency with which each participant correctly performed each aspect of the proper carrying technique. Each participant was observed unobtrusively more than 20 times, so that on any given workday, Sara, Mike, and Tanya did not know whether they were being observed. Importantly, each observer was kept blind as to the timing of when Sara, Mike, and Tanya received their individual safety training.

You can see the key aspects of the experimental design, along with the results, in **Figure 12.6.** Note that the behavior of each participant was observed both before and after the training program, the total number of observations (24 to 27) was similar for each participant, but the length of the baseline period for each cocktail server was different. Prior to receiving the safety training, Sara was observed for 3 baseline sessions, Mike for 12 baseline sessions, and Tanya for 18 baseline sessions. Note also that during baseline observation, Sara, Mike, and Tanya each displayed considerable variability in the percentage of tray-carrying behaviors that they performed safely.

Each participant showed a marked change in behavior immediately after being trained. Not only did the percentage of correct carrying behaviors increase, but the day-to-day variability in their behavior also decreased. For example, after training, Sara consistently performed 90% to 100% of her safety behaviors correctly. At the end of the study, Tanya and Sara indicated that they experienced less soreness in their arms and hands when they carried the trays properly; Mike said the proper technique made it easier to carry the trays.

Before we conclude that the training program was successful, we need to consider whether any confounding factors might plausibly explain the results. Suppose that at the same time the researchers gave Sara her safety training, the federal government launched a "National Job Safety Awareness Campaign," or one of the cocktail servers at the bar developed a serious injury due to improper tray carrying. Such events could easily have heightened Sara, Mike, and Tanya's concern about, and attention to, job safety. Perhaps the mere act of volunteering to participate in a job safety experiment, or the mere expectation of

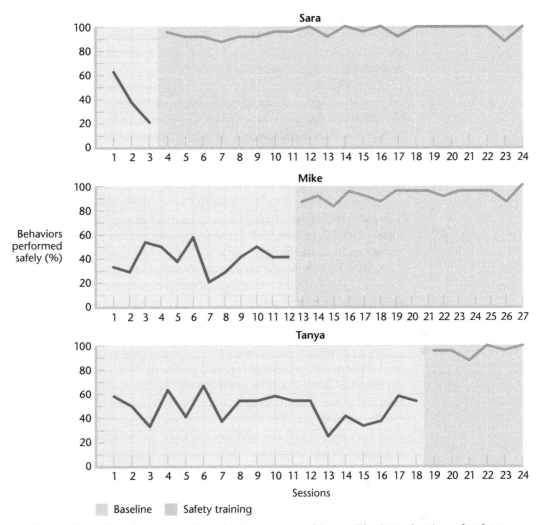

Figure 12.6 A multiple-baseline design across subjects. The introduction of safety training was staggered across three cocktail servers, creating baseline periods of three different lengths. (Data from Scherrer & Wilder, 2008.)

receiving safety training, heightened their attention to carrying trays safely. But, if you want to propose any one of these factors as a plausible confounding variable, you'll have to explain why it only affected Sara's performance starting with the 4th observation session, and also why it did not affect Mike's performance until the 13th session, or Tanya's performance until the 19th session. That's a tall order, making it implausible that any of those factors were confounding variables.

Multiple-Baseline Design Across Behaviors

In a **multiple-baseline design across behaviors**, *the same treatment is applied to two or more distinct behaviors of the same individual and the switch from baseline to treatment periods is staggered across behaviors.* This design is nicely illustrated in a study by clinical psychologist Kim Mueser and his colleagues, who attempted to improve the social skills of a 28-year-old man in order to help him keep his job (Mueser, Foy, & Carter, 1986). This man, whom I'll call Bill, had recently been treated in a hospital for depression and several sleep disorders. After his discharge from the hospital, he eventually landed a job with an office machine repair company in which he was dispatched on service calls to repair machines at business offices. A few months into the job, some customers complained to Bill's supervisor about his rudeness and outbursts of temper. To save his job, Bill agreed to participate in a training program to improve his interpersonal skills.

An ABAB design seemed a poor choice to assess the program's effectiveness because the goal was to enhance social skills that, once improved, would not be expected to revert to baseline levels during a withdrawal phase. Moreover, because Bill was the only participant, a multiple-baseline design across subjects was not feasible. A multiple-baseline design across behaviors, however, can be used when there is only one participant.

The researchers identified seven social skills that Bill needed to improve. These represented the target behaviors. During each of 13 training sessions, Bill engaged in multiple role-plays with a confederate who acted as a customer, a supervisor, or a security guard. Bill received verbal instructions on how to respond appropriately, watched a model demonstrate correct social behaviors, and received praise for correct performance. He also was instructed to practice his skills while on the job.

Figure 12.7 shows the experimental design and results. In the top graph, the three data points to the left of the vertical dashed line represent three baseline observation sessions that were held prior to any training. Training was initiated on the fourth session, but only for three of the target behaviors: voice volume, eye contact, and Bill's emotional response (affect). After six baseline sessions, the training also started to focus on improving Bill's responsiveness (e.g., providing reassurance to customers) and teaching him how to elicit suggestions from other people to solve unexpected problems. Finally, after 11 baseline sessions, the training program also focused on getting Bill to ask for clarification when other people criticized him, and to make appropriate self-assertions if he believed that a criticism was unfair.

The topmost graph of Figure 12.7 shows that when the training program for voice volume, eye contact, and emotion was initiated on the fourth session, these combined behaviors immediately improved. Moreover, this improvement persisted. Similarly, persistent changes in responsiveness, eliciting suggestions, requesting clarification, and self-assertion only occurred after the training program began to target those behaviors. Although some of these behaviors didn't change as immediately and strongly after training began as did voice volume, eye contact, and emotion, the overall pattern of findings from the multiple baselines supports the conclusion that the training program was effective. Any alternative explanation would need to explain why each set of behaviors reliably changed only after the training program was initiated for that particular behavior.

Multiple-Baseline Design Across Settings

When using a **multiple-baseline design across settings**, *the same treatment is applied to the same target behavior in two or more settings, and the switch from baseline to treatment is staggered across settings.* Consider a study of an 8-year-old boy with autism named Jason. Jason frequently put nonfood objects in his mouth, including foam puzzle pieces and plastic items. Although he did not intentionally ingest these objects, such "object mouthing" carries the risk of accidental swallowing, choking, contracting an infectious disease, and other negative health consequences. To reduce Jason's object mouthing, clinical psychologist Henry Roane and his colleagues developed a treatment that consisted of having Jason wear a fanny pack around his waist that contained marshmallows, candy, and chewing gum (Roane, Kelly, & Fisher, 2003). This gave him continuous access to food items to place in his mouth. (We can save the debate over whether marshmallows, candy, and gum are "foods" for another day.) The researchers picked these items because previous observations had indicated that when Jason had them in his mouth, they interfered with his tendency to mouth nonfood objects.

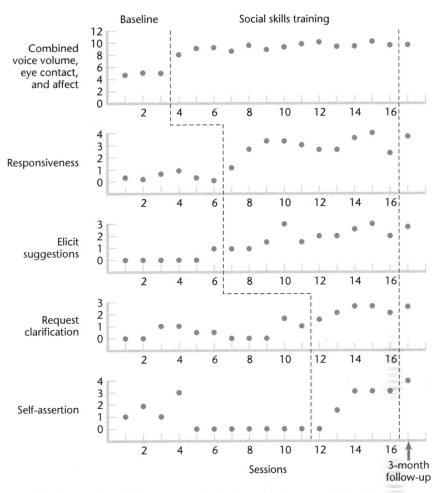

Figure 12.7 A multiple-baseline design across behaviors with one participant.
The introduction of social skills training for a male employee is staggered across
different behaviors, creating baseline periods of five different lengths. (Adapted with
permission from "Social Skills Training for Job Maintenance in a Psychiatric Patient," by K. T. Mueser,
D. W. Foy, and M. J. Carter, 1986, *Journal of Counseling Psychology, 33*, p. 361. Copyright 1986 by the
American Psychological Association.)

As **Figure 12.8** shows, Jason was observed for several days in three settings: a classroom,
a playroom, and outdoors. A total of three to five observation sessions were conducted each
day, with each session lasting 10 minutes. The treatment was first implemented in a classroom
setting after three sessions of baseline observation, and it was initiated in the playroom and
outdoors settings after five and seven baseline sessions, respectively. During the baseline
phase, food items were not available to Jason, and the researchers recorded the number of
nonfood object mouthing responses that Jason made per minute. After the treatment began in
a particular setting, the researchers recorded the frequency of Jason's nonfood object mouthing as well as how many times per minute he placed a food item in his mouth. The results
indicate that Jason's nonfood object mouthing decreased dramatically in each setting when
the treatment was initiated in that specific setting, and not before. The researchers noted that
their study only examined the treatment's short-term effectiveness, and that the consumption
of foods such as candy and marshmallows might pose long-term difficulties of its own.

Compared to a design in which the treatment would have been initiated at the same time
in each setting, the staggered initiation across settings makes it much more difficult to argue
against the conclusion that the treatment was the cause of Jason's behavior change. To be

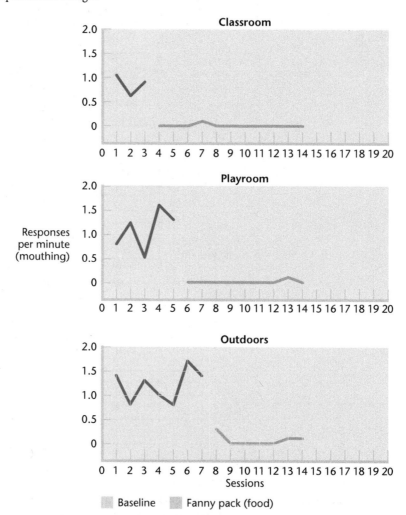

Figure 12.8 A multiple-baseline design across settings. Object-mouthing treatment for a single participant was staggered across three settings, creating baseline periods of three lengths. (Data from Roane et al., 2003.)

plausible, any alternative explanation that you propose would have to account for the unique temporal pattern of results shown in Figure 12.8.

Special Concerns

Unlike ABAB designs, in applied research, multiple-baseline designs avoid the troublesome ethical quandary of withdrawing a potentially effective treatment from the participant. Still, to permit causal conclusions, these designs require the treatment to be applied in a staggered fashion across different participants, behaviors, or settings. Thus, for example, in a multiple-baseline design across subjects, after treatment begins for the first participant, it will be delayed for the others. Is this ethical, especially if it seems that the first or first few participants are benefiting from the treatment?

A second issue pertains to the following question: "To be confident in drawing a causal conclusion, how many baselines (across subjects, behaviors, or settings) should the design include?" In principle, it takes a minimum of two baselines to create a multiple-baseline design. In practice, experts recommend having a minimum of three or four baselines (Barlow et al., 2009; Kazdin, 1982).

Contamination is another potential concern when using multiple-baseline designs. To illustrate, recall that in Scherrer and Wilder's (2008) safety training experiment, Sara was the first cocktail server to receive the training. Suppose that Sara, after being trained, told Tanya and Mike how to carry a tray safely. Or, suppose that Mike and Tanya knew that Sara had just received the training, and then one evening while working the same shift as Sara, decided to imitate her tray-carrying behavior. Either of these events would contaminate the measurements taken during the extended portion of Mike's and Tanya's baseline phases. Subsequently, those extended baselines could no longer be viewed as "pure" baselines. Researchers must take care that when they initiate the treatment for one participant, behavior, or setting, that treatment does not prematurely influence the other participants, behaviors, or settings while those baseline phases are still ongoing.

CHANGING-CRITERION DESIGNS

In a **changing-criterion design**, *an initial baseline phase is followed by a treatment phase that lasts until the target behavior reaches a criterion level and becomes stable. Treatment then continues in a series of additional phases, with a new (and typically, more demanding) performance criterion set in each phase.* Developmental psychologists R. Vance Hall (who gave this design its name) and Donald Hartmann used this design to assess the effectiveness of a treatment for chronic cigarette smoking (Hartmann & Hall, 1976).

The participant was a chain smoker who during a 7-day baseline phase averaged about 48 cigarettes per day. The baseline and first six treatment phases (each 2 weeks long) spanned 91 days, during which time the changing criterion required him to smoke fewer and fewer cigarettes. For example, in Phase B the criterion was set at 46 cigarettes per day, and in Phase C it was set at 43 per day. For each day, the first cigarette smoked that was "over the limit" resulted in a $1.00 fine; a second cigarette over the limit led to a $2.00 fine; and so on. In addition, bonuses were paid for smoking fewer cigarettes than the allowable limit: a 10-cent bonus for the first cigarette under the limit, 20 cents for the next cigarette under the limit, and so forth. (Remember, this was 1976—back then, you could really buy something useful for a dime.) The study lasted 52 weeks and involved a total of 20 criterion changes. **Figure 12.9** shows the results only for the initial baseline and first six treatment phases. You can see that the participant met or bettered the criterion every single day during these treatment phases, and by the end of this period he was smoking 34 or fewer cigarettes per day. By the end of the experiment, he had reduced his smoking to 15 cigarettes per day and continued to successfully meet the criterion every day.

The primary concern when using a changing-criterion design pertains to the difficulty of interpreting the findings when the pattern of behavior change does not closely follow the steadily changing pattern of more stringent criteria (Kazdin, 1982). Suppose that in Figure 12.9, the average daily number of cigarettes smoked changed from 48 during the baseline phase to 23 during treatment Phase B (thereby greatly surpassing the criterion), and then remained at 23 in Phases C through G, while the criterion kept shifting downward. Did this huge initial decrease in Phase B result from the treatment, or some confounding factor that also happened to persist throughout Phases C through G? It's not clear. As another example, suppose that the chain smoker met the changing criterion in the first two treatment phases, but never decreased his cigarette usage after that. Is this sufficient evidence to conclude that the treatment caused those changes that did occur? Again, the answer is not clear.

COMBINED DESIGNS

In addition to ABAB, multiple-baseline, and changing-criterion designs, there are many other categories of single-case designs. Moreover, researchers sometimes combine designs

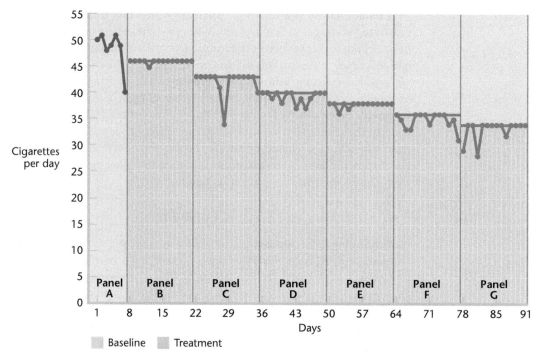

Figure 12.9 A changing-criterion design After an initial baseline phase (panel A), treatment for a chronic, heavy smoker was implemented in 20 phases, six of which are shown here (panels B–G). In each successive phase, a progressively stricter performance criterion (e.g., smoking fewer cigarettes) is set. (Data from Hartmann & Hall, 1976.)

within a single experiment. Consider this example. Suppose that Karl, a 3-year-old boy, chronically pulls his hair so often and forcefully that he has developed large bald patches on his head. His parents have asked us to develop a treatment that will get Karl to stop doing this. We'll base our treatment and our research design to assess its effectiveness on a study by behavior analysts Cristine Deaver, Raymond Miltenberger, and Jason Stricker (2001), who successfully treated a 2½-year-old girl who chronically pulled her hair. Their treatment involved placing thin cotton mittens on the girl's hands, making it difficult for her to twirl and pull her hair.

To gather data on treatment effectiveness, we could observe Karl's behavior over multiple days, at several randomly chosen times each day, and record the percentage of time during each session that he spends pulling his hair. As the upper left graph in Figure 12.10 illustrates, in our study it would be feasible to use an ABAB design to assess the treatment's effectiveness. Or, as the upper right graphs illustrate, we could instead choose to use a multiple-baseline design across settings. Each design is appropriate, but following Deaver et al.'s (2001) approach, we could employ an even more rigorous design that combines the ABAB and multiple-baseline approaches. For example, as the bottom graphs in Figure 12.10 show, we could use a multiple-baseline design across two settings—Karl's home and his daycare facility—and embed an ABAB design within each setting.

Turning first to the home setting, you can see that Karl frequently pulled his hair during the two baseline stages, but virtually not at all during the two treatment phases. Next, you can see that this pattern was replicated in the daycare setting. Finally, looking across the multiple baselines, you can see that while Karl was in the first treatment phase at home and rarely pulling his hair, at daycare he was still in the first baseline phase and pulled his hair a lot. Then, while the treatment was first applied at daycare and he stopped pulling

Infographic: **Figure 12.10**

ABAB, MULTIPLE-BASELINE, AND COMBINED SINGLE-CASE DESIGNS

The Problem: Karl is a 3-year-old boy who chronically pulls his hair, and often pulls it out. This creates large areas of hair loss.

The Proposed Treatment: Based on prior clinical research (Deaver et al., 2001), the plan is to have Karl wear thin mittens during most of the day (e.g., excluding mealtimes).

POTENTIAL RESEARCH DESIGNS

Karl is the only participant and hair pulling is a single target behavior. Therefore, it is possible to use an ABAB design, a multiple-baseline design across settings, or a combined design.

1 ABAB (WITHDRAWAL) DESIGN:
Alternate phases in which the treatment is absent or present. The second baseline phase also could be labeled as a "withdrawal" or "reversal" phase.

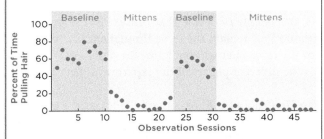

After an initial baseline period of no treatment, Karl wears the mittens while he is awake. The treatment is then withdrawn during a second baseline period and is followed by a second treatment phase. Results like those above would support the treatment's effectiveness, but the treatment may need to be gradually phased out so that Karl does not revert to hair pulling.

2 MULTIPLE-BASELINE DESIGN ACROSS SETTINGS
In different settings, start with baseline observations and stagger the introduction of the treatment.

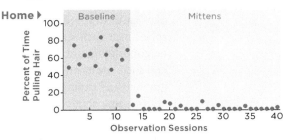

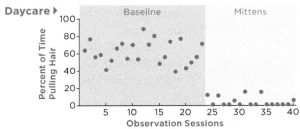

After a baseline period, Karl wears the mittens at his home. At daycare, a longer baseline phase is used and then the treatment is introduced in that setting. Results like those above would support the treatment's effectiveness, but the treatment may need to be gradually phased out in each setting so that Karl does not revert to hair pulling.

3 A COMBINED DESIGN: INTEGRATING AN ABAB DESIGN WITH A MULTIPLE-BASELINE DESIGN ACROSS SETTINGS

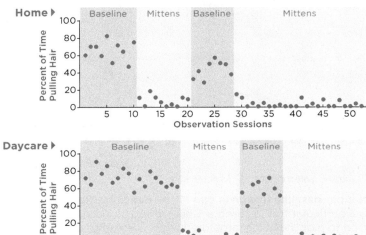

A multiple-baseline design is modified by adding a second baseline and second treatment phase in each setting. This creates an ABAB design within each setting, but the treatment phases and second baseline phase begin at different times across the settings.

This pattern of results offers strong support for the treatment's effectiveness, but the treatment may need to be phased out in each setting so that Karl does not revert to hair pulling.

his hair there, the treatment was withdrawn at home and his hair pulling returned in that setting. In sum, staggering the presentation of the ABAB phases across multiple settings, each with an initial baseline of a different length, provided the opportunity to gather data that strongly supported the conclusion that the treatment, rather than some other factor, has caused the change in Karl's behavior. In other words, identifying an alternative explanation that could plausibly account for this complex pattern of results becomes even more difficult than would be the case if either an ABAB or multiple-baseline design had been used alone.

EXTENDING SINGLE-CASE DESIGNS TO SOCIAL UNITS

The "case" in single-case experiments need not be an individual person, but can be a larger social unit such as a business establishment, a classroom of students, an entire school, a neighborhood, unrelated people who happen to be in the same location, and so forth. If several social units are examined, each would be treated as a separate case and its data would be graphed and examined separately.

In some single-case experiments, the sample of people that constitutes the unit (such as the students in a particular classroom) may remain the same throughout the study. But often, this either won't be the case, or the researcher will not know the degree to which the composition of the unit varies across the different phases of the experiment. Let's consider an example.

Behavioral psychologists Ron Van Houten and J. E. Malenfant (2004) used a multiple-baseline design across settings to assess the effectiveness of a traffic safety enforcement program instituted by the city of Miami Beach, Florida. The program's immediate goal was to

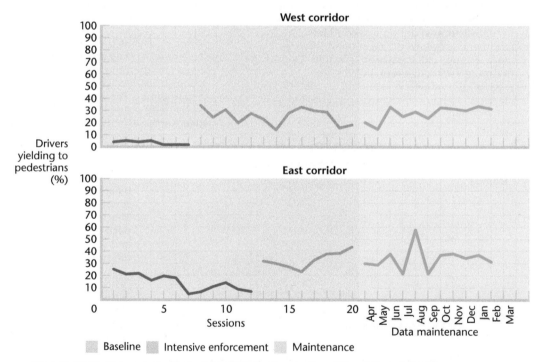

Figure 12.11 Using a multiple-baseline design in two Miami Beach traffic corridors. Drivers using a particular traffic corridor were viewed as a social unit, and a single data point was used to plot the unit's target behavior (yielding to pedestrians) for each observation session. Longer-term findings (i.e., maintenance phase) were plotted with a single data point per month. (Data from Van Houten & Malenfant, 2004.)

get drivers to slow down or stop at crosswalks and yield the right of way to pedestrians. The researchers pointed out that 20% of traffic fatalities in Florida involved automobiles colliding with pedestrians.

Van Houten and Malenfant (2004) identified two settings—two traffic corridors—that had high rates of automobile–pedestrian accidents. One corridor was on the east side of Miami Beach and the other was on the west side. Within each corridor, four crosswalks that did not have traffic lights were observed daily. The main component of the enforcement program involved a plainclothes police officer who, when real pedestrians were not present, acted as a decoy pedestrian and entered a crosswalk as a car approached. If the driver failed to yield, this information was radioed to other officers who pulled over the driver, gave the driver a printed flyer describing the law about yielding for pedestrians, and issued either a warning or a ticket, depending on the severity of the driver's infraction. During a subsequent "maintenance phase" of this program that lasted for a full year, the police periodically conducted this type of enforcement operation once every 6 weeks at each of the crosswalks.

The researchers recorded drivers' behavior at times of the day when the police were not present. **Figure 12.11** reveals that when the enforcement program was initiated in the West Corridor, the percentage of drivers who yielded for pedestrians immediately increased. Yielding in the East Corridor consistently increased only when the program was subsequently introduced in that corridor. Moreover, in both corridors the increase in yielding persisted throughout the maintenance phase. Although it would have been ideal to replicate this pattern in one or two more corridors, this option may not have been available to the researchers. Nevertheless, as compared to studying only one corridor, the use of staggered baselines across the two corridors increases confidence that the program was responsible for the change in drivers' behavior.

 CONCEPT CHECK 12.2 TYPES OF SINGLE-CASE DESIGNS

Match each concept on the left to one of the three items on the right. Answers appear on page 407.

1. also called "withdrawal" or "reversal" designs
2. one type requires at least two participants
3. the most basic single-case designs
4. contamination is a potential concern
5. performance target is progressively more stringent

a. changing-criterion designs
b. ABAB designs
c. multiple-baseline designs

ISSUES CONCERNING SINGLE-CASE DESIGNS

Learning Objectives

After studying this section, you should be able to:

- Discuss ethical issues that arise when using single-case designs.
- Describe concerns regarding the internal and external validity of single-case designs.
- Identify key issues pertaining to the data analysis and examination of interactions in single-case designs.

Single-case experimental designs provide important benefits and offer researchers creative options for evaluating how independent variables affect the behavior of individuals and social units. Like other research methods, however, single-case experimentation has limitations and potential drawbacks.

ETHICAL ISSUES

When traditional between-subjects designs are used to assess treatment effectiveness, some participants receive the treatment and others—those assigned to a standard control or placebo-control group—do not. With single-case designs, each participant serves as her or his own control and receives the potentially beneficial treatment at some point. Proponents of single-case designs emphasize that this represents an ethical advantage of single-case designs: Everyone gets the treatment (Rapoff & Stark, 2008).

We've seen, however, that single-case designs involve their own ethical issues when used to assess treatment effectiveness. With ABAB designs, if a person's behavior clearly changes for the better once the treatment is introduced, is it ethical to remove that treatment during the withdrawal phase? With multiple-baseline designs, is it ethical to keep extending the baseline phase of some participants if the data reveal an immediate posttreatment improvement for participants who had shorter baselines? For both ABAB and multiple-baseline designs, is it ethical to conduct a lengthy initial baseline phase—or any initial baseline phase at all—particularly when the treatment is designed to reduce the frequency of a behavior that carries the risk of serious harm for the participant or other people (e.g., self-injurious behavior, aggression toward others)?

The scientific rationale for these procedures is clear: They maximize our ability to properly evaluate whether the treatment truly was effective. Ethical considerations, however, often necessitate methodological compromises, such as shortening an initial baseline or withdrawal phase. For example, Banda et al. (2012) noted that the withdrawal phase (i.e., the second baseline phase) in their experiment with Travis only involved two measurement sessions, fewer than ideal in terms of demonstrating a reliable reversal of behavior once a treatment is removed. But given the high rate of self-injurious behavior that Travis exhibited immediately upon treatment withdrawal, the researchers believed that a short withdrawal phase was justifiable.

INTERNAL VALIDITY

Recall that an experiment has high internal validity when confounding variables can be ruled out and changes in the dependent variable can therefore be unambiguously attributed to the independent variable. Because each participant in a single-case experiment is exposed to all the conditions, single-case designs essentially reflect a within-subjects approach to experimentation. But unlike the group within-subjects designs described in Chapter 8, which counterbalance the sequence of conditions over multiple participants to control for order effects, single-case experiments in applied settings are rarely counterbalanced. This leaves them vulnerable to potential order effects. For example, in an ABAB design in which A and B each represent a different treatment, if treatment B produces a greater change in a participant's (or several participants') behavior, we are left to wonder whether this would still be true if the phases had been ordered differently (e.g., BABA).

Basic researchers who conduct single-case laboratory experiments in fields such as psychophysics or cognitive neuroscience typically have more control over order effects. For example, when presenting each of several participants with different types of stimuli that represent the independent variable (e.g., types of words, sentences, visual images), each type of stimulus may appear many times within a large total number of stimulus presentations. In such experiments, researchers can randomize the entire order of presentation for each participant (Herbert & Kübler, 2011).

Some psychologists have argued that randomization procedures should be used in applied single-case research, and that without them single-case experiments might best be viewed as quasi-experiments rather than as true experiments (Edgington, 1996; Onghena & Edgington,

2005). For example, suppose an independent variable has two conditions (e.g., baseline and treatment, or treatment A and treatment B), and the study involves one session per day when the dependent variable is recorded. Rather than using a standard ABAB sequence with each phase lasting several consecutive days, the researcher can randomly determine the days on which each condition is applied.

Despite some benefits of randomization, relatively few applied single-case experimenters use it. Among several reasons, they view randomization as interfering with the flexibility of single-case designs. One example of flexibility concerns the length of each phase of the design. Ideally, each phase will continue until there is evidence that the participant's behavior has stabilized—that a steady response level occurs over several measurement sessions—prior to switching to another phase (Barlow et al., 2009). Such stability makes it easier to detect any immediate impact of switching to a new phase. Often, however, participants' behavior displays considerable variability for periods of time within a particular research phase. By not randomly or otherwise predetermining the particular days or sessions on which phase switches will occur, the researcher has the flexibility to extend the length of the current phase in the hope that the participant's behavior will stabilize.

But even without randomization or other counterbalancing techniques, applied single-case experiments typically involve more control over independent and dependent variables than do quasi-experiments. Single-case experimenters usually develop the intervention themselves and have the ability to repeatedly present and withdraw it, or incorporate other design features (e.g., multiple baselines, changing criteria) through which they gain additional control over participants' exposure to the various experimental conditions. The single-case experimenter is also able to choose the behaviors to be measured as well as how and when they will be measured, and to establish measurement reliability (e.g., by having two observers independently record the participants' responses). Quasi-experiments often lack one or more of these aspects of control.

DATA ANALYSIS

With most single-case designs, the ability to rule out alternative explanations for the findings hinges, in part, on obtaining a *temporal pattern of behavior change* that corresponds properly to the sequence of phases in the experiment. The mere fact that a target behavior occurs much more (or less) frequently during the treatment phases than during the baseline stages is not sufficient to conclude unambiguously that the treatment was effective.

Compare the hypothetical data in **Figure 12.12**, shown on the next page, to the actual data (orange bars) in Figure 12.4 on page 388. Both graphs reveal that, overall, the child spent much more time on the climbing frame when he was reinforced for this behavior (i.e., the average of the two reinforcement phases vs. the average of the two baseline phases). But, based on the pattern of the data in Figure 12.12, we would not feel confident in concluding that the reinforcement intervention was effective. This pattern reveals at least one plausible alternative explanation: maturation. Even during the first baseline phase, this child was steadily become more physically active, and the rate at which his activity increased throughout the entire study simply continued this trend. Thus, it is easy to imagine that the results would have come out this way even if the reinforcement had never been presented, and the data from the second baseline phase support such an assertion.

Data from single-case experiments can be analyzed by using statistical tests, although researchers disagree as to which tests are most appropriate (Campbell, 2004). Even more fundamentally, single-case experimenters disagree about whether statistical tests are needed at all. Particularly in applied behavior analysis, other applied fields, and the experimental analysis of behavior, many researchers believe that inferential statistical analyses are not necessary to determine whether an independent variable had an effect. They argue that meaningful

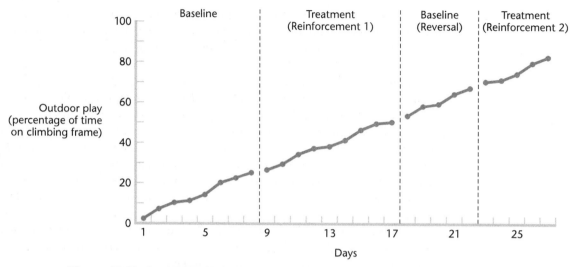

Figure 12.12 An ABAB design with hypothetical results showing a constant trend
The average time spent climbing on the bars is 14% for Baseline Phase 1, 39% for Treatment Phase 1, 60% in Baseline Phase 2, and 75% in Treatment Phase 2.

effects should be strong enough to detect by visual analysis. Tate et al. (2008) examined a sample of 85 published single-case experiments in clinical neuropsychology, each of which examined the effectiveness of a treatment in helping people recover psychological functioning after suffering brain damage. Only 40% of the studies contained inferential statistical analyses.

Reliance on visual data analysis brings its own set of issues. In a treatment effectiveness experiment, for example, an ideal set of data (from the standpoint of ruling out alternative explanations) would reveal a stable level of response in the initial baseline and a large, persistent improvement in behavior that begins immediately when the treatment is introduced. In ABAB designs, the participant's behavior would immediately revert to initial baseline levels each time the treatment is withdrawn, and immediately show large persistent improvement each time the treatment is reintroduced. In multiple-baseline designs, a large, persistent improvement in behavior would occur immediately when, and not before, the treatment is introduced for each particular participant, behavior, or setting.

In the real world, data are rarely ideal. One common problem occurs when behavior shows excessive variability, especially during an initial baseline phase. If the level of response changes when the treatment is introduced, but falls within the range of responses displayed in the baseline phase, this can muddy the conclusion that the treatment caused the change. In principle, the researcher can extend the baseline phase and hope that behavior stabilizes, but due to ethical considerations or other practical constraints, this may be difficult to implement. Similarly, suppose it's unclear whether the last few data points in a baseline phase reflect a changing trend, and then this trend reliably emerges in the treatment phase. Did the treatment have an effect? In sum, how much of a deviation from an ideal pattern does it take, based on visual analysis, to cast doubt on the conclusion that the treatment affected behavior?

EXAMINING INTERACTIONS

You learned in Chapter 9 that factorial designs excel as a method for examining interactions between two, three, or even more independent variables. Moreover, factorial designs can easily assess person × situation interactions, as well as interactions solely between environmental variables. In comparison, single-case designs are much less effective in their ability to examine potential interactions. Single-case designs do exist for examining interactions between two environmental variables, such as between two treatments or treatment components (Barlow et al., 2009). Overall, however, these designs are complicated and not particularly efficient (Kazdin, 1982).

To see why, imagine that we have two different drug treatments—Drug 1 and Drug 2—for a disorder. To determine whether the drugs interact, we would have to expose the participant to a no-drug baseline phase (Phase A); Drug 1 alone (Phase B); Drug 2 alone (Phase C); and Drug 1 and Drug 2 together (Phase BC). Furthermore, with only one participant, we would need to expose him or her to these four conditions at least twice, to determine whether any drug effects on behavior are replicable. Thus, one of many possible designs might be the following sequence of conditions: A-B-C-BC-B-BC-C-A.

Not only is this design complicated (more so if we include additional baseline phases), we are still left with two interpretative problems. First, if the effect on behavior in Phase BC differs from that in B or C alone, we need to determine whether this difference truly reflects an interaction of the two drugs, or merely represents the simple addition of the main effect from each drug. Based on visual analysis alone, this may be difficult. How much, for example, does behavior have to differ in BC versus the separate addition of effects in B and in C, to inspire causal confidence that an interaction occurred? Second, the inclusion of two drugs opens the door to treatment carryover effects; these can't be eliminated as a possible order confound when we only have a single participant exposed to one particular sequence of conditions. To improve internal validity, some single-case experimenters have attempted to examine interactions by exposing a few participants to different sequences of conditions. However, even some experts in single-case designs question the effectiveness of this approach (Kazdin, 1982).

EXTERNAL VALIDITY

Because single-case experiments typically involve few participants, concerns about the generalizability of the findings to other people, settings, and behaviors are often raised as a major limitation of this research approach. Advocates of single-case experimentation argue that findings from experiments that use traditional group designs may also end up having poor external validity. Although this is true, it doesn't change the fact that when an experiment involves only one or a few (as opposed to many) participants, there is a greater risk that the sample of people studied may be atypical of the population from which they are drawn. Ultimately, however, the external validity of psychological principles, treatment effects, or other findings gleaned from single-case experiments is established in the same way as for other experiments: through a process of replication. Single-case researchers often take an initial step toward establishing external validity by replicating their design across several participants within a single study.

Kazdin (1982) pointed out that because single-case experimenters frequently examine independent variables that have powerful effects on behavior, their findings often demonstrate good external validity. In basic research, for example, operant conditioning principles that Skinner and other behaviorists discovered in single-case laboratory experiments with nonhuman animals have shown robust external validity when applied to other nonhuman species and to humans in both laboratory and real-world settings. In educational psychology, Leslie Rogers and Steven Graham (2008) meta-analyzed 88 single-case experiments that examined the effectiveness of various interventions to teach writing skills to first- through twelfth-grade students. Several types of interventions, such as those that focused on teaching students how to plan their writing and produce drafts, were found to produce replicable effects across multiple school grades and across both struggling and typical writers.

In closing this chapter and section of the book, I encourage you to keep in mind that each of the experimental approaches covered—traditional group experimental designs, quasi-experimental designs, and single-case experimental designs—has important benefits and limitations. The same can be said, of course, about the descriptive research methods discussed in other chapters. Psychologists and other behavioral scientists are in the enviable position of having a broad set of sophisticated research methods at their disposal. Tor Wager, a psychologist in the field of cognitive neuroscience, states this point nicely: "There are fundamental tradeoffs involved in different approaches to science. But the beautiful thing about psychological science being a collective enterprise is that, as a field, we can encourage a diverse set of approaches with complementary strengths" (2009, March, para 15).

✓ **CONCEPT CHECK 12.3** ISSUES CONCERNING SINGLE-CASE DESIGNS

Fill in each of the blanks below. Answers appear on page 407.

1. If a serious problem behavior rapidly improves when a treatment is first introduced after baseline observations, then in an ABAB design an ethical issue is _____.

2. Some researchers propose that randomly determining the trials on which a treatment is or is not presented would improve the _____ of single-case experiments. Critics argue that such randomization decreases the _____ of single-case designs.

3. Compared to factorial designs, single-case designs are poorly suited for examining _____ between independent variables.

CHAPTER SUMMARY

- Single-case experimental designs allow researchers to systematically examine how an independent variable influences the behavior of an individual organism. These designs share five central features: (1) Each participant serves as her or his own control; (2) the dependent variable is repeatedly measured within each phase of the experiment; (3) such experiments feature built-in replications; (4) when multiple participants are studied, the data are examined separately for each participant; and (5) although some single-case experimenters employ statistical tests to analyze their data, others rely solely on visual inspection of the data.

- Single-case designs enable researchers to conduct experiments when they are only interested in the behavior of a specific individual, or when only one or a few participants are available. These designs allow researchers to tailor the intervention to the individual participant. Analyzing data separately for each participant avoids the potential problem of masking individual differences.

- ABAB designs involve a sequence of phases in which a treatment is either absent or present. They are also called withdrawal designs or reversal designs and should not be used when (1) it would be unethical to withdraw a potentially effective treatment from a participant during the experiment, and (2) the target behavior would not be expected to revert to baseline levels during withdrawal phases.

- In a multiple-baseline design across subjects, two or more individuals receive the same treatment, and the baseline-to-treatment switch is staggered across subjects. In a multiple-baseline design across behaviors, an individual has a treatment applied to two or more behaviors, and the baseline-to-treatment switch is staggered across behaviors. In a multiple-baseline design across settings, a treatment is applied to a behavior in two or more settings, and the baseline-to-treatment switch is staggered across settings.

- Multiple-baseline designs involve the potential ethical issue of delaying the start of a treatment for certain participants, behaviors, or settings. The risk also exists that once a treatment is introduced for one participant, behavior, or setting, this may contaminate the baseline periods for the remaining participants, behaviors, or settings.

- In a changing-criterion design, an initial baseline phase is followed by a treatment period that lasts until the target behavior reaches a criterion level and becomes stable. Treatment then continues in a series of additional stages, with a new criterion level of performance set in each stage. Different single-case designs—such as multiple-baseline and ABAB designs—may be combined within one study. Single-case designs are also used to study social units: Each unit represents a "single case."

- Concerns about single-case experiments include: (1) ethical issues involving the withdrawal or delay of a potentially beneficial treatment; (2) difficulty drawing clear causal conclusions when the temporal pattern of behavior change doesn't correspond closely to the sequence of phases in the experiment; (3) debate over whether visual analysis of the data is sufficient or whether statistical tests should be used; (4) difficulty in examining interaction effects; and (5) concerns about external validity.

KEY TERMS

ABAB design (p. 386)
applied behavior analysis (p. 385)
baseline phase (p. 382)
changing-criterion design (p. 397)
experimental analysis of behavior (p. 385)
multiple-baseline design (p. 391)

multiple-baseline design across behaviors (p. 393)
multiple-baseline design across settings (p. 394)
multiple-baseline design across subjects (p. 391)
psychophysics (p. 384)

single-case experimental designs (p. 381)
target behavior (p. 387)
treatment phase (intervention phase) (p. 382)
withdrawal design (reversal design) (p. 387)

ASSESS YOUR KNOWLEDGE

1. Describe five key characteristics of single-case experimental designs.
2. What are some advantages of single-case experimentation?
3. What are the experimental analysis of behavior and applied behavior analysis, and how did they foster the use of single-case designs?
4. Describe the basic features of ABAB designs, the rationale of drawing causal inferences based on ABAB designs, and concerns about them.
5. Explain the key features common to multiple-baseline designs, and the logic behind drawing causal inferences from multiple-baseline designs across (a) subjects, (b) behaviors, and (c) settings.
6. Identify three concerns about multiple-baseline designs.
7. What are the key features of a changing-criterion design? Provide an example.

8. Provide an example of how different types of single-case designs can be combined within one study.
9. Illustrate how a single-case design can be used to examine an intervention that is applied to a social unit.
10. Discuss concerns about the internal validity of single-case designs.
11. Describe the controversy over how data from single-case experiments are analyzed. To conclude that a treatment was effective, is it sufficient to demonstrate an average difference in behavior between treatment versus baseline conditions? Explain.
12. Discuss concerns about single-case designs with regard to (a) examining interaction effects and (b) external validity.

CONCEPT CHECKS: ANSWERS

12.1 A Single-Case Approach to Experimentation

1. false   2. true   3. true   4. false   5. false

12.2 Types of Single-Case Designs

1. b   2. c   3. b   4. c   5. a

12.3 Issues Concerning Single-Case Designs

1. whether it is appropriate to remove the treatment by conducting a withdrawal phase   2. internal validity; flexibility   3. interactions

THINKING CRITICALLY AND APPLYING YOUR KNOWLEDGE

EXERCISE 1   Increasing Donations to a Food Bank

Psychologists Samantha Farrimond and Louis Leland Jr. (2006) conducted an experiment in a suburban supermarket in New Zealand. They used an ABAB design with an additional follow-up phase that occurred 2 months later. During the treatment and follow-up phases, signs asking, "HOW ABOUT BUYING ONE FOR THE FOODBANK BIN?" were hung from the shelves in front of various food items. During the baseline phases, the signs were removed. A food bank bin was made available during all phases of the experiment.

Each of the five phases lasted 2 weeks. The researchers counted the donations every Thursday, Saturday, and Tuesday, and the food bank picked up the donated items on Wednesdays. This exercise focuses on one of their dependent variables: the number of items deposited into the food bank bin.

(a) Draw a graph to represent the design of this experiment. You can use the label "No Signs" for the baseline phases, "Signs" for the treatment phases, and "Follow-up" for the follow-up phase. Label the *x*-axis "Counting Session." There were six counting sessions per 2-week phase and five phases. For simplicity, label all the counting sessions consecutively, starting with Session 1 and ending with Session 30. Alternatively, to avoid a crowded *x*-axis, number the *x*-axis with every other value (i.e., 1, 3, 5, etc.), although you will still be plotting 30 data points. The values on the *y*-axis should begin at zero and increase by two units (e.g., 0, 2, 4, 6) up to a maximum of 18.

(b) Plot the following data in your graph. These data are from the actual experiment.
First baseline phase:	2, 1, 3, 2, 0, 2
First treatment phase:	8, 6, 5, 11, 8, 7
Second baseline phase:	4, 3, 2, 3, 2, 1
Second treatment phase:	9, 6, 12, 9, 6, 7
Follow-up phase:	11, 1, 8, 13, 4, 16

(c) Based on a visual inspection of your completed graph, what conclusion do you draw about whether the presence of the signs increased the number of items donated to the food bank? Justify your answer.

EXERCISE 2   A Treatment for Chronic Hair Pulling

Andy, Eddie, and Katy were 12-year-olds who chronically pulled their own hair. For Eddie and Katy, this behavior resulted in visible hair loss on their scalp. Psychologist John Rapp and his colleagues (Rapp, Miltenberger, Long, Elliott, & Lumley, 1998) developed a treatment to reduce these children's chronic hair pulling. The treatment had several components, such as increasing the children's awareness of their own hair pulling and teaching them to make an alternative response (e.g., folding their arms) whenever they became aware that they were pulling their hair. Rapp et al. (1998) used a multiple-baseline design across subjects. Over the course of many days, the children were video-recorded during 10-minute afternoon and evening sessions, and the percentage of time that each child spent pulling his or her hair during each observation session was calculated.

(a) Draw a graph that illustrates how a multiple-baseline design across subjects could be used to assess the effectiveness of the treatment. For simplicity, assume that each child is observed for 40 sessions and that the treatment is applied to the three children in the following order: Andy, Eddie, Katy. Be sure to label your *x*- and *y*-axes. Plot a set of data in your graph that, upon visual inspection, clearly supports the conclusion that the treatment was effective.

(b) Do you believe that using a multiple-baseline design across subjects was a wise choice, or would it have been better to use an ABAB design for each participant? Explain your answer, taking into account the ethical and practical issues involved in each design.

EXERCISE 3   Is There a Treatment Effect?

The data from four hypothetical ABAB experiments are presented in graphs on the next page. Assume that a single adult is the participant in each study. In each experiment, two baseline and two treatment phases are implemented, and behavior is observed during five afternoons per phase. For each observation session, the frequency of a particular target behavior is recorded. In Experiments 1, 2, and 3, assume that the researcher is attempting to increase the frequency of the target behavior. In Experiment 4, assume that the researcher is attempting to decrease the frequency of the target behavior. For each of the four experiments portrayed, (a) decide whether the findings support the hypothesis that the treatment is effective and (b) explain the reasoning behind your conclusion.

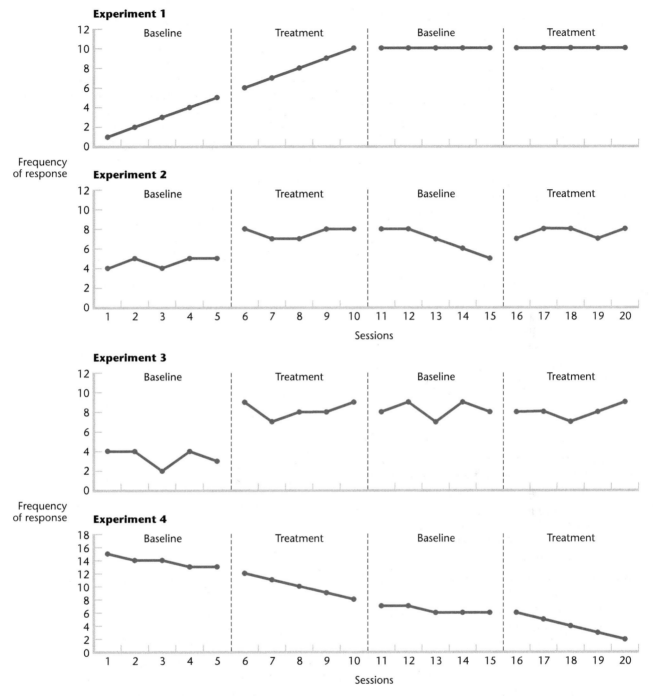

Data from hypothetical ABAB experiments in Exercise 3. In each graph, do the data support a conclusion that the treatment was effective? Explain your reasoning.

To practice key concepts from this chapter, visit the LaunchPad Solo for Research Methods at **launchpadworks.com.**

STATISTICS MODULES

MODULE OUTLINE

s the story is told:

> A researcher tried jalapeños on a stomach ulcer patient, and the ulcer went away. The researcher published an article "Jalapeños Cure Stomach Ulcers." The next patient subjected to the same treatment died. The researcher published a follow-up article "More Detailed Study Reveals That Jalapeños Cure 50% Of Stomach Ulcers." (Kovarik, n.d.)

This fictitious tale illustrates two key points about how research and statistics are intertwined. First, conducting research typically involves some degree of statistical analysis. Second, conclusions drawn from statistical analyses must be evaluated in the context of sound research design. The "50%" cure rate statistic is accurate, but lacking experimental controls and with a sample of only two patients, the researcher cannot conclude that jalapeños were the cure. Numbers may just be numbers, but a solid understanding of research methodology is needed to place them in the proper context.

Statistical analysis is an important tool that most researchers use to help them evaluate their findings. Some analyses may involve only calculating simple statistics (e.g., percentages, means), whereas others may involve advanced statistical procedures. The textbook's main chapters have briefly discussed several basic statistical concepts to help you better understand certain aspects of research methodology. Collectively, the modules in this section expand on some of those concepts, introduce new concepts, and illustrate statistical computations. Although they cannot provide the breadth and depth of coverage of a dedicated statistics textbook, their goal is to enhance your understanding of some fundamental statistical concepts and provide initial practical guidance if your coursework involves performing basic statistical analyses.

These modules are structured differently from Chapters 1 through 12. Numbered learning objectives correspond to numbered subsections within each module. Your instructor may ask you to study only certain modules or subsections of modules, study them in a different order, or study them as you cover particular chapters in the research methods course.

Statistical calculations and statistical tests are typically performed today using computer software. In the behavioral sciences, popular software packages such as SPSS and SYSTAT perform many types of statistical analyses. Even widely available database programs such as Microsoft Excel offer many statistical analysis functions. Why, then, should you bother to learn about statistical concepts or possibly perform statistical calculations by hand? The answer is simple: to better understand the purpose and meaning of statistics that you may encounter in your readings or need to use if you are analyzing data for a class project or other research.

MODULE 1 DESCRIPTIVE AND INFERENTIAL STATISTICS

Learning Objectives

After studying this module, you should be able to:

- Describe why researchers use descriptive statistics.
- Describe why researchers use inferential statistics.

1.1 DESCRIPTIVE STATISTICS

Imagine that you're one of 200 students in my research methods class. Yesterday, graded papers from a writing assignment worth 50 points were returned to students. In lecture today, you raise your hand and ask, "How did the class perform on the assignment?" I reply, "The scores were 38, 41, 47, 22, 31" and so on, continuing to read aloud the remaining 195 scores.

When you asked the question, you probably did not expect me to list all 200 **raw scores:** *the original, individual scores obtained for a particular variable.* If instead I had said, "The average score was 37.5 and 30% of the class had scores of 41 to 50, 47% had scores of 31 to 40," and so forth, this likely is the type of efficient feedback you expected.

Descriptive statistics *organize and summarize a set of data.* They help researchers identify and communicate basic characteristics of the data they collect. For example, look at Figure 7.3 on page 213. The descriptive statistics (percentages) used to create Figure 7.3 summarize the responses of approximately 45,000 students at American colleges studied in nationally representative surveys between 1980 and 2014 (Johnston et al., 2015). The findings indicate that the percentage of students who reported using cocaine at least once yearly dropped substantially between the mid-1980s and the mid-1990s, but has risen somewhat since then. Trying to determine such trends in cocaine use by looking at 45,000 individual responses would be an impossible task.

In many studies, researchers use descriptive statistics to summarize raw scores obtained from participants under various conditions. For example, in one memory experiment, cognitive psychologists exposed undergraduates to word lists that contained (1) only short words, (2) only long words, (3) alternating short and long words, or (4) alternating long and short words (Jalbert, Neath, Bireta, & Suprenant, 2011). These four types of lists represented the four conditions of the experiment. Although there were only 16 participants, each one engaged in all the conditions and was exposed to many word lists within each condition. Descriptive statistics—the proportion of short and/or long words recalled in the correct order in each condition—allowed the researchers to efficiently summarize the raw data. Overall, recall accuracy was best for the lists containing only short words and worst for the lists containing only long words.

Descriptive statistics are the focus of Module 2 (Frequency Distributions), Module 3 (Measures of Central Tendency), and Module 4 (Measures of Dispersion). The concepts covered in Module 5 (Correlation), Module 6 (The Normal Curve), and Module 7 (z Scores) also are important in descriptive statistical analysis, and they are used in inferential statistical analysis as well.

1.2 INFERENTIAL STATISTICS

Ideally, to determine the percentage of American college students who have used cocaine within the past year, we would study all American college students. Similarly, to assess how word length affects adults' ability to remember words, we ideally would study all adults. But, monetary costs, the time and effort involved, and possible barriers to gaining access would prevent us from studying everyone in these groups. Instead, we would do what researchers almost always must do out of necessity: study a subset of the cases we are interested in.

Populations and Samples

A **population** *consists of all the cases or observations of interest to us.* A **sample** *is a subset of cases or observations from a population.* In research methods, the terms *population* and *sample* often refer to people or other entities being studied (e.g., chimpanzees, schools). Thus, in the drug surveys just discussed, "students at American colleges" are the population of interest and the approximately 1,000 to 1,500 students selected for each survey represent the samples.

More technically, as statisticians speak of populations and samples, these terms refer to scores or other observations. For example, with regard to cocaine use, the population of interest would be the entire set of annual cocaine use scores of all American college students. The sample would be the subset of 1,500 scores that we actually obtained. Similarly, within the same drug survey, students' responses to questions about alcohol and marijuana use might yield a sample of 1,500 scores for each of those questions, and the populations of interest would be, respectively, the entire set of alcohol use and marijuana use scores of all American college students.

Although behavioral researchers almost always study samples, they typically are interested in drawing conclusions about populations. **Inferential statistics** *allow researchers to draw conclusions about a population based on data from a sample.* These conclusions are called inferences; hence, the name "inferential" statistics. For example, combined across gender, 4.4% of the randomly sampled college students who were surveyed in 2014 reported using cocaine within the prior 12 months (Johnston et al., 2015). This percentage is called a **statistic,** *which is a number that pertains to a sample.* Using inferential statistics, we might estimate that 4.4% of American college students used cocaine annually. Here, the value of 4.4% is called a **parameter,** *which is a number that refers to a population.*

Inferential statistics allow researchers to make statements, called inferences, about population parameters based on statistics from a sample. Modules 8 through 16 focus on inferential statistical concepts. Keep in mind that some statistics discussed in earlier modules, such as correlation and linear regression in Module 5, and z scores in Module 7, are used in both descriptive and inferential statistical analysis. For example, correlation coefficients are used to describe the strength and direction of a linear relation between two variables (i.e., between two samples of scores). Correlational analysis is also used to draw inferences about population parameters and to test hypotheses about the relation between variables. This brings us to the two major applications of inferential statistics.

Applications of Inferential Statistics

There are two common reasons why behavioral scientists use inferential statistics to draw conclusions about population parameters. First, in many studies, the researcher's primary goal is to estimate the numerical values of those parameters (e.g., "In the past year, 4.4% of American college students used cocaine" "Among registered voters, 38% believe that Congress is doing a good job"). Surveys and polls that examine representative samples of the population are often conducted for this purpose.

Population parameters cannot be estimated from sample statistics with absolute certainty because of *sampling variability:* chance fluctuations in the numerical value of a statistic (e.g., a mean score, a percentage) that occur when different samples are randomly drawn from the same population. Consider an analogy. If we obtain a sample of 100 coin flips, then a second sample, and a third sample of 100 flips using the same coin, merely by chance the number of Heads in each sample of flips is likely to differ: The numerical value (i.e., number of Heads) will fluctuate. Similarly, in a survey studying a nationally representative college student sample, some fluctuation will occur in the statistics we obtain (e.g., the percentage of students reporting annual cocaine use) depending on the particular sample of 1,500 students that we happen to randomly select. Inferential statistics enable scientists and pollsters to determine the degree of certainty with which any parameter estimate can be made (e.g., "We are 95% confident that in 2014, between 1.4% and 7.4% of American college students used cocaine at least once").

Another reason why researchers use inferential statistics is to help them determine whether the findings they obtain in a study are "statistically significant"; that is, unlikely to be due solely to chance. Inferential statistics are often used for this purpose in experiments and other types of studies in which researchers examine relations between variables. For example, in Jalbert et al.'s (2011) memory experiment, when participants were exposed to lists that contained only short words or only long words, they correctly recalled 75% of the short words and 55% of the long words (i.e., correct recall proportions of .75 and .55, respectively). Here, the researchers' goal typically is not to determine and report specific numeric values for population parameters, such as "We estimate from our sample that, for these sets of word lists, the general adult population will accurately recall 75% of short words and 55% of long words." Rather, the researchers' goal is to draw a general conclusion about the relation between word length and memory: "When people are exposed to lists containing only short or only long words, short words are better remembered."

Before we can conclude that this difference in memory performance was caused by the difference in word length, we must first rule out the alternative possibility that it was caused merely by sampling variability. To modify the coin analogy slightly, suppose we conduct an experiment. We ask 16 people to flip a coin 20 times; this is the control condition. Out of 320 total flips, the result is 155 Heads. We also ask these 16 people (or another 16 people) to flip the same coin 20 times, saying "Abracadabra" before each flip. This is the experimental condition. The result is 162 Heads. Should we conclude that saying "Abracadabra" increases the likelihood of flipping a Heads? Of course not; simply by chance, the odds are high that the proportion of Heads obtained in these two conditions will not be identical. Similarly, if you expose people to lists of short words and lists of long words, then even if word length truly has no influence on memory, you are still likely to get some differences in memory performance simply due to chance fluctuations.

The process of performing inferential statistical tests to determine whether a research finding is statistically significant actually does involve the use of sample statistics to estimate certain population parameters, but how this occurs is a technical discussion that need not concern us here. For now, it's more important to keep these two points in mind. First, as Statistics Module 9 discusses, inferences about statistical significance cannot be made with absolutely certainty. Second, even if inferential statistics indicate that a finding is unlikely to be due to chance, this alone does not mean that we can draw a clear conclusion that one variable influenced another variable. Such conclusions depend heavily on the type of study (e.g., an experiment vs. a correlational study) and the quality with which the study was designed and executed (e.g., the absence of confounding variables).

MODULE 2 FREQUENCY DISTRIBUTIONS

Learning Objectives

After studying this section, you should be able to:

- Understand frequency and relative frequency distributions.
- Organize raw data into a table that displays frequencies and relative frequencies.
- Understand several types of graphs used to display frequency and relative frequency distributions.

Have you ever heard an instructor give exam feedback in the following manner: "For the first exam, there were 7 *As*, 15 *Bs*, 18 *Cs*, 6 *Ds*, and 4 *Fs*"? Or perhaps the feedback was given in percentages: "On the exam, 14% of the grades were *As*, 30% were *Bs*," and so forth. If so, then you are familiar with frequency distributions and relative frequency distributions.

2.1 | TYPES OF FREQUENCY DISTRIBUTIONS

A **frequency distribution** *portrays how often each value of a variable occurs within a set of data.* Suppose that we administer a questionnaire to 40 college students. One item asks, "How many hours of nighttime sleep do you typically get on weekdays (not weekends)?" Another item asks students to indicate the type of residence in which they currently live. We also gather long-term data on the number of days during the semester on which each student drinks alcohol.

Quantitative Variables

Quantitative variables are attributes that can differ in "amount" or "quantity." Hours of sleep is a quantitative variable. Here are the raw scores for the item measuring hours of sleep:

6 8 8 7 7 6 7 5 8 6 6 7 6 4 8 9 6 6 6 7 6 8 6 6 7 9 7 6 6 7 7 8 6 6 5 7 8 5 8 5

To organize these data into a frequency distribution, we would count how many students reported sleeping for 4 hours, 5 hours, 6 hours, and so forth. Doing so, we see that the scale value *4* appears once; *5* appears 4 times; *6* appears 15 times; *7* appears 10 times; *8* appears 8 times; and *9* appears twice.

We also could describe the distribution of 40 scores efficiently by creating a **relative frequency distribution,** *which depicts the proportion or percentage of times that each value occurs within a data set.* For example, for the scale value of 4 hours, the proportion is .025 (i.e., one score of 40 total scores) and the percentage is 2.5 (i.e., 1/40 total scores × 100). For the scale value of 5 hours, the proportion is .10 (i.e., 4/40), which equates to 10% of the scores (i.e., 4/40 × 100).

A **cumulative frequency distribution** *portrays the total number of cases that occur at or below (or, at or above) each value in a data set.* For example, working from the smallest to largest scale values, there is one score of *4*, five scores representing 5 hours or less of sleep (i.e., one score of *4* plus four scores of *5*), 20 scores representing 6 hours or less of sleep (i.e., one score of *4* plus four scores of *5* plus 15 scores of *6*), and so forth. We also can express these cumulative frequencies as a **relative cumulative frequency distribution,** *which depicts the total proportion or percentage of cases that occur at or below (or, at or above) each value in a data set.* For example, a score of *4* occurs 2.5% of the time (1/40 cases), a score of *5* or less occurs 12.5% of the time (5/40 cases), a score of *6* or less occurs 50% of the time (20/40 cases), and so forth.

Rather than describing distributions in sentences, it's often simpler to present them in a table, such as Table SM.1. Column 1 presents the values of the variable (e.g., hours of sleep). Column 2 presents how frequently each value occurs among the 40 scores. Columns 3 and 4 illustrate relative frequencies as proportions and percentages. Presented as proportions, the numbers in the column should total to 1.00. Presented as percentages, they should total to 100%. In an actual report or paper, you typically would report relative frequencies either as proportions or percentages, but not as both. Columns 5 and 6 present a cumulative frequency distribution and a relative cumulative frequency distribution.

Table SM.1 Frequency Distributions of a Quantitative Variable

Hours of Sleep	Frequency	Relative Frequency (proportion of observations)	Relative Frequency (percentage of observations)	Cumulative Frequency (lowest to highest scale values)	Relative Cumulative Frequency (e.g., percentage; lowest to highest scale values)
9	2	.050	5.0	40	100.0
8	8	.200	20.0	38	95.0
7	10	.250	25.0	30	75.0
6	15	.375	37.5	20	50.0
5	4	.100	10.0	5	12.5
4	1	.025	2.5	1	2.5
Total	**40**	**1.000**	**100.0**		

One more point. Hours of sleep is a continuous variable that can assume an endless number of values. We chose to measure hours of sleep in full hours, not tenths, hundredths, or smaller units of an hour. Thus, the values in the left column of Table SM.1 actually represent broader intervals that must cover the entire range of possible continuous values. For this reason, *4* actually represents an interval of 3.5 to 4.5 hours, *5* represents 4.5 to 5.5 hours, and so forth. The fact that *4.5 hours* represents the top of the implied range for our scale value of *4* and the bottom of the implied range for our scale value of *5* signifies that the intervals truly are continuous. In other words, there is no possible value—no matter how many decimal points we measure to—that could fall in between the intervals.

Qualitative Variables

Qualitative variables represent properties that differ only in the "type" of some attribute. Suppose that in our questionnaire we measured students' current place of residence by offering the following response options: *Dormitory, Fraternity/sorority house, At home with parent or other caregiver,* and *Other off-campus residence.* In this case, current residence would be a qualitative variable. The four response choices are categories that represent different types of residences.

The raw data could be presented several ways, such as by listing the 40 responses in their complete form:

> *Dormitory   At home   Dormitory   Other off-campus . . .,*   and so on

Alternatively, for efficiency, we could use numeric codes as follows: 1 = *Dormitory*, 2 = *Fraternity/sorority house*, 3 = *At home with parent or other caregiver*, and 4 = *Other off-campus residence*. Here are the numerically coded raw data:

> 1 3 1 4 1 1 2 1 4 4 1 1 3 3 4 1 1 4 1 1 1 3 1 1 3 4 4 4 2 1 4 1 2 1 1 1 1 4 1 3

Note that although we have used a numeric code to represent each category, this does not magically transform current residence into a quantitative variable. For example, it makes no sense to say that a response of 4 (*Other off-campus residence*) is greater than a response of 1 (*Dormitory*). The numbers are merely codes used for convenience.

Table SM.2 shows the frequency and relative frequency distributions for current residence.

Table SM.2 Frequency and Relative Frequency Table for a Qualitative Variable

Place of Residence (and arbitrary numeric code)	Frequency	Relative Frequency (proportion of observations)	Relative Frequency (percentage of observations)
Dormitory (1)	21	.525	52.5
Fraternity/sorority house (2)	3	.075	7.5
At home with parents or other caretaker (3)	6	.150	15.0
Other off-campus (4)	10	.250	25.0
Total	**40**	**1.000**	**100.0**

Grouping Raw Scores Into Intervals

Notice in the left column of Table SM.1 that each scale value (i.e., 4, 5, 6, 7, 8, and 9 hours) is listed separately in its own row. Because there are only six values, the table is efficient and easy to read. Many quantitative variables, however, have a large number of possible values and thus the raw scores may display a wide range. Consider the following 40 raw scores for the variable representing the number of days in a semester that each student consumed alcohol:

22 41 47 32 33 35 9 23 39 15 0 41 37 44 11 72 23 0 4 44
42 17 0 83 20 26 40 49 35 29 57 0 0 12 31 35 55 32 51 30

Because the raw scores range from 0 to 83, we would need to create a frequency table with 84 rows to cover all the possible values within this range. Moreover, because we only have 40 scores in this raw data set and some of those score values occur more than once (e.g., *35* occurs three times), most of the values in the left column of this table (i.e., "Days Alcohol Consumed") would show a frequency of zero in the second column. Creating such a table would be an inefficient way to portray the data. A better alternative would be to group the raw scores into intervals, which would make the frequency table easier to digest. Table SM.3, which is called a grouped frequency table, provides such an example.

Table SM.3 A Grouped Frequency and Relative Frequency Table

Days Alcohol Consumed (interval)	Frequency	Relative Frequency (proportion of observations)	Relative Frequency (percentage of observations)
78–83	1	.025	2.5
72–77	1	.025	2.5
66–71	0	.000	0.0
60–65	0	.000	0.0
54–59	2	.050	5.0
48–53	2	.050	5.0
42–47	4	.100	10.0
36–41	5	.125	12.5
30–35	8	.200	20.0
24–29	2	.050	5.0
18–23	4	.100	10.0
12–17	3	.075	7.5
6–11	2	.050	5.0
0–5	6	.150	15.0
Total	**40**	**1.000**	**100.0**

In Table SM.3, there are 14 intervals, with each spanning 6 days. Some statisticians recommend that grouped frequency tables should have between 10 and 20 intervals; others recommend 5 to 10 intervals (Nolan & Heinzen, 2012). Having fewer intervals makes the table easier to read, but creates a greater loss of information. For example, the first interval (0–5 days) includes five students who didn't drink at all and one who drank on 4 days. If we used wider intervals, such as 12 days instead of 6 (e.g., 0–11, 12–23), Table SM.3 would now have only 7 rows and be easier to read, but students who didn't drink at all would be lumped together with students who drank up to 11 days during the semester.

Ultimately, a researcher must decide how many intervals are needed to best capture the distribution of raw scores. Whatever the decision, common guidelines for constructing grouped frequency intervals recommend that all intervals should have the same width, and the lowest value within each interval should be a multiple of the interval width. For example, in Table SM.3, each interval has a width of six, and once you move beyond the initial interval of 0–5, the lowest value in each interval is a nonzero multiple of six (6, 12, 18, 24, and so forth).

2.2 GRAPHS OF FREQUENCY DISTRIBUTIONS

A **histogram** *is a graph that uses bars to portray the distribution of a continuous quantitative variable.* Values of the variable (which represent an interval or ratio scale; see Chapter 4) are plotted on the *x*-axis, and the width of each bar represents the range of scores covered by the particular interval. (Recall that for a continuous variable such as hours of sleep, each scale value actually represents a range of possible scale values.) In the most common case, where the width of all bars is the same, the frequency, relative frequency, or cumulative relative frequency of each value is plotted on the *y*-axis. By converting the information in the second column of Table SM.1 into a graph, we get a histogram for hours of sleep (**Figure SM.1a**). Notice that adjacent bars in the histogram touch each other. This indicates that there are no gaps in the values plotted along the *x*-axis.

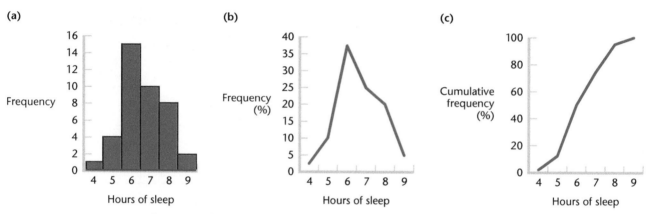

(a) **(b)** **(c)**

Figure SM.1 A (a) histogram, (b) relative frequency polygon, and (c) cumulative relative frequency polygon for hours of sleep.

A **frequency polygon** *is a line graph that shows the distribution of a quantitative variable.* Values of the variable (which represent an interval or ratio scale) are plotted on the *x*-axis, and the frequency, relative frequency, or cumulative relative frequency of each value is plotted on the *y*-axis. Figures SM.1b and SM.1c show two examples (called, more specifically, a *relative frequency polygon* and a *cumulative relative frequency polygon*). Some researchers prefer to use frequency polygons rather than histograms to graph distributions for continuous quantitative variables. Frequency polygons are especially useful when researchers want to compare two or more distributions of the same variable on a single graph. For example, suppose we want to compare the percentage of women and men who sleep for various lengths of time. We could devise a separate histogram or line graph for each gender, but creating a single polygon with two distinctive data lines (e.g., red and blue)—one for the women's distribution and one for the men's—makes it easier to compare the two distributions.

For quantitative variables that are measured on an interval or ratio scale, but which are discrete, bar graphs typically are used to display frequency, relative frequency, and cumulative frequency distributions. For variables measured on an ordinal scale and for qualitative variables, bar graphs can be used to display frequency and relative frequency distributions. We discussed bar graphs in Chapter 4, and because they portray many types of descriptive statistics, not just distributions, we can define them generally as follows: In a **bar graph** *values of a variable are plotted on the x-axis and the descriptive statistic we are interested in is plotted along the y-axis.*

For example, **Figure SM.2a** shows a bar graph of the relative frequency distribution for students' current place of residence. The values on the *x*-axis are the names of the residence categories. The frequency or relative frequency of each category is indicated by the height of the bars. In plotting frequency distributions for noncontinuous quantitative variables and for qualitative variables, the bars typically are shown as nonadjacent: They don't touch one another. This reflects the fact that the *x*-axis values represent discrete quantitative values or, for qualitative variables, different types of a particular characteristic, rather than a continuous quantitative dimension.

Pie charts are another way to portray relative frequency distributions for qualitative variables. A **pie chart** *is a circular graph that is divided into segments.* Each segment represents a

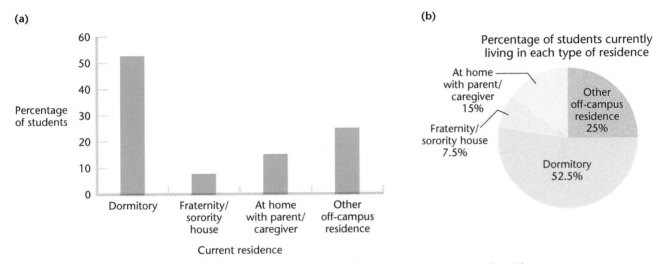

Figure SM.2 **(a) A bar graph and (b) pie chart for place of residence.**

category of the variable and the size of each segment corresponds to the percentage or proportion of scores in that category. Figure SM.2b portrays the same relative frequency distribution shown in the bar graph. Because all the segments combined equal the total area of the circle, the percentages within the segments should add up to 100%. If proportions are used, they should add up to 1.00.

MODULE 3 MEASURES OF CENTRAL TENDENCY

Learning Objectives

After studying this section, you should be able to:

- Define and determine the mode, mean, and median of a set of scores.
- Describe advantages and disadvantages of the mode, mean, and median.

3.1 | THE MODE, MEAN, AND MEDIAN

Measures of central tendency *identify the "typical values" or "center" of a distribution of scores.* The mode, mean, and median are three common measures of central tendency.

Suppose we have a sample of 11 scores. The scores represent the number of errors that each of 11 participants made in the same laboratory task:

4 7 7 9 6 3 5 9 8 5 5

To illustrate the distribution of values, let's place the scores in ascending order:

3 4 5 5 5 6 7 7 8 9 9

The Mode

The **mode** *is the most frequently occurring score in a distribution.* The score 5 occurs three times and other scores only occur once or twice. Thus, the mode is 5. The symbol for the mode of a sample of scores is *Mo*, and it is italicized.

3 4 **5 5 5** 6 7 7 8 9 9

A distribution may have more than one mode. For example, a *bimodal distribution* has two modes. In the distribution below, scores of 4 and 7 each occur three times:

3 **4 4 4** 5 5 6 **7 7 7** 8 9 9

The Mean

The **mean** *is the arithmetic average of a distribution of scores.* Calculating the mean takes only two steps. First, add together all the scores in a distribution. This is called the "sum of scores" and it is represented by the symbol ΣX, in which X represents each individual score and the symbol Σ (sigma) stands for "the sum of." Second, after adding all the scores, you divide by the total number of scores (N) in the distribution. For the original distribution of task errors above, we calculate the mean as follows:

$$\text{Mean} = \frac{\Sigma X}{N} = \frac{3+4+5+5+5+6+7+7+8+9+9}{11} = \frac{68}{11} = 6.18$$

The symbol for the mean of a sample of scores is M (italicized). Thus, $M = 6.18$.

The Median

The **median** *is the midpoint of a distribution.* In a distribution with an odd number of scores, to determine the median, you first order the scores from lowest to highest (or highest to lowest), as we have already done. Then you identify the middle score. In our distribution of 11 scores, the sixth score will be the middle score: Five scores occur to the left of it and five scores occur to the right of it. This middle score has a value of 6:

3 4 5 5 5 **6** 7 7 8 9 9

The symbol for the median of a sample of scores is *Mdn* (italicized). Therefore, *Mdn* = 6.

In a distribution with an even number of scores, there will be two middle scores. The median is found by taking the average of the two middle scores. For example, in a distribution of eight scores, the scores in the 4th and 5th position are the middle scores, as shown below:

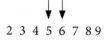

2 3 4 5 6 7 8 9

The median is the halfway point between these scores, namely, 5.5.

3.2 ADVANTAGES AND DISADVANTAGES

Overall, in behavioral research the mode typically is the least commonly used measure of central tendency. The mean is the most commonly used measure. Still, each measure has advantages (+) and disadvantages (−).

The Mode

- (+) The mode is the only central tendency measure that is appropriate to use for qualitative variables (i.e., variables measured on a nominal scale). For example, if we have data about the eye color of 100 students, we can determine which color occurs most frequently.

- (+) For any distribution, if your goal is to guess any specific, individual score, the mode is your best bet (i.e., you will be correct most often).

- (−) The mode may be extremely unrepresentative of the overall distribution and thus highly misleading. Consider the following distribution of course grades. Despite the vast majority of high grades, the mode is 0.0.

  0.0, 0.0, 3.0, 3.1, 3.2, 3.4, 3.6, 3.8, 3.9, 4.0

- (−) When you draw different samples from the same population, the mode usually shows greater fluctuations from sample to sample than do the mean and median.

The Mean

- (+) The mean is the only measure of central tendency that uses all the numeric information in the distribution. If you change the value of any single score, the mean will change to reflect that new information.

- (+) When you draw different samples from the same population, the mean usually shows less fluctuation from sample to sample than do the mode and median.

- (−) A mean cannot be calculated for a qualitative (i.e., nominal scale) variable.

- (−) The mean is very sensitive to extreme scores. In the distribution of 10 grades presented above, the mean grade is 2.80. Among the eight students who passed the class, the mean is 3.50. Especially in distributions with a small number of scores, extreme scores (e.g., the two 0.0 grades) strongly influence the mean and can distort conclusions about the "typical" score.

The Median

- (+) The median is less sensitive to extreme scores than the mean. A small to moderate percentage of extreme scores don't affect it all. In the distribution of 10 grades above, the median grade is 3.3, which does a reasonable job of capturing the "typical" score despite the two extreme grades of 0.0.

- (+/−) When you draw different samples from the same population, the median usually fluctuates less than the mode, but more than the mean.

- (−) A median cannot be calculated for a qualitative (i.e., nominal scale) variable.

- (−) The median does not use all the specific information in a distribution. This is the downside to its advantage of being insensitive to extreme scores. In the distribution of 10 grades, as long as 3.2 and 3.4 remain the middle two scores, then the median will not reflect changes to any scores below or above it. For example, if the top four students had all received a 4.0, the median would remain the same.

The question of which measure best portrays central tendency depends in part on the particular set of scores involved. This is one reason why it is important to examine the frequency distribution of any data you collect. For example, if the mean has been substantially influenced by extreme scores, you may want to report the median and perhaps the mode.

MODULE 4 MEASURES OF DISPERSION

Learning Objectives

After studying this section, you should be able to:

- Understand the concepts of range, variance, and standard deviation.
- Calculate the range, variance, and standard deviation of a set of scores.

4.1 THE RANGE, VARIANCE, AND STANDARD DEVIATION

Measures of dispersion (also called **measures of variability**) *assess how much the scores in a distribution are spread out.* They can let us know whether scores are tightly clustered or spread far apart from one another. The range, variance, and standard deviation are three common measures of dispersion. To illustrate these measures, let's use the data from the Party 1 example in Chapter 2 (p. 59), but here let's imagine that the scores in the Party 1 column of Table SM.4 are the ages of a sample of eight people attending a large party.

Table SM.4 Data Used in Calculating the Variance for People's Age at Party 1

Column				
1	2	3	4	5
Person	Age	Mean	Deviation Score (age – mean)	Deviation Squared
1	20	22	−2	4
2	23	22	1	1
3	22	22	0	0
4	24	22	2	4
5	22	22	0	0
6	24	22	2	4
7	20	22	−2	4
8	21	22	−1	1
Sum	**176**	**176**	**0**	$SS = 18$
Mean	**22**	**22**	**0**	

Note: SS = sum of squares.

The **range** *describes the highest and lowest scores in a distribution; it can also be expressed as the distance between them.* In Party 1, the range is 24 to 20 years of age, which can also be expressed as a range of 4 years (i.e., 24 − 20 = 4). The range is the simplest measure of variability to calculate. However, it also is the crudest and typically the least useful because it only takes the two most extreme scores into account. For example, the following two distributions have a range of 8, yet they are very different:

$$10 \ 10 \ 10 \ 9 \ 9 \ 9 \ 9 \ 2 \quad \text{Range} = 10 - 2 = 8$$
$$10 \ \ 5 \ \ 4 \ 2 \ 2 \ 2 \ 2 \quad \text{Range} = 10 - 2 = 8$$

In contrast to using the range to assess dispersion, we might want to calculate a statistic that is more sensitive to all the scores in a distribution. A simple solution may seem to be this: Why not measure how much each score deviates from the mean (this is called a *deviation score*) and then calculate the average deviation score for the distribution? If a set of scores is generally spread far away from its mean, the average deviation would be large. If the scores are tightly clustered around their mean, the average deviation would be small.

This is a great idea, except for one big problem: The average deviation from the arithmetic mean will always be zero. Simply, when you have a set of scores and subtract the arithmetic mean from each score, the positive deviations (from scores above the mean) and negative deviations (from scores below the mean) cancel each other out. To avoid this, we could ignore the plus and minus signs from each deviation score (i.e., just take the absolute value), and determine the average absolute amount of deviation.

Another alternative—the one typically used in behavioral statistics—is to eliminate the problem of summing to zero by squaring each deviation score. The sum of these squared deviation scores will always produce a positive number. There are two statistics that build on this idea and provide a more sensitive measure of dispersion than the range: the variance and the standard deviation.

The **variance** *measures how much the scores in a distribution are spread out in relation to their mean. It is the average of the squared deviations about the mean.* Essentially, to determine the variance, you take each score, subtract the mean from it, square the resulting number, add up all the squared numbers, and divide by the number of scores.

Another statistic, the **standard deviation,** *is the square root of the variance. It measures how much the scores in a distribution are spread out in relation to their mean, as expressed in the original units of measurement.* For example, suppose we measure how many seconds it takes participants to complete a task. The variance of those scores will give us information about how much those scores are spread out from the mean, but as we will see shortly, that spread will be represented in squared units (i.e., the number of seconds squared). Taking the square root of the variance gives us the standard deviation, which expresses the amount of spread in the original units of measurement (i.e., seconds).

The concepts of variance and the standard deviation are of great importance in many sciences, including psychology, so keep these key points in mind:

- The greater the spread of scores within a distribution, the larger the variance and standard deviation will be.

- It is technically incorrect to say that for a set of scores, the standard deviation simply is the average deviation from the mean. As noted earlier, the average deviation score is always 0. Even if we use absolute values to calculate deviation scores, the standard deviation will almost always be different from the average absolute deviation. However, you can think of the standard deviation as providing one type of estimate of the typical deviation from the mean.

- Some inferential statistical tests that you may learn about in upcoming modules are based on the variance or standard deviation statistic.

4.2 CALCULATING MEASURES OF DISPERSION

The Range

For a set of scores:

$$\text{Range} = \text{highest score to lowest score}$$

Thus, in Table SM.4, the range of ages is 24 to 20. As noted earlier, we can also express the range as the highest score minus the lowest score (i.e., the range is 4). No symbol is used to designate the range; it is simply written as a full word.

The Variance

There are different formulae for calculating the variance. We will use the "definitional formula" because it is best suited to helping you understand the concept of variance. It also is easy to use for simple data sets. For a distribution of scores:

$$\text{Variance} = \frac{\Sigma(X - M)^2}{N}$$

where
Σ = "the sum of" $\qquad$ X = each score in the distribution
N = the number of scores $\qquad$ M = mean of the distribution

Procedure. Refer to Table SM.4 as we perform the following steps:

Step 1 Create a table with five columns and label them in a manner similar to Table SM.4. If you are calculating the variance for a variable other than *age*, use the name of that variable in Column 2.

Step 2 Enter all the scores in Column 2, one score per row.

Step 3 Calculate the mean of the scores and enter this number into each row of Column 3.

Step 4 In Column 4, take each score and subtract the mean from it. Be sure to enter a minus sign if the resulting score is negative. This is a very important statistic called a **deviation score,** *the arithmetic difference between each score in a distribution and the mean of that distribution* (i.e., $X - M$).

Step 5 In Column 5, square each deviation score: $(X - M)^2$.

Step 6 Add up all the squared deviation scores: $\Sigma(X - M)^2$. This is another very important statistic called the **sum of squares (SS):** *the sum of squared deviations of scores from the mean of their distribution.* In Table SM.4, the sum of squares is 18.

Step 7 Divide the sum of squares by the number of scores in the distribution (N). The resulting number is the variance of this set of scores. In this example, the variance is 2.25.

When the variance of a set of scores is calculated as a descriptive statistic, it is represented by the symbol S^2 (not italicized).

The Standard Deviation

The standard deviation is the square root of the variance. Thus, to calculate the standard deviation, you first calculate the variance and then take its square root. When we are interested only in describing the standard deviation of a set of scores, the formula is

$$\text{Standard deviation} = \sqrt{\frac{\Sigma(X - M)^2}{N}}$$

Thus, for the sample of Party 1 scores, the standard deviation = $\sqrt{2.25}$ = 1.50. When the standard deviation of a set of scores is calculated as a descriptive statistic, it is represented by the symbol *SD* (italicized).

Sample Variance and Standard Deviation as Estimates of the Population Variance and Standard Deviation

When data from a sample are used to estimate the variance and standard deviation of a population, the formula for calculating these statistics is slightly different. Specifically, the denominator is $N - 1$ rather than N, as shown below:

$$\text{Variance} = \frac{\Sigma(X - M)^2}{N - 1} \qquad \text{Standard deviation} = \sqrt{\frac{\Sigma(X - M)^2}{N - 1}}$$

The reason for this change is that the amount of variance in a sample of scores tends to underestimate the amount of variance in the population. Dividing by $N - 1$ makes the sample variance and standard deviation better statistics for estimating the population variance and standard deviation. Some inferential statistical tests use these sample statistics to estimate the population variance and standard deviation. In such estimates, $N - 1$ is the denominator. Because the variance and standard deviation are most often calculated as steps in inferential analyses, from this point forward in the statistics modules, we will use $N - 1$ in their denominators. In this case, the variance in the Party 1 example is $18/7 = 2.57$ and the standard deviation $= \sqrt{2.57} = 1.60$.

When the standard deviation and variance of a sample of scores are calculated as estimates of the population standard deviation and variance, the symbol *s* (italicized) represents the sample standard deviation and the symbol s^2 (only the "s" is italicized) represents the sample variance. In addition, the lowercase Greek character σ (not italicized, and pronounced "sigma") represents the population standard deviation, and $σ^2$ (not italicized) is used to represent the population variance. Another important Greek character to know is μ (not italicized, and pronounced "mu"), which represents the population mean.

MODULE 5 CORRELATION

Learning Objectives

After studying this section, you should be able to:

- Identify two common correlation statistics and when they are used.
- Calculate a Pearson correlation and determine whether it is statistically significant.
- Explain the concept of regression and of a regression line.

5.1 COMMON CORRELATION STATISTICS

Chapter 5 discusses the concept of correlation and characteristics of correlational research. Here, we address some additional aspects of correlational analysis. First, however, recall that correlation coefficients describe relations between pairs of variables. **Pearson's *r*** (i.e., the **Pearson product-moment correlation coefficient**) *measures the direction and strength of the linear relation between two variables that have been measured on an interval or ratio scale.* It is the most frequently used correlation statistic. For example, we would compute Pearson's *r* to assess the correlation between adults' height and weight.

Another common statistic, **Spearman's rho** (i.e., the **Spearman rank-order correlation coefficient**), *is used to measure the relation between two quantitative variables when one or both variables have been measured on an ordinal scale (i.e., the scores represent ranks).* For example, if we ranked all the members of a sports team in terms of their popularity and athletic skill, we would calculate Spearman's rho to examine whether popularity and athletic skill are correlated. If all the scores were initially recorded as ranks, then the Spearman's coefficient will indicate the direction and strength of the linear relation between the two sets of ranks. Both Pearson's r and Spearman's rho have a range of values from +1.00 to −1.00. Although we don't have space to discuss them, be aware that other correlation statistics exist for certain types of data.

5.2 | CALCULATING A PEARSON CORRELATION COEFFICIENT

Suppose we conduct a study to examine whether there is a correlation between the number of hours students spend daily playing video games and their exam performance. We will focus on Pearson's r. The formula has several versions. The version here will help you understand why a correlation ends up being positive or negative:

$$r = \frac{[\Sigma(X - M_X)(Y - M_Y)]/N - 1}{\sqrt{(Variance_X)(Variance_Y)}} = \frac{Covariance_{XY}}{\sqrt{(Variance_X)(Variance_Y)}}$$

X = each score on variable X M_x = the mean of X N = number of score pairs
Y = each score on variable Y M_y = the mean of Y

$$Variance_X = \frac{\Sigma(X - M_X)^2}{N - 1} \qquad Variance_Y = \frac{\Sigma(X - M_Y)^2}{N - 1}$$

Look at the numerator of the formula. For each pair of X and Y scores, we first calculate the amount that each score deviates from its mean and then multiply these deviation scores. If a pair of X and Y scores deviate from their means in the same direction—both are above or both are below their respective means—then the cross product of their deviation scores will be a positive number. If a pair of X and Y scores deviate from their means in opposite directions—one is above its mean and the other is below its mean—then the cross product of their deviation scores will be a negative number. Thus, the total (Σ) of these cross products reflects the overall degree to which pairs of scores in the data set deviate from their means in the same direction (leading to a positive correlation) or the opposite direction (leading to a negative correlation).

When the sum of the cross products is divided by $N - 1$, this yields an inferential statistic called the *covariance* of X and Y. Covariance is a measure of the extent to which X and Y vary together, and it is the numerator of the correlation equation. In the Pearson's r equation, the effect of the denominator is to keep all r values within a range of +1.00 to −1.00, regardless of the units of measurement used in a particular study. If, for example, a set of scores revealed a +.48 correlation between people's height and weight, that correlation will remain the same regardless of whether height is measured in inches, feet, centimeters, or meters, and weight in ounces, pounds, grams, or kilograms.

An Example. Suppose we have a sample of 10 college students. We record two variables for each student: X, the average number of daily hours spent playing video games, and Y, their Exam 1 score (maximum possible score = 40). In Table SM.5, Columns 2 and 3 contain the raw scores. Columns 4 through 8 show the results of calculations that need to be made.

Table SM.5 Data Used Calculating a Correlation (Pearson's *r*)

					Column		
1	2	3	4	5	6	7	8
Student ($N = 10$)	Video Games (hours/day) X	Exam 1 Score Y	$X - M_X$	$Y - M_Y$	$(X - M_X)$ × $(Y - M_Y)$	$(X - M_X)^2$	$(Y - M_Y)^2$
KC	0	35	−2	5	−10	4	25
BT	0	28	−2	−2	4	4	4
WT	0	37	−2	7	−14	4	49
JR	1	31	−1	1	−1	1	1
BN	1	36	−1	6	−6	1	36
TJ	2	25	0	−5	0	0	25
ZB	3	27	1	−3	−3	1	9
LW	3	31	1	1	1	1	1
HC	4	27	2	−3	−6	4	9
PJ	6	23	4	−7	−28	16	49
Sum	**20** $M_X = 2.00$	**300** $M_Y = 30.00$	**0**	**0**	**−63** Covariance$_{XY}$ = −7.00	$SS_X = 36$ Variance$_X$ = 4.00	$SS_Y = 208$ Variance$_Y$ = 23.11

Step 1 Calculate the mean of X in Column 2 and the mean of Y in Column 3. In our example, $M_X = 20/10 = 2.00$ and $M_Y = 300/10 = 30.00$.

Step 2 Subtract M_X from each X score and M_Y from each Y score. Enter these deviation scores in Columns 4 and 5, respectively.

Step 3 Multiply each pair of deviation scores from Columns 4 and 5 and enter the cross product in Column 6. Add the cross products and enter this amount at the bottom of Column 6 (the sum is −63). Dividing by $N - 1$ (i.e., $10 - 1 = 9$) gives us the covariance: −7.00.

Step 4 Square the deviation scores for X (Column 4), enter the results in Column 7, and sum these scores ($SS_X = 36$). Square the deviation scores for Y (Column 5), enter the results in Column 8, and sum these scores ($SS_Y = 208$). Dividing each sum of squares by $N - 1$ gives us the variance of X (4.00) and variance of Y (23.11).

Step 5 We now have all the values we need to calculate a correlation:

$$r = \frac{Covariance_{XY}}{\sqrt{(Variance_X)(Variance_Y)}} = \frac{-7.00}{\sqrt{(4.00)(23.11)}} = \frac{-7.00}{9.61} = -.73$$

Step 6 To determine whether a correlation is statistically significant, we can use Table 1 in Appendix C. Based on 10 pairs of scores, a correlation of −.73 is statistically significant ($df = 8$, two-tailed test, $p < .05$). Our results support the hypothesis that greater time spent playing video games is associated with lower exam grades.

5.3 REGRESSION ANALYSIS

Regression analysis (i.e., **simple linear regression**) *explores the quantitative, linear relation between two variables,* and is often used to predict the scores of one variable based on the scores of another variable. Chapter 5 introduced the concepts of regression analysis and a regression line, and an example in which high school students' SAT scores (variable X, the predictor) were used to estimate their first-year college GPAs (variable Y, the criterion). This module discusses the regression equation produced by a regression analysis, which is visually portrayed by the regression line. We will use the previous data set in Table SM.5 as an example.

Suppose we want to use students' scores for daily hours of video game play (variable X) to predict their Exam 1 scores (variable Y). **Figure SM.3** shows a scatter plot of the data and the regression line, which provides the best overall fit to the data according to one statistical criterion that we'll discuss shortly. The regression line visually portrays a *regression equation*, expressed by the following formula:

$$\hat{Y} = a + bX$$

where

$\hat{Y}$ = the predicted value of Y
a = the intercept where the regression line crosses the y axis
b = the slope of the line (i.e., the amount that Y changes when X changes by 1 unit)
X = the value of X

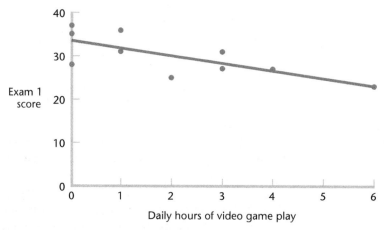

Figure SM.3 Scatter plot with a regression line.

In our data, the correlation between X and Y is negative. Thus, the slope of the regression line is negative, which makes b a negative value and changes the regression equation to $\hat{Y} = a - bX$. Specifically, our regression equation (determined by a software package) is

$$\hat{Y} = 33.50 - 1.75X$$

To illustrate, if we apply this equation to a student, say, LW (who plays video games for 3 hours a day, on average), we get

$$\hat{Y} = 33.50 - 1.75(3) = 33.50 - 5.25 = 28.25$$

LW's actual Exam 1 score was 31, so although our prediction isn't bad, it still is off by almost 3 points. This error in prediction reflects the fact that the correlation between X and Y, although strong, is far from perfect. Had it been perfect, then for this sample the students' Y scores could be predicted precisely by their X scores. The difference between each actual Y score and predicted Y score is called a *residual*. For LW, the residual is 2.75 (31.00 − 28.25) points. Suppose we calculate the residual for each student, square it, and then add all the squared residuals. The total of the squared residuals will be smaller for this regression line than for any other straight line that could be drawn to fit these data. This is the sense in which the regression line provides the best fit to the data.

Of course, our main interest is not to predict Y from X for the original sample; we already know their precise Y scores. Rather, as when using SAT scores to predict college grades, a regression equation generated from one sample will be used to estimate how future applicants will perform in college. Technical adjustments usually are made when a regression equation generated from an original sample is applied to predict values of Y from new samples of data, but that's an advanced topic that we need not discuss here.

Although we can predict Y from X, this does not mean we can conclude that more hours spent playing video games caused students to perform more poorly. Remember the general rule that causal conclusions cannot be drawn from correlation data. Finally, our regression equation used X to predict Y. If for some reason we wanted to use Y to predict X, the regression equation would likely be different.

MODULE 6 THE NORMAL CURVE

Learning Objectives

After studying this section, you should be able to:

- Describe key properties of the normal distribution.
- Understand why the normal distribution is important.
- Understand the concept of skew.

6.1 BASIC CONCEPTS

The normal distribution, also called the normal curve, is a special type of distribution of scores. Specifically, the **normal distribution (normal curve)** *is a theoretical distribution for a population of scores. It is symmetrical, bell-shaped, and has other unique mathematical properties.*

Figure SM.4 presents an example of a normal distribution. Along the *x*-axis, you will notice two rows of scale values. In the top row, the Greek letter μ represents the population mean and is located at the center of the distribution. The Greek letter σ represents the population standard deviation. As scores move away from the population mean, to left or right along the *x*-axis, scale values are located at minus and plus 1, 2, 3, and 4 standard deviations from the mean, respectively. The second row of value labels along the *x*-axis is based on a statistic called a *z* score, which is the focus of Statistics Module 7. In that module, you will be asked to refer back to Figure SM.4.

Look over Figure SM.4 as we discuss the following properties of the normal curve.

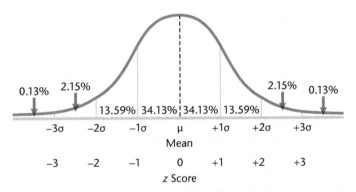

Figure SM.4 A normal curve. The midpoint along the *x*-axis represents the population mean, μ, as well as the mode and median of the distribution. The top set of values along the *x*-axis represent the number of standard deviations (σ) away from the mean. The bottom set of numbers along the *x*-axis are *z* scores.

- *Theoretical.* The normal curve is theoretical; it is a mathematical concept. It portrays a hypothetical distribution of scores that has certain useful mathematical properties important in statistical inference. The normal curve does not represent any particular variable in the natural world.

- *Distribution of a population of scores.* The x-axis portrays a range of score values. The height of the curve on the y-axis between any two points on the x-axis portrays the relative frequency of the scores within that range.

- *Represents a continuous variable.* A continuous variable can assume an infinite number of values within its range of scores. The normal curve is a theoretical distribution of a continuous variable.

- *A "family" of distributions.* A normal distribution can have any mean and any standard deviation. Thus, there are many normal curves. For example, some may have a taller or shorter peak, and be narrower or wider than the curve portrayed in Figure SM.4. But, any distribution that meets the criteria listed here (and other criteria) represents a normal curve.

- *The mean, median, and mode are the same.* The mean, median, and mode are different ways of measuring the "center" of a distribution. A key statistical property of a normal distribution is that the mean, median, and mode have the same numerical value. The peak of the curve occurs at the mean, median, and mode.

- *Symmetrical and bell-shaped.* The normal curve is symmetrical: Along the x-axis, 50% of the cases fall on either side of the mean. It also is bell shaped, and as we move along the x-axis in either direction away from the mean, the relative frequency of cases becomes progressively smaller. Notice that the left and right tails of the curve never touch the x-axis (i.e., they are "asymptotic" to the x-axis).

- *The 68-95-99.7 Rule.* The total area underneath the entire normal curve (i.e., between the curve line and the x-axis) represents 100% of the cases in the distribution. For any normal distribution, approximately 68% of the cases fall within the range of +1 to −1 standard deviations from the mean. Further, approximately 95% and 99.7% of cases will fall within 2 or 3 standard deviations of the mean, respectively.

6.2 | IMPORTANCE OF THE NORMAL CURVE

The most important application of the normal curve is that it allows us to estimate the probability that a particular outcome will occur. For example, suppose we find that 25 participants randomly assigned to perform a task in front of an audience average 5.4 errors, and 25 participants randomly assigned to perform the same task alone average 9.1 errors. We want to conclude that this particular outcome—this difference in performance—was caused by the different environmental conditions (audience vs. alone) to which participants were exposed. However, we must first answer a basic question: What is the probability that this outcome could have occurred simply by chance? In other words, if you randomly divide 50 people into two groups of 25 and have them perform the task under *identical* conditions, it is unlikely that their performance will be exactly the same. So, how big does the difference in errors made by the two groups have to be before it clearly exceeds what we would expect by chance? The normal curve provides the foundation for many statistical tests that researchers use to answer this type of question.

Being able to estimate the probability of particular outcomes has other uses, such as in neuropsychological and educational testing. Here, psychologists administer various tests to assess people's cognitive, perceptual, motor, and intellectual functioning. If the distribution for a particular trait approximates a normal curve and the mean and standard deviation of the population are known, then it is easy to determine the percentile rank of that score. A **percentile rank** is *the percentage of scores in a distribution that fall below a particular score.* Consider a simple example. The Wechsler Adult Intelligence Scale (WAIS) is a commonly used psychological test for measuring intelligence. It provides scores on several subtests (e.g., verbal comprehension, perceptual reasoning) and also yields an overall IQ score. In the adult population, the distribution of IQ scores on the WAIS approximates a normal curve, with a mean score of 100 and a standard deviation of 15 points. Given this information, we can answer questions such as these:

1. "My friend has an IQ score of 130, so just how high a score is that?" Your friend's score of 130 is 2 standard deviations above the mean. In a normal distribution, 50% of the scores fall below the mean, and looking at Figure SM.4, we see that 34.13% of scores fall between the mean and +1 standard deviation (i.e., $+1\sigma$) and 13.59% fall between $+1\sigma$ and $+2\sigma$. By adding these percentages (i.e., 50.00% + 34.13% + 13.59% = 97.72%), we calculate that your friend's percentile rank is 97.72. Thus, at least as defined by the WAIS test, your friend's IQ is higher than that of just over 97% of the population.

2. "My IQ score is 115, so how do I compare to other people?" An IQ score of 115 is +1 standard deviations from the WAIS mean of 100. In a normal distribution, 50% of the scores fall below the mean, and 34.13% fall between the mean and $+1\sigma$. Thus, your IQ score of 115 puts your percentile rank at 84.13%.

Shortly, we'll discuss a concept called *z* scores, and you will learn that there are tables that greatly simplify the task of answering questions such as those above.

6.3 | SKEWED DISTRIBUTIONS

Unlike the normal distribution, which has a symmetrical shape, many distributions are asymmetrical. A **skewed distribution** is *an asymmetrical distribution.* As **Figure SM.5** illustrates, in a *positively skewed distribution,* the right tail of the distribution extends further from the mean than does the left tail, and the bulk of the scores fall to the left of the mean. In a *negatively skewed distribution,* the left tail of the distribution extends further from the mean than does the right tail, and the bulk of the scores fall to the right of the mean.

(a)   (b)

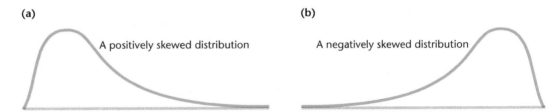

A positively skewed distribution   A negatively skewed distribution

Figure SM.5 Examples of (a) a positively skewed distribution and (b) a negatively skewed distribution.

In a class of 300 students, suppose an instructor gives a very easy exam worth 100 points. A few students receive perfect scores, most get excellent or very good grades, but some receive very poor or failing grades. Would this score distribution be positively or negatively skewed? If an instructor gave an extremely difficult test, in which most students did very poorly and progressively fewer got higher and higher scores, would the distribution be positively or negatively skewed? Assume the *x*-axis ranges left to right from 0 to 100. Here are the answers. The distribution for the easy exam would more closely resemble Figure SM.5b than SM.5a. For a difficult exam, the distribution would more closely resemble the distribution in SM.5a.

MODULE 7 z SCORES

Learning Objectives

After studying this section, you should be able to:

- Describe the general purpose of z scores.
- Calculate a z score.
- Explain how z scores can be used in conjunction with the normal curve.

7.1 | BASIC CONCEPTS

Suppose that Amy is one of 127 students taking a college research methods course. So far there has been one exam and one major paper assignment. Amy received a score of 40 out of 50 on the exam and 19 out of 28 on the paper. On which grading component did she do better? In terms of percentages, Amy scored 80% on the exam and 68% on the paper, suggesting that her exam performance is in some sense better than her performance on the paper. But, this isn't the only way to judge how well she performed, and it could even be misleading. For example, what if her exam score is well below the class average, but her score on the paper is far above the class average?

If we could somehow convert both variables (exam performance, paper performance) to a common measurement scale, we could make a more direct comparison about her performance within the class. A statistic called a *z score* allows us to do this. A **z score** *transforms an original score into a number that represents how many standard deviations that score is from the mean.* The basic concept is simple:

$$z = \frac{original\ score - mean\ of\ the\ distribution}{standard\ deviation\ of\ the\ distribution}$$

Thus, a raw score that is 1 standard deviation above the mean would convert to a z score of +1.00. A raw score that is 2 standard deviations below the mean would be a z score of −2.00. A raw score that falls precisely at the mean would be transformed into a z score of 0.00.

Psychologists study diverse variables that are measured on different scales: speed (e.g., milliseconds, minutes), weight (e.g., milligrams), the number of task errors or problems correctly solved, psychological traits such as IQ (e.g., scores on intelligence and personality tests), and so forth. There are many instances in which it is useful to make comparisons among variables that were measured on a different scale, and z scores provide one method of doing this.

7.2 | CALCULATING A z SCORE

Amy received a score of 40 out of 50 on her exam and 19 out of 28 on the paper. In this example, the 127 students in the class represent the population of interest to us (and to Amy!). The formula for computing a z score in a population is

$$z = \frac{X - \mu}{\sigma}$$

where

X = a particular score in the distribution μ = the mean of the population
σ = the standard deviation of the population

Suppose that the exam mean was 42.35 and the standard deviation was 5.20. For the paper, the mean was 16.00 and the standard deviation was 3.46. Therefore,

$$z_{exam} \frac{40 - 42.35}{5.20} = -.45 \qquad z_{paper} \frac{19 - 16.00}{3.46} = .87$$

These z scores tell us that, relative to her classmates, Amy performed almost 1 standard deviation above the mean on her paper, but performed about half a standard deviation below the mean on her exam. By this definition of "better" (i.e., relative to the class), Amy did better on the paper than on the exam, even though she attained a higher percentage of points on the exam. If the course instructor uses a curve grading system, as some instructors do, then one way this can be implemented is to convert students' scores on each grading component into z scores. Thus, in a curve graded class, Amy's performance on the paper will help to raise her overall standing in the class, whereas her exam grade will lower her relative standing.

7.3 | z SCORES AND THE NORMAL CURVE

Any distribution of scores, whether it approximates the shape of a normal curve or not, can be transformed into z scores. The resulting distribution of z scores will have the same shape as the original distribution of raw scores, but it will always have a mean of 0 and a standard deviation of 1.

In a normal distribution, we can express the values along the x-axis as z scores. Notice that in Figure SM.4, the second row below the x-axis is expressed in z scores. This has the useful property of transforming the mean of any normal distribution to a score of 0. Moreover, because z scores directly represent units of standard deviations, then about 68% of the scores in a normal distribution will fall within a z score range of -1.00 to $+1.00$, 95% will fall within the range of -2.00 to $+2.00$, and 99.7% will fall within a range of -3.00 to $+3.00$.

A detailed table called a standard normal table (or sometimes a z table) describes the proportion of cases that fall to the left and to the right of a particular z score, which we can then convert to percentages (i.e., by multiplying by 100). For example, suppose that in Amy's class the exam and paper scores each approximate a normal distribution. Looking at Table 2 in Appendix C, we see that about 33% of the cases in a normal curve fall to the left of a z score of $-.45$, and almost 81% fall to the left of a z score of .87. This tells us that Amy did better on her exam than only about a third of her classmates, but on the paper, she outperformed most of them. In other words, her percentile ranks (with rounding) were 33% and 81%, respectively.

Table 2 in Appendix C also simplifies the task of answering questions (asked in Module 6) such as, "If my WAIS IQ score is 115, where does that place me relative to other people?" WAIS scores have a mean of 100, a standard deviation of 15, and approximate a normal distribution. Thus, a score of 115 equates to $z = +1.00$. Table 2 in Appendix C informs us that in a normal distribution, 84.13% (i.e., a proportion of 0.8413) of the scores fall to the left of $z = +1.00$. Thus, your percentile rank would be 84.13.

MODULE 8 SAMPLING ERROR

Learning Objectives

After studying this section, you should be able to:

- Describe the concept of sampling error.
- Describe the standard error of the mean.

8.1 | SAMPLING VARIABILITY AND SAMPLING ERROR

Suppose that the mean Exam 1 score in a class of 60 students is 78 out of 100 possible points, and the standard deviation is 3.52. If the class is the entire population of interest to us, then

78 and 3.52 represent the population mean (symbol = μ, pronounced "mu") and population standard deviation (symbol = σ, pronounced "sigma"). We randomly draw a sample of 10 students from the class and obtain a sample mean of 82.4. We return the names of these students to the entire pool of 60 students and randomly draw a second sample of 10 names. The mean is 85.8. We repeat this procedure 28 more times and find means of 75.3, 78.4, 81.2, 77.6, and so forth.

Although the true population mean remains the same (i.e., $\mu = 78$), when we repeatedly draw random samples from a population, chance fluctuations will occur in the statistics we obtain (e.g., the sample means will fluctuate). These fluctuations reflect *sampling variability,* and are due to the "luck of the draw" in terms of the particular 10 cases we happen to select for each sample.

Of course, in this example, we know the Exam 1 population parameters (e.g., mean, standard deviation) precisely, because we have the entire population of scores. But typically, in psychological research, we only have samples available to us and must estimate population parameters when we perform inferential statistical analyses. Sampling variability introduces the potential for error when we make these estimates. This is called **sampling error:** *chance fluctuations that introduce a degree of error when using sample statistics to estimate population parameters.* For example, because of sampling error, the mean of any one sample can only be used to estimate the population mean. We can't view it with certainty as being precisely equal to the population mean.

8.2   STANDARD ERROR OF THE MEAN

In inferential statistics, to use a sample statistic to estimate a population parameter, we need to know how much fluctuation—how much variability—is expected to occur in that statistic when a sample of a particular size is drawn over and over again. To illustrate how this variability is determined, let's focus on the mean and our example in which we have Exam 1 scores for a population of 60 students. Suppose that we draw 30 samples, each containing 10 scores from the full set of 60. We calculate a mean score for each sample. This generates a set of 30 sample means, and just like any set of scores, we can create a frequency distribution of these 30 sample means (graphing them in a histogram, if we wish). We also can compute the average of the 30 means.

Now imagine that we draw all the possible samples that could be drawn from this population. Just as we did when we had 30 samples, we can create a frequency distribution of the mean scores of all these possible samples. In statistics, this distribution is called a *sampling distribution of the mean,* and the term **standard error of the mean (SEM)** *refers to the standard deviation of a sampling distribution of the mean.* The standard error (as it is often called) is one way to represent the overall degree to which sample means vary from the population mean. The more tightly clustered the means in a sampling distribution, the smaller the standard error.

One reason sampling distributions and standard errors are important is because they are used in calculating other inferential statistics. Additionally, an extremely important property of the sampling distribution of the mean is that even if a sample is drawn from a population whose distribution of raw scores deviates substantially from a normal curve, the sampling distribution of the mean will usually approximate the shape of a normal curve as long as the sample size is large enough. Although not all statisticians agree, in practice, this allows researchers to conduct certain inferential statistical tests on variables that are not normally distributed, depending on how severely those distributions deviate from normality.

The formula for calculating the standard error of the mean is

$$SEM = \frac{\sigma}{\sqrt{n}}$$

where

σ = the population standard deviation
n = the sample size

In our exam example, the standard deviation of all exam 60 scores was 3.52, and each sample comprised 10 scores. Therefore,

$$SEM = \frac{3.52}{\sqrt{10}} = 1.11$$

Once again, in research we typically don't know the population parameters and use sample statistics to estimate them. For example, to calculate an estimate of the *SEM*, we would use the standard deviation of our sample to estimate the population standard deviation, and then divide by the square root of the sample size.

MODULE 9 INFERENTIAL ANALYSIS: NULL HYPOTHESIS TESTING AND STATISTICAL SIGNIFICANCE

Learning Objectives

After studying this section, you should be able to:

- Explain what a null hypothesis is and its role in inferential statistical tests.
- Describe the concepts of probability value, alpha level, and statistical significance.
- Explain the concepts of Type I error, Type II error, and power.

Chapter 2 introduced you to the concept of statistical significance. It also discussed how, after performing an inferential statistical test, a risk of error is always present when researchers draw a conclusion as to whether their findings have uncovered a "real" effect, or instead could plausibly be attributed to chance. Here, we take a closer look at these concepts.

9.1 | THE NULL HYPOTHESIS

An approach called null hypothesis testing is the most common form of inferential analysis to determine statistical significance. In null hypothesis testing, we set up two competing hypotheses: a null hypothesis and an alternative hypothesis. (Statistically, these hypotheses are expressed in terms of population parameters.)

The **null hypothesis** (represented by the symbol H_0) *is the hypothesis that is directly examined by a statistical test.* The **alternative hypothesis** (H_1) *is a hypothesis that is contrary to the null hypothesis.* To illustrate this, suppose that we conduct an experiment to examine whether sleep deprivation influences working (i.e., short-term) memory. In a sleep laboratory, volunteer participants are randomly assigned to either of two sleep conditions: Condition 1, a deprivation condition in which they are kept awake all night, or Condition 2, a no-deprivation condition (i.e., control condition) in which they are allowed their normal sleep. Operationally, these two conditions constitute the independent variable. Afterward, participants are presented with lists of words and the researcher measures the number of words participants correctly recall after a brief time delay. Operationally, this is the dependent variable.

For our statistical analysis, we create a null hypothesis that sleep deprivation does not influence word recall. (In other words, we hypothesize that the mean for word recall in the population of scores [μ_1] from which our Condition 1 sample of scores will be drawn does not differ from the mean for word recall in the population of scores [μ_2] from which the Condition 2 sample of scores will be drawn.) Our alternative hypothesis is that sleep deprivation influences word recall (i.e., that the population means for word recall in the two conditions differ). Thus, we have

H_0: Sleep deprivation does not influence word recall (i.e., $\mu_1 = \mu_2$).

H_1: Sleep deprivation influences word recall (i.e., $\mu_1 \neq \mu_2$).

This type of alternative hypothesis is called a nondirectional hypothesis because it states only that sleep deprivation influences (i.e., impairs or enhances) word recall. Even though researchers often form conceptual hypotheses and make predictions about the direction of the expected findings (e.g., we predict that sleep deprivation will impair word recall), in setting up null hypothesis testing, the most conservative and common approach is to treat H_1 as a nondirectional hypothesis. The reason is that the results may turn out to fall in the direction opposite to what we expect, and a nondirectional hypothesis leaves open the possibility of drawing conclusions about discoveries (e.g., about how variables influence one another) regardless of their direction.

In null hypothesis testing, researchers sometimes form a directional H_1. An example would be H_1: Sleep deprivation impairs word recall (i.e., $\mu_1 < \mu_2$). The corresponding null hypothesis would be H_0: Sleep deprivation does not impair word recall (i.e., $\mu_1 \geq \mu_2$). However, we won't explore this approach because many statisticians propose that it should be used very cautiously, and it is much less common than using a nondirectional H_1 (Nolan & Heinzen, 2012).

But, let's step back a minute. Why do we need some strange-sounding concept called the null hypothesis? And why, as is often done, have we set up H_0 to be a hypothesis that essentially states our independent variable has no effect, that it produces no differences in the dependent variable? Why don't we simply test H_1 directly? Let me illustrate this by challenging you to a contest. I'm going to flip a coin 10 times. Each time it comes up Heads, you owe me $5.00. For each Tails, I owe you $5.00. Now I flip the coin and it comes up 10 Heads in 10 flips. You owe me $50, thank you very much, and understandably, you question whether the coin was fair. You think (i.e., you hypothesize) that something was going on, that the coin might have been rigged and thus was not fair. Therefore, let's set up a null hypothesis and alternative hypothesis, as follows:

H_0: The coin is fair (i.e., per flip, probability of Heads = probability of Tails).

H_1: The coin is not fair (i.e., per flip, probability of Heads $\neq$ probability of Tails).

Because we know that a fair coin has a 50% probability of coming up Heads on each flip, we can easily perform a statistical analysis to determine the probability of each possible outcome—0, 1, 2, 3, 4, 5, 6, 7, 8, 9, or 10 Heads—in a series of 10 flips. **Figure SM.6** shows those probabilities. The odds of obtaining 10 Heads in 10 flips are just less than 1 in 1,000. With 10 flips, there are 1,024 possible sequences of Heads (H) and Tails (T), and only one of them—H H H H H H H H H H—will yield 10 Heads. Likewise, only one of the possible 1,024 sequences could result in 0 Heads: T T T T T T T T T T. This is an equally extreme event, just in the other direction. We need to take the probability of this extreme outcome into account as well because if a coin is not fair, in principle, it could be unfair in favor of Heads or Tails.

Now here's the most important point: Our statistical analysis directly tested the notion that the coin is fair; it did not directly test the hypothesis that the coin is unfair. That is, the analysis began by assuming the coin was fair. This is what enabled us to assume as our starting point that the odds of getting a Heads on each flip were equal to the odds of getting a

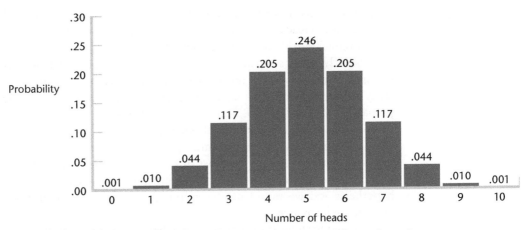

Figure SM.6 The probability of various outcomes in 10 flips of a coin (rounded to 3 decimal places).

Tails, namely, 50% to 50%. From there, we used the laws of probability to calculate the likelihood of obtaining either 10 or 0 Heads in 10 flips.

Suppose we wanted to directly test the hypothesis that the coin is unfair. What would our starting point be? If the coin isn't fair, should we assume that the probability of getting Heads on any single flip is 51%, 64%, 64.3%, 64.4%, 64.41%, 94.48%, or so on. The possibilities are endless, and the value we choose will determine the shape of the distribution in Figure SM.6. Unfortunately, we don't have prior knowledge of just how biased the coin might be. Moreover, if we had such prior knowledge, we wouldn't need to run a statistical analysis!

Analogously, when conducting research, our inferential statistical analysis begins with the assumption that H_0 is true. In our case, we assume that sleep deprivation does not influence word recall. Then, when our actual findings in the sleep deprivation and no-deprivation conditions deviate from having equal means, we can take advantage of known laws of probability to calculate the likelihood that the size of this deviation falls within a range that plausibly could be due solely to chance.

9.2 PROBABILITY VALUES AND STATISTICAL SIGNIFICANCE

Our statistical analysis has revealed that the combined probability of flipping either 10 or 0 Heads (the two most extreme events) in 10 trials is less than 2 in 1,000. This statistic is called a **probability value (p value),** *the probability that an outcome or one more extreme is due simply to chance.* In a research report, these values usually are reported to two or three decimal places, so with rounding this becomes $p = .002$.

Clearly, if the coin truly was fair, then flipping 10 or 0 Heads is a rare outcome. The question is, what do you do with this information? Do you conclude that the coin was not fair, that I cheated you, and demand your money back? Or, do you conclude that the coin was fair, and I was just extremely lucky? How low does a probability value have to be to let us confidently conclude that the null hypothesis (i.e., the coin was fair) simply is not plausible, and therefore that our hypothesis (i.e., the coin was not fair) is correct?

To make this decision, we need a criterion, and it is called the **significance level,** or **alpha (α) level:** *the probability level below which a result is considered to be sufficiently unlikely to be due to chance.* Historically, in psychology, the significance level has been set at $\alpha = .05$ (i.e., 5 in 100). When an inferential statistical analysis produces a p value that is lower than .05, the result is considered to be **statistically significant:** *unlikely to be due to chance,* and we would say we have obtained a "statistically significant" finding. Thus, in our coin flip example, the value of $p = .002$ is lower than the alpha level of .05, and we therefore would conclude that the outcome of 10 Heads in 10 trials is statistically significant. We would reject the null hypothesis and conclude that the coin was not fair.

Similarly, in our sleep deprivation experiment, suppose that out of 100 possible instances of correct word recall, the mean correct recall of the normal sleep and deprivation conditions are 61 words and 43 words, respectively. Further, suppose a statistical test yields a probability value of $p = .03$. Because this value is lower than the criterion for statistical significance ($\alpha = .05$), we would treat our finding as statistically significant. We would reject the null hypothesis and, by examining the mean scores, conclude that sleep deprivation impaired performance. In contrast, if our analysis yielded a value of $p = .12$, the results would not be considered statistically significant. In this case, we would not reject the null hypothesis and we would not have enough evidence to conclude that sleep deprivation affected performance.

To reemphasize a key point noted in Chapter 2, statistical significance only means that it is unlikely our findings are due to chance. It does not mean that the findings are conceptually, theoretically, or practically important. It also does not certify that sleep deprivation truly was the cause of impaired word recall. The overall difference in participants' recall between the conditions probably is not due to chance, but we must evaluate the study's methodological soundness to assess whether this difference was truly caused by the intended independent variable (sleep deprivation) or by some confounding factor.

9.3 | TYPE I AND TYPE II ERROR

In our coin flip contest, we determined that the outcome of 10 or 0 Heads in 10 flips was statistically significant. We therefore rejected the null hypothesis as being implausible: An extreme outcome like ours should rarely occur if the coin was fair. We concluded that the more plausible hypothesis was that the coin was not fair (i.e., it was biased). Is this a good decision? Did our analysis prove that the coin was biased?

If, in reality, the coin truly was biased, then we have indeed made a good decision by rejecting H_0. But, there is some risk, however small, that this decision could be in error. Again, even with a fair coin, roughly two times in a thousand we should expect to obtain an outcome as extreme as 10 Heads or 0 Heads in 10 flips. Thus, if you claim the coin was rigged, you probably are correct, but there is a remote chance that you are sounding a false alarm: that you're falsely concluding the coin was biased when, in fact, it was fair. This type of error is called a **Type I error:** *rejecting the null hypothesis when, in fact, the null hypothesis is true.* In the coin flip example, we have sounded a false alarm by concluding that the coin is biased when, in fact, it was a fair coin. Because the possibility exists of making a Type I error, we cannot say that we have proven the coin is biased.

Conversely, suppose in our coin flip example that even after obtaining an outcome of 10 Heads in 10 flips, you are highly concerned about the risk of a Type I error and don't want to sound a false alarm that the coin is rigged. Therefore, you don't reject the null hypothesis: The hypothesis that the coin is fair remains in play. In this case, if the coin truly is fair, if I just happened to be extremely lucky, then you have made a good decision in failing to reject the null hypothesis. But, if in the real world, the coin truly is biased, then you've made an erroneous decision. This type of error is called a **Type II error:** *failing to reject the null hypothesis when, in fact, it is false.* A Type II error is analogous to a missed opportunity. Something really was going on—the coin was rigged—but you failed to reach this conclusion.

Now let's consider what happens when we use inferential statistics to draw a conclusion based on our sleep experiment. **Table SM.6** summarizes four possible decision-making outcomes that can occur.

First, in terms of how the world actually operates—"Reality" or the "True State of the World" in the table—sleep deprivation either does or does not affect memory on this type of

Table SM.6 Four Possible Outcomes in Null Hypothesis Testing

Our Decision	Reality (True State of the World)	
	H_0 **Is True** (sleep deprivation does not influence memory)	H_0 **Is False** (sleep deprivation does influence memory)
Fail to Reject H_0	**Correct Decision**	**Type II Error** "Missed Opportunity"
Reject H_0	**Type I Error** "False Alarm"	**Correct Decision**

word recall task. Second, based on our data analysis, we will decide either to reject H_0, or we will fail to reject H_0. This produces two possible outcomes in which we have made a correct decision:

- We reject H_0 because our findings are statistically significant. We conclude that sleep deprivation influences memory and, in fact, the true state of the world is that sleep deprivation does indeed influence memory.

- We fail to reject H_0 because our findings are not statistically significant. We are unable to conclude that sleep deprivation influences memory and, in fact, the true state of the world is that sleep deprivation does not influence memory.

There also are two possible outcomes in which our decision will be incorrect:

- **Type I error.** *We reject H_0 when, in fact, H_0 is true.* We've sounded a false alarm by claiming that sleep deprivation influences memory when, in the true state of the world, there is no such relation. Recall that when results are statistically significant, a small probability still exists that the findings are actually due to chance; this is one of those times.

- **Type II error.** *We fail to reject H_0 when, in fact, H_0 is false.* We've missed an opportunity to discover a causal relation between sleep deprivation and memory that really does exist in the natural world.

What is the likelihood of making these errors? For Type I error, the answer is straightforward: It's the *alpha level,* the level below which we judge a finding to be statistically significant. If a researcher uses the traditional alpha level of .05, then if the results are statistically significant, the probability of making a Type I error—of sounding a false alarm—is 5%.

Why not, then, set a very strict alpha level—say, 1 in a million—so that there's virtually no chance of sounding a false alarm? The answer is that the more we try to protect ourselves from making a Type I error and sounding a false alarm, the greater the risk will be of making a Type II error and missing the opportunity to accurately proclaim to our friends and fellow scientists, "Hey, look what I found!" The probability of making a Type II error also depends on other factors, which brings us to a brief discussion of a concept called *power.*

Power

The probability of making a Type II error is called beta (β). Unfortunately, whereas we can determine the precise probability of making a Type I error by setting a particular alpha level, we can't directly know the probability of making a Type II error. In part, the probability of a Type II error will depend on the strength of the relation between two variables (e.g., sleep deprivation and working memory performance) in the true state of the world. If sleep deprivation has a huge effect on memory performance, then it is more likely that our statistical test will detect this relation than would be the case if sleep deprivation only has a small, subtle effect on performance. Prior research on this topic, if any exists, may help us estimate whether sleep deprivation is likely to have a strong, moderate, or weak influence on memory performance. But because we do not have a direct personal pipeline into the true state of affairs in the natural world, we can't know precisely how strong that relation is.

If a relation truly exists between two variables in the real world, then the goal of our inferential statistical test is to detect that relation and reject the null hypothesis. For a statistical test, **power** *is the probability of correctly rejecting the null hypothesis (H_0); that is, rejecting H_0 when it indeed is false.* A test with high power will detect relations that actually exist between variables. As power increases, the likelihood of making a Type II error—of missing an opportunity to find an actual relation—decreases. This is expressed as Power = $1 - \beta$ (i.e., 1 – probability of Type II error).

Researchers can take several steps to increase the power of their tests, and the most common and direct step is to increase the size of the sample that they study. Large sample sizes increase the odds a relationship that truly exists between two variables will have an opportunity to be detected in the data. There is a *power analysis* procedure that researchers use to help estimate how many participants they will need to study in order for their statistical test to have the power that they desire (see Module 14).

MODULE 10 THE CHI-SQUARE TEST FOR GOODNESS OF FIT

Learning Objectives

After studying this section, you should be able to:

- Describe the purpose and nature of the chi-square test for goodness of fit.

- Perform a chi-square test for goodness of fit involving one variable.

10.1 BASIC CONCEPTS

Suppose that a university is expecting a large budget shortfall next year. Administrators propose three possible solutions: a large tuition raise, large cutbacks in educational services (e.g., program eliminations), or combining a moderate tuition increase with moderate cutbacks. We survey a random sample of 900 students (the student body is 12,000) and ask them which budget solution they prefer.

This variable, *preferred budget solution,* is a qualitative variable: It is measured on a nominal scale. The response options represent different types of solutions and people's responses are placed into one category or another. To analyze the data, we count the frequency of responses in each category. **Table SM.7** presents the data.

Table SM.7 Data Analyzed Using a Chi-Square Test for Goodness of Fit

Number of Students Preferring Each Budget Crisis Solution			
Large Tuition Raise	Large Service Cutback	Moderate Tuition Raise and Moderate Service Cutback	Total Sample
305	228	367	**900**

The response frequencies differ across the three categories, suggesting that some options are favored more than others in this sample. However, we can't automatically draw this conclusion for the entire population just because the frequencies in the three categories aren't equal. Perhaps, by chance, by bad luck of the draw, we happened to select an unusual sample of 900 students whose views were not representative of the overall population.

The **chi-square (χ^2) goodness-of-fit test** *is an inferential statistical test used to determine the likelihood that an obtained pattern of results is consistent with the pattern expected from a hypothesized distribution.* It is often used with qualitative variables. In the university budget example, we start by stating a hypothesis, called the *null hypothesis* (see p. 435), that in the population there are no preferences for one category over another. In other words, we assume the response frequencies for each category of the variable are equal in the population. If this assumption is true, we can determine the frequencies that we should expect, on average, to find in a random sample. With 900 students and three categories for our variable, on average, we should expect to find 900/3 = 300 scores in each category. These are the *expected frequencies* under the assumption that the null hypothesis is true, and the symbol for them is f_e (f stands for "frequency," and the subscript e for "expected"). The χ^2 test compares these expected frequencies to the *observed frequencies* (f_o) that we actually obtained in our results. In other words, it examines the goodness of fit between what we observed and what we expect if the null hypothesis is true. The poorer the fit between what was expected and what we observed, the larger the χ^2 statistic will be. After computing the χ^2 statistic for our data, we examine whether the value of χ^2 is large enough to meet the criterion for statistical significance.

When applied to a single variable, the recommended minimum number of expected cases should be 10 per cell if there are only two cells and 5 per cell if there are three or more cells. The categories of the variable must be mutually exclusive, and every score in the sample must be from a different individual.

10.2 PERFORMING A CHI-SQUARE GOODNESS-OF-FIT TEST

The formula for the χ^2 test is

$$\chi^2 = \Sigma \frac{(f_o - f_e)^2}{f_e}$$

where

f_o = the observed frequency in a cell (305, 228, and 367 in our example)
f_e = the expected frequency in a cell (300 in our example, i.e., 900/3)

We now apply these numbers to the formula, as follows:

$$\chi^2 = \frac{(305 - 300)^2}{300} + \frac{(228 - 300)^2}{300} + \frac{(367 - 300)^2}{300}$$

$$= \frac{(5)^2 + (-72)^2 + (67)^2}{300} = \frac{25 + 5184 + 4489}{300} = \frac{9698}{300} = 32.33$$

So, what does a χ^2 value of 32.33 mean? To answer this, we consult Table 3 in Appendix C, which statisticians developed specifically for χ^2 tests. The leftmost column is labeled *degrees of freedom* (*df*). (See the next section of this module to learn about the concept of degrees of freedom.) When there is one variable, *df* = the number of categories − 1. Because we have three categories, *df* = 2. The remaining columns provide what are called the *critical values* of χ^2 necessary for various levels of statistical significance (i.e., alpha levels). In the behavioral sciences, the criterion to consider a finding statistically significant typically is set at α = .05. In the second row of the table (corresponding to *df* = 2), we see that the critical value for α = .05 is 5.99. Our χ^2 value of 32.33 is larger than this critical value of 5.99. In fact, it exceeds the critical value of 13.82 needed for statistical significance at the .001 level. Thus, the table informs us that the probability our pattern of observed results is due to chance is less than 1 in 1,000 (i.e., $p < .001$). (Statistical software informs us more precisely that $p = .00000001$.) Because this probability is less than the alpha level of .05, we reject the null hypothesis that an equal number of students prefer each budget crisis option.

10.3 DEGREES OF FREEDOM

Inferential statistical tests take into account factors such as the number of observations or groups (e.g., levels or categories of an independent variable) upon which the data are based. In an inferential statistical computation, the degrees of freedom reflect the number of numerical values that are free to vary. For example, in some inferential tests, the sample variance is used to estimate the population variance. But to compute the sample variance, the sample mean must first be calculated. Suppose we have a sample of 10 scores and calculate that their mean is 7.00. Next, we use those 10 scores and the mean to calculate an estimate of the population variance. Because we now know the mean, only nine of those 10 scores are free to assume different values. So, if nine scores are 0, 1, 1, 3, 8, 9, 9, 12, and 13, then the last score must be 14 (i.e., all scores must total to 70 and nine scores total to 56; the remaining score must be 14). Thus, in calculating the sample variance as an estimate of the population variance, our data provide us with only nine independent values; that is, there are nine degrees of freedom in the variance estimate.

Similarly, in Table SM.7, we have three data entries (305, 228, 367), one per budget crisis solution category. To calculate chi-square, we must use the total sample size (900) to determine the estimated frequencies. Given that we know the total sample size, the numbers in any two budget solution categories could, in principle, take on various values. But once those values are specified, the value for the remaining budget category is fixed because the numbers must sum to 900. If 305 students prefer a large tuition raise and 228 prefer a large service cutback, then 367 students must prefer the third option. Thus, for this inferential test, because our variable has three categories, there are two degrees of freedom: $df =$ number of categories $- 1$.

Table C.3 illustrates why it is important to know the degrees of freedom. For any particular p level—say, .05—as you look down the column, the critical values of chi-square that must be exceeded in order to conclude that a finding is statistically significant change as the degrees of freedom change. Similarly, in Tables C.1 (Pearson's r, Module 5), C.4 (t test, Module 12), and C.5 (F test, Module 16), to identify the appropriate critical value, the degrees of freedom used in calculating that statistic from the sample of data must be determined. (The reason why this occurs is a technical discussion beyond our current scope.)

MODULE 11 THE CHI-SQUARE TEST FOR INDEPENDENCE

Learning Objectives

After studying this section, you should be able to:

- Describe the purpose of the chi-square test for independence and when it is appropriate to use.
- Perform a chi-square test to determine whether two variables are independent.

11.1 BASIC CONCEPTS

In Module 10, we examined the overall responses of 900 college students when asked which of three options they preferred for addressing a campus budget crisis. Suppose, however, that we want to know whether there is an association between students' budget crisis preferences and their sex, ethnicity, college major, and residence status (out-of-state students pay higher tuition than in-state students at this university). All these variables, including the preference variable, are qualitative.

The **chi-square (χ^2) test for independence** *is an inferential statistical test most commonly used to determine whether two qualitative variables are independent or associated.* The general logic of this test is similar to that of the χ^2 goodness-of-fit test described in Module 10. We begin by creating a null hypothesis that there is no association between the two variables (i.e., the two variables are independent of one another). We then compare the frequencies that we actually obtain in each cell with the frequencies that we would expect to obtain if the null hypothesis is true.

If each variable has only two categories, the suggested minimum number of expected cases should be 10 per cell. As long as one variable has more than two categories, it is suggested that the expected frequencies should be 5 per cell. The categories of each variable must be mutually exclusive, and there can be only one score from each participant.

11.2 PERFORMING A CHI-SQUARE TEST FOR INDEPENDENCE

Table SM.8 is called a *contingency table.* It shows the in-state and out-of-state students' responses separately. At this campus, 60% of students come from within the state, and this is reflected in the sample.

Table SM.8 Data Analyzed Using a Chi-Square Test for Independence

	Number of Students Preferring Each Solution ($N = 900$)			
	Large Tuition Raise	Large Service Cutback	Moderate Raise + Moderate Cutback	Row Totals
In-State Students	224	122	194	**540**
Out-of-State Students	81	106	173	**360**
Column Totals	**305**	**228**	**367**	

The formula for the χ^2 test is the same as that shown in Module 10:

$$\chi^2 = \sum \frac{(f_o - f_e)^2}{f_e}$$

where

f_o = the observed frequency in a cell
f_e = the expected frequency in a cell

We can perform the test in four steps:

Step 1 Give each cell a number label. This will help to organize our calculations. From left to right in the top row, we'll call them Cell 1, Cell 2, and Cell 3. From left to right in the bottom row, we'll label them Cell 4, Cell 5, and Cell 6.

Step 2 Calculate the expected frequencies for each cell. To do this, for the column and row in which the cell is located: (1) Multiply the total number of cases in the column by the total number of cases in the row, and then (2) divide by the total number of cases in the sample. Therefore,

Cell 1 expected frequency $= \dfrac{(305 \times 540)}{900} = 183.0$

Cell 2 expected frequency $= \dfrac{(228 \times 540)}{900} = 136.8$

$$\text{Cell 3 expected frequency} = \frac{(367 \times 540)}{900} = 220.2$$

$$\text{Cell 4 expected frequency} = \frac{(305 \times 360)}{900} = 122.0$$

$$\text{Cell 5 expected frequency} = \frac{(228 \times 360)}{900} = 91.2$$

$$\text{Cell 6 expected frequency} = \frac{(367 \times 360)}{900} = 146.8$$

Step 3 Insert the observed and expected frequencies for each cell into the formula, and calculate the value of χ^2:

$$\chi^2 = \frac{(224-183)^2}{183} + \frac{(122-136.8)^2}{136.8} + \frac{(194-220.2)^2}{220.2} + \frac{(81-122)^2}{122}$$
$$+ \frac{(106-91.2)^2}{91.2} + \frac{(173-146.8)^2}{146.8}$$
$$= 9.19 + 1.60 + 3.12 + 13.78 + 2.40 + 4.68$$
$$= 34.77$$

Step 4 We use Table 3 in Appendix C to determine whether the value of χ^2 is statistically significant. For contingency tables (such as ours in Table SM.8), the degrees of freedom $(df) = (\text{number of rows} - 1) \times (\text{number of columns} - 1)$. Thus, $df = 1 \times 2 = 2$. (See Statistics Module 10.3 for a discussion of the concept of degrees of freedom.) Because our χ^2 value of 34.77 is larger than the critical value of 5.99 needed for statistical significance at the .05 level, our findings are statistically significant. In fact, our χ^2 value exceeds the critical value of 13.82 needed for statistical significance at the .001 level. Thus, the table informs us that the probability our findings are due solely to chance is $p < .001$. (Statistical software informs us more precisely that $p = .000000003$.) Therefore, based on an alpha level of .05, we reject the null hypothesis that students' budget crisis preferences are independent of their in-state/out-of-state status, and conclude that these two variables are associated.

MODULE 12 THE t TEST

Learning Objectives

After studying this section, you should be able to:

- Explain when a t test is used and the concept behind it.
- Perform a t test.

12.1 BASIC CONCEPTS

The **t test** *is an inferential statistical test often used to determine whether there is a statistically significant difference between the means of two groups of scores for the same variable.* For example, in a memory experiment, half the participants may be exposed to lists of short words, and the other half to lists of long words. A t test can determine whether a statistically significant difference exists in the mean number of words recalled between these two conditions. There also are t tests for other purposes, such as to test hypotheses about a single mean. We will not cover that test here.

The *t* test is appropriate for variables measured on an interval or ratio scale, and it also assumes that the groups were drawn from populations in which the scores follow a normal distribution. The formula for the *t* test differs depending on whether the two groups (1) are independent or dependent (more on this distinction shortly), and (2) have similar or dissimilar variances. However, no matter the version, the *t* test employs the same general concept: It reflects the size of the difference between two means relative to the variability of scores within the two groups and their sample sizes. Thus, for two groups of a particular size, as the difference between their two means becomes larger, or as the variability of the scores within the groups becomes smaller, the *t* statistic becomes larger.

t Test for Independent Versus Dependent Groups

When two groups of participants (i.e., two samples of scores) are independent of one another, the *t* test for independent groups is used. In practice, this occurs for between-subjects designs in which researchers (1) manipulate an independent variable and randomly assign participants to one condition or the other, or (2) use a naturally occurring subject variable to create two conditions (e.g., male–female) of unrelated participants.

When the groups are not independent, the *t* test for dependent groups is used. In practice, this occurs in (1) within-subjects (i.e., repeated-measures) designs, in which both conditions involve the same participants, and (2) between-subjects designs that compare two naturally paired groups (e.g., mothers, children) or that use matching to pair participants (e.g., on task ability) before assigning them to conditions.

12.2 PERFORMING A *t* TEST

To illustrate performing a *t* test, we will use the *t* test for independent groups. That is, we will assume that the two groups are independent, have equal sample sizes, and have similar variances. Suppose we randomly assign college students to perform a driving simulation task either while talking on a hand-held cell phone (Group 1) or not talking on a cell phone (Group 2). We measure the number of driving errors they make. We test the null hypothesis that cell phone use does not influence driving performance. The alternative hypothesis is that cell phone use influences driving performance. In the formula for calculating *t*, the denominator can be expressed in several ways. The formula below uses the sum of squares (*SS*) for each group, as follows:

If the two sample sizes are equal,   If the two sample sizes are not equal,

$$t = \frac{M_1 - M_2}{\sqrt{\dfrac{SS_1 + SS_2}{n(n-1)}}} \qquad t = \frac{M_1 - M_2}{\sqrt{\dfrac{SS_1 + SS_2}{(n_1 - 1) + (n_2 - 1)}\left(\dfrac{1}{n_1} + \dfrac{1}{n_2}\right)}}$$

where

M_1 = mean of Group 1
SS_1 = sum of squares of Group 1; this equals $\Sigma(X_1 - M_1)^2$
M_2 = mean of Group 2
SS_2 = sum of squares of Group 2; this equals $\Sigma(X_2 - M_2)^2$
n = the number of cases per condition

For simplicity, in **Table SM.9** on page 446, there are 10 participants per condition. Columns 2 and 3 present the raw scores and group means. Columns 4 and 5 show the deviation scores and sum of squares (i.e., SS_1 and SS_2) for each group. We see that

Table SM.9 Data Analyzed Using a t Test for Independent Samples

	Column			
1	2	3	4	5
Participant (per condition)	Cell Phone (Group 1) X_1	No Phone (Group 2) X_2	$(X_1 - M_1)^2$	$(X_2 - M_2)^2$
1	9	9	1	9
2	5	4	9	4
3	10	8	4	4
4	8	7	0	1
5	11	3	9	9
6	6	5	4	1
7	8	7	0	1
8	6	6	4	0
9	7	4	1	4
10	10	7	4	1
Sum	**80** $M_1 = 8.00$	**60** $M_2 = 6.00$	$SS_1 = 36$	$SS_2 = 34$

$$M_1 = \frac{80}{10} = 8.00 \qquad M_2 = \frac{60}{10} = 6.00 \qquad SS_1 = 36 \qquad SS_2 = 34$$

$$t = \frac{M_1 - M_2}{\sqrt{\dfrac{SS_1 + SS_2}{n(n-1)}}} = \frac{8.00 - 6.00}{\sqrt{\dfrac{36 + 34}{10(9)}}} = \frac{2.00}{0.88} = 2.27$$

To determine whether the difference between the two means is statistically significant, we compare our t value of 2.27 to the critical values in Table 4 of Appendix C for a two-tailed test. The degrees of freedom (df) when comparing two means are $n_1 + n_2 - 2$, which equals 18 (i.e., $10 + 10 - 2$) in our example. (See Statistics Module 10.3 for a discussion of the concept of degrees of freedom.) For a significance level of .05, the critical value of t when $df = 18$ is 2.101. Thus, to be considered statistically significant, a positive t value must be greater than +2.101, and a negative t value (indicating that the no-phone group made more errors than the cell phone group) would have to be −2.101 or a more extreme negative number than −2.101. Our t value of 2.27 exceeds the +2.101 critical value and therefore is statistically significant. (Statistical software indicates that $p = .036$.) We reject the null hypothesis in favor of the alternative hypothesis and, by inspecting the means, we conclude that cell phone use impairs driving performance.

MODULE 13 EFFECT SIZE

Learning Objectives

After studying this section, you should be able to:

- Explain effect size and how it differs from statistical significance.

- Be able to calculate the effect size for the difference between two independent means.

13.1   BASIC CONCEPTS

Effect size *is a statistical measure of the strength of a relation between two variables. In experiments, effect size measures the strength of a treatment effect (i.e., how strongly an independent* variable has influenced a dependent variable). Effect sizes typically accompany tests of statistical significance to provide a more complete picture of the results. Statistical significance tests are highly dependent on sample size. For example, in an experiment, a tiny difference between the means of two groups can be statistically significant if the samples are large enough, whereas a moderate or even a large difference may not reach statistical significance if the samples are too small.

The reason for this is that statistical significance tests only inform us of the likelihood that a particular set of results is due solely to chance. Large samples provide more reliable estimates of population characteristics than small samples. The larger the sample, the less likely it is that a sample statistic (e.g., a mean, an r value) will deviate significantly from the corresponding population parameter (i.e., the mean or correlation in the population). Thus, although it's important to know about statistical significance, it's also important to know about how strongly variables are related. Common effect size statistics express the strength of a relation in a way that is independent of the sample size. Under certain conditions, this enables us to compare effect sizes from different studies that have measured the same variable.

As with tests of statistical significance, measures of effect size do not speak to the internal validity of a study. We may obtain a statistically significant and strong effect, but this does not reveal whether the findings were truly caused by the independent variable or a confounding factor. Conversely, flaws in a study may be the reason we fail to find a statistically significant or sizable effect. This is why it is essential to design the highest-quality study possible given the available resources. In addition, the ultimate decision as to whether a particular effect size is important rests largely on the study's context. For example, in an experiment examining the effects of a drug on reaction time, decision making, or the shrinkage of cancer tumors, even a small effect size may translate into important real-world consequences.

13.2 CALCULATING EFFECT SIZE

Cohen's d (1988) *is a commonly used statistic to report effect sizes in experiments.* The Cohen's d formula differs depending on several factors, including the number of independent variables and groups (i.e., conditions), and whether the groups are completely independent (e.g., randomly assigned to different conditions). For simplicity, we will use the same raw data and calculations for the cell phone experiment discussed in Module 12. If you haven't read that module, just refer to Table SM.9 when indicated below. In this between-subjects experiment, randomly assigned participants performed a driving simulator task while either talking on a hand-held cell phone or not using a phone. The dependent variable was their number of driving errors. Columns 2 and 3 in Table SM.9 show the raw data. Using a statistic called a t test, we found that the difference between the means of the cell phone (8 errors) and no phone (6 errors) groups was statistically significant. But, how large is this effect?

Cohen's d is a measurement of effect size for a population of scores. Because we are working with samples, our computations will yield an estimated d statistic. The formula is

$$d = \frac{M_1 - M_2}{\sqrt{\dfrac{SS_1 + SS_2}{n_1 + n_2 - 2}}}$$

where

M_1 = mean of Group 1

SS_1 = sum of squares of Group 1; this equals $\Sigma(X_1 - M_1)^2$

M_2 = mean of Group 2

SS_2 = sum of squares of Group 2; this equals $\Sigma(X_2 - M_2)^2$

n_1, n_2 = the number of cases in Group 1 and Group 2, respectively

Table SM.9 shows that $M_1 = 8.00$, $M_2 = 6.00$, $SS_1 = 36$, and $SS_2 = 34$. Therefore,

$$d = \frac{8.00 - 6.00}{\sqrt{\dfrac{36 + 34}{10 + 10 - 2}}} = \frac{2.00}{\sqrt{3.89}} = 1.01$$

As a general guideline, Cohen (1988) suggests that a d value of .20 reflects a small effect size, a value of .50 reflects a medium effect size, and .80 or larger reflects a large effect size. In our example, given an estimated d value of 1.01, it appears we have a large effect size.

Correlation Statistics as an Alternative to Cohen's *d*

A correlation coefficient is another way to express an effect size, even for experiments. Correlation coefficients are discussed in Chapter 5 and Statistics Module 5. If you have not read either of those yet, here are two key points. First, a Pearson's correlation coefficient (r) can assume a value from −1.00 to +1.00. Second, the absolute value of r indicates the correlation's strength, and r^2 represents the proportion of variance in one variable (e.g., the dependent variable) that is accounted for by the other variable (e.g., the independent variable).

Let's return to the cell phone data in Table SM.9, for which we performed a t test. We found a statistically significant t value of 2.27. Once we know the value of t and the degrees of freedom ($df = n_1 + n_2 - 2$), the formula for r is

$$r = \sqrt{\frac{t^2}{t^2 + df}} = \sqrt{\frac{2.27^2}{2.27^2 + 18}} = \sqrt{\frac{5.15}{23.15}} = .47$$

(See Statistics Module 10.3 for a discussion of the concept of degrees of freedom.) For this type of study, which involves two independent groups, Cohen (1988) suggests that $r = .10$ reflects a small effect size, $r = .30$ a medium effect size, and $r = .50$ a large effect size. Thus, our value of $r = .47$ reflects a medium to strong effect size when judged against Cohen's suggested criteria. Moreover, squaring r gives us $r^2 = .22$. This indicates that talking versus not talking on a cell phone while driving accounted for a sizable proportion—22%—of the variance in the amount of driving errors participants made.

MODULE 14 POWER AND POWER ANALYSIS

Learning Objectives

After studying this section, you should be able to:

- Explain power and the benefits of a power analysis.
- Use a power table to estimate the expected power of a statistical test.
- Use a power table to calculate the sample size needed for a statistical test.

14.1   BASIC CONCEPTS

Power *is the probability of correctly rejecting the null hypothesis (H_0); that is, rejecting H_0 when it indeed is false.* If the null hypothesis is false but we fail to reject it, then we have committed a Type II error. This means we have missed an opportunity to infer, for example, that one variable influences another when, in fact, such a relation exists. We want to avoid Type II errors, so the more power the better.

Several factors affect the power of a statistical test, including:

- *Sample size.* The larger the sample, the greater the power. Larger samples provide a more reliable estimate of population parameters than do smaller samples.

- *Effect size.* The stronger the relation between two variables in the population (e.g., the larger the effect that an independent variable has on a dependent variable), the greater the power. Stated differently, it's easier to hit a target—detecting a true relation between variables—when the target is large rather than small.

- *Extraneous variability and research design sensitivity.* Eliminating or reducing factors that produce extraneous variance, such as unreliable measurement procedures, increases the sensitivity of a research design and increases the power of a chosen statistical test. In experiments, other factors (e.g., sample size) being equal, within-subjects designs generally are more sensitive—are more likely to reveal the potential effect of an independent variable—than are between-subjects designs. That is, extraneous variability (i.e., error variance) caused by differences in subjects' personal characteristics is reduced when each condition involves the same sample of subjects, rather than different samples of subjects.

- *The criterion chosen for statistical significance (i.e., alpha level).* An alpha level of .05 is typically used as the criterion for judging statistical significance. If we choose a more liberal criterion, say, $\alpha = .10$, then in essence we are casting a wider net in our attempt to capture something that is present. However, the more liberal the alpha level, the greater the risk of Type I error if, in fact, the null hypothesis is true.

- *Properties of the chosen statistical test.* Some statistical tests are inherently more powerful than others. In general, to be used appropriately, these more powerful tests involve stricter requirements about the nature of the data to be examined. In addition, in null hypothesis testing, if H_1 is set up as a directional hypothesis (e.g., H_1 = sleep deprivation impairs memory) rather than as a nondirectional hypothesis (e.g., H_1 = sleep deprivation influences memory), this leads to what is called a *one-tailed test* of statistical significance, rather than a nondirectional *two-tailed test*. If a directional H_1 accurately reflects the state of affairs in the real world, then a one-tailed test increases statistical power. But, it would have a very serious disadvantage in excluding our inferential analysis from testing for the possibility that the world really operates in an opposite way to what the directional H_1 predicts. In practice, null hypothesis testing typically involves two-tailed tests and many statisticians urge caution in using one-tailed tests (Nolan & Heinzen, 2012).

Power Analysis

Power analysis *examines the relation between power, effect size, and sample size for a given statistical test and alpha level.* It has two common, practical uses in research:

- to determine the power of a statistical test;

- to help plan a study by determining the sample size needed to achieve a particular level of power.

To illustrate the first use, in our experiment, we plan to randomly assign 10 participants to drive while talking on a hand-held cell phone, and 10 to drive while not using a cell phone. We will use the conventional alpha level of .05 when conducting a *t* test to assess statistical significance. Suppose that, based on reviewing previous cell phone driving studies in the scientific literature, we expect cell phone use to have a medium-size effect (e.g., $d = .50$) on driving errors. Under these conditions, we want to know what the power of our *t* test will be. As you'll learn in the next section, the statistical power will only be .18. This means that if the null hypothesis (H_0 = cell phone use does not influence driving errors) is false, our test will only have an 18% chance of correctly rejecting the null hypothesis. This leaves us with a high probability of committing a Type II error.

To illustrate power analysis' second use, suppose we are planning the cell phone experiment described in Module 12. We want our test to have good power. Although it would be ideal to have an extremely high power level that approaches 1.00, in most research this would require us to have sample sizes that are difficult to attain. Cohen (1988) suggests that, in general, seeking power of .80 is a reasonable goal. To achieve this in our experiment requires 64 cases (i.e., observations, participants) per condition. If we believe that this is too difficult, then to achieve power of .70 or .60, we would need 50 or 40 cases per condition, respectively. In any event, our current plan of having only 10 participants per condition will leave us with woefully inadequate power. If our results fail to reach statistical significance, we should not be surprised.

14.2 CALCULATING POWER AND SAMPLE SIZE

Although calculations for a power analysis can be done using formulas, statisticians have developed *power tables*, graphs (called *power curves*), and software tools for many statistical tests. This makes conducting power analyses much easier.

Table SM.10a presents a portion of the power tables for a *t* test, where we have a traditional statistical significance criterion of $\alpha = .05$ and are performing a two-tailed (i.e., nondirectional) test. The leftmost column represents the number of cases in each of the two conditions of the study. We've planned for 10 participants per condition. Different *d* values run across the top row: We have used our best judgment to estimate that our effect size will be moderate (e.g., .50). Looking within the table at the intersection of $n = 10$ and $d = .50$, we see that power = .18, which is very low.

Table SM.10b presents a portion of power tables for a *t* test that are used to determine sample size. The leftmost column lists desired power, and the top row of numbers lists

Table SM.10 Tables for Calculating Power and the Sample Size Needed to Achieve Various Power Levels

(a) Calculating power for a given sample size and an estimated effect size

n (per condition)	Nondirectional Hypothesis (two-tailed test, $\alpha = .05$) d (estimated effect size)		
	.20	.50	.80
10	.07	.18	.39
20	.09	.33	.69
30	.12	.47	.86
40	.14	.60	.94
50	.17	.70	.98
80	.24	.88	>.995
100	.29	.94	>.995
200	.51	>.995	>.995
400	.81	>.995	>.995

Data from Cohen (1988, pp. 36–37, Table 2.3.5).

(b) Calculating the sample size needed per condition to achieve various levels of power, based on an estimated effect size

Desired Power	Nondirectional Hypothesis (two-tailed test, $\alpha = .05$) d (estimated effect size)		
	.20	.50	.80
.25	84	14	6
.50	193	32	13
.60	246	40	16
.70	310	50	20
.80	393	64	26
.90	526	85	34
.99	920	148	58

Data from Cohen (1988, p. 55, Table 2.4.1).

estimated effect sizes. If we desire power of .80 and expect a medium effect size (e.g., .50), then the intersection of those two values within the table indicates that we will need to have 64 cases per condition. In practice, this means that we may actually have to recruit somewhat more participants than that, because typically, there will be some people who fail to show up or to complete the experiment.

Notice that if we anticipated that cell phone use would only have a small effect size (e.g., $d = .20$), we would need 393 cases in each condition to achieve power of .80! Unfortunately, many variables that behavioral scientists study only produce small effect sizes, and recruiting a large number of participants often is not feasible. This frequently leaves researchers with inadequate power to avoid a Type II error.

MODULE 15 CONFIDENCE INTERVALS

Learning Objectives

After studying this section, you should be able to:

- Explain the concept of confidence intervals.
- Calculate a confidence interval.

15.1 BASIC CONCEPTS

A **confidence interval (CI)** *is a range of values within which a population parameter (e.g., a population mean) is estimated to fall, with a particular level of confidence.* One type of confidence interval relates to the margin of sampling error and confidence level reported in surveys. Suppose that a survey using a nationally representative sample of 1,200 adults reports that "27% of Americans feel that Congress is doing a poor job," with a margin of error of ±3% and confidence level of 95%. This means we are 95% confident that the percentage of Americans (a population parameter) who disapprove of Congress' job falls within the range of 24% to 30%. Stated differently, if we drew a sample of 1,200 adults 100 times, and kept repeating this procedure, then we would expect, on average, to find that in 95 of the 100 samples the approval rating of Congress falls within the 24% to 30% range. The number 24% represents the *lower limit of the confidence interval;* 30% represents the *upper limit of the confidence interval.* (See Chapter 7 for more discussion of the margin of sampling error in surveys.)

Note that, in reality, the true population percentage either does or does not fall within this interval: It's all or nothing. What the 95% refers to is our level of confidence that the interval we have calculated will contain the true value of the population parameter.

The concept of confidence intervals also applies to mean scores, such as when we conduct an experiment and obtain mean scores from the sample of cases in each condition. As in survey research, confidence intervals for means typically are calculated for a 95% level of confidence. The shorthand term for this is "the 95% confidence interval."

15.2 CALCULATING CONFIDENCE INTERVALS

We will use summary data from our hypothetical cell phone experiment (see Table SM.9, p. 446) to calculate the 95% confidence interval for each of the two means. The formula for calculating the upper and lower limits of a 95% confidence interval for each group is

$$CI = M \pm t_{.05} SEM$$

where

- M is the sample mean: $M_1 = 8.00$ and $M_2 = 6.00$.

- SEM is the standard error of the sampling distribution of the mean. We compute an estimate of the SEM by using the standard deviation (SD) of the sample, as follows:

$$\text{Estimated } SEM = \frac{SD}{\sqrt{n}} \qquad \text{where } SD \sqrt{\frac{SS}{n-1}}$$

Therefore, for the cell phone group (Group 1, $n_1 = 10$),

$$SD_1 = \sqrt{\frac{SS_1}{n_1 - 1}} = \sqrt{\frac{36}{9}} = 2.00 \qquad \text{and} \qquad \text{Estimated } SEM_1 = \frac{SD_1}{\sqrt{n_1}} = \frac{2.00}{\sqrt{10}} = .632$$

For the no phone group (Group 2, $n_2 = 10$),

$$SD_2 = \sqrt{\frac{SS_2}{n_2 - 1}} = \sqrt{\frac{34}{9}} = 1.94 \qquad \text{and} \qquad \text{Estimated } SEM_2 = \frac{SD_2}{\sqrt{n_2}} = \frac{1.94}{\sqrt{10}} = .613$$

- $t_{.05}$ = the critical value of t needed for statistical significance at $\alpha = .05$ (two-tailed, $n - 1$ degrees of freedom; thus, $df = 9$). (See Statistics Module 10.3 for a discussion of the concept of degrees of freedom.) We look up this value in Appendix C, Table 4, Thus,

$$t_{.05} = 2.262$$

Here are the confidence interval calculations:

Cell Phone Condition

$M_1 = 8.00$, $SEM_1 = .632$, $t_{.05} = 2.262$

$CI = M \pm t_{.05}SEM$

$\quad = 8.00 \pm (2.262)(.632) = 8.00 \pm 1.430$

LL (lower limit of CI) = 6.57

UL (upper limit of CI) = 9.43

No Phone Condition

$M_2 = 6.00$, $SEM_2 = .613$, $t_{.05} = 2.262$

$CI = M \pm t_{.05}SEM$

$\quad = 6.00 \pm (2.262)(.613) = 6.00 \pm 1.387$

LL (lower limit of CI) = 4.61

UL (upper limit of CI) = 7.39

Therefore, we are 95% confident that the interval 6.57 to 9.43 captures the population mean for the number of errors for the cell phone condition, and the interval 4.61 to 7.39 captures the population mean for the number of errors for the no-phone condition. Remember that in statistics the word "population" refers to the population of scores from which sample scores are drawn.

Error Bars and Statistical Significance: A Common Misunderstanding

In scientific publications, you may come across many bar graphs that present thin bars (looking like the uppercase letter "I" overlapping with the main bars of the graph; e.g., see Figure 8.1, p. 243). These thin bars are typically called "error bars" or "interval bars." Unfortunately, different graphs may contain different types of error bars; they may represent confidence intervals, the standard error of the mean, or standard deviations. However, all these types of error bars have a common property: They are functions of the degree of variability in the scores within each particular condition. The less the variability, the shorter the bars.

Let's focus on confidence intervals in an experiment such as ours with two independent means. If the intervals of the two groups do not overlap, this suggests that there is a statistically significant difference between the means. But, if the two confidence intervals do overlap, we should not automatically conclude that the difference between the means fails to reach statistical significance. In fact, when the difference between two means is statistically significant, their confidence intervals (and thus, error bars portrayed in a graph) may overlap (Schenker & Gentleman, 2001). This is the case in our hypothetical cell phone data. A study by Belia, Fidler, Williams, and Cumming (2005) suggests than many researchers erroneously believe that if two confidence interval bars overlap, the difference between the means is not statistically significant. The interpretation for other types of error bars (e.g., standard errors bars) differs and is beyond what we can discuss here. Again, a key point is that all error bars provide information about the degree of variability in the set of scores they represent.

MODULE 16 ANALYSIS OF VARIANCE (ANOVA)

Learning Objectives

After studying this section, you should be able to:

- Describe why and when analysis of variance (ANOVA) is used.
- Understand the main principle behind a one-way ANOVA.
- Perform a one-way ANOVA.

16.1 THE PURPOSE OF ANALYSIS OF VARIANCE

Analysis of variance (ANOVA) *determines whether the overall pattern of differences between the means of two or more groups is statistically significant.* Like a *t* test, ANOVA is used when (1) the dependent variable is measured on an interval or ratio scale; (2) groups are created by experimental manipulation or by using a natural subject characteristic; (3) group sizes are equal or unequal (within limits); and (4) the design is between subjects or within subjects (i.e., repeated measures).

When ANOVA is used to compare two groups, the results essentially are equivalent to performing a *t* test. But unlike the *t* test, ANOVA is far more flexible because it can be used when:

- an independent variable has more than two groups;
- there is more than one independent variable (i.e., a factorial design is used).

These properties make ANOVA an extremely versatile and common inferential test in the behavioral sciences.

As with a *t* test, certain assumptions underlie the optimal use of ANOVA. These assumptions are that the samples of scores are randomly drawn from their populations, the dependent variable has a normal distribution in each of the populations, and the samples come from populations with equal variances. However, ANOVA is often performed when one or more of these assumptions are not met. Depending on which assumption is violated and how severe the violation is, the amount of distortion caused to the ANOVA test may be problematic. (This issue is typically covered in statistics courses.)

We will focus on basic ANOVA used to examine findings from a between-subjects experiment that has only one independent variable. Performing an ANOVA on data from a within-subjects experiment or from an experiment that examines multiple independent variables is more complicated; for more detail on such applications, you will want to consult a statistics textbook.

16.2 ## UNDERLYING PRINCIPLES

When a study involves only two groups, you can subtract one group's mean from the other to gauge their difference and test the overall effect of the independent variable. The t test described in Module 12 uses this approach. But, when we have means from three or more groups, this approach doesn't work well. For example, with one independent variable and three means—A, B, and C—we could subtract B from A, C from A, and C from B, and test whether each difference is statistically significant. With four means, we would need six tests (i.e., $A - B$, $A - C$, $A - D$, $B - C$, $B - D$, $C - D$). The problem is, as we perform more and more tests in this manner, it progressively inflates the overall risk of making a Type I error (i.e., the risk of falsely rejecting the null hypothesis that the independent variable had no effect). For example, although each test may employ a standard significance criterion of $\alpha = .05$, when we perform three tests, there is up to a 15% chance of committing at least one Type I error. For four tests, the risk can approach 20%.

ANOVA uses a different approach. In studies with one independent variable, no matter how many groups exist, the ANOVA generates just one statistic called the F statistic. The letter F is designated in honor of a brilliant English statistician, Sir Ronald Fisher (1890–1962), who developed ANOVA and many other widely used statistical tests. When used with three or more groups, an ANOVA does not tell you whether differences between specific pairs of means are statistically significant. Rather, the F statistic is used to determine whether the overall pattern of results is statistically significant.

The F statistic is a ratio that reflects the variability in the scores between the different groups relative to the variability in the scores within those groups. In ANOVA, we use the scores from our samples (i.e., the scores obtained in the various conditions) to estimate the variance in their respective populations. Specifically,

$$F = \frac{\text{between-groups variance}}{\text{within-groups variance}}$$

where "between-groups variance" and "within-groups variance" are estimates of population variance.

The variability in scores within groups provides us with a reference point. It helps us estimate how much a particular characteristic—the dependent variable in this case—naturally fluctuates in a population. For example, in **Table SM.11**, the three columns of raw scores (i.e., the first, third, and fifth columns) present the number of times that three groups of participants smiled while watching a comedy movie segment. Each group was exposed to a different experimental manipulation (a sad, neutral, or happy movie segment) before watching the comedy segment. You can see that the raw scores within each group vary. This variability cannot be due to the independent variable because all participants within each condition received the same experimental treatment. Rather, it is due to inherent differences among people in how much they smile when exposed to the comedy segment. This natural variation is sometimes called *error variance* because it essentially represents chance background variability against which we have to detect whether our independent variable had an effect.

Now look at that table again and notice there are also differences in the raw scores between the groups. Scores in the sad condition, for example, are lower overall than those in the other conditions. This variability between groups provides the numerator for the F

Table SM.11 Data Analyzed in a One-Way Analysis of Variance (ANOVA)

	Experimentally Induced Mood					
	Condition 1: Sad		Condition 2: Neutral		Condition 3: Happy	
	Raw Scores (X_1)	$(X_1 - M_1)^2$	Raw Scores (X_2)	$(X_2 - M_2)^2$	Raw Scores (X_3)	$(X_3 - M_3)^2$
	9	0	18	25	15	1
	6	9	12	1	11	9
	7	4	10	9	13	1
	10	1	15	4	11	9
	10	1	12	1	17	9
	8	1	13	0	18	16
	13	16	11	4	13	1
Sum	63	$SS_{within1} = 32$	91	$SS_{within2} = 44$	98	$SS_{within3} = 46$
Mean	9		13		14	

statistic and comes from two sources. First, imagine that our independent variable (induced prior mood) has absolutely no effect on the dependent variable (smiling). In this case, the variability between groups will be a function of the natural variability for smiling in the population. That is, through random luck of the draw, the participants who happen to end up in each group differ naturally to some extent from the other groups in their smiling behavior.

A second source of between-groups variance derives from the potential treatment effect: the possible influence of the independent variable. For example, if manipulating people's prior mood does influence their smiling when viewing the comedy segment, then this will cause the overall variation in scores between the groups to increase. This increased variation will be reflected in a larger overall difference among the three means.

We can therefore express the F ratio as follows:

$$F = \frac{\text{variance due to treatment effect + natural variance across people (error variance)}}{\text{natural variance across people (error variance)}}$$

For ANOVA, the null hypothesis (H_0) is that the independent variable has no influence on the dependent variable. In other words, regarding the dependent variable, H_0 is that the means of the populations from which our samples of scores were obtained are equal to one another. If an independent variable has absolutely no influence on the dependent variable, then the treatment effect is zero and the F ratio theoretically would be (natural variance)/(natural variance) = 1.00. In reality, due to random fluctuations in samples, the F ratio will almost always be greater than 1.00 even if H_0 is true. But when the F statistic becomes large enough, we conclude it is unlikely that H_0 is true and infer that a treatment effect is present.

16.3 PERFORMING A ONE-WAY ANOVA

We will illustrate a basic one-way, between-subjects ANOVA. For simplicity, there are only 7 participants per condition. Our experiment examines the effects of mood on humor perception. Individually, randomly assigned participants watch a 10-minute movie segment that induces either a sad, neutral, or happy mood. They then watch a 10-minute segment from a comedy movie. The main dependent variable is the number of times they smile during the comedy segment. Trained observers blind to participants' induced mood condition measure the number of smiles. In Table SM.11, the first, third, and fifth columns present the raw data. The other columns present the squared deviation scores within each condition.

Part 1: Determine the Between-Groups Variance Estimate ($MS_{between}$)

Step 1   Calculate the mean of each group, as follows:

$$M = \frac{\Sigma X}{n}$$

where for each group,

$$\Sigma X = \text{sum of scores} \qquad n = \text{number of cases}$$

Thus,

$$M_1 = \frac{63}{7} = 9.00 \qquad M_2 = \frac{91}{7} = 13.00 \qquad M_3 = \frac{98}{7} = 14.00$$

Step 2   Determine the *grand mean* (M_{grand}) of all the scores. Because the groups have equal sample sizes and we already have calculated the sum of scores (ΣX) for each group in Step 1, we simply add these sums and divide by N:

$$M_{grand} = \frac{\Sigma X_1 + \Sigma X_2 + \Sigma X_3}{N} = \frac{63 + 91 + 98}{21} = \frac{252}{21} = 12$$

Step 3   Calculate the between-groups sum of squares ($SS_{between}$). This is a measure of the variability between groups that we will use in the next step to estimate the between-groups variance:

$$SS_{between} = \Sigma n(M - M_{grand})^2$$

where for each group,

$$n = \text{the number of cases} \qquad M = \text{the mean} \qquad M_{grand} = \text{the grand mean}$$

Thus,

$$SS_{between} = 7(9 - 12)^2 + 7(13 - 12)^2 + 7(14 - 12)^2 = (63 + 7 + 28) = 98$$

Step 4   Calculate the between-groups variance estimate, represented by the symbol $MS_{between}$ (which stands for "mean square between groups"). To do this, we need to know the between-group sum of squares, which we calculated in Step 3, and a value called "between groups degrees of freedom" ($df_{between}$), which in a one-way ANOVA is the number of groups − 1. (See Statistics Module 10.3 for a discussion of the concept of degrees of freedom.) In our experiment, we have three groups. Thus,

$$MS_{between} = \frac{SS_{between}}{df_{between}} = \frac{SS_{between}}{(\text{the number of groups}) - 1} = \frac{98}{2} = 49$$

Part 2: Determine the Within-Groups Variance Estimate (MS_{within})

Step 1   In each condition, take each raw score (X), subtract the mean (M) from it, and square the resulting number, that is, $(X - M)^2$. These are squared deviation scores. As Table SM.11 shows, we place each deviation score in the column alongside the corresponding raw scores.

Step 2   Add the squared deviations for each condition. This is the within-groups sum of squares for each condition (i.e., $SS_{within1} = 32$, $SS_{within2} = 44$, $SS_{within3} = 46$).

Step 3   Calculate the *total within-groups sum of squares* (SS_{within}) by adding the within-groups sum of squares for each condition. In our example,

$$SS_{within} = (SS_{within1} + SS_{within2} + SS_{within3}) = (32 + 44 + 46) = 122$$

Step 4   Calculate the within-groups variance estimate (MS_{within}). To do this, we need to know the total within-group sum of squares, which we calculated in Step 3, and a value called the "within-groups degrees of freedom" (df_{within}), which in a one-way ANOVA is the total number of cases minus the number of groups (i.e., number of conditions):

$$MS_{within} = \frac{SS_{within}}{df_{within}} = \frac{SS_{within}}{(total\ number\ of\ cases) - (number\ of\ groups)} = \frac{122}{21 - 3} = 6.78$$

Part 3: Determine the *F* Value and Its Level of Significance

Now that we have determined the between-group and within-group population variance estimates, we determine a statistic called the *F* ratio, as follows:

$$F = \frac{MS_{between}}{MS_{within}} = \frac{49}{6.78} = 7.23$$

Next, we use Table 5 in Appendix C to determine whether our *F* value meets the criterion for statistical significance. Given our degrees of freedom (2, between groups; 18, within groups), we see that the critical values for statistical significance at $p < .05$ and $p < .01$ are $F = 3.56$ and $F = 6.01$, respectively. Our *F* value of 7.23 is larger than these, so our findings are statistically significant. (The more specific output from a software ANOVA test indicates that $p = .005$.) Because the probability is less than 5% that our findings are due solely to chance, we reject the null hypothesis and conclude that, overall, the number of smiles differed across the induced mood conditions.

When performing the calculations for an *F* test, it is standard to create a summary table like the one below. Software programs that perform a one-way, between-groups ANOVA typically provide a similar summary table.

Source	Sum of Squares (SS)	df	Mean Square (MS)	F	p Value
Between groups	98	2	49.00	7.23	.005
Within groups	122	18	6.78		
Total	220	20			

KEY TERMS

alternative hypothesis (p. 435)

analysis of variance (ANOVA) (p. 453)

bar graph (p. 419)

chi-square (χ^2) goodness-of-fit test (p. 441)

chi-square (χ^2) test for independence (p. 443)

Cohen's *d* (p. 447)

confidence interval (CI) (p. 451)

cumulative frequency distribution (p. 415)

descriptive statistics (p. 412)

deviation score (p. 424)

effect size (p. 446)

frequency distribution (p. 414)

frequency polygon (p. 418)

histogram (p. 418)

inferential statistics (p. 413)

mean (p. 420)

measures of central tendency (p. 419)

measures of dispersion (measures of variability) (p. 422)

median (p. 420)

mode (p. 420)

normal distribution (normal curve) (p. 429)

null hypothesis (p. 435)

parameter (p. 413)

Pearson's *r* (Pearson product-moment correlation coefficient) (p. 425)

percentile rank (p. 431)

pie chart (p. 419)

population (p. 412)

power (pp. 440, 448)

power analysis (p. 449)

probability value (*p* value) (p. 437)

range (p. 422)

raw scores (p. 412)

regression analysis (simple linear regression) (p. 427)

relative cumulative frequency distribution (p. 415)

relative frequency distribution
(p. 415)
sample (p. 412)
sampling error (p. 434)
significance level (alpha [α] level)
(p. 437)
skewed distribution (p. 431)

Spearman's rho (Spearman rank-
order correlation coefficient)
(p. 426)
standard deviation (p. 423)
standard error of the mean (*SEM*)
(p. 434)
statistic (p. 413)

statistically significant (p. 437)
sum of squares (*SS*) (p. 424)
t test (p. 444)
Type I error (p. 438)
Type II error (p. 438)
variance (p. 423)
z score (p. 432)

COMMUNICATING RESEARCH RESULTS
Contributed by Dr. Pam Marek, Kennesaw State University

As a research methods text, this book is a guide to understanding, evaluating, and conducting psychological research. But for research to make a contribution, it must be shared with the scientific community, and that usually means it must be written up in an article, paper, or poster. As this appendix describes, psychological scientists use a specific scientific writing style to communicate their findings in a way that generalizes across many disciplines. This style enables them to effectively organize their material; communicate with clarity, precision, and logic; and cite source materials to avoid plagiarism. Familiarity with the elements of scientific writing in the field of psychology—specifically, American Psychological Association (APA) style—will enhance successful report writing and assignment preparation in psychology courses. An understanding of scientific writing is also a valuable tool for the consumer of scientific information; it sharpens critical thinking about ideas and evaluation of conclusions. Accordingly, this appendix is designed to promote your understanding of how to organize ideas about science and express science-related thoughts in clear, formal language. It should serve as a reference to guide formal scientific writing in general, and APA style in particular.

In writing for any discipline, the principal goals are clarity, continuity, and logical flow of ideas. These goals can be attained by following three steps: (1) planning, which encompasses locating and reading source materials; (2) writing a rough draft; and (3) editing and making corrections. In scientific writing, all ideas must be supported by evidence, with appropriate citations to the source of the evidence. Because different instructors have different requirements for writing assignments, it is important for you as a student to be thoroughly familiar with the criteria for specific assignments and to assume responsibility for seeking clarification if you have questions about what a given assignment requires.

In psychology courses, the ultimate source for appropriate writing style is the Publication Manual of the American Psychological Association, 6th edition (American Psychological Association, 2010b). The guidelines for APA style include instructions for formatting, organization, content, citations, language, and sentence construction. Because APA-style papers are typically written for an audience that includes researchers and academics, they should be written in formal language (unless your instructor says otherwise). Precise and clear writing is crucial.

When students learn about APA style, they are sometimes surprised to realize that many psychology textbooks do not use it, or at least do not follow every element of APA style. For example, to engage a student such as yourself, many textbooks (including this one) use a more conversational tone, often addressing the reader as "you." Therefore, keep in mind that the goal of this appendix is not to help you learn to write in the style of this research methods text, but rather to help you become proficient in scientific writing according to APA style.

To illustrate APA style in an actual research report, this appendix includes a Sample Article: an annotated manuscript for an article published in the Psi Chi Journal of Undergraduate Research. The annotated comments point out ways in which science writing may or may not meet APA criteria, and they emphasize correct APA style.

APA-STYLE RESEARCH ARTICLES AND REVIEW ARTICLES

Learning Objective

After studying this section, you should be able to:

- Describe the purpose and main sections of a research article and a review article.

The types of writing assignments that instructors may ask you to complete will vary across courses. For example, in research methods, experimental psychology, and laboratory courses (e.g., some cognitive psychology, social psychology, or learning and behavior courses), your instructor may require article summaries, a laboratory report, a research report on a group project you have completed, or a research proposal. In senior-level courses, instructors may also require a research report on an individual project, or they may require that you prepare a comprehensive literature review paper to compare and contrast different theoretical perspectives on a particular topic. Thus, during your academic career, you will most likely be using APA style to prepare a variety of different types of reports and papers.

To prepare for most of the assignments described above, you will be reading articles from professional journals. Typically, these articles will be classified as either research articles or review articles. A **research article** (also known as an **empirical report**) describes original research that the authors have conducted, typically with human participants or nonhuman animals. In APA-style reports, authors provide a structured framework for their new research by first presenting a literature review that integrates key findings from prior studies and describes the theory (if any) that is being tested. The authors then present their hypotheses, describe their methodology and results, and conclude with a discussion that reiterates their key findings and positions these findings in the context of existing knowledge. In contrast, a **review article** (also called a **literature review**) integrates, summarizes, and provides suggestions for extending prior research on a particular topic. Rather than initiating a new research investigation of their own, authors of review articles study the existing literature on a topic and describe this literature in much greater detail than would occur in the introductory section of a research article. As we described in Chapter 2, some review articles utilize a statistical procedure called meta-analysis to combine the results of different studies that examine the same topic. Although undergraduate students are rarely assigned to conduct meta-analysis in the research methods course, you may need to read meta-analysis review articles when you perform the literature search for your writing assignment.

APA style assists both readers and writers by providing specific guidelines for the order of report sections. Similar to the description in Chapter 2, the main sections of a research report are as follows.

Abstract An abstract is a brief, one-paragraph summary of the report. Typically, it mentions some key details about the study's general purpose, hypotheses, methodology, findings, and conclusions.

Introduction There's no official heading labeled "Introduction," but this section begins the narrative by describing the general topic and specific questions under study, explaining why the topic is important, and summarizing the literature of prior research and theories that bear on the topic. It typically includes a statement of any hypotheses that are being tested.

Method This section provides sufficient information about participants, design, materials, and procedures that interested readers may replicate the research. It is typically divided into subsections that describe the overall research design, the participants' general characteristics (e.g., "72 pairs of mothers and their 4- to 8-month-old infants"), how they were selected, the specific procedures used, and how variables were manipulated or measured. If subsections are short, the authors may combine them (e.g., "Design and Participants").

Results The authors describe how they analyzed their data, and they present their results. Statistical findings may also be shown in tables and graphs.

Discussion This section reiterates the key findings at greater length but in nonstatistical or less statistical terms. It includes interpretation of the results and their theoretical or practical implications, limitations of the study, potential applications, and issues to be resolved in future research. The discussion also states whether the results supported any hypotheses that were tested and explains why the hypotheses were (or were not) supported.

References The authors list the sources they cited in the article, using standard APA format, so that readers can locate the original sources.

APA style also provides guidelines for the main sections of a review article, which are as follows.

Abstract In a review article, this brief, one-paragraph summary identifies the topic of the literature reviewed and summarizes the findings.

Introduction As in a research article, there's no official heading labeled "Introduction." In a review article, this section describes the general topic and specific questions under study, explaining why the topic is important and outlining the scope of the literature review.

Body Review articles often divide the body into topical subsections; in each one, the authors describe key findings from their review of relevant studies. Authors may present a summary table listing key features (e.g., the number and type of participants studied; the tasks used) and major findings of each study reviewed. Each subsection may include a discussion of relevant findings.

Summary or **Conclusions** This section may include interpretation of the findings from the literature review, their theoretical or practical implications, limitations of the study, and directions for future research.

References The authors list the sources they cited in the article, using standard APA format, so that readers can locate the original sources.

In both research articles and review articles, there may be supplementary information (e.g., appendices, tables) that follows the References section. It is generally organized in the following order: tables, figures, and then appendices. In a published article, these sections are integrated within the text rather than appearing in a separate section.

STEP 1. PLANNING YOUR REPORT

Learning Objectives

After studying this section, you should be able to:

- Describe how to plan a writing assignment.
- Use databases such as PsycINFO to find appropriate source material for a writing project.
- Compose an outline and take proper notes on source material to support the outlined points.

Scientific papers are not written in a vacuum; rather, they build on and extend prior research. Thus, becoming familiar with existing scientific literature on the topic of interest is a crucial first step in planning a paper. Planning a scientific writing assignment involves locating appropriate source articles, reading the articles, and taking notes in a manner that will be useful in preparing a first draft with accurate citations.

LOCATING APPROPRIATE SOURCE MATERIAL

When locating appropriate source material, it is important to distinguish between scientific material and articles written for the general public, which may or may not be firmly based on scientific research. It may be tempting to use some of the countless resources available on the Internet, in books, in newspapers, and in trade publications as sources for your paper. However, unlike articles in professional, peer-reviewed literature, these sources often do not contain citations to support their claims, may be based on anecdotal evidence such as personal experience, and may reach conclusions that are not justified by the data presented. In other words, there may be no check on the accuracy of the facts or the logic of the arguments.

The peer-review process is a safeguard against these weaknesses. If an article is published in a peer-reviewed journal, it means that professionals who are experts in the pertinent field have carefully evaluated the article on dimensions such as inclusion and citation of relevant background material, methodology, analysis, and interpretation of results. Thus, the planning phase of a scientific writing project begins with searching the professional, peer-reviewed literature on the chosen topic. As described in Chapter 2, PsycINFO and PsycARTI-CLES are two comprehensive databases for psychology-related sources; they each allow users to limit their searches to peer-reviewed sources. After logging into the database and typing search terms, you will retrieve a listing of published articles, books, and book chapters. In PsycINFO, as in many other databases, searches can be restricted to terms found in specific fields (e.g., author, title, abstract, source) of database records. As shown in **Figure A.1**, a search for the term "writing" in the title and "assessment" in the abstract yielded 541 results.

These results suggest that the initial topic of writing assessment may be too broad to cover in a single paper. Generally, the literature review of a research article is more effective if it probes deeply into a more limited topic rather than skimming over a wide range of material, as this allows the writer to compare and contrast different approaches or theories rather than merely describing them. Careful selection of articles will make it easier to write a cohesive literature review. Reading the abstract of each article that appears to be relevant will indicate how closely a given article relates to your specific topic of interest. Often, you may decide to restrict your database search to specific subtopics or populations. For example, narrowing the PsycINFO results above by adding the term "college students" in the "subjects" field narrowed the list of results from 541 to 31 potential items.

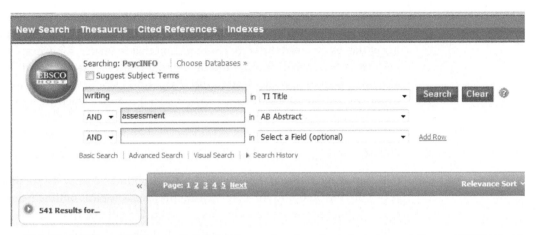

Figure A.1 PsycINFO search fields. (Source: American Psychological Association and EBSCO Host.)

After locating appropriate sources, the next step is to obtain the full text of the material. In some instances, full text articles are available for downloading directly from the database. When given the choice between .html and .pdf, the .pdf version is preferable because it integrates tables and figures in the text for ease of reference. Although some students are tempted to limit their sources to those that are available for immediate download, yielding to that temptation often means that highly relevant information will be omitted from the literature review. To avoid this problem, attempt to locate the material that cannot be immediately downloaded by checking the catalog at your school's library. If your library does not have the material, consult a librarian or a library web page to determine how to order it through interlibrary loan. The time needed to obtain materials from other libraries varies across institutions and by the type of resource requested—one of many reasons to begin your search for relevant source material as early as possible, well before the writing assignment is due.

Before searching for sources or after reading the first few, it is helpful to develop a topical outline for the literature review. This outline can guide the search process and you can refine it as the search progresses. Then, when reading and taking notes about theories, findings, and relevant terms in the source articles, you can position your notes in the appropriate section of the outline.

READING SOURCE MATERIAL

It takes considerable time to select and collect sources and to extract the appropriate material from each source. Professional articles can be demanding to read and digest. Reading the abstract first will give you an idea of what to expect. However, the abstract definitely does not provide sufficient depth to facilitate integrating information into the literature review section of a paper. It is important to read each article thoroughly.

After reading the abstract, familiarize yourself with the article's structure—the information contained in each section. As you read the article more carefully, direct your attention to issues such as the research purpose and importance, how it relates to prior research on the topic, the hypotheses, general methodology, major findings, and interpretation of the findings. As you read, consider how the material relates to what you plan to write.

Students often find their first experience reading articles from the professional literature to be quite challenging as they confront possibly unfamiliar terminology and theories. If this happens to you, do not be discouraged; give yourself time to understand the material and how it relates to the topic of your assignment. Gaining this understanding will enable you to express the ideas from the source accurately in your own words and to integrate them with related material in your report. For students, the material in the Results section, which often includes multiple statistical tests, is often particularly daunting. To gain a better understanding of the results, read the verbal information that indicates, for example, whether one group performed better than another did or whether one variable predicted another variable. It is also often helpful to read ahead to the Discussion section, where authors often reiterate key results in a straightforward (i.e., nonstatistical) manner when they examine support for a hypothesis or explain the findings.

CONSTRUCTING AN OUTLINE AND TAKING NOTES

It is important to begin developing a topical outline as early as possible in the process of reviewing the literature for your writing project. A topical outline helps overcome the tendency to summarize one article after another. Organizing information by topic encourages you to compare and contrast the findings from one study to those of other studies on the same topic in a single paragraph (integrating information from multiple sources). Your topical outline serves as a framework for presentation of past research and provides an underlying structure for writing.

If your writing assignment is a literature review paper, you may choose to use your outline to develop topical headings for subsections of your report. For example, in a review article examining research on the relation between pain and smoking, psychologists developed major topical headings of "introduction to pain and smoking," "effects of smoking on pain," "effects of pain on smoking," "an integrative reciprocal model of pain and smoking," and "summary" (Ditre, Brandon, Zale, & Meagher, 2011). Most of these sections (e.g., effects of smoking on pain) were broken down into more specific subsections (e.g., smoking as a risk factor for chronic pain; acute effects of smoking and nicotine on pain). If you are writing a literature review report, this type of topical outline can provide the structure and headings for your entire report, leading to a final section in which you provide an overall summary and/or conclusions.

If your writing assignment is a research report, such a topical outline will help you structure the introductory section of the report. In this case, the introductory section will be much briefer than a full-blown literature review, and you may end up using only a few (or even none) of the outline headings as actual titles for subsections. Still, the outline will guide the flow of information that you present in your introduction as you describe the research question of interest, briefly summarize key prior research relevant to your topic, and provide a rationale for your research hypothesis.

Taking good notes during your review of the literature is essential if the resulting paper is to be of high quality. Because a source article may address one or more topics, it is helpful to categorize notes by topic and to include identifying information from source articles for citation purposes. Do not copy phrases directly from articles, and do not simply change one or two words in a sentence when you add the information to your notes. Instead, describe the ideas and findings in your own words; this will make it easier to avoid **plagiarism** (*taking credit for someone else's work or ideas*) when the time comes to write your paper. Be sure that your notes include all the information you need for citations: A citation will be required for each factual item in your paper that is not very common knowledge. If in doubt, cite! Although using quotations in psychological writing is discouraged, if it seems absolutely necessary to use a brief quote (and the criteria for your assignment permit doing so), remember to include quotation marks and a page number as well as a citation. Highlighting the sections of source articles from which you draw information will be useful later when you check your paper for signs of plagiarism. (See pp. A-11 through A-15 for more details about using quotations and avoiding plagiarism.)

STEP 2. WRITING A FIRST DRAFT

Learning Objectives

After studying this section, you should be able to:

- Describe the principal formatting guidelines for APA-style manuscripts.
- Use quotations correctly and avoid plagiarism.
- Compose the first draft of a writing assignment according to APA style and format.

This section focuses on the types of information that you need to organize and include in each section of a research report. It begins with general guidelines for formatting and provides additional information about formatting for each individual part of the paper. To emphasize the importance of citations in APA-style writing, it includes a special section about citations and their formatting both in the text of the report and in the References section.

GENERAL INFORMATION ABOUT APA-STYLE FORMATTING

APA-style formatting includes guidelines for margins, line spacing, alignment, and font as outlined in the table below. Using the options provided by word processing software, select the appropriate formatting choices before starting your first draft. When typing the paper, adjust the formatting options for the abstract and references as noted in **Table A.1**.

APA style includes five levels of headings; as a writer, you will use headings and subheadings to subdivide the material you are presenting so that your readers can easily navigate through your paper and follow your arguments. **Table A.2** shows an example of the first three heading levels from a research article. Level 1, used for the main section heading (Method), is centered and in boldface font. If there were multiple words in the Level 1 heading, all words of four letters or more would begin with a capital letter. Level 2, used for

Table A.1 How to Format APA-Style Manuscripts

Line spacing	- Double space all lines of text, including titles. - No extra spaces between paragraphs; tables may be single or double spaced.
Spacing after punctuation	- Use two spaces after punctuation at the end of a sentence; otherwise, use one space after punctuation.
Alignment	- Left for all paragraphs and most headings, but Level 1 headings (headings for major sections) are centered.
Margins	- All (top, bottom, left, right) set at 1 inch (2.54 cm) for the body of the manuscript with header .5 inch (1.27 cm) from top.
Typeface	- 12-point font, Times New Roman.

First line of paragraph	- Set indent at .5 inch.
	- Exceptions:
	  - The abstract is a single block paragraph (without .5 inch indent for the first line).
	  - Reference items are formatted using a "hanging" indent (the first line of each citation begins at the margin and subsequent lines are indented by .5 inch).

Page number and running head	The running head title appears at top left of all pages, and the page number appears at top right on the same line.

Table A.2 Example of Level 1, 2, and 3 Headings

Method

Participants

Participants included 301 individuals from a community sample (180 women and

115 men, M_{age} = 38.64, SD_{age} = 14.15). Participants had a variety of ethnic [text continues]

Materials

  Scenarios and related questions. Participants read a brief scenario about a mother (Maggie)

who was offered the measles, mumps, and rubella (MMR) vaccine for [text continues]

---

the Participants and Materials subsections in the example, is also in boldface font, but it is positioned flush with the left margin. Capitalization rules are the same as those for Level 1 headings. Level 3, used for the Scenarios and related questions subsection in the example, is positioned .5 inch (1.27 cm) from the left margin (as is the indent for the first line of a new paragraph), is in boldface font, and is followed by a period (with text beginning thereafter). Only the first word of Level 3 headings is capitalized unless the heading includes proper nouns, which would also be capitalized.

Level 4 and Level 5 headings, if needed, would also be positioned .5 inch from the left margin and would be followed by a period. Level 4 and Level 5 headings are italicized and follow the same capitalization rules used for Level 3 headings. However, the font style used for Level 4 and Level 5 headings differs: boldface for Level 4 and regular for Level 5.

THE TITLE PAGE

The title should clearly and concisely indicate the topic of the manuscript; it should consist of no more than 12 words. For a research article, it should include the primary variables that you are studying. For a review article, it should contain the major issue that you are investigating. Use Table A.3 as a guide for the title page.

In manuscripts submitted for publication, title pages also contain an Author's Note. Guidelines specify that an Author's Note should include departmental affiliation, acknowledgments, and contact information for the author. However, your instructor may not require an Author's Note on student papers.

THE ABSTRACT

An abstract summarizes the report in 150 to 250 words; maximum length requirements vary across journals (and instructors). When you search databases, the abstract is the only section of a manuscript shown in the database record. Reading the abstract typically enables you to tell whether a source is directly relevant to your paper.

When you actually write a report, you prepare the abstract last because it summarizes the entire paper (Table A.4). The abstract should not contain any information that is not included in the actual paper. Moreover, information in the abstract should be consistent with information that is included in the body of the report. Abstracts are concise, specific, and self-explanatory.

Table A.3 What to Include on a Title Page

Title	• Centered horizontally on upper half of page • Capitalize first letters of important words and all words of four or more letters.
Author's name	• Centered, on a line double spaced below title, including first name, middle initial, and surname • If there are two authors from the same institution, both names are typed on the same line with "and" between them.
Institutional affiliation	• Centered • On a line double spaced below author's name
Running head (appears at top of page in published articles) IMPORTANT NOTE	• In header area (use header feature in word-processing programs) • Type the words *Running head*: left justified; do not use italics. • After the words *Running head*: (on the same line in the header area) type an abbreviated title in all capital letters (maximum 50 characters including spaces and punctuation). • The actual running head appears on all pages, but the words *Running head*: appear on the title page only.
Page number	• In header on every page, on same line as running head, on right • Title page is page 1 • Do not use dashes or the word *page*, just the number. • Use automatic page-numbering feature in word-processing programs.

In manuscripts submitted for publication, authors itemize keywords used for database searches. To do so, double space after the last line of the abstract, indent .5 inch (1.27 cm), and type *Keywords:* (italicized and followed by a colon). Then, type a few words that indicate key topics of your manuscript. For example, keywords for the manuscript in the Sample Article at the end of this appendix might include *violent media* and *aggression* (the actual keywords are not italicized). Your instructor may not require keywords in student papers.

THE INTRODUCTION

The introduction of a research article or the body of a review article begins on page 3 (after the title page and abstract) with the title of the paper. The opening paragraphs highlight general information about the issue under investigation and prepare readers for the detailed literature review that follows. For example, in the Sample Article by Miranda, McCluskey, Silber, von Pohle, and Bainum (2009), the opening paragraphs of the introduction incorporate key facts about the development of research about aggressive modeling that suggest why modeling is

Table A.4 What to Include in an Abstract

Research Article	Review Article
Purpose/problem investigated	Topic/Purpose or thesis
Number, type, age, sex (or species) of participants	Types of sources used
Method (materials used, basic procedures)	Method (basic procedure of meta-analysis, or how studies were grouped or examined in a qualitative review)
Major findings	Major findings
Conclusions and implications	Conclusions and implications

important. The paragraphs include specific statements rather than broad generalities and are supported by citations. The introduction often also includes a statement of the goal or purpose of the research. In the Sample Article, the explicit statement of purpose is positioned as a lead-in to the hypothesis at the end of the introduction.

The Thesis Statement. When you write a review article (or an analytical, explanatory, or argumentative paper), you typically begin with a thesis statement: a short, precise statement that indicates what issue you are analyzing, what you are explaining to readers, or what argument you are making. The thesis statement presents the main idea of your paper. If you have prepared an outline, check to be sure that it includes information relevant to your thesis statement. You may need to add topics (perhaps searching for additional sources), or you may need to eliminate topics that are only peripherally related to your thesis. An outline that conforms to your thesis will serve as an effective framework for your paper.

The Literature Review. The purpose of a literature review is "to convey to your reader what knowledge and ideas have been established on a topic, and what their strengths and weaknesses are" (Taylor, n.d., para. 1). In a literature review, do not simply summarize a series of articles sequentially. Rather, integrate material from multiple articles into paragraphs focused on specific subtopics linked to the purpose of your research. In the Sample Article, Miranda et al. (2009) integrate information about aggressive modeling, parenting styles, and media effects on aggression in their literature review. For articles published in professional, peer-reviewed journals, literature reviews are quite comprehensive. For student papers, instructors' expectations for literature reviews typically reflect the extent of your experience with reading professional literature and preparing scientific reports. Regardless of requirements for length or a minimum number of sources, typical expectations include thorough reading of source articles, precise and accurate reporting, appropriate organization, proper citations, and use of formal grammar and sentence construction.

Your outline will help you integrate the information from multiple articles into a series of paragraphs about a specific topic rather than summarizing one article after another. If coverage of a particular topic area seems weak, the weakness should be a cue that you need to search for additional articles on the topic. If you do not understand something that seems important when you read, make sure to clarify the meaning before using the information in a written assignment. Avoid simply trying to reorganize the original author's words without understanding them: Such "reorganization without understanding" tends to result in plagiarism. If there are conflicting findings or opinions on a topic, compare and contrast them in the same paragraph, perhaps commenting on the possible reason for the conflict (e.g., different methodologies). It often is unnecessary to report detailed information about the number of participants or methodology in a literature review unless the methodology relates to a point about a particular finding. Instead, emphasize the research findings and their theoretical underpinnings. In a research article, the literature review provides information needed to justify the hypotheses. In a review article, the literature review provides evidence to support the conclusion.

Concluding the Introduction of a Research Article. The final paragraphs of the introduction of a research article typically lead in to the Method section. To do so, they provide a brief description of the research design, a rationale for the hypotheses, and the specific hypotheses themselves. A rationale is a statement that indicates the reasoning that underlies a hypothesis based on prior findings or theories introduced in the literature review. In the Sample Article, Miranda et al. (2009) indicate that existing research leaves several questions unanswered about how parental presence influences children's reactions to media violence. They briefly describe what they manipulated (disapproval of aggression) and the types of aggression they measured. This information is followed by two hypotheses that specify how the manipulation will influence the measures of aggression. Although Miranda et al. do not provide an explicit rationale for these hypotheses, the predictions are consistent with prior research that they have reviewed.

CITATIONS AND AVOIDING PLAGIARISM

Scientific writing relies heavily on providing evidence from existing research and theoretical perspectives. One of the most important requirements for scientific writing is the obligation to cite the original sources of ideas and findings. Not only is proper citation an indication of academic courtesy, but the lack of citation for ideas and/or quoted words is considered plagiarism.

Avoiding Plagiarism

APA Principle 8.11, Plagiarism, of the Ethical Principles of Psychologists and Code of Conduct, states, "Psychologists do not present portions of another's work or data as their own, even if the other work or data source is cited occasionally" (APA, 2010a, p. 11). Be aware that the phrase "portions of another's work" refers to short quotations, even single sentences. Moreover, although it may be tempting to adapt someone else's sentence from a source article by changing a few words, such minor changes are not permissible, even if you cite the source article. Rather, in addition to citing sources, use paraphrasing (expressing ideas using your own words and sentence structure).

Citation Format

In all sections of any scientific report, APA style calls for providing citations of the sources used. Citations identify the authors' surnames (i.e., last names, family names) and publication date of the source material. The application of this author–date citation system varies slightly depending on several factors, such as whether a source is being cited for the first time or a subsequent time and whether the citation is placed in the body of the narrative (i.e., woven into the flow of a sentence) or inside parentheses.

Initial Citation: One Author. For narrative citations, the date is placed within parentheses and follows the author's name. In parenthetical citations, a comma is placed after the author's name to separate it from the date.

- *Example 1: a single-author citation placed in the narrative.* Groves (2006) pointed out that, in survey research, the relation between nonresponse rates and nonresponse bias is not straightforward.

- *Example 2: a single-author parenthetical citation.* In survey research, the relation between nonresponse rates and nonresponse bias is not straightforward (Groves, 2006).

Initial Citation: Two Authors. For citations in the narrative, when an article has two authors, the word "and" is placed between the two names, followed by the date, placed in parentheses. If the entire citation is parenthetical, the word "and" is replaced by an ampersand ("&" without quotation marks). A comma is placed after the last author's name to separate it from the date.

- *Example 3: a two-author citation placed in the narrative.* Groves and Peytcheva (2008) used meta-analysis to assess the relation between nonresponse rates and nonresponse bias.

- *Example 4: a two-author parenthetical citation.* Meta-analysis has been used to examine the relation between nonresponse rates and nonresponse bias (Groves & Peytcheva, 2008).

Initial Citation: Three to Five Authors. A comma separates each author's surname from the one before it. If the citation is in the narrative, the word "and" is placed before the last author's name, and after the last author's name the date is placed in parentheses. If the citation is parenthetical, an ampersand ("&" without quotation marks) is placed before the last author's name and a comma separates the last author's surname from the date.

- *Example 5: a five-author citation placed in the narrative.* Roehrs, Burduvali, Bonahoom, Drake, and Roth (2003) examined the effects of sleep loss on memory.
- *Example 6: a five-author parenthetical citation.* Experiments have examined the effects of sleep loss on memory (Roehrs, Burduvali, Bonahoom, Drake, & Roth, 2003).

Initial Citation: Six or More Authors. If a source has six or more authors, the citation format is: first author's surname, comma, the term *et al.* (not set in italics), and then the date either placed in parentheses (for narrative citations) or separated from "et al." by a comma (for parenthetical citations). For the term *et al.* there is no period after "et," but there is a period after "al" because it is an abbreviation for the Latin word *alia*, meaning "others." Here are two examples. The original article has eight authors.

- *Example 7: initial citation for six or more authors, placed in the narrative.* In a cross-cultural study, Weisfeld et al. (2012) examined sex differences in partners' relationship satisfaction.
- *Example 8: initial parenthetical citation for six or more authors.* In a cross-cultural study, sex differences in partners' relationship satisfaction were examined (Weisfeld et al., 2012).

Subsequent Citations: One or Two Authors. When a source has one or two authors, each author's surname is included in all subsequent citations. The publication year also is included, with one exception: If an initial citation and subsequent citation occur within the same paragraph and both are narrative citations, then the year may be omitted from the subsequent citations.

- *Example 9: subsequent narrative citation, one or two authors.* Groves and Peytcheva (2008) included 59 studies in their meta-analysis.
- *Example 10: subsequent parenthetical citation, one or two authors.* The meta-analysis included 59 studies (Groves & Peytcheva, 2008).
- *Example 11: initial narrative citation and a subsequent narrative citation in the same paragraph, one or two authors.* Groves and Peytcheva (2008) used meta-analysis to assess the relation between nonresponse rates and nonresponse bias. Groves and Peytcheva included 59 studies in their meta-analysis.

Subsequent Citations: Three or More Authors. When a source has three or more authors, all subsequent citations include the first author's surname followed by *et al.* (nonitalicized) and the publication year. For narrative citations, the publication year is placed within parentheses. If an initial narrative citation and subsequent narrative citation occur within the same paragraph, then the year does not need to be included.

- *Example 12: subsequent narrative citation, three or more authors.* Roehrs et al. (2003) also examined how alcohol consumption affected memory.
- *Example 13: subsequent parenthetical citation, three or more authors.* In this experiment, the effects of alcohol consumption on memory also were examined (Roehrs et al., 2003).
- *Example 14: initial narrative citation followed by a subsequent narrative citation in the same paragraph, three or more authors.* Roehrs, Burduvali, Bonahoom, Drake, and Roth (2003) examined the effects of sleep loss on memory. Roehrs et al. also examined how alcohol consumption affected memory.

Citing Multiple Sources in the Same Sentence. For narrative citations, format each one as a separate citation. For parenthetical citations, if you include more than one citation within the same parentheses, put the citations in alphabetical order (by surname of first author) and separate them with semicolons. Do not change the order of authors for any citation. (In the following two examples, assume each is a first citation.)

- *Example 15: two narrative citations in the same sentence.* Pedersen, Miller, Putcha-Bhagavatula, and Yang (2002) disagreed with the conclusions of Buss and Schmitt (1993).

- *Example 16: two parenthetical citations placed with the same parentheses.* Researchers disagree about whether this study's findings support Sexual Strategies Theory (Buss & Schmitt, 1993; Pedersen, Miller, Putcha-Bhagavatula, & Yang, 2002).

Quotations

A quotation is an exact copy of the language from a source. If you use a quotation, be sure to encase it in quotation marks, cite the source, and include a page number (unless the material comes from an unpaginated source). Quotations are rare in scientific writing. Overuse of quotations may detract from a paper in both style and content. On occasion, instructors may perceive that use of quotations reflects a lack of effort or understanding. If your instructor permits you to use quotations, remember the quotation marks, citation, and page number. If you do not include quotation marks, the material may be considered plagiarized even if the source is cited.

Examples of the format for quotations appear below. These quotes are based on the following original source material:

- *Original source (Fallahi, Wood, Austad, & Fallahi, 2006, p. 174):* "In conclusion, we recommend that instructors of undergraduate psychology courses incorporate a student-friendly didactic model into their course curricula. Our findings demonstrate that the instructors' time and effort is well spent because it improved students' basic writing skills. Writing proficiency is an essential element of effective communication for future psychology clinicians or academicians that requires ongoing training and feedback, and students are unlikely to master it in a single college-level English course."

- *Correct quotation version 1 (illustrates quotation of a complete sentence):* "Writing proficiency is an essential element of effective communication for future psychology clinicians or academicians that requires ongoing training and feedback, and students are unlikely to master it in a single college-level English course" (Fallahi, Wood, Austad, & Fallahi, 2006, p. 174).

Pay attention to where you place the period at the end of the quote. In the original source, the period ends the sentence after the word "course." However, using APA style, for quotes of less than 40 words, the period is placed after the source information is cited, outside the end-parenthesis mark.

Note that quotes of 40 or more words are called block quotes and have a different format. You can find examples of block quotes on pages 155, 183, and 193.

- *Correct quotation version 2 (quotation of a continuous portion of a sentence that starts at the beginning of the sentence):* "Writing proficiency is an essential element of effective communication for future psychology clinicians or academicians" (Fallahi, Wood, Austad, & Fallahi, 2006, p. 174).

Even though this quote ends mid-sentence, you typically would not use ellipsis dots (i.e., "clinicians or academicians . . .") before the end-quote mark. Similarly, as version 3 of a correct quotation shows below, if your quotation does not start at the beginning of an original source sentence (e.g., it starts mid-sentence), you typically would not begin the quote with ellipsis dots. Using APA style, you would insert ellipsis dots in such quotes only if you wished to emphasize to the reader that your quote omits earlier or later portions of the original sentence in the source material.

- *Correct quotation version 3 (quotation of a continuous portion that falls after the beginning of a sentence):* The skill of academic writing "requires ongoing training and feedback, and students are unlikely to master it in a single college-level English course" (Fallahi, Wood, Austad, & Fallahi, 2006, p. 174).
- *Correct quotation version 4 (illustrates use of ellipsis dots when material in the interior of a sentence is omitted):* "Writing proficiency is an essential element of effective communication . . . that requires ongoing training and feedback" (Fallahi, Wood, Austad, & Fallahi, 2006, p. 174).

Paraphrasing

Paraphrasing involves reading something that someone else has written (i.e., the original source) and digesting it, synthesizing it, and otherwise integrating the material with other topically relevant information. It is extremely important that you thoroughly understand the material you incorporate into your manuscripts; otherwise, it will be difficult to paraphrase accurately and integrate the material into a written report without using quotes. By paraphrasing you show accurate understanding of the material by presenting it in your own words. Rather than attempting to paraphrase a single sentence, carefully read an entire paragraph and make sure you understand its meaning. Then present the gist of the paragraph in your own words. Inappropriate paraphrasing can occur in several ways, including:

- "patch writing" or "connect-the-dots" plagiarism: verbatim use of words, phrases, and sentences without quotation marks and without ellipsis dots (three dots with spaces between them) to indicate omitted material;
- "dictionary" or "thesaurus" plagiarism: substitution of synonyms for words in the original, with the original structure and flow of ideas unchanged.

Following are three examples from the same original source (Fallahi, Wood, Austad, & Fallahi, 2006); the first two indicate inappropriate paraphrasing (plagiarism) and the third illustrates acceptable paraphrasing.

- *Plagiarized version 1 (missing quotation marks and ellipsis dots to indicate omitted interior material):* Writing proficiency is an essential element of effective communication that requires ongoing training and feedback (Fallahi, Wood, Austad, & Fallahi, 2006).
- *Plagiarized version 2 (a few words changed, sentence structure not changed):* Writing well is a key component of meaningful communication that entails continuous training and feedback (Fallahi, Wood, Austad, & Fallahi, 2006).
- *Acceptable paraphrase:* Because writing is an important communication skill, instructors should incorporate writing assignments and provide feedback in multiple courses (Fallahi, Wood, Austad, & Fallahi, 2006).

Citing Unread Sources

Instructors may require that you obtain copies of all sources cited in your writing. However, in some instances, instructors may permit you to cite a source mentioned in your textbook (or in another publication) when you are unable to obtain the source itself. In such instances, you must distinguish what you actually read from the item cited (the original source of the information). For example, suppose you were reporting information from a textbook by Richard Griggs that included coverage of an article by Schwarz (1999). Although textbooks are seldom cited in formal APA writing, suppose your instructor permits you to do so without obtaining the primary source article. In that case, the citation would read as follows:

- When constructing a survey, researchers should remember that question wording may influence participants' answers (Schwarz, 1999, as cited in Griggs, 2012).

The unread, original source is not included in the reference list. Before citing a source that you did not personally read, check the criteria for your assignment. Keep in mind that such citations, whether they are from a textbook, another article, an edited book, or a book chapter, are seldom found in published manuscripts.

METHOD SECTION OF A RESEARCH ARTICLE

The Method section provides enough information for readers to replicate the research and to determine if findings are valid and reliable. This section is typically divided into three subsections: Participants, Materials (or Apparatus), and Design and Procedures. Although content of specific subsections may vary somewhat, the paragraphs below highlight typical content, as does the Sample Article.

Participants. This subsection includes information about the number of participants, the overall group to which they belong (e.g., college students, workers at Company ABC, children from a specific day-care center), and basic demographic characteristics (e.g., age, gender, ethnicity). In addition, this section often includes information about recruiting participants (e.g., random sample from registrar's list, convenience sample of adults, sign-up sheet posted in a particular area) and incentive offered to them (e.g., entered in drawing for prize, small amount of money or credit, no incentive). In some manuscripts, information about recruiting and incentive is included in a Design and Procedures subsection instead of in the Participants subsection.

Materials (or **Apparatus**). The description of materials or apparatus provides sufficient detail for readers to replicate the research. For an experiment, the Materials section includes a description of the stimuli, and explicitly identifies differences in materials used for different groups. For a survey, the Materials section includes a description of the overall questionnaire (number of questions asked, type of answer options), and identifies key topics covered. For each existing scale (a series of items measuring the same construct) included in a questionnaire, descriptions often encompass the following information: what it measures, original source/citation, number of items, type of answer options, anchor points and descriptions, sample item, and reliability and validity data.

Design and Procedures. The subsection on Design and Procedures describes how the investigation was conducted. For an experiment, it indicates whether the design was between subjects (each participant was in only one condition) or within subjects (each participant was in all conditions). For a between-subjects design, it clarifies how you assigned participants to conditions. For a within-subjects design, it clarifies how you counterbalanced the order of conditions (systematically changed the order for different participants). It includes information about participants' tasks, the order in which tasks were completed, instructions, and time limits if applicable. For a survey, this section includes information about how questionnaires were distributed and collected, instructions given to participants, and the approximate time it took participants to complete the questionnaire.

RESULTS SECTION OF A RESEARCH ARTICLE

The Results section contains verbal and statistical information describing the findings. Section organization varies according to the types of analysis involved and the research hypotheses. An opening paragraph often includes information about the types of analysis used and clarification of variables analyzed. Next, a Results section typically includes verbal statements (with descriptive statistics) and the results of inferential tests that pertain directly to the hypotheses. For example, in the Sample Article, Miranda et al. (2009) verbally report differences between the two groups, including means and standard deviations, followed by the results of an independent-samples *t* test. For *t* tests, if a difference is statistically significant, your verbal statement should indicate which mean is larger or smaller. If a difference is not significant, your verbal statement should still include the appropriate means and standard deviations, but it should indicate that the difference between them is not statistically significant.

In addition to reporting the results of tests of statistical significance, which provide the probability (*p* value) that a difference or relationship will occur by chance if the null hypothesis is true, APA guidelines indicate that results should also include a measure of effect size. An effect-size statistic indicates the strength of an effect or association. Unlike the results of significance tests, measures of effect size, such as Cohen's *d,* are not dependent on sample size. The results of an inferential test are more likely to be significant if the sample size is large. Thus, particularly if a sample size is large, the results of an inferential test may be statistically significant even when the effect size is small. (See Statistics Modules 9 and 13 for more detail about statistical significance and effect size, respectively.)

When interpreting your results, keep in mind what statistical significance does and does not mean. As we first discussed in Chapter 2, although statistical significance suggests that a difference or association is unlikely to occur by chance, it does *not* provide information on the quality of the research design. In other words, if a confounding variable (a variable other than the independent variable) in an experiment systematically influences a dependent variable, you will be unable to draw a strong conclusion about the effect of the independent variable itself, *even if there is a statistically significant difference between conditions.* It is too late to correct design problems after you have collected data, so be sure to evaluate a design carefully *before* you begin data collection.

If your report includes multiple variables, you might choose to include descriptive statistics in a table rather than in the text of the Results section. A table may make it easier for readers to compare results for different variables. For example, in the Sample Article, Miranda et al. (2009) have used a table to report descriptive statistics for several behavioral measures. Their table illustrates appropriate use of abbreviations, column spanners, and column headings in an APA-style table. It also includes an example of a note (used to provide information about sample size) and a probability note (to indicate statistically significant differences between conditions). Although the use of a table eliminates the need to include the actual descriptive statistics in the Results section, you should still provide a verbal description of the relevant findings and refer readers to the table.

To highlight key findings, Miranda et al. (2009) have also included a figure. In this rather unusual case, the authors have included some of the same data in the figure that appeared in the table. Typically, journals discourage such duplication; however, their use of a figure in this manuscript provides an opportunity to examine the elements of an APA-style figure. Note that both axes are clearly labeled and that the legend is clear. Beneath the figure, there is a clear caption to identify the information conveyed in the graph. As is the case for tables, even though there is no need to duplicate your reporting of the values shown in the figure in your results, you should still provide a verbal description and refer readers to the figure.

As you review your Results section, be sure that you have included data for all findings that you plan to discuss, even those findings that do not relate directly to your hypothesis. To reiterate, data pertaining to all findings that you subsequently discuss must initially be presented in the results. Be sure the information is organized in a manner that facilitates readers' understanding.

DISCUSSION SECTION OF A RESEARCH ARTICLE

The Discussion section serves as an arena for interpreting the results. It often begins with an explicit statement regarding whether results supported the hypotheses. Subsequent discussion positions the results in the context of theoretical perspectives and explains similarities to and differences from prior research on the topic. The discussion also contains information about the limitations of the study (e.g., the generalizability of findings). It includes coverage of the implications of the findings and potential applications of the results. The Discussion section often concludes by indicating how the research extends the existing literature and by offering suggestions for future investigations to address questions raised by the results of the current study. In the Sample Paper, annotations identify the elements of a Discussion section.

THE REFERENCES

The References section contains a listing in a standardized format (with hanging indent) of all the sources that you have read and cited in your paper. Unlike a bibliography, the References section does *not* include any material that you read but do not cite in the manuscript. Alphabetize reference entries by the surname of the first author. Do not change the order of authors for any source. The APA publication manual (American Psychological Association, 2010b) specifies how to construct reference entries for many types of sources, including periodicals, books, technical reports, meetings and conference presentations, dissertations and theses, audiovisual media, and others.

Individual Reference Entries. Authors' names appear in the same order as they appear on the original source because the ordering of names typically reflects the extent to which authors' contributed to the article or book. The components of each reference entry typically include the authors' names, year of publication, title, and publisher-related information. Authors' names include both surnames and initials. For the most common types of references used in scientific writing, the year is shown within parentheses and then followed by a period.

Increasingly, newly published materials carry a digital object identifier (doi), a reference component designed to facilitate location of items on the Internet. It is most often applicable to articles in professional journals rather than other types of sources. When citing a source that has a doi, place the doi at the end of the citation.

The order of reference components varies somewhat. Following are APA style instructions for reference entries to three common sources (journal article, book, and chapter in an edited book) and to an online resource. Additional examples of references to journal articles, books, and an online newsletter are included in the Sample Paper.

Citing a Journal Article. Include the following components in the following order: author(s) name(s), year, article title, journal name, volume number, page numbers and doi (digital object identifier). As illustrated, when there are multiple authors, an ampersand (&) is used before the name of the last author. The date and title are also followed by a period. In the title, only proper nouns, the first word, and the first word after a colon (if there is one) are capitalized. The journal name, followed by a comma and a volume number (also followed by a comma) are both italicized, but the page numbers are not. The letters *doi* are not capitalized. They are followed by a colon and then the actual doi number. There is no space before or after the colon, and there is no period after the doi number. Here is an example of a reference to a journal article.

Luttrell, V. R., Bufkin, J. L., Eastman, V. J., & Miller, R. (2010). Teaching scientific writing: Measuring student learning in an intensive APA skills course. *Teaching of Psychology, 37*, 193–195. doi:10.1080/00986283.2010.488531

If a publication (e.g., article, book, chapter) has eight or more authors, APA style follows a somewhat unusual guideline for the citation in the References section. The citation should include the surnames and initials for the first six authors followed by an ellipsis (three periods with a space between them . . .) and the surname and initials of the last author. Note that no ampersand is used. Here is an example.

Siegler, R. S., Duncan, G. J., Davis-Kean, P. E., Duckworth, K., Claessens, A., Engel, M., . . . Chen, M. (2012). Early predictors of high school mathematics achievement. *Psychological Science, 23,* 691–697. doi:10.1177/0956797612440101

Finally, if you accessed an article online (rather than, say, going to a library and reading a print copy), and if a doi is not available, include the words "Retrieved from" followed by the URL (website address) of the journal's publisher. In the References section of the Sample Paper, the citation for Chiou (2006) illustrates use of a journal URL when a doi has not been assigned.

Citing a Book. Include the following components in the following order: author(s) name(s), year, book title, publisher's location, and publisher's name. Information about the publisher is found in database records and on one of the first pages in a book. The title of the book is italicized and follows the same capitalization rules used for article titles. Regarding publisher location (city and state, if within the United States), standard (postal code) abbreviations are used for American states (e.g., GA for Georgia). If the location is outside the United States, provide the city and country of the publisher's location (e.g., Toronto, Canada). If the publisher is an association or a press, as in the example below, the publisher's name should be complete; however, if the publisher's name ends with *Publishers, Company,* or *Incorporated,* these words are not included in the citation.

Graham, S., MacArthur, C. A., & Fitzgerald, J. (2007). *Best practices in writing instruction: Solving problems in the teaching of literacy.* New York, NY: Guilford Press.

Citing a Chapter in an Edited Book. Include the following components in the following order: author(s) name(s), year, chapter title, editors' names, book title, pages for chapter, publisher's location, and publisher's name. For editors' names, first and middle initials precede surnames. The editors' names are followed by the abbreviation *Eds.* within parentheses and followed by a comma. The title of the book is italicized and follows the same capitalization rules used for article titles. Unlike a reference to an article, the abbreviation *pp.* precedes the chapter page numbers that are in parentheses. Here are two examples of a reference for a chapter in an edited book. Note that the second example follows the format for eight or more authors, and that this particular chapter had a doi number.

Schmidt, M. E., & Dunn, D. S. (2007). Teaching writing in statistics and research methods: Addressing objectives, intensive issues, and style. In D. S. Dunn, R. A. Smith, & B. Beins (Eds.), *Best practices for teaching statistics and research methods in the behavioral sciences* (pp. 257–273). Mahwah, NJ: Erlbaum.

Rijlaarsdam, G., Van den Bergh, H., Couzijn, M., Janssen, T., Braaksma, M., Tillema, M., . . . Raedts, M. (2012). Writing. In K. R. Harris, S. Graham, T. Urdan, A. G. Bus, S. Major, & H. Swanson (Eds.), *APA educational psychology handbook, Vol 3: Application to teaching and learning* (pp. 189–227). Washington, DC: American Psychological Association. doi:10.1037/13275-009

Citing an Online Resource. To cite a webpage or nonperiodical web document, include the following components in the following order: author(s) name(s), year, title of resource, and URL (website address).

Seas, K., & Brizee, A. (2010). *APA style workshop.* Retrieved from http://owl.english.purdue.edu /owl/resource/664/01/

STEP 3. EDITING AND MAKING CORRECTIONS

Learning Objectives

After studying this section, you should be able to:

- Apply the general rules of grammar and punctuation to a writing assignment.
- Edit and correct the first draft of a writing assignment according to APA style.

After the first draft is written, the next step is the initial edit, which involves a review of content, grammar, sentence construction, punctuation, spelling, and use of APA style. It is especially important to check that you have cited all sources accurately and that all articles cited in the body of the report are included in the manuscript. The following sections illuminate general rules that apply to all formal writing and other rules that are specific to APA-style writing.

GRAMMAR AND PUNCTUATION RULES FOR ALL WRITING

The principles outlined in **Table A.5** are applicable to scientific writing across disciplines; they include fundamental rules of formal English grammar and punctuation. In addition, **Table A.6** provides some rules and guidelines pertaining specifically to APA style. After completing the first draft of your manuscript, it is particularly important to leave sufficient time to check these items and correct any errors.

CONCLUDING THOUGHTS ABOUT WRITING A MANUSCRIPT

When you have edited and made corrections in your manuscript, read it over once more—a step often referred to as proofreading—to make sure it reads smoothly with your corrections. Once that is done, you have completed your first writing cycle. Ideally, if you have time, put the manuscript away for a few days. After some time has elapsed, read it again. Some sources even suggest that you print out your report and read it aloud in order to locate possible discontinuities or awkward phrases. Overall, although you may find these guidelines cumbersome at first, continued practice with formal, scientific APA-style writing, complemented by

Table A.5 General Grammar and Punctuation

Grammar Principles

- Construct complete sentences and avoid sentence fragments.
- Use parallel construction.
- Make sure the subject agrees with the verb.
- Make sure a pronoun agrees with the noun to which it refers.
- Make sure a pronoun clearly refers to a specific noun or noun phrase.
- Don't confuse a word for its homonym or another similar word.
- Use apostrophes appropriately.

Punctuation Principles

- Use a comma before a coordinating conjunction that connects two independent clauses.
- Use a comma after introductory phrases, clauses, or words before the main independent clause, but not if the dependent clause follows the main clause.
- Use a comma after each item in a series of three or more items.
- Avoid comma splices.
- Avoid using commas when they are not necessary.
- Use semicolons correctly.
- Use colons correctly.

instructors' feedback and the material included in this chapter, should enable you to develop and enhance your scientific writing skills. In turn, you may approach your writing assignments with greater confidence and with heightened potential for academic success.

Table A.6 Rules and Guidelines Pertaining Specifically to APA Style

APA Style Recommendations		
What to Use	**Clarification**	**Comment**
Economy of expression	Avoid redundancy by using as few words as possible to express your ideas.	Remember that the goal is clarity.
Numerals versus numbers expressed as words	When referring to numbers 10 and above, use numerals except when the number begins a sentence (in which case use words to express the number).	For more details about the use of numbers, see www.apastyle.org.
Active voice	In general, APA style prefers active voice over passive voice.	For example, "The task was performed by the men" is in passive voice, whereas "The men performed the task" is in active voice.
While and *since* to refer only to time	APA guidelines suggest that the word *while* should be used only when referring to events that occur simultaneously.	When not referring to time, use *whereas* or *although* instead of *while*, and *because* or *given that* instead of *since*.

Things to Avoid in APA Style		
What to Avoid	**Clarification**	**Comment**
Using sexist language	Do not use *he* to refer to a person in general.	Unless you are specifically referring to a man or to a woman, it is often easier to work with plurals (with the nouns *participants* or *people*) and the gender-neutral pronoun *they*.
Using informal language and colloquial expressions	Phrases such as *kind of, sort of, lots of, pretty much,* and *write up,* although used in conversation, are not appropriate in formal writing.	Be as precise as possible. Find data that allow you to specify numbers or percentages if possible, or use words such as *many* or *few*.
Using the word *prove*	Seek alternatives such as *support the hypothesis* or *gathered evidence for.*	In psychology, conclusions are generally probabilistic, not certain, which is why we avoid the use of *prove*.
Writing in the second person	In the second person, the reader is addressed as *you*.	For example, rather than stating "it is important for you to exercise regularly," write "it is important for people to exercise regularly."
Using the *words we, us,* or *our* to refer to people in general	Seek alternatives such as *individuals, students, respondents,* or *people.*	*We* or *our* is appropriate only to refer to the opinions or behaviors of the authors if there is more than one author (e.g., "We recruited a convenience sample.").
Using phrases such as "The first article indicated . . . ," "The next article demonstrated . . ."	Use citations such as "Myers (2011) reported."	In a literature review, integrate material topically, using meaningful transitions such as *Similarly, In contrast,* or *Moreover.*
Using titles of articles (except in references) or authors' first names	Use APA-style citations.	
Using *males* and *females* as nouns	Use *men* and *women* as nouns (e.g., 30 men and 30 women).	Use *male* and *female* as adjectives (e.g., Male participants read a scenario.)
Using contractions	Write "have not" rather than "haven't."	

POSTER PRESENTATIONS

Although students are often required to communicate their research results via formal written reports, there are alternative modes for disseminating research findings. In addition to national and regional conferences sponsored by the American Psychological Association and the Association for Psychological Science, individual colleges may sponsor conferences for students to share their work. At these conferences, participants have the opportunity to network with other researchers and to present their work either by giving an oral presentation or by creating a poster.

At conferences, poster sessions typically occur in a large room with posters displayed on large portable dividers arranged in rows. Participants typically stand by their posters as those attending the poster session browse the various offerings. People who are browsing often stop at posters of particular interest to them and ask the presenters to give a brief summary of their work or to answer questions. This section includes information on how to plan, prepare, organize, and present a poster.

POSTER CONTENT

A poster includes only the *highlights* of relevant background information, research design, results, and conclusions of your research. Although organized into sections analogous to those of a research report, a poster contains only the most important information from these sections, often in the form of bullet points. To prominently display and emphasize key results, posters typically contain figures or graphs. A summary of items included in each major section follows.

- In the Background or Introduction section, include the purpose of the research, the elements of the literature review (with appropriately formatted citations) that most directly provide a framework for the research and that provide a rationale for your hypothesis(es), and the hypothesis(es) themselves.

- In the Method section, include the number and key characteristics of participants (although not necessarily in complete sentences), basic information about materials (e.g., stimuli, scales), and your research design (e.g., prospective correlational study, 2×4 mixed-factorial experiment).

- In the Results section, include figures or tables that highlight the key findings accompanied by brief verbal descriptions.

- In the Discussion section, indicate whether results supported your hypothesis(es), a brief explanation of why your results occurred, a connection between your results and prior findings or a theoretical framework, applications or implications of your findings, and, in some cases, a specific direction for future research.
  Posters frequently also include Abstract and References sections.

- For most conferences that include poster presentations, participants submit an abstract for approval prior to the conference. Some conference sponsors provide a printed copy of poster session programs that include abstracts for all accepted posters. In such situations, it may be acceptable not to include an abstract on the actual poster.

- References are sometimes included on a separate handout that participants create and distribute at poster presentations. One reason for this is to conserve space on the poster for information about the research itself. If you do not provide complete references for cited material on the poster, you should include them on a handout to credit the researchers appropriately and to facilitate access to the source material.

POSTER LAYOUT

Posters are typically designed so that a reader can easily follow the flow of the material from top to bottom and left to right. Each section includes a prominent heading, enabling readers to focus quickly on areas of interest. A poster for a research study might include headings for Abstract, Background (ending with hypotheses), Method, Results, and Discussion (or Conclusion). Some sources suggest that the width of a column should be limited to 60 to 80 characters to maximize readability. If a poster includes graphs, they should have clear legend and axis labels. Note that there are a variety of graph types to choose from (e.g., bar, line, pie chart) depending on the nature of the data; however, you are cautioned to avoid three-dimensional graphs because they tend to distort perceptions of the data. In addition to graphs, posters may include other illustrations either to depict stimuli or to attract readers' attention to the topic. **Figure A.2** shows a sample poster.

Poster Template and Printing Options. Although multiple software programs are available for making posters, Microsoft PowerPoint seems to be one of the most frequently used for presentations of psychological research. In fact, prior to starting a poster, you might check to determine if your institution has any templates available, which may already include an appropriate school logo. If your school does not have a template, there are several free templates available online (try searching "PowerPoint presentations").

Printing of PowerPoint or other computer-created posters requires access to a wide-format printer at your institution or at a public printing facility. However, in some cases, budget constraints may limit the feasibility of these alternatives. For example, if poster presentations are incorporated into classes or an end-of-semester activity, the costs of printing multiple posters may be prohibitive. In such instances, you may use a trifold board to present your poster. Regardless of the type of poster you create, guidelines for content and layout are similar. What differs is that for a trifold board, you would prepare your content on separate sheets, print them, and paste or pin them on the board, perhaps using construction paper as a frame for individual sections.

Poster Size and Font: Design Suggestions. Conferences vary in their specific guidelines for poster size. Recommendations are typically available on the conference website, often near the requirements for submitting your abstract for approval. If reviewers accept your poster presentation, be sure to adhere to the guidelines provided; otherwise, your poster may not fit in the allotted space. Typical poster sizes range from 40" × 30" (102 cm × 76 cm) to 48" × 36" (122 cm × 91 cm) to 48" × 96" (122 cm × 244 cm) for large meetings.

Suggestions for font size vary somewhat, but the overall idea is that your poster should be readable from a viewing distance of approximately 3 to 5 feet (.91 to 1.5 meters). The size of the font in the title (perhaps 60 to 80 points) should be larger than that of the section headings (perhaps 36 to 48 points), which in turn should be larger than that of the body text (perhaps 24 to 36 points). Do not try to cram more text into a poster by using small font. It is important to leave ample blank space between blocks of text or illustrations.

Remember, creating a poster does *not* involve copying sections of a paper onto a PowerPoint slide. Rather, you must put forth the effort to consolidate the most important information in a manner that results in a poster that is self-explanatory. "Self-explanatory" means that people will be able to understand the material on your poster without any prior knowledge of a paper that you may have written. An effective poster conveys research findings clearly and concisely and is not cluttered with nonessential information. You can discuss interesting yet nonessential information informally with conference attendees who stop to view your poster.

Preparing a Handout. At many poster sessions, presenters provide handouts so that those viewing the poster have a clear "take-home" message. Often, one side of the handout is simply a replica of the poster. The other side may include an abstract and references. One item you

Figure A.2 **A sample poster.** (Adapted from Fraune, 2013. Reproduced by courtesy of the author.)

Who Can Trust a Machine? Effects of Human Loneliness and Avatar Gaze on Anthropomorphism and Social Trust

Marlena R. Fraune

Beloit College

Introduction

- Robots are now being used in more social situations, making social trust critical for human-computer interaction (HCI) [5]
- Anthropomorphism increases social trust [2,3,5]

Etiquette:
- During interactions, people act politely and expect reciprocation [8]
- "Polite" gazes enhance interactions [1]

Loneliness:
- Feeling lonely increases anthropomorphism [3,7]

Hypothesis:
- Direct gaze will increase anthropomorphism and trust of artificial agents, especially for lonely participants

Predicted results

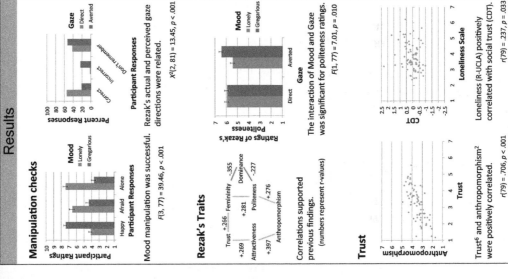

Method

Participants: 81 Beloit college students
- Loneliness/gregariousness was primed with a 3-min video clip (Cast Away or Major League, respectively) [4]
- Introduced computer avatar "Rezak"
- Rezak's gaze was either **direct** or **averted**

Measures:
- Choice-Dilemma Task (CDT) for social trust [5]
  - Modified from risky shift paradigm
  - "Should Ms. K. go to music conservatory or medical school?"
  - Participants' conformity toward Rezak's answer was used to measure social trust
- Rezak's traits (familiarity, femininity, dominance, politeness)
- Trust [6]
- Anthropomorphism (Godspeed Questionnaire) [2]
- Loneliness (R-UCLA) [9]

Results

Manipulation checks

Mood manipulation was successful.
$F(3, 77) = 39.46, p < .001$

Rezak's Traits

Correlations supported previous findings.
(numbers represent r-values)

$r(79) = .706, p < .001$

Rezak's actual and perceived gaze directions were related.
$X^2(2, 81) = 13.45, p < .001$

The interaction of Mood and Gaze was significant for politeness ratings.
$F(1, 77) = 7.01, p = .010$

Trust [6] and anthropomorphism [2] were positively correlated.
$r(79) = .706, p < .001$

Loneliness (R-UCLA) positively correlated with social trust (CDT).
$r(79) = .237, p = .033$

Discussion

- Loneliness and avatar gaze did not impact trust and anthropomorphism
  - Few (40%) consciously noticed Rezak's gaze
  - For minimalistic, static avatars, direction of static gaze does not affect social trust
- Loneliness and avatar gaze affected perceptions of Rezak's etiquette
  - Extends findings of the impact of loneliness on social interaction to HCI
- Survey measures of trust and anthropomorphism correlated
  - Indicate a strong relationship between the two when interacting on a social task
- Loneliness and social trust correlated
  - When lonely, people may be more receptive to social advice, even from artificial agents

Overall Conclusion

- Human loneliness and static avatar gaze do not directly affect anthropomorphism or social trust of the avatar.

References

1. Bee, N. André, E., & Tober, S. (2009). Breaking the Ice in Human-Agent Communication: Eye-Gaze Based Initiation of Contact with an Embodied Conversational Agent Export. *9th International Conference on Intelligent Virtual Agents* (5773), 229-242.
2. Burghart, C. R., Kulic, D., & Croft, E. (2008) Measuring the anthropomorphism, animacy, likeability, perceived intelligence, and perceived safety of robots. *Proceedings of Metrics for Human-Robot Interaction 12*, 37-44.
3. Epley, Nicholas; Waytz, Adam; Cacioppo, John T. (2007). On seeing human: A three-factor theory of anthropomorphism. *Psychological Review 114*(4), 864-886.
4. Epley, N., Akalis, S., Waytz, A., & Cacioppo, J. T. (2008). Creating Social Connection Through Inferential Reproduction Loneliness and Perceived Agency in Gadgets, Gods, and Greyhounds. *Psychological Science, 19*(2), 114-120.
5. Lee, E. J., & Nass, C. (2002). Experimental tests of normative group influence and representation effects in computer-mediated communication: When interacting via computers differs from interacting with computers. *Human Communication Research, 28*(3), 349-381.
6. Mayer, R. C., & Davis, J. H. (1999). The effect of the performance appraisal system on trust for management: A field quasi-experiment. *Journal of Applied Psychology, 84*, 123-136.
7. McConnell, A. R., Brown, C. M., Shoda, T. M., Stayton, L. E., & Martin, C. E. (2011). Friends with benefits: On the positive consequences of pet ownership. *Journal of Personality and Social Psychology, 101*(6), 1239.
8. Reeves, B. & Nass, C. (1996). How people treat computers television and new media like real people and places. *The Media Equation.* Stanford, CA: CSU Publications.
9. Russell, D., Peplau, L. A., & Cutrona, C. E. (1980). The revised UCLA Loneliness Scale: Concurrent and discriminant validity evidence. *Journal of Personality and Social Psychology, 39*(3), 472-480.

Sponsor

Alexis Grosofsky, Ph.D.

should be sure to include is your contact information (name, institution, and email address at a minimum). If questions arise about your research after the conference, clear contact information makes it easy for people to get in touch with you. If your supply of handouts is depleted, post a sheet of paper on which people who want further information can fill in their names and email addresses. After the conference, you can then send them additional materials.

DISCUSSING YOUR POSTER

Most people who attend the poster session will likely walk by without stopping or will stop only briefly to glance at the poster. However, some will stop and look at your poster more closely. Some may ask you to describe your project briefly; thus, you should be prepared to do so, without reading from your poster. Consider the summary as an informal conversation in which you are explaining—preferably in just 1 or 2 minutes—what you have worked on for several months or more. When applicable, point to results or illustrations on your poster to highlight key points. Those who stop to talk are already interested in your topic, so there is no need to be anxious about impressing them. If someone asks a question about your analyses, interpretation, or conclusion, answer it as best you can, but do not be afraid to inquire about alternative possibilities, or acknowledge that the question raises new ideas you haven't thought of. Consider the discussion a chance to elaborate on what you have put on the poster and a learning experience.

Keep in mind that a convention is an excellent setting for networking, meeting others with whom you share interests. Both discussions and handouts can help to expand your circle of contacts with researchers in similar areas. They may even lead to opportunities to collaborate on future research!

KEY TERMS

Research article
(or empirical report) (A-2)

Review article
(or literature review) (A-2)

Plagiarism (A-6)

SAMPLE ARTICLE

On the following pages, you will find a sample article that follows APA style. Read the notes to see each of the features and how they should be presented. Additional sample papers are available at www.apastyle.org.

Running head: EFFECT OF ADULT DISAPPROVAL OF CARTOON VIOLENCE

1

Effect of Adult Disapproval of Cartoon Violence

on Children's Aggressive Play

Priscilla Miranda, Nicholas McCluskey, Benjamin J. Silber,

Christian M. D. von Pohle, and Charlene K. Bainum

Pacific Union College

Annotations (margin callouts):

Page numbering starts on the title page, right justified in the header area.

The running head is left justified. The words *Running head* (followed by a colon, with only the *R* capitalized) appear in the header area for the title page only. The actual running head that appears on all pages is typed in all capital letters in a roman font. The running head should be no more than 50 characters long (including spaces, excluding the label "Running Head:").

Key words (and all words with four or more letters) in the title begin with capital letters. The title, authors' names, and byline (affiliation) are all centered.

Authors' names are on a line or lines double spaced below the title, and affiliation is on the next double-spaced line (if all authors are affiliated with the same institution).

EFFECT OF ADULT DISAPPROVAL OF CARTOON VIOLENCE   2

Abstract

Studies show that children's exposure to violent media increases aggression (Browne & Hamilton-Giachritsis, 2005). Alternatively, in some cases parental involvement suppresses aggression (Singh et al., 2006). We hypothesized that children's behavior would be less aggressive after viewing a violent cartoon with an aggression-disapproving adult (ADA) than with a silent adult (control condition). Second and third graders (6 boys, 10 girls) were randomly assigned to either the ADA or control condition to watch a violent cartoon clip. Afterwards, children played with a variety of toys while observers recorded their behaviors using a 30-s time-sampling method. Children in the ADA condition showed significantly less toy and verbal aggression than those in the control. The parental role in children's media viewing is discussed.

The Abstract section is a single block paragraph. Length limits vary for different journals.

Information from the introduction followed by hypothesis. Some abstracts include the purpose of the study without explicitly stating the hypothesis.

In the Abstract section, *all* numbers are expressed as numerals. Do not begin a sentence with a number in the abstract section. Elsewhere in the manuscript, any number greater than or equal to 10 is also expressed as a numeral (unless it begins a sentence). However, numbers less than 10, with some exceptions, are expressed in words.

Units of time are abbreviated in APA style: min (minute), hr (hour), and s (second).

Information from Method section

In manuscripts submitted for publication, title pages also contain an Author's Note. Guidelines specify that an Author's Note should include departmental affiliation, acknowledgments, and contact information for the author. Author's Notes are usually not required for theses or dissertations.

Information from Results section

Information from Discussion section

A list of keywords can be inserted on the line immediately following the abstract to ensure that your paper can be easily found in databases and through search engines. The word *Keywords* should be indented five spaces from the left margin, italicized, and followed by a colon. Each keyword should be lowercase, and the list should not terminate with a period.

EFFECT OF ADULT DISAPPROVAL OF CARTOON VIOLENCE   3

Effect of Adult Disapproval of Cartoon Violence

on Children's Aggressive Play

In the classic Bobo doll study, Bandura, Ross, and Ross (1961) demonstrated that aggressive behavior modeled by authoritative adults would elicit this same behavior from the observing children. From this study, a virtual cottage industry of research using variations on the theme of aggressive modeling emerged. For example, in a study conducted by O'Carroll, O'Neal, McDonald, and Hori (1977), children who observed a child confederate play with toys aggressively were more likely to act aggressively later in the presence of that child than in the presence of a different child. This suggests that the actual child modeling aggression contains cues for aggression over and above the modeled aggressive behavior. In some way, the presence of this aggressive model affects the amount of later aggression.

Although aggressive modeling has been the primary focus of the Bandura et al. (1961) study, the often-ignored non-aggressive models in that study are central to understanding how to reduce violence. Children who observed non-aggressive models spent significantly more time sitting passively than those exposed to the aggressive models. Also noteworthy is research by Singh et al. (2006) examining autistic children and parenting style. Mothers of autistic children were given training on mindful parenting, which

---

The introduction begins with the title, not the word *Introduction*.

If a citation contains three to five authors, all are included in the first citation in the text, with a comma between them.

There are two spaces between sentences.

Note the comma after the introductory phrase.

If a citation includes more than two authors, only the first author's name (followed by "et al.") is used after the initial citation. "Et al." means "and others." There is a period after "al" (because it is an abbreviation for the Latin word *alia*) but not after "et" (because it is an unabbreviated word).

For this source "et al." is used in the first citation because there are six or more authors.

EFFECT OF ADULT DISAPPROVAL OF CARTOON VIOLENCE   4

consisted of remaining calm and dealing with the actions and attitudes of the child in a nonjudgmental way, as well as considering alternative options for situational responses. This specialized form of intervention, implemented across an extended part of the child's day, was found to have a direct effect on reducing the children's noncompliant behavior. Most relevant to the present study, mindful parenting styles exhibited by the authoritative figures reduced prior aggressive behavior.

However, more studies note the impact parenting styles have on children's increased aggressive behavior. For example, Carroll (1977) reported that children who experienced a physically punitive environment were more likely to display the same type of physically punitive behaviors with others. Similarly, Comstock (2005), who monitored children of abusive parents, found that a major contributing factor to whether these children became abusive themselves as adults was their direct exposure to physical violence in the home. Further, Williams, Conger, and Blozis (2007) focused on adolescents and found that the amount of parental hostility predicted interpersonal aggression among siblings.

Other studies examined whether television would provide the same effect as a live model. In particular, Boyatzis, Matillo, and Nesbitt (1995) found that children exposed to the Power Rangers television show committed

Example of use of citation in narrative

EFFECT OF ADULT DISAPPROVAL OF CARTOON VIOLENCE   5

more aggressive acts per interval than children in the control group. Browne

and Hamilton-Giachritsis (2005) thoroughly investigated 108 studies linking

aggression and media on children and adults. Children who were exposed

to violent scenes in video games, television shows, and movies experienced

aggressive and violent behavior. Browne and Hamilton-Giachritsis concluded

that violent or aggressive media produced short-term effects in individuals'

arousal, emotions, and thoughts, as well as their relative frequency of both

aggressive and fearful behaviors. In short, numerous studies evaluating the

effects of an aggressive model on the subsequent aggressive behavior of the

observing child provide consistent evidence that exposure to violence, whether

live or electronic media, increases violent behavior (Anderson et al., 2003;

Bushman & Anderson, 2001; Huesmann, Moise-Titus, Podolski, & Eron, 2003).

Despite these established findings, television continues to provide

aggressive programming, and parents continue to allow their children to view

these programs. Although parents are often urged to sit down and watch

television with their children in order to explain what is viewed, exactly how

parents help to counteract the impact of media violence and whether their

efforts are effective is unclear. Who has a greater impact as a model? Will

the child be more influenced by the aggressive action figure who obliterates

> Although the year is always required for parenthetical citations, for citations in the narrative, as is this one, the year is used only the first time an article is cited in a particular paragraph.

> Note the correct use of an apostrophe to indicate possession.

> Example of use of ampersand in parenthetical citation

> When multiple citations are included in the same overall parenthetical citation, they are placed in alphabetical order according to the surnames of the first authors.

> Note the use of a comma before a conjunction that connects two independent clauses.

EFFECT OF ADULT DISAPPROVAL OF CARTOON VIOLENCE   6

the bad guy, or the parent who explains to the child that violence is not the best solution?   If a child witnesses aggressive television, but an authority figure models disapproval of violence, how then would the child respond?

Statement of purpose for research

The present study sought to determine how the modeling of aggression disapproval by an adult watching a violent cartoon with a child influences the child's later behavior during separate play activity.   To this end,

Brief description of study to lead in to hypotheses

we examined four types of aggressive behavior as well as the incidence of neutral and prosocial play.   These four aggressive behaviors included verbal aggression, physical aggression, toy aggression, and aggression toward toy.

An abbreviation is initially introduced by putting it in parentheses after the term to which it refers. In subsequent mentions of the concept, only the abbreviation is used. APA guidelines suggest that it is preferable not to introduce an abbreviation for a term that is subsequently used fewer than three times.

It was hypothesized that children who viewed the violent cartoon in the presence of an actively aggression-disapproving adult (ADA) would show

The introduction ends with hypotheses, which identify specific variables and indicate how they are expected to relate to or influence each other.

less of all four types of aggressive behaviors in subsequent play than those who viewed the same cartoon with a silent adult.   Additionally, it was hypothesized that children in the ADA condition would exhibit more prosocial

The heading of the Method section is centered and is in boldface type.

play than those with the silent adult.

Method

This Level 2 heading is flush left and boldface. This Participants section contains basic demographic information about number of participants, approximate age (as inferred from grade), and gender. Ethnicity is often included in the Participants section as well.

Participants

There were 16 participants from the second and third grades (six boys, 10 girls), attending a small private elementary school in northern

Note that numbers less than 10 are expressed in words whereas numbers 10 or greater are expressed in numerals. However, numbers less than 10 are expressed with numerals when they refer to specific units of time, age, scores, points on a scale, and numbers that indicate a position in a series (such as "Table 2").

EFFECT OF ADULT DISAPPROVAL OF CARTOON VIOLENCE   7

California.   Although all children whose parents signed parental con-sent forms were selected as participants, the children signaled their additional consent when asked if they would like to play with toys in another classroom.

Materials

The video clip consisted of the last 5 min of the *Justice League of America* episode entitled *"For the Man Who Has Everything."* The clip was downloaded onto a laptop for portability when connected to the classroom television for viewing.   The toys with which the children were allowed to play in the observation room included several stuffed animals, a set of plastic dinosaurs, several dolls, and a set of Justice League of America action figures: Superman, Batman, Wonder Woman, Bizzaro, and Amazo.   A pre-recorded track providing audio cues for ten 30-s time increments was downloaded onto three iPods for the time-sampling observation.   Observers who were blind to the child's condition used an aggression behavior data recording sheet to mark the occurrence of six categories of behavior.   The following operational definitions were used: a) verbal aggression—name call-ing or yelling at another person; b) physical aggression—touching another person with negative intent to hurt or humiliate; c) toy aggression—using a toy with negative intent toward another person or toy; d) aggression toward

Numerals used to express time are an exception to the general rule regarding the use of words for numbers less than 10. However, when referring to an approximate number of days, months, or years, numbers less than 10 are expressed as words (e.g., "She will return in about six days").

Units of time are abbreviated in APA style: min (minute), hr (hour), and s (second).

Note the appropriate use of commas for items in a series.

Note the use of a colon after an independent clause that is extended with additional information.

Notice the precision with which the authors provide operational defini-tions for recording instances of specific behaviors. Such clarification is a valuable aid to those who may at-tempt to replicate the research or to compare its results to those of other studies.

toy—inflicting violence or harm on the toy; e) prosocial play—playing with or using toys in a positive or helpful way; and, f) neutral play—playing in a way that is neither aggressive nor prosocial (see Appendix).

Procedure

The children were randomly assigned to one of two conditions. The control group was exposed to a 5-min video clip of the *Justice League* cartoon with a silent female adult present. This adult merely sat with the children and watched the cartoon without comment or judgment. In the experimental group, children were exposed to the identical 5-min clip of the *Justice League* cartoon in the presence of the same female adult. However, this time, the female confederate made the following aggression-disapproving remarks after each aggressive act in the cartoon, while watching with the children: "Oh, how terrible!", "Well, that's not very nice!", "They shouldn't do that!", or "He shouldn't hit him like that." Immediately following the video clip, the children were escorted to a nearby classroom for observation while they played with toys. The toys in the room included both neutral toys, such as dolls, plastic dinosaurs, a soccer ball, a football, and stuffed animals unrelated to the cartoon, as well as toys explicitly related to the recently viewed cartoon, like plastic figures of Bizarro, Superman, Wonder Woman, and Batman. In the classroom, four male observers recorded the

In this series of examples, contractions (e.g., *that's, shouldn't*) are used to precisely describe what confederates said. However, in APA style, writers typically avoid the use of contractions.

EFFECT OF ADULT DISAPPROVAL OF CARTOON VIOLENCE   9

occurrence of four types of aggressive behavior, as well as neutral and prosocial play, using a 30-s time sampling format.

Before live observation began, observers trained on a videotape in the laboratory using the aggression behavior data sheet until they attained a minimum of .75 inter-observer reliability. Further, inter-observer reliability of .80 was established on observations of a selected sample of children before actual data collection occurred. Although the children were in the playroom for 10 min, each child was only observed for 5 min. The order that the children entered the playroom determined which observer was assigned to observe their play. The observers were blind to which condition the children were in when in the playroom. As the children entered the playroom, the observers knew which child to observe through a previously established order (e.g., the 1st, 5th, 9th, and 13th child to enter the classroom were assigned to Observer 1).

Results

Initial Analyses

Descriptive Statistics. Table 1 contains means, standard deviations, and comparisons among all study variables. In general, there were significantly fewer instances of aggression in all categories for the experimental group.

EFFECT OF ADULT DISAPPROVAL OF CARTOON VIOLENCE   10

Primary Analyses

The first hypothesis, that children who viewed the violent cartoon in the presence of an ADA would show less of all four types of aggressive behaviors in subsequent play than those who viewed the same cartoon
with a silent adult, was examined by using an independent-samples t test. An
analysis of the data revealed significant differences between the ADA and
control conditions in two categories. Specifically, the children in the ADA
condition demonstrated significantly fewer instances of verbal aggression
($M = 0.25$, $SD = 0.46$) than those in the control condition ($M = 1.38$,
$SD = 1.30$), $t(14) = -2.30$, $p = .04$ (see Figure 1). A measure of effect size
also demonstrated a relationship between adult disapproval of aggression and later incidence of verbal aggression, Cohen's $d = 1.21$. Additionally, children showed less toy aggression in the ADA condition ($M = 0.13$,
$SD = 0.35$), than in the control condition ($M = 1.25$, $SD = 1.04$), $t(14) =$
2.01, $p < .01$. A measure of effect size also demonstrated a relationship
between adult disapproval of aggression and later incidence of toy aggression, Cohen's $d = 1.35$. Although there were no significant differences
found for the other two aggression categories, children showed less physical
aggression in the ADA condition ($M = 0.25$, $SD = 0.46$) compared with the
control ($M = .75$, $SD = 1.17$), $t(14) = 1.13$, $p = .29$.

Note the use of italics for names of statistical tests as well as for specific statistics (e.g., mean and standard deviation).

This sentence describes the results of one type of inferential statistical test, a t test. This type of t test is used to determine whether the difference between two means is likely to be attributable solely to random fluctuation (chance). The authors state that the difference was statistically significant, indicating that it is unlikely that the mean difference in verbal aggression between the ADA and control groups was due solely to chance.

A measure of effect size should be reported for all inferential tests in addition to the probability (p) values. Whereas a significance test indicates the likelihood that a difference is due to chance if the null hypothesis is true, measures of effect size, which are independent of sample size, indicate the magnitude of an effect.

Notice that the exact p value is reported even if a difference is not statistically significant. APA guidelines suggest that effect size should also be reported for differences that are not statistically significant.

EFFECT OF ADULT DISAPPROVAL OF CARTOON VIOLENCE   11

The second hypothesis was that children in the ADA condition would exhibit more prosocial play than those with the silent adult. When analyzed with an independent samples t-test, our second hypothesis was not supported. There was no difference in prosocial play between children in the ADA (M = 1.13, SD = .84) and control conditions (M = 2.25, SD = 2.77), $t(14)$ = 1.10, p = .30.

Discussion

As predicted, less aggressive behavior was exhibited in the ADA condition than in the control condition. In particular, verbal aggression and toy aggression occurred significantly less often. These findings are consistent with previous research by Boyatzis et al. (1995) showing the effects of authoritative modeling of television violence on children's aggression. By introducing an ADA model into our study, we sought to create a similar condition to the home environment. In this way, our adult model would be comparable to the parent or guardian who watches an aggressive television program along with the child and remarks negatively about aggressive actions.

Consequently, if we were to generalize from these findings, even children who watch an aggressive television program with an adult present will later display more aggressive play than will children who watch the same program with an adult who actively disapproved of the aggressive

> The authors explicitly state whether the hypothesis was supported.

> Current findings are placed in the context of existing literature.

> In this paragraph, the authors present implications of the results and discuss key details about the findings.

EFFECT OF ADULT DISAPPROVAL OF CARTOON VIOLENCE   12

actions on the screen. In our study, adult attempts to counteract the aggres-

sive cartoon seemed successful because there was less subsequent aggression

by these children and verbal agreement with the adult's disapproving state-

ments. When the adult made aggression-disapproving comments, several

children audibly agreed, making such statements as "Yeah, he shouldn't do

that, huh?", "Oh wow, that IS terrible!", and "He's not nice, is he?" The

children's agreement could be seen as evidence that the children were aware

that the adult did not approve of the cartoon violence and were influenced

by the adult. In contrast, the children did not say anything while watching

the cartoon violence with a silent adult.

In this paragraph, the authors elaborate further on how the results may apply to behavior and cite the literature to support their speculation.

    Although the children in the ADA condition may have displayed

less aggressive behavior in the short term, we did not measure long-term

effects. They may have been affected by the aggressive programming later,

and especially if they experience repeated viewing of violent media, they may

become desensitized to future violence. A longitudinal study by Huesmann

et al. (2003) has shown this effect. They found that exposure to media

violence in childhood is highly correlated with young adult aggressive

behavior in men and women. This behavior persists even when influences

such as socioeconomic status, intellectual ability, and several parenting fac-

tors are controlled.

EFFECT OF ADULT DISAPPROVAL OF CARTOON VIOLENCE   13

A statement released by six major professional societies declared that over 1,000 studies up to that year pointed to a causal connection between media violence and aggressive behavior among children (Joint Statement, 2000). In addition, the statement indicated that based on over 30 years of research, the public health community concludes that viewing media violence can increase aggressive attitudes and behavior, mostly among children. Anderson et al. (2003) reported that violent television and films increase the likelihood of aggressive and violent behavior both in short-term (aggressive behavior, thoughts, and emotions) and long-term (physical attacks, domestic abuse) situations.

> The information in this paragraph highlights the importance of the research topic.

Perhaps in an ideal world, parents would restrict their children's television viewing to nonviolent educational and entertainment programming and provide alternative activities to enrich their children's development. However, because many children are not monitored while watching violent programs on television, it is important for parents to realize that they can lessen the impact of this exposure through vigilant involvement. Although some parents may counteract the negative influence of media violence through banning violent programs, others are unaware of the negative effects of violent cartoons or prefer to be actively involved in their child's moral development. Ceballo, Ramirez, Hearn, and Maltese (2003) found that increased parental

> Note that no comma is needed after programming because the *and* separates components of a compound predicate rather than two independent clauses.

EFFECT OF ADULT DISAPPROVAL OF CARTOON VIOLENCE   14

monitoring positively affected the psychological health of children who were less exposed to actual violence; however, parental monitoring diminished as exposure to violence increased. Ceballo et al.'s findings further led Singer, Flannery, Guo, Miller, and Leibbrandt (2004) to suggest that monitoring children's television viewing is beneficial and important in reducing violent behavior, anxiety, and fear.

Note the appropriate use of a semicolon between two closely related independent clauses.

It is possible that an even larger effect would have been found had the observation room been a more sterile environment. For example, a number of distractions such as a piano and a whiteboard seemed to promote more neutral play in both conditions. Future studies would need to ensure a more distraction-free room. In addition, the inclusion of another control group that did not watch a violent cartoon, or one with no adult present in the room would provide a comparative baseline for aggression behavior in play.

In this paragraph and the one that follows, the authors discuss limitations of the study and suggest how future research might overcome these limitations.

Although the children were randomly assigned to the ADA and control conditions, the small sample size and uneven gender distribution prevented us from analyzing a gender effect. Future studies should strive for a larger sample size that is balanced for gender.

In this final paragraph, the authors emphasize how the results of the study may be applied to situations in the home.

Despite the limitations of this study, it is clear that exposure to media violence leads to increased aggression in children (Joint Statement, 2000). Parents can oversee the media's exposure to their children by helping

EFFECT OF ADULT DISAPPROVAL OF CARTOON VIOLENCE   15

them to make wise viewing choices when living in today's socio-cultural environment. Rather than becoming censors of the media, today's parents might recognize their limitations and choose critical thinkers over V-chip robots. Parents can teach, discuss, and argue as they purvey the values of critical thinking to their children. Yet, parents who allow their children to watch media violence either in their home or at the neighbor's must understand that distracted or passive adult supervision is not sufficient to counteract exposure to aggressive media content. Rather, active parental disapproval of media violence and family dialogue are needed to lessen children's subsequent aggressive behavior.

The concluding sentence includes the take-home message from the research.

EFFECT OF ADULT DISAPPROVAL OF CARTOON VIOLENCE   16

References

- Every reference included in the article is listed in the References section.
- References are listed in alphabetical order by the surname of the first author.
- Citations use a hanging indentation.
- There is only a single space after the period that follows each reference element (e.g., year, title).
- If there is more than one author, an ampersand (preceded by a comma) is used before the last author's surname.

American Academy of Pediatrics, American Academy of Child

and Adolescent Psychiatry, American Psychological Associa-

tion, American Medical Association, American Association

of Family Physicians, & American Psychiatric Association.

(2000, July 26). *Joint Statement on the Impact of Entertain-*

ment Violence on Children, Congressional Public Health

Summit. Retrieved March 4, 2009, from http://www.aap.org

/advocacy/releases/jstmtevc.htm

If a journal article has more than seven authors, include the first six, followed by three ellipses, and then the last author. This article has eight authors. Thus, the name of the seventh author (Neil M. Malamuth) is not included. If the article had 12 authors, the names of seventh through 11th authors would be omitted.

Anderson, C. A., Berkowitz, L., Donnerstein, E., Huesmann,

L. R., Johnson, J., Linz, D., ... Wartella, E. (2003). The influ-

ence of media violence on youth. *Psychological Science in*

the Public Interest, 4, 81–110. doi:10.1111/j.1529-1006.2003

.pspi_1433.x

This citation is an example of a reference to a journal article with between two and seven authors, the most common type of source in a typical article.
- Note that for each author, the surname is listed first, then the initials of the first name. If the author uses a middle name, include the middle name initial as well.
- Note that in the title of the journal, each major word is capitalized.
- In contrast, note that in the title and subtitle of the article, only the first word is capitalized. Other words in the title are lowercase unless they are proper nouns.
- Note the order of reference elements, the use of capitalization in the article compared to the journal title, and the use of italics for the journal name and volume number (but *not* for the article title or page numbers).
- There is a period after the page numbers, but not after the doi (digital object identifier) or a URL.

Bandura, A., Ross, D., & Ross, S. A. (1961). Transmission of aggres-

sion through imitation of aggressive models. *Journal of Abnor-*

mal and Social Psychology, 63, 575–582. doi:10.1037/h0045925

EFFECT OF ADULT DISAPPROVAL OF CARTOON VIOLENCE   17

Boyatzis, C. J., Matillo, G. M., & Nesbitt, K. M. (1995). Effects of

'The Mighty Morphin' Power Rangers' on children's aggression

with peers. *Child Study Journal, 25,* 45–56.

Browne, K. D., & Hamilton-Giachritsis, C. (2005). The influence

of violent media on children and adolescents: A public-health

approach. *Journal of Child Psychology and Psychiatry, 365,*

702–710.

Bushman, B. J., & Anderson, C. A. (2001). Media violence and the

American public: Scientific facts versus media misinformation.

American Psychologist, 56, 477–489. doi:10.1037

/0003-066X.56.6-7.477

Carroll, J. C. (1977). The intergenerational transmission of family

violence: The long-term effects of aggressive behavior. *Aggres-

sive Behavior, 3,* 289–299. doi:10.1002/1098-2337(1977)3:3

[289::AID-AB2480030310]3.0.CO;2-O

Ceballo, R., Ramirez, C., Hearn, K. D., & Maltese, K. L. (2003).

Community violence and children's psychological well-being:

Does parental monitoring matter? *Journal of Clinical Child and

Adolescent Psychology, 32,* 586–592. doi:10.1207/S15374424

-JCCP3204_11

Be sure to include a middle initial if one is known.

EFFECT OF ADULT DISAPPROVAL OF CARTOON VIOLENCE   18

Comstock, G. (2005). Commentary and discussion on imitation and culture: Media violence and aggression, properly considered. In S. Hurley & N. Chater (Eds.), *Perspectives on imitation: From neuroscience to social science: Vol. 2: Imitation, human development, and culture* (pp. 371–380). Boston, MA: MIT Press.

Congressional Research Service. (1995, May). *Television violence: A survey of selected social science research linking violent program viewing with aggression in children and society* (CRS Rep. No. 95-593). Retrieved April 15, 2009, from Congressional Research Service via Lexis-Nexis Access: http://www.lexisnexis .com:80/us/lnacademic/results/docview/docview.doc

Huesmann, L. R., Moise-Titus, J., Podolski, C., & Eron, L. D. (2003). Longitudinal relations between children's exposure to TV violence and their aggressive and violent behavior in young adulthood: 1977–1992. *Developmental Psychology, 39,* 201–221. doi:10.1037/0012-1649.39.2.201

O'Carroll, M., O'Neal E., McDonald P., & Hori, R. (1977). Influence upon imitative aggression of an imitating peer. *Journal of Social Psychology, 101,* 313–314. doi:10.1080/00224545.1977.9924024

For books and book chapters, include city and state (or city and country, if place of publication is not in the United States). Note that book titles follow the same capitalization rules as article titles, not journal titles.

Singer, M. I., Flannery, D. J., Guo, S., Miller, D., & Leibbrandt,

S. (2004). Exposure to violence, parental monitoring, and televi-

sion viewing as contributors to children's psychological trauma.

Journal of Community Psychology, 32, 489–504. doi:10.1002

/jcop.20015

Singh, N. N., Lancioni, G. E., Winton, A. S., Fisher, B. C., Wahler,

R. G., McAleavey, K., & Sabaawi, M. (2006). Mindful parenting

decreases aggression, noncompliance, and self-injury in children

with autism. *Journal of Emotional & Behavioral Disorders, 14,*

169–177. doi:10.1177/0145445507300924

Williams, S. T., Conger, K. J., & Blozis, S. A. (2007). The develop-

ment of interpersonal aggression during adolescence: The impor-

tance of parents, siblings, and family economics. *Child Develop-

ment, 78,* 1526–1542. doi:10.1111/j.1467-8624.2007.01081.x

In most journals, pages are numbered consecutively across different issues. For example, if the January issue of a journal (Issue 1) ended on page 132, the February issue (Issue 2) would begin on page 133. Some journals, however, begin each new issue by numbering the first page as "1." If you reference an article from such a journal, you need to include the *issue number* directly after the *volume number*. The issue number is placed inside parentheses, the number and parentheses are not italicized, and there is no space between them and the volume number. Because none of the references in this Sample Paper come from such a journal, an example is provided below.

Sokol, M. B. (1992). Time boundaries, task commitment, and the illusion of group immortality. *Consulting Psychology Journal: Practice and Research, 44*(3), 28–32. doi:10.1037/ h009472

EFFECT OF ADULT DISAPPROVAL OF CARTOON VIOLENCE   20

Table 1

Means and Standard Deviations of Aggressive, Neutral, and Prosocial Incidents per 5 Min Interval Between ADA and Control Groups

Behavior	ADA[a]		Control[a]	
	M	*SD*	*M*	*SD*
Verbal*	.25	.46	1.38	1.30
Physical	.25	.46	.75	1.17
Toy*	.13	.35	1.25	1.04
Towards Toy	.13	.35	.25	.71
Neutral*	9.50	1.07	7.88	.99
Prosocial	1.13	.84	2.25	2.77

[a]*n* = 8 for each condition.

*p < .05

Annotations:

Table title is italicized.

The headings ADA and Control are called column spanners because they apply to two or more columns in the table.

Be sure to include a stub head that appropriately describes the items in the first column of the table.

Include column headings for each column.

This is an example of a specific note.

Asterisks are used to indicate probability notes. APA guidelines suggest, if possible, including exact probability values in a table, rather than using a probability note.

EFFECT OF ADULT DISAPPROVAL OF CARTOON VIOLENCE   21

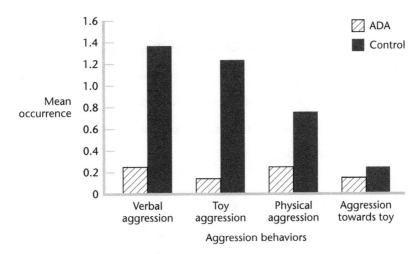

Figure 1. Mean occurrence of aggression behaviors observed for ADA and control conditions.

Figures includes clearly labeled axes and a legend.

The figure number (italicized) and caption (not italicized) are positioned below the figure.

> If a manuscript has more than one appendix, the first one is labeled "Appendix A," the second "Appendix B," etc. Because this manuscript has only one appendix, it is simply labeled "Appendix."

Appendix

Aggressive Behavior Time Sampling Data Sheet

Check the set of behaviors as to its occurrence in a 30-s time interval. If one or more of the behaviors listed below occur during that time interval, check the box. You are not concerned with the number of times it occurs in the interval, only if it did or did not occur.

Operational definitions:

Verbal aggression – name-calling or yelling at another person

Physical aggression – touching another person with negative intent, to hurt or humiliate

Toy aggression – using toy with negative intent toward another person or toy

Aggression toward toy – inflicting violence or harm on toy

Neutral play – neither aggressive nor prosocial play

Prosocial play – playing or using toy in a positive or helpful way

Gender_____ Age/Grade_____ Condition_____

Time Interval/Behavior	1	2	3	4	5	6	7	8	9	10
Verbal Aggression										
Physical Aggression										
Toy Aggression										
Aggression Toward Toy										
Neutral Play										
Prosocial										

B

AMERICAN PSYCHOLOGICAL ASSOCIATION ETHICAL PRINCIPLES OF PSYCHOLOGISTS AND CODE OF CONDUCT

In this Appendix we have reproduced the portions of the APA code of ethics that most directly pertain to the process of conducting research.

GENERAL PRINCIPLES

This section consists of General Principles. General Principles, as opposed to Ethical Standards, are aspirational in nature. Their intent is to guide and inspire psychologists toward the very highest ethical ideals of the profession. General Principles, in contrast to Ethical Standards, do not represent obligations and should not form the basis for imposing sanctions. Relying upon General Principles for either of these reasons distorts both their meaning and purpose.

PRINCIPLE A: BENEFICENCE AND NONMALEFICENCE

Psychologists strive to benefit those with whom they work and take care to do no harm. In their professional actions, psychologists seek to safeguard the welfare and rights of those with whom they interact professionally and other affected persons, and the welfare of animal subjects of research. When conflicts occur among psychologists' obligations or concerns, they attempt to resolve these conflicts in a responsible fashion that avoids or minimizes harm. Because psychologists' scientific and professional judgments and actions may affect the lives of others, they are alert to and guard against personal, financial, social, organizational, or political factors that might lead to misuse of their influence. Psychologists strive to be aware of the possible effect of their own physical and mental health on their ability to help those with whom they work.

PRINCIPLE B: FIDELITY AND RESPONSIBILITY

Psychologists establish relationships of trust with those with whom they work. They are aware of their professional and scientific responsibilities to society and to the specific communities in which they work. Psychologists uphold professional standards of conduct, clarify their professional roles and obligations, accept appropriate responsibility for their behavior, and seek to manage conflicts of interest that could lead to exploitation or harm. Psychologists consult with, refer to, or cooperate with other professionals and institutions to the extent needed to serve the best interests of those with whom they work. They are concerned about the ethical compliance of their colleagues' scientific and professional conduct. Psychologists strive to contribute a portion of their professional time for little or no compensation or personal advantage.

PRINCIPLE C: INTEGRITY

Psychologists seek to promote accuracy, honesty, and truthfulness in the science, teaching, and practice of psychology. In these activities psychologists do not steal, cheat, or engage in fraud, subterfuge, or intentional misrepresentation of fact. Psychologists strive to keep their promises and to avoid unwise or unclear commitments. In situations in which deception may be ethically justifiable to maximize benefits and minimize harm, psychologists have a serious obligation to consider the need for, the possible consequences of, and their responsibility to correct any resulting mistrust or other harmful effects that arise from the use of such techniques.

PRINCIPLE D: JUSTICE

Psychologists recognize that fairness and justice entitle all persons to access to and benefit from the contributions of psychology and to equal quality in the processes, procedures, and services being conducted by psychologists. Psychologists exercise reasonable judgment and take precautions to ensure that their potential biases, the boundaries of their competence, and the limitations of their expertise do not lead to or condone unjust practices.

PRINCIPLE E: RESPECT FOR PEOPLE'S RIGHTS AND DIGNITY

Psychologists respect the dignity and worth of all people, and the rights of individuals to privacy, confidentiality, and self-determination. Psychologists are aware that special safeguards may be necessary to protect the rights and welfare of persons or communities whose vulnerabilities impair autonomous decision making. Psychologists are aware of and respect cultural, individual, and role differences, including those based on age, gender, gender identity, race, ethnicity, culture, national origin, religion, sexual orientation, disability, language, and socioeconomic status, and consider these factors when working with members of such groups. Psychologists try to eliminate the effect on their work of biases based on those factors, and they do not knowingly participate in or condone activities of others based upon such prejudices.

STANDARD 3: HUMAN RELATIONS

3.04 AVOIDING HARM

Psychologists take reasonable steps to avoid harming their clients/patients, students, supervisees, research participants, organizational clients, and others with whom they work, and to minimize harm where it is foreseeable and unavoidable.

3.10 INFORMED CONSENT

(a) When psychologists conduct research or provide assessment, therapy, counseling, or consulting services in person or via electronic transmission or other forms of communication, they obtain the informed consent of the individual or individuals using language that is reasonably understandable to that person or persons except when conducting such activities without consent is mandated by law or governmental regulation or as otherwise provided in this Ethics Code. (See also Standards 8.02, Informed Consent to Research; 9.03, Informed Consent in Assessments; and 10.01, Informed Consent to Therapy.)

(b) For persons who are legally incapable of giving informed consent, psychologists nevertheless (1) provide an appropriate explanation, (2) seek the individual's assent, (3) consider such persons' preferences and best interests, and (4) obtain appropriate permission from a legally authorized person, if such substitute consent is permitted or required by law. When consent by a legally authorized person is not permitted or required by law, psychologists take reasonable steps to protect the individual's rights and welfare.

(c) When psychological services are court ordered or otherwise mandated, psychologists inform the individual of the nature of the anticipated services, including whether the services are court ordered or mandated and any limits of confidentiality, before proceeding.

(d) Psychologists appropriately document written or oral consent, permission, and assent. (See also Standards 8.02, Informed Consent to Research; 9.03, Informed Consent in Assessments; and 10.01, Informed Consent to Therapy.)

STANDARD 4: PRIVACY AND CONFIDENTIALITY

4.01 MAINTAINING CONFIDENTIALITY

Psychologists have a primary obligation and take reasonable precautions to protect confidential information obtained through or stored in any medium, recognizing that the extent and limits of confidentiality may be regulated by law or established by institutional rules or professional or scientific relationship. (See also Standard 2.05, Delegation of Work to Others.)

4.02 DISCUSSING THE LIMITS OF CONFIDENTIALITY

(a) Psychologists discuss with persons (including, to the extent feasible, persons who are legally incapable of giving informed consent and their legal representatives) and organizations with whom they establish a scientific or professional relationship (1) the relevant limits of confidentiality and (2) the foreseeable uses of the information generated through their psychological activities. (See also Standard 3.10, Informed Consent.)

(b) Unless it is not feasible or is contraindicated, the discussion of confidentiality occurs at the outset of the relationship and thereafter as new circumstances may warrant.

(c) Psychologists who offer services, products, or information via electronic transmission inform clients/patients of the risks to privacy and limits of confidentiality.

4.03 RECORDING

Before recording the voices or images of individuals to whom they provide services, psychologists obtain permission from all such persons or their legal representatives. (See also Standards 8.03, Informed Consent for Recording Voices and Images in Research; 8.05, Dispensing with Informed Consent for Research; and 8.07, Deception in Research.)

STANDARD 5: ADVERTISING AND OTHER PUBLIC STATEMENTS

5.01 AVOIDANCE OF FALSE OR DECEPTIVE STATEMENTS

(a) Public statements include but are not limited to paid or unpaid advertising, product endorsements, grant applications, licensing applications, other credentialing applications, brochures, printed matter, directory listings, personal resumes or curricula vitae, or comments for use in media such as print or electronic transmission, statements in legal proceedings, lectures and public oral presentations, and published materials. Psychologists do not knowingly make public statements that are false, deceptive, or fraudulent concerning their research, practice, or other work activities or those of persons or organizations with which they are affiliated.

(b) Psychologists do not make false, deceptive, or fraudulent statements concerning (1) their training, experience, or competence; (2) their academic degrees; (3) their credentials; (4) their institutional or association affiliations; (5) their services; (6) the scientific or clinical basis for, or results or degree of success of, their services; (7) their fees; or (8) their publications or research findings.

(c) Psychologists claim degrees as credentials for their health services only if those degrees (1) were earned from a regionally accredited educational institution or (2) were the basis for psychology licensure by the state in which they practice.

STANDARD 8: RESEARCH AND PUBLICATION

8.01 INSTITUTIONAL APPROVAL

When institutional approval is required, psychologists provide accurate information about their research proposals and obtain approval prior to conducting the research. They conduct the research in accordance with the approved research protocol.

8.02 INFORMED CONSENT TO RESEARCH

(a) When obtaining informed consent as required in Standard 3.10, Informed Consent, psychologists inform participants about (1) the purpose of the research, expected duration, and procedures; (2) their right to decline to participate and to withdraw from the research once participation has begun; (3) the foreseeable consequences of declining or withdrawing; (4) reasonably foreseeable factors that may be expected to influence their willingness to participate such as potential risks, discomfort, or adverse effects; (5) any prospective research benefits; (6) limits of confidentiality; (7) incentives for participation; and (8) whom to contact for questions about the research and research participants' rights. They provide opportunity for the prospective participants to ask questions and receive answers. (See also Standards 8.03, Informed Consent for Recording Voices and Images in Research; 8.05, Dispensing with Informed Consent for Research; and 8.07, Deception in Research.)

(b) Psychologists conducting intervention research involving the use of experimental treatments clarify to participants at the outset of the research (1) the experimental nature of the treatment; (2) the services that will or will not be available to the control group(s) if appropriate; (3) the means by which assignment to treatment and control groups will be made; (4) available treatment alternatives if an individual does not wish to participate in the research or wishes to withdraw once a study has begun; and (5) compensation for or monetary costs of participating including, if appropriate, whether reimbursement from the participant or a third-party payor will be sought. (See also Standard 8.02a, Informed Consent to Research.)

8.03 INFORMED CONSENT FOR RECORDING VOICES AND IMAGES IN RESEARCH

Psychologists obtain informed consent from research participants prior to recording their voices or images for data collection unless (1) the research consists solely of naturalistic observations in public places, and it is not anticipated that the recording will be used in a manner that could cause personal identification or harm, or (2) the research design includes deception, and consent for the use of the recording is obtained during debriefing. (See also Standard 8.07, Deception in Research.)

8.04 CLIENT/PATIENT, STUDENT, AND SUBORDINATE RESEARCH PARTICIPANTS

(a) When psychologists conduct research with clients/patients, students, or subordinates as participants, psychologists take steps to protect the prospective participants from adverse consequences of declining or withdrawing from participation.

(b) When research participation is a course requirement or an opportunity for extra credit, the prospective participant is given the choice of equitable alternative activities.

8.05 DISPENSING WITH INFORMED CONSENT FOR RESEARCH

Psychologists may dispense with informed consent only (1) where research would not reasonably be assumed to create distress or harm and involves (a) the study of normal educational practices, curricula, or classroom management methods conducted in educational settings; (b) only anonymous questionnaires, naturalistic observations, or archival research for which disclosure of responses would not place participants at risk of criminal or civil liability or damage their financial standing, employability, or reputation, and confidentiality is protected; or (c) the study of factors related to job or organization effectiveness conducted in organizational settings for which there is no risk to participants' employability, and confidentiality is protected or (2) where otherwise permitted by law or federal or institutional regulations.

8.06 OFFERING INDUCEMENTS FOR RESEARCH PARTICIPATION

(a) Psychologists make reasonable efforts to avoid offering excessive or inappropriate financial or other inducements for research participation when such inducements are likely to coerce participation.

(b) When offering professional services as an inducement for research participation, psychologists clarify the nature of the services, as well as the risks, obligations, and limitations. (See also Standard 6.05, Barter with Clients/Patients.)

8.07 DECEPTION IN RESEARCH

(a) Psychologists do not conduct a study involving deception unless they have determined that the use of deceptive techniques is justified by the study's significant prospective scientific, educational, or applied value and that effective nondeceptive alternative procedures are not feasible.

(b) Psychologists do not deceive prospective participants about research that is reasonably expected to cause physical pain or severe emotional distress.

(c) Psychologists explain any deception that is an integral feature of the design and conduct of an experiment to participants as early as is feasible, preferably at the conclusion of their participation, but no later than at the conclusion of the data collection, and permit participants to withdraw their data. (See also Standard 8.08, Debriefing.)

8.08 DEBRIEFING

(a) Psychologists provide a prompt opportunity for participants to obtain appropriate information about the nature, results, and conclusions of the research, and they take reasonable steps to correct any misconceptions that participants may have of which the psychologists are aware.

(b) If scientific or humane values justify delaying or withholding this information, psychologists take reasonable measures to reduce the risk of harm.

(c) When psychologists become aware that research procedures have harmed a participant, they take reasonable steps to minimize the harm.

8.09 HUMANE CARE AND USE OF ANIMALS IN RESEARCH

(a) Psychologists acquire, care for, use, and dispose of animals in compliance with current federal, state, and local laws and regulations, and with professional standards.

(b) Psychologists trained in research methods and experienced in the care of laboratory animals supervise all procedures involving animals and are responsible for ensuring appropriate consideration of their comfort, health, and humane treatment.

(c) Psychologists ensure that all individuals under their supervision who are using animals have received instruction in research methods and in the care, maintenance, and handling of the species being used, to the extent appropriate to their role. (See also Standard 2.05, Delegation of Work to Others.)

(d) Psychologists make reasonable efforts to minimize the discomfort, infection, illness, and pain of animal subjects.

(e) Psychologists use a procedure subjecting animals to pain, stress, or privation only when an alternative procedure is unavailable and the goal is justified by its prospective scientific, educational, or applied value.

(f) Psychologists perform surgical procedures under appropriate anesthesia and follow techniques to avoid infection and minimize pain during and after surgery.

(g) When it is appropriate that an animal's life be terminated, psychologists proceed rapidly, with an effort to minimize pain and in accordance with accepted procedures.

8.10 REPORTING RESEARCH RESULTS

(a) Psychologists do not fabricate data. (See also Standard 5.01a, Avoidance of False or Deceptive Statements.)

(b) If psychologists discover significant errors in their published data, they take reasonable steps to correct such errors in a correction, retraction, erratum, or other appropriate publication means.

8.11 PLAGIARISM

Psychologists do not present portions of another's work or data as their own, even if the other work or data source is cited occasionally.

8.12 PUBLICATION CREDIT

(a) Psychologists take responsibility and credit, including authorship credit, only for work they have actually performed or to which they have substantially contributed. (See also Standard 8.12b, Publication Credit.)

(b) Principal authorship and other publication credits accurately reflect the relative scientific or professional contributions of the individuals involved, regardless of their relative status. Mere possession of an institutional position, such as department chair, does not justify authorship credit. Minor contributions to the research or to the writing for publications are acknowledged appropriately, such as in footnotes or in an introductory statement.

(c) Except under exceptional circumstances, a student is listed as principal author on any multiple-authored article that is substantially based on the student's doctoral dissertation. Faculty advisors discuss publication credit with students as early as feasible and throughout the research and publication process as appropriate. (See also Standard 8.12b, Publication Credit.)

8.13 DUPLICATE PUBLICATION OF DATA

Psychologists do not publish, as original data, data that have been previously published. This does not preclude republishing data when they are accompanied by proper acknowledgment.

8.14 SHARING RESEARCH DATA FOR VERIFICATION

(a) After research results are published, psychologists do not withhold the data on which their conclusions are based from other competent professionals who seek to verify the substantive claims through reanalysis and who intend to use such data only for that purpose, provided that the confidentiality of the participants can be protected and unless legal rights concerning proprietary data preclude their release. This does not preclude psychologists from requiring that such individuals or groups be responsible for costs associated with the provision of such information.

(b) Psychologists who request data from other psychologists to verify the substantive claims through reanalysis may use shared data only for the declared purpose. Requesting psychologists obtain prior written agreement for all other uses of the data.

8.15 REVIEWERS

Psychologists who review material submitted for presentation, publication, grant, or research proposal review respect the confidentiality of and the proprietary rights in such information of those who submitted it.

Source: American Psychological Association (2010). *Ethical principles of psychologists and code of conduct (2002, Amended June 1, 2010)*. Retrieved from http://www.apa.org/ethics/code/principles.pdf

STATISTICAL TABLES

Table C.1 The Pearson Correlation Coefficient

For a Pearson correlation to be considered statistically significant at a probability level of .05 or .01, the absolute value of r must be equal to or greater than the value shown in the row that corresponds to the appropriate number of degrees of freedom ($df = N - 2$). Values are shown for two-tailed and one-tailed tests.

	LEVEL OF SIGNIFICANCE FOR ONE-TAILED TEST p level			LEVEL OF SIGNIFICANCE FOR TWO-TAILED TEST p level	
$df = N - 2$	.05	.01	$df = N - 2$	.05	.01
1	.988	.9995	1	.997	.9999
2	.900	.980	2	.950	.990
3	.805	.934	3	.878	.959
4	.729	.882	4	.811	.917
5	.669	.833	5	.754	.874
6	.622	.789	6	.707	.834
7	.582	.750	7	.666	.798
8	.549	.716	8	.632	.765
9	.521	.685	9	.602	.735
10	.497	.658	10	.576	.708
11	.476	.634	11	.553	.684
12	.458	.612	12	.532	.661
13	.441	.592	13	.514	.641
14	.426	.574	14	.497	.623
15	.412	.558	15	.482	.606
16	.400	.542	16	.468	.590
17	.389	.528	17	.456	.575
18	.378	.516	18	.444	.561
19	.369	.503	19	.433	.549
20	.360	.492	20	.423	.537
21	.352	.482	21	.413	.526
22	.344	.472	22	.404	.515
23	.337	.462	23	.396	.505
24	.330	.453	24	.388	.496
25	.323	.445	25	.381	.487
26	.317	.437	26	.374	.479
27	.311	.430	27	.367	.471
28	.306	.423	28	.361	.463
29	.301	.416	29	.355	.456
30	.296	.409	30	.349	.449
35	.275	.381	35	.325	.418
40	.257	.358	40	.304	.393
45	.243	.338	45	.288	.372
50	.231	.322	50	.273	.354
60	.211	.295	60	.250	.325
70	.195	.274	70	.232	.302
80	.183	.256	80	.217	.283
90	.173	.242	90	.205	.267
100	.164	.230	100	.195	.254

Data from Nolan and Heinzen, 2012.

Table C.2 The Standard Normal Distribution (*z* Distribution)

Each entry in the table represents the proportion of area under the standard Normal curve that falls to the left of a particular *z* score. To determine the proportion of area that falls to the right of that *z* value, subtract the table entry from 1.0000. Consider Amy's *z* score of −0.45 on her exam (see p. 433). First, in the leftmost column, scroll down to the row for the blue *z* value of −0.4. Next, across the top row of blue *z* values, find the column for the value of 0.05. The intersection of this row and column represents a *z* score of −0.45. The table entry is .3264. Thus, 32.64% of the area in a standard Normal curve falls to the left of a *z* score of −0.45. The proportion of area to the right of this *z* score is 1.00 − .3264 = .6736 (i.e., 67.36%).

Z	0.00	0.01	0.02	0.03	0.04	0.05	0.06	0.07	0.08	0.09
−3.4	0.0003	0.0003	0.0003	0.0003	0.0003	0.0003	0.0003	0.0003	0.0003	0.0002
−3.3	0.0005	0.0005	0.0005	0.0004	0.0004	0.0004	0.0004	0.0004	0.0004	0.0003
−3.2	0.0007	0.0007	0.0006	0.0006	0.0006	0.0006	0.0006	0.0005	0.0005	0.0005
−3.1	0.0010	0.0009	0.0009	0.0009	0.0008	0.0008	0.0008	0.0008	0.0007	0.0007
−3.0	0.0013	0.0013	0.0013	0.0012	0.0012	0.0011	0.0011	0.0011	0.0010	0.0010
−2.9	0.0019	0.0018	0.0018	0.0017	0.0016	0.0016	0.0015	0.0015	0.0014	0.0014
−2.8	0.0026	0.0025	0.0024	0.0023	0.0023	0.0022	0.0021	0.0021	0.0020	0.0019
−2.7	0.0035	0.0034	0.0033	0.0032	0.0031	0.0030	0.0029	0.0028	0.0027	0.0026
−2.6	0.0047	0.0045	0.0044	0.0043	0.0041	0.0040	0.0039	0.0038	0.0037	0.0036
−2.5	0.0062	0.0060	0.0059	0.0057	0.0055	0.0054	0.0052	0.0051	0.0049	0.0048
−2.4	0.0082	0.0080	0.0078	0.0075	0.0073	0.0071	0.0069	0.0068	0.0066	0.0064
−2.3	0.0107	0.0104	0.0102	0.0099	0.0096	0.0094	0.0091	0.0089	0.0087	0.0084
−2.2	0.0139	0.0136	0.0132	0.0129	0.0125	0.0122	0.0119	0.0116	0.0113	0.0110
−2.1	0.0179	0.0174	0.0170	0.0166	0.0162	0.0158	0.0154	0.0150	0.0146	0.0143
−2.0	0.0228	0.0222	0.0217	0.0212	0.0207	0.0202	0.0197	0.0192	0.0188	0.0183
−1.9	0.0287	0.0281	0.0274	0.0268	0.0262	0.0256	0.0250	0.0244	0.0239	0.0233
−1.8	0.0359	0.0351	0.0344	0.0336	0.0329	0.0322	0.0314	0.0307	0.0301	0.0294
−1.7	0.0446	0.0436	0.0427	0.0418	0.0409	0.0401	0.0392	0.0384	0.0375	0.0367
−1.6	0.0548	0.0537	0.0526	0.0516	0.0505	0.0495	0.0485	0.0475	0.0465	0.0455
−1.5	0.0668	0.0655	0.0643	0.0630	0.0618	0.0606	0.0594	0.0582	0.0571	0.0559
−1.4	0.0808	0.0793	0.0778	0.0764	0.0749	0.0735	0.0721	0.0708	0.0694	0.0681
−1.3	0.0968	0.0951	0.0934	0.0918	0.0901	0.0885	0.0869	0.0853	0.0838	0.0823
−1.2	0.1151	0.1131	0.1112	0.1093	0.1075	0.1056	0.1038	0.1020	0.1003	0.0985
−1.1	0.1357	0.1335	0.1314	0.1292	0.1271	0.1251	0.1230	0.1210	0.1190	0.1170
−1.0	0.1587	0.1562	0.1539	0.1515	0.1492	0.1469	0.1446	0.1423	0.1401	0.1379
−0.9	0.1841	0.1814	0.1788	0.1762	0.1736	0.1711	0.1685	0.1660	0.1635	0.1611
−0.8	0.2119	0.2090	0.2061	0.2033	0.2005	0.1977	0.1949	0.1922	0.1894	0.1867
−0.7	0.2420	0.2389	0.2358	0.2327	0.2296	0.2266	0.2236	0.2206	0.2177	0.2148
−0.6	0.2743	0.2709	0.2676	0.2643	0.2611	0.2578	0.2546	0.2514	0.2483	0.2451
−0.5	0.3085	0.3050	0.3015	0.2981	0.2946	0.2912	0.2877	0.2843	0.2810	0.2776
−0.4	0.3446	0.3409	0.3372	0.3336	0.3300	0.3264	0.3228	0.3192	0.3156	0.3121
−0.3	0.3821	0.3783	0.3745	0.3707	0.3669	0.3632	0.3594	0.3557	0.3520	0.3483
−0.2	0.4207	0.4168	0.4129	0.4090	0.4052	0.4013	0.3974	0.3936	0.3897	0.3859
−0.1	0.4602	0.4562	0.4522	0.4483	0.4443	0.4404	0.4364	0.4325	0.4286	0.4247
−0.0	0.5000	0.4960	0.4920	0.4880	0.4840	0.4801	0.4761	0.4721	0.4681	0.4641

Data from Larose, 2010.

Z	0.00	0.01	0.02	0.03	0.04	0.05	0.06	0.07	0.08	0.09
0.0	0.5000	0.5040	0.5080	0.5120	0.5160	0.5199	0.5239	0.5279	0.5319	0.5359
0.1	0.5398	0.5438	0.5478	0.5517	0.5557	0.5596	0.5636	0.5675	0.5714	0.5753
0.2	0.5793	0.5832	0.5871	0.5910	0.5948	0.5987	0.6026	0.6064	0.6103	0.6141
0.3	0.6179	0.6217	0.6255	0.6293	0.6331	0.6368	0.6406	0.6443	0.6480	0.6517
0.4	0.6554	0.6591	0.6628	0.6664	0.6700	0.6736	0.6772	0.6808	0.6844	0.6879
0.5	0.6915	0.6950	0.6985	0.7019	0.7054	0.7088	0.7123	0.7157	0.7190	0.7224
0.6	0.7257	0.7291	0.7324	0.7357	0.7389	0.7422	0.7454	0.7486	0.7517	0.7549
0.7	0.7580	0.7611	0.7642	0.7673	0.7704	0.7734	0.7764	0.7794	0.7823	0.7852
0.8	0.7881	0.7910	0.7939	0.7967	0.7995	0.8023	0.8051	0.8078	0.8106	0.8133
0.9	0.8159	0.8186	0.8212	0.8238	0.8264	0.8289	0.8315	0.8340	0.8365	0.8389
1.0	0.8413	0.8438	0.8461	0.8485	0.8508	0.8531	0.8554	0.8577	0.8599	0.8621
1.1	0.8643	0.8665	0.8686	0.8708	0.8729	0.8749	0.8770	0.8790	0.8810	0.8830
1.2	0.8849	0.8869	0.8888	0.8907	0.8925	0.8944	0.8962	0.8980	0.8997	0.9015
1.3	0.9032	0.9049	0.9066	0.9082	0.9099	0.9115	0.9131	0.9147	0.9162	0.9177
1.4	0.9192	0.9207	0.9222	0.9236	0.9251	0.9265	0.9279	0.9292	0.9306	0.9319
1.5	0.9332	0.9345	0.9357	0.9370	0.9382	0.9394	0.9406	0.9418	0.9429	0.9441
1.6	0.9452	0.9463	0.9474	0.9484	0.9495	0.9505	0.9515	0.9525	0.9535	0.9545
1.7	0.9554	0.9564	0.9573	0.9582	0.9591	0.9599	0.9608	0.9616	0.9625	0.9633
1.8	0.9641	0.9649	0.9656	0.9664	0.9671	0.9678	0.9686	0.9693	0.9699	0.9706
1.9	0.9713	0.9719	0.9726	0.9732	0.9738	0.9744	0.9750	0.9756	0.9761	0.9767
2.0	0.9772	0.9778	0.9783	0.9788	0.9793	0.9798	0.9803	0.9808	0.9812	0.9817
2.1	0.9821	0.9826	0.9830	0.9834	0.9838	0.9842	0.9846	0.9850	0.9854	0.9857
2.2	0.9861	0.9864	0.9868	0.9871	0.9875	0.9878	0.9881	0.9884	0.9887	0.9890
2.3	0.9893	0.9896	0.9898	0.9901	0.9904	0.9906	0.9909	0.9911	0.9913	0.9916
2.4	0.9918	0.9920	0.9922	0.9925	0.9927	0.9929	0.9931	0.9932	0.9934	0.9936
2.5	0.9938	0.9940	0.9941	0.9943	0.9945	0.9946	0.9948	0.9949	0.9951	0.9952
2.6	0.9953	0.9955	0.9956	0.9957	0.9959	0.9960	0.9961	0.9962	0.9963	0.9964
2.7	0.9965	0.9966	0.9967	0.9968	0.9969	0.9970	0.9971	0.9972	0.9973	0.9974
2.8	0.9974	0.9975	0.9976	0.9977	0.9977	0.9978	0.9979	0.9979	0.9980	0.9981
2.9	0.9981	0.9982	0.9982	0.9983	0.9984	0.9984	0.9985	0.9985	0.9986	0.9986
3.0	0.9987	0.9987	0.9987	0.9988	0.9988	0.9989	0.9989	0.9989	0.9990	0.9990
3.1	0.9990	0.9991	0.9991	0.9991	0.9992	0.9992	0.9992	0.9992	0.9993	0.9993
3.2	0.9993	0.9993	0.9994	0.9994	0.9994	0.9994	0.9994	0.9995	0.9995	0.9995
3.3	0.9995	0.9995	0.9995	0.9996	0.9996	0.9996	0.9996	0.9996	0.9996	0.9997
3.4	0.9997	0.9997	0.9997	0.9997	0.9997	0.9997	0.9997	0.9997	0.9997	0.9998

Data from Larose, 2010.

Table C.3 The Chi-Square Distribution: Critical Values

Determine the degrees of freedom (*df*), shown in the first column, and the criterion for statistical significance, shown as *p* levels in the blue top row. At the intersection of each row and column, the table entry is the critical value of chi-square that must be exceeded in order to reject the null hypothesis and conclude that a finding is statistically significant.

			p Level		
df	.10	.05	.01	.005	.001
1	2.71	3.84	6.63	7.88	10.83
2	4.61	5.99	9.21	10.60	13.82
3	6.25	7.81	11.34	12.84	16.27
4	7.78	9.49	13.28	14.86	18.47
5	9.24	11.07	15.09	16.75	20.51
6	10.64	12.59	16.81	18.55	22.46
7	12.02	14.07	18.48	20.28	24.32
8	13.36	15.51	20.09	21.95	26.12
9	14.68	16.92	21.67	23.59	27.88
10	15.99	18.31	23.21	25.19	29.59
11	17.28	19.68	24.72	26.76	31.26
12	18.55	21.03	26.22	28.30	32.91
13	19.81	22.36	27.69	29.82	34.53
14	21.06	23.68	29.14	31.32	36.12
15	22.31	25.00	30.58	32.80	37.70
16	23.54	26.30	32.00	34.27	39.25
17	24.77	27.59	33.41	35.72	40.79
18	25.99	28.87	34.81	37.16	42.31
19	27.20	30.14	36.19	38.58	43.82
20	28.41	31.41	37.57	40.00	45.31
21	29.62	32.67	38.93	41.40	46.80
22	30.81	33.92	40.29	42.80	48.27
23	32.01	35.17	41.64	44.18	49.73
24	33.20	36.42	42.98	45.56	51.18
25	34.38	37.65	44.31	46.93	52.62
26	35.56	38.89	45.64	48.29	54.05
27	36.74	40.11	46.96	49.64	55.48
28	37.92	41.34	48.28	50.99	56.89
29	39.09	42.56	49.59	52.34	58.30
30	40.26	43.77	50.89	53.67	59.70
40	51.81	55.76	63.69	66.77	73.40
50	63.17	67.50	76.15	79.49	86.66
60	74.40	79.08	88.38	91.95	99.61
80	96.58	101.9	112.3	116.3	124.8
100	118.5	124.3	135.8	140.2	149.4

Data from Moore, Notz, and Fligner, 2013.

Table C.4 The *t* Distribution: Critical Values

Determine the degrees of freedom (*df*), shown in the first column, and the criterion for statistical significance, shown as *p* levels in the blue top row. At the intersection of each row and column, the table entry is the critical value of *t* that must be exceeded in order to reject the null hypothesis and conclude that a finding is statistically significant. Values are shown for two-tailed and one-tailed tests.

| | One-Tailed Tests | | | Two-Tailed Tests | | |
| | *p* level | | | *p* level | | |
df	.10	.05	.01	.10	.05	.01
1	3.078	6.314	31.821	6.314	12.706	63.657
2	1.886	2.920	6.965	2.920	4.303	9.925
3	1.638	2.353	4.541	2.353	3.182	5.841
4	1.533	2.132	3.747	2.132	2.776	4.604
5	1.476	2.015	3.365	2.015	2.571	4.032
6	1.440	1.943	3.143	1.943	2.447	3.708
7	1.415	1.895	2.998	1.895	2.365	3.500
8	1.397	1.860	2.897	1.860	2.306	3.356
9	1.383	1.833	2.822	1.833	2.262	3.250
10	1.372	1.813	2.764	1.813	2.228	3.170
11	1.364	1.796	2.718	1.796	2.201	3.106
12	1.356	1.783	2.681	1.783	2.179	3.055
13	1.350	1.771	2.651	1.771	2.161	3.013
14	1.345	1.762	2.625	1.762	2.145	2.977
15	1.341	1.753	2.603	1.753	2.132	2.947
16	1.337	1.746	2.584	1.746	2.120	2.921
17	1.334	1.740	2.567	1.740	2.110	2.898
18	1.331	1.734	2.553	1.734	2.101	2.879
19	1.328	1.729	2.540	1.729	2.093	2.861
20	1.326	1.725	2.528	1.725	2.086	2.846
21	1.323	1.721	2.518	1.721	2.080	2.832
22	1.321	1.717	2.509	1.717	2.074	2.819
23	1.320	1.714	2.500	1.714	2.069	2.808
24	1.318	1.711	2.492	1.711	2.064	2.797
25	1.317	1.708	2.485	1.708	2.060	2.788
26	1.315	1.706	2.479	1.706	2.056	2.779
27	1.314	1.704	2.473	1.704	2.052	2.771
28	1.313	1.701	2.467	1.701	2.049	2.764
29	1.312	1.699	2.462	1.699	2.045	2.757
30	1.311	1.698	2.458	1.698	2.043	2.750
35	1.306	1.690	2.438	1.690	2.030	2.724
40	1.303	1.684	2.424	1.684	2.021	2.705
60	1.296	1.671	2.390	1.671	2.001	2.661
80	1.292	1.664	2.374	1.664	1.990	2.639
100	1.290	1.660	2.364	1.660	1.984	2.626
120	1.289	1.658	2.358	1.658	1.980	2.617
∞	1.282	1.645	2.327	1.645	1.960	2.576

Data from Nolan and Heinzen, 2012.

Table C.5 The *F* Distribution: Critical Values

Determine the degrees of freedom *(df)* within groups (first column), the criterion for statistical significance (second column), and the degrees of freedom between groups (top row of blue numbers). At the intersection of each row and column, the table entry is the critical value of *F* that must be exceeded in order to reject the null hypothesis and conclude that a finding is statistically significant.

df for Denominator (within groups)	Significance level (*p*)	*df* for Numerator (between groups)					
		1	2	3	4	5	6
1	.01	4,052	5,000	5,404	5,625	5,764	5,859
	.05	162	200	216	225	230	234
2	.01	98.50	99.00	99.17	99.25	99.30	99.33
	.05	18.51	19.00	19.17	19.25	19.30	19.33
3	.01	34.12	30.82	29.46	28.71	28.24	27.91
	.05	10.13	9.55	9.28	9.12	9.01	8.94
4	.01	21.20	18.00	16.70	15.98	15.52	15.21
	.05	7.71	6.95	6.59	6.39	6.26	6.16
5	.01	16.26	13.27	12.06	11.39	10.97	10.67
	.05	6.61	5.79	5.41	5.19	5.05	4.95
6	.01	13.75	10.93	9.78	9.15	8.75	8.47
	.05	5.99	5.14	4.76	4.53	4.39	4.28
7	.01	12.25	9.55	8.45	7.85	7.46	7.19
	.05	5.59	4.74	4.35	4.12	3.97	3.87
8	.01	11.26	8.65	7.59	7.01	6.63	6.37
	.05	5.32	4.46	4.07	3.84	3.69	3.58
9	.01	10.56	8.02	6.99	6.42	6.06	5.80
	.05	5.12	4.26	3.86	3.63	3.48	3.37
10	.01	10.05	7.56	6.55	6.00	5.64	5.39
	.05	4.97	4.10	3.71	3.48	3.33	3.22
11	.01	9.65	7.21	6.22	5.67	5.32	5.07
	.05	4.85	3.98	3.59	3.36	3.20	3.10
12	.01	9.33	6.93	5.95	5.41	5.07	4.82
	.05	4.75	3.89	3.49	3.26	3.11	3.00
13	.01	9.07	6.70	5.74	5.21	4.86	4.62
	.05	4.67	3.81	3.41	3.18	3.03	2.92
14	.01	8.86	6.52	5.56	5.04	4.70	4.46
	.05	4.60	3.74	3.34	3.11	2.96	2.85
15	.01	8.68	6.36	5.42	4.89	4.56	4.32
	.05	4.54	3.68	3.29	3.06	2.90	2.79
16	.01	8.53	6.23	5.29	4.77	4.44	4.20
	.05	4.49	3.63	3.24	3.01	2.85	2.74
17	.01	8.40	6.11	5.19	4.67	4.34	4.10
	.05	4.45	3.59	3.20	2.97	2.81	2.70
18	.01	8.29	6.01	5.09	4.58	4.25	4.02
	.05	4.41	3.56	3.16	2.93	2.77	2.66
19	.01	8.19	5.93	5.01	4.50	4.17	3.94
	.05	4.38	3.52	3.13	2.90	2.74	2.63
20	.01	8.10	5.85	4.94	4.43	4.10	3.87
	.05	4.35	3.49	3.10	2.87	2.71	2.60
21	.01	8.02	5.78	4.88	4.37	4.04	3.81
	.05	4.33	3.47	3.07	2.84	2.69	2.57
22	.01	7.95	5.72	4.82	4.31	3.99	3.76

		1	2	3	4	5	6
23	.05	4.30	3.44	3.05	2.82	2.66	2.55
	.01	7.88	5.66	4.77	4.26	3.94	3.71
24	.05	4.28	3.42	3.03	2.80	2.64	2.53
	.01	7.82	5.61	4.72	4.22	3.90	3.67
25	.05	4.26	3.40	3.01	2.78	2.62	2.51
	.01	7.77	5.57	4.68	4.18	3.86	3.63
26	.05	4.24	3.39	2.99	2.76	2.60	2.49
	.01	7.72	5.53	4.64	4.14	3.82	3.59
27	.05	4.23	3.37	2.98	2.74	2.59	2.48
	.01	7.68	5.49	4.60	4.11	3.79	3.56
28	.05	4.21	3.36	2.96	2.73	2.57	2.46
	.01	7.64	5.45	4.57	4.08	3.75	3.53
29	.05	4.20	3.34	2.95	2.72	2.56	2.45
	.01	7.60	5.42	4.54	4.05	3.73	3.50
30	.05	4.18	3.33	2.94	2.70	2.55	2.43
	.01	7.56	5.39	4.51	4.02	3.70	3.47
35	.05	4.17	3.32	2.92	2.69	2.53	2.42
	.01	7.42	5.27	4.40	3.91	3.59	3.37
40	.05	4.12	3.27	2.88	2.64	2.49	2.37
	.01	7.32	5.18	4.31	3.83	3.51	3.29
45	.05	4.09	3.23	2.84	2.61	2.45	2.34
	.01	7.23	5.11	4.25	3.77	3.46	3.23
50	.05	4.06	3.21	2.81	2.58	2.42	2.31
	.01	7.17	5.06	4.20	3.72	3.41	3.19
55	.05	4.04	3.18	2.79	2.56	2.40	2.29
	.01	7.12	5.01	4.16	3.68	3.37	3.15
60	.05	4.02	3.17	2.77	2.54	2.38	2.27
	.01	7.08	4.98	4.13	3.65	3.34	3.12
65	.05	4.00	3.15	2.76	2.53	2.37	2.26
	.01	7.04	4.95	4.10	3.62	3.31	3.09
70	.05	3.99	3.14	2.75	2.51	2.36	2.24
	.01	7.01	4.92	4.08	3.60	3.29	3.07
75	.05	3.98	3.13	2.74	2.50	2.35	2.23
	.01	6.99	4.90	4.06	3.58	3.27	3.05
80	.05	3.97	3.12	2.73	2.49	2.34	2.22
	.01	6.96	4.88	4.04	3.56	3.26	3.04
85	.05	3.96	3.11	2.72	2.49	2.33	2.22
	.01	6.94	4.86	4.02	3.55	3.24	3.02
90	.05	3.95	3.10	2.71	2.48	2.32	2.21
	.01	6.93	4.85	4.01	3.54	3.23	3.01
95	.05	3.95	3.10	2.71	2.47	2.32	2.20
	.01	6.91	4.84	4.00	3.52	3.22	3.00
100	.05	3.94	3.09	2.70	2.47	2.31	2.20
	.01	6.90	4.82	3.98	3.51	3.21	2.99
200	.05	3.94	3.09	2.70	2.46	2.31	2.19
	.01	6.76	4.71	3.88	3.41	3.11	2.89
1000	.05	3.89	3.04	2.65	2.42	2.26	2.14
	.01	6.66	4.63	3.80	3.34	3.04	2.82
∞	.05	3.85	3.00	2.61	2.38	2.22	2.11
	.01	6.64	4.61	3.78	3.32	3.02	2.80
	.05	3.84	3.00	2.61	2.37	2.22	2.10

Data from Nolan and Heinzen, 2012.

Table C.6 Random Numbers

Line/Column	(a)	(b)	(c)	(d)	(e)	(f)	(g)	(h)
01	19223	95034	05756	28713	96409	12531	42544	82853
02	73676	47150	99400	01927	27754	42648	82425	36290
03	45467	71709	77558	00095	32863	29485	82226	90056
04	52711	38889	93074	60227	40011	85848	48767	52573
05	95592	94007	69971	91481	60779	53791	17297	59335
06	68417	35013	15529	72765	85089	57067	50211	47487
07	82739	57890	20807	47511	81676	55300	94383	14893
08	60940	72024	17868	24943	61790	90656	87964	18883
09	36009	19365	15412	39638	85453	46816	83485	41979
10	38448	48789	18338	24697	39364	42006	76688	08708
11	81486	69487	60513	09297	00412	71238	27649	39950
12	59636	88804	04634	71197	19352	73089	84898	45785
13	62568	70206	40325	03699	71080	22553	11486	11776
14	45149	32992	75730	66280	03819	56202	02938	70915
15	61041	77684	94322	24709	73698	14526	31893	32592
16	14459	26056	31424	80371	65103	62253	50490	61181
17	38167	98532	62183	70632	23417	26185	41448	75532
18	73190	32533	04470	29669	84407	90785	65956	86382
19	95857	07118	87664	92099	58806	66979	98624	84826
20	35476	55972	39421	65850	04266	35435	43742	11937
21	71487	09984	29077	14863	61683	47052	62224	51025
22	13873	81598	95052	90908	73592	75186	87136	95761
23	54580	81507	27102	56027	55892	33063	41842	81868
24	71035	09001	43367	49497	72719	96758	27611	91596
25	96746	12149	37823	71868	18442	35119	62103	39244
26	96927	19931	36809	74192	77567	88741	48409	41903
27	43909	99477	25330	64359	40085	16925	85117	36071
28	15689	14227	06565	14374	13352	49367	81982	87209
29	36759	58984	68288	22913	18638	54303	00795	08727
30	69051	64817	87174	09517	84534	06489	87201	97245
31	05007	16632	81194	14873	04197	85576	45195	96565
32	68732	55259	84292	08796	43165	93739	31685	97150
33	45740	41807	65561	33302	07051	93623	18132	09547
34	27816	78416	18329	21337	35213	37741	04312	68508
35	66925	55658	39100	78458	11206	19876	87151	31260
36	08421	44753	77377	28744	75592	08563	79140	92454
37	53645	66812	61421	47836	12609	15373	98481	14592
38	66831	68908	40772	21558	47781	33586	79177	06928
39	55588	99404	70708	41098	43563	56934	48394	51719
40	12975	13258	13048	45144	72321	81940	00360	02428
41	96767	35964	23822	96012	94591	65194	50842	53372
42	72829	50232	97892	63408	77919	44575	24870	04178
43	88565	42628	17797	49376	61762	16953	88604	12724
44	62964	88145	83083	69453	46109	59505	69680	00900
45	19687	12633	57857	95806	09931	02150	43163	58636
46	37609	59057	66967	83401	60705	02384	90597	93600
47	54973	86278	88737	74351	47500	84552	19909	67181
48	00694	05977	19664	65441	20903	62371	22725	53340
49	71546	05233	53946	68743	72460	27601	45403	88692
50	07511	88915	41267	16853	84569	79367	32337	03316

Data from Nolan and Heinzen, 2012.

ANSWERS TO THINKING CRITICALLY AND APPLYING YOUR KNOWLEDGE QUESTIONS

This appendix presents answers to the odd-numbered Thinking Critically and Applying Your Knowledge items at the end of each chapter. Answers to even-numbered items are available to course instructors in the Instructor's Resource Manual.

CHAPTER 1 SCIENCE AND PSYCHOLOGY

EXERCISE 1. IDENTIFYING EMPIRICAL AND NONEMPIRICAL QUESTIONS

The following are the answers to the 10 items in Table 1.3 and the reason behind each answer. For each item where the answer is *"nonempirical,"* one or two examples are given of how that item can be converted into an empirical question.

1. Empirical. We can measure whether a relation exists between how wealthy and happy people are.

2. Nonempirical. As typically used in a religious or spiritual sense, the soul is metaphysical: It cannot be measured scientifically. Empirical versions would include: "What percentage of people believe that humans have a soul?" and "What personal characteristics are associated with whether people believe in a human soul?"

3. Nonempirical. Judging what constitutes a good life involves personal values. An empirical version would be: "What factors do people believe make up a good life?"

4. Nonempirical. We can measure wealth and wisdom, but "better" involves a value judgment. Empirical questions would be: "Which factor—wealth or wisdom—correlates more strongly with longevity/happiness/life satisfaction?" and so forth.

5. Empirical. We can measure personality traits and biological and environmental factors that may contribute to their development.

6. Nonempirical. The answer clearly involves personal moral values. Empirical versions would include "Under what circumstances, if any, do people believe that stealing is morally justified?" and "Are there cross-cultural differences in whether people believe stealing is ever morally justified?"

7. Empirical. We can test whether songbirds will demonstrate their species' songs if they are raised in isolation from birth, thus never having environmental exposure to those songs.

8. Empirical. We can measure what people perceive to be beautiful or whether their beauty ratings of the same stimulus differ depending on their gender, ethnicity, personality traits, and so forth.

9. Nonempirical. An empirical version would be: "Are people's age, sex, and ethnicity associated with whether they support the death penalty for committing murder?"

10. Empirical. We can measure naturally occurring associations between how often or severely children are spanked and the future likelihood that they will engage in various aggressive behaviors. In principle, to gain a clearer causal picture, we also can envision how an experiment could be designed to test whether spanking increases children's aggression, but we would not conduct such an experiment for ethical reasons.

EXERCISE 3. CLAIMS, COMETS, AND CRITICAL THINKING

1. What claim is being made? The claim is that *Deep Impact*'s spacecraft–comet crash ruined the natural balance of forces in the universe.

2. What is the source of the claim? Russian astrologer Marina Bai made the claim and filed the lawsuit against NASA.

3. Can I gather information about the credibility of that source? Online news reports (e.g., BBC News) provide no information that establishes her as a scientifically credible source.

4. What evidence is presented to support the claim? Ms. Bai did not actually present the following true events as evidence, but hypothetically, if she had, the events claimed as evidence are a strong earthquake, a hurricane, and the collapse of a famous rock formation that occurred within days of the *Deep Impact* collision.

5. What is the quality of the evidence? The evidence is poor, as explained below.

6. Are there plausible alternative explanations? You bet: coincidence. It was hurricane season in North America. And, worldwide in 2005, the magnitude 6.7 Indonesian earthquake was one of 151 earthquakes of magnitude 6.0 or higher. In 2004 and 2006, there were 157 and 153 such earthquakes. That's about one per 2.5 days (United States Geological Survey, July 22, 2011). Moreover, suppose that natural disasters on Earth significantly increased long term following the *Deep Impact* collision. In this case, we would have to consider alternative explanations, such as natural geological and weather cycles.

7. Are the interpretations of the findings reasonable? No. Due to plausible alternative explanations, it is unreasonable to conclude that these three events were caused by the *Deep Impact* collision.

8. What additional evidence is needed to reach a clearer conclusion? Unfortunately, Ms. Bai's claim about "forces in the universe" being disrupted was incredibly vague. She did state, however, that the *Deep Impact* collision "obviously" would change the comet's orbit. NASA's analyses predicted and confirmed that the collision had no noticeable effect on the comet's orbit: It was

"like a moving truck hitting a pebble" (National Aeronautics and Space Administration, June 28, 2010).

9. Given the current state of the evidence, what conclusion is most reasonable? Ms. Bai's claim is unacceptably vague and not supported by good evidence. A Russian court eventually ruled against her claim.

CHAPTER 2 THE PROCESS OF CONDUCTING RESEARCH

EXERCISE 1. IDENTIFY THE TYPE OF RESEARCH AND THE MAIN VARIABLES

(a) Dr. Gutiérrez' study is an experiment. The independent variable is the type of stimulus to which participants are exposed; Dr. Gutiérrez manipulates this factor. The dependent variable is the level of neural activity that occurs in response to these stimuli in each of the brain regions that are studied.

(b) Dr. Jackson's study is an experiment. The main independent variable is the therapy condition (behavioral, cognitive-behavioral, or none). Dr. Jackson manipulates this factor. The dependent variable is the strength of the children's phobia, and Dr. Jackson will examine whether exposure to the different experimental conditions produces a change in this dependent variable.

(c) Dr. Lieberman's study is descriptive; it seeks to determine whether there is a naturally occurring relation between two variables: job satisfaction and job productivity. Both of these variables are measured; neither is manipulated by the researcher.

(d) Dr. Wu's study is an experiment. The independent variable is the type of interview procedure (new, standard). Dr. Wu manipulates this variable by assigning each detective to use one interview technique or the other. The dependent variable, which Dr. Wu measures, is the accuracy of the information recalled by the eyewitnesses.

EXERCISE 3. SEARCHING FOR SOMETHING?

Compared to the search terms in Search A, the terms in Search B will produce a search that is:

1. narrower. Articles will be identified only if they include both *phobia* and *depression* in their title, list of key terms, or abstract. 2. broader. Articles will be identified if they include either *phobia* or *depression* in their title, list of key terms, or abstract. 3. narrower. Journal articles on schizophrenia published before or after 2012 will not be identified. 4. broader. The search will identify articles on schizophrenia, as well as others that have used terms such as "schizoid," "schizotypal," "schizoaffective," and "schizophreniform." 5. broader. The term *depress** will pick up the word "depression" as well as words such as "depressive," "depressed," and "depressing." 6. narrower. The search will only identify articles that mention all three terms: *phobia*, *therapy*, and *experiment*.

CHAPTER 3 CONDUCTING ETHICAL RESEARCH

This chapter has emphasized the fact that research ethics are complex and generate honest disagreements and debate. Realize that, with regard to these critical thinking exercises, your judgments, your classmates' and instructor's judgments, and my judgments may differ. The discussion of Exercise 1 illustrates the variability that can occur in judgments about research ethics.

EXERCISE 1. SHYNESS AND HELP: A DECEPTION EXPERIMENT

The summary of the study mentions three deceptive procedures. Participants were (1) misled about the purpose of the experiment; (2) misled into believing that the "stranger" was another student, when in fact the stranger was another experimenter (i.e., a confederate); and (3) not told that one stick in the experimental task was rigged so as to be impossible to stand up.

Fisher and Fyrberg (1994) presented 30 college students with the summary of the shyness–help study that you read. Students used rating scales to indicate their opinions about various issues. See how your judgments correspond to theirs.

Most students believed that (a) the hypothesis was important (73%), (b) the experimental procedures effectively tested the hypothesis (77%), and (c) the participants in the experimental condition would experience psychological discomfort (93%). Most students also felt that during debriefing, when participants learned they were deceived, the participants would feel annoyed (77%) or embarrassed (87%). Nonetheless, (d) they felt that the researchers' ability to use deception in a study like this was important (76%), even though other methods to study shyness and helping (e.g., filling out questionnaires, having students role-play) were available. Overall, most students (e) felt that the benefits of the research to society outweighed the costs to the participants (73%) and (f) approved of the fact that the study was actually conducted (76%). It is important to keep in mind, however, that there was diversity of opinion—a significant minority of the students did not feel the study should have been permitted.

Fisher and Fyrberg (1994) propose that in planning a deception study, researchers might benefit by assessing reactions to the planned study from members of the population that will be studied. Information could be gathered on issues, such as those you were asked about, that might prove useful to the researchers in considering modifications to their procedures or in developing their debriefing protocols. This type of planning study, of course, would itself have to conform to ethics regulations.

EXERCISE 3. A GREAT RESEARCH IDEA

This scenario focuses on potential plagiarism. Standard 8.11 of the APA Ethics Code deals with plagiarism and states that "psychologists do not present portions of another's work or data as their own, even if the other work or data source is cited occasionally" (APA, 2010a, p. 11). This raises the question of whether Darla's research idea and proposed study constitute "work." At present, there is no physical "work product" (such as a paper or article that Darla wrote) to plagiarize. Yet, although we might debate the meaning of "work" as written in the APA code, in common usage plagiarism clearly includes stealing other people's ideas and presenting them as if they were one's own ideas (American Heritage Dictionary, 1980, p. 1001).

Several general principles in the APA Ethics Code (2010a, p. 3) are relevant, including beneficence and nonmaleficence ("Psychologists seek to safeguard the welfare and rights of those with whom they interact professionally," para. 2); fidelity and responsibility ("Psychologists establish relationships of trust with those with whom they work," para. 3); and integrity ("Psychologists seek to promote . . . honesty and truthfulness in the science, teaching and practice of psychology. In these activities psychologists do not steal," para. 4). Even after Darla's departure, does the psychology professor have an obligation to safeguard her intellectual rights and maintain the trust that she undoubtedly placed in the professor by meeting to discuss her idea? My answer would be yes, and I feel this does represent a case of idea plagiarism in which the professor and graduate student are at fault.

The ethical response would be to locate Darla through the departmental advising office, psychology honors program director, college registrar, alumni association, or a web search. If the professor doesn't remember her name, some "detective work" with the advising office or honors program director may turn up her identity.

Perhaps Darla will be accepted into graduate school and will conduct this research for a first-year project or something beyond. Perhaps her interest in graduate school will turn to some other topic, or she will not get accepted into a graduate program and will pursue some other career. In any event, the professor and/or graduate student should discuss the situation with her. At a minimum, if the graduate student still wishes to pursue this idea (or more appropriately, a variation on her idea into which he imparts his own creative scientific thought), he should properly cite Darla's contribution as the originator of the idea. Personally, if I were in this graduate student's shoes and learned there was a possibility that Darla might pursue this research, I would find another topic for my research.

Finally, although this case involving Darla is hypothetical, actual instances of plagiarized ideas can put the originator of the idea in a real professional bind. Consider the following incident, which was submitted to the committee that developed the first APA Ethics Code (1953, p. 134):

> A psychologist in an informal theoretical discussion
> with a colleague expressed an idea clearly and in
> detail, an idea which seemed quite novel to the second
> psychologist. In fact, the second man had considerable
> difficulty in understanding the idea so that it had
> to be explained several times. Soon afterwards the
> second psychologist published the idea as part of an
> experimental article without acknowledging its source.
> As the originator of the idea was conducting research
> and about to publish on the same topic, he was forced
> to choose between publicly accusing his colleague of
> stealing the idea, citing his colleague as the source of
> his own idea, or appearing unethical or ignorant [i.e., by
> not making any reference to the colleague's published
> paper]. (APA, 1953, p. 133)

You can imagine how Darla would feel if she were to pursue her research idea only to find out that, for example, this graduate student and the professor eventually coauthored a published article based on the idea and design she had suggested to the professor.

CHAPTER 4 DEFINING AND MEASURING VARIABLES

EXERCISE 1. INDEPENDENT AND DEPENDENT VARIABLES

In each answer, the independent variable is listed first, the dependent variable second.

(a) (degree of) sleep deprivation; mood

(b) amount of alcohol consumed; reaction time

(c) age of first exposure to a second language; the ease with which a second language is acquired

(d) (degree of) practice of physical task; structural changes in brain neurons

(e) (degree of) smoking while pregnant; risk of newborn having a low birth weight

(f) type of culture (individualistic/collectivistic); preference for team or individual sports

(g) rate of word presentation; number of words recalled

(h) number of bystanders; likelihood that victim will receive help

(i) reinforcement schedule; resistance to extinction

(j) degree to which people have opposite characteristics; physical attraction

EXERCISE 3. RELIABILITY AND VALIDITY

Scenario A

This scenario most directly illustrates the concept of good criterion validity. The job-skills test has good criterion validity because it predicts future job performance, and the main concern in this applied context involves selecting those job applicants who will perform best on the job. Secondarily, this good criterion validity will help to establish the construct validity of this job-skills test.

Scenario B

This scenario most directly illustrates the concept of good reliability. Unconscious prejudice is not a characteristic that would be expected to fluctuate a lot over 3 weeks, so the high correlation between scores on the two administrations of the test are yielding high test–retest reliability. If you answered "poor face validity" based on reasoning such as "On the face of it, a computer-based test might not look like it measures unconscious prejudice," that's an understandable response. But the main point of this scenario is to illustrate high reliability.

Scenario C

This scenario illustrates the concept of good construct validity. The strong correlations between Dr. Suzuki's optimism test and other optimism tests suggest that his test has good convergent validity. The fact that Dr. Suzuki's test correlates weakly with tests that measure people's tendency to give socially desirable responses helps to demonstrate the discriminant validity of his test: In other words, it appears that his test is measuring people's true optimism, rather than people's tendency to state that they are optimistic merely because they believe it is more socially appropriate to say that you are optimistic rather than pessimistic.

CHAPTER 5 CORRELATION AND CORRELATIONAL RESEARCH

EXERCISE 1. HAPPINESS AND FRIENDSHIPS

(a) Happiness and time spent with friends appear to be positively correlated. For example, the five students (Erin, Claire, Sheridan, Maliah, Shih-Fen) who have lower happiness ratings (2, 3, 3, 5, and 5, respectively) spent between 20 and 50 minutes per day with friends. The remaining students, who have higher happiness ratings (6, 7, 7, 8, and 9), spent between 50 and 80 minutes per day with friends. Indeed, the difference in minutes spent per day with friends is most pronounced for students with the lowest versus highest happiness scores: Erin, Claire, and Sheridan versus Rachel and Camila.

(b) On the following page is the scatterplot. It should make it easier to detect that there is a positive correlation between happiness and minutes spent with friends.

Data from Farrimond & Leland (2006).

(c) The answer is number 4: We cannot assume from this study that there is a causal relation between happiness and time spent with friends.

(d) The *bidirectionality problem* is that greater happiness might be the cause of why people spend more time with friends (e.g., compared to less happy people, happier people may be more motivated, or may more often be in a mood, to see their friends)—or, alternatively, that spending more time with friends causes people to become happier. It's also possible that the causal influence might occur in both directions; this study does not enable us to decide among these possibilities. The *third-variable problem* is that some other factor might be entirely responsible for the correlation between happiness and time spent with friends. One example of a third variable might be self-esteem. Perhaps greater self-esteem causes people to be happier, and also to seek out time with friends. Another example of a third variable might be physical health: Greater physical health may contribute to happiness and also to people's ability to spend time with friends. To help rule out these factors as plausible third variables, Dr. Alvarez could measure them, assess whether they are associated with happiness and time spent with friends, and if so, examine whether happiness and time spent with friends remain correlated after statistically controlling for their associations with self-esteem and physical health.

EXERCISE 3. CORRELATION AND CAUSATION

(a) *Bidirectionality problem:* More frequent corporal punishment by parents might cause children to misbehave more frequently at school. Conversely, more frequent child misbehavior might cause parents to respond more frequently with the use of corporal punishment. *Third-variable problem:* There are many possible third variables. For example, perhaps greater family economic stress, or greater interpersonal conflict between parents, causes parents to become more frustrated and therefore they punish their children more harshly. At the same time, greater family economic stress or parental conflict may increase children's misbehavior at school.

(b) *Bidirectionality problem:* Employees who perform better may cause their managers to give more praise (i.e., their better performance provides managers with more opportunities to give praise). Conversely, greater praise provided by managers may motivate employees to perform better. *Third-variable problem:* Many possible third variables may exist. Greater job experience, or greater job satisfaction, may cause better employee

performance and also increase the odds that managers will adopt an interpersonal style that involves praising employees. In a real study, we would want to statistically control for possible third variables such as employees'/managers' experience, age, and job satisfaction.

(c) *Bidirectionality problem:* Having fewer friends may lead teenagers to spend more time playing video games. Conversely, spending more time playing video games may cause them to have fewer friends. *Third-variable problem:* There are many possible third variables. For example, personality traits such as greater shyness or greater anxiety may cause teenagers to have fewer friends and may also cause them to spend more time playing video games (e.g., to spend their time alone, to distract them from things they worry about).

CHAPTER 6 CASE STUDIES AND OBSERVATION RESEARCH

EXERCISE 1. SPACED OUT: REGIONAL DIFFERENCES IN INTERPERSONAL SPACE

(a) For at least two reasons, Dr. Zola's choice of locations is poor. First, the geographic region of the United States is completely confounded with the type of setting. Suppose the study reveals that, on average, people's interpersonal space boundaries differ from one region to the next. Is this a regional difference, or is it a difference caused by diverse settings (i.e., a park, airport, mall, and amusement park) that we might have found even within a single geographic area? There's no way to know. Second, each location is likely to have a significant mix of people who live within and outside the region, especially during the summer travel season. Many tourists, business travelers, and family visitors from all over the country (and world) are likely found in these locations. I would recommend choosing the same type of setting, and a more local setting, within each region. First, I would suggest studying the same type of population center (e.g., a large, medium, or small city, or suburb thereof; a town) within each region. Second, the same type of site, such as a park that is not a tourist spot but that is used by residents from multiple neighborhoods, could be chosen for observation within each population center.

(b) One viewpoint is that Dr. Zola's top priority should be to observe behavior in more geographic regions, because dividing the United States into only four regions is too broad. I would argue, however, that Dr. Zola's top priority should be to sample more sites within the four initial locations that she ends up choosing. For example, if she studies four mid-sized cities, then she could observe behavior not only in local parks, but also in large shopping malls and the lobbies of public buildings. This would enable Dr. Zola to examine whether regional differences (or lack thereof) replicate across different types of sites. In other words, rather than knowing that "on average, differences in interpersonal space were found across 12 regions when people were observed conversing in parks," I would rather know that "on average, differences in interpersonal space were found across four regions, regardless of whether observations were made in parks, shopping malls, or building lobbies." If studying different types of sites yields similar results, then this makes cross-regional comparisons more meaningful, and from there Dr. Zola can conduct further research that examines a greater number of regions.

EXERCISE 3. EVALUATING A BEHAVIORAL CODING SYSTEM

(a) At a minimum, I would add two categories. One would represent "Other" verbal remarks that the parent addresses to the child. This would enable Dr. Brunell to examine not only the absolute amount of verbal praise, encouragement, and criticism that each child receives, but also the percentage of overall comments from the mother that fall into each category. If, for example, children with high self-esteem receive a greater absolute amount of praise than children with low self-esteem, context would be provided by knowing whether this is simply because their mothers are more communicative in general or because a greater percentage of the mothers' communications involves praise. The second additional category, something like "Mother Ignores," would code instances when a mother completely ignores comments (e.g., "Look, mommy") or actions (the child holds out something for the mother to look at) that the child explicitly directs to her.

There are many ways to further expand the coding system. Building on some of the ideas represented in the coding system in Table 6.2, general maternal encouragement, praise, and criticism could be distinguished from encouragement, praise, and criticism in response to specific child behaviors (e.g., the child solves a problem or makes a mistake); the category of "Mother Ignores" could likewise be broken down in terms of the type of child behavior that is being ignored (e.g., the child has made a mistake or successfully completed a task). Maternal comments that are merely requests or instructions could be recorded.

(b) In general, as conceptually useful categories are added, coding systems can allow for a more comprehensive analysis of behavior. However, they also become more complex to use because observers must make finer discriminations (e.g., generally distinguishing praise from encouragement is no longer sufficient; the observer must also decide if the mother's remark was spontaneous or in reaction to the child's behavior). Observer training is always crucial; as coding categories are added, researchers need to ensure that observers can reliably use each category.

CHAPTER 7 SURVEY RESEARCH

EXERCISE 1. WOULD YOU LIKE A SAMPLE?

Survey 1

(a) nonprobability sampling **(b)** self-selected sampling ("convenience sampling" also would be a correct answer) **(c)** The conclusions are not appropriate. Despite the large sample of 150,000 respondents, probability sampling was not used, and there is no way to know whether the sample is representative of the population of fully employed adults in Canada, or even representative of the population of fully employed adults in Canada who are Internet users. Neither a margin of sampling error nor a confidence level can be determined.

Survey 2

(a) nonprobability sampling **(b)** purposive sampling (expert sampling) **(c)** Although the sample is not random, the conclusion is appropriate. The editors avoid stating that the findings represent the views of all American liberal arts college presidents. Instead, they note that the findings reflect the views of the sample that was contacted.

EXERCISE 3. WHAT ARE YOU ASKING? CRITIQUING SURVEY ITEMS

(a) This is a poorly worded, double-barreled question. It asks about two issues—poverty and hunger—but only permits one response. Poverty and hunger are related, but a person might believe that only one of them is among the world's most important problems. In addition, "among the most important problems" is vague. It would be clearer to state a specific number, such as "among the five most important problems."

(b) This is poorly worded. The word *not* makes the question unnecessarily complex and creates a double negative when combined with *unlikely*. A simpler phrasing would be "Do you believe you will be likely or unlikely to find a good job?"

(c) The item is clear but needlessly long. Here's one possible rewording: "The state government has proposed raising the legal drinking age from 21 years to 22 years of age. Do you support or oppose this proposal to raise the legal drinking age?"

(d) This is poorly worded. First, it is unbalanced and should read, "Do you agree or disagree. . . ?" Second, it is vague: "a higher priority" than what? A higher priority than it currently is, or than some other specific issue (e.g., a higher priority than improving mass transit). Third, "public school system" could be defined more clearly (e.g., does it refer specifically to kindergarten through high school?).

(e) This is poorly worded. The "past few months" refers to how many months? A number should be specified (e.g., "past 2 months").

(f) The question is clear, but the answer options overlap. For example, if your GPA is 3.0, do you choose answer option 1 or 2? The options should be changed to 4.0 to 3.00, 2.99 to 2.00, 1.99 to 1.00, less than 1.00. Additionally, these are broad categories, so further subdivisions might be considered. Finally, the question assumes a 0.0 to 4.0 grade scale and would need to be modified if the target population includes colleges that use a different grading system.

CHAPTER 8 SINGLE-FACTOR EXPERIMENTAL DESIGNS

EXERCISE 1. ANALYZE THE EXPERIMENT

Bowl Me Over: The Original

(a) independent variable: presence or absence of an audience; dependent variable: task performance (i.e., bowling score) **(b)** within-subjects design **(c)** all possible orders (That is, if an experiment only has two conditions, *A* and *B*, then there are two possible orders: *AB* and *BA*. Half the participants perform one order and half perform the other order. Note that the answer is not "reverse counterbalancing" because each woman is exposed to each audience condition only once.)

Bowl Me Over: The Sequel

(a) independent variable: audience size (zero, four, eight); dependent variable: task performance (i.e., bowling score) **(b)** between-subjects design **(c)** independent-groups design using block randomization

EXERCISE 3. THE FACE OF EMOTION

Experiment 1. all possible orders

Experiment 2. a Williams Latin Square

Experiment 3. random starting order with rotation

Experiment 4. reverse counterbalancing

CHAPTER 9 FACTORIAL DESIGNS

EXERCISE 1. DESCRIBE THE FACTORIAL DESIGN

Experiment 1. (a) two **(b)** two levels and six levels **(c)** 12 conditions

Experiment 2. (a) three **(b)** three levels, three levels, and two levels **(c)** 18 conditions

Experiment 3. (a) four **(b)** three levels, two levels, two levels, two levels **(c)** 24 conditions

Experiment 4. (a) three **(b)** two levels, two levels, four levels **(c)** 16 conditions

EXERCISE 3. IDENTIFY THE MAIN EFFECTS AND INTERACTIONS

Line Graph

(a) There is a main effect of sleep length. As sleep length increases, the average number of errors (i.e., averaged across age of participant) decreases. The averages are: 2 hours (45 errors); 4 hours (40 errors); 6 hours (30 errors); 8 hours (25 errors).

(b) There is an age of participant main effect. The yellow line is consistently above the orange line. On average, older adults (45 errors) make more errors than younger adults (25 errors).

(c) There is an Age of Participant × Sleep Length interaction. The lines are not parallel. As sleep length increases, the performance difference between younger and older adults grows larger. Another way to say this is that the increases in sleep length had a larger effect on younger adults' performance than on older adults' performance.

Bar Graph

(a) There is a main effect of sleep length. As sleep length increases, the average number of errors decreases. The averages are: 2 hours (50 errors); 4 hours (40 errors); 6 hours (30 errors); 8 hours (20 errors).

(b) There is an age of participant main effect. On average, older adults (45 errors) make more errors than younger adults (25 errors).

(c) There is no interaction. For each of the four sleep length conditions, older adults made 20 more errors than younger adults: The difference didn't grow larger or smaller. Another way to say this is that sleep length had the same effect on younger and older adults; overall, each age group progressively made 10 fewer errors for every additional 2 hours of sleep deprivation.

CHAPTER 10 EXPERIMENTATION AND VALIDITY

EXERCISE 1. LET'S GET PHYSICAL

(a) The change in self-esteem scores may partly or fully (1) reflect statistical regression to the mean (participants were selected based on having extremely low self-esteem scores), or (2) have been caused by a testing effect (taking the same self-esteem test twice). The scenario describing Dr. Adams's study does not mention any attrition, or any factor that might have caused a history confound. Still, Dr. Adams should consider whether outside events might have taken place that plausibly could account for the findings. Instrumentation is not a confounding variable because the same psychological test was used to measure self-esteem both times, and selection is not an internal validity threat because the study only involved one condition. Maturation would be a plausible internal validity threat if there was some reason to expect that among adults, self-esteem would generally rise over any given 10-week period. However, I don't know of any such plausible reason.

(b) Dr. Adams's exercise program (the "treatment") was implemented to represent the construct of "regular exercise." However, the program did more than just increase people's exercise exposure. Over 10 weeks, it provided them with (1) something new in their lives—it broke up their typical routine, (2) opportunities to socialize with fellow participants three times per week, and (3) attention from the researchers and/or exercise trainers. The mere fact of being selected for the study may have made participants feel special and/or caused the participants to expect that the program would make them feel better about themselves (i.e., a placebo effect). To Shadish et al. (2002), and others (Brewer, 2000), this adds up to the fact that the exercise program was a very impure (i.e., confounded) manipulation of the construct of "regular exercise." Perhaps the 10-week program—as implemented—truly did enhance participants' self-esteem, but if so, we cannot conclude that it was the exercise per se that was responsible. In addition, if the exercise trainers were aware of Dr. Adams's self-esteem hypothesis, this could create an experiment expectancy effect in their interactions with participants. Finally, the fact that participants took a self-esteem test before and after the program may have tipped them off to Dr. Adams's hypothesis and created a demand characteristic.

(c) At a minimum, after selecting a sample of participants on the basis of low self-esteem scores, I would want to randomly assign them across the following three conditions: (1) an exercise treatment condition, similar to the one Dr. Adams implemented; (2) a nonexercise treatment condition (alternative activity control group), in which participants likewise meet three times weekly for 2 hours and engage in activities other than physical exercise (e.g., arts and crafts; watching and then discussing a movie); and (3) a wait-list control group in which participants' self-esteem is measured at the same two times as the other participants' self-esteem—this control group does not meet or receive any treatment during that 10-week period. If present, we would expect threats to internal validity such as regression to the mean, testing, history, and so forth to be equivalent in all three groups. Potential confounding factors such as receiving attention, engaging in new activities, social interaction, expectancy effects, and demand characteristics would affect the exercise and alternate activity groups. If the self-esteem of the exercise group increases beyond that of the other groups, this design allows us to infer with greater confidence (as compared to Dr. Adams's original design) that regular exercise enhances self-esteem.

EXERCISE 3. A DIRTY SALES PITCH

(a) This vacuum cleaner test is grossly flawed. There is a Vacuum Cleaner (the owner's, the salesperson's) × Order of Cleaning confound. For example, if the Mega-Suck had been used first on the carpet, and the owner's vacuum had been used second, the results might have been the same: The owner's vacuum might have picked up just as much dirt that the Mega-Suck failed to pick up. Another way to conceptualize this is that, after the owner's vacuum was used first, we would want to compare how the Mega-Suck and the owner's vacuum would perform in getting a chance to pick up any residual dirt. Second, we would want to ensure that both vacuum cleaners perform each part of this test starting with an empty vacuum bag (or, if bagless, clean filters).

(b) One approach would be to clean two small areas of the carpet, measure two equivalent amounts of dirt, place the dirt on each of the carpet areas, and then counterbalance the order in which the two vacuums are used: Clean one area with the Mega-Suck first and the owner's vacuum cleaner second, and vice versa for the other area. The amount of dirt picked up on the first pass and second pass from each vacuum cleaner can be compared. Again, for each part of each test, start with a clean vacuum bag or clean filter. In real life, if I'm the homeowner and following all these filter-cleaning and dirt-measuring procedures would be impractical, I would at least repeat the test with the order of the vacuum cleaners reversed. And, if my vacuum can pick up residual dirt that the Mega-Suck leaves behind, I'd look forward to hearing the salesperson try to wiggle out of that result.

CHAPTER 11 QUASI-EXPERIMENTAL DESIGNS

EXERCISE 1. IDENTIFY THE QUASI-EXPERIMENTAL DESIGN

Study 1

(a) The college students were not randomly assigned to hurricane and no-hurricane conditions! This study compares nonequivalent groups (students at two colleges) and, of course, the researchers did not manipulate the independent variable. **(b)** pretest-posttest design with a nonequivalent control group

Study 2

(a) Each year, from 2005 through 2014, the students are not randomly assigned to computer lab and no lab conditions. At each measurement period, this study involves two nonequivalent groups (Grade 5 and Grade 6) that differ in age and amount of schooling. The researcher also has little to no control over potential selection × history or selection × instrumentation effects that—over a 20-year period—could differentially affect fifth- and sixth-graders' performance. For example, the researcher will need to pay careful attention to whether, from 1995 to 2014 or years within that range, sixth-graders were exposed to events (e.g., changes in other teaching methods, changes in the standardized tests used to measure achievement) to which the fifth-graders were not exposed. **(b)** time-series design with a nonequivalent control group

Study 3

(a) There is no randomly assigned control group or, alternatively, counterbalanced order of participation in the diet without pill versus diet with pill conditions. The researcher also has little to no control over history effects (e.g., medical news about the importance of weight loss, growing availability of fitness centers) that might occur in the second year of the study and affect participants' weight loss. **(b)** simple interrupted time-series design

EXERCISE 3. BIG BROTHER IS WATCHING

(a) Regression to the mean is one possible alternative explanation. These three intersections were chosen for red light camera installation because of their extreme scores on the dependent variable: number of accidents. These 2 months may have reflected a rare, chance spike in the accident rate at these particular intersections. Even without the installation of cameras, a decrease back toward the normal rate may have occurred. There is evidence even in this small data set that, at each intersection, scores from

Month 1 to Month 2 began to regress toward the mean even before the red light cameras were installed.

History would be another important, potentially confounding factor. Perhaps in the first 2 months, the road conditions suddenly took a turn for the worse (e.g., many jolting potholes) after unusually bad weather, but then were improved as the cameras were being installed. Perhaps construction was occurring near these intersections for those 2 months and traffic signage was altered, causing a spike in accidents. Perhaps there were more cars on the road at these intersections than usual due to events in the local community. The evidence may also indicate that nothing unusual occurred in the vicinity of these intersections, but possible history effects need to be examined.

(b) At a minimum, a longer simple interrupted time-series design would yield better information. Accident rates should be examined for several prior years and post-camera observations should likewise be charted for a longer period of time. Adding a nonequivalent control group (four other intersections with the next highest accident rates over those same 2 months) would improve upon this. Assuming we judge it ethical, a better option would be to randomly divide the four intersections into two groups and use a time-series design with a switching replication (i.e., delay the introduction of the cameras at two intersections). In fact, the introduction of the cameras could be staggered across the intersections one at a time, say, with 4 months in between each installation. If the accident rate remained high at each intersection (hence, the key ethical issue) and then dropped only after the camera was introduced at that particular intersection, this would be convincing evidence. This staggered approach represents a type of research design (called a multiple-baseline design) that we will discuss in Chapter 12.

CHAPTER 12 SINGLE-CASE EXPERIMENTAL DESIGNS

EXERCISE 1. INCREASING DONATIONS TO A FOOD BANK

(a) and **(b)** Your graph may look similar to the one shown below. Line graphs are often used in research articles based on single-case experimental designs. This enhances visual clarity (there usually are many data points) and the x-axis variable (e.g., days, sessions, trials) typically corresponds to the passage of time. In this exercise, each three consecutive observations represent 1 week, but within each week the individual observations occurred at different time intervals (i.e., 2 days, 3 days, and 2 days apart). Thus, a more conservative approach to graphing these data would be to create a bar graph rather than a line

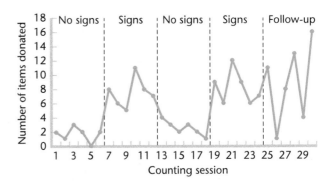

graph. Another approach used in single-case research is to plot the data points but not connect them with lines.

(c) The data support the conclusion that the treatment had an effect. Donations increased when the signs were posted, decreased when the signs were withdrawn, and increased when the signs were posted again. This pattern represents a classic ABAB treatment effect. The large degree of variability in the follow-up phase is not ideal, but overall, donations remained at a higher level than during either of the baseline periods. Farrimond and Leland's (2006) analysis indicated that the difference in the number of items donated in the treatment versus baseline phases was statistically significant.

EXERCISE 3. IS THERE A TREATMENT EFFECT?

Experiment 1

(a) The findings do not support a conclusion that the treatment was effective. (b) The target response did not decline; it increased steadily during the first baseline phase and introducing the treatment did not change the rate of increase, nor did it produce an overall jump in the level of response. What's more, during the second baseline phase, the response level did not decrease. The most conservative conclusion is that the frequency of this behavior rose on its own, hit a ceiling, and remained there.

Experiment 2

(a) The data support a conclusion that the treatment had an effect. (b) The frequency of the target response increased noticeably when the treatment was introduced and remained steady at that higher level. Within two sessions of withdrawing the treatment, the response rate started to steadily decline. Reintroduction of the treatment was accompanied, once again, by a rapid increase in the frequency of the response.

Experiment 3

(a) The data are inconclusive. (b) As in Experiment 2, the frequency of the target response increased noticeably as soon as the treatment was introduced. However, when the treatment was withdrawn, the target response did not decline; it remained steady and did not increase beyond that level when the treatment was reintroduced. It is possible that initial introduction of the treatment did cause the behavior to increase and that, once this occurred, other factors (e.g., other reinforcers in the situation) were sufficient to maintain the behavior at its new level. Alternatively, a confounding variable that coincided with the initial introduction of the treatment may have caused the behavior change, and its continued influence during the rest of the study may be responsible for the steady response rate during the last three phases of the study. Thus, the withdrawal and reinstatement of the treatment would be expected to have no effect. Given the available information, we cannot conclude that the treatment caused the behavior change.

Experiment 4

(a) These data provide cautious support for the conclusion that the treatment had an effect. (b) The frequency of the target response decreased slightly during the first baseline phase, but introduction of the treatment led to a steadier and steeper rate of decrease. Then the response rate did not revert to its prior, higher level when the treatment was withdrawn, which works against the conclusion that the treatment had an effect. However, the response frequency did not continue to decline once the treatment was withdrawn: It remained steady; the decline only continued after the treatment was reintroduced. Overall, the data suggest that (1) if there had been no treatment, the response might have decreased somewhat on its own over time, and (2) the treatment appears to have accelerated the rate of decline.

ABAB design a type of single-case design that involves a sequence of phases in which a treatment is either absent or present; *see also* **withdrawal design.**

ABBA-counterbalancing design *See* **reverse-counterbalancing design.**

accuracy (of a measure) the degree to which a measure yields results that agree with a known standard.

all-possible-orders design (also called **complete counterbalancing**) a within-subjects design in which the conditions of an independent variable are arranged in every possible sequence, and an equal number of participants are assigned to each sequence.

alpha (α) level *See* **significance level.**

alternative hypothesis (H₁) a hypothesis that is contrary to the null hypothesis; used in inferential statistical tests.

American Psychological Association (APA) Ethics Code a document that describes general ethical principles and specific ethical standards to guide psychologists' professional behavior.

analysis of variance (ANOVA) a statistical test that determines whether the overall pattern of differences between the means of two or more groups is statistically significant.

anecdotal evidence a type of evidence in which anecdotes—brief stories or descriptions about personal experiences, other people, or events—are offered as facts to support or refute a claim.

Animal Welfare Act U.S. federal law that regulates the use of warm-blooded vertebrates (except mice, rats, and birds) in scientific research.

anonymity in a study, the fact that a participant's identity is unknown, even to the researcher.

applied behavior analysis the application of principles from the experimental analysis of behavior to socially significant problems.

applied research scientific inquiry that directly focuses on helping to solve or evaluate a specific real-world problem; *compare* **basic research.**

archival records previously existing documents or other data that were produced independently of the current research.

assent evidence provided by a participant of willingness to participate in a study even though the participant might not be able to comprehend details of the study to the degree listed on the consent form.

at risk describes participants in a proposed study that involves more than minimal risk; *compare* **minimal risk.**

attrition (also called **subject loss**) the loss of participants in the course of a study when they fail to complete it.

authority (as a method of knowing) relying on other people as the source of our knowledge and beliefs.

bar graph a visual representation of data in which values of a variable are plotted on the *x*-axis and the descriptive statistic of interest is portrayed by the height of bars plotted along the *y*-axis.

baseline phase a phase of an experiment during which the treatment or intervention is not presented; often refers to an initial phase in which data are recorded prior to introducing a treatment.

basic research scientific inquiry that examines the fundamental nature of phenomena; *compare* **applied research.**

behavioral coding systems classifications of participants' responses into mutually exclusive categories; a component of many observational studies.

Belmont Report an ethics code that provides the foundation for U.S. federal regulations governing research on human subjects.

beneficence, principle of a principle in the APA Ethics Code stating that psychologists "should strive to benefit those with whom they work" (APA, 2010a, p. 3).

between-subjects design an experimental design in which different participants are assigned to each of the conditions in the experiment.

between-subjects factorial design a factorial design in which each subject engages in only one condition.

bias *See* **systematic error.**

biased sample *See* **nonrepresentative sample.**

bidirectionality problem (also called **two-way causality problem**) ambiguity about whether X has caused Y or Y has caused X.

blind observation an observational technique in which observers are kept unaware of (i.e., "blind" to) the hypotheses being tested and/or any key information about participants that relates to those hypotheses.

blinding *See* **masking.**

block randomization an experimental procedure in which researchers conduct a round of all the conditions, then another round, then another, for as many rounds as needed to complete the experiment. Within each round, the order of conditions is randomly determined.

block-randomization design a within-subjects design in which every participant is exposed to multiple blocks of trials, with each block for each participant containing a newly randomized order of all the conditions.

carryover effects order effects that occur when participants' responses in one condition are uniquely influenced by the particular condition or conditions that preceded it.

case study an in-depth analysis of an individual, social unit, event, or other phenomenon.

causal inference the conclusion that variable *X* caused variable *Y*.

ceiling effect the effect that occurs when scores on a dependent variable bunch up at the maximum score level; *compare* **floor effect.**

changing-criterion design a single-case experimental design in which an initial baseline phase is followed by a treatment phase that lasts until the target behavior reaches a criterion level and becomes stable; treatment then continues in a series of additional phases, with a new (and typically more demanding) performance criterion set in each phase.

chi-square (χ²) goodness-of-fit test an inferential statistical test used to determine the likelihood that an obtained pattern of results is consistent with the pattern expected from a hypothesized distribution.

chi-square (χ²) test for independence an inferential statistical test most commonly used to determine whether two qualitative variables are independent or associated.

closed-ended question an item, as in a questionnaire or survey, that provides specific response options.

cluster sampling a sampling procedure in which units (e.g., geographic regions, schools) that contain members of the population are identified. These units—called "clusters"—are then randomly sampled, and within each sampled cluster either all members or randomly chosen members are selected to participate in the study.

Cohen's *d* a statistical measure of effect size; commonly used to report effect sizes in experiments.

cohort sequential research design a design in which several cohorts are tested longitudinally.

collective case study A case study in which each of several cases is studied in depth for the purpose of learning about a broader phenomenon.

Common Rule U.S. federal policy that specifies ethics regulations for human subjects research.

complete counterbalancing *See* **all-possible-orders design.**

complete replication (also called **full replication**) replication that includes all the conditions of the original study.

conceptual replication replication that examines the same question investigated in the original study but operationalizes the constructs differently.

confederate an accomplice of the investigator who is trained to act a certain way.

confidence interval (CI) a range of values within which a population parameter (e.g., a population mean) is estimated to fall, with a particular level of confidence.

confidence level the degree of confidence that a true population value resides within a particular margin of sampling error.

confidentiality in a study, the fact that participants' identities will not be released without their consent, and data from the study will be reported in a way that does not identify individual participants.

confirmation bias (also called **congeniality bias**) the tendency to selectively seek information that supports one's views and avoid disconfirming information.

confounding variable an extraneous factor that covaries with an independent variable in such a way that we can no longer determine which one has caused the changes in the dependent variable; a confounding variable provides a potential alternative explanation for the results.

congeniality bias *See* **confirmation bias.**

construct validity the degree to which the constructs (the conceptual variables) that researchers claim to be studying are, in fact, the constructs that they are manipulating and measuring.

contamination (in a study) occurs when knowledge, services, or other experiences intended for one group are unintentionally received by another group (e.g., when future participants learn information from previous participants that they are not supposed to know until after data collection is completed).

content analysis an analysis of the different types of content found within or represented by a set of data.

content validity the degree to which the items on a measure adequately represent the entire range or set of items that could have been appropriately included.

context effects in administering a survey (or questionnaire), a situation in which responses to a survey item are influenced by the particular items that occur directly or soon before it.

continuous variables variables for which, in principle, intermediate values are possible between any two adjacent scale values.

control the ability to regulate research settings and procedures and to guide the application of scientific knowledge.

control condition in an experiment, the circumstance in which participants do not receive the treatment of interest or are exposed to a baseline level of an independent variable; *see also* **control group.**

control group the participants in an experiment who do not receive the treatment of interest or are exposed to a baseline level of an independent variable; *see also* **control condition.**

convenience (or **haphazard**) **sampling** a sampling method in which members of a population are selected nonrandomly for inclusion in a sample on the basis of convenience.

convergent validity the principle that scores on a measure should correlate highly (i.e., converge) with scores on other measures of the same construct.

correlation a statistical association between variables.

correlational research (also called **relational research**) research that involves examining potential associations between naturally occurring variables by measuring those variables and determining whether they are statistically related.

counterbalancing in a within-subjects design, a procedure in which the order of conditions is varied so that no condition has an overall advantage relative to the other conditions.

criterion validity the degree to which a measure predicts an outcome that it is expected to predict.

criterion variable a variable that a researcher is trying to estimate or predict.

cross-lagged panel design a research design that involves three steps: (1) measure X and Y at Time 1; (2) measure X and Y again, at Time 2; and (3) examine the pattern of correlations among X_1, X_2, Y_1, and Y_2.

cross-sectional research design (also called **one-shot correlational study**) a descriptive research design in which each person in the study participates on one occasion and all variables are measured at that time; in developmental research, a study in which participants of different ages are compared at the same point in time; *compare* **longitudinal research.**

cumulative frequency distribution a distribution that portrays the total number of cases that occur at or below (or, at or above) each value in a data set.

debriefing a conversation with a participant, after data are gathered from that participant, in which the researcher conveys additional information about the study.

deception the intentional withholding by researchers of information from potential participants that might influence their decision to provide informed consent (so-called passive deception) or intentionally misleading participants about some aspect of a study (so-called active deception).

deductive reasoning using a general principle to reach a more specific conclusion.

demand characteristics cues that influence participants' beliefs about the hypothesis being tested and the behaviors expected of them.

dependent variable in an experiment, the behavior or outcome that the researcher measures to determine whether the independent variable has produced an effect. In a cause–effect relation between two variables, the dependent variable is the presumed effect.

descriptive research (also called **nonexperimental research**) a research method in which researchers measure variables but do not manipulate them.

descriptive statistics statistics that organize and summarize a set of data.

deviation score   the arithmetic difference between each score in a distribution and the mean of that distribution (i.e., $X - M$).

diary   a self-report technique in which participants record their behaviors or experiences for defined periods of time or whenever certain events take place.

differential attrition   significantly different rates of or reasons for participants' discontinuing a study across the various conditions in that study.

direct (or **"exact"**) **replication**   replication in which the researchers follow the procedures used in the original study as closely as possible.

discrete variables   variables for which no intermediate values are possible between any two adjacent values (e.g., number of children).

discriminant validity   the principle that scores on a measure should not correlate too strongly with scores on measures of other constructs.

disguised observation   an observational technique in which the individuals being studied are not aware that they are being observed; *compare* **undisguised observation.**

distal causes   remote causes; in a chain of interrelated events that lead to a given result, the events that are remote from the result; *compare* **proximal causes.**

double negative (question)   a questionnaire item whose phrasing contains two negative words.

double-barreled question   a survey item that asks about two issues within one question, forcing respondents to combine potentially different opinions into one judgment.

double-blind procedure   in experiments, a procedure in which neither the participants nor the experimenters are aware of who is receiving the actual treatment and who is receiving a placebo.

ecological validity   the degree to which responses obtained in a research context generalize to behavior in natural settings; also refers to how well a research setting (e.g., tasks, procedures) corresponds to what people encounter in daily life.

effect size   a statistical measure of the strength of a relation between two variables. In experiments, effect size measures the strength of a treatment effect.

efficiency assessment   in program evaluation, the process of weighing the program's benefits and effectiveness in relation to its costs to determine whether it is an efficient method for addressing the problem at hand.

empirical knowledge   knowledge that is based on the senses—on experiences with the world.

empirical question (also called **empirical claim**)   a question or claim that, in principle, can be tested empirically through observation.

empiricism   the process of acquiring knowledge directly through observation and experience; the philosophical viewpoint that all knowledge is derived from experience.

ethics   a system of moral principles and standards.

ethnography   a qualitative research approach that often combines participant observation with interviews to gain an integrative description of social groups.

evidence-based treatments (also called **empirically supported treatments**)   interventions that scientifically controlled studies have demonstrated to be effective in treating specific conditions.

exact replication   *See* **direct replication.**

experiment   a research method in which the researcher manipulates one or more variables, attempts to control extraneous factors, and then measures how the manipulated variables affect participants' responses.

experimental analysis of behavior   the intensive study, under controlled conditions, of how environmental stimuli and consequences regulate an individual organism's behavior.

experimental condition   in an experiment, the circumstance in which participants receive the treatment or "active" level of the independent variable; *see also* **experimental group.**

experimental control   the ability to (1) manipulate one or more independent variables; (2) choose the types of dependent variables that will be measured, and how and when they will be measured, so that the effects of the independent variables can be assessed; and (3) regulate other aspects of the research environment, including the manner in which participants are exposed to the various conditions in the experiment.

experimental group   participants who are exposed to a treatment or "active" level of the independent variable; *see also* **experimental condition.**

experimenter expectancy effects   unintentional ways in which researchers influence their participants to respond in a manner consistent with the researchers' hypothesis.

expert sampling   a type of purposive sampling in which researchers identify experts on a topic and ask them to participate.

external validity   the generalizability of the findings beyond the circumstances of the present study.

extraneous variable   a factor that is not the focus of interest in a particular study, but that could influence the outcome of the study if left uncontrolled.

face validity   the degree to which the items on a measure appear to be reasonable.

factorial design   an experimental design that includes two or more independent variables and crosses (i.e., combines) every level of each independent variable with every level of all the other independent variables.

falsifiability   a criterion for judging testability; an assertion is testable if we can envision some type of empirical evidence that will reveal it to be false.

fatigue effect   a performance decline that results from becoming tired, inattentive, or less motivated to perform well with repeated exposure to a task.

fidelity, principle of   a principle in the APA Ethics Code stating that psychologists should behave in a trustworthy manner.

field experiment   a study in which researchers manipulate an independent variable in a natural setting and exercise some control over extraneous factors.

field study   research that takes place in a real-world ("field") setting.

floor effect   an effect that occurs when scores on a dependent variable bunch up at the minimum score level; *compare* **ceiling effect.**

focal sampling   a sampling technique in which researchers select a particular member (or unit, such as a parent-infant dyad) who will be observed at any given time.

focus group   a procedure for gathering data in which a moderator leads a group of people through an interview and discussion of a set of topics.

frequency distribution   a distribution that portrays how often each value of a variable occurs within a set of data.

frequency polygon   a line graph that shows the distribution of a quantitative variable.

full replication   *See* **complete replication.**

habituation   a decrease over time in the strength of a response to a repeated stimulus.

haphazard sampling   *See* **convenience sampling.**

histogram   a graph that uses bars to portray the distribution of a quantitative variable.

history (with regard to a study)   events that occur while a study is being conducted and that are not a part of the experimental manipulation or treatment.

hypothesis   a tentative proposition about the causes or outcome of an event or, more generally, about how variables are related.

hypothetical construct   underlying characteristics or processes that are not directly observed but instead are inferred from measurable behaviors or outcomes.

independent replication   a replication conducted by researchers who were not part of the original research group.

independent variable   the manipulated variable in an experiment; a factor that the researcher manipulates, or systematically varies. In a cause–effect relation between two variables, it is the presumed causal factor.

independent-groups design (also called **random-groups design**)   a between-subjects design in which participants are randomly assigned to the various conditions of the experiment.

inductive reasoning   using specific facts to reach a general conclusion or general principle.

inferential statistics   statistics that allow researchers to draw conclusions about a population on the basis of data from a sample.

informed consent   the principle that prospective participants have the right to make a voluntary, informed decision about whether or not to participate in a study.

Institutional Animal Care and Use Committee (IACUC)   a legally mandated committee that reviews animal research proposals for compliance with federal regulations.

Institutional Review Board (IRB)   a legally mandated independent committee that evaluates whether an institution's proposed research with human participants complies with federal ethics regulations.

instrumental case study   a case study in which the case is analyzed in depth because it is an example of, or otherwise provides information about, a broader phenomenon.

instrumentation (as a potential confounding variable)   changes that occur in a measuring instrument during the course of data collection (e.g., pretest to posttest changes in the observer's criteria for rating depression).

integrity, principle of   a principle in the APA Ethics Code stating that psychologists should be honest and truthful, and should not engage in fraud.

interaction (also called **interaction effect**)   in a factorial design, occurs when the way in which an independent variable influences behavior differs depending upon the level of another independent variable.

internal replication   occurs when researchers follow up their initial study with one or more replications and present this series of studies in a single research report.

internal validity   the degree to which we can be confident that a study demonstrated that one variable had a causal effect on another variable.

interobserver reliability (also called **interrater reliability**)   the degree to which independent observers show agreement in their observations. It occurs, for example, when different raters using the same coding system agree in how they classify or otherwise score participants' responses.

interval scale   a type of measurement in which equal distances between values on the scale reflect equal differences in the amount of the attribute being measured.

intervention phase   See **treatment phase.**

interviewer effects   aspects of the interviewer's presence that distort participants' responses.

intrinsic case study   A case study in which the case is examined in depth due to some inherent interest in learning about that particular individual or phenomenon.

justice, principle of   a principle in the APA Ethics Code calling upon psychologists to recognize that the benefits of their research, and of psychological science as a whole, should be made available to all persons.

Latin Square   in a single-factor experiment with n conditions, an n (number of positions in a series) × n (number of orders) matrix in which each condition will appear only once in each column and each row.

law of parsimony   a guiding rule stating that explanations should use the minimum number of principles necessary to account for the greatest number of facts.

leading question   a questionnaire item presented in an unbalanced way that can overtly or subtly suggest that one viewpoint or response is preferable to another.

Likert scale   a rating scale that measures participants' attitudes by combining scores on several items, each of which records how positively or negatively a participant feels about a statement (e.g., "strongly agree," "agree," "neither agree nor disagree").

loaded question   a questionnaire item containing emotionally charged words that suggest one viewpoint or response is preferable to another, or containing assumptions with which the option to disagree is not provided.

longitudinal research   a research design in which the same participants are tested across different time periods (i.e., data are gathered on the same individuals or groups on two or more occasions over time); *compare* **cross-sectional research.**

main effect   in a factorial design, occurs when an independent variable has an overall effect on a dependent variable.

manipulation check   an approach that seeks to improve the validity of an experiment by determining whether the procedures used to manipulate an independent variable successfully captured the intended construct.

margin of sampling error   a range of values within which the true population value is presumed to reside; *see also* **sampling error.**

masking (also called **blinding**)   a procedure in which the parties involved in an experiment are kept unaware of the hypothesis being tested and/or the condition to which each participant has been assigned.

matched-groups design   a between-subjects design in which each set of participants that has been matched on one or more attributes is randomly assigned the various conditions of the experiment.

matching variable   in a matched-groups design, a characteristic on which sets of individuals are matched as closely as possible.

maturation   the ways in which people naturally change over time, independent of their participation in a study.

mean   the arithmetic average of a distribution of scores.

measurement   the process of systematically assigning values (numbers, labels, or other symbols) to represent attributes of organisms, objects, or events.

measures of central tendency   calculations that identify the typical values or "center" of a distribution of scores; the mode, mean, and median are three common measures of central tendency.

measures of dispersion (also called **measures of variability**) calculations that assess how much the scores in a distribution are spread out; the range, variance, and standard deviation are three common measures of dispersion.

median   the midpoint of a distribution.

mediator variable   a variable that provides a causal link in the sequence between an independent variable and a dependent variable.

meta-analysis   a statistical procedure for combining the results of different studies that examine the same topic.

minimal risk   defined as risk in which "the probability and magnitude of harm or discomfort anticipated in the research are not greater in and of themselves than those ordinarily encountered in daily life or during the performance of routine physical or psychological examinations or tests" (U. S. Department of Health and Human Services, 2009, Section 46.102.i); *compare* **at risk.**

mixed-factorial design   a factorial design that includes at least one between-subjects variable and at least one within-subjects variable.

mixed-methods case study design   An approach to conducting a case study in which researchers rely substantially on both qualitative and quantitative data and analyses to explore a case.

mode   the most frequently occurring score in a distribution.

moderator variable   a factor that alters the strength or direction of the relation between an independent and a dependent variable.

multiple regression   a statistical analysis that explores the linear relation between one variable and a set of two or more other variables.

multiple-baseline design   a type of single-case design in which (1) behavior is repeatedly measured, first during a baseline period and then during a treatment period; (2) this procedure is replicated with at least one other participant or behavior, or in one other setting; and (3) the time at which the treatment is introduced (and thus, typically, the length of the baseline period) varies across the different participants, behaviors, or settings.

multiple-baseline design across behaviors   a type of single-case design in which the same treatment is applied to two or more distinct behaviors of the same participant, and the switch from baseline to treatment periods is staggered across behaviors.

multiple-baseline design across settings   a type of single-case design in which the same treatment is applied to the same target behavior in two or more settings, and the switch from baseline to treatment is staggered across settings.

multiple-baseline design across subjects   a type of single-case design in which two or more participants are exposed to the same treatment, and the switch from baseline to treatment periods is staggered across participants.

multiple-case study design   an approach to conducting a case study in which researchers examine two or more cases and perform an in-depth analysis of each case.

multistage sampling   the use of two or more stages to select progressively smaller samples.

natural-groups design   an approach in which a researcher measures a subject variable, forms different groups based on participants' level of that variable, and then measures how the different groups respond on other variables.

naturalistic observation   an observational technique in which researchers passively observe behavior in a natural setting.

needs assessment   the process of determining whether there is a need for a social program and the general steps required to meet that need.

negative correlation   correlation in which higher scores or levels of one variable tend to be associated with lower scores or levels of another variable.

nominal scale   a type of measurement that occurs when the scale values represent only qualitative differences (i.e., differences of type rather than amount) of the attribute of interest.

nonexperimental research   *See* **descriptive research.**

nonmaleficence, principle of   a principle in the APA Ethics Code stating that psychologists should be careful not to cause harm.

nonprobability sampling   a sampling technique in which each member of the population either does not have a chance of being

selected into the sample, the probability of being selected cannot be determined, or both.

nonrepresentative (or **biased**) **sample**   a sample that does not reflect important characteristics of the population.

nonresponse bias   bias that occurs when people who were selected but didn't participate in a survey would have provided significantly different answers (or other data) from those provided by participants.

normal distribution (also called **normal curve**)   a theoretical distribution for a population of scores; the curve is symmetrical and bell shaped, and has other unique mathematical properties.

null hypothesis (H_0)   the hypothesis that is directly examined by a statistical test.

Nuremberg Code   a code established in 1947 by military tribunal judges that sets forth the ethical principles essential if a medical experiment is to be "permissible."

observational research   research that encompasses different types of nonexperimental studies in which behavior is systematically watched and recorded.

observer bias   bias that occurs when researchers have expectations or other predispositions that distort their observations.

observer rating and ranking scales   measures in which observers record their own quantitative judgments that evaluate participants' behavior or other characteristics.

one-group posttest-only design   a design in which a treatment occurs and afterward the dependent variable is measured once.

one-group pretest-posttest design   a design in which a dependent variable is measured once before and once after a treatment occurs.

one-shot correlational study   *See* **cross-sectional research design.**

open-ended question   an item, as in a questionnaire or survey, that asks participants to respond in their own terms.

operational definition   the specific procedures (i.e., the specific "operations") used to measure or manipulate a variable in a particular study; refers to defining a variable in terms of the procedures used to measure or manipulate it.

operationism   defining a concept in terms of the specific procedures (or "operations") used to represent it.

order effects (also called **sequence effects**)   effects that occur when participants' responses are affected by the order of the conditions to which they are exposed.

ordinal scale   a scale in which the different scale values represent relative differences in the amount of some attribute.

outcome evaluation   a type of program evaluation that assesses a program's effectiveness in achieving its goals.

parameter   a number that describes a population (e.g., the percentage of Americans who hold a given political opinion).

partial correlation   a statistical approach in which a correlation between variable X and variable Y is computed while statistically controlling for their individual correlations with a third variable, Z.

partial replication   replication that includes only some of the conditions of the original study.

participant observation   an observational technique in which the observer becomes a part of the group or social setting being studied.

Pearson's *r* (also called **Pearson product-moment correlation coefficient**)   a statistic that measures the direction and strength of the linear relation between two variables that have been measured on an interval or ratio scale.

peer-reviewed journal   a professional journal in which reports submitted for publication first undergo a screening process by several experts.

percentile rank   the percentage of scores in a distribution that fall below a particular score.

person × situation (or **person × environment**) **factorial design** an experimental design that incorporates at least one subject variable along with at least one manipulated situational variable.

physical trace measures unobtrusive measures in which researchers examine traces of behavior that people create or leave behind.

pie chart a circular graph that is divided into segments.

pilot study a trial run, usually conducted with a smaller number of participants, prior to initiating the actual experiment.

placebo control group the group of participants in an experiment who do not receive the core treatment but are led to believe that they are (or may be) receiving it.

placebo effect the effect that occurs when participants' expectations about how a treatment will affect them influence their responses (on the dependent variable) to that treatment.

plagiarism presenting someone else's work or ideas as one's own.

plausible alternative explanations credible reasons for why something has occurred, that differ from our belief or conclusion about it.

population all the cases or observations of interest in a given study.

positive correlation correlation in which higher scores or levels of one variable tend to be associated with higher scores or levels of another variable.

posttest-only design with a nonequivalent control group a design in which participants in one condition are exposed to a treatment, a nonequivalent group is not exposed to the treatment, and scores from both groups are obtained after the treatment ends.

power (of a statistical test) the probability of correctly rejecting the null hypothesis (H_0); that is, rejecting H_0 when it indeed is false.

power analysis examines the relation between power, effect size, and sample size for a given statistical test and alpha level.

practice effect a performance improvement due to gaining greater experience with a task.

predictor variable a variable whose scores are used to estimate scores of a criterion variable.

pretest-posttest design with a nonequivalent control group a design in which pre- and posttreatment scores are obtained for a treatment group and a nonequivalent control group.

probability sampling a sampling technique in which each member of the population has a chance of being selected into the sample and in which the probability of being selected can be specified.

probability value (also called **p value**) the probability that an outcome or one more extreme is due simply to chance.

process evaluation a type of program evaluation that determines whether a program is being implemented as intended.

program diffusion the process of implementing and maintaining effective programs in other settings or with other groups.

program evaluation the use of research methods to assess the need for, and the design, implementation, and effectiveness of, a social intervention.

program theory and design assessment a type of program evaluation that examines the rationale for why a program has been, or will be, designed in a particular way.

progressive effects changes in participants' responses that result from their cumulative exposure to prior conditions.

prospective design a longitudinal design in which variable X is measured at an earlier point in time than variable Y.

proximal (or **proximate**) **causes** immediate causes; in a chain of interrelated events that lead to a given result, the events that are close to the result; *compare* **distal causes**.

psychophysics a subfield of the study of sensation and perception that examines the relation between physical properties of stimuli (such as their intensity) and sensory-perceptual responses.

purposive sampling a sampling technique in which researchers select a sample according to a specific goal or purpose of the study rather than at random.

qualitative analysis nonmathematical analysis of data, which often involves identifying, classifying, and describing different types of characteristics, outcomes, or behaviors.

qualitative case study a case study in which the central goal is to examine an individual case in depth, within its real-life context, using qualitative methods.

qualitative research research that seeks to achieve a relatively holistic or thematic description and understanding of behavior, primarily through the nonstatistical analysis of data.

qualitative variables variables representing properties that differ in "type" (i.e., a type of attribute or quality), such as sex, religious affiliation, eye color, and marital status.

quantitative analysis mathematical analysis of data, which typically involves using statistics to aid in summarizing and interpreting those data.

quantitative case study a case study in which researchers rely primarily on numerical assessments and analysis to describe and understand a case.

quantitative research research that relies primarily on numerical data and numerical (e.g., statistical) analysis to describe and understand behavior.

quantitative variables variables representing properties that differ in amount (e.g., height, weight, degree of shyness, time spent learning a task, or blood alcohol levels on a Saturday night).

quasi-experiment a study that has some features of an experiment but lacks key aspects of experimental control.

quota sampling a sampling technique in which a sample is nonrandomly selected to match the proportion of one or more key characteristics of the population.

random assignment a procedure in which each participant has an equal probability of being assigned to any one of the conditions in the experiment.

random measurement error random fluctuations in the measuring situation that cause the obtained scores to deviate from a true score.

random-groups design *See* **independent-groups design.**

randomized controlled trial (also called **randomized clinical trial**) an experiment in which participants are randomly assigned to different conditions for the purpose of examining the effectiveness of an intervention.

random-selected-orders design a within-subjects design in which a subset of orders is randomly selected from the entire set of all possible orders, and each order is administered to one participant.

range a statistic that describes the highest and lowest scores in a distribution; it can also be expressed as the distance between them.

range restriction the artificial limiting of the range of scores obtained for a variable.

ratio scale measurement in which equal distances between values on the scale reflect equal differences in the amount of the attribute being measured and the scale has a true zero point.

raw scores the original individual scores obtained for a particular variable.

reactivity a change in behavior that occurs as a result of the process of observing (or otherwise measuring) behavior.

reason the use of logic and rational (i.e., intellectually sound) argument to reach a conclusion about how things "must be."

regression analysis (also called **simple linear regression**) a statistical analysis that explores the quantitative linear relation between two variables.

regression to the mean the statistical concept that when two variables are not perfectly correlated (e.g., scores on a pretest and posttest), more extreme scores on one variable will be associated overall with less extreme scores on the other variable. In experimental design, regression to the mean refers to the fact that when a group is selected because of their above- or below-average scores on a measure, the group's average score on a retest (or on another related measure) will tend to regress toward (i.e., become closer to) the mean score of the overall population.

relational research See **correlational research.**

relative cumulative frequency distribution a distribution that depicts the total proportion or percentage of cases that occur at or below (or, at or above) each value in a data set.

relative frequency distribution a distribution that depicts the proportion or percentage of times that each value occurs within a data set.

reliability (of a measure) the degree of the consistency of measurement.

replication the process of repeating a study to determine whether the original findings will be upheld.

replication and extension (also called **replication with extension**) a replication that adds a new design element to the original study.

representative sample a sample that reflects the important characteristics of the population.

research protocol a standardized set of procedures that a researcher will follow with each participant.

respect, principle of a principle in the APA Ethics Code calling for psychologists to "respect the dignity and worth of all people, and the rights of individuals to privacy, confidentiality, and self-determination" (APA, 2010a, p. 3).

response rate (of a survey) the percentage of those who participate in a survey out of all those who were selected to participate.

responsibility, principle of a principle in the APA Ethics Code that calls for adhering to professional codes of conduct and not exploiting participants.

reversal design See **ABAB design; withdrawal design.**

reverse-counterbalancing design (also called **ABBA-counterbalancing design**) a within-subjects design in which each participant receives a random order of all the conditions and then receives them again in the reverse order.

risk/benefit ratio the comparison of risks and benefits. To approve a study, an IRB first must be convinced that the researcher has minimized any scientifically necessary risks to participants; and, second, regardless of the level of risk, that such risk is outweighed by the study's potential benefits.

sample a subset of cases or observations from a population.

sampling error chance fluctuations that introduce a degree of error when using sample statistics to estimate population parameters; see also **margin of sampling error.**

sampling frame a list—of names, phone numbers, addresses, or other units—from which a sample will be selected.

sampling variability chance fluctuations in the characteristics of samples that occur when randomly selecting samples from a population.

scales of measurement rules for assigning scale values to measurements.

scan sampling a sampling technique in which the observer rapidly scans each member of a group at preselected times so that the entire group is observed within a relatively short period.

scatter plot (also called **scattergram**) a graph in which data points portray the intersection of X and Y values.

science a process of systematically gathering and evaluating empirical evidence to answer questions and test ideas.

selection a potential threat to internal validity in which, at the start of a study, participants in the various conditions already differ on a characteristic that can partly or fully account for the eventual results.

selection interactions the interaction of selection with another threat to internal validity.

self-selection the selection that results when participants place themselves into a sample rather than being chosen for inclusion by a researcher.

semi-structured interview an approach to interviewing in which the researcher identifies in advance a set of topics or themes to be discussed with the interviewee, but the way and sequence in which questions are asked remain flexible.

sensitivity (of a measure) the ability of a measure to detect an effect that actually is present.

sensitization effect a type of order effect in which exposure to multiple conditions increases participants' awareness of, or sensitivity to, the variable that is being experimentally manipulated.

sequence effects See **order effects.**

sequential research design a research design in which several age cohorts are tested longitudinally.

significance level (also called **alpha (α) level**) the probability level below which a result is considered to be sufficiently unlikely to be due to chance.

simple interrupted time-series design a design in which a dependent variable is repeatedly measured at periodic intervals before and after a treatment.

simple interrupted time-series design with a nonequivalent control group a design in which a series of pre- and posttreatment scores are obtained for a treatment group and a non-equivalent control group.

simple linear regression See **regression analysis.**

simple main effect in a factorial experiment, the effect of one independent variable at a particular level of another independent variable.

simple random sampling a sampling technique in which every member of the sampling frame has an equal probability of being chosen at random to participate in the survey.

single-blind procedure in experiments, a procedure in which either the participants or the experimenters, but not both, are kept unaware of who is receiving the actual treatment and who is receiving a placebo.

single-case experimental designs an approach to experimentation that allows researchers to systematically examine how an independent variable influences the behavior of an individual case.

single-case study design an approach to conducting a case study in which researchers analyze one case in depth.

single-factor design an experimental design that has only one independent variable.

single-stage cluster sampling a form of probability sampling in which all the participants in the randomly selected clusters are chosen to participate in the survey.

situation sampling a sampling technique in which behavior is observed in a variety of settings.

situational variable a characteristic that differs across environments or stimuli.

skepticism an outlook that questions the validity of claims before deciding whether to accept them.

skewed distribution an asymmetrical distribution.

snowball sampling a type of purposive sampling in which people contacted to participate in a survey are asked to recruit or to provide contact information (names, locations) for other people who meet the criteria for survey inclusion.

social desirability bias in a study, a participant's tendency to respond in a way that the participant feels is socially appropriate, rather than as she or he truly feels.

Spearman's rho (also called **Spearman rank-order correlation coefficient**) a statistic used to measure the relation between two quantitative variables when one or both variables have been measured on an ordinal scale (i.e., the scores represent ranks).

split-half reliability a method of estimating reliability in which the items that compose a test are divided into two subsets, and the correlation between subsets is determined.

standard deviation the square root of the variance; the standard deviation measures how much the scores in a distribution are spread out in relation to their mean as expressed in the original units of measurement. *See also* **variance**.

standard error of the mean (*SEM*) the standard deviation of a sampling distribution of the mean.

statistic a number that pertains to a sample.

statistical conclusion validity the degree to which the statistical treatment of data is proper and the researchers' statistical conclusions are sound.

statistically significant describes a result that is unlikely to be due to chance.

stratified random sampling a sampling technique in which a sampling frame is divided into groups (called strata; singular = stratum), and then within each group random sampling is used to select the members of the sample.

structured observation an observational technique in which the researcher fully or partly configures the setting in which behavior will be observed.

subject loss *See* **attrition**.

subject variable a personal characteristic that differs from one individual to another.

sum of squares (*SS*) the sum of squared deviations of scores from the mean of their distribution.

survey a research technique that uses questionnaires and/or interviews to gather information about participants.

switching replication design a design in which one group receives a treatment and a nonequivalent group initially does not receive the treatment but is then exposed (i.e., "switched") to it at a later point in time.

systematic error (also called **bias**) a constant amount of error that occurs with each measurement.

t **test** an inferential statistical test often used to determine whether there is a statistically significant difference between the means of two groups of scores for the same variable.

target behavior the behavior that a treatment is designed to change.

tenacity (as a method of knowing) holding a belief simply because it is what has long been believed.

testing a potential threat to internal validity in which the act of measuring participants' responses affects how they respond on subsequent measures.

test–retest reliability a method of measuring reliability determined by administering the same measure to the same participants on two or more occasions, under equivalent test conditions.

theory a set of formal statements that specifies how and why variables or events are related.

third-variable problem an ambiguity in correlational research whereby a third variable, Z, may be the true cause of why X and Y appear to be related.

Three Rs in nonhuman animal research, three general principles to which many federal ethical standards and regulations pertain: reduction, refinement, and replacement.

three-way interaction an effect in which the interaction of two independent variables depends upon the level of a third independent variable.

time sampling a sampling technique in which researchers select a representative set of time periods during which observations will occur.

treatment phase (also called **intervention phase**) in applied research, the condition that involves the presentation of a specific treatment or other intervention; the experimental condition.

two-way causality problem *See* **bidirectionality problem**.

two-way interaction an effect in which the way that one independent variable influences a dependent variable depends upon the level of a second independent variable.

Type I error rejecting the null hypothesis when, in fact, the null hypothesis is true.

Type II error failing to reject the null hypothesis when, in fact, the null hypothesis is false.

undisguised observation an observational technique in which the individuals being studied are aware that they are being observed; *compare* **disguised observation**.

unobtrusive measure a technique that assesses behavior without making people aware that the behavior is being measured or studied.

validity the degree to which a measure truly assesses what it is claimed to assess.

variable any factor or attribute that can assume two or more values.

variance the average of the squared deviations about the mean; variance measures how much the scores in a distribution are spread out in relation to their mean. *See also* **standard deviation**.

wait-list control group a group of randomly selected participants who do not receive a treatment, but expect to and do receive it after treatment of the experimental group(s) ends.

withdrawal design (also called **reversal design**) a type of single-case design in which, after the initial A phase, the subsequent A phases involve a "withdrawal" of the treatment or a "reversal" of the procedures; *see also* **ABAB design**.

within-subjects design an approach to designing experiments in which each participant engages in every condition of the experiment one or more times.

within-subjects factorial design a factorial design in which each participant engages in every condition.

yoked control group an experimental design in which each control group member is procedurally linked (i.e., "yoked") to a particular experimental group member whose behavior will determine how both of them are treated.

z **score** a statistic that transforms an original score into a number that represents how many standard deviations that score is from the mean.

Aamodt, M. G. (1991). *Applied industrial/organizational psychology.* Belmont, CA: Wadsworth.

Abidin, R. (1995). *Parenting stress index (PSI)* (3rd ed.). Odessa, FL: Psychological Assessment Resources.

Achenbach, T. M. (1992). *Manual for child behavior checklist/2–3 and 1992 profile.* Burlington: University of Vermont, Department of Psychiatry.

Achenbach, T. M., & Rescorla, L. A. (2001). *Manual for ASEBA school-age forms & profiles.* Burlington: University of Vermont, Research Center for Children, Youth, & Families.

Ader, R., & Cohen, N. (1975). Behaviorally conditioned immunosuppression. *Psychosomatic Medicine, 37,* 333–340. doi:10.1097/00006842-197507000-00007

Ader, R., & Kelley, K. W. (2007). A global view of twenty years of *Brain, Behavior, and Immunity. Brain, Behavior, and Immunity, 21,* 20–22. doi:10.1016/j.bbi.2006.07.003

Allan, V. (2006, May 12). The mild bunch. *Sunday Herald.* Retrieved from http://www.heraldscotland.com/

Allen, A. P., & Smith, A. P. (2012). Demand characteristics, pre-test attitudes and time-on-task trends in the effects of chewing gum on attention and reported mood in healthy volunteers. *Appetite, 59,* 349–356. doi:10.1016/j.appet.2012.05.026

Ally, B. A., Hussey, E. P., & Donahue, M. J. (2013). A case of hyperthymesia: Rethinking the role of the amygdala in autobiographical memory. *Neurocase, 19,* 166–181. doi:10.1080/13554794.2011.654225

Altmann, J. (1974). Observational study of behavior: Sampling methods. *Behaviour, 49,* 227–267. doi:10.1163/156853974X00534

American Association for Public Opinion Research. (2011). *Standard definitions: Final dispositions of case codes and outcome rates for surveys.* Retrieved from http://www.aapor.org/Standards_and _Ethics.htm

American Association for Public Opinion Research. (n.d.). *Question wording.* Retrieved from http://www.aapor.org/Resources.htm

American Heritage Dictionary of the English Language (3rd ed.). (1980). Boston: Houghton Mifflin.

American Psychological Association, Committee on Animal Research and Ethics. (n.d.). *Research with animals in psychology.* Retrieved from http://www.apa.org/research/responsible/research-animals.pdf

American Psychological Association. (1953). *Ethical standards of psychologists.* Washington, DC: Author.

American Psychological Association. (1973). *Ethical principles in the conduct of research with human participants.* Washington DC: Author.

American Psychological Association. (2010a). *Ethical principles of psychologists and code of conduct* (2002, amended June 1, 2010). Retrieved from http://www.apa.org/ethics/code/principles.pdf

American Psychological Association. (2010b). *Publication manual of the American Psychological Association* (6th ed.). Washington, DC: Author.

American Psychological Association. (2012). *Guidelines for ethical conduct in the care and use of nonhuman animals in research.* Retrieved from http://www.apa.org/science/leadership/care /guidelines.aspx

American Psychological Association. (2013). *APA guidelines for the undergraduate psychology major: Version 2.0.* Retrieved from http://www.apa.org/ed/precollege/undergrad/index.aspx

American Psychological Association. (2015a). *PsycARTICLES.* Retrieved from http://www.apa.org/pubs/databases/psycarticles /index.aspx

American Psychological Association. (2015b). *PsycINFO.* Retrieved from http://www.apa.org/pubs/databases/psycinfo/index.aspx

American Psychological Association. (2016). Summary report of journal operations, 2015. *American Psychologist, 71,* 455–456. doi:10.1037/amp0000014

Amit, Z., & Smith, B. R. (1992). Differential ethanol intake in Tryon maze-bright and Tryon maze-dull rats: Implications for the validity of the animal model of selectively bred rats for high ethanol consumption. *Psychopharmacology, 108,* 136–140. doi:10.1007/BF02245298

Anderson, B. A., Silver, B. D., & Abramson, P. R. (1988). The effects of the race of the interviewer on race-related attitudes of Black respondents in SRC/CPS national election studies. *Public Opinion Quarterly, 52,* 289–324. doi:10.1086/269108

Anderson, C. J., Bahnik, S., Barnett-Cowan, M., Bosco, F. A., Chandler, J., Chartier, C. R., . . . Zuni, K. (2016). Response to comment on "Estimating the reproducibility of psychological science." *Science, 351*(6277), 1037c. doi:10.1126/science .aad9163

Anderson, J. Q., & Rainie, L. (2010). *The future of the Internet.* Retrieved from Pew Internet and American Life Project website: http://www .pewinternet.org/Reports/2010/Future-of-the-Internet-IV.aspx

Anderson, S. F., & Maxwell, S. E. (2016). There's more than one way to conduct a replication study: Beyond statistical significance. *Psychological Methods, 21,* 1–12. doi:10.1037/met0000051

Aronson, E. (2004). Reducing hostility and building compassion: Lessons from the jigsaw classroom. In A. G. Miller (Ed.), *The social psychology of good and evil* (pp. 469–488). New York, NY: Guilford.

Aronson, E., Wilson, T. D., & Brewer, M. B. (1968). Experimentation in social psychology. In L. Gardner & E. Aronson (Eds.), *The handbook of social psychology* (2nd ed., pp. 99–142). Reading, MA: Addison-Wesley.

Asch, S. E. (1955). Opinions and social pressure. *Scientific American, 193*(5), 31–35. doi:10.1038/scientificamerican1155-31

AskMen. (2012, July 24). *Great Male Survey: 2012 edition* (Part 1: Dating and sex). Retrieved from http://www.askmen.com /specials/great_male_survey/

Associated Press. (2005, July 6). Russian astrologer sues NASA over *Deep Impact. Seattle Post-Intelligencer,* p. A4.

Associated Press. (2015, August 27). Many psychology studies fail reproducibility test. *CBC News.* Retrieved from http://www.cbc .ca/news

Aubrey, A. (2015, June 19). Chocolate, chocolate, it's good for your heart, study finds. *NPR: National Public Radio.* Retrieved from http://www.npr.org/sections/thesalt/2015/06/19/415527652 /chocolate-chocolate-its-good-for-your-heart-study-finds

Baldwin, V. N., & Powell, T. (2015). Google Calendar: A single case experimental design study of a man with severe memory problems. *Neuropsychological Rehabilitation, 25,* 617–636. doi:10.1080/09602011.2014.956764

Ball, S. (2007, March 5). Despite allure of Internet surveys, old-fashioned, face-to-face interview still best, Stanford expert says. *Cornell University Chronicle Online.* Retrieved from http://www.news.cornell.edu/

Banaji, M. R., & Crowder, R. G. (1989). The bankruptcy of everyday memory. *American Psychologist, 44,* 1185–1193. doi:10.1037/0003-066X.44.9.1185

Banda, D. R., McAfee, J. K., & Hart, S. L. (2009). Decreasing self-injurious behavior in a student with autism and Tourette syndrome through positive attention and extinction. *Child & Family Behavior Therapy, 31,* 144–156. doi:10.1080/07317100902910604

Banda, D. R., McAfee, J. K., & Hart, S. L. (2012). Decreasing self-injurious behavior and fading self-restraint in a student with autism and Tourette syndrome. *Behavioral Interventions, 27,* 164–174. doi:10.1002/bin.1344

Barlow, D. H., & Nock, M. K. (2009). Why can't we be more idiographic in our research? *Perspectives on Psychological Science, 4,* 19–21. doi:10.1111/j.1745-6924.2009.01088.x

Barlow, D. H., Nock, M. K., & Hersen, M. (2009). *Single case experimental designs: Strategies for studying behavior change* (3rd ed.). Boston, MA: Allyn & Bacon.

Baron, R. M., & Kenny, D. A. (1986). The moderator–mediator variable distinction in social psychological research: Conceptual, strategic, and statistical considerations. *Journal of Personality and Social Psychology, 51,* 1173–1182. doi:10.1037/0022-3514.51.6.1173

Baumeister, A. A. (2006). Serendipity and the cerebral localization of pleasure. *Journal of the History of the Neurosciences, 5,* 92–98. doi:10.1080/09647040500274879

Baumeister, A. A., Hawkins, M. F., & López-Muñoz, F. (2010). Toward standardized usage of the word serendipity in the historiography of psychopharmacology. *Journal of the History of the Neurosciences, 19,* 253–270. doi:10.1080/09647040903188205

Baumeister, R. F. (2008). Free will in scientific psychology. *Perspectives on Psychological Science, 3,* 14–19. doi:10.1111/j.1745-6916.2008.00057.x

Baumrind, D. (1985). Research using intentional deception: Ethical issues revisited. *American Psychologist, 40,* 165–174. doi:10.1037/0003-066X.40.2.165

Beel, J., & Gipp, B. (2009). Google Scholar's ranking algorithm: The impact of citation counts (an empirical study). In A. Flory & M. Collard (Eds.), *Proceedings of the 3rd IEEE International Conference on Research Challenges in Information Science,* 429–446. doi:10.1109/RCIS.2009.5089308

Belia, S., Fidler, F., Williams, J., & Cumming, G. (2005). Researchers misunderstand confidence intervals and standard error bars. *Psychological Methods, 10,* 389–396. doi:10.1037/1082-989X.10.4.389

Bem, D. J., & Lord, C. G. (1979). Template matching: A proposal for probing the ecological validity of experimental settings in social psychology. *Journal of Personality and Social Psychology, 37,* 833–846. doi:10.1037/0022-3514.37.6.833

Benson, E. (2003, January). The unexpected benefits of basic science. *Monitor on Psychology, 34*(1). Retrieved from http://www.apa.org/monitor/

Bernard, H. R. (1996). Qualitative data, quantitative analysis. *Field Methods, 8,* 9–11. doi:10.1177/1525822X960080010401

Bernstein, D. A., Clarke-Stewart, A., Penner, L. A., Roy, E. J., & Wickens, C. D. (2000). *Psychology* (5th ed.). Boston, MA: Houghton Mifflin.

Berry, C. M., & Sackett, P. R. (2009). Individual differences in course choice result in underestimation of the validity of college admissions systems. *Psychological Science, 20,* 822–830. doi:10.1111/j.1467-9280.2009.02368.x

Birnbaum, M. H. (2004). Human research and data collection via the Internet. *Annual Review of Psychology, 55,* 803–832. doi:10.1146/annurev.psych.55.090902.141601

Bjork, E. L., & Bjork, R. A. (2011). Making things hard on yourself, but in a good way: Creating desirable difficulties to enhance learning. In M. A. Gernsbacher, R. W. Pew, L. M. Hough, & J. R. Pomerantz (Eds.), *Psychology and the real world* (pp. 56–64). New York, NY: Worth.

Blumberg, S. J., & Luke, J. V. (2015). *Wireless substitution: Early release of estimates from the National Health Interview Survey, January–June 2015.* Retrieved from the National Center for Health Statistics website: http://www.cdc.gov/nchs/data/nhis/earlyrelease/wireless201512.pdf

Boesch, C. (1991). Teaching among wild chimpanzees. *Animal Behaviour, 41,* 530–532. doi:10.1016/S0003-3472(05)80857-7

Bolton, D., William, T., Perrin, S., Atkinson, L., Gallop, C., Waite, P., & Salkovskis, P. (2011). Randomized controlled trial of full and brief cognitive-behaviour therapy and wait-list for paediatric obsessive-compulsive disorder. *Journal of Child Psychology and Psychiatry, 52,* 1269–1278. doi:10.1111/j.1469-7610.2011.02419.x

Bonanno, G. A., Galea, S., Bucciarelli, A., & Vlahov, D. (2006). Psychological resilience after disaster: New York City in the aftermath of the September 11th terrorist attack. *Psychological Science, 17,* 181–186. doi:10.1111/j.1467-9280.2006.01682.x

Bond, F. W., & Bunce, D. (2001). Job control mediates change in a work reorganization intervention for stress reduction. *Journal of Occupational Health Psychology, 6,* 290–302. doi:10.1037/1076-8998.6.4.290

Bond, R. M., Fariss, C. J., Jones, J. J., Kramer, A. D., Marlow, C., Settle, J. E., & Fowler, J. H. (2012). A 61-million-person experiment in social influence and political mobilization. *Nature, 489,* 295–298. doi:10.1038/nature11421

Bottge, B. A., Rueda, E., LaRoque, P. T., Serlin, R. C., & Kwon, J. (2007). Integrating reform-oriented math instruction in special education settings. *Learning Disabilities Research & Practice, 22,* 96–109. doi:10.1111/j.1540-5826.2007.00234.x

Brandt, A. M. (2000). Racism and research: The case of the Tuskegee syphilis experiment. In S. M. Reverby & J. H. Jones (Eds.), *Tuskegee's truths: Rethinking the Tuskegee syphilis study* (pp. 15–33). Chapel Hill: University of North Carolina Press.

Brevard Times. (2012, July 24). Great Male/Female Survey 2012: Dating, politics, technology. Retrieved from http://news.brevardtimes.com

Brewer, M. B. (2000). Research design and issues of validity. In H. T. Reis & C. M. Judd (Eds.), *Handbook of research methods in social and personality psychology* (pp. 3–16). Cambridge, UK: Cambridge University Press.

Brown, R. E. (2007). Behavioural phenotyping of transgenic mice. *Canadian Journal of Experimental Psychology, 61,* 328–344. doi:10.1037/cjep2007033

Buhle, J. T., Stevens, B. L., Friedman, J. J., & Wager, T. D. (2012). Distraction and placebo: Two separate routes to pain control. *Psychological Science, 23,* 246–253. doi:10.1177/0956797611427919

Buss, D. M., & Schmitt, D. P. (1993). Sexual strategies theory: An evolutionary perspective on human mating. *Psychological Review, 100,* 204–232. doi:10.1037/0033-295X.100.2.204

Buss, D. M., & Schmitt, D. P. (2011). Evolutionary psychology and feminism. *Sex Roles, 64,* 768–787. doi:10.1007/s11199-011-9987-3

Calaprice, A. (2005). *The new quotable Einstein.* Princeton, NJ: Princeton University Press.

Callender, K. A., Olson, S. L., Choe, D. E., & Sameroff, A. J. (2012). The effects of parental depressive symptoms, appraisals, and physical punishment on later child externalizing behavior. *Journal of Abnormal Child Psychology, 40,* 471–483. doi:10.1007/s10802-011-9572-9

Campbell, D. T., & Fiske, D. W. (1959). Convergent and discriminant validation by the multitrait-multimethod matrix. *Psychological Bulletin, 56,* 81–105. doi:10.1037/h0046016

Campbell, D. T., & Stanley, J. C. (1966). *Experimental and quasi-experimental designs for research.* Chicago, IL: Rand McNally.

Campbell, J. M. (2004). Statistical comparison of four effect sizes for single-subject designs. *Behavior Modification, 28,* 234–246. doi:10.1177/0145445503259264

Campbell, W. K., Goodie, A. S., & Foster, J. D. (2004). Narcissism, confidence, and risk attitude. *Journal of Behavioral Decision Making, 17,* 297–311. doi:10.1002/bdm.475

Canadian Press. (2009, May 5). Telemarketing survey scams widespread in Canada: Poll. *CBC News.* Retrieved from http://www.cbc.ca/news/

Canadian Psychological Association. (2000). *Canadian code of ethics for psychologists* (3rd ed.). Retrieved from http://www.cpa.ca/cpasite/userfiles/Documents/Canadian%20Code%20of%20Ethics%20for%20Psycho.pdf

Canadian Psychological Association. (2016). *Canadian code of ethics for psychologists* (4th ed.; Second full draft for comment—March 2016). Retrieved from http://www.cpa.ca/docs/File/Ethics/CPA_Code_March2016FINALDraftDIST.pdf

Carey, B. (2015, August 27). Many psychology findings not as strong as claimed, study says. *The New York Times.* Retrieved from http://www.nytimes.com

Carifio, J., & Perla, R. J. (2007). Ten common misunderstandings, misconceptions, persistent myths and urban legends about Likert scales and Likert response formats and their antidotes. *Journal of Social Sciences, 3,* 106–116. doi:10.3844/jssp.2007.106.116

Cavazos-Rehg, P. A., & DeLucia-Waack, J. L. (2009). Education, ethnic identity, and acculturation as predictors of self-esteem in Latino adolescents. *Journal of Counseling and Development, 87,* 47–54. doi:10.1002/j.1556-6678.2009.tb00548.x

CBS News. (2000, February 14). The truth about push polls. Retrieved from http://www.cbsnews.com/news/the-truth-about-push-polls/

Ceci, S. J., & Bruck, M. (2009). Do IRBs pass the minimal harm test? *Perspectives on Psychological Science, 4,* 28–29. doi:10.1111/j.1745-6924.2009.01084.x

Ceci, S. J., Peters, D., & Plotkin, J. (1985). Human subjects review, personal values, and the regulation of social science research. *American Psychologist, 4,* 994–1002. doi:10.1037/0003-066X.40.9.994

Cedernaes, J., Brandell, J., Ros, O., Broman, J.-E., Hogenkamp, P. S., Schiöth, H. B., & Benedict, C. (2014). Increased impulsivity in response to food cues after sleep loss in healthy young men. *Obesity, 22,* 1786–1791. doi:10.1002/oby.20786

Center for Open Science. (n.d.). *The reproducibility project: Cancer biology.* Retrieved from https://osf.io/e81xl/wiki/home/

Child, N. D., & Benarroch, E. E. (2013). Anterior nucleus of the thalamus: Functional organization and clinical implications. *Neurology, 81,* 1869–1876. doi:10.1212/01.wnl.0000436078.95856.56

Chiou, W. (2006). Adolescents' sexual self-disclosure on the Internet: Deindividuation and impression management. *Adolescence, 41,* 547–561. Retrieved from http://www.vjf.cnrs.fr/clt/php/va/Page_revue.php?ValCodeRev=ADO

Christian, K. M., Song, H., & Ming, G. (2014). Functions and dysfunctions of adult hippocampal neurogenesis. *Annual Review of Neuroscience, 37,* 243–262. doi:10.1146/annurev-neuro-071013-014134

Cohen, J. (1960). A coefficient of agreement for nominal scales. *Educational and Psychological Measurement, 20,* 37–46. doi:10.1177/001316446002000104

Cohen, J. (1988). *Statistical power analysis for the behavioral sciences* (2nd ed.). Hillsdale, NJ: Erlbaum.

Cohen, N. J., & Squire, L. R. (1980). Preserved learning and retention of pattern-analyzing skill in amnesia: Dissociation of knowing how and knowing that. *Science, 210,* 207–210. doi:10.1126/science.7414331

Coile, D. C., & Miller, N. E. (1984). How radical animal activists try to mislead humane people. *American Psychologist, 39,* 700–701. doi:10.1037/0003-066X.39.6.700

Committee for the Update of the Guide for the Care and Use of Laboratory Animals. (2011). *Guide for the care and use of laboratory animals* (8th ed.). Washington, DC: National Academies Press. Retrieved from http://www.nap.edu/catalog.php?record_id=12910

Corazzini, L., Filippin, A., & Vanin, P. (2015). Economic behavior under the influence of alcohol: An experiment on time preferences, risk-taking, and altruism. *PLoS ONE, 10,* e0121530. doi:10.1371/journal.pone.0121530

Cotter, P. R., Cohen, J., & Coulter, P. B. (1982). Race-of-interviewer effects in telephone interviews. *Public Opinion Quarterly, 46,* 278–284. doi:10.1086/268719

Crabtree, J. W., & Riesen, A. H. (1979). Effects of the duration of dark rearing on visually guided behavior in the kitten. *Developmental Psychobiology, 12,* 291–303. doi:10.1002/dev.420120404

Creswell, J. W., Hanson, W. E., Clark, V. L. P., & Morales, A. (2007). Qualitative research designs: Selection and implementation. *Counseling Psychologist, 35,* 236–264. doi:10.1177/0011000006287390

Cronbach, L. J. (1970). *Essentials of psychological testing* (3rd ed.). New York, NY: Harper.

Cronbach, L. J., & Meehl, P. E. (1955). Construct validity in psychological tests. *Psychological Bulletin, 52,* 281–302. doi:10.1037/h0040957

Crowe, S., Cresswell, K., Robertson, A., Huby, G., Avery, A., & Sheikh, A. (2011). The case study approach. *BMC Medical Research Methodology, 11,* article 100. doi:10.1186/1471-2288-11-100

Crowley, K., Callanan, M. A., Tenenbaum, H. R., & Allen, E. (2001). Parents explain more often to boys than to girls during shared scientific thinking. *Psychological Science, 12,* 258–261. doi:10.1111/1467-9280.00347

Curtin, R., Presser, S., & Singer, E. (2005). Changes in telephone survey nonresponse over the past quarter century. *Public Opinion Quarterly, 69,* 87–98. doi:10.1093/poq/nfi002

Curtis, B., Smith, R. E., & Smoll, F. L. (1979). Scrutinizing the skipper: A study of leadership behaviors in the dugout. *Journal of Applied Psychology, 64,* 391–400. doi:10.1037/0021-9010.64.4.391

CustomInsight.com. (n.d.). *Survey random sample calculator.* Retrieved from http://www.custominsight.com/survey-research-articles.asp

Dahl, L. C., & Price, H. L. (2012) "He couldn't have done it, he was with me!": The impact of alibi witness age and relationship. *Applied Cognitive Psychology, 26,* 475–481. doi:10.1002/acp.2821

The Daily. (2013, October 28). Individual Internet use and e-commerce, 2012. *Statistics Canada.* Retrieved from http://www.statcan.gc.ca

Darley, J. M., & Latané, B. (1968). Bystander intervention in emergencies: Diffusion of responsibility. *Journal of Personality and Social Psychology, 8,* 377–383. doi:10.1037/h0025589

Deary, I. J., & Brett, C. E. (2015). Predicting and retrodicting intelligence between childhood and old age in the 6-day sample of the Scottish Mental Survey 1947. *Intelligence, 50,* 1–9. doi:10.1016/j.intell.2015.02.002

Deaver, C. M., Miltenberger, R. G., & Stricker, J. M. (2001). Functional analysis and treatment of hair twirling in a young child. *Journal of Applied Behavior Analysis, 34,* 535–538. doi:10.1901/jaba.2001.34-535

Dennis, W. (1935). The effect of restricted practice upon the reaching, sitting and standing of two infants. *Pedagogical Seminary and Journal of Genetic Psychology, 47,* 17–32. doi:10.1080/08856559.1935.9943882

DePaulo, B. M., Dull, W. R., Greenberg, J. M., & Swaim, G. W. (1989). Are shy people reluctant to ask for help? *Journal of Personality and Social Psychology, 56,* 834–844. doi:10.1037/0022-3514.56.5.834

Derogatis, L., & Melisaratos, N. (1983). The Brief Symptom Inventory: An introductory report. *Psychological Medicine: A Journal of Research in Psychiatry and the Allied Sciences, 13,* 595–605. doi:10.1017/S0033291700048017

Derogatis, L. R. (1993). *Brief symptom inventory: Administration, scoring, and procedures manual.* Minneapolis, MN: National Computer Systems.

Desbonnet, L., O'Tuathaigh, C., Clarke, G., O'Leary, C., Petit, E., Clarke, N., . . . Waddington, J. L. (2012). Phenotypic effects of repeated psychosocial stress during adolescence in mice mutant for the schizophrenia risk gene neuregulin-1: A putative model of gene-environment interaction. *Brain, Behavior, and Immunity, 26,* 660–671. doi:10.1016/j.bbi.2012.02.010

DeVito, C. (2008). *Yogi: The life and times of an American original.* Chicago, IL: Triumph.

de Waal, F. (1982). *Chimpanzee politics: Power and sex among apes.* Baltimore, MD: Johns Hopkins University Press.

Dillman, D. A., Smyth, J. D., & Christian, L. M. (2014). *Internet, mail, and mixed-mode surveys: The tailored design method* (4th ed.). Hoboken, NJ: Wiley.

Dillon, K. P., & Bushman, B. J. (2015). Unresponsive or un-noticed?: Cyberbystander intervention in an experimental cyberbullying context. *Computers in Human Behavior, 45,* 144–150. doi:10.1016/j.chb.2014.12.009

Ditre, J. W., Brandon, T. H., Zale, E. L., & Meagher, M. M. (2011). Pain, nicotine, and smoking: Research findings and mechanistic considerations. *Psychological Bulletin, 137,* 1065–1093. doi:10.1037/a0025544

Doob, A. N., & Macdonald, G. E. (1979). Television viewing and fear of victimization: Is the relationship causal? *Journal of Personality and Social Psychology, 37,* 170–179. doi:10.1037/0022-3514.37.2.170

Dodge, K. A., Pettit, G. S., & Bates, J. E. (1994). Socialization mediators of the relation between socioeconomic status and child conduct problems. *Child Development, 65,* 649–665. doi:10.2307/1131407

Durlak, J. A., & DuPre, E. P. (2008). Implementation matters: A review of research on the influence of implementation on program outcomes and the factors affecting implementation. *American Journal of Community Psychology, 41,* 327–350. doi:10.1007/s10464-008-9165-0

Eagly, A. H., & Wood, W. (1999). The origins of sex differences in human behavior: Evolved dispositions versus social roles. *American Psychologist, 54,* 408–423. doi:10.1037/0003-066X.54.6.408

Edgington, E. S. (1996). Randomized single-subject experimental designs. *Behaviour Research and Therapy, 34,* 567–574. doi:10.1016/0005-7967(96)00012-5

Elbert, T., Pantev, C., Wienbruch, C., Rockstroh, B., & Taub, E. (1995). Increased cortical representation of the fingers of the left hand in string players. *Science, 270*(5234), 305–307. doi:10.1126/science.270.5234.305

Elliot, A. J. (2015). Color and psychological functioning: A review of theoretical and empirical work. *Frontiers in Psychology, 6* (April), 1–8. doi:10.3389/fpsyg.2015.00368

Elliot, A. J., Maier, M. A., Moller, A. C., Friedman, R., & Meinhardt, J. (2007). Color and psychological functioning: The effect of red on performance attainment. *Journal of Experimental Psychology: General, 136,* 154–168. doi:10.1037/0096-3445.136.1.154

Elliot, A. J., Payen, V., Brisswalter, J., Cury, F., & Thayer, J. (2011). A subtle threat cue, heart rate variability, and cognitive performance. *Psychophysiology, 48,* 1340–1345. doi:10.1111/j.1469-8986.2011.01216.x

Enchautegui-de-Jesús, N., Hughes, D., Johnston, K. E., & Oh, H. J. (2006). Well-being in the context of workplace ethnic diversity. *Journal of Community Psychology, 34,* 211–223. doi:10.1002/jcop.20091

Enserink, M. (2011, September 7). Dutch university sacks social psychologist over faked data. *ScienceInsider.* Retrieved from http://news.sciencemag.org/scienceinsider/

Epley, N., & Huff, C. (1998). Suspicion, affective response, and educational benefit as a result of deception in psychology research. *Personality and Social Psychology Bulletin, 24,* 759–768. doi:10.1177/0146167298247008

Erceg-Hurn, D. M., & Mirosevich, V. M. (2008). Modern robust statistical methods: An easy way to maximize the accuracy and power of your research. *American Psychologist, 63,* 591–601. doi:10.1037/0003-066X.63.7.591

Eron, L. D., Huesmann, L. R., Lefkowitz, M. M., & Walder, L. O. (1972). Does television violence cause aggression? *American Psychologist, 27,* 253–263. doi:10.1037/h0033721

Fallahi, C. R., Wood, R. M., Austad, C., & Fallahi, H. (2006). A program for improving undergraduate psychology students' basic writing skills. *Teaching of Psychology, 33,* 171–175. doi:10.1207/s15328023top3303_3

Farrimond, S. J., & Leland, L. S., Jr. (2006). Increasing donations to supermarket food-bank bins using proximal prompts. *Journal of Applied Behavior Analysis, 39,* 249–251. doi:10.1901/jaba.2006.10-05

Ferdinand, A. O., & Menachemi, N. (2014). Associations between driving performance and engaging in secondary tasks: A systematic review. *American Journal of Public Health, 104*(3), e39–e48. doi:10.2105/AJPH.2013.301750

Festinger, L., Riecken, H., & Schachter, S. (1956). *When prophecy fails.* Minneapolis: University of Minnesota.

Fiedler, K., & Schwarz, N. (2016). Questionable research practices revisited. *Social Psychological and Personality Science, 7,* 45–52. doi:10.1177/1948550615612150

Finkel, S. E., Guterbock, T. M., & Borg, M. J. (1991). Race-of-interviewer effects in a preelection poll: Virginia 1989. *Public Opinion Quarterly, 55,* 313–330. doi:10.1086/269264

Fischer, M. J. (2007). Settling into campus life: Differences by race/ethnicity in college involvement and outcomes. *Journal of Higher Education, 78,* 125–161. doi:10.1353/jhe.2007.0009

Fisher, C. B. (2005). Deception research involving children: Ethical practices and paradoxes. *Ethics & Behavior, 15,* 271–287. doi:10.1207/s15327019eb1503_7

Fisher, C. B., & Fyrberg, D. (1994). Participant partners: College students weigh the costs and benefits of deceptive research. *American Psychologist, 49,* 417–427. doi:10.1037/0003-066X.49.5.417

Fisher, C. B., & Vacanti-Shova, K. (2012). The responsible conduct of psychological research: An overview of ethical principles, APA Ethics Code standards, and federal regulations. In S. J. Knapp, M. C. Gottlieb, M. M. Handelsman, & L. D. VandeCreek (Eds.), *APA handbook of ethics in psychology: Vol. 2. Practice, teaching and research* (pp. 335–369). Washington, DC: American Psychological Association. doi:10.1037/13272-016

Flyvbjerg, B. (2006). Five misunderstandings about case-study research. *Qualitative Inquiry, 12,* 219–245. doi:10.1177/1077800405284363

Fouts, H. N., Roopnarine, J. L., Lamb, M. E., & Evans, M. (2012). Infant social interactions with multiple caregivers: The importance of ethnicity and socioeconomic status. *Journal of Cross-Cultural Psychology, 43,* 328–348. doi:10.1177/0022022110388564

Frank, M. G., & Feeley, T. H. (2003). To catch a liar: Challenges for research in lie detection training. *Journal of Applied Communication Research, 31,* 58–75. doi:10.1080/00909880305377

Fraune, M. R. (2013, April). *Who can trust a machine? Effects of human loneliness and avatar gaze on anthropomorphism and social trust.* Poster session presented at the 37th Annual Beloit College Symposium Day, Beloit, WI.

Fuchs, L. S., Compton, D. L., Fuchs, D., Hollenbeck, K. N., Hamlett, C. L., & Seethaler, P. M. (2011). Two-stage screening for math problem-solving difficulty using dynamic assessment of algebraic learning. *Journal of Learning Disabilities, 44,* 372–380. doi:10.1177/0022219411407867

Gardner, H. (2006). *Multiple intelligences: New horizons.* New York, NY: Basic Books.

Gardner, P. L. (1975). Scales and statistics. *Review of Educational Research, 45,* 43–57. doi:10.3102/00346543045001043

Gazzaniga, M. S., Bogen, J. E., & Sperry, R. W. (1965). Observations on visual perception after disconnexion of the cerebral hemispheres in man. *Brain, 88,* 221–236. doi:10.1093/brain/88.2.221

George, W. H., Gilmore, A. K., & Stappenbeck, C. A. (2012). Balanced placebo design: Revolutionary impact on addictions research and theory. *Addiction Research and Theory, 20,* 186–203. doi:10.3109/16066359.2012.680216

Gerbner, G., & Gross, L. (1976). Living with television: The violence profile. *Journal of Communication, 26,* 172–199. doi:10.1111/j.1460-2466.1976.tb01397.x

Gerbner, G., Gross, L., Eleey, M. F., Jackson-Beeck, M., Jeffries-Fox, S., & Signorielli, N. (1977). TV violence profile no. 8: The highlights. *Journal of Communication,* 171–180. doi:10.1111/j.1460-2466.1977.tb01845.x

GFK Knowledge Networks. (2013). *KnowledgePanel® design summary.* Retrieved from http://www.knowledgenetworks.com

Gilbert, D. T., King, G., Pettigrew, S., & Wilson, T. D. (2016). Comment on "Estimating the reproducibility of psychological science." *Science, 351*(6277), 1037a. doi:10.1126/science.aad7243

Gluck, J. P., & Bell, J. (2003). Ethical issues in the use of animals in biomedical and psychopharmocological research. *Psychopharmacology, 171,* 6–12. doi:10.1007/s00213-003-1478-y

Goodall, J. (1986). *The chimpanzees of Gombe: Patterns of behavior.* Cambridge, MA: Harvard University Press.

Goodman, S. H. (2007). Depression in mothers. *Annual Review of Clinical Psychology, 3,* 107–135. doi:10.1146/annurev.clinpsy.3.022806.091401

Gortmaker, V. J., Daly, E. J. III, McCurdy, M., Persampieri, M. J., & Hergenrader, M. (2007). Improving reading outcomes for children with learning disabilities: Using brief experimental analysis to develop parent-tutoring interventions. *Journal of Applied Behavior Analysis, 40,* 203–221. doi:10.1901/jaba.2007.105-05

Gottman, J. M., Coan, J., Carrere, S., & Swanson, C. (1998). Predicting marital happiness and stability from newlywed interactions. *Journal of Marriage and the Family, 60,* 5–22. doi:10.2307/353438

Gould, F., Bowie, C. R., & Harvey, P. D. (2012). The influence of demographic factors on functional capacity and everyday functional outcomes in schizophrenia. *Journal of Clinical and Experimental Neuropsychology, 34,* 467–475. doi:10.1080/13803395.2011.651102

Green, D. P. (2015, May 19). Appendix—Green science retraction request. In D. Broockman, J. Kalla, & P. Aronow (Eds.), *Irregularities in LaCour [2014]* (p. 27). Retrieved from http://stanford.edu/~dbroock/broockman_kalla_aronow_lg_irregularities.pdf

Greenwald, A. G. (1976). Within-subjects designs: To use or not to use? *Psychological Bulletin, 83,* 314–320. doi:10.1037/0033-2909.83.2.314

Griffiths, M. D. (2011). A typology of UK slot machine gamblers: A longitudinal observational and interview study. *International Journal of Mental Health and Addiction, 9,* 606–626. doi:10.1007/s11469-010-9291-4

Griggs, R. A. (2012). *Psychology: A concise introduction* (3rd ed.). New York, NY: Worth.

Gross, K., & Aday, S. (2003). The scary world in your living room and neighborhood: Using local broadcast news, neighborhood crime rates, and personal experience to test agenda setting and cultivation. *Journal of Communication, 53,* 411–426. doi:10.1111/j.1460-2466.2003.tb02599.x

Groves, R. M. (2006). Nonresponse rates and nonresponse bias in household surveys. *Public Opinion Quarterly, 70,* 646–675. doi:10.1093/poq/nfl033

Groves, R. M., & Peytcheva, E. (2008). The impact of nonresponse rates on nonresponse bias: A meta-analysis. *Public Opinion Quarterly, 72,* 167–189. doi:10.1093/poq/nfn011

Guadagno, R. E., Okdie, B. M., & Kruse, S. A. (2012). Dating deception: Gender, online dating, and exaggerated self-presentation. *Computers in Human Behavior, 28,* 642–647. doi:10.1016/j.chb.2011.11.010

Guerin, D., & MacKinnon, D. P. (1985). An assessment of the California child passenger restraint requirement. *American Journal of Public Health, 75,* 142–144. doi:10.2105/AJPH.75.2.142

Gute, G., Eshbaugh, E. M., & Wiersma, J. (2008). Sex for you, but not for me: Discontinuity in undergraduate emerging adults' definitions of "having sex." *Journal of Sex Research, 45,* 329–337. doi:10.1080/00224490802398332

Hagelin, J., Carlsson, H.-E., & Hau, J. (2003). An overview of surveys on how people view animal experimentation: Some factors that may influence the outcome. *Public Understanding of Science, 12,* 67–81. doi:10.1177/0963662503012001247

Handwerk, B. (2015, August 27). Scientists replicated 100 psychology studies, and fewer than half got the same results. *Smithsonian Magazine.* Retrieved from http://www.smithsonianmag.com/science-nature/scientists-replicated-100-psychology-studies-and-fewer-half-got-same-results-180956426/

Hart, P. K. (2012, February 18). Hart: Houston docs found leak in Holy Grail of cancer treatment. *Houston Chronicle.* Retrieved from http://www.chron.com

Hartmann, D. P., & Hall, R. V. (1976). The changing criterion design. *Journal of Applied Behavior Analysis, 9,* 527–532. doi:10.1901/jaba.1976.9-527

Hastorf, A. H., & Cantril, H. (1954). They saw a game: A case study. *Journal of Abnormal and Social Psychology, 49,* 129–134. doi:10.1037/h0057880

Healy, M. (2015, June 15). British study links chocolate with fewer heart attacks, strokes. *The Seattle Times.* Retrieved from http://www.seattletimes.com/nation-world/british-study-links-chocolate-with-fewer-heart-attacks-strokes/

Hebb, D. (1949). *The organization of behavior: A neuropsychological theory.* New York, NY: Wiley.

Hedrich, H. J. (2006). Taxonomy and stocks and strains. In M. A. Suckow, S. H. Weisbroth, & C. L. Franklin (Eds.), *The laboratory rat* (2nd ed., pp. 71–92). Burlington, MA: Academic Press.

Hensley, L., & Varela, R. E. (2008). PTSD symptoms and somatic complaints following Hurricane Katrina: The roles of trait anxiety and anxiety sensitivity. *Journal of Clinical Child and Adolescent Psychology, 37,* 542–552. doi:10.1080/15374410802148186

Herbert, C., & Kübler, A. (2011). Dogs cannot bark: Event-related brain responses to true and false negated statements as indicators of higher-order conscious processing. *PLoS ONE, 6,* 1–8. doi:10.1371/journal.pone.0025574

Herman, D. B., Struening, E. L., & Barrow, S. M. (1994). Self-reported needs for help among homeless men and women. *Evaluation and Program Planning, 17,* 249–256. doi:10.1016/0149-7189(94)90002-7

Hersen, M., Michelson, L., & Bellack, A. S. (Eds.). (1984). *Issues in psychotherapy research.* New York, NY: Plenum.

Hess, E. H. (1959). Imprinting: An effect of early experience, imprinting determines later social behavior. *Science, 130*(3368), 133–141. doi:10.1126/science.130.3368.133

Hill, C. E., Kline, K., Bauman, V., Brent, T., Breslin, C., Calderon, M., . . . Knox, S. (2015). What's it all about? A qualitative study of meaning in life for counseling psychology doctoral students. *Counselling Psychology Quarterly, 28,* 1–26. doi:10.1080/09515070.2014.965660

Hirsch, J., & Tryon, R. C. (1956). Mass screening and reliable individual measurement in the experimental behavior genetics of lower organisms. *Psychological Bulletin, 53,* 402–410. doi:10.1037/h0040715

Hoerger, M., & Currell, C. (2012). Ethics issues in Internet research. In S. J. Knapp, M. C. Gottlieb, M. M. Handelsman, & L. D. VandeCreek (Eds.), *APA handbook of ethics in psychology: Vol. 2. Practice, teaching and research* (pp. 385–400). Washington, DC: American Psychological Association. doi:10.1037/13272-018

Holbrook, A. L., Green, M. C., & Krosnick, J. A. (2003). Telephone versus face-to-face interviewing of national probability samples with long questionnaires: Comparisons of respondent satisficing and social desirability response bias. *Public Opinion Quarterly, 67,* 79–125. doi:10.1086/346010

Hooey, B. L., & Foyle, D. C. (2006). Pilot navigation errors on the airport surface: Identifying contributing factors and mitigating solutions. *International Journal of Aviation Psychology, 16,* 51–76. doi:10.1207/s15327108ijap1601_3

Hoyer, W. J., Semenec, S. C., & Buchler, N. E. G. (2007). Acute alcohol intoxication impairs controlled search across the visual field. *Journal of Studies on Alcohol and Drugs, 68,* 748–758. Retrieved from http://www.jsad.com/

Huesmann, L. R., Moise-Titus, J., Podolski, C. L., & Eron, L. D. (2003). Longitudinal relations between children's exposure to TV violence and their aggressive and violent behavior in young adulthood: 1977–1992. *Developmental Psychology, 39,* 201–221. doi:10.1037/0012-1649.39.2.201

Hufford, M. R., Shields, A. L., Shiffman, S., Paty, J., & Balabanis, M. (2002). Reactivity to ecological momentary assessment: An example using undergraduate problem drinkers. *Psychology of Addictive Behaviors, 16,* 205–211. doi:10.1037/0893-164X.16.3.205

InnerTalk. (2016). *InnerTalk: The super center of personal improvement.* Retrieved from www.innertalk.com

Innocence Project. (n.d.). *Know the cases: Maurice Patterson.* Retrieved from http://www.innocenceproject.org/Content/Maurice_Patterson.php

Intons-Peterson, M. J. (1983). Imagery paradigms: How vulnerable are they to experimenters' expectations? *Journal of Experimental Psychology: Human Perception and Performance, 9,* 394–412. doi:10.1037/0096-1523.9.3.394

Jalbert, A., Neath, I., Bireta, T. J., & Suprenant, A. M. (2011). When does length cause the word length effect? *Journal of Experimental Psychology: Learning, Memory, and Cognition, 37,* 338–353. doi:10.1037/a0021804

James, J. E. (1998). Acute and chronic effects of caffeine on performance, mood, headache, and sleep. *Neuropsychobiology, 38,* 32–41. doi:10.1159/000026514

Jensen, L. A., Arnett, J. J., Feldman, S. S., & Cauffman, E. (2004). The right to do wrong: Lying to parents among adolescents and emerging adults. *Journal of Youth and Adolescence, 33,* 101–112. doi:10.1023/B:JOYO.0000013422.48100.5a

John, L. K., Loewenstein, G. F., & Prelec, D. (2012). Measuring the prevalence of questionable research practices with incentives for truth-telling. *Psychological Science, 23,* 524–532. doi:10.1177/0956797611430953

Johnson, M., Thomson, K., & Scholes, S. (2007). *British election study 2005 technical report.* Essex, UK: University of Essex. Retrieved from http://www.essex.ac.uk/bes/2005/Survey%20Documents/bes%20technical%20report%20plus%20internet%202007.pdf

Johnston, L. D., O'Malley, P. M., Bachman, J. G., Schulenberg, J. E., & Miech, R. A. (2015). *Monitoring the future: National survey results on drug use, 1975–2014: Vol. 2. College students and adults ages 19–55.* Ann Arbor: Institute for Social Research, University of Michigan. Retrieved from http://monitoringthefuture.org/

Johnston, M. K., Kelley, C. S., Harris, F. R., & Wolf, M. M. (1966). An application of reinforcement principles to development of motor skills of a young child. *Child Development, 37,* 379–387. doi:10.2307/1126811

Jones, J. H. (1993). *Bad blood: The Tuskegee syphilis experiment.* New York, NY: Free Press.

Joyce, N. R., & Rankin, T. J. (2010). The lessons of the development of the first APA ethics code: Blending science, practice, and politics. *Ethics & Behavior, 20,* 466–481. doi:10.1080/10508422.2010.521448

Jozkowski, K. N., & Wiersma, J. D. (2015). Does drinking alcohol prior to sexual activity influence college students' consent? *International Journal of Sexual Health, 27,* 156–174. doi:10.1080/19317611.2014.951505

Kanoski, S. E., Hayes, M. R., Greenwald, H. S., Fortin, S. M., Gianessi, C. A., Gilbert, J. R., & Grill, H. J. (2011). Hippocampal leptin signaling reduces food intake and modulates food-related memory processing. *Neuropsychopharmacology, 36,* 1859–1870. doi:10.1038/npp.2011.70

Karasik, L. B., Adolph, K. E., Tamis-LeMonda, C. S., & Zuckerman, A. L. (2012). Carry on: Spontaneous object carrying in 13–month-old crawling and walking infants. *Developmental Psychology, 48,* 389–397. doi:10.1037/a0026040

Karau, S. J., & Hart, J. W. (1998). Group cohesiveness and social loafing: Effects of a social interaction manipulation on individual motivation within groups. *Group Dynamics: Theory, Research, and Practice, 2,* 185–191. doi:10.1037/1089-2699.2.3.185

Kaufman, J. S., Crusto, C. A., Quan, M., Ross, E., Friedman, S. R., O'Rielly, K., & Call, S. (2006). Utilizing program evaluation as a strategy to promote community change: Evaluation of a comprehensive, community-based, family violence initiative. *American Journal of Community Psychology, 38,* 191–200. doi:10.1007/s10464-006-9086-8

Kaushall, P. I., Zetin, M., & Squire, L. R. (1981). A psychosocial study of chronic, circumscribed amnesia. *Journal of Nervous & Mental Disease, 169,* 383–389. Retrieved from http://Journals.Lww.Com/Jonmd/Pages/Default.Aspx

Kazdin, A. E. (1979). Unobtrusive measures in behavioral assessment. *Journal of Applied Behavior Analysis, 12,* 713–724. doi:10.1901/jaba.1979.12-713

Kazdin, A. E. (1982). *Single-case research designs: Methods for clinical and applied settings.* New York, NY: Oxford University Press.

Kellegrew, D. H. (2000). Constructing daily routines: A qualitative examination of mothers with young children with disabilities. *American Journal of Occupational Therapy, 54,* 252–259. doi:10.5014/ajot.54.3.252

Kelman, H. C. (1967). Human use of human subjects: The problem of deception in social psychological experiments. *Psychological Bulletin, 67,* 1–11. doi:10.1037/h0024072

Kim, H.-I., Lee, H.-J., Cho, C.-H., Kang, S.-G., Yoon, H.-K., Park, Y.-M., . . . Kim, L. (2015). Association of *CLOCK, ARNTL,* and *NPAS2* gene polymorphisms and seasonal variations in mood and behavior. *Chronobiology International, 32,* 785–791. doi:10.3109/07420528.2015.1049613

Kimmel, A. J. (2012). Deception in research. In S. J. Knapp, M. C. Gottlieb, M. M. Handelsman, & L. D. VandeCreek (Eds.), *APA handbook of ethics in psychology: Vol. 2. Practice, teaching and research* (pp. 401–421). Washington, DC: American Psychological Association. doi:10.1037/13272-019

Kitching, C. (2015, June 20). Pilot error blamed after London-bound British Airways plane crashed into building while using wrong taxiway at airport. *Daily Mail.* Retrieved from http://www.dailymail.co.uk/home/search.html?searchPhrase=3132502

Kleim, J. A., Barbay, S., Cooper, N. R., Hogg, T. M., Reidel, C. N., Remple, M. S., . . . Nudo, R. J. (2002). Motor learning-dependent synaptogenesis is localized to functionally reorganized motor cortex. *Neurobiology of Learning and Memory, 77,* 63–77. doi:10.1006/nlme.2000.4004

Klein, R. A., Ratliff, K. A., Vianello, M., Adams, R. B., Jr., Bahník, S., Bernstein, M. J., . . . Nosek, B. A. (2014). Investigating variation in replicability: A "many labs" replication project. *Social Psychology, 45,* 142–152. doi:10.1027/1864-9335/a000178

Köhler, W. (1925). *The mentality of apes* (2nd rev. ed.; E. Winter, Trans.). New York, NY: Harcourt.

Kolb, B., & Whishaw, I. Q. (2006). *An introduction to brain and behavior* (2nd ed.). New York, NY: Worth.

Koluchová, J. (1972). Severe deprivation in twins: A case study. *Journal of Child Psychology and Psychiatry, 13,* 107–111. doi:10.1111/j.1469-7610.1972.tb01124.x

Koluchová, J. (1991). Severely deprived twins after 22 years of observation. *Studia Psychologica, 33,* 23–28. Abstract retrieved from PsycINFO database (accession no. 1992-16098-001).

Koot, H. M., Van Den Oord, E. J. C. G., Verhulst, F. C., & Boomsma, D. I. (1997). Behavioral and emotional problems in young preschoolers: Cross-cultural testing of the validity of the Child Behavior Checklist/2–3. *Journal of Abnormal Child Psychology, 25,* 183–196. doi:10.1023/A:1025791814893

Kort-Butler, L. A., & Sittner Hartshorn, K. J. (2011). Watching the detectives: Crime programming, fear of crime, and attitudes about the criminal justice system. *Sociological Quarterly, 52,* 36–55. doi:10.1111/j.1533-8525.2010.01191.x

Kovarik, Z. V. (n.d.). United [E-mail message]. In Verhagen, *Science Jokes* (section 1.2, Statistics and Statisticians). Retrieved from http://jcdverha.home.xs4all.nl/scijokes/1_2.html

Kramer, A. D. I., Guillory, J. E., & Hancock, J. T. (2014). Experimental evidence of massive-scale emotional contagion through social networks. *PNAS: Proceedings of the National Academy of Sciences of the United States of America, 111,* 8788–8790. doi:10.1073/pnas.1320040111

Kraut, R., Olson, J., Banaji, M., Bruckman, A., Cohen, J., & Couper, M. (2004). Psychological research online: Report of Board of Scientific Affairs' Advisory Group on the Conduct of Research on the Internet. *American Psychologist, 59,* 105–117. doi:10.1037/0003-066X.59.2.105

Krech, D., Crutchfield, R. S., & Ghiselli, E. E. (1969, May). *In Memoriam. Robert Choate Tryon, Psychology: Berkeley.* Retrieved from University of California Calisphere: http://texts.cdlib.org/view?docId=hb229003hz&doc.view=frames&chunk.id=div00012&toc.depth=1&toc.id

Kreiman, G., Koch, C., & Fried, I. (2000). Category-specific visual responses of single neurons in the human medial temporal lobe. *Nature Neuroscience, 3,* 946–953. Retrieved from http://neurosci.nature.com

Krosnick, J. A. (1999). Survey research. *Annual Review of Psychology, 50,* 537–567. doi:10.1146/annurev.psych.50.1.537

Krosnick, J. A., & Presser, S. (2010). Question and questionnaire design. In P. V. Marsden & J. D. Wright (Eds.), *Handbook of Survey Research* (2nd ed., pp. 263–313). Bingley, UK: Emerald.

Kunert, R. (2016). Internal conceptual replications do not increase independent replication success. *Psychonomic Bulletin & Review, 23*, 1–8. doi:10.3758/s13423-016-1030-9

Kushner, R. F., Kessler, S., & McGaghie, W. C. (2011). Using behavior change plans to improve medical student self-care. *Academic Medicine, 86*, 901–906. doi:10.1097/ACM.0b013e31821da193

Kwok, C. S., Boekholdt, M., Lentjes, M. A. H., Loke, Y. K., Luben, R. N., Yeong, J. K., . . . Khaw, K.-T. (2015). Habitual chocolate consumption and risk of cardiovascular disease among healthy men and women *Heart, 101*, 1279–1287. doi:10.1136/heartjnl-2014-307050

LaCour, M. J. (2015, May 29). Response to irregularities in LaCour & Green (2014). Retrieved from http://retractionwatch.com/wpcontent/uploads/2015/05/LaCour_Response_05-29-2015.pdf

LaCour, M. J., & Green, D. P. (2014; retracted May 28, 2015). When contact changes minds: An experiment on transmission of support for gay equality. *Science, 346*(6215), 1366–1369. doi:10.1126/science.1256151

Landrum, R. E. (2003). Graduate admissions in psychology: Transcripts and the effect of withdrawals. *Teaching of Psychology, 30*, 323–325. doi:10.1207/S15328023TOP3004_05

Laney, C., Kaasa, S. O., Morris, E. K., Berkowitz, S. R., Bernstein, D. M., & Loftus, E. F. (2008). The Red Herring technique: A methodological response to the problem of demand characteristics. *Psychological Research, 72*, 362–375. doi:10.1007/s00426-007-0122-6

Lang, P. J., & Melamed, B. G. (1969). Case report: Avoidance conditioning therapy of an infant with chronic ruminative vomiting. *Journal of Abnormal Psychology, 74*, 1-8. doi:10.1037/h0027077.

Laroche, M., Nepomuceno, M. V., Huang, L., & Richard, M.-O. (2011). What's so funny? The use of humor in magazine advertising in the United States, China, and France. *Journal of Advertising Research, 51*, 404–416. doi:10.2501/JAR-51-2-404-416

Larose, D. T. (2010). *Discovering statistics*. New York, NY: Freeman.

Lashley, K. S. (1944). Studies of cerebral function in learning. XIII. Apparent absence of transcortical association in maze learning. *Journal of Comparative Neurology, 80*, 257–281. doi:10.1002/cne.900800207

Lefkowitz, J. (2012). Ethics in industrial-organizational psychology. In S. J. Knapp, M. C. Gottlieb, M. M. Handelsman, & L. D. VandeCreek (Eds.), *APA handbook of ethics in psychology: Vol. 2. Practice, teaching and research* (pp. 149–167). Washington, DC: American Psychological Association. doi:10.1037/13272-008

Legerski, J. P., & Bunnell, S. L. (2010). The risks, benefits, and ethics of trauma-focused research participation. *Ethics & Behavior, 20*, 429–442. doi:10.1080/10508422.2010.521443

Lemmer, G., & Wagner, U. (2015). Can we really reduce ethnic prejudice outside the lab? A meta-analysis of direct and indirect contact interventions. *European Journal of Social Psychology, 45*, 152–168. doi:10.1002/ejsp.2079

Lemonick, M. D. (1998, April 13). Emily's little experiment. *Time*. Retrieved from http://www.time.com/time/magazine/article/0,9171,988122-1,00.html

Liesen, L. T. (2013). Feminists need to look beyond evolutionary psychology for insights into human reproductive strategies: A commentary. *Sex Roles, 69*, 484–490. doi:10.1007/s11199-012-0153-3

Likert, R. (1932). A technique for the measurement of attitudes. *Archives of Psychology, 140*, 44–53.

Link, M. W., Battaglia, M. P., Frankel, M. R., Osborn, L., & Mokdad, A. H. (2008). A comparison of address-based sampling (ABS) versus random-digit dialing (RDD) for general population surveys. *Public Opinion Quarterly, 72*, 6–27. doi:10.1093/poq/nfn003

Lipsey, M. W., & Cordray, D. S. (2000). Evaluation methods for social intervention. *Annual Review of Psychology, 51*, 345–375. doi:10.1146/annurev.psych.51.1.345

Logel, C., Walton, G. M., Spencer, S. J., Iserman, E. C., von Hippel, W., & Bell, A. E. (2009). Interacting with sexist men triggers social identity threat among female engineers. *Journal of Personality and Social Psychology, 96*, 1089–1103. doi:10.1037/a0015703

Luria, A. R. (1968). *The mind of a mnemonist: A little book about a vast memory* (L. Solotaroff, Trans.). New York, NY: Basic Books.

Lutgendorf, S. K., Russell, D., Ullrich, P., Harris, T. B., & Wallace, R. (2002). Religious participation, interleukin-6, and mortality in older adults. *Health Psychology, 23*, 465–475. doi:10.1037/0278-6133.23.5.465

Lyons, L. (2005, November 1). *Paranormal beliefs come (super) naturally to some*. Gallup. Retrieved from http://www.gallup.com/poll/19588/Paranormal-Beliefs-Come-SuperNaturally-Some.aspx

MacKinnon, D. P., & Fairchild, A. J. (2009). Current directions in mediation analysis. *Current Directions in Psychological Science, 18*, 16–20. doi:10.1111/j.1467-8721.2009.01598.x

MacLean, W. E., & Dornbush, K. (2012). Self-injury in a statewide sample of young children with developmental disabilities. *Journal of Mental Health Research in Intellectual Disabilities, 5*, 236–245. doi:10.1080/19315864.2011.590627

Marczinski, C. A., Fillmore, M. T., Henges, A. L., Ramsey, M. A., & Young, C. R. (2013). Mixing an energy drink with an alcoholic beverage increases motivation for more alcohol in college students. *Alcoholism: Clinical and Experimental Research, 37*, 276–283. doi:10.1111/j.1530-0277.2012.01868.x

Matthews, B. R. (2015). Memory dysfunction. *Continuum, 21*, 613–626.

McBurney, D. H., Zapp, D. J., & Streeter, S. A. (2005). Preferred number of sexual partners: Tails of distributions and tales of mating systems. *Evolution and Human Behavior, 26*, 271–278. doi:10.1016/j.evolhumbehav.2004.09.005

McCarthy, J. (2016). Americans' financial worries edge up in 2016. Gallup. Retrieved from http://www.gallup.com/poll/191174/americans-financial-worries-edge-2016.aspx

McClearn, G. E. (1962). The inheritance of behavior. In L. Postman (Ed.), *Psychology in the making*. New York, NY: Alfred A. Knopf.

McGraw, M. B. (1939). Later development of children specially trained during infancy: Johnny and Jimmy at school age. *Child Development, 10*, 1–19. doi:10.2307/1125336

McKerracher, G., Powell, T. O., & Oyebode, J. (2005). A single case experimental design comparing two memory notebook formats for a man with memory problems caused by traumatic brain injury. *Neuropsychological Rehabilitation, 15*, 115–128. doi:10.1080/09602010443000056

Meddis, R., & Lecluyse, W. (2011). The psychophysics of absolute threshold and signal duration: A probabilistic approach. *Journal of the Acoustical Society of America, 129*, 3153–3165. doi:10.1121/1.3569712

Mehl, M. R., Gosling, S. D., & Pennebaker, J. W. (2006). Personality in its natural habitat: Manifestations and implicit folk theories of personality in daily life. *Journal of Personality and Social Psychology, 90,* 862–877. doi:10.1037/0022-3514.90.5.862

Milgram, S. (1963). Behavioral study of obedience. *Journal of Abnormal and Social Psychology, 67,* 371–378. doi:10.1037/h0040525

Milgram, S. (1964). Issues in the study of obedience: A reply to Baumrind. *American Psychologist, 19,* 848–852. doi:10.1037/h0044954

Milgram, S. (Producer, Director). (1965). *Obedience* [Motion picture]. University Park: Pennsylvania State University Audio-Visual.

Milgram, S. (1974). *Obedience to authority: An experimental view.* New York, NY: Harper & Row.

Miller, N. E. (1985). The value of behavioral research on animals. *American Psychologist, 40,* 423–440. doi:10.1037/0003-066X.40.4.423

Miranda, P., McCluskey, N., Silber, B. J., von Pohle, C. M. D., & Bainum, C. K. (2009). Effect of adult disapproval of cartoon violence on children's aggressive play. *Psi Chi Journal of Undergraduate Research, 14,* 79–84. Retrieved from http://www.psichi.org/pubs/journal/

Moberg, C. A., Weber, S. M., & Curtin, J. J. (2011). Alcohol dose effects on stress response to cued threat vary by threat intensity. *Psychopharmacology, 218,* 217–227. doi:10.1007/s00213-011-2304-6

Mograbi, D. C., Ferri, C. P., Sosa, A. L., Stewart, R., Laks, J., Brown, R., & Morris, R. G. (2012). Unawareness of memory impairment in dementia: A population-based study. *International Psychogeriatrics, 24,* 931–939. doi:10.1017/S1041610211002730

Monaghan, M., Sanders, R. E., Kelly, K. P., Cogen, F. R., & Streisand, R. (2011). Using qualitative methods to guide clinical trial design: Parent recommendations for intervention modification in type 1 Diabetes. *Journal of Family Psychology, 25,* 868–872. doi:10.1037/a0024178

Moore, D. S., Notz, W. I., & Fligner, M. A. (2013). *Essential statistics* (2nd ed.). New York, NY: Freeman.

Moore, D. W. (2005). *Three in four Americans believe in paranormal.* Retrieved from Gallup News Service website: http://www.gallup.com/poll/16915/Three-Four-Americans-Believe-Paranormal.aspx

Moore, J., & Prentice, D. (2013). Collaboration among nurse practitioners and registered nurses in outpatient oncology settings in Canada. *Journal of Advanced Nursing, 69,* 1574–1583. doi:10.1111/jan.12017

Mooshagian, E., Iacoboni, M., & Zaidel, E. (2009). Spatial attention and interhemispheric visuomotor integration in the absence of the corpus callosum. *Neuropsychologia, 47,* 933–937. doi:10.1016/j.neuropsychologia.2008.12.005

Mostert, M. P. (2001). Facilitated communication since 1995: A review of published studies. *Journal of Autism and Developmental Disorders, 31,* 287–313. doi:10.1023/A:1010795219886

Mueller, P. A., & Oppenheimer, D. M. (2014). The pen is mightier than the keyboard: Advantages of longhand over laptop note taking. *Psychological Science, 25,* 1159–1168. doi:10.1177/0956797614524581

Mueser, K. T., Foy, D. W., & Carter, M. J. (1986). Social skills training for job maintenance in a psychiatric patient. *Journal of Counseling Psychology, 33,* 360–362. doi:10.1037/0022-0167.33.3.360

Nash, K., Stevens, S., Greenbaum, R., Weiner, J., Koren, G., & Rovet, J. (2015). Improving executive functioning in children with fetal alcohol spectrum disorders. *Child Neuropsychology, 21,* 191–209. doi:10.1080/09297049.2014.889110

National Aeronautics and Space Administration. (2008). *Deep Impact: Mission to a comet.* Retrieved December 19, 2008, from http://www.nasa.gov/mission_pages/deepimpact/main/

National Aeronautics and Space Administration. (2010, June 28). *Deep Impact. Discovery zone: Fun facts.* Retrieved from http://solarsystem.nasa.gov/deepimpact/disczone/funfacts.cfm

National Commission for the Protection of Human Subjects of Biomedical and Behavioral Research. (1979). *The Belmont report: Ethical principles and guidelines for the protection of human subjects of research.* Retrieved from http://ohsr.od.nih.gov/guidelines/belmont.html

National Council on Youth Sports. (2008). *Report on trends and participation in organized youth sports.* Stuart, FL: Author. Retrieved from http://www.ncys.org/index.php

National Highway Traffic Safety Administration. (2001). *Evaluation of the Illinois .08 law: An update with the 1999 FARS data.* U.S. Department of Transportation (DOT HS 809 392). Retrieved from http://www.nhtsa.dot.gov/people/injury/research/Illinois08/index.htm

National Institutes of Health. (2000). *Required education in the protection of human research participants* (NIH Notice OD-00–039). Retrieved from http://grants.nih.gov/grants/guide/notice-files/not-od-00–039.html

National Statistical Service. (n.d.). *Sample size calculator.* Australian Bureau of Statistics. Retrieved from http://www.nss.gov.au/nss/home.NSF

National Weather Service. (2012). *Heat: A major killer.* National Oceanic and Atmospheric Administration. Retrieved from http://www.nws.noaa.gov/os/heat/index.shtml doi:10.3758/APP.71.1.194

Nesic, J., & Duka, T. (2014). Effects of stress and dietary tryptophan enhancement on craving for alcohol in binge and non-binge heavy drinkers. *Behavioural Pharmacology, 25,* 503–517. doi:10.1097/FBP.0000000000000067

Neville, R., & Dey, M. (2012, January). Innovative 787 flight deck designed for efficiency, comfort, and commonality. *Aero Quarterly,* 10–17. Retrieved from http://www.boeing.com/commercial/aeromagazine

Nic Dhonnchadha, B. Á., Lovascio, B. F., Shrestha, N., Lin, A., Leite-Morris, K. A., Man, H. Y., . . . Kantak, K. M. (2012). Changes in expression of c-Fos protein following cocaine-cue extinction learning. *Behavioural Brain Research, 234,* 100–106. doi:10.1016/j.bbr.2012.06.010

Nichols, A. L., & Maner, J. K. (2008). The good-subject effect: Investigating participant demand characteristics. *Journal of General Psychology, 135,* 151–165. doi:10.3200/GENP.135.2.151-166.

Nicholson, I. (2011). "Torture at Yale": Experimental subjects, laboratory torment, and the "rehabilitation" of Milgram's "Obedience to Authority." *Theory and Psychology, 21,* 737–761. doi:10.1177/0959354311420199

Niu, G. C., & Arean, P. A. (2015). Refining evidence-based treatments for late-life depression. *GeroPsych: The Journal of Gerontopsychology and Geriatric Psychiatry, 28,* 67–76. doi:10.1024/1662-9647/a000127

Nolan, S. A., & Heinzen, T. E. (2012). *Statistics for the behavioral sciences.* New York, NY: Worth.

Nolen-Hoeksema, S. (2011). Lost in thought: The perils of rumination. In M. A. Gernsbacher, R. W. Pew, L. M. Hough, & J. R. Pomerantz (Eds.), *Psychology and the real world* (pp. 189–195). New York, NY: Worth.

Norcross, J. C., Hanych, J. M., & Terranova, R. D. (1996). Graduate study in psychology. *American Psychologist, 51,* 631–643. doi:10.1037/0003-066X.51.6.631

Norcross, J. C., Kohout, J. L., & Wicherski, M. (2005). Graduate study in psychology: 1971–2004. *American Psychologist, 60,* 959–975. doi:10.1037/0003-066X.60.9.959

Novick, M. R. (1966). The axioms and principal results of classical test theory. *Journal of Mathematical Psychology, 3,* 1–18. doi:10.1016/0022-2496(66)90002-2

Nuernberg Military Tribunals. (October 1946–April 1949). Permissible medical experiments. In *Trials of war criminals before the Nuremberg military tribunals under Control Council Law No. 10* (Vol. 2, pp. 181–182). Washington, DC: U.S. Government Printing Office.

Nykamp, K., Rosenthal, L., Folkerts, M., Roehrs, T., Guido, P., & Roth, T. (1998). The effects of REM sleep deprivation on the level of sleepiness/alertness. *Sleep, 21,* 609–613. Retrieved online from http://www.journalsleep.org/

Ohashi, G. (2015). Pestle-pounding and nut-cracking by wild chimpanzees at Kpala, Liberia. *Primates, 56,* 113–117. doi:10.1007/s10329-015-0459-1

Olson, S. L., Bates, J. E., & Bayles, K. (1982). Maternal perceptions of infant and toddler behavior: A longitudinal, construct validation study. *Infant Behavior & Development, 5,* 397–410. doi:10.1016/S0163-6383(82)80049-0

Onghena, P., & Edgington, E. S. (2005). Customization of pain treatments: Single-case design and analysis. *Clinical Journal of Pain, 21,* 56–68. doi:10.1097/00002508-200501000-00007

Open Science Collaboration. (2015). Estimating the reproducibility of psychological science. *Science, 349*(6521). doi:10.1126/science.aac4716

Orne, M. T. (1962). On the social psychology of the psychological experiment: With particular reference to demand characteristics and their implications. *American Psychologist, 17,* 776–783. doi:10.1037/h0043424

Orne, M. T., & Scheibe, K. E. (1964). The contribution of nondeprivation factors in the production of sensory deprivation effects: The psychology of the "panic button." *Journal of Abnormal and Social Psychology, 68,* 3–12. doi:10.1037/h0048803

Orne, M. T., & Whitehouse, W. G. (2000). Demand characteristics. In A. E. Kazdin (Ed.), *Encyclopedia of psychology* (Vol. 2, pp. 469–470). Washington, DC: American Psychological Association.

Orvis, B. R., McDonald, L. L., Raymond, B., & Wu, F. (2005). *Increasing participation in Army Continuing Education: eArmyU and effects of possible program changes.* Santa Monica, CA: RAND Corporation. Retrieved from http://www.rand.org/ard/pubs/monographs/2005.html

Pace-Schott, E. F., Germain, A., & Milad, M. R. (2015). Effects of sleep on memory for conditioned fear and fear extinction. *Psychological Bulletin, 141,* 835–857. doi:1037/bul0000014

Pail, G., Huf, W., Pjrek, E., Winkler, D., Willeit, M., Praschak-Rieder, N., & Kasper, S. (2011). Bright-light therapy in the treatment of mood disorders. *Neuropsychobiology, 64,* 152–162. doi:10.1159/000328950

Pan, S. C., Pashler, H., Potter, Z. E., & Rickard, T. C. (2015). Testing enhances learning across a range of episodic memory abilities. *Journal of Memory and Language, 83,* 53–61. doi:10.1016/j.jml.2015.04.001

Pavlov, I. P. (1928). *Lectures on conditioned reflexes: Twenty-five years of objective study of the higher nervous activity (behaviour) of animals* (W. H. Gantt, Trans.). New York, NY: International (Original work published 1923.)

Pedersen, W. C., Miller, L. C., Putcha-Bhagavatula, A. D., & Yang, Y. (2002). Evolved sex differences in the number of partners desired? The long and the short of it. *Psychological Science, 13,* 157–161. doi:10.1111/1467-9280.00428

Pedersen, W. C., Putcha-Bhagavatula, A., & Miller, L. C. (2011). Are men and women really that different? Examining some of Sexual Strategies Theory (SST)'s key assumptions about sex-distinct mating mechanisms. *Sex Roles, 64,* 629–643. doi:10.1007/s11199-010-9811-5

Peirce, C. S. (1877, November). Illustrations of the logic of science. The fixation of belief. *Popular Science Monthly, 12,* 1–15. Retrieved from https://en.wikisource.org/wiki/Popular_Science_Monthly/Volume_12/November_1877/Illustrations_of_the_Logic_of_Science_I

Pellegrini, A. D., & Bartini, M. (2000). A longitudinal study of bullying, victimization, and peer affiliation during the transition from primary school to middle school. *American Educational Research Journal, 37,* 699–725. doi:10.2307/1163486

Peña, P. A. (2015). A not so happy day after all: Excess death rates on birthdays in the U.S. *Social Science & Medicine, 126,* 59–66.

Peng, L., Zhang, J., Li, M., Li, P., Zhang, Y., Zuo, X., . . . Xu, Y. (2012). Negative life events and mental health of Chinese medical students: The effect of resilience, personality and social support. *Psychiatry Research, 196,* 138–141. doi:10.1016/j.psychres.2011.12.006

Perrin, A., & Duggan, M. (2015). *Americans' Internet access: 2000–2015.* Retrieved from Pew Research Center Internet, Science, and Tech website: http://www.pewinternet.org/2015/06/26/americans-internet-access-2000-2015/.

Perry, G. (2013). *Behind the shock machine: The untold story of the notorious Milgram psychology experiments.* New York, NY: New Press.

Perry, J. L., & Dess, N. K. (2012). Laboratory animal research ethics: A practical, educational approach. In S. J. Knapp, M. C. Gottlieb, M. M. Handelsman, & L. D. VandeCreek (Eds.), *APA handbook of ethics in psychology: Vol. 2. Practice, teaching and research* (pp. 423–440). Washington, DC: American Psychological Association. doi:10.1037/13272-020

Pew Research Center. (2015, January 29). *U.S. survey research: Questionnaire design.* Retrieved from http://www.pewresearch.org/methodology/u-s-survey-research/questionnaire-design/

Pew Research Center. (2016). *Political typology: Quiz.* Retrieved from the Pew Research Center for the People & the Press website: http://www.people-press.org/quiz/political-typology

Phillips, D. P., & Feldman, K. A. (1973). A dip in deaths before ceremonial occasions: Some new relationships between social integration and mortality. *American Sociological Review, 38,* 678–696. doi:10.2307/2094131

Phillips, J. P., Cole, C., Gluck, J. P., Shoemaker, J. M., Petree, L. E., Helitzer, D. L., . . . Holdsworth, M. T. (2015). Stakeholder opinions and ethical perspectives support complete disclosure of incidental findings in MRI research. *Ethics & Behavior, 25,* 332–350. doi:10.1080/10508422.2014.938338

Piaget, J. (1930). *The child's conception of physical causality* (M. Gabain, Trans.). New York, NY: Harcourt. (Original work published 1927.)

Picheansathian, W., Pearson, A., & Suchaxaya, P. (2008). The effectiveness of a promotion programme on hand hygiene compliance and nosocomial infections in a neonatal intensive care unit. *International Journal of Nursing Practice, 14,* 315–321. doi:10.1111/j.1440-172X.2008.00699.x

Pincock, S. (2012). Robert Ader. *The Lancet, 379,* 308. doi:10.1016/S0140-6736(12)60134-2

Pitts, M., & Rahman, Q. (2001). Which behaviors constitute "having sex" among university students in the UK? *Archives of Sexual Behavior, 30,* 169–176. doi:10.1023/A:1002777201416

Plous, S. (1996a). Attitudes toward the use of animals in psychological research and education: Results from a national survey of psychologists. *American Psychologist, 51,* 1167–1180. doi:10.1037/0003-066X.51.11.1167

Plous, S. (1996b). Attitudes toward the use of animals in psychological research and education: Results from a national survey of psychology majors. *Psychological Science, 7,* 352–358. doi:10.1111/j.1467-9280.1996.tb00388.x

Pope, K. S., Tabachnick, B. G., & Keith-Spiegel, P. (1987). Ethics of practice: The beliefs and behaviors of psychologists as therapists. *American Psychologist, 42,* 993–1006. doi:10.1037/0003-066X.42.11.993

Powell, L. H., Shahabi, L., & Thoresen, C. E. (2003). Religion and spirituality: Linkages to physical health. *American Psychologist, 58,* 36–52. doi:10.1037/0003-066X.58.1.36

Pritchard, I. A. (2011). How do IRB members make decisions? A review and research agenda. *Journal of Empirical Research on Human Research Ethics, 6*(2), 31–46. doi:10.1525/jer.2011.6.2.31

Public Works and Government Services Canada. (2014, November 11). *Secondary research into cell phones and telephone surveys.* Retrieved from http://www.tpsgc-pwgsc.gc.ca/rop-por/rstcst-srcpts-eng.html#a3

Puschmann, C., & Bozdag, E. (2014). Staking out the unclear ethical terrain of online social experiments. *Internet Policy Review, 3*(4). doi:10.14763/2014.4.338

Rajsic, J., Wilson, D. E., & Pratt, J. (2015). Confirmation bias in visual search. *Journal of Experimental Psychology: Human Perception and Performance, 41,* 1353–1364. doi:10.1037/xhp0000090

Rapoff, M., & Stark, L. (2008). Editorial: Journal of Pediatric Psychology statement of purpose: Section on single-subject studies. *Journal of Pediatric Psychology, 33,* 16–21. doi:10.1093/jpepsy/jsm101

Rapp, J. T., Miltenberger, R. G., Long, E. S., Elliott, A. J., & Lumley, V. A. (1998). Simplified habit reversal treatment for chronic hair pulling in three adolescents: A clinical replication with direct observation. *Journal of Applied Behavior Analysis, 31,* 299–302. doi:10.1901/jaba.1998.31-299

Rasch, D., & Guiard, V. (2004). The robustness of parametric statistical methods. *Psychology Science, 46,* 175–208. Retrieved from http://www.pabst-publishers.de/psychology-science/index.html

Razel, M. (1988). Call for a follow-up study of experiments on long-term deprivation of human infants. *Perceptual and Motor Skills, 67,* 147–158. doi:10.2466/pms.1988.67.1.147

Remland, M. S., Jones, T. S., & Brinkman, H. (1995). Interpersonal distance, body orientation, and touch: Effects of culture, gender, and age. *Journal of Social Psychology, 135,* 281–297. doi:10.1080/00224545.1995.9713958

Resick, P. A., Galovski, T. E., Uhlmansiek, M. O., Scher, C. D., Clum, G. A., & Young-Xu, Y. (2008). A randomized clinical trial to dismantle components of cognitive processing therapy for posttraumatic stress disorder in female victims of interpersonal violence. *Journal of Consulting and Clinical Psychology, 76,* 243–258. doi:10.1037/0022-006X.76.2.243

Rhoades, L. J. (2004). *New institutional research misconduct activity: 1992–2001.* Office of Research Integrity, Office of Public Health and Science, Department of Health and Human Services. Retrieved from http://ori.dhhs.gov/documents/NewInstitutionalResearchMisconductActivity.pdf

Rieger, S., Göllner, R., Trautwein, U., & Roberts, B. W. (2016). Low self-esteem prospectively predicts depression in the transition to young adulthood: A replication of Orth, Robins, and Roberts (2008). *Journal of Personality and Social Psychology, 110,* e16–e22. http://dx.doi.org/10.1037/pspp0000037

Riegle-Crumb, C., & King, B. (2010). Questioning a White male advantage in STEM: Examining disparities in college major by gender and race/ethnicity. *Educational Researcher, 39,* 656–664. doi:10.3102/0013189X10391657

Roane, H. S., Kelly, M. L., & Fisher, W. W. (2003). The effects of noncontingent access to food on the rate of object mouthing across three settings. *Journal of Applied Behavior Analysis, 36,* 579–582. doi:10.1901/jaba.2003.36-579

Robles, T. F., Shaffer, V. A., Malarkey, W. B., & Kiecolt-Glaser, J. K. (2006). Positive behaviors during marital conflict: Influences on stress hormones. *Journal of Social and Personal Relationships, 23,* 305–325. doi:10.1177/0265407506062482

Roehrs, T., Burduvali, E., Bonahoom, A., Drake, C., & Roth, T. (2003). Ethanol and sleep loss: A "dose" comparison of impairing effects. *SLEEP: Journal of Sleep and Sleep Disorders Research, 26,* 981–985. Retrieved from http://www.journalsleep.org/

Rogers, E. M. (2003). *Diffusion of innovations* (5th ed.). New York, NY: Free Press.

Rogers, L. A., & Graham, S. (2008). A meta-analysis of single subject design writing intervention research. *Journal of Educational Psychology, 100,* 879–906. doi:10.1037/0022-0663.100.4.879

Roh, Y. S., & Issenberg, S. B. (2014). Association of cardiopulmonary resuscitation psychomotor skills with knowledge and self-efficacy in nursing students. *International Journal of Nursing Practice, 20,* 674–679. doi:10.1111/ijn.12212

Rosa, L., Rosa, E., Sarner, L., & Barrett., S. (1998). A close look at Therapeutic Touch. *Journal of the American Medical Association, 279,* 1005–1010. doi:10.1001/jama.279.13.1005

Rosenbloom, S. R., & Way, N. (2004). Experiences of discrimination among African American, Asian American, and Latino adolescents in an urban high school. *Youth & Society, 35,* 420–451. doi:10.1177/0044118X03261479

Rosenhan, D. L. (1973). On being sane in insane places. *Science, 179,* 250–258. doi:10.1126/science.179.4070.250

Rosenthal, R. (1994.) Science and ethics in conducting, analyzing, and reporting psychological research. *Psychological Science, 5,* 127–134. doi:10.1111/j.1467-9280.1994.tb00646.x

Rosenthal, R., & Fode, K. L. (1963). The effect of experimenter bias on the performance of the albino rat. *Behavioral Science, 8,* 183–189. doi:10.1002/bs.3830080302

Rosenzweig, M. R. (1984). Experience, memory, and the brain. *American Psychologist, 39,* 365–376. doi:10.1037/0003-066X.39.4.365

Rosenzweig, M. R. (2007). Historical perspectives on the development of the biology of learning and memory. In J. L. Martinez & R. P. Kesner (Eds.), *Neurobiology of learning and memory* (2nd ed., pp. 3–55). Burlington, MA: Academic Press.

Rossi, P. H., Lipsey, M. W., & Freeman, H. E. (2004). *Evaluation: A systematic approach* (7th ed.). Thousand Oaks, CA: SAGE.

Rote, J. A., & Dunstan, D. A. (2011). The assessment and treatment of long-standing disruptive behavior problems in a 10-year-old boy. *Clinical Case Studies, 10,* 263–277. doi:10.1177/1534650111410228

Rudder, C. (2014, July 28). We experiment on human beings! [Web log post]. Retrieved from http://blog.okcupid.com/index.php/we-experiment-on-human-beings/

Russell, W. M. S., & Burch, R. L. (1959). *The principles of humane experimental technique.* London, England: Methuen.

Sacks, O. (1985). *The man who mistook his wife for a hat, and other clinical tales.* New York, NY: Summit.

Saxton, T. K., Lyndon, A., Little, A. C., & Roberts, S. C. (2008). Evidence that androstadienone, a putative human chemo-signal, modulates women's attributions of men's attractiveness. *Hormones and Behavior, 54,* 597–601. doi:10.1016/j.yhbeh.2008.06.001

Schacter, D. L., Gilbert, D. T., Wegner, D. M. & Nock, M. K. (2014). *Psychology.* New York, NY: Worth.

Schellinck, H. M., Cyr, D., & Brown, R. E. (2010). How many ways can mouse behavioral experiments go wrong? Confounding variables in mouse models of neurodegenerative diseases and how to control them. In H. J. Brockmann, T. J. Roper, M. Naguib, K. E. Wynne-Edwards, J. C. Mitani, & L. W. Simmons (Eds.), *Advances in the study of behavior* (Vol. 41, pp. 255–366). doi:10.1016/S0065-3454(10)41007-4

Schenker, N., & Gentleman, J. F. (2001). On judging the significance of differences by examining the overlap between confidence intervals. *American Statistician, 55,* 182–186. doi:10.1198/000313001317097960

Scherrer, M. D., & Wilder, D. A. (2008). Training to increase safe tray carrying among cocktail servers. *Journal of Applied Behavior Analysis, 41,* 131–135. doi:10.1901/jaba.2008.41-131

Schmuckler, M. A. (2001). What is ecological validity? A dimensional analysis. *Infancy, 2,* 419–436. doi:10.1207/S15327078IN0204_02

Scholten, A. Z., & Borsboom, D. (2009). A reanalysis of Lord's statistical treatment of football numbers. *Journal of Mathematical Psychology, 53,* 69–75. doi:10.1016/j.jmp.2009.01.002

Schry, A. R., Roberson-Nay, R., & White, S. W. (2012). Measuring social anxiety in college students: Comprehensive evaluation of the psychometric properties of the SPAI-23. *Psychological Assessment. 24,* 846–854. doi:10.1037/a0027398

Schulz, R., & Bazerman, M. (1980). Ceremonial occasions and mortality: A second look. *American Psychologist, 35,* 253–261. doi:10.1037/0003-066X.35.3.253

Schwarz, N. (1999). Self-reports: How the questions shape the answers. *American Psychologist, 54,* 93–105. doi:10. 1037/0003-066X.54.2.93

Seaton, K. A., Bowie, K. E., & Sipes, W. A. (2009). Behavioral and psychological issues in long-duration head-down bed rest. *Aviation, Space, and Environmental Medicine, 80*(5, Suppl.) A55-A61. doi:10.3357/ASEM.BR08.2009

Secretary's Advisory Committee on Human Research Protections. (n.d.). *Appendix: Understanding minimal risk.* Retrieved from http://www.hhs.gov/

Secretary's Advisory Committee on Human Research Protections. (2008, January 31) . *SACHRP letter to HHS Secretary: Recommendations related to waiver of informed consent and interpretation of "minimal risk."* Retrieved from http://www.hhs.gov/

Secretary's Advisory Committee on Human Research Protections. (2013, March 12–13). *Attachment B: Considerations and recommendations concerning Internet research and human subjects research regulations, with revisions.* Retrieved from http://www.hhs.gov/

Shadish, W. R., & Cook, T. D. (2009). The renaissance of field experimentation in evaluating interventions. *Annual Review of Psychology, 60,* 607–629. doi:10.1146/annurev.psych.60.110707.163544

Shadish, W. R., Cook, T. D., & Campbell, D. T. (2002). *Experimental and quasi-experimental designs for generalized causal inference.* Boston, MA: Houghton Mifflin.

Shadish, W. R., Hedges, L. V., & Pustejovsky, J. E. (2014). Analysis and meta-analysis of single-case designs with a standardized mean difference statistic: A primer and applications. *Journal of School Psychology, 52,* 123–147. doi:10.1016/j.jsp.2013.11.005

Shannon-Missal, L. (2014, March 13). U.S. teens more likely than adults to believe in God, heaven and angels. *The Harris Poll #25.* Retrieved from http://www.theharrispoll.com/

Sheikh, A., Conford, T., Barber, N., Avery, A., Takian, A., Lichtner, V., . . . Cresswell, K. (2011). Implementation and adoption of nationwide electronic health records in secondary care in England: Final qualitative results from prospective national evaluation in "early adopter" hospitals. *BMJ, 343* (d6054), 1–14. doi:10.1136/bmj.d6054

Shimizu, M., & Pelham, B. W. (2008). Postponing a date with the Grim Reaper: Ceremonial events and mortality. *Basic and Applied Social Psychology, 30,* 36–45. doi:10.1080/01973530701866482

Sidman, M. (1960). *Tactics of scientific research.* New York, NY: Basic Books.

Sieber, J. E. (2012). Research with vulnerable populations. In S. J. Knapp, M. C. Gottlieb, M. M. Handelsman, & L. D. VandeCreek (Eds.), *APA handbook of ethics in psychology: Vol. 2. Practice, teaching and research* (pp. 371–384). Washington, DC: American Psychological Association. doi:10.1037/13272-017

Siegel, S., & Castellan, J. N. Jr. (1988). *Nonparametric statistics for the behavioral sciences* (2nd ed.). New York, NY: McGraw-Hill.

Siler, K., Lee, K., & Bero, L. (2015). Measuring the effectiveness of scientific gatekeeping. *PNAS Proceedings of the National Academy of Sciences of the United States of America, 112,* 360–365. doi:10.1073/pnas.1418218112

Singer, E., Hoewyk, J. V., & Maher, M. P. (2000). Experiments with incentives in telephone surveys. *Public Opinion Quarterly, 64,* 171–188. doi:10.1086/317761

Skinner, B. F. (1938). *The behavior of organisms: An experimental analysis.* New York, NY: Appleton-Century.

Skitka, L. J., Bauman, C. W., & Mullen, E. (2004). Political tolerance and coming to psychological closure following the September 11, 2001, terrorist attacks: An integrative approach. *Personality and Social Psychology Bulletin, 30,* 743–756. doi:10.1177/0146167204263968

Slavin, R. E. (2012). *Educational psychology: Theory into practice* (10th ed.). Boston, MA: Allyn & Bacon.

Smith, J. D. (2012, July 30). Single-case experimental designs: A systematic review of published research and current standards. *Psychological Methods, 17,* 510–550. doi:10.1037/a0029312

Smith, R. E., Smoll, F. L., & Hunt, E. (1977). A system for the behavioral assessment of athletic coaches. *Research Quarterly, 48,* 401–407.

Smith, S. S., & Richardson, D. (1983). Amelioration of deception and harm in psychological research: The important role of debriefing. *Journal of Personality and Social Psychology, 44,* 1075–1082. doi:10.1037/0022-3514.44.5.1075

Squire, L. R., Amaral, D. G., Zola-Morgan, S., Kritchevsky, M., & Press, G. A. (1989). Description of brain injury in the amnesic patient N.A. based on magnetic resonance imaging. *Experimental Neurology, 105,* 23–35. doi:10.1016/0014-4886(89)90168-4

Society for the Experimental Analysis of Behavior. (2012). *Journal of Applied Behavior Analysis.* Retrieved from: http://seab.envmed.rochester.edu/jaba/index.html

Solutions Research Group (2014, June 10). *Massive competition in pursuit of the $5.7 billion Canadian youth sports market* [Web media release]. Retrieved from http://www.srgnet.com/

Spearman, C. (1923). *The nature of "intelligence" and the principles of cognition.* London, England: Macmillan.

Spitzer, R. L. (1975). On pseudoscience in science, logic in remission, and psychiatric diagnosis: A critique of Rosenhan's "On being sane in insane places." *Journal of Abnormal Psychology, 84,* 442–452. http://dx.doi.org/10.1037/h0077124

Squire, L. R., Amaral, D. G., Zola-Morgan, S., Kritchevsky, M., & Press, G. A. (1989). Description of brain injury in the amnesic patient N.A. based on magnetic resonance imaging. *Experimental Neurology, 105,* 23–35. doi:10.1016/0014-4886(89)90168-4

Stake, R. (1994). Case studies. In N. K. Denzin & Y. S. Lincoln (Eds.), *Handbook of qualitative research* (pp. 236–247). Thousand Oaks, CA: SAGE.

Stanovich, K. E. (2013). *How to think straight about psychology* (10th ed.). Boston, MA: Pearson.

Stark, L. (2010). The sciences of ethics: Deception, the resilient self, and the APA code of ethics, 1966–1973. *Journal of the History of the Behavioral Sciences, 46,* 337–370. doi:10.1002/jhbs.20468

Statistics Canada. (2014, June 23). *Residential telephone service survey, 2013.* Retrieved from http://www.statcan.gc.ca/daily-quotidien/140623/dq140623a-eng.htm

Stavrova, O., & Ehlebracht, D. (2016). Cynical beliefs about human nature and income: Longitudinal and cross-cultural analyses. *Journal of Personality and Social Psychology, 110,* 116–132. doi:10.1037/pspp0000050

Stephens, N. M., Fryberg, S. A., Markus, H. R., Johnson, C. S., & Covarrubias, R. (2012). Unseen disadvantage: How American universities' focus on independence undermines the academic performance of first-generation college students. *Journal of Personality and Social Psychology, 102,* 1178–1197. doi:10.1037/a0027143

Stewart, D. W., Shamdasani, P. N., & Rook, D. W. (2007). *Focus groups: Theory and practice* (2nd ed.). Thousand Oaks, CA: SAGE

Stratton, G. M. (1896). Some preliminary experiments on vision without inversion of the retinal image. *Psychological Review, 3,* 611–617. doi:10.1037/h0072918

Strayer, D. L., Drews, F. A., & Johnston, W. A. (2003). Cell phone-induced failures of visual attention during simulated driving. *Journal of Experimental Psychology: Applied, 9,* 23–32. doi:10.1037/1076-898X.9.1.23

Stukenberg, K. W., Dura, J. R., & Kiecolt-Glaser, J. K. (1990). Depression screening scale validation in an elderly, community-dwelling population. *Psychological Assessment: A Journal of Consulting and Clinical Psychology, 2,* 134–138. doi:10.1037/1040-3590.2.2.134

Suzuki, L. A., Ahluwalia, M. K., Mattis, J. S., & Quizon, C. A. (2005). Ethnography in counseling psychology research: Possibilities for application. *Journal of Counseling Psychology, 52,* 206–214. doi:10.1037/0022-0167.52.2.206

Taber, K. H., & Hurley, R. A. (2006). Functional neuroanatomy of sleep and sleep deprivation. *Journal of Neuropsychiatry & Clinical Neurosciences, 18,* 1–5. doi:10.1176/appi.neuropsych.18.1.1

Tate, R. L., McDonald, S., Perdices, M., Togher, L., Schultz, R., & Savage, S. (2008). Rating the methodological quality of single-subject designs and *n*-of-1 trials: Introducing the single-case experimental design (SCED) scale. *Neuropsychological Rehabilitation, 18,* 385–401. doi:10.1080/09602010802009201

Taylor, D. (n.d.). *The literature review: A few tips on conducting it.* University of Toronto Health Writing Centre. Retrieved from http://www.writing.utoronto.ca/advice/specific-types-of-writing/literature-review or http://tinyurl.com/mt22ly

Teachman, B. A. (2006). Aging and negative affect: The rise and fall and rise of anxiety and depression symptoms. *Psychology and Aging, 21,* 201–207. doi:10.1037/0882-7974.21.1.201

Teddlie, C., & Tashakkori, A. (2009). *Foundations of mixed-methods research.* Thousand Oaks, CA: SAGE.

Teuber, H. L., Milner, B., & Vaughan, H. G., Jr. (1968). Persistent anterograde amnesia after stab wound of the basal brain. *Neuropsychologia, 6,* 267–282. doi:10.1016/0028-3932(68)90025-0

Therapeutic Touch International Association. (2015). *The process of Therapeutic Touch.* Retrieved from http://therapeutic-touch.org/what-is-tt/history-of-tt/

Thorndike, E. L. (1898). *Animal intelligence: An experimental study of the associative processes in animals.* New York, NY: Macmillan.

Thorndike, E. L. (1911). *Animal intelligence: Experimental studies.* New York, NY: Macmillan.

Thurman, S. (2015). Ethical considerations in longitudinal studies of human infants. *Infant Behavior & Development, 38,* 116–125. doi:10.1016/j.infbeh.2014.12.012

Thurstone, L. L. (1938). *Primary mental abilities.* Chicago, IL: University of Chicago Press.

Tilburg University. (2011, October 31). *Interim report regarding the breach of scientific integrity committed by Prof. D. A. Stapel.* Retrieved from http://www.tilburguniversity.edu/nl/nieuws-en-agenda/commissie-levelt/interim-report.pdf

Tolman, E. C. (1925). Purpose and cognition: The determiners of animal learning. *Psychological Review, 32,* 285–297. doi:10.1037/h0071472

Tolman, E. C. (1948). Cognitive maps in rats and men. *Psychological Review, 55,* 189–208. doi:10.1037/h0061626

Toplak, M. E., West, R. F., & Stanovich, K. E. (2014). Assessing miserly processing: An expansion of the Cognitive Reflection Test. *Thinking & Reasoning, 20,* 147–168. doi:10.1080/13546783.2013.844729

Tourangeau, R., Singer, E., & Presser, S. (2003). Context effects in attitude surveys: Effects on remote items and impact on predictive validity. *Sociological Methods and Research, 31,* 486–513. doi:10.1177/0049124103251950

Towles-Schwen, T., & Fazio, R. H. (2003). Choosing social situations: The relation between automatically activated racial attitudes and anticipated comfort interacting with African Americans. *Personality and Social Psychology Bulletin, 29,* 170–182. doi:10.1177/0146167202239042

Trei, L. (2006, September 27). *Social science researcher proposes overhaul of survey methodology.* Stanford News Service. Retrieved from http://news.stanford.edu/pr/2006/pr-krosnick-092706.html

Trotter, J. L., & Allen, N. E. (2009). The good, the bad, and the ugly: Domestic violence survivors' experiences with their informal social networks. *American Journal of Community Psychology, 43,* 221–231. doi:10.1007/s10464-009-9232-1

Tryon, R. C. (1930). Studies in individual differences in maze ability. I. The measurement of the reliability of individual differences. *Journal of Comparative Psychology, 11,* 145–170. doi:10.1037/h0071525

Tryon, R. C. (1940). Studies in individual differences in maze ability. VII. The specific components of maze ability, and a general theory of psychological components. *Journal of Comparative Psychology, 30,* 283–335. doi:10.1037/h0054238

Tryon, R. C. (1942). Individual differences. In F. A. Moss (Ed.), *Comparative psychology review* (Rev. ed., pp. 330–365). New York, NY: Prentice-Hall.

United States Geological Survey. (2011, July 22). *Earthquake facts and statistics.* Retrieved from http://earthquake.usgs.gov/earthquakes/eqarchives/year/eqstata.php

U.S. Department of Health and Human Services. (1998). *Protection of human subjects: Categories of research that may be reviewed by the Institutional Review Board (IRB) through an expedited review procedure.* Retrieved from http://www.hhs.gov/ohrp/policy/63fr60364.html

U.S. Department of Health and Human Services. (2004). *Human subjects regulations decision charts.* Retrieved from http://www.hhs.gov/ohrp/policy/checklists/decisioncharts.html

U.S. Department of Health and Human Services. (2009). *Code of Federal Regulations, Title 45: Public Welfare, Part 46, Protection of human subjects.* Retrieved from http://www.hhs.gov/ohrp/humansubjects/guidance/45cfr46.html

U.S. Department of Health and Human Services. (2010). *Mandatory reporters of child abuse and neglect: Summary of state laws.* Retrieved from http://www.childwelfare.gov/systemwide/laws_policies/statutes/manda.cfm

U. S. Department of Health and Human Services, National Institutes of Health, Office of Extramural Research. (2011, B1). *Frequently asked questions: Certificates of confidentiality.* Retrieved from http://grants.nih.gov/grants/policy/coc/faqs

U.S. Department of Labor, Bureau of Labor Statistics. (2015). *Employer-reported workplace injuries and illnesses—2014* (USDL Publication No. 15-2086). Retrieved from http://www.bls.gov/news.release/pdf/osh.pdf

Uziel, L. (2007). Individual differences in the social facilitation effect: A review and meta-analysis. *Journal of Research in Personality, 41,* 579–601. doi:10.1016/j.jrp.2006.06.008

Van Houten, R., & Malenfant, J. E. L. (2004). Effects of a driver enforcement program on yielding to pedestrians. *Journal of Applied Behavior Analysis, 37,* 351–363. doi:10.1901/jaba.2004.37-351

Van Iddekinge, C. H., Roth, P. L., Raymark, P. H., & Odle-Dusseau, H. N. (2012). The criterion-related validity of integrity tests: An updated meta-analysis. *Journal of Applied Psychology, 97,* 499–530. doi:10.1037/a0021196

VandenBos, G. R. (Ed.). (2007). *APA dictionary of psychology.* Washington, DC: American Psychological Association.

Vaughan, P. W., Rogers, E. M., Singhal, A., & Swalehe, R. M. (2000). Entertainment-education and HIV/AIDS prevention: A field experiment in Tanzania. *Journal of Health Communication, 5*(Supplement), 81–100. doi:10.1080/10810730050019573

Volbrecht, M. M., & Goldsmith, H. H. (2010). Early temperamental and family predictors of shyness and anxiety. *Developmental Psychology, 46,* 1192–1205. doi:10.1037/a0020616

Vollmer, C., & Randler, C. (2012). Circadian preferences and personality values: Morning types prefer social values, evening types prefer individual values. *Personality and Individual Differences, 52,* 738–743. doi:10.1016/j.paid.2012.01.001

vos Savant, M. (2006). *Game show problem.* Retrieved February 11, 2009, from http://www.marilynvossavant.com/articles/gameshow.html

Wager, T. D. (2009, March). A view from the rising academic's office. *Observer, 22,* 3. Retrieved from http://www.psychologicalscience.org/index.php/publications/observer

Walker, E., Shapiro, D., Esterberg, M., & Trotman, H. (2010). Neurodevelopment and schizophrenia: Broadening the focus. *Current Directions in Psychological Science, 19,* 204–208. doi:10.1177/0963721410377744

Ward, G., Grenfell-Essam, R., & Tan, L. (2010). Examining the relationship between free recall and immediate serial recall: The effects of list length and output order. *Journal of Experimental Psychology: Learning, Memory, and Cognition, 36,* 1207–1241. doi:10.1037/a0020122

Warden, R. (n.d.). Maurice Patterson. *Center on Wrongful Convictions: Northwestern University Law, Bluhm Legal Clinic.* Retrieved from http://www.law.northwestern.edu/wrongfulconvictions/exonerations/ilpattersonmSummary.html

Webb, E. J., Campbell, D. T., Schwartz, R. D., Sechrest, L., & Grove, J. B. (1981). *Nonreactive measures in the social sciences.* Boston, MA: Houghton Mifflin.

Wegner, D. M. (2011). When you put things out of mind, where do they go? In M. A. Gernsbacher, R. W. Pew, L. M. Hough, & J. R. Pomerantz (Eds.), *Psychology and the real world* (pp. 114–120). New York, NY: Worth.

Weick, K. E. (1990). The vulnerable system: An analysis of the Tenerife air disaster. *Journal of Management, 16,* 571–593. doi:10.1177/014920639001600304

Whiteford, H. A., Harris, M. G., McKeon, G., Baxter, A., Pennell, C., Barendregt, J. J., & Wang, J. (2013). Estimating remission from untreated major depression: A systematic review and meta-analysis. *Psychological Medicine, 43,* 1569–1585. doi:10.1017/S0033291712001717

Whiten, A., Goodall, J., McGrew, W. C., Nishida, T., Reynolds, V., Sugiyama, Y., . . . Boesch, C. (2001). Charting cultural variation in chimpanzees. *Behaviour, 138,* 1481–1516. doi:10.1163/156853901317367717

Whittington, B. (1986). Life skills for single-parent women: A program note. *Canadian Journal of Community Mental Health, 5,* 103–109. Retrieved from http://cjcmh.metapress.com/

Wilson, B. A., Hinchcliffe, A., Okines, T., Florschutz, G., & Fish, J. (2011). A case study of locked-in-syndrome: Psychological and personal perspectives. *Brain Injury, 25,* 526–538. doi:10.3109/02699052.2011.568034

Wilson, B. J. (1999). Entry behavior and emotion regulation abilities of developmentally delayed boys. *Developmental Psychology, 35,* 214–222.

Wilson, B. J., Petaja, H. S., Stevens, A. D., Mitchell, M. F., & Peterson, K. M. (2011). Children's responses to entry failure: Attention deployment patterns and self-regulation skills. *Journal of Genetic Psychology: Research and Theory on Human Development, 172,* 376–400. doi:10.1080/00221325.2010.547233

Wondra, J. D., & Ellsworth, P. C. (2015). An appraisal theory of empathy and other vicarious experiences. *Psychological Review, 122,* 411–428. doi:10.1037/a0039252

Wood, J. M., Bootzin, R. R., Rosenhan, D., Nolen-Hoeksema, S., & Jourden, F. (1992). Effects of the 1989 San Francisco earthquake on frequency and content of nightmares. *Journal of Abnormal Psychology, 101,* 219–224. doi:10.1037/0021-843X.101.2.219

Woodzicka, J. A., & LaFrance, M. (2005). The effects of subtle sexual harassment on women's performance in a job interview. *Sex Roles, 53,* 67–77. doi:10.1007/s11199-005-4279-4

Woollaston, V. (2013, July 29). What does your handwriting say about you? Study finds more than 5,000 personality traits are linked to how we write. *Daily Mail.* Retrieved from http://www.dailymail.co.uk

Yeater, E., Miller, G., Rinehart, J., & Nason, E. (2012). Trauma and sex surveys meet minimal risk standards: Implications for institutional review boards. *Psychological Science, 23,* 780–787. doi:10.1177/0956797611435131

Yin, R. K. (2003). *Case study research: Design and methods* (3rd ed.). Thousand Oaks, CA: SAGE.

Yong, E. (2013, November 26). Welcome to the era of big replication [Web log post]. Retrieved from http://phenomena.nationalgeographic.com/2013/11/26/welcometotheeraofbigreplication/

Yu, C. K.-C., (2015). One hundred typical themes in most recent dreams, diary dreams, and dreams spontaneously recollected from last night. *Dreaming, 25,* 206–219. doi:10.1037/a0039225

Zahed, S. R., Prudom, S. L., Snowdon, C. T., & Ziegler, T. E. (2008). Male parenting and response to infant stimuli in the common marmoset (Callithrix jacchus). *American Journal of Primatology, 70,* 84–92. doi:10.1002/ajp.20460

Zawacki, T. (2011). Effects of alcohol on women's risky sexual decision making during social interactions in the laboratory. *Psychology of Women Quarterly, 35,* 107–118. doi:10.1177/0361684310384106

NAME INDEX

SUBJECT INDEX

Note: Page numbers followed by f indicate figures; those followed by t indicate tables; and those preceded by A, B, or C indicate Appendices.